10/03

Managing White Supremacy

WELCOME
Our School Board Has Vetoed THE BILL OF RIGHTS
The School Board's Method of Dealing with Colored Teachers Is Un-American
QUALIFY TO VOTE SCHOOL BOARD MUST GO!

J. DOUGLAS SMITH

Managing White Supremacy

Race, Politics, and Citizenship in Jim Crow Virginia

THE UNIVERSITY OF NORTH CAROLINA PRESS

Chapel Hill & London

© 2002 The University of North Carolina Press
All rights reserved

Set in Granjon with Bodoni display
by Tseng Information Systems, Inc.

Manufactured in the United States of America

The paper in this book meets the guidelines for
permanence and durability of the Committee on
Production Guidelines for Book Longevity of
the Council on Library Resources.

Library of Congress Cataloging-in-Publication Data
Smith, J. Douglas.
Managing white supremacy : race, politics, and citizenship
in Jim Crow Virginia / by J. Douglas Smith.
p. cm.
Includes bibliographical references and index.
ISBN 0-8078-2756-8 (cloth : alk. paper) —
ISBN 0-8078-5424-7 (pbk. : alk. paper)
1. Virginia — Race relations.   2. Virginia — Race relations —
Political aspects.   3. Virginia — Politics and government —
1865–1950.   4. Whites — Virginia — Politics and
government — 20th century.   5. Elite (Social sciences) —
Virginia — History — 20th century.   6. African Americans —
Civil rights — Virginia — History — 20th century.   7. African
Americans — Segregation — Virginia — History — 20th century.
8. Citizenship — Virginia — History — 20th century.   I. Title.
F235.A1 S65   2003
305.896'0730755'09042 — dc21   2002006437

Portions of this work appeared previously, in somewhat different
form, as "The Campaign for Racial Purity and the Erosion of
Paternalism in Virginia, 1922–1930: 'Nominally White,
Biologically Mixed, and Legally Negro,'" *Journal of Southern
History* 68 (February 2002): 65–106, and are reprinted here with
permission of the journal.

cloth   06 05 04 03 02   5 4 3 2 1
paper   06 05 04 03 02   5 4 3 2 1

For my parents,

John and Eleanor Smith

Contents

Illustrations and Maps

Acknowledgments

Nearly eight years have passed since the genesis of this project. The memories are vague as to what I first proposed to a gathering of faculty and graduate students at the University of Virginia, but at best those early ideas bear little resemblance to the finished product. Along the way, as chapters became a dissertation and the dissertation a book, numerous individuals provided wisdom, support, and vast reservoirs of generosity and friendship for which I am deeply grateful. For quite some time I have looked forward to thanking them, and I do so now.

It is difficult to imagine a better graduate mentor than Ed Ayers. From the time I arrived in Charlottesville, Ed provided an example of what it means to combine excellence in scholarship and teaching. His infectious enthusiasm may draw the crowds of students, but his creative insight and rigorous analysis into the complexities of southern history are what open minds and force students and readers to think in new ways. As a thesis advisor, Ed always provided honest criticism, but he made certain that the process was enjoyable, not arduous. I am particularly indebted to Ed for allowing me to determine the development of this project; always supportive, he never tried to shape or twist my interests to fit his agenda. I remember well the day that I stopped referring to Ed as Mr. Ayers. I was grateful then for his mentorship. I am even more grateful now for his friendship.

I am equally appreciative of the role that Paul Gaston has played in shaping and transforming my understanding of southern history. More important, Paul has taught generations of his students that academia and activism are not mutually exclusive. His personal commitment to racial and social justice continues to inspire me in countless ways. Paul and his wife, Mary, also deserve special thanks for making so many of his students feel welcome in their home. Whether for a seminar, dinner, or a casual afternoon chat, the Gaston home was, and remains, a source of hospitality and friendship.

Nelson Lichtenstein supported this project from its inception and provided invaluable insight at every step along the way. In addition, the seeds of my dissertation were developed while sitting on the back porch of Nelson's home, where I lived for a year while he was on sabbatical. Among the faculty at the University of Virginia, I owe a final thanks to Grace Hale. Grace arrived in Charlottesville as I was finishing the dissertation from afar in Los Angeles. Although not a formal member of my committee, Grace nevertheless carved out time in her own hectic schedule to give the entire dissertation a close and critical reading. Along with Ed, Paul, and Nelson, Grace helped smooth the edges and make this a better book.

Among my classmates in Charlottesville, I am particularly indebted to Andy Lewis and Matt Lassiter for their intellectual and extracurricular camaraderie. Matt read the entire dissertation and portions of the manuscript. Andy read portions of the dissertation and the entire manuscript. More often than not, each of them was able to articulate the substance of my thoughts more clearly than I was. Phil Troutman read portions of the manuscript and saved me from several errors. Joe Rinkevich and Michael Mauney—neither a historian, both great friends—enriched my time in Charlottesville, kept me balanced, and taught me a great deal, nothing so important as the intricacies of home brewing.

Trying to finish a dissertation and write a book about the South while living in southern California was no easy task. I could not have done so without the help of a number of archivists, institutions, and individuals. The staffs at the University of Virginia Library, the Virginia Historical Society, and the Library of Virginia patiently fielded my requests, answered my queries, and suggested new avenues of investigation. In particular, Minor Weisiger and Gregg Kimball at the Library of Virginia shared with me their vast knowledge of the library's holdings, while their colleague Brent Tarter deserves special thanks for spending so much of his time helping younger scholars find their footing. The interlibrary loan staff at the California Institute of Technology, where I spent three years after finishing graduate school, never failed to track down a request, including some that were quite obscure.

The University of Virginia provided generous financial assistance during graduate school, while the Andrew Mellon Foundation, the Virginia Historical Society, and the Organization of American Historians eased the pain of traveling between the coasts on research trips. My debt to the National Academy of Education and the Spencer Foundation is unsurpassed; a National Academy of Education/Spencer Postdoctoral Fellowship allowed me a full year to finish the manuscript. The California Institute of Technology, and in particular Susan Davis, provided me an office during the fellowship year. In addition to financial assistance, I would not have completed this project without the hospitality of friends and relatives throughout Virginia who provided room, and often board, on my annual research trips. My deepest thanks go to my late aunt, Misty Davis, whose home in Richmond more often than not served as my headquarters. I am sure that I spent the equivalent of six or eight weeks with Misty. My last visit came as she courageously battled cancer yet somehow still evinced an interest in my work.

As I discussed at length with Misty, the biggest surprise in researching this book occurred when I stumbled across the name of her father and my grandfather, Armistead Boothe. Despite an intimate knowledge of his role in Virginia politics in the 1950s and 1960s, I had no inkling until the final stages of research that as city attorney of Alexandria, he prosecuted the five young men who attempted to desegregate the city's library in 1939 (see Chapter 9).

A number of other individuals deserve special thanks for helping make this a better book. David Perry of the University of North Carolina Press saw promise in a dissertation and nurtured it into a publishable manuscript. Mary Reid provided expert guidance throughout the copyediting process. Jeff Norrell read the entire manuscript for the Press; his insightful comments pushed me to extend the narrative in directions I had not initially planned. Peter Wallenstein read portions of the dissertation and helped clarify points of confusion. Neither Brian Ward nor Bryant Simon has actually read a page, but both of them have provided encouragement and real friendship at crucial times. My thanks to Tony Badger for providing an entrée into a community of scholars that has evolved into a circle of friends. The 1999 Tulane-Cambridge conference, which Tony organized, remains without a doubt the most enjoyable professional meeting I have attended. At various points in this project, I crossed paths with Peter Hardin, the Washington correspondent for the *Richmond Times-Dispatch*, Matt Spangler, a documentary filmmaker, and Stephen Ackerman, a freelance writer. Each of them shared with me the results of his own work and, in the process, enhanced my conclusions.

I owe a particular debt of gratitude, one that I can never repay, to John Kneebone at the Library of Virginia. In addition to answering questions, mailing me information from the library's archives, and serving as a commentator on a conference panel that I organized, John read the entire manuscript for the University of North Carolina Press not once, but twice. Perhaps more than anyone else, John understands the transformation that this manuscript underwent. Many of the most significant changes came in response to his initial set of comments. He also saved me from errors of fact and interpretation; any that remain are, of course, my responsibility. Without a doubt, John's knowledge of Virginia's twentieth-century racial and political history deeply influenced this book on many levels.

I am blessed with a wonderful family and group of friends who have provided me with more support than any individual deserves. At Caltech, Miriam Feldblum listened to every twist and turn in the book's gestation during our daily, or even twice daily, breaks. More often than not, Bill Deverell joined us. As indebted as I am to Bill for supporting my professional development, and those debts are enormous, I owe him a great deal more for introducing me to Philip Goff and David Igler. Over the past four years, Bill, Philip, and David have taught me more than I really need to know about western, religious, and environmental history, but their camaraderie, friendship, and support, forged on all those early morning walks, has meant more than words can adequately express.

Rudi Colloredo-Mansfeld, one of my oldest and dearest friends, has taught me how to endure the inanities of academic life with grace and humor. Peter Hatcher's continued interest in my work and unquestioned faith in my abilities remain an invaluable source of comfort.

My sisters, Katherine and Sarah, have never let me forget what is most important in life. For a lifetime of unconditional love and support, this book is dedicated to my parents, John and Eleanor Smith.

Julie Lynn has been my greatest friend and champion for more than a decade. I gladly followed her from the foothills of the Blue Ridge to the Hollywood Hills. I eagerly await the next chapter in our life together.

Acknowledgments

Managing White Supremacy

White people in their fear, built protective barriers, so they thought, against the "encroachments of Negroes upon the special prerogatives of the whites." What they really built were road blocks to democracy and justice and equal opportunity. In so doing, they hurt all the South and all the people. The evil weeds that grow from oppression, poverty, and ignorance spread in many directions. Trying to "keep the Negro in his place," the white man darkened and impoverished the society in which he lived, and narrowed his own soul.

—LUCY RANDOLPH MASON, 1952

Introduction

> In Virginia, the powers that be were a little more sophisti-
> cated than they were in the deeper South, and they'd always
> apparently been. And as a consequence, you didn't have as
> much physical violence in Virginia as you had in the deeper
> South. . . . [But] Virginia and the whole South were police
> states. There isn't a question about that. Negroes didn't serve
> on juries, they didn't serve on grand juries or petit juries.
> You saw no blacks in places like city hall, or public buildings,
> unless, except, maybe an elevator operator or janitor. And
> that's the way it was. — OLIVER HILL, 1985

In March 1929 Douglas Southall Freeman, the editor of the *Richmond News Leader*, worried that he and other white elites were losing their ability to manage the city's race relations. His concern prompted him to ask William Reed, a Richmond tobacco magnate and the most important and trusted advisor to then-governor Harry F. Byrd, to quietly contribute to a legal defense fund that would help black citizens of Richmond fight a residential segregation ordinance recently passed by the city council. Freeman mentioned that increased antagonism had resulted from the ordinance's passage and added that "anything that disturbs good race-relationships is inimical to Richmond." A firm opponent of the measure from the beginning, Freeman preferred to have the matter "worked out by friendly conference, rather than by law." But given the council's contrary view, Freeman suggested that "we may be able to allay bad feelings if a few of us quietly contribute to the fund the Negroes are raising for a test of this ordinance. By doing this, we could give the Negroes evidence that we were determined to see that they got absolute justice."[1]

On the surface, the developments described by Freeman appear extraordinary: white southerners at the height of Jim Crow did not make a habit of raising money to help blacks fight segregation ordinances. Freeman's motives, however, were suffused with self-interest. He opposed the Richmond ordinance not because he sought an end to segregation, but rather because he considered it self-defeating. A pragmatist, he knew the statute could not pass constitutional review; given the inevitable, he saw no point in unnecessarily arousing racial bitterness and animosity. To this end, Freeman iterated in newspaper columns and private correspondence "that the memory of this support would dispose the Negroes to cooperate in the right sort of residential separation, by consent," an arrangement by which blacks would agree to lead separate lives as long as whites provided more equitable treatment and services.[2]

Freeman's notion of "separation by consent" embodied the commitment of white elites to what Freeman repeatedly referred to as "the Virginia Way." Perpetually suspicious of democracy and fervently convinced that only the upper orders should govern, white elites in Virginia embraced a concept of managed race relations that emphasized a particularly genteel brand of paternalism. Intent on maintaining order and stability, practitioners of the idea of managed race relations wholeheartedly supported segregation and disfranchisement but rejected the rigid racial oppression and violence trumpeted elsewhere in the South. Emphasizing civility and their friendship for black Virginians, paternalists promised to provide a modicum of basic services and even encouraged a certain amount of black educational and economic uplift. In return, white elites demanded complete deference and expected blacks to seek redress of their grievances only through channels deemed appropriate by whites. In one respect, white elites did keep their end of the bargain: the violence and physical coercion that defined the culture of segregation throughout much of the South was less prevalent in Virginia. Consequently, white Virginians enjoyed a reputation throughout the first half of the twentieth century for managing race relations that were, in the words of political scientist V. O. Key, "perhaps the most harmonious in the South."[3]

White Virginians who claimed to preside over harmonious race relations shared a great deal with their counterparts in North Carolina who believed in their own "progressive mystique." Committed to a "paternalism so unconscious that it would never be called such by whites," writes historian William Chafe, elites in North Carolina accepted their "moral obligation to help those who are worse off." As in Virginia, however, these

4

whites postponed meaningful reform with an unremitting emphasis on civility, which served as "a way of dealing with people and problems that made good manners more important than substantial action."[4]

From World War I through the end of the 1920s, it became evident that this genteel paternalism had become increasingly irrelevant in a modern, urban world. Ironically, the apotheosis of the New South creed of industrial and mercantile development exposed the limitations and inherent contradictions of paternalism and contributed to an erosion of managed race relations in the Old Dominion. Black and white Virginians crowded into the commonwealth's cities and towns, straining municipal resources, altering traditional housing patterns, and increasing competition for jobs. In response, elite whites joined leading blacks on interracial committees and discussed the most pressing concerns but finessed professions of civility and amity to evade any meaningful reform. As throughout the United States, the Ku Klux Klan expressed anxiety over the implications of modernization and made inroads in Virginia in the postwar years. Although white elites almost universally condemned the Klan, many lent their support in the 1920s to the Anglo-Saxon Clubs, an umbrella organization devoted to the absolute purity of the white race. The group's extremist ideology and successful legislative campaign challenged claims of harmonious race relations, exposed splits within elite ranks, and contributed to the further erosion of paternalism.[5]

By the time Richmond's city council passed a segregation ordinance in 1929, Douglas Southall Freeman understood just how difficult the management of white supremacy had become. He and other leading whites found themselves on the defensive, confronted with challenges to their authority on all fronts. Ideological extremists rejected the path chosen by genteel whites and attempted to redefine race relations in rigidly exclusionary terms. Working- and lower-class whites, who competed with blacks for jobs, housing, and seats on buses, increasingly exhibited disdain for their social superiors, whose advocacy of harmonious race relations offered little of relevance to meet their own concerns. For their part, black Virginians openly rejected the terms of the paternalistic bargain central to managed race relations. Emboldened by their experiences during World War I and tired of enduring what one white newspaper editor referred to as the "little tyrannies and petty skullduggeries" of Jim Crow, blacks in Virginia recognized that they could not depend on the unreliable whims of the so-called "good white people" to enact meaningful change.[6] Freed from the constraints of personal contact and control that defined race relations in the rural South, African Americans in Virginia's urban areas turned to the federal courts and joined organizations such as the National

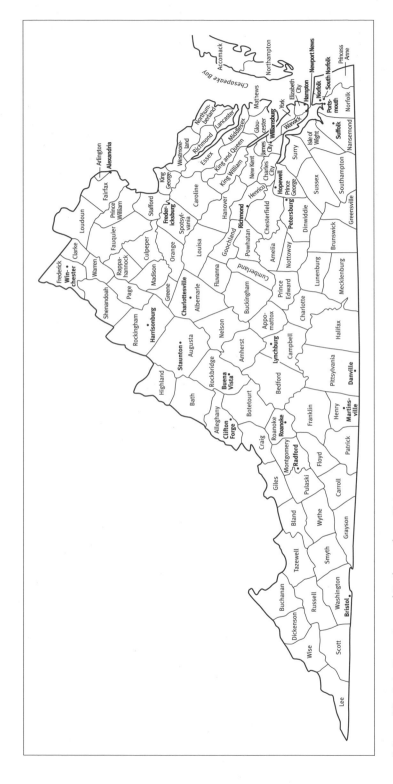

Map 1. Virginia Counties and Independent Cities, 1930

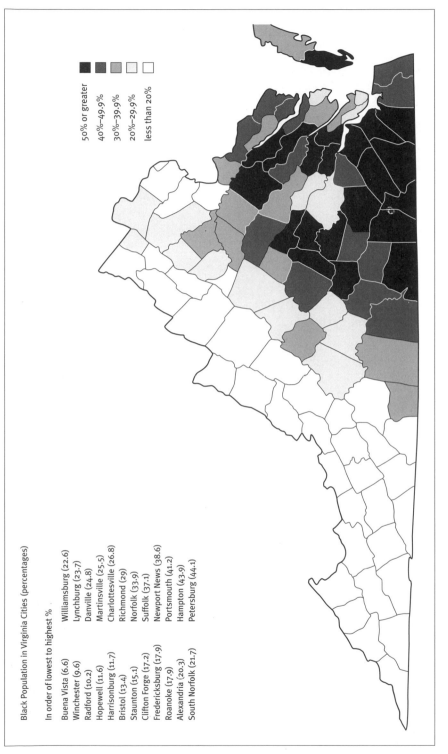

Black Population in Virginia Cities (percentages)

In order of lowest to highest % .

Buena Vista (6.6)	Williamsburg (22.6)
Winchester (9.6)	Lynchburg (23.7)
Radford (10.2)	Danville (24.8)
Hopewell (11.6)	Martinsville (25.5)
Harrisonburg (11.7)	Charlottesville (26.8)
Bristol (13.4)	Richmond (29)
Staunton (15.1)	Norfolk (33.9)
Clifton Forge (17.2)	Suffolk (37.1)
Fredericksburg (17.9)	Newport News (38.6)
Roanoke (17.9)	Portsmouth (41.2)
Alexandria (20.3)	Hampton (43.9)
South Norfolk (21.7)	Petersburg (44.1)

Legend:
- 50% or greater
- 40%–49.9%
- 30%–39.9%
- 20%–29.9%
- less than 20%

Map 2. Black Population of Virginia Counties and Cities, 1930 (U.S. Bureau of the Census, *Fifteenth Decennial Census of the United States, 1930, Population*, vol. 3, pt. 2, *Reports by States*, 1161–68)

Association for the Advancement of Colored People (NAACP) in order to take possession of their rights of citizenship.

During the 1930s education emerged as the most salient issue around which blacks and whites contested the future of Jim Crow. Throughout the commonwealth, blacks filed petitions and organized protest marches and "sit-down" strikes, demanding equal access to schools and libraries. As long as these claims could be addressed safely within the bounds of segregation, a handful of white elites emphasized that the state had an obligation to provide equal facilities and salaries. In fact, the more prescient understood that they must meet this responsibility in order to ensure that the courts would continue to sanction segregation. Black Virginians, however, recognized that separate would never be equal and indicated that they intended to attack the broader manifestations of Jim Crow. In response, even the most progressive white elites, considered the best that the white South had to offer in race relations, announced that black demands had become "too radical for us."[7]

By the eve of World War II, elite paternalism had ceased to function as an effective means of managing race relations in the Old Dominion. Leading whites continued to denounce rabble-rousers who sanctioned violence to keep blacks in their place, but they also labeled as extremist any individual who pushed for change outside the limits mandated by paternalism. In the process, white elites lumped together as equal threats to civil society the most virulent racists and the most cautious advocates of the NAACP. In remaining devoted to a conception of race relations that encouraged black advancement but denied the possibility of equality, white elites ran up against a conundrum to which paternalism offered no solution. They had always relied on a "better class" of black leaders to counsel prudence and ensure that change would occur as whites saw fit. But by the early 1940s, even the most cautious black leaders signaled their intention to push for an end to Jim Crow. Those whites considered most moderate on racial matters were stunned by the realization that this "better class" of blacks had ambitions for black Virginians that could not be contained within the framework of managed race relations.

Virginia's reputation for good race relations remained relatively intact until the mid-1950s, when white Virginians led the white South down the path of massive resistance rather than comply with the Supreme Court's *Brown v. Board of Education* decision. Embarrassed by this response in later years, eminent Virginians attempted to dismiss massive resistance as an aberration from Virginia's heritage of sound leadership and good race relations. Massive resistance, however, was not an aberration at all, but rather a response to black demands for change that can only be understood in the context of decisions made in the two decades prior to World War II. During this period, as the heart of this narrative examines, white Virginians clung to their paternalism, emphasizing civility in order to circumscribe the civil rights of black Virginians. By the 1950s, however, white Virginians could no longer paper over the accumulated weight of more than a half-century of irresolvable contradictions. Massive resistance gave the lie to Virginia's system of managed race relations, but the emptiness of paternalism had been evident for some time. Although less violent than in other southern states, whites in Virginia proved to be just as committed to segregation, and often less honest with themselves and the black citizens of the commonwealth.[8]

While massive resistance shattered the myth of harmonious race relations in the Old Dominion, it ultimately failed and in this sense did not represent the future of Virginia or the South. Whites from the Southside counties of the more rural black belt, who enjoyed disproportionate political power, refused to accept any integration anywhere in the state; consequently, state and federal courts overturned Virginia's massive resistance laws. In North Carolina, by contrast, where political power was more evenly divided between rural and urban interests, metropolitan whites eschewed massive resistance, in large part by continuing to emphasize civilities, and instead opted for token integration to meet the demands of the courts. In the process they forestalled meaningful change even longer than their counterparts in Virginia. Before long, a new generation of power brokers in the Old Dominion, mostly lawyers and businessmen in the state's booming metropolitan areas, recognized that North Carolina's more subtle form of resistance offered a blueprint for controlling the pace and limiting the scope of future demands for social justice.[9]

Central to the argument of this book, and evident in each chapter, is a belief in political efficacy; the emphasis here is on the effect that the words, phrases, and actions of well-placed persons had on the management of white supremacy. Although identifying labels such as "elite" and "non-elite" are imprecise at best, shifting from place to place and across time, throughout this study the term "elite" refers to those persons whose opinions, whether because of wealth, social prestige, occupation, political office, or appointment, made the most difference in shaping the commonwealth's political, social, economic, and cultural climate. More so than in any other state in the South in the first half of the twentieth century, an oligarchic elite dominated Virginia in this respect. As few as a thousand state and local officials controlled the Old Dominion's political machinery. Wealthy industrialists, lawyers, doctors, dentists, bankers, businessmen, and railroad executives offered their support in exchange for favorable tax and labor laws. Influential newspaper editors, especially in Virginia's largest cities, used their columns to boost the state's economic fortunes, ratify the leadership of those in power, and encourage continued social order. University professors and educators lent intellectual credibility to the ruling class, while a corps of theologians and clergymen added spiritual sanction. Their wives, daughters, mothers, and sisters staffed and ran library and school boards, charitable associations, and cultural institutions.[10]

Black Virginians had their own elites. These leaders formed the nucleus of a growing middle and professional class; like whites, they were lawyers, doctors, dentists, ministers, newspaper editors, and educators. Because they had significantly less wealth and lacked the political power of the white elites, I have at times referred to them as leaders or leading citizens rather than as elites. Although most blacks were disfranchised at the turn of the century, a majority of these leaders continued to vote. Without a doubt, this group of blacks, almost all men, were the ones with whom white elites communicated and discussed grievances and through whom they attempted to manage white supremacy.[11]

White elites embraced disfranchisement and segregation as a means of limiting and controlling the electorate, while simultaneously affirming what Douglas Southall Freeman called "the first law of the South—that a white man is a white man and must be treated as such regardless of his station." Although devoted wholeheartedly to this essential principal of white supremacy, Virginia's leadership disavowed the race-baiting and violence so prevalent elsewhere in the South. Such behavior simply did not promote social stability and order. Consequently, as V. O. Key observed in 1949, political leadership in Virginia was "reserved for those who can qualify as gentlemen. Rabble-rousing and Negro-baiting capacities, which in Georgia or Mississippi would be a great political asset, simply mark a person as one not of the manner born." In this context, elites in Virginia were not unjustified in imagining that they presided over a less extreme form of racial management than that envisioned and practiced by other southerners.[12]

Elite whites in Virginia not only imagined themselves more genteel than whites elsewhere in the South, they also lauded black Virginians as the "blue-blood" of their race. Echoing a refrain shared by black and white Virginians, Freeman reasoned that Virginia had essentially ceased to import slaves after 1750; from that point until the Civil War, the most aggressive slaves, who tended to work in the fields, were sold to the newer states of the Deep South, while the most highly skilled remained in Virginia.

Consequently, according to this narrative, blacks in Virginia were better positioned after emancipation to develop and support a commercial and professional class that became "indisputably the most prosperous of their race in the South." Furthermore, Virginia's black residents enjoyed the "moral support of nearly all the whites," who shared with blacks a deep sense of mutual understanding. Throughout the era of Jim Crow Freeman argued that if not for the agitation of black extremists in the North and white radicals in the Deep South, blacks and whites in Virginia "could live side by side through the centuries and have no strife."[13]

More so than most of his contemporaries, Freeman acknowledged that managed race relations entailed a responsibility toward, not a rejection of, the state's black residents. He also recognized that the continued co-operation of African Americans in Richmond and elsewhere in Virginia depended upon the ability of white elites to meet their end of the bargain, and that a failure to do so undermined the harmony and negated the sense of mutual understanding essential to managed race relations. Cognizant of black grievances and demands, Freeman struggled to provide relief to the situation, faithfully urging city and state authorities to provide better schools, improve living conditions, and ensure equitable treatment in the criminal justice system. At all times, however, Freeman and his peers insisted that they manage the pace of such change.[14]

Although he expressed views seconded by most of his contemporaries, Douglas Southall Freeman was not, by any means, a spokesman for all white elites in racial matters. Expressing a range of opinions from the most draconian to the most progressive, elite attitudes changed over time and reflected deep and important differences. A look at some of these individuals, what they shared in common, and how they differed offers a blueprint for understanding the management of white supremacy in Virginia.

Few elites paid as heavy a price for expressing their views as did Robert Kerlin. A theologian and professor at the Virginia Military Institute, Kerlin's commitment to challenging racial violence and injustice set him apart from the vast majority of whites in Virginia. His condemnation of authorities in another southern state ultimately cost him his job and any voice of legitimacy in the Old Dominion. Once fired, he openly denounced segregation and called for an end to Jim Crow, further isolating him from those in power.

Lucy Randolph Mason came as close as any Virginian to denouncing the injustices endemic to segregation while simultaneously maintaining her standing in elite circles. A tireless champion of African Americans, women, and laborers, Mason committed her life to ending the oppression that resulted from white supremacy and the South's low-wage economy.

Blacks in Richmond recognized Mason, a descendant of illustrious Virginians, as one of the few whites genuinely committed to their well-being. In a state devoted to ancestor worship, her impressive family tree allowed her to negotiate a narrow path along the edge of the acceptable.[15]

While Freeman and more mainstream elites easily marginalized Kerlin and more or less put up with Mason, they had a much more difficult time responding to the threats posed by a group of racial extremists led by John Powell, a native of Richmond and a staple in elite social circles. Like most elites, Powell and his followers explicitly denounced the Ku Klux Klan and racial violence; on the other hand, they pursued a legislative agenda as draconian as any in the United States. Powell's organization, the Anglo-Saxon Clubs, derived its membership and support from both male and female elites. Although some white elites denounced the legislative program of this group, none of them objected to the underlying assumption that drove the organization's agenda: the necessity and desirability of maintaining pure Anglo-Saxon bloodlines. The vast majority of elites shared with Powell a fixation on the importance of genealogy in defining an individual's worth.

As Powell and his most fervent supporters pursued their legislative agenda, the commonwealth's political leadership stood by silently, a clear abdication of their paternalistic responsibility. The most important such politician, Harry Byrd, governor during the 1920s and later a U.S. senator, followed the contours established by persons such as Freeman but proved less willing to denounce the racial extremism that arose in the 1920s. Byrd subscribed to elite notions of goodwill and harmony between the races, condemned mob violence and the Ku Klux Klan, and lent his support to the Commission on Interracial Cooperation. But as an elected official, he considered it more expedient to refrain from taking a position on controversial racial issues; both as a state senator and as governor, Byrd remained neutral on legislation supported by Powell and his followers. Unlike Freeman, Byrd chose not to denounce those who favored such measures. Although Byrd ultimately authored Virginia's antilynching law in 1928, he moved hesitantly, acting only after others had convinced him that such a measure would enhance the state's reputation.[16]

Like Freeman, Mary-Cooke Branch Munford saw a need to improve the living conditions of Virginia's black citizens. An advocate of educational reform for blacks and women, she had worked toward those ends for many years. Munford also shared Freeman's predilection for demanding that elites such as herself control the pace of racial and social change in the Old Dominion. Although a committed supporter of early interracial efforts, the Richmond native preferred to work on behalf of blacks rather than with them.[17]

Throughout the 1920s and 1930s, no white Virginian in a position of public leadership challenged so thoroughly the state's commitment to white supremacy as did Louis Jaffé, the editor of the *Norfolk Virginian-Pilot* from November 1919 until his death in 1950. Unlike Kerlin, Jaffé remained safely within the boundaries of acceptable behavior as he argued on behalf of blacks for better schools, improved housing and sanitation, access to recreational facilities, and an antilynching law. Jaffé understood that a frontal assault on segregation would cost him readers and possibly his job. Instead, he gently chided municipal and state authorities as he reminded them of their corporate responsibilities under Jim Crow, a system that he believed would ultimately fade away. Born in the North and educated in North Carolina, Jaffé worked with black leaders yet maintained considerable influence in white-elite circles.[18]

Although Freeman and Jaffé wrote editorials that, for the most part, advocated the same course of action, they differed in their personal commitment to segregation. Freeman never considered that segregation was wrong, only that its application was often extreme. Jaffé, on the other hand, though never openly calling for an end to segregation, recognized its inherent incompatibility with democratic ideals and institutions. Whereas Freeman reacted to events that threatened managed race relations, Jaffé actively sought out opportunities to alleviate the worst injustices, an important distinction recognized by blacks at the time.

A decade-and-a-half younger than Freeman and Jaffé, Virginius Dabney emerged in the 1930s as one of the most consistent and persistent advocates for the equitable treatment of African Americans. Dabney rejected a core tenet of white supremacy, the horizontal color line, which mandated that all whites were considered superior to all blacks. Instead, he envisioned a vertical color line that allowed blacks and whites to live parallel lives, equal yet divided, each with their own intraracial hierarchy. As the editor of the *Richmond Times-Dispatch*, Dabney supported a federal antilynching statute, promoted the equalization of salaries for black teachers, and advocated the loosening of franchise restrictions. Although far ahead of most white Virginians in the 1930s in terms of recognizing the inherent worth of African Americans, Dabney proved unable to shed the constraints of his own heritage. His inability to envision a world without segregation revealed with striking clarity the limits of managed race relations and boded poorly for the future course of racial interaction in the Old Dominion.[19]

In the wake of World War I, all of these elites, with the exception of Powell, supported the Commission on Interracial Cooperation (CIC). The organization, active throughout the southeast, encouraged an interracial dialogue and sought to alleviate the worst injustices, put an end to lynching, and provide a modicum of basic public services to blacks in the Old Dominion. On the surface, none of these goals appeared at odds with paternalistic notions of goodwill. Over time, however, black members challenged whites over the appropriate pace and breadth of change. As a result, many white elites proved willing to lend only limited support.

Among the most prominent and active black members of the CIC were Gordon Blaine Hancock, a Baptist minister and professor of sociology at Virginia Union University in Richmond, and P. B. Young, the editor and publisher of the *Norfolk Journal and Guide*, the largest black newspaper in the South. Hancock and Young loathed the oppression and discrimination endemic to segregation but reasoned that pragmatism demanded civility and required their cooperation with white elites in the management of white supremacy. Cautious and conservative in the style of Booker T. Washington, Hancock and Young emphasized self-help, solidarity, and patience while awaiting the day when blacks might attack segregation head on.[20]

Born in Alexandria just before World War I, Samuel Wilbert Tucker stood out among a younger generation of African Americans in the 1930s who challenged the leadership of figures such as Young and Hancock, and who made clear their rejection of the racial status quo. Tucker came of age during the 1920s, infused with the spirit of the Harlem Renaissance and the "New Negro." Well-educated, raised in an urban environment that proved fertile ground for challenges to white supremacy, Tucker chafed at the accommodation of older blacks. In 1939, more than twenty years before the sit-ins in Greensboro, North Carolina, he organized a sit-down strike at the Alexandria Public Library, an audacious move that stunned white elites, who had never considered the possibility of such defiance.

White elites responded to the actions of African Americans like Tucker by labeling them overzealous or extremist and comparing them unfavorably with Young, Hancock, and other black leaders on whom they relied to manage white supremacy. Emphasizing harmony and civility, the hallmarks of their paternalism, Freeman and other whites spoke of black Virginians as "blue bloods" and as a "superior class of negroes" precisely because they viewed them as cooperative and easily managed. White elites, however, erred mightily in assuming that they understood their black neighbors.[21]

This very assumption, in fact, contained the essential contradiction at the heart of Virginia's system of managed race relations. So long as white elites remained secure at the top of the hierarchical ladder, they encouraged black education and advancement in a way that extremists did not. But paternalists refused to recognize that the ultimate implication of continued black progress was the development of a larger, more prosperous, and independent black middle class more able to vocalize its dissatisfaction with inequality. Consequently, they attempted to impose limits on black advancement that even black leaders like Young and Hancock eventually rejected. Extremist elites like John Powell, on the other hand, avoided the essential contradiction of paternalism by advocating the near-total political and social exclusion of African Americans, a damnable but in some respects more consistent position.

As more established black leaders began to openly reject the emptiness of white elite paternalism, they joined a younger generation in announcing that only the abandonment of Jim Crow could resolve the contradictions inherent in managed race relations. In expressing that their rights as citizens in a democratic society were incompatible with the dictates of segregation, African Americans made clear that few whites understood them or their desires. Unprepared to consider an end to segregation, and unwilling to sanction violence to keep blacks in their place, the majority of white elites in Virginia found it easier to affirm the rightness of their approach to managing race relations than to comprehend the disintegration of their cooperative relationship with black leaders. Only a handful of whites acknowledged the degree to which their understanding extended no further than the myth of contented blacks of bygone days who remained fixed in their assigned place.

In certain respects, the emptiness and failure of paternalism reflected the transformation of Virginia, the South, and the nation from a highly localized, largely agrarian world to a modern, urban, consumer-oriented world. More suited to a rural way of life, paternalism required enough personal contact and knowledge for both blacks and whites to accept unwritten promises. But in the commonwealth's growing and increasingly anonymous cities and towns, the setting for much of this narrative, white elites lacked the necessary intimacy to control the aspirations of either blacks or non-elite whites. As paternalism eroded, urban whites increasingly turned to the state legislature and city councils to redefine the terms of white supremacy; rural whites, who dominated the state's politics, enthusiastically embraced such measures. Additional segregation statutes, of course, only deepened the distance between blacks and whites, both in physical and psychological terms, and ensured that whites knew and understood even less about their black neighbors than they had before.[22]

In Virginia this transformation evolved slowly but accelerated in the two decades after World War I. Consequently, the most significant of Virginia's Jim Crow statutes were adopted not in the 1900s and 1910s, but in the 1920s and 1930s, a sign to historian Charles Wynes that whites "knew that their world was changing." This does not suggest that white Virginians had lost their grip on power, but rather that the management of that power had become increasingly difficult. Dominant whites failed to control their social inferiors, their own unity proved elusive, and they discovered that they no longer enjoyed the crucial support of leading black Virginians. Left to shore up an inherently unstable institution already riddled with contradictions, white elites appeared increasingly uncertain as they lost some of what Dan Carter refers to as the "racial self-confidence" constructed in the years prior to World War I. Over time, of course, the sustained persistence of African Americans and the democratic rhetoric of the Second World War further undermined whatever confidence remained.[23]

The activities described in these pages argue against popular and historiographical notions of the 1920s and 1930s as a relatively static period in race relations. Historians of the American South have produced a rich body of work that emphasizes the contested nature of race relations in the late nineteenth and early twentieth centuries as whites employed every imaginable device to divest blacks of the promises made by the Fourteenth and Fifteenth Amendments. During these years each of the southern states adopted Jim Crow and disfranchisement laws, the Democratic Party began seventy-five years of unparalleled dominance, and lynchings occurred with alarming frequency.[24]

Historians have not, however, portrayed the decades between the establishment of segregation and disfranchisement and the demise of Jim Crow after the Second World War with the same fluidity; as a result, the classical period of segregation has been portrayed as one during which little of consequence occurred, at least in terms of race relations. George Tindall, for instance, writes that "in the 1920's the new peculiar institution of Negro subordination had reached its apogee as an established reality in law, politics, economics, and folkways—under attack from certain minorities in the North, to be sure, but not effectively menaced and virtually taboo among respectable whites as a subject for serious discussion. The question was settled." Similarly, Joel Williamson describes the pitched battle that pitted southern white conservatives and racial radicals against one another between 1890 and 1915 but concludes that such divisions had given way to a consensus on race after 1915.[25]

More recently, Grace Elizabeth Hale has described a culture of segregation and violence that whites used to dominate black southerners and to construct an identity of whiteness in the late nineteenth and early twentieth centuries. Although she portrays the degree to which race relations remained deeply contested throughout the era of segregation, Hale also lends support to Tindall's conclusion when she writes that "by 1930 white southerners felt so secure within the new racial order of segregation that white supremacy, often politely expressed as interest in 'the Negro question,' received much less public attention."[26]

There is, of course, a great deal of evidence to support the conclusions of these historians. As Tindall notes, respectable whites did not debate the wisdom of segregation; nor did political candidates in Virginia or elsewhere in the South. In a sense, therefore, the question was settled. But as I emphasize throughout this narrative, a variability and uncertainty concerning race relations did exist. By looking at politics as a sphere of directed activity larger than what happens in elections, it becomes clear that dominant whites in Virginia struggled on a daily basis to figure out how best to manage white supremacy. They knew that the race question was not settled, nor likely ever to be. Cultural and ideological inertia did not ensure the perpetuation of segregation; instead, a panoply of issues, from the distribution of municipal resources to the application of criminal justice, demanded constant negotiation and involved continual contestation. Eventually, these quotidian interactions among and between white and black Virginians eroded the patina of civility that had faithfully served the interests of Virginia's ruling class. With heightened intensity, black and white Virginians at midcentury looked toward the South of the future, some with expectation and hope for a more just and equitable society, others with a sense of fear and uncertainty about what such a world would look like.

1

A Fine Discrimination Indeed

PARTY POLITICS AND WHITE SUPREMACY FROM

EMANCIPATION TO WORLD WAR I

> The destinies of the two races, in this country, are
> indissolubly linked together, and the interests of both require
> that the common government of all shall not permit the seeds
> of race hate to be planted under the sanction of law. . . . If
> evils will result from the commingling of the two races upon
> public highways established for the benefit of all, they will be
> infinitely less than those that will surely come from state
> legislation regulating the enjoyment of civil rights upon the
> basis of race. We boast of the freedom enjoyed by our people
> above all other peoples. But it is difficult to reconcile that
> boast with a state of law which, practically, puts the brand of
> servitude and degradation upon a large class of our fellow
> citizens,—our equals before the law.
> —JOHN MARSHALL HARLAN, dissenting
> in *Plessy v. Ferguson* (1896)

A majority of white Virginians who assumed positions of leadership in the
1920s and 1930s were born into a late-nineteenth-century political culture
dominated by chaos, electoral fraud, and racial violence. Educated by their
fathers and mothers to distrust democracy in general, and the postemancipation political alliance of blacks and whites known as Readjusters in particular, Douglas Southall Freeman, Harry Byrd, and their contemporaries
learned well the lessons of their childhood. Throughout their lives, they

sanctioned segregation and disfranchisement as necessary to prevent a return to the embittered days of Virginia's experiment with manhood suffrage and interracial political cooperation. As one-party democracy and white supremacy became the guiding principles of twentieth-century politics in the Old Dominion, white Virginians defined blacks out of the body politic. Only at this point, after silencing the political voice of African Americans, did white elites in Virginia reconfigure their management of white supremacy along paternalistic lines.

Virginia became the only state of the former Confederacy to avoid postwar military rule by agreeing to a new constitution in 1869 that granted the suffrage to black men. During that year's elections, the first since the end of the Civil War, black men flocked to the polls. Consequently, the 180 new members of the Virginia General Assembly included twenty-seven blacks, not an overwhelming number given that blacks outnumbered whites in forty of the commonwealth's ninety-nine counties. In the words of one historian, "an appearance of moderation and amiability" developed among the black and white legislators. Members of the ruling Conservative Party, however, soon revealed their true colors. In addition to pushing through a series of laws that chipped away at black political rights, conservatives played the race card with greater intensity in subsequent campaigns, successfully warning of the danger of black domination.[1]

In part, the effective use of racial rhetoric allowed the Conservative Party to downplay class differences that otherwise might have erupted sooner than they did; the party's policies consistently ignored the needs of the state as a whole and instead favored the agenda of the railroad and large business interests that controlled most of the wealth in the state. Rather than earmarking scarce funds for the public school system provided for by the new constitution, for instance, the legislature directed monies to pay off the state's debt. At the same time, corporations paid minimal taxes. Not surprisingly, most supporters of the Conservative Party resided in Virginia's cities and small towns, the hubs of commercial and industrial activity; bankers, lawyers, and railroad executives from Richmond, all of whom served on one another's boards of directors, dominated the party's leadership.[2]

In 1870 and 1871 the legislature passed a series of laws that committed the state to paying in full a $46 million debt incurred prior to the Civil War. Proponents, known as Funders and representative of the financial and corporate interests most likely to benefit from full payment, argued on behalf of maintaining the state's honor and credit rating. Opponents considered the measures excessive and asked why the state's corporations should not assume a share of the commonwealth's financial burdens. Enormous sums

A Fine Discrimination Indeed

of money were spent in procuring this legislation, which, in the words of one historian, resulted from "'an unholy combination of the forces of the bankers, brokers, speculators, and railroads.'"[3]

The two sides continued to differ on a fair settlement of the debt issue throughout the 1870s. When the Conservative governor vetoed a bill passed in 1877 to provide for a mild readjustment of the debt and instead slashed funding for schools and other state services, the most significant political revolt in Virginia's postbellum history erupted. The Readjusters, led by former Confederate general William Mahone, took control of the legislature in 1879 and elected the state's governor two years later. Mahone himself went to the U.S. Senate. The Readjusters funneled money into the nascent public school system, eliminated the poll tax, raised taxes on corporations, lowered property taxes that had become burdensome to farmers, and readjusted the state debt to coincide, in the words of one student of the movement, with their belief that "'the state's creditors should be compelled to share in the general loss occasioned by war and reconstruction.'"[4]

Black voters remained in the background during the initial Readjuster victory in 1879, but many soon joined the nascent movement, drawn to the party's platform and its openness to all persons "without distinction of color." African Americans enthusiastically supported two tenets at the core of the Readjuster agenda: opposition to debt payment and the establishment of a vibrant public school system. They believed that decades of enslavement constituted more than their fair share of the state's obligations and recognized education as absolutely essential for the full realization of their citizenship. Mahone, according to the most recent historian of the Readjusters, "never intended to challenge white supremacy," but he quickly recognized that his success depended upon black votes; as white Virginians divided their support between the Conservatives and Readjusters, the black vote became decisive. Unlike the Republican Party, which had effectively ignored blacks in Virginia since 1870, Mahone and the Readjusters rewarded the black members of their coalition with a share of the patronage appointments that came under their control. For their part, blacks understood that patronage entailed not only material benefits, but also the recognition of their electoral influence.[5]

Highly dependent on the votes of black men, white Readjusters recognized their vulnerability to charges leveled by many southern whites that black political power would lead to social equality, often a code phrase for interracial sexual relations. Consequently, white Readjusters went to great lengths to distinguish between the presence of blacks in the public and private spheres. Acknowledging their support for African American political, legal, and commercial rights, Readjusters simultaneously affirmed their commitment to white supremacy and argued for the sanctity of segregation in the home. Opponents of the Readjusters, however, refused to accept any such distinction and instead emphasized that black gains in the public sphere, particularly in the schools, threatened the private sphere. Conservatives turned the appointment of two black men to the Richmond school board into a major election issue in 1883 by stressing that most teachers were women and that the black members of the board therefore exercised direct control over white women. Not only did the situation, in the minds of conservative whites, pose an obvious and menacing sexual threat, it also raised specific fears of "Negro domination."[6]

In that same 1883 election, Mahone's Readjusters lost at the polls, ending for the next eighty years any chance of significant interracial political cooperation in the Old Dominion. Amidst charges of corruption, bossism, and catering to blacks, scores of supporters deserted the insurgent party. The Conservative Party reconstituted itself as the Democratic Party, adopted many of the changes instituted by the Readjusters, including debt readjustment and support for the public schools, and organized efficiently in every precinct in the state. Focusing on Mahone's corrupt practices and on his support of black political participation, the Democrats received a boost to their efforts when a race riot erupted in Danville just days before the November election. While ostensibly precipitated by white perceptions that blacks increasingly failed to show proper deference in public, the riot's deeper causes stemmed from the inclusion of blacks in the Readjuster coalition. At the time of the riot, blacks in Danville sat on the city council, served on the police force, and held other public positions. Although white incumbency in the offices of mayor, commonwealth's attorney, judge, city sergeant, commissioner of the revenue, and chief of police made it unlikely that blacks ever exercised significant control over Danville's government, whites lost no opportunity to warn against such domination. Word of the riot spread throughout the state, blacks were intimidated and forced from the polls, and the Democrats swept two-thirds of the seats in the legislature.[7]

Virginia's big-city and small-town newspapers eagerly supported the determination of the Democratic Party to "redeem" the state from the "vice, venality, corruption, and unscrupulous rapacity" of Mahoneism. The new legislature passed statutes that weakened the powers of the Readjuster governor and placed the state's election machinery firmly in the hands of the Democratic Party. Nevertheless, elections remained hotly contested for the rest of the decade, and both sides openly sought the support of black voters. Ballot-box stuffing, vote buying, and other forms of fraud, usually justified as necessary to avoid "Negro domination," led to no less than twenty contested congressional elections in Virginia between 1874 and 1900.[8]

The most contentious of these elections occurred in 1888 in the Fourth District, the heart of Virginia's heavily black Southside. John Mercer Langston, the son of a white planter and a freed slave, educated at Oberlin College and Howard Law School, a former U.S. minister to Haiti and president of Virginia State College for Negroes, rejected Mahone's uneven treatment of blacks and ran as an independent in a three-way race. Mahone condemned Langston as an enemy of the Readjusters and of blacks. Democrats warned of the danger of black rule and left no stone unturned in an effort to win the seat. In an election rife with fraud and vote buying, Langston came in second to the Democratic nominee but demanded a recount. In 1890 the Republican-controlled House of Representatives declared him the winner by the smallest of margins, and Langston served out the remaining months of the term, becoming the Old Dominion's first black member of Congress, and the last for nearly a century.[9]

When Langston ran for reelection in 1890, the Democrats and their allies in the press announced that party politics no longer mattered, "'but rather whether intelligence or ignorance should rule, whether civilization should be preserved, in short, whether the white man or the negro should rule the Commonwealth of Virginia.'" The *Richmond Dispatch* acknowledged that Langston "'is one of the best educated men of his race'" but then declared that "'he is still a negro, with all of a negro's conceit, pomposity, credulity, and stupidity.'" Langston lost decisively, and one year later, in 1891, all remaining black candidates for the Virginia General Assembly lost for the first time since 1869.[10]

Events of the 1870s and 1880s convinced supporters of the Democratic Party that they ought to eliminate blacks from politics in the Old Dominion. Although white elites most feared another insurgent movement like the one led by Mahone, they chose to make blacks the scapegoats. As long as blacks remained enfranchised, many whites were able to deny responsibility for their own culpability in demeaning the electoral process. Nearly twenty years after he was first elected to the U.S. Senate in 1893, Thomas Staples Martin, the recognized head of the Virginia Democratic Party until his death in 1919, defended his corrupt use of railroad money as the necessary price of restoring white supremacy and ending fear of black domination. Although such fears were unfounded, pedaling to them paid remarkable political dividends for the Democratic Party.[11]

Backed fully by railroad and corporate interests desirous of political and social calm, Martin and his cronies proceeded to build a machine with almost total control over political affairs in each of Virginia's counties. Using election laws and appointive powers, the Democratic Party worked through county chairmen who tapped election boards that were confirmed by the legislature. Election boards then appointed election judges and clerks, but only after consulting with the county chairman. Such control over the machinery ensured the election of favored candidates to the state legislature and to the major local offices: treasurer, sheriff, clerk of court, commissioner of revenue, and county supervisor. These "courthouse cliques" dominated Virginia politics for the next seventy-five years.[12]

In 1894 the Democratic Party took a significant step toward disfranchising black Virginians when the General Assembly passed the Walton Act, a secret ballot measure aimed at illiterates, who were disproportionately black. The statute ordered the use of ballots that contained no symbols or other designations of party affiliation. Voters were instructed to vote in secret and to cross out the names of the candidates they did not support, leaving only the name of the candidate of their choice. Although the legislation allowed special constables to assist illiterates, the Democratic Party's control of the election machinery ensured that whites received far more help than the 50 percent of black Virginians who were illiterate. One Democratic stalwart deemed the law "the Democratic salvation," and the subsequent plunge in black voting confirmed the assessment.[13]

Firmly in control, Martin and the Democratic Party set out to reclaim Virginia's antebellum tradition of responsible political and social leadership exercised by a small elite on behalf of the majority. Ignoring their own complicity in the past quarter-century of political chicanery, Democrats blamed the Underwood Constitution of 1869, the rapaciousness of Mahone and the Readjusters, and the presence of black voters. By the late 1890s, in the words of one historian, the Democrats came to recognize "complete white supremacy" as the most effective means of achieving their ends. Although legislation had already limited the participation of most black voters in the Old Dominion, sentiment among elites favored a constitutional restriction that offered a greater degree of permanency. Efforts in this direction were greatly aided by the decision of the U.S. Supreme Court in *Williams v. Mississippi*, a ruling that sanctioned Mississippi's use of the poll tax and literacy tests to restrict its electorate.[14]

During the 1900 legislative session, the Virginia General Assembly called for a referendum on the holding of a constitutional convention. A handful of partisan newspapers came out strongly in favor of the convention, which they perceived would destroy the flawed constitution forced upon Virginia during Reconstruction. During a party meeting held several weeks before the referendum, some critics worried that new suffrage

A Fine Discrimination Indeed

restrictions would disfranchise illiterate whites as thoroughly as blacks. To allay such fears, the Democratic Party convention pledged that no whites would be stripped of the franchise. Just as significantly, the Democratic convention instructed that the constitutional convention submit its work to the voters of the whole state for ratification.[15]

A small percentage of Virginia voters turned out for the May referendum, barely half the number who would vote in that November's presidential election. One historian cites the low turnout as evidence that the Old Dominion's white populace never demanded a new constitution or new suffrage laws, but that, rather, a handful of politicians and newspapers pushed the cause. Of those who did vote, large numbers of whites from the mountains and valleys of the west and from the Northern Neck along the Chesapeake Bay voted against the referendum. Both constituencies, long supporters of the Readjusters, distrusted the effect of new suffrage laws on the high numbers of poor and illiterate whites in their populations. Nevertheless, sufficient support existed in the cities and the Southside, home to the heaviest concentrations of blacks, to carry the day for those in favor.[16]

Despite earlier reassurances, delegates to the constitutional convention adopted suffrage restrictions that not only decimated what remained of the black vote but substantially reduced the white vote as well. A handful of delegates openly acknowledged their desire to disfranchise illiterate and lower-class whites as well as blacks. Most, however, admitted only that these restrictions were essential for eliminating the black electorate, a necessary first step in cleaning up the electoral process. Democrats argued that the very presence of black voters tempted unscrupulous politicians of both parties to commit illegal acts. One Republican delegate mocked Democrats who "say the negro . . . has irritated them and caused them to sin." Instead, remarked the same delegate, these self-styled "best people" sought "to take the government out of the hands of the common people and to organize a highly-paid aristocracy." To blunt the effect of these claims, the convention adopted a number of literacy, understanding, and grandfather clauses that left open the possibility that generous registrars might allow illiterate whites to register while denying the privilege to black aspirants.[17]

No individual in Virginia matched the determination or commitment of Lynchburg's Carter Glass in achieving these goals. A newspaper editor and state senator at the time, Glass was propelled to the forefront of Virginia politics by his leadership at the convention; after serving as Woodrow Wilson's secretary of the treasury, he represented Virginia in the U.S. Senate for more than a quarter-century before his death in 1946. In bringing to a vote the debate on the state's new suffrage law, Glass proclaimed that "there stands out the uncontroverted fact that the article of suffrage which the Convention will to-day adopt does not necessarily deprive a single white man of the ballot, but will inevitably cut from the existing electorate four-fifths of the negro voters." Pausing only to acknowledge applause, the delegate declared without equivocation, "That was the purpose of this Convention; that will be the achievement." When asked by another member of the assembled body if the new law resorted to fraud and discrimination to achieve the desired ends, Glass perfectly articulated the position of Virginia's dominant white elites when he thundered:

> By fraud, no; by discrimination, yes. But it will be discrimination within the letter of the law, and not in violation of the law. Discrimination! Why, that is precisely what we propose; that, exactly is what this Convention was elected for—to discriminate to the very extremity of permissible action under the limitations of the Federal Constitution, with a view to the elimination of every negro voter who can be gotten rid of, legally, without materially impairing the numerical strength of the white electorate. As has been said, we have accomplished our purpose strictly within the limitations of the Federal Constitution by legislating against the characteristics of the black race, not against the "race, color or previous condition" of the people themselves. It is a fine discrimination, indeed, that we have practiced in the fabrication of this plan; and now, Mr. President, we ask the Convention to confirm our work and emancipate Virginia.[18]

Concerned that a majority of Virginians might reject the new constitution, delegates ignored the pledge made earlier by the Democratic Party to submit their work for ratification and instead proclaimed the new document as law. Glass and his contemporaries succeeded spectacularly in their mission. While 264,095 Virginians voted in the presidential election of 1900, only half that number, almost all of them white, bothered four years later. By the end of 1902, determined registrars and literacy tests had eliminated all but 21,000 of an estimated 147,000 blacks of voting age from the registration lists; three years later, the new poll tax cut that number in half. The electorate was so thoroughly eviscerated that throughout the first half of the twentieth century the Democratic Party regularly elected its gubernatorial candidates with the support of less than 10 percent of the adult population. From 1905 to 1948, state employees and officeholders accounted for one-third of the votes in state elections. So few Virginians voted in the first half of the twentieth century that political scientist V. O. Key quipped that "by contrast Mississippi is a hotbed of democracy."[19]

In 1905 the Democratic Party adopted a primary method of nominating candidates, thereby ensuring that any disagreements would be settled behind closed doors and not within public view. The primary, therefore, enhanced the already significant power of local and state officeholders and further distanced the majority of Virginians from the political process. As the Democrats tightened their grip on the electoral and political machinery of the state, party leaders claimed that relative calm had descended over Virginia politics for the first time in decades. Claude Swanson, the winner in the 1905 gubernatorial race and later a U.S. senator, explained, "'We have no Negro problem here. . . . The suffrage question has been determined with justice and fairness and has ceased to be a subject of discussion or agitation.'"[20]

Although black Virginians clearly would have challenged Swanson's notion of justice and fairness, his remark reflected in part a consensus that white Virginians did better by their black neighbors than did whites in other southern states. In 1880, at the height of the Readjuster movement, Henry Adams told a U.S. Senate committee that he and five hundred other black men had examined race relations in the South and determined that the Old Dominion, followed by Kentucky and Tennessee, ranked highest. Other observers noted that political hostilities did not necessarily enter the realm of interpersonal relations. Blacks continued to rely on white patronage for employment, while whites understood that their self-interest necessitated a willing labor force that could, if unhappy, migrate north.[21]

Historian Charles Wynes has argued that white treatment of blacks in Virginia depended on several critical historical and economic factors. First, more free blacks lived in Virginia during the antebellum period than in states to the south. In 1860 half of the 260,000 free blacks in the slave states resided in Virginia and Maryland. Many white Virginians, therefore, were better able to cope with the social adjustments necessitated by emancipation. Second, Virginia lacked the huge plantations and high prevalence of absentee landownership that characterized the cotton states. As a result, blacks and whites developed less physically oppressive relationships. Third, Virginia had a more diversified economy and one whose cash crop, tobacco, did not dominate the economy as did cotton in the Deep South. Furthermore, tobacco and other crops in Virginia required a more highly skilled labor force than did cotton. Many less skilled slaves in Virginia were sold south. Consequently, after emancipation, Virginia had both a more skilled labor force and better labor relations relative to states farther south.[22]

More recently, historian Fitzhugh Brundage has cited similar economic factors to explain Virginia's lower rate of lynching between 1880 and 1930. In particular, he notes that white farmers, especially those involved in truck farming and livestock husbandry, could afford to grant laborers a greater degree of independence. The absence of a dominant cash crop requiring high intensity, low-skilled, often coercive labor allowed white farmers to develop a "system of labor that was exploitative, stable, and lucrative and yet did not rest upon the steady application of coercive methods."[23]

While Virginia may indeed have enjoyed a better record than other southern states in certain racial matters, Claude Swanson's logic embodied the deftness with which Virginia's political leaders chose, as one observer has noted, to "legislate away" the political and civil rights of black citizens and then "deny that a problem existed." In addition to circumscribing the political rights of black Virginians, white elites at the turn of the century began to remove blacks physically into separate spaces. Armed with the sanction of the U.S. Supreme Court's decision in *Plessy v. Ferguson*, the General Assembly in 1900 passed Virginia's first Jim Crow law, which required separate cars for whites and blacks on railroads. No widespread demand for such legislation ever arose, but the press and the state's political leadership exaggerated a series of minor racial incidents on Virginia's trains to garner support for the statute. Before long, Virginia extended Jim Crow from railroads to streetcars and residential neighborhoods. As separation and exclusion came to govern the management of white supremacy in the Old Dominion, white elites began to convince themselves that they had, indeed, solved the "Negro problem."[24]

For black Virginians, however, their political and social exclusion did not entail willful accommodation or acceptance of the status quo, a revelation that whites failed to comprehend for decades. Throughout Virginia, African Americans struggled persistently not just for autonomy, but for empowerment. As one historian has noted, a wide spectrum of blacks, often at odds with one another, often in agreement, "fought for equal treatment, sometimes quietly and sometimes visibly. They never abided racism, 'polite' or otherwise, well; instead, they boycotted, rioted, petitioned, cajoled, demonstrated, and sought legal redress." Indeed, in the immediate aftermath of disfranchisement and segregation, African Americans in Norfolk and Richmond boycotted the Jim Crow streetcars, others filed suit challenging the constitutionality of the 1902 constitution, and still others voted with their feet and abandoned the state altogether.[25]

These protests, boycotts, and legal challenges, however, did not alter the contours of white supremacy in Virginia. While blacks never accepted second-class citizenship, they understood too well the restrictive power of the forces arrayed against them—the multiple institutions of state and municipal governments, the courts, the press, and white public opinion. As

A Fine Discrimination Indeed

their political power reached its nadir in the first two decades of the twentieth century, black leaders, especially in the state's urban areas, emphasized education, economic development, and self-help. Individuals such as John Mitchell and Maggie Walker in Richmond and P. B. Young Jr. in Norfolk devoted their energies to the development of insurance companies, fraternal organizations, banks, newspapers, and, perhaps most important, better schools. While often in disagreement with one another over tactics, these African American leaders prepared for the day when new political opportunities might arise.[26]

After first reestablishing firm political control at the turn of the twentieth century, elite men and women in Virginia embraced southern progressivism, which, at its core, entailed a commitment to paternalism. For some elites, political power itself had been the goal of disfranchisement. For others, elite leadership alone guaranteed social stability and avoided a return to the chaos, electoral fraud, and racial violence of the late nineteenth century. In this sense, in fact, disfranchisement was understood by some whites as a progressive measure. Blacks, of course, recognized a different reality. Guided by self-interest and a core set of values that included "order, morality, benevolence, and efficiency," white elites never for a moment doubted that blacks required guidance and supervision. But they also worried about working-class and rural whites, the "other half of the race peril" who, according to a contemporary clergyman, lived in "ignorance, poverty, and irresponsibility." Southern progressives promoted education and social welfare for the masses, albeit mostly for whites, yet remained deeply distrustful of them.[27]

Most of these reformers hailed from the South's urban environs, tied their fortunes to a modernizing South, and recognized that traditional, physically coercive forms of racial control threatened the social stability necessary for regional advancement. Distilled to its essence as one part white supremacy and one part white responsibility, paternalism offered an alternative means of managing race relations that promoted, rather than hindered, the modernization of the commonwealth and the region. The South as a whole, reasoned progressives, would never achieve its potential if overwhelming numbers of people remained uneducated, prone to disease, and unprepared for modern life. White elite reformers thus accepted the advancement and uplift of African Americans as their responsibility. Lila Meade Valentine of Richmond and many of her contemporaries, for example, who remained devoted to white supremacy and considered blacks inferior, still recognized their potential for improvement, so long as they accepted the guidance of whites. Although patronizing and deeply limiting, such attitudes, as Marjorie Spruill Wheeler has explained, were "enlightened compared to the attitudes of most white Southerners."[28]

While white paternalists in Virginia and elsewhere in the South condemned racial violence and took seriously their responsibility for promoting black uplift, they ultimately blamed racial hostility on the failures and shortcomings of African Americans. Drawing support and sustenance from northerners who subscribed to the tenets of scientific racism popular in academic circles at the time, southern white elites imagined slavery as civilizing. They believed that emancipation, by contrast, eroded all vestiges of proper behavior among African Americans, and that it was the consequent collapse in etiquette that led to riots and lynchings. White elites therefore envisioned paternalism, in which they would dictate the terms of black uplift and advancement, as the only viable solution. They reasoned that racial peace required, in the words of one historian, "development under complete subservience and white control."[29]

In many respects, progressivism served first and foremost to satisfy the needs of business boosters who dominated the South's urban landscape in the early twentieth century. Desperate for a veneer of civility to cloak the dark underbelly of white supremacy, these businessmen and their wives agitated for better schools, prisons, and asylums, although never for enhanced political rights for African Americans. In this sense, the needs of Virginia's business elites dovetailed with those of the Democratic Party. No longer concerned with challenges to their political dominance, party leaders wholeheartedly supported the economic development of the Old Dominion. Beginning at the municipal level in the early 1900s, state officials prepared the way for "business progressivism," a form of governance championed by Westmoreland Davis, elected governor in 1917, and embodied in the values of Harry Byrd, elected eight years later. A businessman with extensive and profitable apple orchards, Byrd perfectly represented the monied interests of the commonwealth. Committed to low taxes and labor laws that favored employers over workers, Byrd and his supporters limited the expenditure of public funds on critical state services such as highways and education. Disfranchisement and segregation ensured that whatever resources were begrudgingly allocated to the larger body politic went almost exclusively to middle-class whites. At its best, therefore, paternalism meant benign neglect toward African Americans, and at its worst, exploitation and degradation.[30]

Although deeply neglectful of essential public services, Virginia's political and business leadership did preside over a growing economy between

A Fine Discrimination Indeed

1900 and the eve of World War I. In many respects, the tremendous diversity of the commonwealth's geography, climate, and natural resources contributed to this growth. From the coastal plains, rivers, and natural harbors of the Tidewater region in the east, across the extensive Piedmont, to the foothills of the Blue Ridge, into the soil-rich Shenandoah Valley, down through the mountains and valleys of Southwest Virginia, the Old Dominion possessed advantages not seen farther south. In addition, the state's farmers and manufacturers could rely upon an extensive railroad network to ferry their products quickly to the urban centers of Baltimore, Philadelphia, and New York. Eighty-five of Virginia's one hundred counties had access to rail transportation; ten of the fifteen that did not were located in the Tidewater area and had access to navigable waterways. Nearly half the population of the United States lived within five hundred miles of Richmond.[31]

Although still overwhelmingly rural on the eve of World War I, the Old Dominion's economy had already begun to rely less on agriculture.[32] The growth of manufacturing in Virginia was not centered in the state's few large urban areas, but rather in scattered small towns throughout the state. Access to water, railroads, and labor proved sufficient as rayon, chemical, and machine tool plants sprung up in places as diverse as Hopewell, Waynesboro, and Abingdon. Small villages arose in the neighborhood of the coal mines in the Southwest. Because Virginia's soil and climate proved unfavorable to cotton production, the Old Dominion was home to few of the textile mills that drove the economic development of North Carolina and other southern states; the Dan River Mills in Danville, situated on the North Carolina border, proved the exception. Consequently, few Virginians lived in the mill villages that so dominated the experiences of many southerners of the time.[33]

World War I accelerated the economic trends already under way in Virginia. In particular, shipbuilding, the only heavy industry in the state, swelled dramatically. The Tidewater region received another boost when Norfolk was selected as one of two embarkation points for the European front; that city's population rose 72 percent from 1910 to 1920. Although a predictable recession followed the war's end, the shipbuilding industry soon recovered and remained vibrant. Less directly affected by the war, but more generally influenced by broader war-related needs, Richmond saw its number of manufacturing plants increase, its banking assets double, and its population grow by 22 percent from 1910 to 1920. Coal production in Virginia's Southwest also rose to meet war-generated demand.[34]

The uneven but steady rise in the fortunes of Virginia's industrial development, combined with the overall decline in agricultural profitability, spurred tremendous demographic movement, which ultimately affected the management of race relations in the Old Dominion. Virginia's black population since antebellum times had been centered in the Tidewater and Southside regions, those counties in the eastern and southeastern parts of the state closest to the Chesapeake Bay and those counties between Richmond and Lynchburg in the north, North Carolina to the south, and Martinsville to the west. Tobacco and smaller vegetable farms, those most in need of cheap labor, dominated this portion of the state. In 1920 nearly three-quarters of Virginia's black population lived in this region.[35]

Virginia's modest population growth of 4.8 percent between 1920 and 1930 hid a more significant development: during the decade Virginia's farm population declined by 111,167, more than 10 percent. More whites than blacks left Virginia's farms in absolute numbers during the twenties, but blacks deserted at a much higher rate: 9 percent of white farmers moved away, while nearly 16 percent of blacks did so.[36] Virginia's urban population grew by roughly the same number that left the farms. The state's rural nonfarm population, comprised of those who settled in the small towns that dominated the state's politics, grew by a similar number. Almost all of this growth, however, occurred among the white population. The majority of whites who did leave their farms stayed in Virginia, swelling the urban population by more than 16 percent and the rural nonfarm population by more than 20 percent. Very few blacks, on the other hand, moved into Virginia's cities and small towns in the 1920s. Instead, they fled the state's farms for the more promising environs of Baltimore, Philadelphia, and New York. In fact, the number of blacks in Virginia actually declined in the 1920s from 690,017 to 650,165, a drop of nearly 6 percent. While blacks in Virginia had made up over 35 percent of the population as recently as 1900, that number had dropped below 30 percent by 1920 and fell to 27 percent by 1930.[37]

Significant numbers of black migrants, however, had settled in Virginia's cities during World War I; between 1910 and 1920, the number of blacks living in Virginia's urban centers grew by 32 percent, most of the increase occurring during the war. In Norfolk the black population swelled more than 73 percent, the majority of newcomers arriving from neighboring rural counties in Virginia and North Carolina. Although Virginia's population became whiter in the 1920s, interracial antagonisms worsened as blacks and whites found themselves living in tighter quarters and competing for jobs and municipal resources in an unfamiliar environment devoid of the personal relations that governed rural life. Blacks who had moved to the cities the decade before remained fixed there, while whites who left the farms after the war now crowded into the urban centers as well, ensuring that available housing, sewage and power, space for recreation, and funding for education failed to keep pace with demand. Local leaders, unaccustomed to providing much of anything in the way of public services, proved unprepared to handle the influx of new residents and their competing claims.[38]

Although rates of tenancy, demographic statistics, and migration patterns for the 1910s and 1920s suggest that conditions faced by blacks in Virginia may have been better than those in other southern states, Virginia's white populace continued to share assumptions about their black neighbors that prevented them from ever treating blacks on truly fair and equitable terms. Virginius Dabney, later a Richmond newspaper editor but a teenager during World War I, once wrote that Virginians grew up inundated with "the thesis that the white race not only is superior to the black race, but that every individual white is superior to every individual black." This lesson was taught, learned, and reinforced in homes, schools, and churches throughout Virginia. White children absorbed the lessons of this hierarchical relationship and expected deference from those blacks with whom they came in contact. Although white elites pledged themselves to treat blacks fairly, the line between paternalism and antipathy too often blurred and even vanished.[39]

Dabney's observation echoed the experience of J. A. Brinkley of Smithfield, Virginia. Just after World War I, Brinkley wrote to the editor of the *Norfolk Journal and Guide* and related the story of "a bright-eyed, sunny faced, poorly clad, white lad of ten summers" who greeted a passing black motorist with a cheerful "Hello Nigger!" As Brinkley pointed out, it made no difference to the white child that the black man in question held a college degree, had graduated from seminary with honors, and had become a nationally recognized priest. The white youth considered his greeting to be friendly, for this man was just a "plain nigger." Brinkley proceeded to emphasize that "instinct teaches a child to fear, to cry and to take nourishment. But instinct knows nothing about germs and 'niggers.' At millions of American firesides, determined teachers with a dogged ideal are indoctrinating white faced, white hearted babes with the thought of Negro inferiority and inoculating their young souls with the virus of race antipathy."[40]

W. O. Saunders, a journalist and native of North Carolina, explained in *Collier's National Weekly* his own education with regard to blacks. "When I was a child I loved my 'ole black mammy' and played with Negro children without prejudice," he wrote. "But I grew up to dislike Negroes generally, just as almost everybody in the South does, for no particular reason at all except that a 'nigger is a nigger.' I came to manhood with a Southerner's dislike and contempt for black folks. Once or twice I searched my heart and mind for some basis of this dislike. At such times I satisfied myself by contemplating only the vicious, indolent, shiftless, improvident, dirty, ragged, ignorant, offensive type of Negro. I did not give much thought to any other kind."[41]

The inability of most white Virginians to see blacks as anything other than servile or puerile provided Richard Bowling, a black minister in Norfolk and occasional newspaper columnist, an opportunity to parody the position of blacks. Most people, he figured, "must commit a crime, hazard an air flight across an ocean, roll a wheelbarrow across a continent, be photographed in an aboriginal costume, or jump from a twenty-story window, that is, if they desire the thrill that comes from being studied and psycho-analyzed as a being separate and apart from the average. . . . But being a Negro, one gets a thrill almost every day." Whites looked upon poor, tenement-dwelling blacks as "raw, little better than heathen, untouched by American love of cleanliness and ease." But, Bowling pointed out, "let that same Negro continue to save his money, educate his children, improve his tastes, until finally he leaves the old shack and goes to live in a decent home. Do you think he will thereby become an average American and drop out of notice? I tell you, he will be eyed all the more."[42]

Many whites among the well-to-do, on the other hand, asserted their own fondness for and fair treatment of blacks in general, but in fact the feelings they described were reserved for particular mammies or servants. Mary Burnley Gwathmey wrote an unpublished manuscript about "Aunt" Sylvia Hill, born a slave to Gwathmey's grandparents in eastern Virginia. Gwathmey assigned to Aunt Sylvia certain characteristics to separate her from the mass of blacks. She emphasized that Sylvia was the granddaughter of an African princess and that such bloodlines proved significant in the advancement of civilization. Indeed, she concluded that blacks of less royal ancestry "are the ones who will drag our people down." Furthermore, Gwathmey related the story of climbing onto Sylvia's lap as a child and having Sylvia say to her, "'[Y]ou better not touch me I'm so black.'" After Sylvia stroked Mary's cheek, the young girl replied, "Aunt Sylvia *you* are not black, you are white." As the older narrator of her manuscript, Gwathmey added, "And she was. With a soul so pure, a heart so kind and a mind tuned to the finest and best, what has color to do with it?" Whatever color had to do with it, Sylvia's perceived whiteness set her apart.[43]

In addition to lessons learned around the hearth and kitchen table, the educational curriculum of white children in Virginia shaped their images of blacks. In the fifth grade, all boys and girls in the Old Dominion took their first official course in state history. Throughout the 1920s, they read *A History of Virginia for Boys and Girls* by John Walter Wayland, a professor at the State Teachers College in Harrisonburg. Young children read a great deal about the exploits and heroics of Virginia's favorite sons. At almost no time, however, did Virginia's fifth-graders learn about blacks in any capacity other than as slaves.

White schoolchildren in Virginia learned first that in August 1619 Dutch traders brought twenty slaves to Virginia's shores. "Thus began a traffic," they were told, "that was unfortunate in many ways," although how so remained unclear. Wayland explained that the prosperity of Virginia's early years developed as a result of the success of tobacco as a staple crop, which in turn depended upon slave labor. Schoolchildren were taught that tobacco continued to turn "green to gold" into the 1920s and that black labor remained crucial to tobacco-related industries. Referring to black tobacco workers, Wayland offered that "with many of them it is a habit to sing from day to day, keeping a sort of happy time in their tunes to the motions of their hands and bodies. Often the music is weird and beautiful. To hear it is worth a journey of miles." Young boys and girls, however, learned little about what sort of work slaves actually did, or under what conditions they toiled. At no time did Wayland suggest that the songs of tobacco workers masked back-breaking, mind-numbing, and highly exploitative labor.[44]

Fifth-graders learned about the Civil War in terms that would be reemphasized and amplified throughout their formal and informal education. Virginia, like the North, wanted desperately to preserve the Union, but "tried to withdraw from it only because she saw no other honorable course." Virginia's ten-year-olds learned volumes about the battles of the Civil War, but not a bit about emancipation or Reconstruction, and next to nothing about the status of the freed slaves. At no time in their history course did white schoolchildren learn of the existence of free blacks before the war.[45]

Five years after studying the history of their state, Virginia schoolchildren took a survey in U.S. history that emphasized slavery and secession. In addition to the regular text in U.S. history, Virginia's tenth-graders read Beverley Bland Munford's *Virginia's Attitude toward Slavery and Secession*. First published in 1909, Munford's text remained required reading throughout the 1920s.

Munford's message to Virginia's tenth-graders allowed them to maintain a vision of Virginia as a moral high ground. Not only did Munford emphasize that the federal government coerced a reluctant Virginia to secede, and hence that slavery was not the issue, he also argued that Virginia had actually opposed slavery and wanted to end it long before the advent of the Civil War. Munford conceded that slavery had created conditions that ultimately led to war, but he insisted that Virginia would never have seceded had not Lincoln and the federal government forced the issue.

Virginia's high school history students learned from Munford's book that since colonial times "the institution of slavery was regarded with disfavor by a majority" of Virginians who "tolerated its existence as a *modus vivendi* to meet the dangers and difficulties of the hour" but hoped to "render feasible its abolition, with a maximum of benefit to the slaves and their owners, and a minimum of danger to society and the state." Virginia's delegates to the Constitutional Convention therefore vociferously opposed the provision for continued importation of slaves until 1808.[46]

Unable to extend the state's ban on the importation of slaves to the entire country, white Virginians, according to Munford, considered the gradual emancipation of their slaves. At the same time, they continued "day by day the work of teaching these children of the Dark Continent an intelligible language, the use of tools, the necessity for labor and the rudiments of morality and religion." For twenty years, Virginia adopted a series of laws that allowed masters to manumit their slaves. As more and more slave owners did just that, the Old Dominion became concerned about the increasing number of free blacks who lacked the "privileges of the whites" but were "not amenable to the restrictions imposed upon the great mass of the blacks." As a result, in 1806 the General Assembly passed a statute requiring all freed slaves to leave the state. Thirteen years later, the same body amended the law to allow certain "sober, peaceful, orderly and industrious" persons to remain.[47]

Munford taught his readers that white Virginians would have emancipated their slaves if not for two factors: the Nat Turner rebellion in Southampton County in August 1831, and the increasing hostility of northern abolitionists. Turner's insurrection forced lawmakers to adopt "repressive legislation to nullify the dangers of slave insurrection." At the same time, abolitionists "not only attacked the institution of slavery but the morality of slaveholders." Thus, concluded Munford, "thousands sincerely desiring the abolition of slavery were driven to silence or into the ranks of its apologists in the widespread and indignant determination of Virginians to resent these libels upon their character and defeat these attempts to excite servile insurrections."[48]

Munford emphasized that, despite such affronts, Virginia still voted against secession. Only in April 1861, after President Lincoln ordered the states of the Union to take up arms against those who had seceded, did Virginia vote to join the Confederacy. Munford's emphasis on federal coercion, as opposed to slavery, as the cause of secession and the Civil War represented a fundamental component in the education of several generations of Virginia children. This distinction allowed boys and girls, as well as men and women, to celebrate the Lost Cause decades after slavery became insupportable on moral grounds.[49]

Historian Fred Arthur Bailey has concluded that "Munford's work perfectly articulated Virginia's patrician definition of the past," and that the author himself, a devoted member of the Sons of Confederate Veterans, "typified that organization's commitment to a suitable past." Critical voices outside of Virginia blasted Munford's omission of fact and his one-sided defense of secession. But Virginia's establishment, according to Bailey, fully supported the message in his work, and the "state senate thanked Munford for 'fairly representing Virginia in the light of history.'"[50]

Undoubtedly, Douglas Southall Freeman was among those elites who praised Munford's work. Although too old to have read Munford's history in high school, Freeman absorbed the "patrician definition of the past" in his youth and championed it as an adult. Born in 1886, Freeman came of age in Richmond at the height of the disfranchisement movement. As the Democratic Party eliminated blacks from the political process, Richmond's white citizens renewed their devotion and commitment to the Lost Cause. The future newspaper editor and civic leader shared in this communal enthusiasm, watched in awe as his father marched in parades of Confederate veterans, and applauded as the city's matrons unveiled monuments to the commonwealth's war heroes: Robert E. Lee, Jefferson Davis, J. E. B. Stuart, and Matthew Fontaine Maury. This childhood reverence for and worship of the Confederate past, combined with a belief in the wisdom of disfranchisement, guided Freeman and many of his contemporaries throughout their lives. A Pulitzer Prize–winning biographer of Lee, Freeman claimed to know where the general had spent every day of his life. Each morning on his way to work for nearly forty years, Freeman reportedly saluted Lee's statue on Monument Avenue.[51]

Although Freeman and his contemporaries acknowledged and even acted upon their paternalistic responsibility to improve the lives of black Virginians, they never freed themselves from a belief in the inherent inferiority of African Americans. The Reverend M. Ashby Jones, a white Baptist minister from Atlanta and a founding member of the Commission on Interracial Cooperation in 1919, explained that this guiding principle, which lay at the root of white racial ideology, derived from a still palpable belief that blacks were less than fully human and instead constituted a slave race "with fixed and predetermined limitations of physical and spiritual accomplishments." In order to address such limitations, whites carved out a separate "place" for blacks, demarcated by a psychological and increasingly physical barrier that hindered African Americans from realizing their potential or determining their own destiny. A handful of white elites accepted the idea that blacks might one day advance beyond their inferior status, but such progress was envisioned in terms of centuries.[52]

Jones agreed that non-elite whites were responsible for the lynchings and other acts of violence that besmirched the South's reputation. The Georgia cleric, however, did not absolve elite whites of blame. Jones argued, in effect, that the dehumanization of blacks in the minds of the "better class" granted permission for the mass of southern whites to view blacks in the same manner. Untrained in the etiquette and niceties of paternalism, the "lower class" of whites interpreted their perceived superiority as a literal license to kill. Any genuine improvement in southern race relations required that whites, elite and non-elite, recognize the full humanity of their African American neighbors and remove all barriers to their development.[53] Citing one example, Jones condemned voter registration laws in the South that denied even the most-educated blacks the right to vote but allowed many whites to vote without the benefit of education. Such a dichotomy, according to Jones, "gives to nearly all of our white people a false sense of values, and contributes at the same time to a false racial pride in the superior privileges, which they have done nothing to earn."[54]

Jones recognized that a majority of southern whites justified the very barriers he disdained as absolutely necessary to ensure "no social equality," an oft-repeated phrase that really meant that "the integrity of the two races is to be preserved." But unlike most white southerners at the time, Jones believed that the full recognition of African American humanity need not threaten racial integrity, which he embraced as "perfectly justifiable" and in the best interest of both whites and blacks. "For this reason," explained the clergyman, "the races should be separated by such social barriers as are necessary to preserve the purity of the blood of the two peoples. . . . But no other barriers or discriminations are justified." The distinction between necessary and unjustified may have seemed obvious to Jones, standing at the forefront of the southern interracial movement in the early 1920s. Over the course of the next two decades, however, Jones and his colleagues on the cic, including Douglas Southall Freeman and Virginius Dabney, appeared less certain; ultimately, they were unable to divorce their own fears of racial amalgamation from the implications of full citizenship for blacks in Virginia and the South.[55]

White Virginians in the era of Jim Crow expected complete deference from their black neighbors. In the state's more rural areas, blacks had little choice but to comply. But in the Old Dominion's growing cities and towns, deference and place became harder to define and manage. In some instances, violence erupted. More often, whites relied on exclusionary legislation to define not only place and deference, but the very meaning of whiteness itself. Stripped of the ballot, blacks lacked the political means to challenge the racial status quo. Emerging in a louder and more articulate voice in the years after World War I, however, blacks insisted that whites take seriously their stated ideology and treat them in more equitable terms. Over time, of course, even the most forward looking white elites in Virginia proved incapable of maintaining that fiction known as separate but equal.

2

Opportunities Found and Lost

RACE AND POLITICS AFTER WORLD WAR I

> [In Virginia] inter-racial relations are close to the
> ideal. States to the south of us and states to the north
> of us are looking to Virginia for guidance in the handling of
> the delicate race problem, for here, more than in any other
> state, it has ceased to be a problem. — *Richmond Times-
> Dispatch* editorial, 1921
>
> The War has made our group restless all through
> the South, much to his benefit, and perhaps, as the southern
> white man sees more clearly "the hand-writing on the wall,"
> he will awake to a sense of justice and fair play towards
> the Negro. — THE REVEREND C. M. LONG, 1922

World War I dramatically altered the social and economic markers that
guided southerners in the second decade of the twentieth century. In some
respects, the war accelerated change already under way; in other respects,
it created new dynamics that produced unintended consequences. The
army drafted or enlisted nearly a million southerners, black and white,
who were trained miles from their homes with people from places they
had never imagined. War-related industries provided new economic opportunities and wrought demographic upheaval in certain locales. Agricultural production rose to meet demand. While white southerners welcomed the boon to their economy and used the opportunity to proudly
assert their national identity, they preferred to ignore the fact that for black
Americans the war served as a vivid reminder that American democracy
remained a work in progress.[1]

The decision of the United States to answer President Woodrow Wilson's call to "save the world for democracy" and enter World War I gave pause to many African Americans, who were all too cognizant of their own status as second-class citizens. The vast majority of blacks in Virginia and throughout the United States, however, seized upon the war as a "golden opportunity" to prove once again their patriotism and dedication to the American body politic. African Americans returned from the war expecting more equal treatment, only to face racially motivated riots and lynchings across the country. In the South, a handful of white elites responded to the violence by forming the Commission on Interracial Cooperation, an organization dedicated to the elimination of the worst forms of discrimination and degradation. Over time, many of these same elites sought to limit the pace and extent of postwar racial change and to guide it in their own image.[2]

The growing determination of many blacks to loosen the shackles of segregation and Jim Crow occurred as increasing numbers of black and white Virginians left the state's farms and moved into cities and towns. Tensions mounted as blacks and whites came into ever greater contact and competed for limited municipal resources. Schooled in the rhetoric and practice of white supremacy, local authorities across the state implemented new segregation statutes. Other whites turned to the Ku Klux Klan in an attempt to establish more effective control. Ironically, few whites understood that most blacks had no interest in integrating neighborhoods, playgrounds, and other public facilities. Instead, blacks asked that whites take seriously their own avowed devotion to separate but equal and provide facilities for blacks commensurate with those enjoyed by the state's whites.

Unlike their counterparts in many other states, Virginia's political elites never supported the Ku Klux Klan, objecting specifically to the secretive nature of the organization as a violation of law and order. The state's white press, especially the *Norfolk Virginian-Pilot*, condemned its activities from the start. The Klan's very presence threatened paternalistic notions of noblesse oblige that formed the foundation of Virginia's claim to friendly race relations. In short, elites considered the Klan crass and embarrassing. These same elites, however, had long manipulated race to maintain the loyalty of marginalized whites now threatened with black encroachment in employment, housing, and the distribution of municipal resources. White elites found themselves in a difficult position as they struggled to maintain that allegiance while at the same time eliminating the worst excesses of racial discrimination.

The transformative effect of the First World War on race relations in Virginia and throughout the United States actually preceded Congress's declaration of war in April 1917. Beginning in 1916, massive labor shortages in northern factories spurred the decision of hundreds of thousands of black southerners to migrate north. Within three years, nearly 500,000 blacks participated in what has become known as the Great Migration. Most of these migrants left the Deep South states of Mississippi, Alabama, Louisiana, and Georgia. Some blacks in Virginia took advantage of the Old Dominion's geographic proximity and made the trip to northern industrial areas in a matter of hours. But parts of Virginia, especially Norfolk and the adjacent Hampton Roads area, also became destinations, home to key war-related industries that attracted migrants on a daily basis.[3]

Black leaders in Virginia were split on the wisdom of the migration. John Mitchell, editor of the *Richmond Planet*, joined northern leaders who urged African Americans to take advantage of the opportunity to flee the low wages, segregation, disfranchisement, and mob violence endemic to the South. P. B. Young, the editor of the more conservative *Norfolk Journal and Guide*, urged blacks to remain in the South and warned that they would not be welcomed in the North once the war ended and the flood of European immigration resumed. Week after week, Young editorialized about new industrial and agricultural opportunities in Virginia. In particular, he cited the increase in war-related manufacturing jobs in Norfolk and Hampton Roads and the demand for labor for the harvesting and marketing of truck crops in neighboring counties. The Norfolk editor stressed that wages for blacks in the Old Dominion were on the rise and that such money would support a growth in black business enterprises.[4]

Despite strong differences of opinion on the relative merits of the Great Migration, black leaders throughout Virginia offered near unanimous support once Wilson asked for a declaration of war. Mitchell, Young, and their contemporaries provided assurances of their loyalty and denied repeated reports that a pro-German movement had developed among African Americans. Norfolk's black paper exaggerated the extent of enthusiasm when it opined that blacks would forget the multiple injustices of segregation and disfranchisement, but the *Journal and Guide* no doubt underscored the feeling of many when it stressed the multiple instances of black patriotism dating back to the American Revolution. Just weeks after the United States officially joined the European conflict, however, a race riot tore through East St. Louis, Illinois, killing and injuring scores of people, most of them black. The incident reminded many blacks, as well as some whites, that the definition of democracy as practiced at home remained tenuous. Writing to the editor of the *Richmond Planet*, Uzziah Miner declared himself "completely disgusted with America's hypocrisy and insincerity. . . . I fail to see how I can conscientiously volunteer to fight for a 'World Democracy' while I am denied the fruits and blessings of a Democracy at home."[5]

While blacks did not forget such injustices at home, most rallied to the call of W. E. B. Du Bois, the editor of the *Crisis*, the monthly journal of the NAACP, who implored blacks to "forget our special grievances and close our ranks shoulder to shoulder with our white fellow citizens and the allied nations that are fighting for democracy." Considered one of the nation's most outspoken and articulate opponents of racial inequality and a frequent critic of the accommodationism favored by Booker T. Washington and his disciples, Du Bois angered some blacks who read his editorial as a sign that he, like Washington before him, had bowed to the wishes of influential whites with whom he associated. Their suspicions were further aroused when word spread that Du Bois had authored the editorial in exchange for a commission in military intelligence. Du Bois, however, wrote the editorial not to curry favor or receive a commission, but rather because he was a pragmatist who believed that African Americans had more to gain by supporting the war than opposing it. His call to "close ranks" struck a chord with and became a rallying cry for blacks throughout the United States.[6]

Whites in cities, towns, and counties throughout Virginia commented upon the support blacks gave to the war effort. In the Southside county of Mecklenburg, whites praised the "loyal and patriotic attitude of the negroes." Blacks contributed to Liberty Loan drives and War Savings Stamp campaigns. Although segregated, black women formed Red Cross auxiliaries, which made clothing for the troops and sent Christmas cards to the boys in France. Black families joined whites in limiting their consumption of meat, sugar, and flour, all needed for the soldiers. Whites noted the involvement of black schools and churches in emphasizing patriotic themes. The thorough involvement of blacks in the war effort provided whites from the governor on down the opportunity to praise the Old Dominion's race relations as the best in the nation.[7]

The shift to a wartime economy and the conscription of thousands of men in the Old Dominion afforded blacks the chance to enter new occupations and work for higher wages. Black women replaced conscripted men in Greensville County's lumber mills and in factories throughout the state. The high demand for labor even put blacks in Northumberland County on the Northern Neck in a position to refuse to work for a farmer known to have participated in a lynching. Enough work at high wages existed elsewhere.[8]

Black Virginians also demonstrated their support for the war effort by registering for the draft and entering the army. The very notion of arming and training young black men, however, frightened many white southerners. Mississippi senator James Vardaman drew the wrath of African Americans when he warned that arming blacks was more dangerous than a German victory. Joel Springarn of the NAACP explained the Mississippi demagogue's reaction as the embodiment of a general southern feeling that nothing could be worse than "the thought of black millions disciplined, organized, and dangerously effective."[9]

Whites in Virginia did not react so strongly to the notion of armed blacks. One resident of Fluvanna County in the central Piedmont admitted that "it came somewhat as a shock to know that the colored men were to be included in the draft." Nevertheless, many whites in Virginia, especially in the area around Petersburg, focused more on the economic benefits to the region of the army's decision to establish a training facility for black and white conscripts at Camp Lee. The threat of 10,000 armed black men paled in comparison to their impact on the local economy.[10]

Once black men in Virginia began to register for the draft by the thousands, the state's black press turned its attention to lauding the capabilities of black servicemen. Segregated from white draftees, black conscripts received far inferior training, which led to poor performance evaluations and the denial of promotion. The *Norfolk Journal and Guide* devoted many columns to refuting the "prejudiced and skeptical attitudes" of most southern whites, who considered blacks insufficiently courageous to lead in battle. While entire regiments of blacks soldiers serving under French commanders were cited for their bravery during World War I, most blacks remained under American commanders who rarely acknowledged their abilities and assigned them primarily to labor battalions and other noncombat positions. The experience disillusioned and frustrated scores of black soldiers. Sent to France as an observer at the end of the conflict, Du Bois observed firsthand the widespread discrimination that faced black soldiers despite their decision to close ranks. In response, with the war safely won and his patriotism beyond question, Du Bois encouraged black Americans to "return fighting" from the war and to demand their rights as American citizens. Many black veterans heeded Du Bois's call; translating their war-related experiences into greater self-assertiveness and a willingness to protest discrimination and injustice, they emerged in the 1920s as the "New Negro."[11]

Service in France during World War I, on the other hand, forced some whites to see blacks in a new light. Soon after arriving in France, Dr. James D. Fife of Charlottesville wrote his sister Ella that he "saw a couple of American coons today," but he lamented that he had not yet encountered "any of our good old Virginia niggers." Ella, also serving in France as a nurse, reported to their mother, "We see soldiers of every nation—French, British, American, and even a few black niggers." Several months later, toward the end of her posting, Ella revealed a new, albeit tempered, admiration for the abilities of certain blacks. She wrote her sister Madgie:

> I've often wondered what you folks would think if you could see the motley procession. . . . Well, you'd fall off your seat to see some things and you'd hardly believe it unless you saw it. We are very democratic. Yours truly would like to have a dollar for every time I'd sat at the next table to the blackest shines you ever saw—We do everything but eat at the same table with them—At first, we used to laugh and wonder what you'd think but we've gotten used to it now and would feel lonesome without them: The boys sit right next to them and sing with them all the time, even many of the Southern boys, but I'm afraid there are going to be some spoiled darkies coming back home—They have made excellent soldiers, tho, and certainly have done their part. They seem very happy and well satisfied all the time.[12]

Immediately after returning from the war, many black Virginians, in fact, did articulate a clear sense of frustration that no one could have mistaken for happiness or satisfaction. Willis Brown Godwin, twenty-three at the end of the war, a former student at Hampton Institute, and a combat veteran, returned from the war and wondered, "[W]hy can't all the men be treated equally. What did we fight for? Democracy. Are we having it?" Experiences in the war taught William Franklin Banks, also a former student at Hampton, "the value of a man as a man in time of war regardless of color and makes me feel it should be the same in time of peace." Judge Goodwin, a twenty-one-year-old farmer from Dinwiddie County, stated, "I was faithful to my duty and was ready to give all for Democracy. As a Negro, I feel that at least I might have full rights of citizenship." James Waverly Crawley, a railroad employee from Petersburg, remarked that he was "patriotic as any man but as a black man I have felt as if my country did not appreciate my service as a true American."[13]

African Americans throughout Virginia, the South, and the nation echoed both the expectation and disappointment felt by returning veterans. After touring the South, the Reverend C. M. Long of Norfolk noted the growing restlessness of blacks who expected more equitable treatment. S. H. Williamson of the Tidewater Council on Sunday Schools wrote that "during the war promises of better things were made our boys, white and colored. The Negro soldier accepted these promises for their face value." Instead, during the summer of 1919 lynch mobs killed eighty blacks in the South, a number of the victims in uniform, and race riots erupted in twenty-five cities across the nation. The deadliest occurred in Chicago, where thirty-eight people died; that fifteen of them were white indicated that blacks, at least in the North, had indeed returned fighting and would defend themselves with force.[14]

The wave of violence that greeted returning veterans in the summer of 1919 led to the formation of the Commission on Interracial Cooperation. Based in Atlanta, and drawing its membership primarily from the ranks of the South's clergy, university professors, big city newspaper editors, and their wives and daughters, the cic sought to lessen prejudice by bringing together blacks and whites of "good will." The cic's leadership, black and white, had a distinctly urban flavor that reflected the shifting nature of race relations in the 1920s. Not only did most black leaders emerge from a growing middle class fostered by urban segregation, but the locus of interracial contact had shifted to the cities. While the cic vehemently denounced the lynchings that remained a staple of the rural South, the organization concerned itself primarily with easing tensions in rapidly growing urban areas in which traditional means of racial control had begun to erode and friction threatened to escalate into riotous proportions.[15]

In Virginia, as elsewhere in the South, white supporters of the cic led comfortable lives among the region's elites. Many found their way into the organization by way of firm religious convictions; the cic attracted white members especially from institutions of higher learning with denominational affiliations—Randolph-Macon, Lynchburg College, and the University of Richmond. Many had been engaged previously in a variety of reform efforts, including women's suffrage and Progressive Era health, welfare, and educational campaigns. Leaders of the cic eschewed the dire language of Progressives, however, who cloaked their support for reform with fearful warnings of "Negro domination." A handful of interracialists emphasized that humanity and justice were central concerns of the social gospel. Few, however, went so far as Will Alexander, the executive director of the cic, or Lucy Randolph Mason, both of whom made known their conviction that segregation was wrong.[16]

Most Virginia members of the cic, on the other hand, consistently supported a dialogue with black leaders as necessary and desirable to reduce tension, but always within the framework of segregation. They worked safely within accepted racial boundaries that assured the support of the state's press and the non-interference of political leaders. For these elites, interracial cooperation provided a means to the proper management of white supremacy. White interracialists envisioned that, in exchange for an improvement in black living conditions and a reduction in violence, they could prevent blacks from turning to organizations such as the NAACP. Clearly ahead of the majority of whites, who continued to believe in the innate inferiority of African Americans, members of the CIC recognized the possibility of black improvement and encouraged the advancement of blacks but insisted on controlling the pace of such change. In the early 1920s, they maintained room to maneuver, able to advocate uplift on behalf of black Virginians without challenging Jim Crow. Over time, however, blacks became increasingly disenchanted as white interracialists threw up barriers to their quest for full citizenship, exposing once and for all the limits of managed race relations.[17]

Early interracialists sought and depended upon the support of people like Homer Ferguson, the president of the Newport News Shipbuilding and Drydock Company, who employed 4,000 black laborers, more than anyone else in the Old Dominion. Ferguson, like other members of Virginia's small ruling class, combined a sense of self-interest with paternalistic pronouncements that emphasized the friendly relations that existed between blacks and whites in Virginia. In particular, Ferguson urged other business leaders to recognize black labor as a "great asset." He stressed the need for better schools and municipal facilities to encourage blacks to remain in the South at a time when hundreds of thousands migrated North.[18]

The necessity of such support required that all interracial efforts and rhetoric remain intentionally nonthreatening. Norfolk's black newspaper repeatedly emphasized this theme. For instance, an editorial cartoon showed a can labeled "Mutual Interest Frank Discussion of Conditions" watering a plant tagged "Friendly Race Relations." The Tidewater city's white paper remarked with approval that "the clear-sighted leaders of the colored people know that the white people of the South are their true friends."[19]

Early interracial efforts were often framed within appeals to Christian righteousness and in terms of improving the morals of the state's black citizens. The Reverend Walter Russell Bowie, rector of St. Paul's Episcopal Church in Richmond, told his congregation in 1921 that "race integrity must be assured, not for one race, but for both; but equally necessary is a determination to secure for the Negro justice, sympathy, and co-operation in the attainment of his legitimate desires for betterment." The Reverend Dr. Peter Ainslie, another white clergyman, told an audience that the amelioration of racial trouble depended upon a "reconsecration" of the principles of Christianity.[20]

Interracial committees in Suffolk, Norfolk, Danville, Richmond, and

THE RIGHT SOLUTION---LET IT FLOW

In this editorial cartoon from July 1921, the *Norfolk Journal and Guide* expressed its support for the city's nascent interracial committee. (Used with permission of the *Norfolk Journal and Guide*)

outlying rural areas sponsored "Health Weeks" and "Clean-Up Weeks." In Caroline County, the local interracial committee met regularly and focused on health and educational issues. In Charlottesville, whites and blacks created separate committees that considered the abolition of the chain gang and the establishment of a playground for black children.[21]

Women, both black and white, played a critical role in Virginia's early interracial movement. Women's committees worked to secure library facilities for blacks and to stimulate among black women an appreciation for better housing conditions. The Virginia State Federation of Colored Women's Clubs worked through churches and clubs to promote interracial cooperation. Mrs. Lee Britt, the president of the white Women's Missionary Society of the Virginia Methodist Conference, admitted that many of her organization's members "are yet afraid of this question and are shy of having anything to do with it, but as the matter is made clear" most of them came to support the aims of the CIC.[22]

Mrs. G. Harvey Clarke, chair of the CIC Women's Committee, emphasized the opportunity afforded to white women in their relations with domestic servants. In an article intended for the religious press, Clarke wrote that the white home provided the most frequent point of contact between the races "and here the largest chance for helping the colored woman by upright living, intelligent interest and kindness of heart." Although never

Opportunities Found and Lost

specifically addressing class implications in her letter, Clarke clearly referred to elite white women, or at least those able to afford a domestic servant. Elite paternalists, of course, envisioned themselves, not all white women, as capable of providing the necessary guidance for black uplift and advancement. Clarke urged white women with black domestic servants to ask themselves:

1. Do we realize that the negro who lives in our home receives there an influence which is not only personal, but which reaches into the lives of other colored people, and makes for harmony and friendliness, or for discord and, perhaps, hatred?

2. Do we as Christian women realize our obligation to be a friend to the maid in our home, and to make the Golden Rule our guide in dealing with her?

3. How much personal interest do we show the colored girl who serves us — as to her associates, her church connections, and her amusements during the hours she is off duty?

4. Do we set an example of moral and Christian conduct before the maid who looks on with observing eyes — an example of truthfulness, temperance, and gentleness of manner?

5. Do we regard the comfort and welfare of those who serve us, requiring of them in this respect no more than we are willing to render to them?

6. In other words — do we the white women of the home feel a responsibility to bring about more friendly relations, and better understanding between the white and colored races, and thus make for greater harmony in our domestic life as well as in our community life?[23]

Clarke, however, did not stress only the paternalistic obligations of white women toward their black maids. She also emphasized that black women had a corresponding "duty to be honest, to be truthful, to be polite, to be cleanly, to be on time in performing her tasks." Clarke added that black girls and women should not expect a full day's wages if late for work and, furthermore, that white women must help them appreciate that better wages would only follow an efficient performance of their duties.[24]

While the very presence of state and local interracial committees signaled an evolution in the Old Dominion's race relations, no amount of "clean-up weeks" or "health weeks" could possibly have addressed the pervasive and persistent neglect of black standards of living perpetuated and reinforced by Jim Crow. Gordon Blaine Hancock, a Baptist minister, a professor of sociology at Virginia Union University, and a black member of Richmond's interracial group, once described segregation as "a form of elimination," citing disease, infant mortality, low life expectancy, and soaring crime rates as examples of eliminative influences that affected the standard of living of African Americans. Black residential areas, almost without exception, lacked paved streets, lighting, and sewage. Black children had minimal access to recreational facilities enjoyed by whites. And even in a seaside community like Norfolk, black families lacked access to the miles of beaches that provided relief from the heat of summer. In the years just after World War I, whites consistently failed to address such needs.[25]

Evidence of neglect permeated the state. Just before World War I, social scientist Gustavus Weber found black housing in Richmond "'poorly lighted, unventilated, damp, imperfectly drained, exposed to undue fire peril, in bad repair, vermin infested, with unclean surroundings, with insufficient water supply, without toilet accommodations adequate for comfort, cleanliness or privacy, with defective plumbing, with over-crowded rooms, and with cellar tenements.'" Little was done in the wake of Weber's findings, as a series of reports and surveys over the next two decades found conditions unchanged. By 1940, some of the worst slum housing in the nation was located in Richmond and Norfolk.[26]

Throughout Virginia, black leaders denounced the failure of municipal administrations to provide basic services. Not one street in the black residential area of Roanoke was paved in 1921. In Portsmouth, the Reverend Dr. O. C. Jones preached about such inequalities and pointed out that streets in white sections of town had been oiled to keep down the dust, but that in black households, residents found it impossible to keep dust out of their homes every time an automobile passed by. In March 1922 some black sections of Norfolk had roads reported as impassable because of rain. By the end of the decade, blacks in Richmond still suffered "the plague of dust in summer and the bane of mud in winter." Black and white children who grew up on Charlottesville's Ridge Street remembered that the road was only half-paved, and that "'of course the blacks lived . . . where the road narrowed and was no longer paved.'" Some black children would leave their homes bound for church in their worn-out shoes and only change into their dress shoes when they reached the paved portion of the street.[27]

Throughout the 1920s blacks and some whites became increasingly vocal in their demand for recreational facilities for black citizens. In April 1921 the Norfolk Kiwanis Club unanimously endorsed the recommendation of Robert Coates, described as a prominent white citizen, to urge the city council to provide recreational facilities for black children. Coates claimed to have been moved by watching black children "'gazing with longing eyes

Opportunities Found and Lost

and envious hearts upon the scenes of gaiety participated in by white children.'" Nearly a year later, the Norfolk City Council voted three to two to purchase land for such a park.[28]

When yet another year passed and no new facilities for blacks had been built, John P. Pitt, described as a "substantial white citizen," objected in a letter to the *Norfolk Virginian-Pilot.* Sympathizing with the frustration felt by African Americans throughout Virginia, Pitt wrote at a time when Norfolk had recently constructed a golf course and tennis courts and had discussed a campground to add to the facilities available to whites yet maintained only four inadequate schoolyard playgrounds for the use of the city's blacks. Pitt underscored the injustice of such an arrangement and condemned "the oversensitive views of those who mistake every step toward fair treatment and a square deal as an advance towards social equality." In conclusion, he suggested that anyone capable of clear thought and reason would recognize his position.[29]

Responding to Pitt's article and the continued refusal of the city manager to approve a site for the new park, Norfolk's black newspaper wrote that "what puzzles and humiliates colored people most is the facility with which the objectors can bob up whenever and wherever a suggestion is made that something be done for the betterment of the condition of the Negroes. It doesn't matter where it is, or what is suggested, whether it be a park, hospital, bathing beach, school, church, residence or what not the objectors are ever there if they see color in it." Whites objected repeatedly that proposed facilities for blacks were too close to white areas or that public funds would be better spent on projects to benefit white taxpayers. Five years later, the park still remained unbuilt while whites enjoyed at least twenty different public facilities, including golf courses, tennis courts, swimming pools, and campgrounds. The delays and frustrations in obtaining a single park reflect what historian Earl Lewis has referred to as the "harsh realities of urban racial paternalism." Lacking significant political influence, African Americans in Norfolk and elsewhere in Virginia found themselves dependent on the always tenuous "good graces of whites."[30]

Most members of Virginia's state and local interracial committees focused their energies on improving basic services, but Robert Kerlin, an early supporter of the cic, understood that any fundamental improvement in race relations required a great deal more than encouraging the moral uplift of the Old Dominion's black citizens. A professor of English at the Virginia Military Institute (vmi) and a former Methodist clergyman, Kerlin recognized a need to drastically transform the practical application of the legal system so that blacks were not solely dependent on the whims of white officials for their physical safety. Kerlin drew upon his perceived Christian duty to demand that whites speak out in opposition to obvious injustice, whenever and wherever it occurred. The Board of Visitors at VMI, however, understood Kerlin's duty in different terms and fired him for his response to an outbreak of racial violence in Phillips County, Arkansas. If the majority of elites involved in interracial work delineated the contours of acceptable interracial behavior, Kerlin overstepped those boundaries.

In October 1919, at the end of a year that witnessed eighty lynchings and at least twenty-five race riots throughout the United States, shooting erupted in Phillips County. When the carnage ended, official reports listed five whites and twenty-five blacks as dead. Other sources suggested that whites had killed as many as one hundred blacks. Whites claimed that they acted to break up a black tenant union that had been "'established for the purpose of banding Negroes together for the killing of white people.'" In fact, the union had formed in an effort to prevent landlords from cheating sharecroppers out of their rightful earnings and to address concerns that many agricultural workers were actually being held in a state of peonage. The white version, however, provided the official explanation, and before long, twelve blacks had been sentenced to death and more than fifty to prison.[31]

In June 1921, soon after a date of execution had been set for six of the condemned tenant farmers, Kerlin wrote "An Open Letter to the Governor of Arkansas" that appeared in *The Nation*. The VMI professor told Governor Thomas C. McRae that the impending execution constituted "a deed to be contemplated with extreme horror" and urged him "to take the matter into your private chamber and give it an hour's earnest consideration, as before the Eternal Judge." Kerlin addressed the gross "iniquities of the peonage system" and reminded the governor that appeals court proceedings proved that the tenant farmers had taken up arms only in self-defense. Furthermore, the trials of ninety-two men had occurred "without legal counsel, without witnesses, without knowledge of court procedures," and a number of the defendants "were whipped, tortured in electric chairs, and terrorized into pleading guilty to murder in the second degree."[32]

Drawing upon Christian imagery, Kerlin urged McRae to resist the weight of white public opinion in Arkansas and in the South and to "stand for the eternal right against all consequence, stand as a champion of human nature, a vindicator of human dignity." The professor informed the governor that "Heaven itself has appointed you for this redemptive act. To thrust it aside were to dent God." A native of Missouri and a child

Opportunities Found and Lost

of two Kentuckians, Kerlin assured McRae that he descended from the "same stock and traditions" as the people of Arkansas and wanted only that "they with you may rise in moral courage to meet this test and stand not in disgrace but in honor before the world."[33]

Less than a week after the letter's publication, Kerlin was hauled before the Board of Visitors at VMI to explain his actions. Unmoved by the professor's interpretation of the gospel, the board told him it felt "inclined to consider your action in criticizing the conduct of the courts in a sister-State . . . as not only indiscreet but most improper and injurious to this Institution." Kerlin responded that he saw "nothing indiscreet or improper" in his actions and considered it a duty to speak up in the face of obvious injustice. He disagreed that he had harmed the Institute in any way and wondered exactly what was meant by such a charge. In fact, Kerlin argued, his actions ought to be viewed as "exemplary," especially in a military school "where the fundamental virtues of manhood, of courage in action, and justice in thought and action are inculcated and developed." Kerlin even suggested that his efforts would benefit VMI, "inasmuch as it will attract to its instruction and discipline parents who desire their sons to be taught by men who stand for right and justice at whatever cost."[34]

The Board of Visitors postponed making any decisions until later in the summer. The Institute's superintendent, however, told Kerlin that he expected the board to ask for his resignation. When the call finally came to reappear before the school's trustees on August 20, Kerlin prepared to lose his job. At the June meeting, board members had refused Kerlin's request to discuss his letter in the broader context of his interracial work in the South. Just before the August meeting, he sent Herbert Seligmann, director of publicity for the NAACP, a copy of the defense that he hoped to put before the board and asked that Seligmann make it public in the event he lost his job. Although clearly expecting to be fired, Kerlin added, almost as an afterthought, "I have no independent income and no capital—I am entirely dependent on my salary and have wife and three young children to support. Dismissal would be materially calamitous."[35]

Three days before the August meeting, Kerlin wrote Seligmann in an attempt to clarify his previous correspondence. He asked that the NAACP not be the first organization to release news of his dismissal, if and when it occurred. His intention, rather, was that Seligmann get the news and Kerlin's defense out through white press organizations. Kerlin explained that "I expect to continue living in the South to the bitter or the triumphant end. I do not wish to lose what advantage there belongs to being a Southerner in birth, rearing, and residence. And I do not wish to seem to alienate myself from the forward-moving enlightened portion of the Southern people." Kerlin's caution reflected the harsh difficulty of his position; in the early 1920s most white elites envisioned interracial work, at least in part, as a means of preventing blacks from cooperating with the NAACP. That a white southerner corresponded with the civil rights organization was tantamount to treason.[36]

Kerlin delivered to the Board of Visitors the defense that he had hoped to present in June. In a seven-page letter, he attempted to place his plea to the governor of Arkansas in the broader context of his own interracial activities, as well as the growing interracial movement in Virginia and the South. Kerlin explained that after ten years of involvement with the University Commission on Southern Race Questions, a group of college professors and students dedicated to bringing thoughtful leadership to questions of racial adjustment, he had recently turned his attention to the work of the CIC. Emphasizing the inherently conservative work of both organizations, Kerlin asserted that he had "never given utterances to a single idea on the question of the Negro and his status and treatment in our civil society which is not in accord with the soundest traditions of the South." Kerlin insisted that his goal "has been solely to promote such inter-racial adjustment as would secure to both races the fullest measure of prosperity and happiness, with mutual good-will and co-operation instead of perpetual friction and frequent outbursts of mob violence that disgrace and imperil our civilization."[37]

So as not to appear a lone voice in a hostile South, the embattled professor attempted to legitimize his own actions by repeatedly emphasizing the involvement of southern governors, university presidents, and church officials in all of these matters. He laid before the Board of Visitors positive press reports of his various speeches and activities. He cited personal commendations from well-known and well-respected white leaders in black education and referred to the enthusiastic reviews and clear sociological value of *The Voice of the Negro*, a compilation of thought from black newspapers that he had edited. Ever mindful of the reason the board sought to dismiss him, Kerlin quoted the *Arkansas Democrat*, which had said of his book: "'In this compilation made with sympathy and knowledge from the colored press of America . . . we have a true cross-section of the Negro mind, which will be admitted of primary importance in the vital and necessary work of getting to know the Negro and of giving him justice and the rights of a citizen.'"[38]

Referring to other well-respected southerners involved in interracial work, Kerlin insisted that "without agitation or appeal to passion, but only by addressing the sense of justice and of Christian duty, these men, with whom I rank myself, are seeking to bring about a juster, safer, and

Opportunities Found and Lost

more Christian order of society as regards the Negroes, to secure for them such fairness and humanity of treatment as will reduce the problem to its lowest possible terms and guarantee ourselves against the reproaches which otherwise we can not escape." Kerlin reminded his judges that his work would not end if he were fired, asserting that "I can safely challenge anyone to adduce a single utterance of mine which goes beyond what I have here cited as representing the growing and prevailing sentiment of the South."[39]

Not swayed by Kerlin's pronouncement, nor by his eleven years of service at the school, the Board of Visitors of VMI fired him for actions it considered "harmful and detrimental," and therefore "embarrassing," to the school. In the days following, Kerlin expressed confidence that the governor of Virginia might not approve the board's action and indicated that he had received numerous professions of support from VMI alumni. He told one supporter that he remained certain that "a double cause — academic freedom and justice to the Negro — will result." The governor, however, refused to overturn the board's decision.[40]

Editorial opinion throughout the nation, including a number of newspapers in the South, defended Kerlin. Two leading dailies in the Old Dominion added their support to the embattled professor. The *Norfolk Virginian-Pilot* praised Kerlin's even-handed approach to racial issues and found him eminently qualified to "discuss our major social problems without prejudice." The *Richmond Times-Dispatch* derided Kerlin's dismissal as an attack on academic freedom and free speech but expressed even greater concern that the episode threatened to undermine Virginia's sound management of race relations.[41]

The *Southern Workman*, published by Hampton Institute, praised the *Times-Dispatch* and other southern papers that came to Kerlin's defense but simultaneously challenged the limited reach of that support. The monthly periodical remarked that "even those who call themselves liberals in the matter of race adjustment move slowly in contrast with those who see clearly certain wrongs and who wish, in the spirit of the martyrs, to see those wrongs wiped out." The definition of a racial liberal in the South evolved in the 1920s and 1930s, but in 1921 a liberal might have been anyone who advocated interracial dialogue and emphasized the need for harmony and understanding. As the *Southern Workman* recognized, these liberals never questioned the rightness of segregation and, as a result, moved ever so slowly. Kerlin, by contrast, witnessed obvious injustice and sought to eliminate it. Despite his best efforts to convince the VMI Board of Visitors that his views remained safely within the mainstream of southern thought, Kerlin's thoughts, words, and deeds suggested otherwise.[42]

After he was fired, freed from the constraints of maintaining his position on the VMI faculty, Kerlin revealed the extent to which he was out of step with acceptable white southern opinion. In June 1922 he appeared before an audience at the True Reformers Hall in Richmond and openly professed his opposition to segregation. He apparently made similar stops in other southern cities. Several days after Kerlin's address, members of the *News Leader* Current Events Class, comprised of Richmond's business and professional elites, gathered for their weekly meeting and discussed the professor's speech. According to the minutes of that night's forum, those in attendance expressed concern over Kerlin's association with the NAACP. Class founder and leader Douglas Southall Freeman, the editor of the *Richmond News Leader*, "explained the actions and utterances of Kerlin by saying that the man was crazy." Freeman, an early and enthusiastic supporter of the CIC who wielded substantial influence in Richmond and throughout the state, spoke for many of his peers, who demanded clear limits to interracial dialogue and activity. Most white elites, even those who championed racial uplift, simply did not contemplate an end to segregation; any suggestion to the contrary could not be explained except as a mental deficiency.[43]

Will Alexander, the executive director of the CIC, well recognized the distinct boundaries within which he and other interracialists had to operate. He generally avoided discussing segregation itself, but in response to a question, Alexander once acknowledged his personal belief that segregation was "unjust" and morally indefensible. His admission stunned a group of white ministers, who denounced him as unsuitable to lead future interracial efforts. Although Alexander was able to salvage his job, the uproar ensured that he did not repeat the remark in public. This circumscribed atmosphere meant that southern interracial activity in the 1920s and 1930s addressed only the most obvious inequities of Jim Crow—substandard housing, education, recreational facilities, and transportation—but never the causes. "Clean-up weeks" and "health days" may have served a useful purpose, but black Virginians remained second-class citizens who lacked access to political and economic power. Robert Kerlin, and one suspects Will Alexander as well, understood that only the eradication of white supremacy in all its vestiges—political, social, and economic—would satisfy a genuine commitment to social justice. While at VMI, Kerlin tried to skate along the narrow line of acceptability, but he ultimately crossed the border. Alexander momentarily stepped over the line but pulled himself back, a pragmatist who thought he could do the most good from within the CIC. Only a handful of southern radicals in the 1920s and 1930s were willing to directly confront segregation and the economic injustice that remained unchanged by the efforts of the CIC. However, in the words of one historian, these individuals always moved "against the grain" of legitimacy in the South, and their voices were never acknowledged by those who made the decisions in the parlors, boardrooms, and legislative halls of the Old Dominion.[44]

Kerlin's firing may have harmed recent gains in interracial cooperation, as one Richmond newspaper suggested, but the reintroduction of blacks as political scapegoats caused far more damage. Beginning in 1915 and increasing in intensity throughout the decade, antisuffragists pandered to racial fears in an attempt to discourage support for women's suffrage. Suffragists saw the inclusion of black female voters as posing no threat to white supremacy; they reasoned that the state's election laws had effectively eliminated black men from the polls and would do the same with women. Despite this commonsense logic, antisuffragists warned of impending danger. Leading newspapers such as the *Newport News Daily Press* and the *Winchester Evening Star* argued that black women would prove more qualified than their male counterparts and register in greater numbers. Historian Suzanne Lebsock has concluded that "the antis as a group were willing to say anything that might strengthen their cause; there were no minimal standards of either decency or truthfulness to which they held themselves or anyone else." Consequently, the more moderate suffragists found themselves boxed into a corner, unable to respond for fear of being charged with endangering white supremacy.[45]

The debate over women's suffrage in Virginia shifted in August 1920 when the requisite number of states adopted the Nineteenth Amendment. Ratification occurred in time for women to register for the November presidential elections. Throughout September, newspapers carried daily counts of the numbers of white and black women who had signed up. Although final tallies revealed that 2,410 black women and 10,645 white women qualified in Richmond, the same newspapers that boasted of Virginia's friendly race relations warned that black women outnumbered whites among new registrants. The *Richmond News Leader* informed its readers, in a tone laced with disapproval over a breach in racial etiquette, that on one occasion black women filled the offices of the registrar while white women waited in the hall. The Richmond dailies appeared particularly troubled by the activities of Maggie Walker, a leading African American activist who poured her energy into registering black women.[46]

In a matter of weeks, the ratification of the Nineteenth Amendment had forced Democratic party leaders and pro-Democratic newspapers to reverse their position. Politicians and newspapers had almost unanimously

opposed women's suffrage, employing explicitly white supremacist arguments to defeat what the *Richmond News Leader* referred to as the "obnox-
ious amendment." But once forced to confront the reality of women's suffrage, the same people used further appeals to white supremacy "to scare
white women into behaving like good Democrats." For instance, John M.
Purcell, the chairman of the Richmond Democratic Committee, issued
a statement to all Democratic women in the city that warned of "an ap-
proaching crisis in the matter of feminine registration" and declared it
"the duty of every woman who regards the domination of the white race
as essential to the welfare of the Southland to qualify for the ballot by paying her poll tax and registering before Oct. 2." Similar appeals went out
from state headquarters.[47]

That white Virginians could have seriously worried that black women
would register in greater numbers than white woman seems unlikely,
given that whites thoroughly controlled every aspect of election machinery, from registration and payment of poll taxes to the appointment of
election judges. As A. W. Hunton discovered in October 1920 when he
visited Hampton on behalf of the NAACP, black registrants faced overwhelming odds. While in Hampton, where a disproportionately large
number of middle-class and professional blacks lived in connection with
Hampton Institute, Hunton interviewed more than twenty black women
who had attempted to register. He reported that no more than fifty out
of over a thousand eligible black women succeeded in registering. Many
aspirants, according to Hunton, "noting the humiliation or anger of their
sisters as they returned from the registration bureau, would not go at all."
Many of those who did attempt to enroll had to return two or three times,
the humiliation increasing with each visit.[48]

Black women watched as their white counterparts, many of them also
affiliated with Hampton Institute, registered in two or three minutes,
while they waited for hours. Hunton explained that all registrants received
a number upon arrival, but white numbers started at one, while black
numbers began at forty. Consequently, white women who arrived after
black women still received lower numbers. More than a few black women
waited until the office closed for the day; they were told to return in the
morning.[49]

Among those black women lucky enough to have their number called,
most were handed a blank application and told to write down all necessary information. White applicants, on the other hand, received a form
listing exactly what was required. Many black women had anticipated
such obstacles, a common practice faced by many of their husbands, and
memorized the necessary information. They then faced a litany of ques-

tions aimed at disqualifying them, most of them irrelevant except that they were successfully used to prevent many blacks from voting.[50]

The experience of Mrs. Charles Isham, the wife of Hampton Institute's electrician, epitomized the obstacles confronted by black women in Hampton. She attempted to register the first possible day, received a blank application form, and was asked a number of questions, including "How many people does it take to make a county?" According to Hunton, Isham "questioned very boldly the right to ask her so many questions and keep her when the white teachers were being registered in about a half minute while she waited." The registrar sent her home with instructions not to return until summoned.[51]

Despite the instructions of the registrar, Isham returned the following day with Mrs. Allen Washington. The two women were greeted by the clerk of court. According to Hunton's reports, the clerk initially "was courteous to Mrs. Washington, thinking she was white." Upon learning the name of her husband, however, the clerk's demeanor changed, "he whispered to the registrar," and "boldly told Mrs. Washington that he did not intend to be bothered with a lot of colored women." Instead, he "intended to just let a few register."[52]

The shabby treatment faced by black aspirants continued until G. W. Fields acted in response to his wife's failed attempt to register. Mrs. Fields had expected difficulty and studied thoroughly the requirements of a successful application. The registrar, she later recounted, actually complimented her "on its perfection." The official, nevertheless, told Mrs. Fields that she had failed to provide correct responses to the questions he had put forward, such as, "1. How is Supt. of public instruction elected? 2. How are vacancies filled and what is his term of office? 3. What is the maximum and minimum number of section districts in the State of Virginia?" No white applicants were asked such questions.[53]

Mr. Fields, an attorney, consulted with a white Republican lawyer and threatened to file a lawsuit. Apparently registration officials feared that the whole county would be disqualified if the threatened suit succeeded. Soon after Mr. Fields appealed the situation, a number of black women received letters from officials stating that they could now register. Many others, however, chose not to endure further humiliation, while still others stayed away after being threatened with a loss of employment. Mrs. Fields remarked that when she was first turned away, the registrar assumed she would not return after suffering "humiliation in the presence of white men and women." Although finally successful in registering, Mrs. Washington and Mrs. Isham expressed extreme bitterness and anger at their treatment. The experience of the black women in Hampton prompted A. W. Hunton to comment that he had found the majority of these people to be among the "most patient and conservative" persons that he knew. "One of the strongest proofs of the enormity of the humiliation and injustice to which the women were subjected," he continued, "is the vehement freedom with which they recite their grievances and the desire not only for redress but in many cases vengeance."[54]

The humiliation and anger suffered by black women attempting to register in 1920 was exacerbated by the decision of the Republican Party in 1921 to sever all ties to the state's black voters. Driven by the personal ambition of a few key individuals and buoyed by stronger than expected results in the 1920 presidential elections, Virginia's moribund Republican Party showed signs of new life in 1921. Insofar as a rigidly restricted electorate had ensured the dominance of the Democratic Party, any Republican renaissance in the Old Dominion depended upon an expansion of the voting pool. Newly enfranchised female voters offered one possibility, but Republican ties to the few qualified black voters in the state, not to mention memories of Reconstruction, continued to discredit the party in the eyes of the white majority.[55]

Both parties stressed the need to register women voters during the 1921 gubernatorial campaign. Democratic party organizers like state senator Harry F. Byrd of Winchester urged fellow Democrats to undertake a "reorganization of the county in a quiet way. It is most necessary that all women who are favorable to our side be registered and that their poll taxes be paid." Byrd's emphasis reflected the experience of William F. Keyser, an attorney and friend of Byrd's in Page County, who found that "our farmers are so bitterly opposed to their women registering that they will not let our canvassers approach them as a rule." Byrd reported that "the intense partisanship and the excessive activity" of a Republican recruiter had damaged that party's cause and underscored the need to handle the issue of female suffrage in a delicate manner.[56]

As Democrats and Republicans competed for female support, the *Norfolk Ledger-Dispatch*, a pro-Democratic paper, reminded its readers that the Republican Party could not easily "rid itself of the incubus it has borne ever since the war between the States." Deeply aware that most white Virginians, especially those who voted, remained suspicious of its motives, the Virginia Republican Party voted in July 1921 to bar black delegates from its convention. On the same day, the party nominated for governor Henry Watkins Anderson, a fifty-year-old lawyer from Richmond who grew up in Dinwiddie County in Virginia's heavily black Southside. In his acceptance speech, the nominee attacked the structure of political rule in Vir-

Opportunities Found and Lost

ginia. Echoing a growing number of southerners concerned with meeting the requirements of a modern society, Anderson argued that the slower rate of economic progress in Virginia as compared to North Carolina, the sorry state of schools and highways, and the disproportionate number of public officials in relation to voters resulted from one-party rule that "leads inevitably to stagnation and inefficiency, the decline of intellectual, political and economic life, and ultimately, unless changed, to the destruction of all freedom." In particular, Anderson objected to the adoption of the 1902 constitution, which he considered antidemocratic and illegal because it had not been submitted to the populace for ratification.[57]

Precisely because he appealed for greater political participation on the part of Virginia's citizenry, in and of itself a matter of concern to the state's small ruling class, the Republican nominee felt compelled to distance himself and his party even further from the state's black voters. In his acceptance speech, Anderson addressed directly "a question, the existence of which is the chief excuse urged for the present Constitution — the Race Question." Acknowledging that the experiments of Reconstruction constituted a grave mistake, Anderson reminded his audience that no African American had held office in Virginia for thirty years, and that no black sought to do so in 1921. The Republican nominee asked that the facts be allowed to speak for themselves and noted that whites in Virginia comprised more than two-thirds of the population, owned 95 percent of the property, were more educated than most blacks, and thoroughly controlled the mechanisms and institutions of local and state government. Black Virginians, in short, had been removed from the political process. In nonthreatening and deeply paternalistic terms, the Republican nominee concluded "that the solution of this question lies in the spirit of mutual sympathy and understanding, not in political agitation; that their future happiness and prosperity is to be attained not through politics, but by hard work, and the development of personal character."[58]

A number of influential Virginians, including Douglas Southall Freeman and his publisher, John Stewart Bryan, admired Anderson personally and shared his belief that a modern industrial state required better government than that which Virginia currently offered. Bryan, in fact, even considered giving the *Richmond News Leader*'s endorsement to the Republican candidate. Freeman, however, prevailed upon Bryan to withhold such an endorsement. Although he acknowledged the shortcomings of the state's Democratic leadership, Freeman rejected the claim of Anderson and the Republicans that they could expand the electorate without threatening the primacy of white supremacy. Republican rule, he editorialized, meant "the reenfranchisement of those who were taken out of politics in

1902." Freeman clearly preferred a flawed Democratic Party that "makes no pretense to be any other than a white man's party."[59]

Although Freeman, like most Democrats, rejected Anderson's contention that the electorate could be expanded without threatening white supremacy, he and Anderson shared essential assumptions about the appropriate "place" for African Americans in the modern industrial state that they both championed. Freeman and Anderson argued for more responsive government that would provide infrastructure and expanded educational opportunities essential for growth and development, but neither saw any contradiction between modernization and segregation. As Freeman articulated editorially, however, such development did require the cooperation of blacks and whites if either race was to advance. His support of the cic followed logically. Although Democrats would not accept African Americans into the body politic, Freeman explained that they did embrace their "duty . . . to see that the negro has decent living conditions, educational facilities and absolute justice in the courts of law." In nearly thirty-five years as editor of the *News Leader*, Freeman rarely stated so succinctly the essence of the paternalism that guided managed race relations in the Old Dominion.[60]

Black Virginians, especially that small number among the professional and middle classes who had continued to vote after the adoption of the 1902 constitution, reacted with disgust, although not necessarily surprise, to the Republican Party's lily-white pronouncement in 1921. At the previous year's state convention, white Republicans had essentially ignored black members of the party. In an unsuccessful attempt to prove that the white Republicans needed their votes, black Republicans ran Joseph Pollard of Richmond for the U.S. Senate when party officials decided not to oppose the Democratic incumbent. By 1921, the anger felt by black Republicans stemmed not only from a sense of betrayal, but also from the fact that the convention barred from participation black delegates selected through regular channels. Dr. Edward T. Morton left the convention hall with a white colleague after officials refused to seat him. John Robinson of Hampton, a former member of the state legislature during Reconstruction, had been elected a delegate by a local gathering dominated by white Republicans; he, too, was barred from participation.[61]

The *Norfolk Journal and Guide* pointed the finger directly at the recently elected Harding administration. No previous administration, explained the Tidewater weekly, had sanctioned such treatment, which in effect allowed Virginia's Republican leadership to endorse precisely the sort of chicanery that Democrats had sanctioned for decades. The *Journal and*

Guide emphasized the small role that blacks had played in the Republican Party the previous twenty years, noted the inconsequential number of minor offices held by blacks, and concluded that the Republican attack on blacks constituted a desire "to manufacture the sort of propaganda that it requires to seduce a Democrat." [62]

Black political leaders, however, could not agree on the most appropriate response and quickly divided into camps led by the editors of Virginia's two leading black newspapers, P. B. Young of the *Norfolk Journal and Guide* and John Mitchell of the *Richmond Planet*. The two men had emerged as rivals during World War I when Mitchell urged blacks to migrate North, while Young insisted that African Americans faced a more certain and prosperous future in the South. Young and Mitchell offered contrasting styles and philosophies of leadership that reflected growing divisions among black southerners as to how best confront the stark realities of white supremacy. Young emerged in the 1910s and 1920s as the leading proponent in Virginia of what his biographer has called "Washingtonian militance." In the columns of his newspaper and in private utterances, Young championed Booker T. Washington's emphasis on self-help and hard work, not political activism, as the key to improving the living conditions of African Americans. For Young, better jobs and higher wages would eventually lead to a stronger political voice. But in the meantime, Young's pragmatism guided his acceptance of a certain amount of accommodation with segregation. He considered it useless to challenge segregation itself and consequently remained ambivalent about the more confrontational approach of labor unions and the NAACP. Young recognized the inequities of Jim Crow and worked passionately for better schools and paved streets, but always without challenging segregation itself. Instead, Young cultivated relationships with influential whites and urged interracial cooperation, although always adhering to the social parameters established by these whites. Prejudice, he believed, would eventually wither away with the right sort of cooperation. For two decades, Young continued to advocate this pragmatic brand of conservative militance. When he shifted gears at the height of World War II, white elites were left speechless, stunned to discover that they did not, in fact, understand Young at all. [63]

John Mitchell, on the other hand, rejected the caution and conservatism of black leaders like Young and advocated a greater degree of activism in fighting the inequities of Jim Crow. Although observers North and South alternately embraced and condemned the emergence of the younger and more militant "New Negro" in the aftermath of World War I, Mitchell's differences with Young were not generational. Born a slave in

1863, Mitchell was actually twenty years older than Young, but he possessed a restless spirit intent on eliminating racial repression and discrimination. At the turn of the century, Mitchell orchestrated a boycott of Richmond's segregated streetcars. Although unsuccessful in integrating public transportation, the boycott did force the transit company into bankruptcy. Mitchell ran advertisements for guns in his newspaper and remarked that armed blacks, willing to use their weapons, would earn the respect of whites. He eagerly embraced the NAACP and used the *Planet* to support its efforts until his death in 1929. Mitchell, however, was not reckless; he understood the need to appear affable and to avoid being labeled a "dangerous Negro." He, too, considered it necessary at times to proclaim the friendship of whites and blacks in the Old Dominion.[64]

After the declaration of the Republican Party in 1921, a number of blacks responded with an all-black convention in Richmond in September and elected a full slate of candidates for the November elections: Mitchell for governor, Theodore Nash of Newport News for lieutenant governor, and Thomas Newsome of Newport News for attorney general. The black convention offered P. B. Young the number two slot on the ticket, but he declined. Young shared with the convention the desire to be heard politically, but he openly denounced the tactics and strategy of the third-party campaign as "political suicide." Young understood that votes mattered most in politics and failed to see how blacks might leverage their weight, no matter how minimal, as a third party. Furthermore, he considered an all-black party no better than an all-white one, both guaranteed to stir racial tensions.[65]

In the weeks following the all-black convention, the cleavage between the two camps widened and the attacks became more personal. Young, driven in part by personal jealousy of Mitchell and wounded pride at not having been offered the top spot on the ticket, claimed "that the small group that is the inspiration of the lily black ticket are seekers after glory, honor, publicity and self-aggrandizement, rather than the good of the whole people, whom they presume to represent." Thomas Newsome challenged Young's conclusion and asked what was so wrong with blacks seeking office, especially once they had been thrown out of the Republican Party. Objecting to claims that they endangered interracial cooperation, the all-black proponents emphasized that they did not advocate social equality but rather demanded "to be treated as other citizens with all the rights, privileges, and immunities accorded them, including the right to vote, and to be voted for." Without naming names, supporters of the all-black ticket hurled invectives at their black opponents, labeled them "'white folks' Negroes,'" and claimed that any self-respecting black would support the ticket. As a result, the two factions nearly came to blows at a rally in Portsmouth in mid-October.[66]

The decision of Virginia's white Republicans to cast aside their black supporters did not deter the Democrats from making race an issue throughout the fall. Democrats understood that Anderson and the Republicans had cut their ties to blacks in an effort to appeal to newly enfranchised white women, just as had occurred in the North Carolina gubernatorial campaign the year before. But rather than granting that the maneuver removed blacks from politics, Democrats argued that Republicans had only worsened the situation by attempting to bring white women into a party with black men, and now black women. Mixing racial and sexual demagoguery, the most potent combination of all, Democrats assailed their opponents, asking, "Who introduced the Black man into politics in the South? Who enfranchised him? Who sat him in the legislatures of the Southern States, including Virginia, during the days of the Carpet-Bagger and of Reconstruction? Who is it now who would introduce the negro woman as a political factor in Virginia?" Democrats charged that Anderson's proposals would allow for the "promiscuous participation" of every black man and woman in the Old Dominion. Most reprehensible of all, according to the Democrats, Anderson appealed to "the white women of Virginia for assistance. Such an invitation is an insult to his own intelligence, to Southern womanhood, and to the State at large."[67]

In his opening campaign speech several weeks later, E. Lee Trinkle, the Democratic nominee, accused the Republicans of pure political expediency "in avowing their purpose to rip the colored man from the body of Virginia Republicanism, and this they did by a scheme of impudent political lawlessness." Trinkle did not make clear, however, why he deemed the new Republican policy lawless when Democrats had long barred blacks from their primaries. He did point out, on the other hand, that Democrats had never enticed African Americans with promises of false hopes, perhaps scoring points for honesty if not for a broad understanding of democracy.[68]

Anderson's campaign literature announced to voters that he had made the Republicans "a party of white citizens" and that he championed a revision of the 1902 constitution, "which was conceived in distrust of the people and born of a breach of faith." Democrats responded that no Virginian was fooled by the Republican nominee's rhetoric, and that, in fact, the very constitution that Anderson attacked was "the bulwark erected to save Virginia from negro participation in politics." This constitution, according to the Democrats, "made Virginia a white man's commonwealth."[69]

In the ensuing weeks, Anderson continued to press for a revision of the election laws, while maintaining that an expanded electorate did not necessitate a reintroduction of blacks into politics. Indeed, the Republican nominee challenged his opponent to a debate on the "race question." In refusing the offer to meet face to face, Trinkle and Congressman Hal D. Flood, the state Democratic Party chairman, claimed that racial matters had not been an issue in Virginia for twenty years until Anderson revived them in his platform and speeches. Trinkle and Flood attacked Anderson's proposals to revise the poll tax and registration requirements. "The Democratic party," the two stated in a joint attack on Anderson, "has erected reasonable barriers to the elective franchise. You would take them down. The Democratic party has succeeded in eliminating from the electorate the bulk of the negro vote in the Commonwealth. You would invite them all back into the electorate, including the women. . . . The only conclusion to be drawn from your platform is that you want every negro to vote." Trinkle and Flood emphasized that blacks constituted a majority of the population in more than one-fourth of the counties of the state. Playing to white fears but ignoring the truth of Reconstruction, when black Republicans served in the Virginia General Assembly and in the U.S. Congress, but never in proportion to their percentage of the population, the Democratic leaders claimed that blacks would assume control of local government in these counties if granted the franchise. "The white people of Virginia need no discussion of the race question," concluded Trinkle and Flood. "They have long ago made up their minds that this State or no county in it shall be dominated and controlled by the colored race."[70]

As the campaign moved into its final week, U.S. senator and former governor Claude A. Swanson joined the fray and summarized all the arguments in favor of white supremacy. "If the Republican candidates should be elected at this time," began the senator, "it means the injection of the negro into politics in Virginia again, it would mean the elimination of all restrictions upon suffrage which have had the effect of disbarring the negro and preventing him from being potential as a voter in politics in Virginia. The return of the negro as a political factor would be a detriment to the State." Swanson reminded his audience that "the Democratic party stands for white supremacy, political and otherwise. The Republican party favors . . . political equality between the races, which means if accomplished negro governors, negro representatives and varied negro officials. The democracy is opposed to this and stands for white supremacy."[71]

Results at the polls left no doubt that the Democratic Party remained firmly in control in Virginia. Despite every effort to disassociate his party from its historical relationship with the state's African Americans, Anderson finished a distant second, receiving only 65,933 votes to Trinkle's 139,416. Several days after the election, Carter Glass, the architect of disfranchisement in the Old Dominion, concluded that Anderson had attempted to revive an issue that was decided long ago and "'now is buried in the same grave with unrestricted Negro suffrage.'" All-black candidate John Mitchell received only 5,046 votes, less than a third of the number garnered in 1920 by a black candidate for U.S. Senate. Although Mitchell's dismal showing suggests that most black voters agreed with P. B. Young, the all-black movement fostered an emerging political militance among African Americans in Virginia that would become more evident in the late 1920s and 1930s.[72]

Although the 1921 gubernatorial campaign deeply divided African American leaders and voters in Virginia, the lily-whitism of the Republican Party forced both factions to reexamine their allegiance to the party of Lincoln, which, at best, had proven indifferent to the concern of African Americans. Throughout the South, as Republicans adopted lily-white strategies in an effort to solicit the votes of newly enfranchised white women, African Americans began an exodus away from the Republican Party. In fits and starts, blacks gravitated toward the Democrats, a process completed in 1936, but whose genesis dates to the early 1920s, long before the onset of the Great Depression. In fact, unsubstantiated rumors intimated that John Mitchell ran in 1921 with the blessing of Democratic leaders to draw votes away from the Republicans. Whether or not this is accurate, Mitchell wasted no time before building bridges to the one party with power in Virginia. Slower than Mitchell to make a clean break with the Republicans, P. B. Young also grew exasperated with what a fellow Norfolk editor deemed a Republican strategy "to absorb the Black vote without paying for it with Colored patronage." After a relatively cordial and inclusive state convention in 1924, which reflected national Republican efforts to win black votes in the North, Young finally abandoned the Republican Party during the presidential election of 1928, an editorial and personal position that moved him closer and closer to the NAACP and more activist blacks whom he had long opposed.[73]

With victory secured, Governor E. Lee Trinkle affirmed his friendship for Virginia's black citizenry. Throughout his term, the chief executive spoke to groups such as the Negro Organization Society and received thanks from black leaders for his words of encouragement. On one occasion, the governor addressed over 7,000 people attending what the *Norfolk Journal and Guide* termed a "monster inter-racial mass meeting." The *Richmond Times-Dispatch* also covered the meeting and reported that Trinkle "advocated and lauded the efforts of negro leaders who are striving for a better understanding between the colored and white people."[74]

The facility with which the governor jumped back and forth between campaigning on behalf of white supremacy and affirming friendship for black Virginians epitomized the essence of Virginia's paternalistic race relations. White and black leaders frequently praised the level of cooperation and mutual goodwill that existed between the races. Norfolk's black newspaper seconded the comments of a white judge who proclaimed that "one of the valuable assets of Norfolk is the kindly cooperative feeling existing between the white and colored races in this city. Colloquially speaking, they get on well together. There are no riots or lynchings, and there is no enmity or spirit of bitterness." The *Richmond Times-Dispatch* echoed the same sentiments in Richmond, noted that both races derided the Ku Klux Klan, and supported better housing and sanitation for blacks "in order that they may remain a happy, contented, and a healthy people." Trinkle told an out-of-state correspondent that "there is no State in the Union that has better colored people than we have and the white and colored people here live in harmony." Even John Mitchell reminded the governor in 1923 that for forty years he had told the state's blacks that "their best friends are here and that the future prosperity of the colored people is to be worked out among these white people with whom we are acquainted."[75]

Such paternalistic pronouncements, however, minimized a stark reality: interracial cooperation was always governed according to terms dictated by whites whose concern stemmed less from a humanitarian impulse than from a desire to do the minimum necessary to ensure that blacks remained happy, content, and, most important of all, easily managed. In practice, therefore, paternalism meant that urban officials and city planners failed to undertake reform meaningful to African Americans, all too often blaming their own negligence on the opposition of working-class and middle-class whites. Furthermore, paternalistic offerings failed to insulate black Virginians from the friction and tension that became more pronounced in urban areas as blacks and whites came into more direct contact.[76]

White supremacy, without a doubt, granted all white people phenomenal privileges; all whites, however, did not experience their enhanced status in the same terms. If elites envisioned segregation as a necessary means of achieving social stability and order, other whites focused more on preserving the quotidian advantages of their whiteness. In the urban South, this distinction was particularly pronounced in disputes over transportation and housing. Streetcars and buses provided a frequent point of physical contact between blacks and whites and afforded whites a daily reminder of the benefits of their whiteness. Elites, on the other hand, drove themselves or hired chauffeurs and thus avoided much of this interaction.

The Virginia General Assembly never insisted that blacks should occupy the rear of streetcars and buses while whites sat forward. All segregation legislation pertaining to common carriers mandated separate accommodations for black and white passengers but did not specify how that should be worked out. Section 3980 of the Code of 1919 provided "that there shall be a complete separation of white and colored passengers upon all urban, interurban and suburban electric railways, and that the conductor or other person in charge of an electric street car shall have the right to require any passenger to change his or her seat as often as it may be necessary or proper." The 1930 legislative act that formally extended segregation to buses also failed to specify the assignation of certain seats to blacks or whites, but it did direct the driver "to change the designation so as to increase or decrease the amount of space or seats set apart for either race" and further mandated that "no contiguous seats on the same bench shall be occupied by white and colored passengers at the same time." In addition, the act authorized bus drivers to act as "the judge of the race of each passenger whenever such passenger has failed to disclose his or her race."[77]

Custom and company policy, however, made sure that blacks occupied the rear. Throughout the 1920s and early 1930s, common carriers in Richmond had signs that read, "White patrons will sit from the front backward; colored patrons will sit from the rear forward. Join the Y.M.C.A." Traveling through the Old Dominion in 1939, black sociologist Ralph Bunche commented that the signs, which the YMCA had later claimed were a mistake, were no longer used "as everyone knows what to do." The force of custom and the assumptions of white supremacy confused even the justices of the Virginia Supreme Court of Appeals. In a 1927 opinion that cited the Code of 1919, the court referred to "the rear of said street car, where, by the statute of Virginia, all negroes are required to be seated."[78]

Although African Americans frequently complained about rude drivers who refused to make change or pulled away from the curb as black passengers were about to board, violations of Virginia's Jim Crow laws on common carriers were rarely reported in the press, a likely indication that few people, especially blacks, openly challenged the terms of the laws. Furthermore, not all of those arrested were black. In July 1921 P. E. Abinoness, a Syrian by birth and a white man according to Virginia law, was fined $20 plus court costs for refusing the directions of a driver in Norfolk. According to evidence presented at trial, a number of black passengers stood on a streetcar while seats toward the front remained unoccupied. The conductor of the car asked Abinoness to take a seat farther forward in order to open up a seat for a black passenger, but he refused and was arrested. Although vehemently opposed to the law, Norfolk's black newspaper praised the fairness of the conductor in applying the law to a white man.[79]

The temperament of individual bus drivers and streetcar conductors had much to do with the enforcement of segregation. Elizabeth Snyder Carter, born in 1912, grew up in Charlottesville, the daughter of a grocer. As a child, she spent most of each day with her sister and the family's black cook, Agnes Winn. Elizabeth and her sister often rode on the streetcar with Agnes, and thanks to the "'broad-broad-minded'" attitude of the driver, sat on the back seat with her. Richard Bowling, a black Norfolk minister and frequent newspaper columnist, often wrote about the vagaries of Jim Crow. In one account, he recalled boarding a city bus and heading to the rear, "precisely what any colored person is supposed to do in these parts." At the same time, however, a white sailor and his family were in the process of taking over the section normally reserved for blacks. The driver saw Bowling's predicament, walked back to him, and suggested that he take a seat toward the front. Bowling praised the driver's sensibility and especially appreciated that he had made a suggestion and not given an order.[80]

Other potential conflicts and friction were not usually so easily resolved. In July 1924 Sarah Deaton, seventy-two years of age and a resident of Norfolk for half of them, boarded a bus and sat in the third seat from the front. A white woman sitting closer to the front complained to the driver, who walked back to Deaton and told her, according to court testimony, "to move back with the rest of the negroes." The driver, acting on the complaint of another passenger, failed to realize that Deaton was, in fact, white. She later sued the streetcar company for damages, but the appeals court ruled that the driver had acted in good faith, mistaking her dark complexion for blackness, and found for the defendant.[81]

Deaton's experience suggested that at least some whites who rode the buses considered it imperative to draw a strict color line. The incantations of the press and a few politicians may have been responsible for the passage of Virginia's initial Jim Crow statutes at the turn of the century, but by the 1920s whites throughout the Old Dominion protected their statutory and customary space with resolve. While buses and streetcars provided one obvious source of tension in this regard, residential neighborhoods increasingly became the focus of interracial friction. As a growing middle class of whites joined elites who built homes in neighborhoods far from

Opportunities Found and Lost

black residential districts, working-class and poorer whites regularly worried that blacks were encroaching onto their turf.[82]

In the early twentieth century, urban officials and city planners, fixated on boosting the fortunes of their municipalities, failed to address the root causes that explained the deterioration of black neighborhoods. Instead, they saw endemic poverty as evidence of black inferiority and zoned blacks into increasingly restrictive and rapidly worsening neighborhoods, while creating suburban enclaves for middle-class and professional whites. Richmond adopted the state's first residential segregation ordinance in April 1911, followed by Roanoke, Portsmouth, Norfolk, and Clifton Forge. Upheld by the Virginia Supreme Court, these municipal statutes were overturned by a 1917 decision of the U.S. Supreme Court. In the years following World War I, the continued expansion of urban commercial districts contributed to a parallel decline in affordable residential housing, especially for African Americans. As whites abandoned their old neighborhoods and fled to the suburbs, blacks moved in, only to find themselves still without paved streets, adequate electricity, proper sanitation, access to parks, and other benefits they deeply desired. Throughout the Old Dominion, the debate over public services, recreational facilities, and housing became irrevocably intertwined with concerns about how best to manage racial segregation in an increasingly urban society.[83]

In Roanoke in the spring of 1921, a meeting between city officials and black leaders ended abruptly when it became clear that the two sides had quite different agendas. The city commissioner, acting in response to the increased encroachment of blacks into previously all-white neighborhoods, had prepared a resolution affirming segregation as best for both races and urging whites not to sell to blacks and blacks not to buy from whites. Black participants, however, had arrived at the meeting with a resolution intended to address the inhumane conditions that existed in the city's black residential areas. Not one street was paved, and most sections completely lacked sewers, gas, and electricity. But, according to one report, blacks expressed the greatest displeasure with the condition of their schools; most were hardly fit for use. The black participants suggested that a recognition of their grievances and progress in addressing them would dramatically improve interracial harmony and understanding. The city commissioner, clearly unprepared for the protest, announced that nothing else could be done at the time and ended the meeting.[84]

Civic officials in Norfolk faced a similar problem as the black population increased and black residents sought new neighborhoods with paved roads, streetlights, and sewers. In 1921 a homeowner in Brambleton, an all-white section of the city inhabited primarily by working-class whites, sold a home to a black couple. The harsh objections of other residents led the city to intervene and resolve the matter by purchasing the property. In addition, black and white real estate agents agreed not to sell or rent any property in Brambleton to blacks. Over the course of the next two years, however, numerous white property owners found themselves with vacant homes; whites did not want to move into the area, blacks were forbidden to do so, and real estate agents felt constrained.[85]

When Norfolk annexed significant sections of the surrounding county on January 1, 1923, more than 8,000 African Americans were added to the city's rolls. Norfolk's black newspaper claimed that most of these new residents lived in middle-class developments whose annexation ensured sufficient room for the expansion of black neighborhoods within the city limits. The paper's prognosis proved too optimistic; by the end of the summer more blacks sought to move into Brambleton, only to be forced out the following day.[86]

In the spring of 1923, agents managed to sell to black buyers property that lay within the district lines of a new high school but still fell within the forbidden areas of Brambleton. One newspaper offered the opinion that real estate agents had begun selling white-owned property to blacks in an attempt to force whites out and to create new black neighborhoods. As prices invariably climbed in the process, agents stood to gain a great deal of money out of such transactions. Tensions flared as whites proved determined not to make any more adjustments.[87]

In July 1923 a gathering of eighty to one hundred white residents of Brambleton informed a black family that they had crossed the "'dead line'" and moved into a section of the city reserved for whites only. Armed and indignant, the crowd never resorted to physical violence but made it clear that the black family would have to move. Press reports also noted that fifty white children witnessed the confrontation, and that the white visitors were all "well known men," including a member of the city council. After the visit, the family agreed to move.[88]

Clearly the white residents of Brambleton considered the recent arrivals to be black, but according to acquaintances of the family, some question had always existed as to their color. The family apparently considered themselves white. The mother and children easily passed as white, but the father did not. His presence, in fact, had tipped off the white residents of Brambleton and led to the confrontation. When a black reporter arrived at the home the following day to speak with the family, one female member said, "'Why don't they send a white man to talk to us, we don't talk to niggers.'" When the reporter persisted, the woman exclaimed, "'No! No! No news for niggers.'"[89]

Opportunities Found and Lost

Whatever motivated the family in question to move into Brambleton, whether driven by a desire to pass completely into the white world or, more than likely, a desire simply to have a decent home in a clean neighborhood, white residents of Brambleton could not abide their presence. For two years, whites had watched blacks increasingly encroach on their neighborhood, and they were determined to put a stop to it. The encroachment continued for at least another two years and ultimately led to the passage of a residential segregation ordinance.[90]

The anger and frustration felt by white residents of Brambleton and other neighborhoods throughout the state paralleled the rise of the Ku Klux Klan in Virginia. From the end of World War I through the early 1920s the Klan attracted members in such growing industrial cities as Norfolk, Newport News, Portsmouth, Lynchburg, Danville, Hopewell, and Roanoke, as well as Staunton and Winchester in the Shenandoah Valley. The most authoritative study on the Ku Klux Klan in the 1920s points out that "these cities handled the coal shipped in by railroad from the mines of Virginia and West Virginia, packed and distributed the seafood of the middle south, built ships, manufactured fertilizer, farm machinery, cotton and silk textiles, chemicals, paints, cottonseed oil, and munitions. They marketed the tobacco, made the shoes and hosiery, fired the foundries, treated the lumber, cut out the furniture, and manned the railroad shops and the cellulose factories." The thousands of blacks and whites who had left the farms during and after World War I swelled the populations of these towns and competed for already insufficient municipal resources.[91]

The secretive nature of the Ku Klux Klan makes it impossible to know how much support the organization actually enjoyed, but clearly the hooded order drew adherents from all over the state. According to one estimate, membership approached 10,000 in Norfolk, a city that enjoyed the most extensive war-related expansion and then suffered through postwar contraction. Rumors connected the chiefs of police in Richmond and Norfolk, the two largest cities in the state, to the order. Some of the white clergy in Danville refused the request of that city's black ministers to prevent the establishment of a local chapter. In Roanoke, on the other hand, a group of white clergy emphasized that good relations existed between whites and blacks and asked the city commission to go on record as opposed to the Klan. The city commission went along in part, objecting to mob rule, but specifically stated its support for the Klan's "benevolent work."[92]

The Klan, in fact, did engage in a variety of pursuits. Unmasked Klansmen and Klanswomen from Lynchburg paraded through the streets of

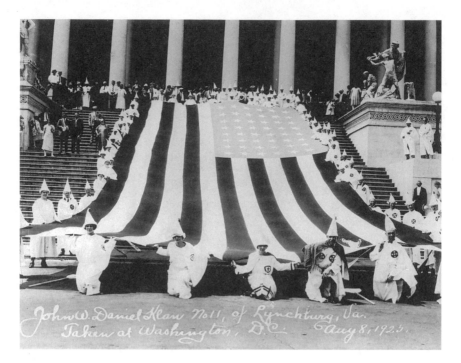

John W. Daniel Klan No 11, of Lynchburg, Va. Taken at Washington, D.C. Aug 8, 1925.

Part of a national gathering that brought 30,000 unmasked Klansmen and Klanswomen to Washington, D.C., in August 1925, members of the John W. Daniel Klan of Lynchburg, Virginia, pose on the steps of the U.S. Capitol. (Photograph by Ed Herbrun; courtesy of the Architect of the Capitol, Washington, D.C.)

Washington, D.C., with 30,000 other adherents from around the nation. Hooded members in Charlottesville appeared during funeral services for the local sheriff and presented a cross of red flowers. Klansmen in Farmville donated $100 to the widow of a slain minister. In Alexandria, fully dressed members delivered fruits, nuts, and cakes to three elderly blacks, and the Ku Klux Klan nine challenged the busmen and other baseball teams. As many as 5,000 Klansmen descended on the College of William and Mary to declare their patriotism with the presentation of an American flag. Afraid of offending the hooded order, the school's president refused to cancel the ceremony but did use the opportunity to deliver a thinly veiled attack on the organization's racial, religious, and social intolerance.[93]

Despite such "benevolent work," the Klan in Virginia could not disguise its true intent or its devotion to terror. In a state with very few immigrants, less than 1 percent of the population, the Klan regularly terrorized African Americans, as well as whites involved in interracial work. In Norfolk,

Opportunities Found and Lost

the organization abducted a Catholic priest who ran a school for black children. In Portsmouth, three robed and hooded Klansmen attempted to kidnap W. B. Trent, a sixty-year-old black man, for no other reason than that he owned "several acres of fine truck land and several head of live stock," more than likely a good deal more than that owned by his abductors. Trent's son foiled the kidnapping attempt by firing six shots in the direction of the Klansmen. The elder Trent claimed to have known one of his assailants since childhood.[94]

Although newspapers such as the *Richmond Times-Dispatch* were slow to recognize the threat posed by the hooded and secret order, Virginia's urban press never supported the Klan. No one in the state more consistently opposed the order than did Louis Jaffé, the editor of the *Norfolk Virginian-Pilot*. Whereas many of his fellow newspapermen offered lukewarm opposition, Jaffé denounced the Klan as having "no place in a free country" and suggested that the organization "leave the various American races to adjust their differences in court." He did not equivocate when clergymen and other Klan supporters emphasized the Klan's commitment to true American values. The Ku Klux Klan of Franklin, Virginia, attempted to assure Jaffé that it stood "for justice to one and all," but the editor understood what that meant in the context of white supremacy. Jaffé's persistent denunciations led the Klan to issue him both threats and pleas to understand its position. A charter member of the Norfolk Klan claimed that the organization did not engage in violent acts and insisted that the group's membership included "men whose standing in this community, for honesty, obedience and respect for law and order are above reproach." On several other occasions, however, Jaffé received explicit threats, including a letter that reminded him, "We see all and know all: so beware!" That letter was signed "K.K.K."[95]

Although the Klan may have been more active in the Tidewater area than in the state capital, nowhere in Virginia did the hooded order have a stranger history than in Richmond. The Klan's Richmond branch disbanded and disavowed any ties with the national organization. In its place, Richmond Klan members offered their allegiance to the Anglo-Saxon Clubs, an umbrella organization started by native Virginians convinced that the Klan was not sufficiently devoted to white supremacy. Drawing upon the pseudo-science of eugenics and the obsession of elite Virginians with genealogy and bloodlines, the organization advertised itself as a respectable alternative to the lower-class Klan. The group's ideology and the activities of its members rigidified Jim Crow in Virginia and made it increasingly difficult for those favoring interracial cooperation to continue their work.

3

Redefining Race

> While nothing can be said against racial integrity, much
> can be said against the un-Christian, undemocratic, and
> inhumane methods too often employed in its attainment.
> The integrity of both the white and Negro races stands better
> chances of preservation through a racial pride begotten of
> spiritual freedom than through force born of fear. There is
> an inverse ratio between race mixture and Negro advance-
> ment and this alone should relieve the morbid fears that
> too generally characterize interracial politics.
> —GORDON BLAINE HANCOCK, 1944

In September 1922 John Powell, a Richmond native and world-renowned
pianist and composer, and Earnest Sevier Cox, a self-proclaimed explorer
and ethnographer, organized Post No. 1 of the Anglo-Saxon Clubs of
America. By the following June, the organization claimed four hundred
members in Richmond alone and had added new groups throughout the
state, all dedicated to "the preservation and maintenance of Anglo-Saxon
ideals and civilization." For the rest of the decade, John Powell and his
supporters dominated racial discourse in the Old Dominion, successfully
challenged the legislature to redefine blacks, whites, and Indians, used
the power of a state agency to enforce the law with impunity and without mercy, and fundamentally altered the lives of hundreds of mixed-race
Virginians. Although few whites questioned the assumptions central to
the Anglo-Saxon ideology, the fulminations of the organization exposed
a fissure in elite ranks as to the most effective means of managing white
supremacy: genteel paternalism or rigid extremism.[1]

Most accounts of the Anglo-Saxon Clubs have emphasized, with good reason, the leading role played by "a small but determined group of racial zealots" who "played effectively on the fears and prejudices of many whites." Fearing that increasing numbers of individuals with traces of black blood were passing as white, these extremists made a "last stand" against racial amalgamation.[2] The leaders of the Anglo-Saxon Clubs could not have succeeded, however, if their views and policies had not resonated with a much broader swath of the white population. The Anglo-Saxon Clubs did not merely manipulate the racial fears and prejudices of whites but rather tapped into the same assumptions that undergirded the entire foundation of white supremacy and championed segregation as a system of racial hierarchy and control. The call for racial purity appealed especially to elite whites in Virginia who were obsessed with genealogy and their pristine bloodlines. Lady Astor, for instance, reportedly informed her English friends that they lacked the purity of the white inhabitants of the Virginia Piedmont. "We are undiluted," proclaimed the native Virginian. Author Emily Clark satirized this prevailing view in Richmond when one of her characters remarked, "[F]or here alone, in all America, flourished the Anglo-Saxon race, untainted, pure, and perfect." White elites across Virginia gave their support to the Anglo-Saxon Clubs and allowed Powell's message a hearing—state senators and delegates approved legislation, governors publicly advocated the aims of the organization, some of the most socially prominent women in Richmond joined the ladies auxiliary, and influential newspapers offered editorial support and provided a public platform for the dissemination of the organization's extreme views.[3]

Ironically, it was the extremists, not the genteel paternalists, who most clearly recognized and acknowledged that Virginia's system of managed race relations had become increasingly unstable in the 1920s. John Powell and others reacted with alarm precisely because they understood that paternalistic support for interracial cooperation and black education—strongest in the state's urban areas—might ultimately lead to the breakdown, not the reinforcement, of white supremacy. That all white Virginians did not share the concerns of John Powell and Earnest Cox only confirmed their worst fears. While those elites most devoted to paternalism considered additional statutes unnecessary, humiliating, and violative of harmonious race relations, Powell and his supporters desperately sought increasingly rigid laws to shore up the foundation of white supremacy.

In addition to exposing a fundamental weakness in the system of managed race relations, the efforts of the Anglo-Saxon Clubs unintentionally revealed the absurdity of the basic assumption that underlay their mission: it proved impossible to divide the state, or, for that matter, the nation, into

Redefining Race

readily identifiable races. The longer the clubs waged their campaign, the more apparent it became that they could not divine the precise amount of nonwhite blood in a given individual. Furthermore, the Anglo-Saxon Clubs met a great deal of resistance from individuals and communities who rejected the clubs' particular construction of racial identity. Communities across the state revealed a variability in race relations that confounded those elites most committed to a discrete, binary definition of race.

The 1924 Racial Integrity Act, the major legislative achievement of the Anglo-Saxon Clubs, did not directly affect the majority of black Virginians who never tried nor had any desire to pass as white. But over time, John Powell and his supporters engendered a great deal of interracial hostility and ultimately contributed to a crack in the edifice of white supremacy and to an erosion of paternalistic race relations. While many members of Virginia's ruling class objected to the rhetoric and tactics of the Anglo-Saxon Clubs as excessive and injurious to otherwise harmonious race relations, they never questioned the essential rightness and necessity of racial integrity. Before long, these elites trotted out the same arguments to denounce the demands of black Virginians for equality and justice, but by then the hollowness and inherent contradictions of paternalism had been exposed. Elite Virginians could not defend the segregationist status quo and simultaneously ensure racial harmony and goodwill, the very hallmarks of their paternalism.

John Powell, Earnest Cox, and Walter Ashby Plecker, the director of Virginia's Bureau of Vital Statistics and the third leading member of the Anglo-Saxon Clubs, drove the organization's agenda, publicized its platform, and formulated legislation. Powell did not act initially, however, until he felt confident that he had the implicit backing of some of the Old Dominion's wealthiest and most powerful citizens. In January 1921, more than eighteen months before the establishment of Post No. 1, Powell wrote to William T. Reed, a tobacco magnate and arguably Virginia's most powerful unelected individual. Powell was pleased to report that John Kerr Branch, one of the wealthiest men in the state and a close friend of Reed's, had "expressed wholehearted approval of the purposes of the Anglo-Saxon Clubs and I believe he will really be willing to help our program along. I am sure his changed attitude is the result of your influence."[4]

From the outset, supporters of the Anglo-Saxon Clubs defined themselves in opposition to the Ku Klux Klan, which never received the support of Virginia's elites, and asserted their intention to achieve their goals "in the spirit of good sportsmanship and fair play." Powell's claim earned him both explicit and tacit support from many of the same elites who condemned the Klan as a threat to law and order. Leading newspapers, especially the *Richmond Times-Dispatch*, added much-needed editorial support. The organization's early history, however, suggests a much closer connection to the Ku Klux Klan than Virginia's elites ever cared to admit.[5]

In fact, just weeks after the establishment of the first post of the Anglo-Saxon Clubs, the *Times-Dispatch* reported that the local chapter of the Klan had seceded from the national organization based in Atlanta. According to J. T. Bethel, an attorney for the Richmond Klansmen, the capital city's lodge had determined that the national Klan was run by "bad characters" whose primary concern was making money. Furthermore, Richmond's membership, including some of the city's "best citizens," found the national organization a "rampant anti-Catholic organization instead of an organization to maintain white supremacy." Consequently, the membership voted to sever its ties with the Klan and to join instead the local chapter of the Anglo-Saxon Clubs in an effort to "retain the best there is in the Klan and to eliminate the worst."[6]

Bethel explained that in Richmond, as in numerous cities throughout the state and country, scores of white residents had rushed to join the Klan in 1920 and 1921. Posing as the American Civic Association, Klan members concealed their identity in order to maintain ties with Richmond's business community. Before long, however, Klansmen in Richmond began to distrust the motives and character of national representatives, several of whom seemed most interested in making money from the sale of memberships, robes, and regalia. The decision of the Richmond Klan to leave the national organization led to a series of suits and countersuits as the national organization attempted to take control of local funds and to enjoin the Richmond lodge's officers from acting as official representatives of the Klan. In response, the Richmond members went before a notary public and swore that they were no longer members of the Ku Klux Klan and that the national organization therefore had no authority over them. The Richmond chapter finally settled the issue by returning over five hundred robes to the national organization.[7]

While no evidence exists to suggest that John Powell himself ever belonged to the Ku Klux Klan, his insistence that he and supporters of the Anglo-Saxon Clubs were in no way connected with the Klan was simply not true. Dr. Lawrence T. Price, W. C. Maddox, and W. I. Stockton Jr., respectively the chairman, president, and secretary of the Anglo-Saxon Clubs, all appeared in the notarized list of former Richmond Klansmen who had renounced their membership. By putting a new face on the Klan, Powell was able to legitimize the Anglo-Saxon Clubs in the minds of respectable, elite Virginians.[8]

Although Powell and Cox initially placed their efforts within the broader nativist context of the national debate over federal immigration policy, they soon ceased to mention immigration at all. Instead, they focused their energies toward "achieving a final solution" to the "negro problem." In July 1923 the *Richmond Times-Dispatch* published lengthy articles by Powell and Cox, both of which ran under the headline "Is White America to Become a Negroid Nation?" Powell argued that the passage of Jim Crow laws and the disfranchisement of blacks had "diverted the minds of our people from the most serious and fundamental peril, that is, the danger of racial amalgamation." Insisting that such laws addressed only the more superficial aspects of the issue, the pianist and composer declared that "it is not enough to segregate the Negro on railway trains and street cars, in schools and theaters; it is not enough to restrict his exercise of franchise, so long as the possibility remains of the absorption of Negro blood into our white population."[9]

Powell acknowledged that Virginia's laws already prevented the intermarriage of blacks and whites, but he warned that such laws did not necessarily "prevent intermixture" and that "numerous individuals with Negro blood are legally white and may not marry Negroes." Powell and his colleagues in the Anglo-Saxon Clubs believed that a 1910 Virginia statute that defined a black person as having at least one-sixteenth black blood no longer maintained the integrity of the white race. Pointing to census figures that showed that the number of mulattos in Virginia decreased from 222,910 in 1910 to 164,171 in 1920, they argued that an increasing number of people with some black blood were therefore passing as white. Consequently, according to Powell, a new, "absolute" color line offered the only "possibility, if not the probability, of achieving a final solution."[10]

Powell's analysis of census data, however, was fraught with problems that point to the absurdity of his campaign to define race in absolute terms. While Powell interpreted the steep drop in mulattos in Virginia in the 1910s as proof of increased passing, historian Joel Williamson argues that mixing between whites and blacks essentially ended after emancipation. By the early twentieth century, the only significant mixing occurred between lighter-skinned blacks and darker-skinned blacks. Even census officials warned in 1920 that "considerable uncertainty necessarily attaches to the classification of Negroes as black and mulatto, since the accuracy of the distinction depends largely upon the judgment and care employed by the enumerators." Mulattos in Virginia did not become white between 1910

JOINT RECITAL WITH SOPHIE BRASLAU
AUSPICES PENINSULA MUSIC CLUB.

To dear Grace,
affectionately
John Powell

JOHN POWELL

A world-renowned pianist and founder of the Anglo-
Saxon Clubs, John Powell inscribed this concert poster
to his childhood friend Grace Copeland (see Chapter 4).
(Courtesy of the Prints File, Albert and Shirley Small
Special Collections Library, University of Virginia)

and 1920, but rather became black. Not surprisingly, the census bureau
did away with mulatto as a category for the 1930 enumeration.[11]

Powell and Cox borrowed much of their rhetoric from the science of
eugenics, and from its counterpart, scientific racism. Although they referred most often to northern eugenicists like New York attorney Madison
Grant and *Saturday Evening Post* contributor Lothrop Stoddard, the clubs'
leading spokesmen need not have looked far from home for intellectual
sanction. Virginia, and in particular the University of Virginia in Charlottesville, had become a hotbed of eugenical studies by the mid-1920s.
According to the leading scholar of the eugenics movement in Virginia,
biology professor Ivey Foreman Lewis and a number of other eugenicists
at the university developed a curriculum that "taught that heredity governed all aspects of life, from anatomical form to social organization." By

definition, therefore, eugenics "reinforced the social hierarchy that elevated the elite, extolled sedate whites as fit, and considered troublesome whites, poor whites, and all others to be genetic defectives in need of control." Firmly rooted in the ethos of Progressive Era reform, Lewis and his compatriots sanctioned white elite rule in scientific terms and "provided generations of educated, self-consciously modern Virginians with a new method of legitimating the South's traditional social order." [12]

The belief of Lewis and other eugenicists in heredity as the determining factor in all aspects of human interaction culminated in the 1924 passage of an involuntary sterilization measure, ultimately upheld by the U.S. Supreme Court. For nearly fifty years, the commonwealth of Virginia sterilized thousands of individuals, white and black, deemed feebleminded, insane, or prone to criminal behavior. Those at the top of Virginia's social order, including Douglas Southall Freeman, commented on the "beneficent effects" of the bill. Many of Lewis's students, especially those who went on to careers in medicine and politics, were directly responsible for the enforcement of the sterilization statute; in this respect alone, Lewis's teachings had a profound and long-lasting effect on public policy in the Old Dominion. [13]

Lewis's beliefs and teachings quite naturally led him to embrace the aims of the Anglo-Saxon Clubs, although he was never a leader of the organization. He never appeared before the legislature on its behalf and did not promote its cause in the state's major newspapers, but he did admire the positions taken by John Powell, Earnest Cox, and Walter Plecker. As late as 1929, as Plecker came under increased pressure to moderate his views, Lewis urged him "to stand firm in the face of ill considered and ill tempered criticism" and referred to Plecker's efforts as "the most important public service being rendered in Virginia." [14]

Though never a serious student of eugenics, Powell recognized an opportunity to whitewash his extreme prejudice with a veneer of respectable intellectualism by clothing his ideology in theories of biology and ethnography. In particular, Powell latched on to Mendel's theories of heredity, arguing that when two races interbred "the more primitive, the less highly specialized, variety always dominates." A widespread belief in the inferiority of blacks allowed the Anglo-Saxons to claim that "every race that has crossed with the Negro has failed to maintain its civilization and culture." Powell warned, therefore, that "one drop of Negro blood makes the Negro." He acknowledged that blacks had been forced to come to the United States against their will and consequently remained "innocent of responsibility for the existence of the Negro problem." Perhaps mindful that he needed at least the passive acquiescence of Virginia's dominant and paternalistic elites, he added that "these considerations should compel us, in any sentiment of the matter, to treat him not only with meticulous fairness but also with large generosity. Noblesse oblige would permit no less."[15]

Powell and Cox underscored the degree to which the Anglo-Saxon movement reflected an admission among whites that they, at the very height of the classical period of segregation, had become powerless to guarantee racial boundaries in absolute terms. "Those of us who live in the South," Cox explained, "will detect with comparative accuracy the presence of colored blood in the individual, but not always are we sure, and in a large number of cases where the race purity of the individual is suspected there is lacking adequate means by which the white race may be protected." Legislation was therefore necessary to "remove the 'suspect' from uncertainty and place him on the right side of the color line."[16] As evidence of the problem in Richmond, Powell reported that he had stood for forty-five minutes at the intersection of Broad and Second Streets. "During this time," observed Powell, "I counted among the passers-by over 200 Negroes, of whom only five were black. In addition, I counted over thirty individuals of whom I could not with any degree of certainty state whether they were white or colored."[17]

Although Powell clearly worried about the biological breakdown of the color line, he was also concerned that interracial cooperation on social welfare committees and in training schools led to inappropriately familiar forms of address that threatened "social and caste distinctions." Knowing that many of his friends in Richmond's elite circles participated in such interracial work, Powell noted the noble motives of these whites but warned of the "advance of social equality under existing conditions." In addition, Powell expressed concern that a younger generation of Virginians lacked the wherewithal to protect the color line. To all these problems, legislation offered the only remedy.[18]

The *Richmond Times-Dispatch*, the most widely read morning paper in the state, enthusiastically embraced the positions taken by the two Anglo-Saxon Club leaders. In an editorial published alongside the pieces by Powell and Cox, the Richmond daily concluded that all "thinking men and women in Virginia" had to give the articles "serious consideration." Acknowledging that the Anglo-Saxon platform alone would not "solve the negro problem," the paper did suggest that the platform "will at least express an ideal, and throw every possible safeguard around racial purity."[19]

Two weeks after the appearance of the Powell and Cox articles, Walter Plecker provided an early glimpse of the zeal with which his department, the Bureau of Vital Statistics, would attempt to define Virginians as white or black. Plecker instructed local registrars in Amherst and Bedford Counties, both home to persons of contested racial heritage, "'to firmly refuse to admit them as white if they have even a trace of negro blood on either side.'"[20] This determination to redefine blackness according to a "one-drop" rule, however, flew in the face of Virginia law, which defined as black those persons with one-sixteenth or more black blood. In essence, Plecker granted himself legislative authority and sought to define race in terms favored by the Anglo-Saxon Clubs before the General Assembly had considered the issue. This attempt to tighten the law in matters of miscegenation resonated throughout the South. Beginning immediately after emancipation, all of the southern states adopted or reinforced preexisting laws against miscegenation. Custom and belief dictated to all white southerners that "one drop" defined a black person, but the law in most states said otherwise. Some states ultimately followed Virginia's lead and adopted a "one-drop" test, but other states kept a "one-eighth" or "one-sixteenth" rule on their books. Some states even maintained one definition of blackness for the purpose of intermarriage and a second definition for all other purposes.[21]

No doubt Plecker's concern was only heightened by the reaction that his instructions prompted from at least one unidentified local registrar, possibly from Bedford County, who expressed a concern with the damage to his own business if he did not register people according to their wishes. The official told Plecker that "these people have their own churches, schools, etc., and do not associate with either class, yet they are registered as white on the voting list, and the only thing I could do without being injurious to my business, was to let the birth registers go on as handed in to me by the midwives as white." Several months later, this registrar resigned rather than choose between the health of his business and complying with Plecker's instructions. Plecker's experience with local registrars not only revealed the degree to which some communities in Virginia rejected his rigid definition of race but also further convinced him of the need for a state law that would leave local officials with no discretion in the matter of racial classification.[22]

With the Virginia legislature not due to convene until January 1924, John Powell and his supporters set about building support for their agenda. In October 1923 the Anglo-Saxon Clubs held their first statewide convention. Representatives from twenty-four posts, including eight colleges, met and declared themselves "for the preservation of racial integrity; for the supremacy of the white race in the United States, without racial prejudice or hatred; and for all principles of liberal Americanism conceived in the spirit of broad patriotism." The convention further decreed the organization open to "all native-born, white, male American citizens, over the age of eighteen years, of temperate habits and good moral character, who are qualified to vote or who will pledge themselves to qualify at the earliest opportunity." To make certain that they were not confused with their robed and hooded cousins, the Anglo-Saxons declared themselves "'in no sense a secret, fraternal organization.'"[23]

Although Powell never realized his grand ambitions of turning the Anglo-Saxon Clubs into a nationwide organization, his influence was nevertheless broad. From its first post in Richmond in September 1922, the club apparently reached its peak in 1925 with thirty-one posts in Virginia, plus three in the North. In addition, the Women's Racial Integrity Club of Richmond had at least forty members. A number of these women gravitated toward Powell because of his influence in Richmond's music circles, but many others were members of the capital's most socially prominent families. Although plans to start chapters in North Carolina and Mississippi apparently never came to fruition, Powell succeeded in garnering support for legislation in other states. He was invited to address the Georgia legislature in 1925; his pleas contributed to that state's adoption of a racial integrity law two years later, the same year that Alabama added a similar statute.[24]

While a number of college chapters appeared on early lists, their membership proved less than reliable. The Hampden-Sydney post objected to the new constitution as "too complicated." Only a week after the first statewide convention, M. O. Williams, president of the chapter at Virginia Polytechnic Institute in Blacksburg, told John Powell that only ten members remained in his post; several months later, just as Powell, Cox, and Plecker prepared to present legislation to the Virginia General Assembly, Williams resigned his presidency and withdrew his membership. The collegian claimed to remain "in accord with the aims" of the organization but decided that "the method followed by the Anglo-Saxon Clubs does not lead to a solution as I see it."[25]

This kind of unreliable support, coupled with other, more threatening campus activities, further convinced Powell that the younger generation of whites lacked the necessary commitment and upbringing to maintain white racial integrity. A front-page story in the January 10, 1924, issue of the student newspaper at Virginia Tech, for example, detailed the proceedings of the Student Volunteer Conference, held in Indianapolis over the Christmas holidays and attended by 7,000 students, including fourteen from Tech. Most of the coverage centered on discussions of race, and no doubt the conclusion of at least half of the participants that racial distinctions should not be drawn terrified Powell. Conference participants proposed to "eliminate the white superiority complex ingrained in the primary schools," to "utilize every opportunity to become friends with members of other races," to "begin tackling the problem by converting our own families!" and to "work for the breaking down of racial discrimination in dormitories, class-rooms, societies, athletics, fraternities, churches — in college life generally." The last two suggestions in particular drew Powell's attention. Although the article did not specify how Virginia Tech's delegates responded to these questions, the student newspaper reported favorably on the convention as a whole and gave full coverage to the discussions on race. To make matters worse, M. O. Williams, the former president of Virginia Tech's Anglo-Saxon Club, had attended as a delegate.[26]

Powell received further evidence of a breakdown of racial decorum on college campuses several months later when W. S. Gooch, a textbook salesman for the Macmillan Company, wrote about alleged interracial activities at Lynchburg College. In one letter, Gooch asserted that black men and women sat at the same table with whites for lunch. "I cannot understand," exclaimed Gooch, "such a meeting being tolerated in Virginia under any circumstances." Several days later, however, the textbook salesman reported to Powell that his earlier account had been wrong and that whites and blacks had not sat at the same table at what he now revealed to be a YMCA-YWCA meeting. Not to fully disappoint Powell, however, Gooch assured him that several months earlier blacks and whites did dine together at Randolph-Macon Woman's College in Lynchburg. "I think," concluded Gooch, "this sort of thing ought to be nipped in the bud."[27]

Whether or not he realized it at the time, Gooch had stumbled upon the genesis of the southern student interracial movement. In early 1924, as a result of discussions at the Indianapolis conference, collegians established interracial groups in a half-dozen southern cities, including Lynchburg, Virginia. When a handful of students from Lynchburg College, Randolph-Macon Woman's College, and the Lynchburg Theological Seminary, a black college, gathered at the Lynchburg YWCA, local citizens and YWCA officials forced them to meet instead in the city's black slums. Although the students did not openly challenge legalized segregation, they proved far more committed to genuine interracial cooperation than did their adult counterparts. In an effort to break down the psychological and physical barriers imposed by segregation, the collegians promoted social interaction, held debates, musicals, literary readings, and, as Gooch discovered, even dined together, an absolute taboo in southern society.[28]

In many respects, the activities of the Lynchburg students reflected the growing awareness of Howard Kester, the group's leader. Although Kester's devout Christianity led him in his youth to denounce bigotry and discrimination, he arrived at Lynchburg College in the fall of 1921 imbued with vestiges of the paternalism that guided the management of white supremacy in the Old Dominion. Kester, like so many well-meaning white elites, believed that he "understood" African Americans, their desires, needs, strengths, and weaknesses. During the summer of 1923, after his sophomore year, Kester traveled to war-ravaged Europe under the auspices of the YMCA. Shown one of the massive locks formerly used to seal off the Jewish ghetto in Krakow, Poland, Kester awoke to a realization that white southerners restricted and exploited blacks in much the same way. Upon his return to college that fall, Kester's continued involvement with the YMCA led him to address a group at the Lynchburg Seminary. Attempting to express his concern for the plight of African Americans in the South, Kester asked his audience "to please be patient" as "progress was slow." His plea, which clearly embodied the essence of cautious paternalism, drew a stinging rebuke from Channing Tobias, the highest-ranking black official with the YMCA. Tobias forced Kester to recognize that, in fact, he did not understand the feelings of blacks, whose patience had already run out. In this respect alone, Kester's awakening set him apart from the vast majority of white elites who supported interracial cooperation, but only on their own terms. Although difficult to accept at first, Tobias's condemnation launched Kester on a path to fight for the absolute equality of African Americans in social, economic, and political terms; the Lynchburg student interracial movement proved to be just the first stop on a lifelong journey that ultimately distinguished Kester as a true radical in racial matters. Howard Kester embodied John Powell's worst nightmare, a white southerner advocating not only interracial cooperation, but the equality of all people.[29]

In February 1924 Powell and other supporters of the Anglo-Saxon Clubs finally had an opportunity to present their case to the Virginia General Assembly. Sponsors in the house and senate introduced legislation based on Powell's stated aims: rigid, mandatory registration of all Virginians under the auspices of Walter Plecker and the Bureau of Vital Statistics; one year in the penitentiary for willfully lying about one's color; mandatory presentation of racial certification to local registrars before a marriage license could be issued; prohibition against whites marrying anyone save another white; and the definition of a white person as one "who has no trace whatsoever of any blood other than Caucasian." This last provision marked the first time Virginia law defined white persons. In addition, to meet the concerns of white elites who descended from Pocahontas and John Rolfe (blood traced to that union was considered a badge of status in the Old Dominion and offered the sole example of acceptable nonwhite ancestry), supporters created a "Pocahontas Exception": persons "'who have less than one sixty-fourth of the blood of an American Indian and have no other non-Caucasic blood shall be deemed to be white persons.'"[30]

John Powell headlined the list of supporters who appeared before a legislative committee on February 12. Citing cases from around the state that showed the danger of racial mixing, Powell quoted leading northern eugenicists Lothrop Stoddard, Madison Grant, and Franklin Giddings, all of whom predicted the downfall of white civilization without proper legislation. Powell claimed that the Anglo-Saxon Clubs had in mind the best interests of both races, and he repeatedly emphasized that racial integrity was more important than rigid racial separation. Yet he simultaneously regarded even the most basic manifestations of racial cooperation as inevitably posing a threat to white racial integrity. Thomas Dabney, a black professor at Virginia Union University, underscored the inherent contradiction in Powell's rhetoric by pointing out how often Powell "'lamented' the degree to which barriers between the races were coming down." In his testimony, for example, Powell argued that blacks would have to receive greater rights and opportunities if they remained in the South. He specifically mentioned that the proposals of the Student Volunteer Conference would likely lead to amalgamation. Powell worried, moreover, because white southern students had attended this convention. While no credible evidence suggested that miscegenation was actually on the increase, student newspapers and interracial groups proved to Powell that interracial cooperation was on the rise.[31]

Virginia's black press remained relatively quiet as the racial integrity measure wound its way through the legislature. Aimed at those mixed-race individuals who were no longer clearly identifiable as black, the proposed statute did not directly affect the vast majority of black Virginians. The *Richmond Planet* opined that "we do not see that it concerns any Negro in this state. . . . Every well-thinking colored person who understands existing conditions wants the line of racial demarcation to remain. They want the white man to 'stay on his side' of the line and they will do the same on their side." Upon the measure's passage, the *Norfolk Journal and Guide* added its regret that the statute was intended to preserve only the integrity of the white race.[32]

Nevertheless, Powell's testimony elicited a strong reaction from Gordon Blaine Hancock, who vehemently denied that blacks in Virginia or anywhere in the South were interested in racial amalgamation. "What the negro wants, therefore, is not gratitude, but a man's chance and simple justice," wrote Hancock in a letter to the *Richmond News Leader*. "The negro is not demanding amalgamation . . . and he resents an implication that he does." Hancock argued that fears of racial mixing had disingenuously been used as a smokescreen to deny to blacks benefits of citizenship such as education and neighborhood improvements. Proponents of racial integrity dismissed such objections as evidence that blacks were "determined to pass over into the white race."[33]

While influential supporters such as the *Richmond Times-Dispatch* fully backed Powell's position, some state senators considered the section of the bill that mandated racial registration an insult to whites. Accordingly, the senate amended the bill to allow for voluntary registration and, in a further nod to elites, raised the allowable amount of Indian blood to one-sixteenth. In March 1924 the General Assembly passed and Governor E. Lee Trinkle signed the Racial Integrity Act, a measure that one historian has termed "the most draconian miscegenation law in American history." Several weeks later, the secretary of Post No. 1 of the Anglo-Saxon Clubs thanked Governor Trinkle not only for his support of the bill but for "the promptness of the registration of yourself and family."[34]

Although John Powell was the Anglo-Saxon Clubs' leading spokesman, Walter Plecker, as director of the Bureau of Vital Statistics, was without a doubt the group's primary enforcer. From 1924 until his retirement twenty-two years later, Plecker waged a campaign of threats and intimidation aimed at classifying all Virginians by race and committed to identifying even the smallest traces of black blood in the state's citizens. In short, the statistician operated on the belief that a person was guilty of being black until he or she could prove otherwise.

Although the Virginia General Assembly had objected to the mandatory registration clause, Plecker considered it his mission to encourage as many Virginians as possible to register with the state. Between 10,000 and 20,000 near-white Virginians, he noted, "possess an intermixture of colored blood, in some cases to a slight extent, it is true, but still enough to prevent them from being white." Such people, declared Plecker, previously had been considered white, which allowed them to demand "admittance of their children to white schools" and "in not a few cases" to marry whites. Plecker reminded his audience that although such people were "scarcely distinguished as colored," they "are not white in reality." Registration, he argued, would enable the Bureau of Vital Statistics to head off such trouble.[35]

Plecker's concern, however, did not stop at the Virginia border. Soon after his plea to Virginians to register, he prevailed upon the governor to send a copy of Virginia's new statute to the chief executives of all other

Walter Ashby Plecker at his desk at the Bureau of Vital Statistics, 1935.
(Courtesy of the *Richmond Times-Dispatch*)

states. He told a Mississippi lawyer that Virginia must get the other states
to pass similar legislation and that a successful effort might hold off amalgamation for five hundred years. In a letter to Earnest Cox, Plecker emphasized that Virginia stood to gain most especially from urging Maryland and North Carolina to follow suit. Plecker went so far as to send U.S.
senator Morris Shepherd of Texas a draft of a bill to preserve racial integrity in Washington, D.C. John Powell also corresponded with other state
legislatures; he praised the efforts of the Ohio house of representatives,
for example, but informed its speaker that a definition of black based on
"distinct and visible" features would prove insufficient.[36]

Within days of the passage of the Racial Integrity Act, Plecker sent instructions to county and city registrars, health professionals, and all other
officials responsible for the administration of the law. He emphasized
the necessity of recording accurately the racial composition of both parents and warned authorities not to accept a person as white if any doubt
existed. He instructed physicians and registrars in the proper usage of
terms such as "mulatto," "quadroon," "octoroon," "mixed," and "issue."
That fall Plecker asked schoolteachers and officials to assist his office in

Redefining Race

preventing children with even a trace of black blood from enrolling in white schools and urged them to report to his office any uncertainties. Relying on birth and marriage records from 1853 to 1896 in his office's possession, Plecker confirmed that some families in the past had been "correctly listed as colored, but have now succeeded in passing as white, and intermarrying with white people who have no knowledge of the facts." Nevertheless, according to Plecker, "under Mendel's law, the children from such marriages are likely, even after many generations, to present clear marks of colored ancestry."[37]

The enforcement of Virginia's Racial Integrity Act produced profound and devastating consequences in the lives of Plecker's targets. Within weeks of the law's passage, Plecker established the tone with which he would use the power of his state agency to enforce the letter of the law. On April 30, 1924, for example, he wrote Mrs. Robert Cheatham of Lynchburg with regard to the racial classification of her child born the previous July, well before the law was passed. According to a birth certificate signed by midwife Mary Gildon, Cheatham and her husband were white. Yet the Lynchburg health department, Plecker revealed, listed her husband as black. "This is to give you warning that this is a mulatto child and you cannot pass it off as white," wrote Plecker. "You will have to do something about this matter and see that this child is not allowed to mix with white children. It cannot go to white schools and can never marry a white person in Virginia. It is an awful thing." Plecker further informed the midwife that "it is a penitentiary offense to willfully state that a child is white when it is colored. You have made yourself liable to very serious trouble by doing this thing." Although John Powell held no state position, Plecker supplied him with copies of agency documents, including this one, at the top of which he scribbled, "This is a specimen of our daily troubles and shows how we are handling them."[38]

Erroneous reports arose as Plecker and his staff worked during the summer to identify families throughout Virginia that should not be considered white. Reid Williams of Dinwiddie claimed that he had information from Plecker that fifty of the most influential families in Russell County had some black blood, were not actually aware of it themselves, and thus had continued to intermarry with the county's best citizens. Plecker assured the superintendent of the Russell County School Board that Williams had misinterpreted his comments, but he did not totally discount the possibility that some leading whites had traces of black blood. "We are now beginning to get in touch with similar conditions throughout the State and are trying to establish a list of all doubtful families," concluded Plecker.

"Of course, I am up against the question of offending and antagonizing individuals which cannot be avoided. We cannot consider the individual but the State." [39]

In late April Plecker received from a local registrar in Amherst County a list of families in both Amherst and neighboring Rockbridge County that the registrar knew to be of mixed blood. Several days later, Plecker urged all clerks in Amherst, Rockbridge, and Augusta Counties to use extreme caution in issuing marriage licenses to members of these families. Never for a moment did he consider the possibility that any family with one of the names in question might not actually be part black. A handwritten note to John Powell indicated that Plecker had sent the same warning to school authorities and local registrars. [40]

The degree to which residents of Amherst and Rockbridge Counties would cause trouble for Plecker became readily apparent in the ensuing weeks. Located in the mountainous western part of the state, these counties comprised one of two regions in the state considered home to significant numbers of mixed-race Virginians. Plecker told Earnest Cox that "our Amherst County colony is up in arms and are on the verge of a race riot, threatening the life of one of our local registrars for giving out information concerning them." Plecker revealed that forty-seven suspected mixed-race people had attempted to register as white, but that he could prove they were not. In a letter to John Powell, Plecker added that the "Amherst crowd are all trying to register as white." In response, the bureau had instructed all local registrars to refund the registration fee rather than accept them as white. As almost an afterthought, or perhaps as a reminder that the Bureau of Vital Statistics was busy all over Virginia, Plecker told Powell, "I struck quite an interesting family in Norfolk County yesterday with ten children, seven of whom are registered with us, three as white, three as colored and one doubtful. Think of the benefit of preventing those ten mixed children from going white." [41]

Plecker's instructions to local registrars led to court challenges in the fall of 1924. A. T. Shields, the clerk of court for Rockbridge County, refused to grant a marriage license to Dorothy Johns and James Connor after he determined that Johns had at least a trace of black blood. Johns took Shields to court, where witnesses on her behalf testified that she had no black blood. But Plecker and Silas Coleman, a resident of Amherst County, effectively used birth records that showed she descended from the Johns family of Amherst County, all of whom had "colored" ancestors. Johns's attorney argued correctly that "colored" had been used in the nineteenth century to describe Indians as well as blacks and provided witnesses who acknowledged her Indian ancestry. Judge Henry Holt sided with the clerk of court and accepted evidence that Johns had at least some black blood. At the same time, he objected to aspects of the law itself. In particular, he found that individuals wrongly accused of having some nonwhite blood would find it nearly impossible to disprove such charges.[42]

Several weeks later, Plecker found himself back in the same court in an almost identical case. This time the clerk of court had refused a marriage license to Atha Sorrells and Robert Painter, believing that Sorrells had at least some black blood, mixed with white and possibly Indian ancestry. Despite the earlier victory, Plecker approached this second case with extreme caution. He urged his star witness in the *Johns* case, Silas Coleman, to testify a second time despite being "afraid that they will burn your barn and do you other injury." Coleman, however, refused Plecker's request.[43]

Now lacking any witnesses to support Plecker's testimony, Judge Holt ruled in favor of the plaintiff and ordered that the clerk grant the marriage license to Sorrells and Painter. While the judge expressed support in his opinion for the intent of the Racial Integrity Act, he nevertheless determined that it depended upon a definition of Caucasian "which in the present state of ethnology has no certain meaning." As Holt noted, a literal interpretation of the statute would deny a marriage license to a white woman and a Hungarian nobleman but would permit the marriage of the same woman to an Arab or North African. The jurist argued, furthermore, that nobody could prove without a doubt that they did not have somewhere, generations back, a drop of black blood. "Half the men who fought at Hastings were my grandfathers," reasoned Holt. "Some of them were probably hanged and some knighted, who can tell?" Holt insisted that the "rule of reason" must be applied to law, and therefore "an appreciable amount of foreign blood" must exist to fall within the bounds of the Racial Integrity Act. In this case, the evidence showed "no strain present in the applicant of any blood other than white, except Indian, and there is not enough of that to come within the statute."[44]

In distinguishing between Hungarians and Arabs and North Africans, Holt understood that contemporary ethnography divided humans into five races: Caucasian, Ethiopian, Mongolian, American, and Malay. Hungarians, along with Finns and Turks, were considered Mongolian in origin, while Arabs and North Africans, as well as numerous other darker-skinned, non-European peoples, were deemed Caucasians. At one point, Powell acknowledged that no such thing as an Anglo-Saxon "race" had ever existed, but he concluded that, without a doubt, the words "Anglo-Saxon Civilization" had a distinct cultural meaning. In attempting to maintain and preserve that culture through legislation, however, Powell and his compatriots failed to recognize that race and color did not necessarily comport with cultural expectations.[45]

Holt's decision stunned Powell, Plecker, and other supporters of the Racial Integrity Act. Newspaper accounts reported that Plecker's office would continue to consider Sorrells and any children as black. An editorial in the *Richmond Times-Dispatch* challenged the judge's authority to insist on an appreciable amount of black blood. Normally prone to caustic and vituperative attacks, Powell suppressed personal criticism of the judge but did express an urgent concern with the implications of his ruling. Referring to the birth and marriage records kept by the Bureau of Vital Statistics, Powell warned that Holt's decision, if upheld, "will mean the complete nullification of our most precious possession, our race records, [those of] 1853–1896, our greatest protection against the infusion of negro blood. If this decision is to stand, any negroid in the state can go before a court and say, 'My ancestors are recorded as colored, but that does not mean negro, they were Indians.' He may then be declared white and may marry a white woman." Consequently, exclaimed Powell, "Indians are springing up all over the state as if by spontaneous generation."[46]

Powell's devotion to the state's race records underscores one of the most troublesome aspects of the entire history of the racial integrity crusade in Virginia. Birth and marriage records were kept from 1853 until 1896 and then discontinued until 1912. Five years later, the old records were transferred to the Bureau of Vital Statistics. But no evidence exists to suggest that the old record keepers were especially careful. Many of the records, in fact, were incomplete. "Colored" may well have meant black to one registrar and Indian to another. Plecker and Powell, however, recognized no such uncertainty.[47]

Anthropologists and genealogists agree that tri-racial mixing did occur with some frequency in certain parts of Virginia in the seventeenth, eighteenth, and early nineteenth centuries. Whites, Indians, free blacks, and slaves lived as neighbors, most especially along the Tidewater peninsulas between the Rappahannock and James Rivers, but also in the western mountain counties that were home to Atha Sorrells and Dorothy Johns. Some of them certainly fell in love, married, and had children. But just as interracial mixing between whites and blacks slowed to a trickle by the Civil War, so, too, did mixing between Indians, many of whom also had white blood, and blacks. In fact, Indians understood all too well the social implications of blackness. Throughout the late nineteenth century, Virginia Indians sought to separate themselves from their black neighbors, establishing their own schools and churches. Over time, some even disavowed cousins with recognizable black features. As late as 1928, Chief George Cook of the Pamunkey tribe proclaimed, "I will tie a stone around my neck and jump in the James River rather than be classed as a Negro."[48]

Not once prior to the passage of the Racial Integrity Act did Powell or Plecker suggest that their efforts would be aimed at Virginia's Indians. But in the aftermath of the *Sorrells* decision, as individuals and families followed Sorrells's tactic and claimed that any mixed blood was Indian, Plecker attempted to define the state's Indians out of existence. Although tri-racial mixing had certainly occurred, all Virginians of Indian descent did not necessarily have a trace of black blood, a distinction lost on Plecker. Armed with his flawed birth and marriage records, he insisted that no Indians existed in Virginia who did not also share black blood.[49]

While the *Johns* and *Sorrells* cases had originated in the western mountain counties of Amherst and Rockbridge, the majority of Virginians claiming Indian status lived in the eastern Virginia Tidewater counties of Charles City, New Kent, King and Queen, and King William. Plecker devoted himself to interviewing white residents of these counties in an effort to determine the racial classification of the Indians. E. H. Marston and his brother George, both lifelong residents of Charles City County, assured Plecker that no one claimed Indian heritage until the passage of Virginia's first Jim Crow laws at the turn of the century. At that time, a group of mixed-race people organized themselves as the Chickahominy Indians; their first action was to buy train passes that allowed them to ride on whites-only cars. A local registrar in Charles City County confirmed the essence of Marston's account with the story of Hill Adkins, who chose not to join the tribe because he could not afford membership fees. According to the registrar, Adkins said, "I am a negro, and stay with the negroes."[50]

The development of Virginia's Jim Crow laws led many of the Chickahominy Indians to understand that their own self-interest lay in establishing institutions separate from those of their black friends and relatives. After organizing as a tribe, however, a number of Chickahominy Indians maintained their membership in black churches before finally establishing their own Indian congregations. Moreover, their children continued to attend black schools until just a few years before the passage of the Racial Integrity Act, when the Charles City County School Board established a school for Indian children, a development that helped the tribe gain a measure of recognition from census officials in Washington. Members of the Rappahannock tribe, by contrast, were slower to establish their own institutions. In 1924 leading white citizens of Richmond asked the General Assembly to appropriate funds for a school for Rappahannock children.

Barred from white schools and unwilling to attend black schools, many of these children did not go to school at all.[51]

The nieces and nephews of William Archer Thaddeus Jones attended the Indian school near Roxbury in January 1925. When Jones attempted to enroll his children in that school, authorities refused on the grounds that he did not appear on the Bureau of Vital Statistics list of "mixed Indians." The superintendent of schools informed Jones's lawyer, however, that the school board would be happy to enroll Jones's children if the Bureau of Vital Statistics would consent to list him as "mixed Indian." In an interview with his legal advisor, Albert O. Boschen, Jones acknowledged that he had not joined the tribe when he had had the chance several years before. During an interview conducted to establish Jones's Indian heritage, Boschen asked, "You understand, Jones, this is simply to get your children into the 'Indian' school, and not to allow you the privilege of riding on the white cars and intermarrying with white people." "Yes sir," responded Jones, "for nothing else."[52]

Plecker seized upon such anecdotal, and highly distorted, evidence to bolster his belief that all Indians in Virginia had black blood. In anticipation of the 1930 enumeration, Plecker unsuccessfully pleaded with the director of the federal census not to recognize any Virginians as Indians. Plecker acknowledged that he could not change the status of the Pamunkey and Mattaponi, who had lived on reservations in King William County since colonial times. Since these groups had not been taxed and normal records had therefore not been kept, Plecker lacked evidence to prove they were black. Yet he used the information acquired from interviews with individuals such as the Marston brothers to disqualify the claims of the Chickahominy of Charles City County and the Rappahannock of King and Queen and Essex Counties. By contrast, Plecker disqualified the mulattos of Amherst and Rockbridge Counties, whom he identified as the largest and "lowest socially" group of blacks trying to gain Indian status, based on his reading of the census: the 1900 enumeration showed no Indians in Amherst, and only seven appeared in 1910, yet there were 304 in 1920. Certainly, reasoned Plecker, these people were not truly Indians.[53]

Throughout 1925 Plecker became increasingly strident in his claims that no Virginia Indians were free from black blood. To combat the success of people claiming Indian ancestry, Plecker concentrated on tightening loopholes in the 1924 statute. A legislative act of 1910 had not defined whites, but it had defined blacks as those with one-sixteenth or more black blood. (Before 1910 blacks had been defined as persons with one-fourth or more black blood.) Hence, according to the law of 1910, a person with at least a drop but less than one-sixteenth black blood was defined as white and prohibited from marrying a black person. The Racial Integrity Act of 1924, however, also prohibited such a person from marrying a white. Plecker became convinced that an amended law, even if it entailed removing the privileges granted under the "Pocahontas Exception," offered the only means of correcting this statutory contradiction and of preventing certain blacks from continuing to pass as whites or Indians.[54]

In late November, Edward P. Bradby, chief of the Charles City and New Kent Chickahominy Indians, whom Plecker considered black, wrote Governor Trinkle concerning Plecker's intentions to introduce this new, amended legislation. Though the disingenuous governor claimed to know nothing of Plecker's plans, Trinkle assured Bradby that the chief would have an opportunity to present his case to the General Assembly. Remarking that "the Indians have certainly given me no trouble since I have been Governor," Trinkle expressed a desire to avoid such trouble in the future. At the same time, Trinkle admonished Plecker "to be conservative and reasonable and not create any ill feeling if it can be avoided between the Indians and the State government. . . . I am afraid sentiment is molding itself along the line that you are too hard on these people and pushing matters too fast."[55]

The governor's warning illuminated the contours of the relationship between Virginia's political leadership and the Anglo-Saxon ideologues. Trinkle and the vast majority of state legislators found it politically expedient to support the agenda of the Anglo-Saxon Clubs. After all, as politicians they had often employed racial imagery successfully in their own campaigns and feared having their own stated devotion to white supremacy questioned. Many of them, however, found certain aspects of the Anglo-Saxon ideology excessive. Enough senators had objected to the mandatory registration statute, for example, to defeat it. As Trinkle realized, Plecker's mission to enforce mandatory registration in his own terms threatened to create a backlash. Yet the nature and power of white supremacy ideology ensured that the governor would only dare to rebuke Plecker in private. Furthermore, the chief executive appears to have been guided more by a reading of public opinion than by personal conviction. Interestingly enough, the perception among whites that Plecker had gone too far extended only to his treatment of those persons claiming Indian ancestry. No whites publicly doubted the essential rightness of the racial integrity measures. At best, Trinkle and the rest of Virginia's political elites chose to offer minimal resistance to expressions of racial extremism. They proved unable and unwilling to turn off the faucet of race hatred from which they so willingly drank.

Despite the governor's warning, Plecker continued to insist that the Chickahominy group had been classified correctly; Trinkle, in turn, assured Plecker that he in no way intended to interfere with Plecker's enforcement of the Racial Integrity Act. At the same time, Trinkle regretted the negative press, which "makes it look as if we are probably working on them pretty hard and continually exposing their misfortune of having colored blood. I know this is humiliating if it is true and I was in hopes that this could be handled in a quiet way so as not to emphasize and embarrass them any more than possible." Plecker, however, considered Trinkle's position an impossibility. His job, regardless of the negative publicity, was to prevent Virginians with any black blood from passing as white. "I am, therefore, unable," Plecker wrote, "to see how it is working any injustice upon them or humiliation for our office to take a firm stand against their intermarriage with white people, or to the preliminary steps of recognition as Indians with permission to attend white schools and to ride in white coaches."[56]

More than likely, Plecker's exchange with the governor only confirmed his belief that Trinkle's attitude constituted part of the problem in the law's enforcement. A month earlier, Plecker had complained to Richmond attorney Hiram Smith about a photograph of Trinkle posing with Chief George Cook of the Pamunkey Indians and his daughter, Pocahontas, that appeared in the *Richmond Times-Dispatch*. Plecker appealed to Smith "and other prominent men to protest against this thing" so that the newspapers would stop running such pictures. Plecker also implicitly criticized Trinkle in a letter to governor-elect Harry Byrd.[57]

Plecker's criticism of Trinkle drew a strong rebuke from his boss, state health commissioner Ennion G. Williams. The reprimand appeared particularly ironic in that Trinkle had consistently supported Plecker's positions and methods in correspondence with both private citizens and public officials. The censure from Williams was not the first time that Plecker overstepped his bounds as a government employee. As director of the state Bureau of Vital Statistics, a division of the public health department, Plecker's duties included the dissemination of modern health information to new parents. His office provided the latest theories on nutrition, the prevention of disease, proper sanitation, and other aspects of health care. Because he held this position, Plecker also was appointed a special agent of the Children's Bureau of the U.S. Department of Labor. Although he was paid only $1 a year by the federal government, Plecker's position provided him a federal title and authorized him to mail certain state publications using federal franking privileges.[58]

In addition to the authorized mailings, however, Plecker sent out a pam-

At the height of Walter Plecker's crusade against the state's Indians in the late 1920s, Governor Harry F. Byrd continued a long-standing tradition of meeting with representatives of Virginia's Indian tribes. (Courtesy of the Harry F. Byrd Sr. Papers [#9700], Albert and Shirley Small Special Collections Library, University of Virginia)

phlet entitled *Eugenics in Relation to the New Family and the Law on Racial Integrity*. In an effort to warn young white newlyweds, especially men, of the dangers that confronted them, Plecker decreed, "Let the young men who read this realize that the future purity of our race is in their keeping, and that the joining of themselves to females of a lower race and fathering children who shall be a curse and a menace to our State and civilization is a crime against society, and against the purity and integrity of their future homes and the happiness of their future loved ones and themselves." Educators, health workers, and ministers snapped up more than 60,000 copies of the pamphlet.[59]

Relatively quiet at the time of the 1924 act's passage, the black press denounced the dissemination of Plecker's pamphlet. African Americans decried Plecker's assertion that they were incapable, even under the best of circumstances, of advancing to the level of whites. Furthermore, blacks roundly denounced Plecker's equation of blacks with the moronic, criminal, and undesirable. "With the sanction and seal of the great State of Virginia upon his utterances," the *Norfolk Journal and Guide* opined, "Dr.

Plecker, as a Virginia health officer, paid by the taxpayers of the State, Negroes included, is industriously engaged in sowing the seeds of bitterest racial discord, from one end of the country to another." Few whites, reasoned the paper, could possibly read Plecker's literature and not develop a bad reaction to blacks. Labor Department officials agreed that Plecker had exceeded his authority in sending out unauthorized materials and terminated his position.[60]

The loss of his federal position did not slow down Plecker for a moment. He joined John Powell and several other colleagues in extending their influence to the censorship of motion pictures through the Board of Censors, established by the Virginia General Assembly in 1922 and charged with reviewing each motion picture submitted for public viewing in the state. Board members understood that their mandate demanded the censorship of films that portrayed blacks and whites in a manner inconsistent with accepted racial norms. In fact, the board stated clearly in an early annual report that it had "scrutinized with peculiar care all films which touch upon the relations existing between whites and blacks. Every scene or subtitle calculated to produce friction between the races is eliminated." In this regard, the censors worked hard to make sure that Virginians saw only stereotypical images of blacks on the screen: the faithful servant, the ignorant child, and the loathsome criminal. After 1924 the censors consistently explained their decisions in light of the Racial Integrity Act. Moreover, Powell and Plecker used the censorship of such films to judge the fealty of white public officials to their agenda.[61]

Most of the films that dared to address racial issues in meaningful terms and to present blacks as fully human were produced by black film entrepreneurs. Historian Thomas Cripps eloquently reveals the degree to which Hollywood productions in the 1910s and 1920s failed to present blacks in ways other than stereotypically subhuman. "At their most well meaning," he concludes, "white movies never really touched the Negro world. That market was supplied by a thin stream of movies created by blacks for black audiences." By the mid-1920s, Oscar Micheaux stood at the forefront of those producing these so-called "race films."[62]

One Micheaux biographer writes that the filmmaker intended his films to "depict accurately the social, economic, and political conditions under which the black man lived in the United States." Although his films were seen almost exclusively by other blacks, Micheaux refused to produce pictures that simply placed blacks in a favorable light. He understood that, just as Hollywood films that portrayed only the innocent "man-child" or the "bad nigger" failed to develop blacks in human terms, films that focused only on the growing black middle and professional class ignored the daily reality of the lives of most African Americans.[63] Historian Charlene Regester emphasizes that, while determined to "portray blacks neither as degraded caricatures, as white filmmakers had done, nor as one-dimensional, angelic caricatures," Micheaux sought to construct "a racial image of which they could be proud." In this pursuit, the black filmmaker settled upon themes that by definition challenged the sensibilities of white censors. As Regester aptly notes, Micheaux's "films often exposed intraracial and interracial prejudice, color consciousness, hypocritical ministers, corrupt politicians, interracial relationships, incestuous relationships, and vices he felt were destructive of the moral fiber of the African American community." In addition, Micheaux indicted "white America's racism by attacking lynching, the Ku Klux Klan, and the denial of economic and educational opportunities to African Americans."[64]

In March 1925 the Virginia Board of Censors screened *The House behind the Cedars*. Just as had occurred with the examination of two previous Micheaux films, the board's consideration of *The House behind the Cedars* engendered significant controversy. Unlike previous deliberations, however, in this case Oscar Micheaux readily agreed to recut the film according to the censors' wishes and thus was not the actual focus of the uproar. Instead, the board's deliberations became a litmus test for the proper allegiance of white civil servants to the Racial Integrity Act. When Arthur James, an assistant commissioner of public welfare, failed to object to the film with sufficient vehemence, John Powell and members of the Anglo-Saxon Clubs threatened to ruin his career.[65]

The House behind the Cedars tells the story of a mulatto woman who successfully passes as white and becomes engaged to a wealthy white North Carolinian. Before they are married, however, the woman decides to return to her black lover. The young white man, apparently deeply in love and now aware of her color, continues to pursue her until she marries the black suitor. Moreover, the film addresses the general mistreatment of blacks in a segregated society. Not surprisingly, the Virginia Board of Censors found the movie "so objectionable, in fact, as to necessitate its total rejection." The three members, however, chose to screen the film a second time in the presence of at least a half-dozen state officials and private citizens. When reviewing particularly controversial films, the board often called in others to help them pass judgment. In this case, the censors were joined by state labor commissioner John H. Hall Jr., Arthur James of the Department of Public Welfare, Walter Plecker, Earnest Sevier Cox,

Louise Burleigh (later the wife of John Powell), a Mrs. Beattie and a Mrs. Staples. Most of these individuals had gone on record as strict advocates of Virginia's Racial Integrity Act.[66]

The board's report concluded that movies were not "the medium" for handling touchy subjects such as black grievances and intermarriage between the races. Members, however, failed to suggest a more appropriate forum. The censors recognized that *The House behind the Cedars* would screen only in black theaters, but they felt that its exhibition would prove especially harmful in those venues since it was "liable to cause friction between the races and might therefore incite to crime." In a nod to the influence of the Anglo-Saxon Clubs, the Virginia Board of Censors noted that "the picture, either purposely or through the maladroitness of the producers, at least indirectly contravenes the spirit of the recently enacted anti-miscegenation law which put Virginia in the forefront as a pioneer in legislation aimed to preserve the integrity of the white race."[67]

As soon as he received word of the board's decision, Oscar Micheaux responded that he had adapted *The House behind the Cedars* from the novel by Charles Chesnutt, which had been published thirty years earlier and "read by over a thousand white people to every colored person." The filmmaker noted that no other state or local censorship board had ordered eliminations, and that the film had run without incident in theaters across the country. Nevertheless, he indicated his willingness to "reconstruct and eliminate so as to destroy that of which you complain." Micheaux concluded by disavowing any personal interest in promoting interracial marriage and assured the Virginia board that he had no interest "in propaganda or of waging any idea that is likely to incite to riot." While complying with the whims of the censors, Micheaux took the opportunity to let the board know that he felt they had overestimated the negative impact his film might have on other blacks. "There has been but one picture that incited the colored people to riot, and that still does," he explained. "[T]hat picture is *The Birth of a Nation*."[68]

Although Micheaux claimed to appreciate the board's attempt to treat him fairly by calling in the group of citizens, he delicately called into question the board's policy of exclusion when he wrote, "I cannot gather from your ruling, however, that you called in any of your representative colored citizens of Richmond to help you sit in judgment. If you regard the colored Tax payers and leaders as being capable of thought, which I am sure you do, I could more fully appreciate your effort." No doubt Micheaux intended his comment as backhanded criticism. He informed the Virginia censors that in several cases in other southern states "representative Colored people were called in to express their opinion," an ar-

Redefining Race

rangement that allayed white fears and reflected growing efforts to achieve interracial cooperation. Micheaux admitted to the Virginia censors that he had initially intended to ask them to allow representative black citizens to screen *The House behind the Cedars* but ultimately decided to "avoid controversy and delay."[69]

The Virginia Board of Censors greeted warmly Micheaux's willingness to make whatever cuts they ordered. In fact, the censors allowed the filmmaker to use their facilities to eliminate a few scenes from his reconstructed version. Micheaux cut one subtitle that implied that a black man would marry a white woman, another that read, "'You are going away and will pass as white and marry a fine white man,'" and a third that contained a derogatory remark of a white doctor toward "trifling negroes" and to the "'pretty women along the borderland' of the race." The board also ordered Micheaux to cut remaining references to the wealthy white man's continued pursuit of the mulatto woman who spurned him for a black man. It is difficult to imagine what remained of the original story, but the board licensed *The House behind the Cedars*, and Micheaux exhibited it in black theaters in the Old Dominion.[70]

Several weeks after the Virginia board reviewed Micheaux's film, John Powell returned to Richmond after a prolonged absence. Upon his return, close friends and colleagues, including Walter Plecker, Earnest Cox, and Louise Burleigh, reported that Arthur James had made inappropriate comments at a meeting of the Board of Censors. Although the official report of the censors gave no indication of the brewing controversy, Burleigh reported that James had expressed opinions "so opposed to the consensus as to indicate that Mr. James' feeling about the proper position of the races differed fundamentally from that of the other people present and from the accepted standard in Virginia." In particular, James reportedly dismissed the need to make certain cuts in the film because "you can at any time, go up to Atlantic City and see the best people in Richmond dancing in cabarets with negresses." James further offended his accusers when he said that he would like to see the most competent black lawyers, doctors, and ministers move to Richmond. Burleigh's report reminded Powell of a visit he made in January 1925 to James's office, where he saw a copy of Plecker's controversial eugenics pamphlet. Powell claimed that when he remarked favorably upon the publication, James "criticized it severely, stating that Dr. Plecker had gone too far and . . . was using his official position to conduct a campaign of propaganda against the negro."[71]

Powell now informed James that "such views and expressions on the part of a State official—especially one connected with the Board of Public Welfare, constituted, in the present delicate and tense situation, a very real menace to the public." While claiming to recognize James's freedom of speech and thought on a personal level, Powell declared, "I shall not hesitate to criticize the actions and expressed views of public servants whenever they may seem to me unsound or dangerous." Powell subsequently convened a closed meeting of Anglo-Saxon Post No. 1, whose members decided to write James and ask him to explain his opinions. James denied making the statements ascribed to him, but Powell's informants offered to provide signed statements to their accounts. Powell appeared to relish his role as self-appointed judge and told James that he would happily publicize the results once James resolved his differences with his accusers. "If, however, you desire," Powell continued, "to institute against me a suit for slander, I must tell you without any hesitation that I should welcome the opportunity to clear up before the public a matter so deeply affecting the public welfare." Several weeks later, Powell sent James the signed statements of Cox and Burleigh and apparently made his point.[72]

Although Powell's antics underscored the lengths to which the Anglo-Saxons went to ensure conformity, his threats and intimidation failed to derail James's career. Several years after the incident, James was promoted to commissioner of the Virginia Department of Public Welfare, and he served with distinction in a number of state and federal posts for several decades to come. Nevertheless, the influence of John Powell, Walter Plecker, and Earnest Cox in the deliberations of the Virginia Board of Censors assured not only that any films addressing serious racial issues would not be seen in the Old Dominion, but that white opponents of the ideological extremism of the Anglo-Saxons would find it difficult to express themselves.[73]

In 1931 northern novelist and essayist George Schuyler published *Black No More*, a brilliant satire in which Junius Crookman, a black medical researcher and doctor, recognized that "if there were no Negroes, there could be no Negro problem. Without a Negro problem, Americans could concentrate their attention on something constructive." Using a new chemical process that he had invented, Crookman offered black men, women, and children an opportunity to become white and therefore to rid themselves of all the barriers that blackness placed in their way. African Americans all over the United States underwent the treatment, causing immense consternation as "one couldn't tell who was who." In response, membership in the Knights of Nordica, a clear reference to the Ku Klux Klan, soared, although it became impossible to ascertain the color of new members.[74]

While Schuyler spared no one — black or white, rich or poor — he saved his sharpest barbs for two white southerners connected with the Anglo-Saxon Association of America. Headquartered in Richmond, its members were "too highbrow" to join the Knights of Nordica; no one could have mistaken the object of Schuyler's wit or wrath. Arthur Snobbcraft, the group's president and a descendant of one of the First Families of Virginia (FFV), had devoted his life to "white racial integrity and Anglo-Saxon supremacy." Dr. Samuel Buggerie, a statistician, "professional Anglo-Saxon," and FFV, believed that millions of lower-class whites had black ancestors. After an intense investigation, Buggerie stunned Snobbcraft with the unexpected and devastating truth that black blood extended deep into the family tree of most FFVs, the two of them included. When a member of Buggerie's research team, a recipient of Crookman's treatment, released the report that identified thousands of upper-class whites as black, Snobbcraft and Buggerie were forced to flee Richmond. When their plane crash-landed in Mississippi, the pair were caught and identified by a rabid mob that recognized them from the newspapers. Snobbcraft and Buggerie, the fiercest advocates of Anglo-Saxon purity and superiority, were lynched for being black.[75]

John Powell and Walter Plecker avoided such an ending, of course, but Schuyler's keen powers of observation penetrated to the heart of the campaign for racial purity. Despite its absurdity, the determination of the Anglo-Saxons to identify even the slightest trace of black ancestry in white Virginians appealed to elites obsessed with their own bloodlines and convinced of their own superiority. A number of more thoughtful whites, including Douglas Southall Freeman, never felt the imminent danger that so concerned Powell and Plecker. But Freeman, like all elites, did support the essential goals of the Anglo-Saxons, as well as the assumptions that undergirded the movement. Moreover, the realities of white supremacy ensured that whites of "good will" did nothing to protect the racial integrity of African Americans. Deeply cognizant that the management of white supremacy was completely one-sided in this respect, as in all others, *Richmond Planet* editor John Mitchell remarked that a revised racial integrity bill "should be amended so as to read that no person, who may have any perceptible trace of white blood in their veins shall be regarded or classified as a Negro." Mitchell's quip drew the enthusiastic praise of George Schuyler.[76]

Before long, members of the Anglo-Saxon Clubs launched an assault that ultimately led to the passage, in 1926, of Virginia's Public Assemblages Act, a statute that mandated the separation of the races in all public places. The agitation over the proposed measure revealed that John Powell and his supporters were not, in fact, concerned primarily with biological interracial mixing, but rather with ensuring that blacks remained second-class citizens. The issue placed white paternalists in a difficult bind and left them struggling to negotiate a middle ground between professions of goodwill for their black neighbors and fealty to the dictates of white supremacy. More important, the passage of the measure further revealed to black Virginians the inherent emptiness of white elite paternalism.

4

Educating Citizens or Servants?

HAMPTON INSTITUTE AND THE DIVIDED MIND

OF WHITE VIRGINIANS

> It is clear that the numerous laws and regulations enacted to
> halt associations between the colored and white people on a
> plane of equality have been written by the few and not the
> many. It was the "pillars of society" who insisted upon racial
> segregation. Jim Crow schools, railroad coaches, bus compart-
> ments and waiting rooms would not exist if those who are
> influential in American society had opposed them.
> —GEORGE SCHUYLER, 1944

On February 21, 1925, Grace B. Copeland of Newport News attended
a dance recital at Hampton Institute's Ogden Hall. Whether or not the
2,000-seat auditorium had sold out because, as one trustee later noted, "the
dancers were practically naked and therefore everybody went," Mrs. Copeland arrived late and discovered that the only remaining seats were next to
a group of black patrons. Three weeks later her husband, newspaper editor Walter Scott Copeland, wrote a blistering piece in the *Newport News
Daily Press* in which he accused the school of teaching and practicing "social equality between the white and negro races." Without mentioning the
specific experience of his wife, Copeland noted the school's wealth, fine
library and facilities, and the presence of an auditorium that hosted "the
highest class" of costly plays, recitals, and concerts. The editor thundered
that "there is no pretense of separating the races in the auditorium. To the
contrary, the whites are informed that if they attend the entertainments

they must come on the same terms as the negroes, and no distinctions made." While Copeland vigorously blamed school officials, he could not escape noting, with evident concern, that white men and women "freely patronized" the auditorium and, therefore, tacitly accepted the school's policy as a small price to pay for cultural enlightenment.[1]

Copeland borrowed extensively from the discourse of the Anglo-Saxon Clubs to explain the threats posed by the situation at Hampton. He acknowledged that blacks had made great strides since emancipation but argued that they remained a "disadvantaged race" eager to "lose itself in the Anglo-Saxon race." He commended the "morals, manners, and handicraft" of the Institute's students, all of whom had comported themselves admirably and not one of whom had run afoul of the law. But this very advancement, warned Copeland, created the danger that the next generation of whites and blacks would not properly respect the color line. The editor worried that Virginia's segregation laws would prove insufficient if black and white children grew up lacking the "sentiments" of their parents. By definition, therefore, Copeland denied African Americans the chance to advance beyond the most rudimentary and deferential point. Insisting that the attitudes fostered at Hampton Institute promoted equality and would lead ultimately to racial amalgamation, Copeland exclaimed that he "would prefer that every white child in the United States were sterilized and the Anglo-Saxon race left to perish in its purity."[2]

Dr. James Gregg, the white principal of Hampton Institute, responded that Copeland had misunderstood the facts of the situation. Gregg denied that policies at the school had changed in recent years and insisted that "there has never been encouragement of the social mingling of the races under circumstances which would lead to embarrassment on either side." Furthermore, Gregg reminded Copeland that blacks objected to interracial sexual relations just as fervently as did whites. "The Institute," explained Gregg, "exists to help the Negro race and to serve the whole nation. It has simply tried to be courteous and fair on the one hand to its white friends, both of the North and of the South, and on the other hand to its Negro constituency."[3]

Gregg's reassurance failed to calm Copeland. Several days later, the sixty-nine-year-old newspaperman penned a second editorial in which he charged that Gregg had not denied that Hampton Institute taught and practiced social equality. Copeland asked in a mocking tone, "Do not the officers and teachers of the institution, white and colored, meet upon terms of social equality? And do not white teachers and colored pupils meet upon such terms? Do they not on occasion sit at the same table and have a sociable meal together without racial distinction? Are not the students of

Hampton Institute taught that the Negro race is in all respects the equal of the white race and that no racial distinctions should be made either in law or society?" Copeland accepted the principal's claim not to believe in amalgamation but responded that "social equality would lead to amalgamation ultimately."[4]

Gregg chose not to respond publicly to Copeland's second editorial, but he did discuss the matter in private with the editor. According to Gregg, Copeland seemed satisfied with the principal's assurances and agreed to pursue the matter no further. But even if Copeland genuinely intended to let the matter drop, neither an enraged black press nor the supporters of the Anglo-Saxon Clubs were willing to follow suit.[5] The *Norfolk Journal and Guide* derided the "venomous appeal to race prejudice" that flowed from Copeland's editorials. The Tidewater weekly, ably edited and published by P. B. Young, found itself unable to comprehend the limits that Copeland wished to place on the training of African Americans. White teachers and administrators interacted with black students in institutions throughout the South. Principals, teachers, and pupils, reasoned the black paper, could not possibly avoid the quotidian interaction that the *Daily Press* derided as social equality. The *Journal and Guide* exposed the fundamental contradiction inherent in managed race relations when it reminded Copeland that "a human being cannot be educated to feel and act inferior. The highest aim of education is to refine, to uplift, to ennoble and to inspire."[6]

The *Journal and Guide* expressed special amazement at the remarks in the *Daily Press* because Copeland had "been regarded by colored citizens as a friend of the race." Copeland had stood in the forefront of educational reform in Virginia at the turn of the twentieth century. Although such efforts served primarily to benefit whites, early reformers acknowledged a need for better black schools as well. Copeland's attack on Hampton Institute appeared particularly inexplicable given his own association with the school. He had served for ten years on the Institute's board of overseers for land-grant funds, a position that brought him and his wife into regular contact with the school, its commencement exercises, and its entertainment functions, all of which involved mixed black and white audiences. But as historian Adam Fairclough has articulated, the involvement of whites such as the Copelands in the affairs of black colleges remained grounded in "the humiliating etiquette of white supremacy." The very sort of events attended by the Copelands, writes Fairclough, were "legendary for their excesses in pampering white visitors; politicians and trustees were treated to mouth-watering feasts, elaborate entertainments, and fawning attention."[7]

The Newport News editor seemed stunned by the response of the *Journal and Guide*. Drawing upon deeply paternalistic language, he declared himself not unfriendly to blacks and cited as proof the love and respect he felt for his mammy. Three years earlier Copeland had drawn an explicit connection between his mammy, the virtues she taught, and the mission of Hampton Institute. In a tribute to Charity Copeland Peele soon after her death, Walter Copeland described her as "the soul of honesty and truth." In particular, he praised her ability and willingness to teach black children "obedience, honesty, truthfulness, fidelity, good manners and handiwork," the very qualities that Copeland understood as fundamental to the Hampton Normal and Agricultural Institute.[8]

Copeland, like so many other whites born in Virginia just before and after the Civil War, believed that true affection for and friendship with a few individual blacks proved his intentions honorable. In a private letter to James Gregg written in late March 1925, Copeland insisted, "I am inspired by no evil motive nor hostile spirit in pursuing this subject. I was brought up in a Southern home, where there were slaves, one of whom was my 'mammy,' who very largely 'raised me.' It would be impossible for a man thus reared to have any but feelings of affection for the negro race." As evidence of his veracity, the editor informed Gregg that he recently took time off from work to visit a black friend whose wife had died, and that he regularly offered advice to black friends in Newport News.[9]

Copeland spoke about his mammy and a few other blacks in terms of affection and respect, but he conceived of black education only in terms of teaching manners, morals, and the skills necessary for assuming subservient roles. Though he described his own mammy as the epitome of honesty, truth, and fidelity, he emphasized her obedience. Developing such qualities in young blacks had been essential in the eyes of the white founders of Hampton Institute at the time of its charter in the late 1860s, but by 1925 mammy's children and grandchildren no longer accepted the premise that the purpose of their training was purely vocational.[10]

Other than the initial flurry of editorials in Copeland's *Daily Press* and the black *Journal and Guide*, Virginia's press ignored the situation at Hampton. Consequently, Grace Copeland sent copies of her husband's editorials to Governor E. Lee Trinkle, termed it a "pity" that no other editors had joined in his denunciations, warned of the inherent danger in educating blacks "beyond a certain point," and appealed to the chief executive for some sort of relief. Acknowledging her views of African Americans in far more overt and honest terms than those of her husband, she declared, "[T]his is a white man's land and God made the Negro race an inferior and a disadvantaged race." Like most of her peers, Grace Copeland sensed

Educating Citizens or Servants?

no contradiction between such declarations of the inferiority of blacks as a race and assertions of personal affection for select individuals. She admitted to the governor that she had not fully digested the "seriousness of the negro problem in America" until her friend John Powell educated her to the facts.[11]

Several weeks later, Governor Trinkle answered that "it looks as if there is nothing that can be done in this matter at this time," a response that proved more than unacceptable to John Powell. An article in the *Crisis* by W. E. B. Du Bois further inflamed the supporters of the Anglo-Saxon Clubs and provided them an additional excuse to issue dire warnings. In the May 1925 issue of the *Crisis*, Du Bois excerpted Copeland's two editorials as well as Gregg's response to the first one. A month later, Du Bois suggested that Gregg issue the following response to Copeland's threatening questions:

> Yes, we do practice social equality at Hampton. We always have practiced it and we always shall. How else can teacher and taught meet but as equals? Yes, we eat together at times. To be sure we have some "Jim Crow" dining halls to appease our Southern friends but we are ashamed of this and try to conceal it. . . . The results of the social equality practiced at Hampton have been fine friendships, real knowledge of human souls, high living and high thinking: and we know of no single racial inter-marriage or mulatto child as a result; while, on the other hand, the result of racial segregation in the state of Virginia was officially reported at 164,171 mulattos in 1920. Hampton endeavors to keep the spirit of the laws of Virginia and for this reason instead of admitting everybody to its course of study it admits only colored people. When white folk, however, come voluntarily as our guests, we welcome them and treat them with every courtesy, although we can expect for our students no reciprocal courtesy from them. But when they demand the right to cross this color line which they themselves have drawn, and then to have a second and internal drawing of race distinctions inside a Negro institution, we say, No. You are not compelled to enter this colored world and it is monstrous when you come as guests to ask us to insult these already twice insulted people within the very bounds you yourselves have set.[12]

Noting that "no other civilized group in the world . . . is asked to accept such personal insult in their own homes and schools and in their own social life as you demand of these Hampton Negroes," Du Bois warned that whites could not expect blacks to continue to meet them on the terms dictated by Copeland. He added that a failure to recognize the full humanity of blacks threatened to create "an impassable gulf" between the races that "foreshadows 'Ku Klux Klans' and 'Anglo-Saxon Leagues' and the continuance of hatred, lynching and war."[13]

For John Powell, Du Bois's perceptive and biting criticism merely confirmed his need to discredit Hampton Institute and equate its practices with the worst possible threats to the integrity of Anglo-Saxon bloodlines. Although Powell was absent from Virginia on concert tour from January until April, at least one correspondent kept him abreast of events and urged him to address the issues as soon as possible. Within days of his return in late April, Powell helped establish a post of the Anglo-Saxon Clubs in Hampton and used the pages of the *Newport News Daily Press* to attack the *Norfolk Journal and Guide*, repeatedly charging its editors with desiring nothing less than racial amalgamation.[14]

That the initial controversy surrounding Hampton Institute involved Walter Copeland, and in particular his wife, Grace, provided John Powell an invaluable source of needed publicity. Powell had grown up in Richmond with Grace Copeland, their parents had moved in the same social circles, and they had even shared a piano teacher as youngsters. According to Grace and Walter Copeland's daughter, a teenager at the time of the controversy, her mother remained enamored of her childhood friend throughout her life. Elizabeth Copeland Norfleet remembered Powell frequently visiting her home. The Richmond pianist was an "engaging, commanding person," possessed of good looks and incredible charm, matched only by an effortless ability to persuade. A firsthand witness to the conversations in her home, the Copelands' daughter insisted that John Powell took advantage of his friendship with Grace in order to gain editorial support for his views and crusades. Walter Copeland, a respected journalist who served four terms as the president of the Virginia Press Association, worshiped his wife, twenty years his junior, and fell under Powell's spell as well.[15]

Over the course of the next year, John Powell and Walter Copeland together kept alive the issue of social equality at Hampton Institute, Powell in frequent speeches and behind-the-scenes maneuvering, Copeland through his editorial pages and in testimony before the Virginia General Assembly. At the outset, black journalist William Pickens suggested in the *Norfolk Journal and Guide* that Copeland's attack on Hampton was motivated by the recent announcement that northern industrialists John D. Rockefeller Jr. and George Eastman had donated a combined $3 million to a campaign aimed at boosting the endowments of Hampton and Tuskegee Institutes. Although Copeland never addressed the issue, John Powell had decided by the end of May that widespread publicity of Copeland's charges might scare off potential donors and torpedo the fund-raising effort. On

Educating Citizens or Servants?

May 15 Governor Trinkle agreed to lend his name to the Southern Advisory Committee of the endowment fund, but only after conferring with Homer Ferguson, the president of the Newport News Shipbuilding and Drydock Company and a Hampton trustee. While acknowledging, in the deeply paternalistic language of the advisory committee, that Hampton provided a valuable resource in developing and training African American leaders who "will return to their own communities and preach to the people their gospel of industry, of morality and respect for law and order," the governor expressed concern that a number of reports indicated that the Institute tolerated social equality. Ferguson assured the governor that throughout his tenure as a trustee he had never witnessed any inappropriate behavior between blacks and whites. In fact, reasoned Ferguson, employing language that embodied the essence of managed race relations, "my chief objective in remaining on the Board of Trustees is to prevent the very thing you write about." Like Trinkle, Ferguson recognized the need to groom African American leaders but sought to control the terms and extent of that education.[16]

Reassured by the Hampton trustee and leading Virginia industrialist, Trinkle rebuffed Powell's initial efforts against the endowment campaign. Instead, the governor invited Powell to stop by his office and discuss the matter in greater detail. By early July, however, Trinkle's level of discomfort had clearly risen in the wake of the Du Bois editorial. In a letter to James Gregg, Trinkle informed the Hampton principal that his support of the advisory committee had begun to cause him "embarrassment and anxiety." Citing Du Bois's suggested response to Copeland, the governor reiterated to Gregg the essence of what he had told Homer Ferguson. In language that reflected the deeply conditional nature of paternalism, Trinkle wrote, "[N]aturally you must know that I do not approve of social equality between the races for I believe nothing worse could happen to the white and black people in this country for this doctrine to prevail."[17]

Several days later, Gregg replied that he would be frank but would prefer to discuss the matter with the governor in person rather than through correspondence. Gregg informed Trinkle that he had no intention of responding to Du Bois but added that he had also heeded the advice of Homer Ferguson and ceased responding to Copeland as well. Despite the attacks in the *Daily Press*, Gregg expressed a belief that "a decided majority of the thoughtful white people of our community have sympathized with the Institute and have regretted the untimely, unwarranted and misleading newspaper utterances which started the reports that have come to you. You need not fear and no one need fear that Hampton Institute either in its teaching or in its practice, will ever do anything to break down the truest and soundest traditions of the South with respect to chivalry, courtesy, self-respect, justice, and Christian peace and good will."[18]

Any reassurance that Gregg had hoped to provide must have vanished as soon as Trinkle read a four-page letter sent by the Anglo-Saxon Clubs to the press and addressed to members of the Southern Advisory Committee of the Hampton-Tuskegee Endowment Fund. Noting that each recipient had publicly lent support to the fund-raising campaign, the letter reprinted Copeland's charges and Gregg's response to the first editorial. The statement from the Anglo-Saxons described Copeland as "famed for the kindliness and generosity of his feelings, as well as for his fairness and impartiality. His attitude toward the negro in general and toward Hampton Institute has always been most cordial." Despite Copeland's good intentions, according to the letter, neither Gregg nor any Hampton trustee had responded to his second editorial. Therefore, reasoned the Anglo-Saxons, "the unavoidable inference is that the charges are well-founded." Resorting to the same sort of threatening language and twisted logic found elsewhere in the correspondence of Walter Plecker and John Powell, the statement encouraged all recipients to withhold continued support of the endowment campaign until Gregg replied to Copeland's charges.[19]

Several members of the advisory committee expressed unease over the situation, one even writing a charged letter to Gregg asking for an explanation. Most members, however, encouraged the committee simply to ignore the charges leveled by the Anglo-Saxon Clubs. The letter led to no resignations, and the endowment drive reached its target by the end of the year.[20]

While members of the advisory committee ignored the threats and challenges that emanated from the Anglo-Saxon Clubs, the Virginia press did not. On July 14 the *Richmond Times-Dispatch* telegrammed Governor Trinkle, noted that he intended to investigate the situation, and asked if he wanted to make a statement. The next day, Douglas Southall Freeman penned an editorial in the *Richmond News Leader* in which he called on Gregg to maintain the "good will" between the college and its white supporters in the South. Racial separation in the auditorium, noted Freeman, would not hinder the financial support of northern whites but would go a long way toward reassuring suspicious whites in the South. Silent upon the launch of Copeland's attack, Freeman embedded his warning to Gregg in deeply paternalistic terms. Avoiding the dire threats favored by Copeland, Powell, and their supporters, Freeman reminded his readers that southern whites had looked favorably upon Hampton because it had offered "proper education and training for the negro." Furthermore, asserted Freeman, "Hampton is designed to achieve two aims: To make

Educating Citizens or Servants?

the negro the best citizen possible and to keep unbroken friendship between the races." As blacks throughout Virginia recognized, however, such friendship came at a steep price.[21]

The following day, Copeland asked the governor if he could be present when Trinkle investigated the charges leveled against Hampton Institute. Reminding the governor that his paper had raised the issue first, the Newport News editor suggested a line of questioning to be directed at Gregg. In addition, he encouraged the governor to ask local residents "if it is not common knowledge in the community that the white and colored teachers are on terms of absolute equality." Copeland insisted that he harbored "no ill will toward the school" but that "the practices in that institution cannot but bring mischief."[22]

Several days later, Grace Copeland, the childhood friend and ardent admirer of John Powell, sent Trinkle her own analysis of the situation. Expressing on the one hand a deep concern that the sequence of events threatened to bring her husband "into very distasteful and perhaps dangerous notoriety," she pronounced herself pleased at the rumored possibility that black teachers might soon replace whites at Hampton. Echoing the sentiments of her husband and so many other white elites in Virginia, Grace Copeland reiterated her "real feeling of affection" for certain blacks who had lived and worked in her home but stated that she saw no reason to train blacks beyond what was necessary for them to assume "their rightful position in life and to keep them in their own place."[23]

The *Norfolk Virginian-Pilot*, the most racially progressive of Virginia's white papers, eschewed the language and logic favored by Grace Copeland but did run an editorial that supported her desire to see the white teachers at Hampton replaced. Such a move, reasoned the daily, might alleviate a "'difficult social situation.'" The *Norfolk Journal and Guide* asked in response why whites singled out Hampton, where white teachers taught black and Indian students, for abuse, when public sentiment in Richmond required that black schools, hospitals, sanitariums, and schools for deaf and blind black children be administered by whites. "Is it because at Hampton," asked the weekly, "Negroes are treated as human beings and at the other places they are treated as inferior human beings?"[24]

Norfolk's black newspaper asked a question that penetrated to the heart of the racial debate in Virginia in the 1920s and 1930s. Hampton was originally conceived as an institute emphasizing vocational training and had represented for decades the embodiment of Virginia's paternalistic approach to race relations. White elites in Virginia, including Walter Copeland, easily supported the school's mission. In this respect, Hampton served the needs of white elites as much as those of its black students. Its presence allowed white elites to assert their support for the educational and economic advancement of blacks; at the same time, rigid control of the Institute by white administrators and trustees made certain that the school's mission and activities would not threaten the Old Dominion's commitment to the social and political segregation of the races. But by the mid-1920s, students at Hampton, like African Americans throughout the South, rejected the restrictions that limited their growth and ultimately went out on strike to demand a more intellectually rigorous education. Many of the same whites who sanctioned and supported manual training, however, refused to see blacks in terms other than as subordinate and therefore balked at the implications of a more classical education that promised further advancement.[25]

Over the next few months, Governor Trinkle took steps to meet privately with officials and trustees of Hampton in an effort to resolve the matter away from the press. In early November, however, the controversy erupted anew when an all-white glee club from the University of North Carolina performed at Hampton's Ogden Hall. Following already established practices, authorities made no effort to provide segregated seating. Incited supporters of the Anglo-Saxon Clubs sent a telegram of protest to North Carolina's governor. Copeland was beside himself with anger and said so in his paper, but the rest of Virginia's white press failed to heed his call. A week after the incident, by contrast, the *Norfolk Virginian-Pilot* criticized the Anglo-Saxon Clubs for needlessly mixing up their quest for racial integrity with "insignificant externals." The Tidewater daily then affirmed the position taken six months earlier by W. E. B. Du Bois when it asked, "Instead of making no end of unpleasantness to induce a negro college to provide them with special seating accommodations for spectacles they are under no compulsion to attend, why do not these white people who object to mixed seating stay away?"[26]

On November 27, three hundred members of the Hampton Anglo-Saxon Club, led by prominent doctors, lawyers, and the judge of the circuit court, gathered at the city courthouse and listened to speeches by John Powell, Earnest Cox, and Walter Copeland. Participants heaped abuse upon James Gregg and criticized him for not attending the meeting. Several faculty members from Hampton Institute, however, attempted to defend the school in Gregg's absence. J. L. Blair Buck acknowledged that the school did not segregate whites and blacks in Ogden Hall and further shocked the audience when he admitted that black and white teachers at times even ate together. Frank Foster was asked to leave the meeting when he referred to the Institute's critics as "mongrels." Having heard enough to confirm their worst suspicions, those gathered passed a resolution calling on their delegate, Alvin Massenburg, to introduce legislation at the upcoming session of the General Assembly that would "prohibit the mixing of audiences at public assemblages." Though the resolution aimed at curtailing the arrangements at Hampton, supporters intended the legislation to cover the entire state.[27]

The *Newport News Star*, a black newspaper, condemned the signatories of the resolution as "the vilest and most consistent enemies" of African Americans. Dismissing the shibboleth of goodwill held by so many white elites, the *Star* declared that "no person can either entertain the commonest degree of respect for another, or wish him the slightest hope of advancement, who continually hounds and persecutes his every effort to rise in the scale of decency, honesty, and self-respect." A handful of white elites, in fact, agreed with the *Star*'s assessment. The *Norfolk Ledger-Dispatch* and *Norfolk Virginian-Pilot* both urged that Hampton Institute be left alone. William Howard Taft, chief justice of the U.S. Supreme Court, a former president of the United States, and at the time the president of the Hampton Board of Trustees, dismissed the "fool declarations of those extremists" and agreed with James Gregg that it was best to "sit tight and let these cranks yell." Taft expressed doubt that the state legislature could actually do much but admitted that "the ingenuity of fools is sometimes very great." Before long, Taft and Gregg realized how gravely they had underestimated the appeal of these extremists to the larger body politic.[28]

On January 20, 1926, thirty-one-year-old Alvin Massenburg, serving his first term in the house of delegates, introduced a bill "requiring the separation of white and colored persons at public halls, theaters, opera houses, motion picture shows and places of public entertainment and public assemblages." More than a decade later, Massenburg contended that leading businessmen and editors had forced him to introduce the bill, but that he had not personally supported the measure. Whether genuine or not in this claim, the young legislator undoubtedly felt enormous pressure from some of his most vocal constituents during his first term in office. Whatever his personal predilections, the Massenburg Bill, as the measure became known, was the first of its kind in the United States; it defined segregation in Virginia for four decades to come.[29]

The bill met its first test at a public hearing before the House Committee on General Laws on January 26. John Powell, Earnest Cox, and Walter Copeland, joined editorially by the *Richmond Times-Dispatch*, urged passage of the measure. Several days before the hearing, the *Times-Dispatch* revealed the extent to which its support for the Massenburg Bill reflected its own lack of confidence with regard to the future of managed race relations. Acknowledging that such a bill should not be necessary in Virginia since whites had always trusted blacks to adhere to the social order, the *Times-Dispatch* simultaneously reasoned that the legislature must act to guard against the pernicious attempts of those who taught and practiced social equality at Hampton Institute. The Richmond daily urged immediate action since the legislature was not scheduled to meet again for two years. The *Norfolk Journal and Guide* suggested that the *Times-Dispatch* had chosen to take such a position because it was bothered by the large sums of money recently bequeathed to Hampton. In the opinion of the black paper, the *Times-Dispatch* resented the tangible benefits that flowed from such largesse and contributed to the continued advancement of the black race.[30]

Unlike the debate in 1924 when the legislature considered the Racial Integrity Act, prominent white speakers denounced the public assemblages measure. The group included J. Scott Parrish, president of the Richmond Chamber of Commerce; Dr. S. C. Mitchell of the University of Richmond; Dr. R. E. Blackwell, president of Randolph-Macon College; the Reverend Beverly Tucker Jr., rector of St. Paul's Episcopal Church in Richmond; and Richard Carrington, a Richmond lawyer and former member of the house of delegates. The *Norfolk Journal and Guide* reported that opponents considered the bill unnecessary and likely only to increase tensions in race relations, now considered healthy. Despite such opposition, the measure sailed through the committee. Several days later, the entire Richmond Chamber of Commerce ratified a resolution that described the Massenburg Bill as "unfortunate" and urged that city's delegates to oppose it; nevertheless, the measure passed the full house of delegates with only three dissenting votes.[31]

Up until this point, only two white papers, the *Norfolk Virginian-Pilot* and the *Lynchburg News*, had come out in opposition to the measure. Louis Jaffé, the editor of the *Virginian-Pilot*, emerged early as the leading white critic of the segregation bill. Jaffé pointed out that all whites believed in racial integrity but not in "Prussianized segregation" that would affect a privately owned assembly hall in a privately endowed black college. Instead, Jaffé advocated "voluntary segregation," which he believed worked well throughout Virginia, and urged those who objected to the conditions at Hampton to stay away. The Lynchburg paper, owned by U.S. senator Carter Glass, considered the legislation an "unjustifiable slap at the Negro race"; it agreed that Hampton's auditorium constituted a private facility, and that people not wanting to come into contact with black patrons should stay home. A day after the house of delegates passed the Massenburg Bill, Louis Jaffé wrote his counterpart at the *Roanoke World-*

Educating Citizens or Servants?

News, Junius Fishburne, and asked why the "clear-sighted and liberal" Roanoke paper had not editorialized against the proposed statute. Offering his opinion that the bill was "a sad move, useless and frighted with distress for the future," Jaffé lamented the silence of most "liberal" papers. Several days later, Fishburne replied that he had not really thought too much about the issue, but that he had been impressed with Jaffé's reasoning in a recent editorial. "Colonel Copeland filled my head full of the opposite side of the question last fall," admitted the Roanoke editor, who now professed to believe that Jaffé's position was correct.[32]

As the senate prepared to consider the Massenburg Bill, opposition grew. First, the *Richmond News Leader* and *Norfolk Ledger-Dispatch* joined the Lynchburg and Norfolk papers in editorializing against the measure. In the pages of the *News Leader*, Douglas Southall Freeman reaffirmed his unshakable belief in racial integrity but simultaneously expressed uncertainty about the appropriate role of the state in managing race relations. The minutes of the *News Leader* Current Events Class reveal that Freeman was deeply troubled by the conditions at Hampton Institute. Freeman praised the founders of the school but despaired that a number of contemporary teachers, and even board members, "do not sympathize with our southern view, but believe that equal rights and privileges should be given the negroes." Whereas Louis Jaffé accepted the practices at Hampton, Freeman worried that a failure to correct the situation would lead to a complete erosion of support for the Institute among white southerners. Despite these grave reservations, Freeman preferred to "have the negro conform to a custom than to compel obedience to a law"; consequently, the editor of the *News Leader* decided to oppose the Massenburg Bill and to give authorities at Hampton more time to fix the problem.[33]

Aside from the newspaper editors, the most prominent opposition to the measure came from several groups of clergy. Members of the Richmond Ministerial Union, the foreign mission board of the Southern Baptist convention, and the Methodist and Baptist ministers' conferences of Richmond argued that, under the proposed legislation, white colleges in the state would have to provide separate seating for Chinese and Japanese students who attended white colleges as part of denominational missionary efforts. The Reverend Dr. J. F. Love, the corresponding secretary of the foreign mission board of the Southern Baptist convention, explained that the legislation would "offer offense to all non-white people and would in China, at this time, cause much irritation and give all Virginia missionaries serious trouble." In particular, Love cited "young women stationed in the interior who have no protection other than that offered by the Chinese themselves."[34]

Love reiterated his position before the Senate Committee on General Laws. Homer Ferguson and Frank Darling, both Hampton trustees and leading industrialists, joined the clergyman in opposition. Ferguson asserted that, as one of the largest employers of blacks in the commonwealth, he felt himself in a unique position to pass judgment. Although he admitted that blacks and whites at Hampton occasionally shared a meal together, he insisted that the school did not teach or practice social equality. The Reverend W. T. Johnson, a black minister in Richmond, drew a sharp distinction between social equality and social justice and denounced those who asserted that African Americans sought the former, when in fact they demanded "social justice, equal rights before the law, and the same privileges that our laws guarantee to other racial groups." Johnson warned that the Massenburg Bill had intensified racial prejudice and hatred and threatened to undo the work of the state's interracial groups.[35]

As expected, Powell, Cox, and Copeland appeared in support of the measure. This time, however, perhaps in response to the growth of public opposition to the Massenburg Bill, their rhetoric reached new levels of extremism. John Powell asserted that the situation at Hampton was part of a broader conspiracy among blacks to achieve social equality, and that mixed audiences merely represented the means to a more dire end. In particular, he blamed the NAACP and the *Norfolk Journal and Guide* for "making this breaking down of the color line a matter of principle." According to J. A. Rogers, a journalist of mixed racial heritage from the North who covered the hearings, Walter Copeland testified to the sincerity of his affection for his mammy and then said, with reference to Hampton Institute, "The niggers in that institution are being taught that there ought not be any distinction between themselves and white people. If you wipe out the color line we are gone. There will be no power on earth to prevent the nigger from entering our homes and marrying your daughter." Referring specifically to the dance troupe whose performance at Hampton ignited the controversy, Copeland summoned images intended to prevent any legislator from opposing the measure. "There they were," began the editor, "beautiful white women in the nude with nigger youths gazing at them and there was the flower of our womanhood seated next to the black. There are a certain amount of our women who cannot resist temptation and it is our duty to protect them by maintaining the barrier that Southern manhood has always stood for."[36]

Rogers concluded after the hearing that blacks in the North could not possibly understand the obstacles faced by blacks in the South. He claimed to have learned more about the psychology of southern whites from three hours of testimony than from years of personal experience. He noted that any similar debate in a northern legislature would have revolved around the desirability of segregation itself. "At that hearing in Richmond," discovered Rogers, "segregation was taken as a prime necessity by both attackers and advocates of the bill." Proclamations of white supremacy and Anglo-Saxon racial purity from both sides led the journalist to wonder which side he found the most objectionable. Recognizing that managed race relations depended upon a degree of self-delusion, Rogers commented that "if anything, my sympathies were with the advocates for they at least were frank."[37]

Rogers particularly objected to the stand taken by Dr. Love, who expressed such concern over the law's impact on Chinese and Japanese students in Virginia that "one would have thought they were the citizens and the Negro the alien." Love's concern with relegating foreign students to Jim Crow cars prompted Rogers to note the injustice inherent in "making a law against a group of citizens which the state is afraid to apply to aliens." Nevertheless, mused Rogers in a moment of prophecy, "later, we might be called upon to be loyal in a struggle with Japan."[38]

After listening to hours of testimony, Rogers met several times with the leaders of the Anglo-Saxon Clubs. Their discussions enabled the journalist to articulate far better than any contemporary the nature of racial demagoguery in the Old Dominion. Finding John Powell "earnest, sympathetic, and very kindly," Rogers admitted that he should have liked the Richmond pianist as much as any of his friends had he not heard his propaganda. The northern journalist considered Powell and Earnest Cox "much moved" as he described the 1919 Chicago race riots and other injustices suffered by blacks. "BUT," warned Rogers, "it is from just such affable sources [that] flow agitation which culminates in lynchings, race-riot and racial discords. . . . As I listened to them . . . I felt, indeed, as if I were having an interview with the Devil, himself." Offering deep insights into the class dimensions of race relations in the South, Rogers acknowledged that uncouth "rag tags and bobtails" perpetrated lynchings and other acts of overt racial violence, but he placed the blame for the actions of these "imps" squarely on the shoulders of the devils — Powell, Cox, and Plecker — who stood "at the fountain head of mischief."[39]

In addition to the Massenburg Bill, John Powell, Walter Plecker, Walter Copeland, and other supporters of the Anglo-Saxon Clubs sought passage of a revised racial integrity law that they deemed necessary to prevent people they considered black from passing as Indians. The new measure, however, ran into immediate trouble when opponents revealed that its terminology would reclassify as black as many as 20,000 whites, many of them considered aristocratic. The *Richmond News Leader* announced that the "Bill Brands 63 'First Families' of Va. 'Colored,'" while members of the *News Leader* Current Events Class speculated without evident concern that half of their number might be subject to racial reassignment. The language in the proposed law maintained the "Pocahontas Exception," but only with regard to persons descended from Indian-white marriages that occurred before 1620. Apparently supporters of the bill failed to recognize that two marriages between whites and Indians in 1644 and 1684 had produced thousands of prominent Virginians, including two U.S. senators, two presidents of the United States, three governors, five generals, several famous novelists, well-respected bishops, and hosts of others.[40]

A house committee amended the racial integrity bill in order to meet the objections of the descendants of the two later marriages. Such changes satisfied many critics, including a cautious *News Leader*. On the other hand, the Reverend R. H. Pitt, a Baptist minister and editor of the *Religious Herald*, wrote Governor Harry F. Byrd that many of his close friends distrusted the intent of the bill's sponsors; he asked the recently inaugurated chief executive "to use your influence to discourage the passage of the bill." The extent of the governor's influence remains unknown, but the senate killed the racial integrity proposal twenty votes to nine. Senator John Henry Johnson of Gate City opposed the bill for its effect on foreign missions. Senator Gray Haddon of Richmond warned against "the far-reaching effects of the bill." Responding in part to a series of articles authored by John Powell in support of the bill, Senator Henry Wickham of Ashland expressed deep resentment over "the advertising which had been given Virginia as a State that was fast becoming mongrelized." In his articles, entitled "The Last Stand," Powell relied on case files from Walter Plecker's Bureau of Vital Statistics to claim that miscegenation occurred in each of the commonwealth's ten congressional districts. Wickham, however, like many of his colleagues, believed that the 1924 Racial Integrity Act adequately ensured the integrity of the Anglo-Saxon race, and he dismissed Powell's latest rantings.[41]

The defeat of the revised racial integrity measure, however, did not portend a similar fate for the Massenburg Bill. In the days leading up to the Virginia senate's final deliberations, Louis Jaffé, James Gregg, and other leading opponents recognized that momentum favored the measure's passage. In private correspondence with R. E. Blackwell, the president of Randolph-Macon College and the chairman of the state interracial committee, Gregg grappled with the implications of the bill's adoption; he told his counterpart that efforts to keep whites from concerts at Hampton would be difficult because large numbers of people "really wish to come

Educating Citizens or Servants?

and do come, both to concerts and lectures." One event over the winter had drawn a sold-out audience, explained Gregg, "and the white people in the audience were *practically* segregated without any compulsory regulation to this effect. . . . it would of course be impossible to be sure that white people and Negroes were not seated near each other at some points."[42]

Practical segregation, of course, was not a viable alternative for Powell, Copeland, and other proponents of the Massenburg Bill. Writing one last editorial to urge passage of the measure, Copeland underscored the great irony of his crusade: white elites, not blacks or working-class whites, threatened the color line in the Old Dominion. "It is well enough to say that the situation can be remedied by the whites remaining away from the entertainments," argued Copeland. "But the enticements are such that some whites go in spite of the mixing, and the objectionable fact is that this institution refuses to conform to the Virginia custom and traditions." The dexterity of Copeland's mind in blaming the institution for the inability of some whites to control themselves matched that of white Virginians at the turn of the century who disfranchised blacks rather than punish their own propensity for fraud and violence.[43]

Debates over the Massenburg Bill, coming on the heels of the campaign for racial integrity, offered evidence that by the 1920s Virginia's elites had become deeply divided over the management of white supremacy. Critics of the Massenburg Bill preferred to think of their opponents as extremists who were out of touch with the racial sympathies of the Old Dominion's respectable and responsible white elites. James Gregg and William Howard Taft, for instance, dismissed Copeland, Powell, and their friends as "fanatics" and "cranks." But numerous leading whites lent critical support to the segregation of public assemblages. In Richmond alone, twenty-six of the city's most influential citizens publicly rejected the sufficiency of voluntary segregation and argued instead that "the present custom has no legal basis; its only sanction is the threat of force," a remarkable admission in a state whose traditions included a disavowal of racial violence. For these elites, a new law offered the only remedy to the "incipient decay of the present custom."[44]

As they awaited final action on the Massenburg Bill by the state senate, the trustees of Hampton Institute met to discuss an appropriate response. In late January, that group had considered issuing a statement in opposition to the legislation but chose to make no public comment at the time. In early March, three white Virginians attended a board meeting in an advisory capacity: Randolph-Macon president R. E. Blackwell; James H. Dillard, an official of the Slater Fund and the Phelps-Stokes Fund, both dedicated to black education; and Mary-Cooke Branch Munford of Richmond. Ironically, Munford and her late husband had worked with Walter Copeland to promote educational reform in Richmond in the early part of the century. A woman who moved easily in Richmond's highest social circles, Munford had championed the admittance of women to the University of Virginia. In the early 1920s she helped establish a Richmond branch of the Commission on Interracial Cooperation. Chief Justice William Howard Taft advised the group not to make any official statements, while Dillard urged those assembled to "'get rid of the idea that Ogden Hall is a *public* theatre or space of entertainment.'"[45]

The day after the trustees adopted a policy of non-interference, John Powell informed Walter Copeland that Mary Munford, whom he described as "the mainspring of the anti-Massenburg lobby," had planned a dinner party and intended "to entice to it all the Senators whom she believes to be amenable to the seductions of her 'liberal' philosophy." Shocked by his discovery, Powell wrote Munford and claimed to "have learned with grief and dismay" that she had advocated the bill's defeat. The founder of the Anglo-Saxon Clubs suggested that only a misapprehension of the facts could explain her position and reiterated that his organization had defused a potentially violent situation in Hampton by pledging to its residents to direct their grievances to the General Assembly. Now, asserted Powell, those same residents "can not understand why any Virginian should object to the legalizing of a custom which is unanimously approved and which the whites of Virginia certainly have no intention of abandoning." Attempting to appeal to Munford's own patrician past, Powell concluded that "the defeat of this bill may bring tragedy and horror upon the oldest English-speaking community in America." Powell, however, need not have worried; several days later, the Virginia senate passed the Massenburg Bill with only five dissenting votes.[46]

At this point, only a veto from Governor Harry Byrd, inaugurated just six weeks earlier, could have prevented the bill from becoming law. Given the breadth of support for the bill, James Gregg feared that any settlement would require Hampton to admit some wrongdoing. Consequently, he thought it best not to ask Chief Justice Taft or other Hampton officials to request a veto from Byrd. Mary Munford, however, decided on an alternative course. Munford first procured from Taft a letter that he allowed her to share with Byrd. The chief justice stressed that Hampton's leaders had never promoted or taught social equality but had instructed their pupils "that their object should be to maintain themselves and secure their rights of life, liberty and property and their prosperity and comfort by developing themselves through hard work, self-restraint, self-sacrifice

Educating Citizens or Servants?

and saving." Such a conservative course, noted Taft, did not please numerous black leaders but rather "accords with the spirit of high-minded Virginians in respect of the progress to be developed in the colored race." The chief justice warned that punitive legislation such as the Massenburg Bill might have the negative effect of harming that long-cultivated spirit acceptable to Virginia's best citizens.[47]

Although Taft doubted that his letter would make any difference in Byrd's deliberations, Munford met with the governor and presented her case. She was joined by the Reverend R. H. Pitt, a close friend of the governor's recently deceased father. Pitt apparently left the meeting under the impression that Byrd might consider a veto if Hampton officials pledged to voluntarily segregate audiences. But Gregg made no such concession, and after consulting with trustees and other interested parties, the Hampton principal chose to meet with Byrd rather than send a statement. The remote possibility that Byrd might consider a veto led at least one supporter of the Massenburg measure to recoil in horror. Dr. J. Wilton Hope, the president of the Hampton Anglo-Saxon Club, told the governor that officials at Hampton Institute were more concerned with donations to their endowment than protecting Virginia traditions. "For God sake," he begged, "do not let them betray our whole state for a few pieces of silver. Judas was a high toned Christian gentleman compared with these people."[48]

On March 22, 1926, the Massenburg Bill became law without the governor's signature. When Gregg and Byrd finally met several days later, the chief executive apparently told Gregg that "'he considered the bill extremely regrettable,'" and that he would not have supported it had he still been in the senate. Nevertheless, the governor expressed an unwillingness to veto legislation passed by such a large majority. More than likely, however, Harry Byrd would have taken no position on the issue had he remained in the senate, just as he had abstained from the vote on the Racial Integrity Act two years before. A public stand against any racially charged measure might have threatened the political future of the ambitious young chief executive.[49]

Virginia's black press and citizenry condemned the passage of the Public Assemblages Act. The *Norfolk Journal and Guide* wondered if its enactment did not foreshadow the introduction of even stiffer Jim Crow legislation at the next session of the General Assembly. The Reverend Richard Bowling of Norfolk proclaimed that many Hampton students did believe in the equality of races, not because of the teachings of the school, but rather because of their upbringing, which emphasized the contributions of blacks to American life. J. H. Baynes, a native of Norfolk living in Connecticut, agreed with Bowling and wrote, "When I was illiterate and a student in an industrial school some years ago, I nevertheless had burning in my soul that flame of equality of all men, and I am sure it was born there and was not the teaching of any school." A. Dodson McWilliams of Norfolk declared that "not since the advent of 'Jim Crowism' have the liberty loving and self respecting Negroes of this state been so deliberately humiliated." McWilliams further asserted that "the young Negro student of today will not willingly comply with a law of this type."[50]

Members of the national press joined in the condemnation of Virginia's General Assembly. *The Nation* urged Hampton to challenge the law's constitutionality all the way to the Supreme Court and suggested that the school should move out of the state in the event that the law remained on the books. In addition, the national weekly directly challenged the complicity of white elites in allowing the law to pass. "If this piece of prejudice is really enacted into law," wrote *The Nation*, "the State should lose the school and the entire country be notified that Virginia is insincere when it declares that it wishes the Negro to be trained along industrial lines and to be treated with justice."[51]

Robert R. Moton, the principal of Tuskegee Institute and the only black member of the Hampton board, agreed with *The Nation* that Hampton should challenge the law in court. Citing recent Supreme Court precedent, he saw cause to expect a favorable decision. Moreover, and even more critical to Moton, Hampton had an obligation to uphold its principles. A failure to fight such an assault on the school's "'peaceful policy of conciliation,'" he argued, "'would constitute a repudiation of all its past'" and would leave African Americans with deep feelings of betrayal. On the other hand, Moton believed that a test case "'would thus become the champion of a cause much larger than itself'" and would produce an overwhelming reservoir of goodwill toward Hampton and its leaders.[52]

The remaining members of the Hampton Board of Trustees, however, disagreed with Moton and vigorously opposed a court challenge as likely to unleash an even greater backlash among the Institute's critics. Insofar as Hampton's mission could not continue in a truly segregated manner, officials searched for a workable solution that complied with the law without compromising essential features of the school's philosophy. After vigorous discussion and consultation with school lawyers, the trustees implemented a new policy that defined all gatherings—including church services, concerts, plays, dance recitals, and exhibits—as private affairs. Henceforward, Hampton held only private meetings open to students, faculty, administrators, and invited guests.[53]

Several months after Virginia passed the nation's first public assemblages act, William Howard Taft reported to Mary Munford that James Gregg felt that conditions had improved at Hampton and "that there really had followed no unpleasant or sinister results from the legislation which we so deprecated." Furthermore, the chief justice added, Gregg "rather thinks that a good many people who acquiesced in it or were led to urge it, are a bit ashamed of themselves now." Gregg, along with local residents and Hampton trustees Homer Ferguson and Frank Darling, had in fact taken steps to eliminate the influence of the Hampton Anglo-Saxon Club in the wake of the statute's passage. George Mallison, a resident of Hampton and fervid supporter of the organization, told John Powell that the "'Hampton Anglo-Saxon Club was, to the best of my belief, killed because the politicians quietly passed the word around that this should be done.'" These politicians, including state senator Saxon Holt, who had supported the Massenburg law, themselves bowed to economic pressures exerted by Gregg and other Hampton officials. According to Mallison, Gregg threatened to close down a black primary school, which would have forced local authorities to educate the children at public expense. In addition, the Institute warned that it would withdraw all funds from local banks and would terminate all business transactions with local vendors.[54]

Despite such behind-the-scenes efforts by Gregg and others, the public acquiescence of Hampton officials caused, as some observers had predicted, a loss of confidence among many of the school's students. Like other white supporters of Hampton Institute, Gregg continued to denounce racial vitriol as "incompatible with democracy and with Christianity," and yet his unwillingness to publicly condemn the Public Assemblages Act underscored yet again the limits and inherent contradictions at the root of managed race relations. As one student remarked in response to the emphasis of the principal and other white friends of the school on avoiding any criticism in the wake of the law's enactment, "'Dr. Gregg and all of his co-workers have spent more time trying to teach the Negroes their places . . . than they have spent trying to give them an education that would make them men and women capable of facing the world and its great problems.'"[55]

Students at Hampton did not forget such grievances. Increasingly restricted by the administration in curricular and disciplinary matters, and infused with the activist spirit of the "New Negro" that transformed African Americans throughout the United States in the decade after World War I, Hampton students went on strike in October 1927. Writing in his *Newport News Daily Press*, Walter Copeland connected the strike to the conditions that had guided his support of the Public Assemblages Act. Terming the strike an expected result of teaching social equality, Copeland wrote that it was "'folly to teach those students that the Negro race is the equal in all respects of the white race, and then tell them that men and women of their own race are not competent to administer the affairs of the institute.'" The editor's position on the strike once again revealed the limitations in his own support for black education and his professions of love and affection for his mammy and other black friends; he believed that blacks ought to be educated to serve their station in life, but he could not understand blacks in terms that made them equal to whites in any way.[56]

For her part, Grace Copeland considered the strike at Hampton "the final outcome of giving the negro a false idea of his place in life." In a letter to Governor Harry Byrd, Mrs. Copeland seconded the belief of former Governor Henry Carter Stuart, who reportedly said, "'I have never seen any good resulting from educating the negro.'" Instead, she told Virginia's chief executive, her father was correct to have believed "that it was impossible to reason with a negro—that the only way to keep him in his place was to keep him under fear." Acknowledging that she had attended events at Hampton with her husband for years, Copeland wrote that eventually "the situation so grated on my sensibilities" that she told her husband she "couldn't mix up with the negroes over there" and hoped never to enter Ogden Hall again. Nevertheless, she and her husband subsequently attended a concert at Hampton, but she became "so nauseated" that she left after ten minutes. For whatever reason, Grace Copeland returned to Hampton yet again, and apparently alone, in February 1925, precipitating the chain of events that resulted in the Massenburg Bill.[57]

Numerous levels of irony abound in the passage of Virginia's Public Assemblages Act. While the act was aimed at specific conditions at Hampton Institute, the school's administrators and trustees sidestepped any practical application of the law by redefining all functions as private. In the narrowest sense, the act most affected those white residents unable to obtain a guest pass and therefore prohibited from attending significant cultural and educational events at the school. Such unintended consequences, however, paled in comparison to the humiliation suffered by black Virginians, especially those who had labored to educate and better themselves within the confines of white supremacy.

Essentially unanimous in their response to the Racial Integrity Act in 1924, white elites divided publicly over the Massenburg Bill. A number of the state's leading newspaper editors, clergy, businessmen, and their wives rejected the ideological extremism of the Anglo-Saxon Clubs and opposed the legislation as unnecessary. In the truest sense of elite paternalism, these critics argued that they could more efficiently provide for the continued separation of the races by alleviating the worst grievances of their black neighbors, not by saddling them with humiliating laws. The majority of white elites, however, accepted the claim of leading proponents that custom no longer effectively guaranteed the color line. In response to such claims, white Virginians adopted new and increasingly restrictive laws to manage and maintain white supremacy. These whites, however, soon discovered that additional statutes proved equally unreliable in finessing the contradictions and inconsistencies of Jim Crow. Moreover, the passage of the Public Assemblages Act reinforced for African Americans a sense that they could not depend on white elites for meaningful support. Determined to redefine the terms of their own citizenship, black Virginians ultimately rejected the limitations of managed race relations.[58]

5

Little Tyrannies

and Petty Skullduggeries

> We get the segregation but we don't get the equal
> accommodations or treatment or appropriations, and any
> white man who takes it upon himself to declare "the better
> class of Negroes know that such separation of the races . . . is
> best for both races," speaks without authority and is simply
> over familiar and insolent. . . . The Afro-American people are
> not a race of cowards. They do not accept wrong and injustice
> because they think such best to preserve the good relations
> between the races; they accept such because they cannot now
> help themselves, and they enter their protest against all such.
> —P. B. YOUNG, 1925

The discourse surrounding the passage of the Racial Integrity and Public Assemblages Acts in the mid-1920s contributed to and reinforced an absence of political accountability on the part of white elites toward black Virginians. State and local leaders understood that they owed no political favors to the Old Dominion's black citizenry. Consequently, they ignored the constitutional mandate spelled out in *Plessy v. Ferguson* that separate facilities be equal and repeatedly neglected the most basic needs of the black populace. Furthermore, the rigid fiscal conservatism of white political and business elites kept taxes low and ensured that spending on services, most especially for blacks, remained negligible. Racial demagoguery and tight wallets proved a difficult combination for Virginia's black citizens to overcome.[1]

No individual in the twentieth century more perfectly represented Virginia's devotion to fiscal conservatism than Harry Flood Byrd, elected governor in 1925. Until 1921, Byrd was an unexceptional state senator from Winchester. But soon after that year's gubernatorial election, Hal Flood, the chairman of the Democratic State Central Committee and Byrd's uncle, died suddenly. Flood's death opened the door for his nephew to assume leadership of the state committee. Byrd worked tirelessly to build a strong organization, writing thousands of letters to party workers all over the state. In 1923 he led the campaign against a bond issue for highways, championing instead the fiscally conservative pay-as-you-go philosophy that guided Virginia for the next forty years and ensured that state services would never meet demand. Byrd's assault on the bond issue and his general fiscal conservatism won him the critical support and admiration of deep-pocketed businessmen like William Reed, a stalwart of the Democratic Party and strong supporter of the racial integrity and public assemblages campaigns.[2]

Most historians of twentieth-century Virginia politics and of Harry Byrd have stressed the significance of political organization, Byrd's devotion to rigid fiscal conservatism, and his application of business principles to state government; rarely has race figured as a critical component in his political makeup. Byrd, however, fully understood the impact and ramifications of racial rhetoric and its place in Virginia politics. After easily winning the 1925 Democratic gubernatorial primary, Byrd laid out the essential components of his platform in a speech before the members of the Democratic State Central Committee. Before he talked about making government more efficient and businesslike, streamlining the tax system, and building better roads and schools, Byrd defended the one-party system that controlled Virginia and the South as absolutely necessary for the maintenance of white rule. "The supremacy of the Democratic party in the South," declared the nominee, "is in a measure due to our peculiar racial conditions, and is the extreme expression of that instinct of self-preservation, which does not desert any people until it is ready to perish." Byrd argued that a black electorate with decisive strength to sway elections constituted a much greater evil than "the continued and unchallenged government by a single political party."[3]

Despite the absence of any meaningful Republican opposition in the 1925 gubernatorial campaign, Byrd unleashed the Democrats' familiar, but apparently still effective, tirade against the opposition. In his keynote address in October, Byrd renewed the attack begun four years earlier against Henry Anderson and savaged the Republican call for an expanded electorate as a ploy to enfranchise 700,000 blacks. The nominee reassured his audience that the citizens of Virginia "will never again enthrone the negro as the arbiter of our political destiny by giving him the balance of

Riding The Usual Hobby

"Riding the Usual Hobby." This editorial cartoon from October 1925 emphasized the propensity of gubernatorial candidate Harry Byrd and the Democratic Party to play the race card. (Used with permission of the *Norfolk Journal and Guide*)

power." Byrd's speech prompted the *Norfolk Journal and Guide* to remark that the Democratic nominee really meant that "there are 700,000 Negroes in Virginia and the most important task of the Democratic party is to keep them poor, so that they will not be able to meet certain economic qualifications, and to keep them ignorant, so that they will not be able to meet certain educational qualifications." An accompanying cartoon, entitled "Riding the Usual Hobby," featured Byrd astride a wooden horse named "Negro Bugaboo."[4]

During his campaign, Byrd paid lip service to the cause of education in the Old Dominion. But in his inaugural address, he reminded his constituency that "the State can do no more than her revenue will permit." A philosophical descendant of the Reconstruction-era Funders, Byrd had won the near-unanimous support of Virginia's business and industrial elites by promising to streamline government, make it more efficient, and keep taxes low. His devotion to fiscal conservatism meant that increased state spending for education would remain a low priority. Consequently, under Byrd's leadership, the Virginia General Assembly continued to neglect its constitutional obligation to "establish and maintain an efficient system of free schools throughout the State." The Democratic Party's fealty to white supremacy ensured that educational opportunities for African Americans remained even more illusory than those for white Virginians.[5]

Little Tyrannies and Petty Skullduggeries

A 1919 report on the status of education in Virginia had detailed the inequality in spending on white and black education. The state paid an amount to each county based on the total number of students, black and white. Almost all of the counties, however, redirected a disproportionate amount of these funds to white schools. In addition, localities consistently refused to use local taxes to pay for black education, a practice that led the authors of the report to conclude that "such conditions are thoroughly unjust and should not be tolerated." In practical terms, the inequality in spending meant that black children attended school in old, cramped, un-lit, and unventilated one- or two-room schoolhouses. Overcrowding in some black schools was so bad that black children went to school in shifts, essentially receiving no more than a part-time education. Salaries for black teachers remained so low that black women could find better work as laborers, and thus many teachers lacked proper training. School terms for black students were usually much shorter than those for white students, often no more than five months a year. In 1919 only three fully accredited high schools for blacks existed in the entire state, one each in Norfolk, Richmond, and Portsmouth. Facilities in the rural parts of the state were nonexistent.[6]

A commission of out-of-state educators appointed by the General Assembly during Byrd's administration found essentially the same conditions noted in the 1919 study. Contrary to Byrd's campaign assertion that Virginia led the South in its commitment to education, the O'Shea Commission, named for the director of the survey staff, concluded otherwise. The commission blamed Virginia's pathetic inattention to public education in general, and to black education in particular, on an unwillingness, not an inability, to provide adequate facilities. In 1928 Virginia ranked nineteenth among all of the states and first among the southern states in tangible wealth, but only forty-fifth out of forty-eight states in the percentage of wealth spent on education. Among the eleven southern states, Virginia ranked next to last in this respect. The report further noted that the state's proportion of educational spending had shrunk over the preceding decade. The O'Shea Commission left little reason to expect that matters would improve when it asserted that the negligence of the state reflected the philosophical leanings of the dominant political party.[7]

In its analysis of black education, the O'Shea Commission noted some improvements from 1919, especially in the increase in the number of four-year black high schools—from three to eight, all but one located in urban areas. Whites, by contrast, attended four hundred high schools in every city and county in the Old Dominion. The commission also found that attendance at black schools had improved in areas with better facilities. In most parts of the commonwealth, however, facilities remained less than adequate. Even in cities with new high schools, students continued to attend in shifts owing to a shortage of space. The failure of state and local governments to provide vocational training for African Americans meant that any such training depended upon northern educational foundations such as the Rosenwald and Jeanes Funds. In many instances, blacks themselves had to bear the cost of building new facilities. Black teachers did their best but suffered from overcrowding and subpar training, which white administrators cited to justify salaries that averaged one-third to one-half of those paid to white teachers. In Richmond, for instance, white nurses in black schools earned more than black teachers in the same school. The situation led the O'Shea Commission to insist that the state and local governments had to spend more on facilities and black teacher salaries if conditions were to improve. "The whole thing," concluded the commission, "is largely a matter of attitude."[8]

As the commission recognized, whites in Virginia had repeatedly balked at appropriating funds for black education. In 1922, when the state adopted a compulsory attendance law in response to the 1919 survey, state senators from a number of Southside counties objected on the grounds that it would require their white constituents to spend money on black education. As an alternative, the Southside legislators proposed a local option bill that would have allowed localities not to require the compulsory education of blacks. Although that alternative failed to win approval from the legislature, the O'Shea Commission found that a number of localities did not enforce the law with respect to African Americans. As late as 1933, the superintendent of Richmond's public schools admitted as much, explaining that he did not enforce compulsory attendance among black pupils because of a shortage of adequate facilities. Furthermore, as many as twenty-six of Virginia's one hundred counties did not spend even the paltry state appropriation of $6.50 per child on black education. Such counties directed not one cent of local funds to black education, and in many cases they redirected state funds for black children to the white schools.[9]

The conclusions of the O'Shea Commission hardly came as a surprise to blacks in Virginia. For years the black press had highlighted the discrepancy in educational spending that resulted from a Jim Crow system in which African Americans had absolutely no voice in determining budgets. The large gap in per pupil expenditures manifested itself in better facilities, newer books, longer school terms, and less crowded buildings for white students. Blacks and whites alike recognized that white teachers were more qualified, but while whites cited inferior credentials as a reason for paying black teachers much lower salaries, blacks argued for better training for their teachers.[10]

Despite claims from white officials that the situation had improved by the mid-1920s, spending priorities suggested a grim reality: in 1925, state and local governments spent an average of $40.27 per white pupil and only $10.47 per black student. In the Deep Creek area of Norfolk County, for example, black children, who comprised about half of the population, attended school in a building constructed in 1869 and last renovated in 1884. Black citizens themselves had paid for the meager improvements in the intervening years. Blacks had even gone so far as to purchase property for a new school and present the land to the county government, but county officials took no steps to build a new facility. Because of a lack of resources and an inability to pay black teachers, the school term for black children in Deep Creek was less than seven months. By contrast, white children attended school in a building constructed twenty years before and enlarged three times, financed in part by a bond issue. White schools remained open for nine months and white children were provided transportation, a luxury unknown to black children. Approximately $100,000 had been spent in the district on white school facilities during the preceding twenty years; only $500 had been spent on black education.[11]

White Virginians frequently attempted to justify the gross inequality in educational spending by claiming that they paid a much greater proportion of taxes and therefore deserved better facilities. In Norfolk County, the superintendent of schools made precisely this argument when he asserted that because white farmers were responsible for most of the tax base, they should benefit accordingly in terms of superior facilities and should not have to pay additional taxes for black schools. One observer reminded the school official that the county's tax base depended not only on revenue from white farmers, but also on the contributions of manufacturing plants and railroads. The *Norfolk Journal and Guide* added that the relative wealth of the county was also determined by the reliable and loyal labor provided mainly by African Americans. Norfolk's black newspaper ruminated that the superintendent's reasoning, carried to its logical extreme, ought to prohibit the county's blacks from using public roads and bridges. Furthermore, the logic and rhetoric of whites failed to acknowledge that blacks did pay their fair share of taxes. In Brunswick County, according to a report carried by the *Journal and Guide*, blacks contributed one-third of that county's tax assessment but received only one-sixteenth of the school funds.[12]

African Americans highlighted the persistent inequality in educational spending in Virginia by repeatedly mentioning the more favorable situation in North Carolina, a canny strategy that undermined white Virginians' exalted view of themselves and their state. In the decade following World War I, North Carolina undertook a massive commitment to improving black education. By 1928, Virginia's neighbor had financed fifty-six black high schools, with another seventy-five on the way, all part of a goal to open a black high school in every county in the state. In particular, black Virginians noted the example set by Nathan C. Newbold, the director of the North Carolina Division of Negro Education. When Newbold publicly called for one standard of education for both races, the *Norfolk Journal and Guide* praised his statement as "the most revolutionary and progressive utterance on the race question that ever came from a Southern white man." While the Tidewater weekly may have exaggerated the significance of Newbold's words, the response underscored the emptiness of elite paternalism in Virginia. Newbold's leadership did lead to appropriations for black education that dwarfed those in Virginia. As a result, North Carolina provided far better elementary and secondary facilities, greater access to higher education, more competent and better paid teachers, and longer school terms for black children than did Virginia. Observers in Virginia pointed out that such commitments in North Carolina had cut crime rates, reduced illiteracy and disease, and promoted better interracial relations.[13]

The unwillingness of state authorities to address seriously the condition of black education paralleled the attitude of officials in counties throughout the state, such as those in Norfolk County, who denied any responsibility for their black neighbors. In rural locales, decisions made by whites met little or no overt resistance. In the state's urban areas, on the other hand, black Virginians increasingly demanded better treatment as they contested white denial and neglect. More often than not, however, ideological extremism and the nuances of Jim Crow won out and blacks continued to receive less than their fair share of municipal resources and access to public spaces.

White officials in Richmond worked harder than those in any other city to deny the benefits of citizenship to blacks. Mayor Fulmer Bright, first elected in 1924 just weeks after the passage of the Racial Integrity Act, campaigned and won on a platform of "'no Negroes on the city payrolls—city jobs for hard working white men.'" Toward the end of Bright's sixteen-year incumbency, *Richmond Times-Dispatch* editor Virginius Dabney referred to the mayor as a "total reactionary" who "thinks Negroes should have no consideration." A black constituent more bluntly stated that the mayor "hates Negroes and maintains the loyalty of the

Little Tyrannies and Petty Skullduggeries

poor whites by declaring himself a defender of their city jobs. He keeps the support of the rich business men by his relative small tax demands on them."[14]

In fact, tax policy distinguished Bright from his predecessor, George Ainslie, more so than did his commitment to white supremacy. Bright advocated what one urban planning expert has referred to as "reform through retrenchment," a policy that represented a firm commitment to limited taxation and spending and appealed to many economically prosperous voters who had tired of the wasteful expenditures of the Ainslie regime. For twelve years, Ainslie's administration had faithfully represented the aspirations of the city's business establishment through the use of taxpayer resources and municipal personnel to oversee the growth of Richmond into an efficient, well-planned metropolis. These self-styled business progressives, however, might more appropriately have been considered civic boosters. Their progressivism was limited to their own self-interest while they ignored the needs of the city's less affluent white citizens and presided over the creation of black ghettoes. Although Bright, a physician, never presented himself as a champion of the laboring classes, he owed his margin of victory to working-class voters who felt increasingly ignored by Ainslie's administration. Any hope that Bright would commit resources to the improvement of working-class neighborhoods, however, soon faded as the new mayor reduced the city's role in all aspects of planning and development.[15]

Nevertheless, Bright maintained the loyalty of non-affluent voters throughout his incumbency, in part because he adhered religiously to his campaign promises to reserve municipal jobs for white workers. For African Americans in Richmond, the change in city leadership made an already dire situation worse. With the exception of black teachers in black schools, Richmond employed no blacks on the city payroll throughout the 1920s. At a time when most of the South began to hire black principals for black schools, Richmond refused to do so. In July 1927 the city added a previously private library to its public system. For many years a black janitor had worked in the building at a salary of $15 per week. When the city took over the facility, a white man announced his desire to have the black janitor's job. Despite firm opposition from library authorities, the city council voted to fire the longtime employee, a decision that prompted an outcry from the state's press. The Norfolk Virginian-Pilot led the way, asking, "What exhibition of rapaciousness, race prejudice and political spoliation could be cheaper, commoner, or meaner? These are the little tyrannies and petty skullduggeries that make bitter the relations between the races."[16]

The observation of Norfolk's morning paper underscored an inherent tension that plagued managed race relations in Richmond and elsewhere. Confined by the demands of their own commitment to Jim Crow, even the most well-intentioned whites could not prevent such mean-spirited actions. For the most part, prominent citizens in Richmond and cities throughout the commonwealth indicated a willingness to leave the running of municipal affairs to others, so long as elected officials kept taxes low and maintained civic order. Such an arrangement, however, proved troubling at times when the city administration's hostility collided with paternalistic notions of noblesse oblige. For instance, the unwillingness of Richmond's municipal government in 1924 to provide recreational facilities for African Americans prompted the *Richmond News Leader* to organize a fund-raising campaign for that purpose. Norfolk's black newspaper commended the initiative of the Richmond white daily but remarked that such an effort was really the job of the municipal administration. This pattern repeated itself in Richmond over the years: when the city refused to provide services for its black citizens, the city's blacks, with help from some white elites, raised private funds to accomplish what they could. In 1929 the board of aldermen voted against purchasing a tract of land for a black recreational facility after white residents of North Richmond complained that blacks traveling to and from the new park would pass through white residential areas. By the end of the summer, private investors had opened a facility for blacks that contained a pool, ferris wheel, merry-go-round, and dancing pavilion. Twenty-five thousand black patrons reportedly visited the park in its first two months of operation; city officials contributed not a cent to the project.[17]

Not every municipality in the Old Dominion denied and neglected the needs of blacks in such absolute terms. In Newport News, for example, a paternalistic commitment to the fairer treatment of African Americans by the state's largest employer assured blacks of better living conditions and a greater degree of civility in public life. At the same time, however, blacks and whites in Newport News remained as separate as in any other part of Virginia.

According to high school principal Lutrelle Palmer, an African American, Newport News Shipbuilding and Drydock Company founder Collis Huntington encouraged and perpetuated "a favorable attitude toward the Negro." Huntington's influence, and that of the shipyard, continued after his death and contributed to the treatment blacks received from municipal authorities as well. The shipyard employed thousands of blacks, many of them skilled laborers, and depended upon a healthy and contented labor force. The company built a recreational facility and community center for its black employees next to the black high school in town, and fifteen blacks served on an Employees Representatives Committee, a grievance board that drew members from every department. Consistent with the shipyard's leadership, blacks in Newport News held jobs on the city payroll, working as janitors, scrubwomen, messengers, watchmen, street cleaners, ashmen, garbage men, and road workers, all positions denied them in Richmond. Most considered schools good, although no library existed, and paving, electricity, and sewage treatment acceptable. George Hardy, a white supporter of interracial cooperation, declared that "'whatever we get, they get a part of it.'" Blacks also voted with more ease in Newport News than elsewhere in the state.[18]

Both black residents and visitors described race relations in Newport News as good or excellent. But just as the attitude and example of the shipyard's ownership set such a tone, shipyard policies also served to control and limit the actions of their employees. Marion Poe, the first black woman to pass the Virginia bar, told an interviewer that the shipyard had advised its employees, by means of a note in their pay envelopes, how to vote in various elections. In addition, blacks and whites remained truly separate away from the work place. Whites did not allow blacks to use the city armory and kept them out of white movie theaters. Furthermore, Newport News's interracial commission maintained no tolerance for "those advocating common cause between blacks and whites." As George Hardy explained, "'[W]henever we find 'em and no matter how long it takes us to find 'em, we kick 'em right out. Nobody decent here wants any part of them radicals.'"[19]

Elected officials in Norfolk lacked both the racial animosity of their counterparts in Richmond and the paternalistic authority of the shipyard ownership in Newport News. Faced with tremendous growth in the years during and after World War I, Norfolk's leaders sought to address problems associated with an increased demand for municipal services. Led by Louis Jaffé, Virginia's most progressive big-city editor, the *Norfolk Virginian-Pilot* prodded the city's leadership to acknowledge an obligation to the black third of the city's population. Unlike the city council in Richmond, which plainly rejected such calls, officials in Norfolk made tentative steps in the right direction, but more often they caved in to mounting pressure from those whites who feared that black gains would come at their expense. Housing remained unfit for human habitation, parks and playgrounds remained off-limits to blacks, and city officials paved streets and installed sewage treatment only in white neighborhoods.[20]

By 1925 Norfolk's black press had begun to articulate a clear sense of the emptiness and limitations of white elite paternalism. For years, *Nor-*

folk Journal and Guide editor P. B. Young had supported the cooperation of blacks and whites within the confines of segregation; he did not publicly call for the abolition of segregation until the 1940s. Nevertheless, the steady refusal of whites to address even the most basic black grievances led Young to denounce assumptions at the heart of managed race relations. Noting that accommodations, transportation, education, wages, employment, housing, and access to municipal appropriations remained thoroughly segregated but in no sense equal, Young warned whites that African Americans did not, in fact, accept the "wrong and injustice" forced upon them.[21]

No doubt events in Norfolk over the next eighteen months only convinced Young more fully that he and other blacks would have to develop new strategies to achieve their goals. Since the early 1920s, tensions had multiplied in the Brambleton section of the city as blacks began to move into the formerly all-white neighborhood. After two years of relative calm following a confrontation between white and black residents in the summer of 1923 (see Chapter 2), the situation worsened in the spring of 1925. Hundreds of white residents, described as descendants of Norfolk's "first settlers," though not among the city's leading citizens, had moved out of the neighborhood, but their homes remained vacant and unsold because of the determination of the remaining whites to keep out blacks. As Norfolk's black district developed in the direction of Brambleton, some of the white homeowners could no longer hold onto empty properties. When two black families purchased homes in Brambleton, one hundred white men, calling themselves the Brambleton Civic League, visited the new residents and told them to leave within twenty-four hours. The group then proceeded to the home of the real estate agent who had sold the properties and reminded him of the agreed upon demarcation line. One newspaper reported that in the absence of any legislation barring such sales, intimidation had been used from time to time.[22]

In response to the continuing troubles in Brambleton, the Norfolk city council passed a residential segregation ordinance in August 1925 that prohibited whites or blacks from living in sections of the city inhabited by the other race "except upon the written consent of a majority of the persons of the opposite race inhabiting such community." Needless to say, members of the Brambleton Civic League did not rush to sign many consent forms. Soon after Norfolk passed its law, other Virginia communities considered the issue. The city council in Falls Church, in the northern part of the state, originally passed a segregation statute and used it to deny a building permit to a black resident. But when the NAACP argued against the ordinance's constitutionality, the city council reversed itself, overturned

Little Tyrannies and Petty Skullduggeries

the ordinance, and granted the building permit. In Portsmouth, Norfolk's neighbor, some residents sought a segregation ordinance as a means of removing unsightly houses, but the city manager opposed any such action as unworkable.[23]

The passage of Norfolk's residential segregation statute provided the needed impetus to jump-start that city's NAACP chapter, dormant since 1921. Several months after the adoption of the Norfolk ordinance, the NAACP challenged the law's constitutionality in court. Rather than waiting for a black person to be arrested for moving into a white neighborhood, however, David H. Edwards, the new president of the local chapter, filed a complaint that resulted in the arrest of a Jewish merchant, Nathan Falls. Falls, who acted in concert with Edwards, apparently moved into and operated a store in a black neighborhood for the sole purpose of testing the law. Several days after the arrest, Justice R. B. Spindle of the Police Court ruled the city's residential segregation ordinance unconstitutional. Despite their victory, NAACP attorneys filed an appeal in order to receive a judgment from a court of record. The following month, in March 1926, Judge Allen Hanckel of Norfolk's Circuit Court upheld the decision of the lower court.[24]

After their first victory in Norfolk's courts, opponents of the segregation ordinance had to fight a second round in July 1926, when white residents of Brambleton swore out a warrant for the arrest of Samuel Costen, a black man who had recently moved into their neighborhood. John B. Gentry and J. John Broudy, attorneys for the city of Norfolk, argued that the Norfolk statute differed from the Louisville, Kentucky, ordinance, which the U.S. Supreme Court had struck down in 1917. Instead, they described the Norfolk law as identical to a New Orleans statute, recently upheld by the Louisiana Supreme Court and headed for hearings before the U.S. Supreme Court. Louisiana's highest court had ruled that the New Orleans statute made no attempt to deny property ownership to anyone but rather prevented a black owner from occupying or renting such property in a white neighborhood, and vice versa. David Edwards, arguing the case on behalf of Costen, challenged this distinction and argued "that the denial of the right of occupancy was effectually a restriction of property rights."[25]

On July 15, 1926, Justice Spindle again ruled Norfolk's segregation ordinance unconstitutional. The following week, Judge John Hart of the Hustings Court in Roanoke declared unconstitutional that city's segregation ordinance, identical in wording to the New Orleans statute to which Norfolk's lawyers had referred. In his opinion, Hart echoed Edwards's claim and declared that "'property is more than a mere thing which a person owns. It is elementary that it includes the right to acquire, use and dispose of it. . . . Property consists of the free use, enjoyment and disposal of a person's acquisitions without control or diminution, save by the law of the land.'" The justices of the U.S. Supreme Court affirmed the decisions of the Norfolk and Roanoke jurists when they overturned New Orleans's segregation ordinance, thereby denying legitimacy to the argument that this latest round of statutes differed from the Louisville ordinance overturned ten years before.[26]

As whites in Brambleton attempted to mandate residential segregation, race was also figuring prominently in the reorganization of Norfolk's transportation system. In the wake of World War I, the city's population, black and white, increased by leaps and bounds. The white-run streetcar company, however, chose not to operate routes in predominately black sections of the city. Consequently, black-owned jitneys began operation and developed their own routes of interest to the city's black population. Although not mandated by law, a dual transportation system developed, and blacks rarely patronized white carriers.[27]

In 1925, however, a measure appeared on the November ballot to merge the two transportation systems. The Virginia Power and Railway Company operated most of the city's transportation network; its officials fully supported the measure and no doubt coveted the extra business that black riders represented. Civic leaders also favored the legislation, citing the efficiency of a unified system. Black opposition, however, appeared on two fronts. Many black passengers suspected that a unified system would fail to provide service in black sections of the city, as had been the case before the black jitneys began operation, and that they would have to walk long distances to catch a bus. Officials at Virginia Power attempted to assuage such concerns in the weeks leading up to the referendum, claiming that they would not discontinue any routes served by the black bus operators; they emphasized the number of black workers they employed and stressed the advantages of a unified system to the city's development.[28]

The most vocal opponents of a unified system were the black busmen themselves, who clearly feared their own loss of business. At first, the black jitney drivers warned that a unified system would mean an increase in fares and a loss of service in black residential areas. In the days leading up to the vote, however, the black busmen adopted a rhetorical strategy laced with irony as they distributed handouts that lauded the dual system as a better guarantor of amicable race relations. The black drivers argued that black citizens of Norfolk had become proud of the black-owned bus system that served them so well. The unified system, they emphasized, would force blacks to ride in the back of Jim Crow buses. Borrowing the language so often employed by white Virginians, but inverting its mean-

Little Tyrannies and Petty Skullduggeries

ing for their own purposes, the busmen warned that such a development threatened the "continued good feeling" that existed between blacks and whites.[29]

In response to the circulars warning of increased racial contact and friction, W. W. Houston, the chairman of the citizens' committee in favor of the ordinance, sought to reassure voters that blacks would continue to ride on their own buses, as well as on streetcars patronized by both races, but not on white buses. Although most of the warnings had originated with the black busmen, Houston attempted to address white fears when he emphasized that blacks were not then banned by law from riding on white buses but rather chose not to, an example that Norfolk's blacks "'are careful not to do anything to agitate racial prejudice.'" The chairman of the citizens' committee assured voters that black bus passengers would not have to ride on routes frequented by white patrons.[30]

Soon after the ordinance passed, the worst fears of black passengers were realized. In the process of unifying the bus system, municipal authorities and officials of the Virginia Power and Railway Company cut service to black residential areas. City manager J. Walker Truxton, who had the final say in the matter, designated two lines as "colored bus routes" and claimed that "careful consideration was given to the desire of the colored people to have their lines operated for their exclusive use and by colored drivers, and the white people to have their lines reserved for white passengers." Relying on the position taken by the colored busmen, who had desired the maintenance of a dual system, Truxton claimed to have the support of African Americans. A group of Norfolk's leading black citizens, however, objected vociferously to the city manager's classic bait and switch. Once the ordinance passed, they argued, the city of Norfolk had an obligation to provide equal access to all transportation facilities. After all, reasoned the black protesters, segregation statutes sufficiently separated blacks and whites on streetcars and on other forms of transportation. They failed to "see the justice, therefore, of virtually closing common carriers on certain public thoroughfares to colored citizens when no other means of transportation are available."[31]

Before long, the white-owned Virginia Power and Railway Company had put black jitney operators in Norfolk out of business, and municipal authorities had approved a plan that excluded blacks entirely from routes designated as white. Segregation of the races gave way to outright exclusion. It did not take long for black residents of Norfolk to comprehend that they had become the "greatest sufferers" of the new unified transportation system. By the following summer, the situation prompted the Reverend Richard Bowling to wonder in print how the city's black citizens could be denied access to public carriers. Blacks and whites rode the same streetcars without incidence, he emphasized, and other cities treated ·buses like streetcars, but not Norfolk. "Norfolk's Negroes," blasted Bowling, "must suffer inconveniences and humiliation in the matter of buses all the while being assured, nevertheless, that they are the finest colored folks anywhere. Does not the chamber of commerce booster literature speak of the contented, dependable labor supply to be found in Norfolk?"[32]

Bowling's words of anger and frustration had hardly reached the printed page when the Ku Klux Klan in neighboring Princess Anne County kidnapped Father Vincent Warren, a Catholic priest who had devoted his life to the education of black children. Since 1916 Warren had been the pastor of St. Joseph's Church in Norfolk and the principal of St. Joseph's Academy. By 1924, more than 700 black students of all ages attended the school, each of them asked to pay one penny per day, although Warren refused to turn away those who could not afford even that. As part of his school's curriculum, Father Warren had established a band, which periodically played concerts for black audiences.[33]

On September 1, 1926, Warren took the school band into Princess Anne County for a community picnic and gathering at the home of a black farmer. When the group arrived, Warren was informed that six hooded men had appeared at the farm earlier and objected to the impending appearance of a white priest with the black musicians. He thereupon withdrew to a car with two other white men who had accompanied the group. Toward the end of the concert, which Warren observed from afar, a gang of between twenty-eight and fifty well-organized and armed Klansmen approached the Catholic priest and forced him into one of their cars. Heading toward the North Carolina line, Warren prepared for death. Finally, after a thirty-minute ride, the entourage stopped deep in the woods and ordered Warren out of the car.[34]

Warren later reported that the Klansmen had questioned his motives for bringing the band into the county; he assured them that the "purpose of the party was to give the colored children a picnic and the country people a concert." Members of the hooded order pressed him as to the purposes of his school in the city. When Warren responded that his intent was merely to train young black children to become solid citizens, qualities he thought that the Klan supported, one of his abductors concluded that they had been misinformed and told Warren that they had received a report that he encouraged the immoral mixing of blacks and whites. Despite the wishes of some of the Klansmen to rough up the priest, the kidnappers released Warren unharmed.[35]

Little Tyrannies and Petty Skullduggeries

The rhetoric of Warren's kidnappers revealed the growing tension and discomfort felt in the years after World War I by whites uncertain about their futures. At a time when demographic and economic changes both pushed and pulled many rural residents into urban environs in search of better wages, the Klansmen expressed disdain for, but also fear of, the influences of the city. Although rural, Princess Anne County was close to the city of Norfolk. Not only was Warren a Catholic priest in a heavily Protestant region, but he trained black children at a time when ideological and racial extremism had ascended into prominence. Although not a single white child attended Warren's school, the Klansmen believed without question the veracity of a report that Warren promoted immoral contact between black and white pupils.[36]

Virginia's press and political leadership condemned the Warren kidnapping. In the *Norfolk Virginian-Pilot*, Louis Jaffé ripped the "indifference" of local authorities whose unwillingness to investigate the incident only encouraged such activity in the future. James E. Allen, a resident of Virginia Beach, echoed Jaffé's sentiments and warned in a letter to the governor that "if mob rule is going to usurp the functions of our courts and dominate the social life, politics and religion of our citizens, the country will soon be in the grasp of Bolshevism." Governor Byrd offered his aid if local authorities requested it, but neither the Princess Anne sheriff nor the commonwealth's attorney appeared interested. Judge B. D. White of the Princess Anne Circuit Court did convene a grand jury and instructed its members to investigate the matter. Although black residents of the area from which Warren was abducted reportedly recognized members of the mob, the jury refused to take action.[37]

In keeping with the emphasis of the white press and state political leaders on law and order, the city of Norfolk passed an antimask ordinance the week following the abduction. At no time, however, did white elites respond to Father Warren's kidnapping in terms of the broader ramifications of his work. Richard Bowling, on the other hand, used the occasion to connect the Catholic priest's ministry with the broader plight of black Virginians. In particular, Bowling emphasized that Warren's determination to educate black children had resulted from the priest's awareness of the overwhelming and persistent neglect of state and local authorities. His school had become all the more necessary precisely because most white Virginians chose to ignore the constitutional mandate of *Plessy*.[38]

No doubt most white elites who emphasized law and order in the wake of the Warren kidnapping considered their condemnations of the Klan evidence of their fair treatment of their African American neighbors. A growing number of white opinion shapers, however, understood and began to articulate the degree to which white authorities had failed the Old Dominion's black citizens. By the mid-1920s, Louis Jaffé had emerged as one of the most outspoken white racial moderates in the state. In his editorials and speeches before black and white audiences, Jaffé crafted a cautious yet optimistic approach designed not only to improve the terms of contact between the races, but also to compel whites to accept responsibility for abusing their disproportionate power. A realist with regard to the prevailing view of white southerners, he believed in the necessity of "relegating to the wisdom of another day and generation the solution of problems that touch the races as social entities and which involve discriminations based on social fear." Unlike most of his contemporaries, however, who used such reasoning as an excuse for inaction, Jaffé identified numerous problems that could be solved and called on whites to muster the will to do so. Jaffé himself did not appear to fear the implications of change that he knew must one day occur; instead, he stressed that "old patterns of thinking about the Negro's place in the American scheme are changing or breaking down, and that a new generation of Americans, white and black, is emerging."[39]

Jaffé emphasized first and foremost the necessity of easing the economic predicament of African Americans in Virginia. Cognizant that equal pay for equal work was perhaps an unrealizable goal in the foreseeable future, he insisted that "it is the standard toward which all economic teaching impels us and to which we are pointed by justice." Referring to the abysmal housing, sewage-laden alleyways, and unpaved roadways endemic to black neighborhoods, Jaffé concluded that "there is something monstrously wrong with an economic system that makes these conditions so unfailingly and so exclusively, the reward of Negro labor." While acknowledging that the average African American laborer lacked the skills and training necessary for higher-paying jobs, Jaffé blamed the situation on "the discrimination practiced against him by the great unions . . . the heartless exploitation of him by the white employing world, and . . . a municipal policy that has failed to do justice to the colored population in the planning and carrying out of public improvements."[40]

In a 1927 speech before a predominately black audience, the Norfolk editor noted in particular that southern cities "are under the most compelling moral obligation to make a fairer distribution of public improvements." Citing Norfolk's erection of a new black high school, Jaffé saw reason for optimism insofar as he believed that public opinion was moving, albeit slowly, toward acceptance of this responsibility. He acknowledged that much remained to be done and chided the city for not building a bathing beach or adequate hospital for Norfolk's blacks. In closing, Jaffé confronted the responsibility of the press in fostering interracial tension and hostility. Despite efforts to ameliorate the situation, he considered the white press "still too prone to exploit Negro crime," too quick to accuse blacks of criminal acts without evidence, and "too timid about giving space and attention to those aspects of Negro life that bear witness to its dignity and its finer aspirations." He pledged his newspaper's best efforts to correct these wrongs, and to contribute toward a condition of "fairness, justice, and mutual respect which all sincere men and women of both races are seeking."[41]

Jaffé's ability to address rightable wrongs remained circumscribed by the second-class political and social status foisted on blacks by Jim Crow. Though more genuinely progressive than most other white elites who evinced an interest in improving the lives of African Americans, Jaffé still worked within the confines of Jim Crow and white supremacy, which limited the opportunity for any fundamental change. In the late 1920s Jaffé did not address the rights of citizenship of black Virginians; rather, he considered improvements in the black standard of living an "obligation" that rested with "the race that controls the machinery of government, the administration of justice and the organization of business and industry." But, as Jaffé knew too well, so long as municipal and state leaders remained politically unaccountable to African Americans, great inequalities in public life would persist. The seriousness of this conundrum could not have been lost on Jaffé, for precisely at the time he most clearly articulated his ideas to a black audience in Norfolk, a dispute erupted that revealed the depth and extent of white resistance to the recognition of African Americans as citizens of the commonwealth and nation.[42]

In November 1927 national opponents of Prohibition began to ask publicly if they might nullify the Eighteenth Amendment in the same manner that the southern states had effectively nullified the Fourteenth and Fifteenth Amendments. In an effort to remain consistent, Senator William Borah of Idaho, a dry, responded to a wet colleague that he would be willing to extend the Republican Party's plank at the following year's convention to include not only the enforcement of Prohibition but also the enforcement of the Fourteenth and Fifteenth Amendments. Meanwhile, a leading opponent of Prohibition questioned the "inconsistency" of Senator Carter Glass in refusing to support the dispatch of federal election monitors to supervise a disputed election in Kentucky while simultaneously sanctioning the use of federal agents to enforce the Prohibition laws.[43]

Glass, Virginia's junior U.S. senator and the author of the state's suffrage provisions, responded with a withering attack. Glass characterized opposition to the Prohibition amendment as an attempt to "facilitate" crime, whereas he defended Virginia's suffrage laws as necessary "to avert the wretched consequences of the unspeakable crime involved in the adoption" of the Fourteenth and Fifteenth Amendments. The passage of black suffrage, Glass argued, "was done in the passions of war, and constituted an attempt to destroy white civilization in nearly one-third of the nation and to erect on its ruins an Ethiopian state ignorant, profligate, corrupt, controlled by manumitted slaves."[44]

Although Glass clearly felt that Virginia and the South were justified in their resistance to black suffrage, he insisted that "there is no constitutional or statutory law in the code of a single southern state that violates the terms of the fifteenth amendment." As evidence, he cited repeated rulings of the U.S. Supreme Court, noting in particular that a challenge to his own election to Congress had resulted in a finding that the Old Dominion's laws did not violate the federal constitution. Consequently, the senator concluded, "the white people of Virginia, within the limitations of the federal constitutions, have complete control of their state affairs, without the least fear of disturbance by the blacks."[45]

Surprisingly enough, given the overwhelming support among white Virginians for disfranchisement, Glass's outburst engendered significant controversy in the commonwealth's press. A handful of editors, most notably Walter Scott Copeland of the *Newport News Daily Press*, took issue with the senator's claims. Copeland, a leading advocate of the Massenburg Bill, agreed with Glass that black suffrage had been foisted upon the South in a "spirit of malice." While he recognized that southern election laws "technically" did not violate the federal constitution, he insisted that the same laws "were ingeniously devised to nullify the Fifteenth Amendment; and nullification was the result."[46]

The *Richmond Times-Dispatch* came to Glass's defense, asserting, in Copeland's words, that the Old Dominion's election law "no more denies illiterate negroes the right to vote than it denies illiterate Caucasians the right to vote." Copeland accepted this argument on technical grounds but reminded his subscribers that Virginia's laws gave tremendous "power and discretion" to election registrars to employ literacy tests and understanding clauses in an effort "to register the whites in general and to exclude the negroes." Lest Carter Glass or anyone else misunderstand the purpose of his dissent, however, Copeland accepted the absolute necessity of Virginia's adoption of such regulations. In other words, he differed with Glass only in his willingness to admit that the state's laws had been designed precisely to "nullify" the Fifteenth Amendment.[47]

Copeland's embrace of the necessity of Virginia's election laws failed to ameliorate Glass. Lashing out on the editorial pages of his own publication, the *Lynchburg News*, the fiery senator continued to deny the veracity of Copeland's allegations, insisted upon the legality of Virginia's statutes, and ignored any discussion of the effective powers of the local registrars. For nearly two weeks, Glass and Copeland traded barbs in their respective papers. For Glass, all that mattered was the Fifteenth Amendment, which "clung to the body politic of the South like the putrid corpse of scriptural anathema. It is fastened there now. It has crabbed the civilization of this section; has warped its intellect; has injured its character; has repressed its aspirations; has driven it to distasteful expedients; has, for sixty-five years, rendered impossible a division of mind or contrariety of action." Copeland, on the other hand, sought only to curb the "smug hypocrisy" of those who condemned every violation of the Prohibition amendment as "treason" or "nullification" but in the same breath defended the South's election procedures.[48]

The exchange left Louis Jaffé dumbfounded, unable to comprehend why some southerners went to such lengths to deny what was commonly known and accepted. In a letter to Copeland, Jaffé asked, "Is it not far more sincere to say: 'Yes, we've excluded the Negro from the polls because we are afraid of him at the polls and don't want him there, and we've done it despite a constitutional mandate imposed on us against our will,' than it is to put on a smirking hypocrisy and pretend that we have faithfully abided by the spirit and letter of the Constitution and that the Negro has committed political suicide of his own free will?"[49]

The debate spilled onto the floor of the U.S. Senate in January 1928. Claude Swanson, Virginia's senior senator, stood before his colleagues and argued that the Fourteenth and Fifteenth Amendments unquestionably allowed for educational requirements and understanding clauses. "It was distinctly understood in both Houses of Congress," he proclaimed, "that the resolution as passed permitted suffrage qualifications to be imposed by the States on any ground except 'on account of race, color, or previous condition of servitude.'" Ignoring the fact that many of Virginia's black voters were as well educated as their white counterparts, Swanson declared that the "South has exercised her constitutional right to eliminate a class of ignorant, shiftless, and corrupt voters who for many years were in charge of her local, municipal, and State affairs, with the result of unspeakable impoverishment and disgrace."[50]

At the conclusion of Swanson's prepared speech, Senator William Cabell Bruce of Maryland, a leading wet, challenged Swanson to explain why such a small percentage of the black population voted in the Old Dominion, especially when compared to the white population. Swanson proved unable to say more than that Virginia did not discriminate based on "race, color, or previous condition of servitude." At this point, Carter Glass entered the fray and asked if Bruce, born and raised in Southside Virginia, counted himself "among those who threaten the South with universal negro suffrage unless the South shall quietly sanction the violation of the eighteenth amendment." Bruce, a good friend of Glass's despite the repartee, replied that if southerners had the right "by the exercise of legal ingenuity" to nullify amendments to which they objected, "we have the right by any lawful means in our power to extricate ourselves from the tyrannous oppression of the eighteenth amendment and the Volstead Act." Glass responded, drawing laughter, "Then why does not the Senator exercise the ingenuity to do it?"[51]

As the two men debated the issue, a clear difference in emphasis emerged. Bruce focused on the administration of the law and remarked at the facility with which whites interpreted and enforced the law in terms that put African Americans at a profound disadvantage. Glass, on the other hand, clung to the legality of Virginia's statutes, proudly claimed authorship of the state's disfranchisement laws, and asked the senator from Maryland to "suggest how the suffrage laws of Virginia could be rendered more generous or more liberal to the Negro race with perfect safety to the Commonwealth itself." As the exchange between the two men heated up, Bruce defended his credentials as a true and loyal southerner but insisted that Glass's position suited a South long since past. "The negro is no longer a slave," began the Virginia native. "He is no longer an ignorant, staggering freedman such as he was just after the Civil War. He is acquiring education, and intelligence along with it. He is acquiring property. He is becoming a better citizen." Concluding that the white South's future no longer depended upon disfranchisement, Bruce added that "the whole attitude of the South toward the negro ought to be a little more liberal than it has in the past. I think it can be without any sacrifice of sound principles or any peril to the social integrity of the white race."[52]

In the ensuing months the issue remained in the news, and Carter Glass rose to defend his and Virginia's reputation. In speech after speech, Glass defined the legality of Virginia's compliance with the Fourteenth and Fifteenth Amendments. After one fiery oration, J. J. Taylor wrote in the *Religious Herald*, a Richmond-based Baptist publication, that the senator's emphasis on the legality of Virginia's laws meant only that they had been "adroitly" written. The author urged that Virginians follow the spirit, as well as the letter, of the law, warning that "the violation of a law because it is distasteful naturally leads to the violation of other distasteful laws. . . . In the end every man does what is right in his own eyes, and anarchy takes the place of orderly government."[53]

In April 1928 the national media picked up the story. *Liberty*, a weekly magazine published in New York City, sent Sidney Sutherland to speak with Glass. According to the reporter, the junior senator from Virginia rejected as "'colossal nonsense'" the notion that wets could nullify the Eighteenth Amendment because southerners had accomplished as much with regard to the Fourteenth and Fifteenth Amendments. "'There is not one single instance of a Southern State passing a law which violates a Federal statute,'" insisted Glass. "'No State in the South has disenfranchised a single colored citizen because he was colored.'" Prodded by Sutherland, Glass eventually lost his composure and declared that the "'people of the original thirteen Southern States curse and deride and spit upon the Fifteenth Amendment—and have no intention of letting the Negro vote.'" Expressing the same sentiments he revealed before Virginia's constitutional convention of 1901–2, Glass finally admitted, "'We obey the letter of the amendments and the Federal statutes, but we frankly evade the spirit thereof—and purport to continue doing so. White supremacy is too precious a thing to surrender for the sake of a theoretical justice that would let a brutish African deem himself the equal of white men and women in Dixie.'"[54]

The publication of Glass's remarks prompted an immediate denunciation from both of Virginia's black newspapers, the *Norfolk Journal and Guide* and the *Richmond Planet*. The Tidewater weekly labeled Glass a "demagogue" whose comments reflected a lifelong rebellion against the Fourteenth and Fifteenth Amendments. An editorial declared, "No more desperate appeal to race prejudice has been uttered by Vardaman, long since retired, or Tillman, now dead, or Blease or Heflin. It is the swan song of dying political and personal bigotry; the wail of one who perceives about his head the giving away of a wall of ignorance which he has fostered, for the dictates of real, not theoretical, justice." The paper reminded its audience, especially its white readers, that African Americans did not seek domination or supremacy but "balanced justice, economic and educational opportunity, and equality before the law." For its part, the Richmond paper read Glass's utterances as proof that he had fallen into "the cess-pool of the ordinary politician vainly endeavoring to bring consistency out of inconsistency and righteousness out of wrong-doing."[55]

Immediately after publication of his remarks, Glass backpedaled, labeling the story "inaccurate and largely fictitious" and asserting that "nobody who knows me or my habit of speech could believe that I had ever been guilty of the coarse utterances attributed to me." Sutherland, however, insisted that if anything he had toned down the tenor of the senator's remarks. Accepting Glass's denial, two major white newspapers in the Tidewater area criticized the response of the *Norfolk Journal and Guide*. The *Norfolk Virginian-Pilot* objected not so much to the content as to the tone of the black weekly and considered extreme the comparison of Glass to other demagogues; the *Newport News Daily Press* and its editor, Walter Scott Copeland, no doubt mindful of the editorial war waged two years earlier with the *Journal and Guide* over the Massenburg Bill, took a harsher stance and labeled the black paper guilty of "false and slanderous assertions." Acknowledging that it may have been a bit harsh in its criticism of Glass, the *Journal and Guide* admitted that the Virginian was indeed more capable than Vardaman but insisted that he had fallen into the habit of race-baiting and that any thorough look at the senator's record would reveal a contempt for the Fourteenth and Fifteenth Amendments.[56]

Journal and Guide subscribers offered varied responses to Glass's comments. W. L. Davis of Norfolk, like the white press, questioned the labeling of Glass as a demagogue. Instead, he considered Glass able, honest, sincere, and consistent, albeit "incapacitated, either from too much pondering over exaggerated fears or a mental derangement in regard to one subject only (the Negro)." Rather than considering the political rights or privileges due Virginia's blacks, Davis wrote, Glass considered only "an arrangement which suits his own convenience." Davis ended on a note of pity, claiming that "while I admire Senator Glass for the courage of his convictions, I am sorry for his affliction."[57]

Gordon Blaine Hancock, on the other hand, termed Glass's remarks "an affront to every Negro citizen of this country." But just as important to the professor and Baptist minister from Richmond, the senator's scornful words ignored the fact that a growing number of white southerners had ceased to "tremble before the ghost of 'Negro domination' when all the laws and all the wealth and all the armies and all the navies are at their command." More specifically, Hancock condemned Glass for encouraging a disrespect for the law. "When the Senator defiantly boasts of adhering to the letter of the law but spurning its spirit," Hancock explained in a moment of devastating prophesy, "he sets a dangerous precedent for the oncoming generations of white men. Whether law can be repudiated today and evoked for protection tomorrow is extremely doubtful, and when Senator Glass assumes such position he is 'sowing to the

wind of law evasion, and the rising generations must reap the whirl-wind'
of lawlessness."[58]

The political rhetoric and demagoguery of officials such as Carter Glass
reflected an attitude among white Virginians that allowed for the constant
and withering neglect of black needs and the denial of black citizenship.
The statewide passage of the Racial Integrity and Public Assemblages
Acts, the commonwealth's continued inattention to black education, the
agitation among marginalized whites for residential segregation in Norfolk, and the commitment of a municipal administration in Richmond to
reserve city jobs for whites only, all served to remind black Virginians of
the inherent emptiness of paternalism. Douglas Gordon, the editor of the
Norfolk Ledger-Dispatch, was among a handful of whites who acknowledged the limitations of managed race relations. Addressing an interracial
audience at Hampton Institute, Gordon reported that he had overheard
the head of a large railway in Richmond say, "'Why don't the people of the
North let us alone! We are the only people who understand the Negro.'"
"Why, bless his heart," Gordon responded to the Hampton audience. "He
knows less than nothing about the Negro.... With deliberation, with what
I believe to be a fairly comprehensive understanding of the old and new
South, I say what I have often said in private: We of Virginia, we of the
South in general, know less about the modern Negro than do the people
of any other section of the entire United States. We have closed our eyes;
we have closed our ears; we have even closed our minds."[59]

Black Virginians understood all too well what Gordon expressed. Unfortunately, the Norfolk editor spoke for few whites. Governor Harry
Byrd better represented the position of Virginia's elite whites in racial
matters. While he did not espouse the meanness and virulence of Richmond mayor Fulmer Bright, the governor essentially ignored the plight
of African Americans in Virginia. Byrd and other elites paid homage to
the friendly relations that existed between whites and blacks but failed
to act in a complementary manner. As a state senator, Byrd chose not to
vote for or against the Racial Integrity Act; as governor, he allowed the
Massenburg Bill to become law without his signature. More concerned
with maintaining support for his program to streamline the state's government, Byrd made no effort either to oppose the rise in ideological extremism or to show support for the fairer treatment of Virginia's blacks.
Furthermore, he proved adept at using white supremacy as a campaign
tool when it suited his needs.

In fact, white elites did not act to pass legislation meaningful to the Old
Dominion's black citizenry until 1928, when an increase in mob violence

threatened the commonwealth's reputation as a state devoted to law, order, and racial harmony. The blot on Virginia's good name came as Byrd and other elites sought to attract business and industry to the Old Dominion. Although black Virginians genuinely applauded the nation's most significant antilynching legislation, they understood that it did not address the "little tyrannies and petty skullduggeries" of Jim Crow. Their lack of political power, perpetuated by Carter Glass and others, allowed white elites to continue to ignore their most basic requests, thereby ensuring continued dissonance between the rhetoric and the reality of Virginia's brand of managed race relations.

6

A Melancholy Distinction

VIRGINIA'S RESPONSE TO LYNCHING

> The indifference on the part of white people generally
> to the crime of lynching is due largely to the fact that the one
> lynched is invariably a Negro. "Just another nigger gone" is
> the usual comment, and the matter is dismissed. . . . Until our
> dominant race of white Virginians come to understand and
> revere the principles of human liberty—not to mention the
> ideal of Christian charity—this notion that a Negro life is
> merely a remnant of an old chattel will persist. And just
> as surely will mob violence continue and justice—in the
> language of the kangaroo court—be dispensed with.
> —BRUCE CRAWFORD, editor of *Crawford's Weekly*, 1927

In February 1950 a group of newcomers to the Virginia legislature noted that the General Assembly had passed but one law in the twentieth century that conferred "upon the Negro any one of the many attributes of Virginia citizenship which we possess, and which he does not possess, although they are guaranteed to him by our Constitution." They referred to an antilynching law passed in 1928 and trumpeted at the time as the nation's most forceful statement against mob law. Newspapers and politicians had lost no time in praising the measure as evidence of Virginia's long-standing commitment to law and order; for years the state's boosters proudly emphasized that no lynchings had occurred since the act's passage. If the Racial Integrity Act in 1924 and the Public Assemblages Act in 1926 revealed an uglier side to managed race relations in Virginia, then the passage of an antilynching measure in 1928 reassured white elites that their paternalism guaranteed racial amity and goodwill. While the bill's enactment proved remarkable for public relations, it did little to advance the interests of African Americans or to address their most pressing concerns.[1]

Fewer African Americans were lynched in Virginia than in any other southern state in the twentieth century, a dubious distinction that nevertheless reinforced for white Virginians the superiority of their system of race relations. While less active than elsewhere in the South, mobs in the Old Dominion did execute at least seventy blacks between 1880 and 1930. As was the case throughout the South, more lynchings occurred in the 1890s than in any other decade, and each succeeding decade saw a drop in the numbers, although often an increase in brutality. In Virginia, no blacks were lynched from 1906 to 1916, before mobs took the lives of two men in 1917 and one in 1918.[2]

In his analysis of lynching in Virginia and Georgia, Fitzhugh Brundage concludes that Virginia experienced fewer lynchings between 1880 and 1930 because the state's diverse economy did not depend upon the more coercive labor control methods found deeper in the South where single-crop farming dominated. Landlords in Virginia could afford to extend a small degree of independence to black workers; in addition, the most disgruntled blacks had an easier time migrating north merely as a result of geographical proximity. Furthermore, the "profoundly conservative inclinations of Virginia's elite," according to Brundage, opposed lynching as a disruption of social order in the same way they objected to labor unrest. Consequently, whites who ultimately supported an antilynching statute emphasized a need for law and order, not a respect for the rights of African Americans.[3]

While Brundage provides a penetrating analysis of the macro forces that explain the frequency of lynching in Virginia, mob violence remained essentially a local affair, virtually unexplainable by larger models of behavior. Local mobs responded to perceived causation, and local officials usually chose to take no action. State officials refused to intervene in local affairs. During the 1920s, however, such local occurrences assumed statewide relevance. While the rest of the South continued to note a decline in mob violence in the 1920s, the frequency of mob deaths in the Old Dominion increased. Virginians lynched at least six black men in the 1920s, double the number of the previous decade. Each instance of mob violence further undermined the commonwealth's reputation at a time when the state's press, political leaders, and business elites worked hard to attract industry and manufacturing. Concurrently, groups such as the Commission on Interracial Cooperation attacked mob violence on moral grounds.

In this climate, lynching emerged as a state issue that required a state solution.[4]

In many respects, the lynching of Allie Thompson just outside Culpeper in the early hours of November 25, 1918, typified mob deaths throughout the South. A young black man, Thompson was jailed for sexually assaulting a white woman. Before he went to trial, a mob kidnapped him from the jail and lynched him. Local officials never identified or brought charges against any mob members. According to news reports and confirmed by Commonwealth's Attorney Edwin H. Gibson, Thompson had been accused of attacking Lelia Sisk and lodged in jail to await the next session of the Circuit Court. Neither Gibson nor Thompson's lawyer, T. E. Grimsley, appeared concerned that a lynching might take place. Both expressed a belief that Mrs. Sisk's neighborhood remained "unusually quiet" and that "a number of the best people of the neighborhood were doing what they could to allay what little feeling there was." Gibson later told the governor that "there seemed no disposition not to allow the law to take its usual course."[5]

Several nights later, a pair of men appeared at the jail carrying a third man tied up with a rope. Explaining that they had taken the bound man into custody, the two captors asked the jailers to allow them into the jail to deposit their prisoner. One jailer later claimed that he looked up and down the street, saw no reason for concern, and told the men to walk around to a side entrance with direct access to the cells. When the jailer opened the side door, twelve to fifteen masked men overwhelmed him and his partner, located Thompson, secured a rope around his neck, and took him from the facility. According to the local newspaper, "the entire proceeding was remarkably quiet and devoid of any exciting circumstances or noise." The mob apparently made no noise on their way out of town; they traveled three miles, found a tree, and hanged Thompson.[6]

In his report to Governor Westmoreland Davis, the commonwealth's attorney accepted the judgment of the coroner and concluded that "it is impossible to find any clue upon which to base an investigation. There is not even local gossip fixing the responsibility upon any particular person." Although all reports indicated that the mob had worn masks, neither the commonwealth's attorney nor any other local official raised the question of the identity of the two men and their supposed prisoner whose ruse had fooled the jailers. Certainly they had not worn masks. As a result of such incomplete information, Governor Davis requested that Gibson continue his investigation and identity the responsible parties.[7]

A few days later, Davis received a letter from Moses A. Summons, a black resident of Amissville, a hamlet not far from Culpeper. In ten pages handwritten in pencil, Summons challenged the certainty of Thompson's guilt and presented a version of events that never appeared in the newspaper. Summons argued that Thompson could not have traveled from the place of the alleged assault to the place of his arrest in the time claimed by his accusers. Furthermore, Summons noted that "no effort was put forward to prove whether the lady's statement was either true or false. No one ever went over the ground to prove whether he made any tracks going to the woods or coming away." Most disturbing of all, Mrs. Sisk had expressed doubt as to whether her assailant was a light-skinned mulatto like Thompson or a white man.[8]

Summons accused William Robson, a local magistrate, of complicity in Thompson's death. Specifically, Summons told the governor that the magistrate had jailed the accused without any corroborating evidence and that Robson "continually made statements calculated to stir up mob violence; he made no secret of his confidence of Thompson's guilt and made no effort to defend the life of the prisoner." Directly contradicting the account of the commonwealth's attorney, Summons explained that Thompson's parents had expressed to Robson their fears of the danger of a lynching, but that the magistrate had dismissed them as unwarranted. Summons concluded that Robson "knew something of the mob."[9]

Summons reminded the governor that whether Allie Thompson was guilty or innocent, the Constitution guaranteed him "a right to a fair and impartial trial." The Amissville resident questioned the commitment of state and local authorities to the rule of law and emphasized the damage done to Virginia's reputation. Expressing particular outrage that Robson had assumed "powers of judge, jury and executioner," Summons informed the governor that he did not "cry for vengeance but for justice and truth" and asked only that those responsible be held accountable.[10]

No record exists to suggest that Governor Davis responded to the impassioned letter from Summons, nor does any record indicate that the commonwealth's attorney pursued the matter. Two months later, however, Allie Thompson's father, Wade, wrote the chief executive a short note. "I saw in the paper," commented the grieving father, "that you were going to take a personal hand in the investigation of the lynching of Allie Thompson my son. So far as nothing has been done towards this. I trust you will see that the Commonwealth Atty. of Culpeper Co. will begin an investigation at once. Please oblige."[11]

Wade Thompson's letter, so eloquent in its simplicity, is remarkable in a number of ways. First, it appears to be the only direct plea from a relative of a lynched man to reach the governor's desk in the years after World War I. More important, Thompson's words reflected at least a basic education: he read the paper and could write at a time when illiteracy rates among black adults in Virginia approached 30 percent. More than likely, his son Allie had received at least as much schooling, a conclusion supported by the *Culpeper Exponent*, which commented that "his face showed more than the average intelligence." The Culpeper mob did not lynch an illiterate transient, but rather an educated young man who lived either with or near both of his parents, at least one of whom also was literate. Finally, Wade Thompson's simple request reflected a continued determination among black Virginians, despite decades of disfranchisement and Jim Crow, to make state and local government work for them as well as for whites.[12]

Although the next officially recognized lynching in the Old Dominion occurred in November 1920, evidence suggests that a mob in Halifax County either lynched Leslie Allen in August 1920 or killed him after an argument in a manner resembling a lynching. According to the *Danville Register*, an unidentified number of whites shot Allen in the head, neck, and throughout the body; the victim's wounds included a shotgun blast in the mouth and another to the side of the head. John M. Royall, a black man living in New York but visiting Halifax County at the time, told the NAACP that he understood that Allen's crime had been to utter a remark after not being allowed to join a game of ten pins. Soon after, a mob overtook Allen and killed him. The newspaper account of Allen's murder indicated that he had in his possession the caliber of revolver considered standard issue in the army. Allen might well have returned from service in France determined not to endure the slights of white men and as a result paid with his life in a manner repeated throughout the South in the years after World War I.[13]

On November 14, 1920, a mob in Wise County, in Virginia's extreme southwestern corner, stormed the jail, removed Dave Hurst, a black prisoner, and lynched him. Held in connection with the rape of Sarah Ball two days before, Hurst's alleged crime and his death appear unremarkable in the annals of southern mob violence except for the determination of Commonwealth's Attorney C. R. McCorkle to prosecute the mob. Upon Hurst's arrest, McCorkle asked the local judge to call a special term of court in order to try the case without delay. Ball's husband appeared satisfied and said "that he would counsel his friends against any resort to violence." Nevertheless, the commonwealth's attorney expressed concern that public sentiment in favor of mob violence would only increase as word of the attack spread. Consequently, he pressed the urgency of the matter upon the judge the following day and secured a definite commitment for a special term of court to convene on November 22. McCorkle publicized this development throughout the county and again felt that relatives and friends of the Ball family "would be satisfied to let the law take its course."[14]

Later that same night, however, an anonymous caller warned the sheriff and commonwealth's attorney that a mob had begun to form and would soon head to the Wise jail. When McCorkle arrived at the jail, he found between fifty and one hundred heavily armed men threatening the sheriff. The commonwealth's attorney learned later that additional mob members guarded the roads going in and out of town. Clearly outnumbered, McCorkle attempted to persuade mob leaders to disperse; a few, including Ball's husband and son, indicated a willingness to comply. At the same time, however, a detachment of the mob had broken into the jail with a sledgehammer. McCorkle then went inside the jail in an effort to reason with that faction of the mob, only to find himself "looking down the barrels of two forty-five's." The commonwealth's attorney later told Governor Davis that he believed the initial willingness of some mob leaders to comply with his request to disperse "was only a ruse to deceive the sheriff and gain time." After locating Hurst, who had reportedly confessed, the mob took him to a site near where he had allegedly assaulted Sarah Ball and lynched him.[15]

Hurst's killers made no attempt to disguise themselves. McCorkle claimed to have known three of the men himself and to have known the identities of at least six other mob members, including Ball and his son. In the immediate aftermath of the lynching, the commonwealth's attorney informed the governor that he intended "to let the matter rest quietly for a few days, so as to give them a chance to do some talking." McCorkle worried that pushing ahead too quickly would force participants to clam up, but unlike so many other local officials confronted with mob violence, he remained resolute in his determination to identify as many mob members as possible and "to go after them with every resource at the command of the Commonwealth." To that end, he asked the governor for help in securing a skilled investigator and welcomed the assistance of the attorney general's office.[16]

McCorkle kept his promise to the governor and won grand jury indictments against fifty members of the mob. On August 16, 1921, one of those fifty, Shaler B. Tate, was convicted of voluntary manslaughter and sentenced to two years, later reduced to fourteen months, in the state penitentiary. The *Norfolk Journal and Guide* described the trial as an extremely difficult one in which "every technicality of the law and human prejudice were appealed to." Although various appeals postponed the start of his sentence, Tate began serving his term on January 4, 1923. In addition, Wise County jurors convicted Al Napier, described by the *Journal and Guide* as a "prominent" citizen, of lesser charges and sent him to jail for one year. Determined to see both men serve time for their crimes, McCorkle and the presiding judge refused to support an initial pardon application. In October 1923, on the other hand, after Tate and Napier had served more than half their sentences, Governor E. Lee Trinkle accepted the recommendation of the trial judge and prosecuting attorney and pardoned both men. In explaining his decision, the chief executive noted that the two men had been punished while dozens of coconspirators had gone free.[17]

Tate and Napier became the first two white men sent to jail in Virginia for lynching a black man. No others ever followed. Their convictions were the result of the determination and persistence of a commonwealth's attorney who defied local pressure, called upon the support of state authorities, and pursued the matter as far as he could. In the wake of Dave Hurst's lynching, officials in Wise County exhibited a willingness to use force to discourage mob violence, even at the risk of killing white men. In early December 1920, only three weeks after Hurst's death, another Wise mob descended upon the jail in an attempt to lynch a black man charged in the death of a white merchant from the town of Appalachia. On this occasion, however, Sheriff A. L. Corder anticipated trouble and placed a half-dozen well-armed deputies around the jail. A mob of thirty-five remained undeterred and attacked the jail but met return fire. Deputies killed two mob members and injured several others. The deaths enraged neighbors of the mob members, six hundred of whom regrouped and headed again for the county jail. Once again, the mob met a determined coterie of local officials and prominent citizens who convinced the vigilantes that an attack would result only in the deaths of more of their number. As the mob dispersed, troops arrived from Lynchburg and Roanoke to spirit the black prisoner away.[18]

Most officials lacked the will to emulate the example of Sheriff Corder and Commonwealth's Attorney McCorkle. Authorities in Brunswick County made no effort to punish any of the estimated 2,000 members of a mob that lynched Lem Johnson in August 1921. Although Governor Davis instructed the commonwealth's attorney to undertake a thorough investigation, local officials may have sympathized with a mob that acted in retaliation for the death of a white man. News reports indicated that most members of the mob had worn masks, therefore providing the commonwealth's attorney an easy excuse for inaction. In addition, the large number of participants might have been accepted as a gauge of popular support.

The size of the mob alone calls into question the report of one news account that "so quietly did the mob carry out its work that few in the neighborhood knew what was going on." More than likely, the entire neighborhood participated, at least in spirit if not directly.[19]

While authorities treated the deaths of Allie Thompson, Dave Hurst, and Lem Johnson as essentially local matters, the lynching of Horace Carter initiated a transformation in white attitudes that ultimately redefined the state's response to mob murder. Although black leaders and newspapers in the Old Dominion had long demanded that the state take steps to eradicate lynching, white authorities paid little attention until forced to do so by the efforts of Louis Jaffé, who wrote the first of many antilynching editorials in October 1923. A member of the Norfolk branch of the Commission on Interracial Commission, Jaffé at first hoped to bring an end to lynching by moving public opinion. The grim reality of repeated mob deaths, however, eventually led Jaffé to endorse a state antilynching law.[20]

On October 12, 1923, a mob of ten people in King and Queen County seized Horace Carter as he was being transported by authorities to the county jail. The forty-year-old black man had been arrested in a neighboring county on charges of assaulting a married white woman almost one year earlier. As sheriff's deputies drove along a dark stretch of road near King and Queen Courthouse, the mob forced the car over, leveled guns at the deputies, and removed Carter from the patrol car. The deputies later reported that Carter had begged "that he not be harmed without a chance to prove his innocence." Nevertheless, the self-appointed executioners shot him six or seven times as he stepped out of the car, not bothering to remove his handcuffs or the cord that bound his legs. Sheriff's deputies claimed that darkness prevented them from getting a good look at those responsible.[21]

Within several days Governor E. Lee Trinkle issued a statement declaring that the persons "guilty of the lynching are guilty of murder, and when brought to justice should be treated according to the severity of the crime." The chief executive wrote privately to state and local officials, indicating a firm desire to punish those responsible. He told the judge of the King and Queen Circuit Court that "I hope you will leave no stone unturned to bring the guilty ones to trial." Trinkle wrote King and Queen sheriff W. H. Eubank that the lynching "grieved" him and that he had hoped to make it through his four-year administration without another one occurring in the Old Dominion. The governor told the sheriff, "[I]t is up to you and your associates to apprehend those guilty of this crime and see that they are punished." Two days later Eubank responded, "I have done all that I can do so far." Ignoring the issue of bringing the murderers to justice, the sheriff informed Trinkle that "every thing is very quiet and the negroes are behaving beautifully. I do not fear a riot."[22]

Despite Trinkle's request, local officials apparently made little effort to punish those responsible for Carter's death. Evidence in the governor's files suggests that an investigation turned up several names of individuals tied to the lynching. One notation even indicates that authorities had spoken with someone who knew who had purchased the ammunition that killed Carter. But the attitude of Sheriff Eubank probably reflected the position of local authorities: as long as African Americans in King and Queen remained quiet, they saw no reason to pursue the matter.[23]

Virginia's black press did not limit condemnation for Horace Carter's death to the ten members of the mob or the citizens of King and Queen. Instead, the *Norfolk Journal and Guide* blamed all white Virginians and white Americans because "lynching could not survive in this country under a righteous national indignation against it. No group of men is mightier than the great public and few evils can withstand a sweeping public condemnation." Furthermore, reasoned the Tidewater weekly, "good white people who oppose and condemn lynching pass the buck by alluding to it as a crime common to ignorant bigots and a low type of white man. This might ease their conscience, but it does not lift from their shoulders the responsibility." Despite Governor Trinkle's stated intentions to punish those responsible, the *Journal and Guide* doubted that anything would come to pass because "there is no public clamor for it."[24]

While exhibiting considerably more restraint than P. B. Young, his counterpart at the *Norfolk Journal and Guide*, Louis Jaffé condemned the lynching of Horace Carter in the strongest terms yet to appear in a white newspaper in Virginia. In an editorial entitled "Besmirching a Good Record," the voice of the *Virginian-Pilot* blasted those who "substituted violence" for "the law and order on which the security of society rests." He even suggested that "it ought to serve some useful purpose to make public the names of the men capable, in the name of 'justice,' of shooting to death an untried and unconvicted man while he lay on the ground handcuffed and hobbled." Jaffé's advocacy of publicizing the names of mob members sprang not only from a desire to punish Carter's murderers but also from a need to restore the damage done to Virginia's reputation. The editor argued that the absence of lynchings on the state's soil had caused Virginians to begin to derive a certain satisfaction. "While it was at best a melancholy distinction to be less savage than other States," he reasoned, "it was a record in which the State was beginning to take pride." Jaffé's acknowledgment that such self-congratulatory praise was not fully warranted reflected a more enlightened view than that found elsewhere in the white press.[25]

As Louis Jaffé matured in his job and increasingly used his editorial page to campaign for basic improvements in the lives of African Americans in Norfolk and throughout Virginia, his attack on lynching assumed a central role. In January 1925, as he reflected on a lynching-free 1924 and looked to the year ahead, he wrote that the greatest problem facing Virginians "is to eradicate racial injustice, to exterminate the lynching practice as something vile, savage and utterly unworthy of a civilized people." Jaffé remained fully cognizant of his audience and attempted to move whites to understand lynching as a violation of their own most civilized instincts. Although a biographer has argued correctly that Jaffé never challenged the basic tenets of white supremacy, the Norfolk editor did insist that whites had an obligation to extend the measures of civilized behavior to their treatment of blacks. "Civilization has pinned its faith to enlightenment," he argued. "That this enlightenment must be confined to certain races and shut away from others, is a theory not to be reconciled with modern thinking."[26]

Whatever hopes Jaffé and others may have entertained that Virginians would adhere to the basics of civilized behavior came to a crashing halt on March 20, 1925, when a mob of between 500 and 2,000 residents of Sussex County and the Southside town of Waverly broke into the city jail and dragged away James Jordan, a twenty-two-year-old sawmill worker who had reportedly confessed to assaulting a young white woman. After hanging Jordan from a tree near the railroad depot, the Southside mob riddled its victim with bullets and then set fire to his body in plain view of an arriving train and its startled passengers.[27]

Jordan's body hung until the fire burned all the way through the rope, dropping him to the ground. Commonwealth's Attorney Thomas H. Howerton pledged to hold an inquest and secure indictments against those responsible for the murder, but his efforts were put on hold the following morning when he learned that Jordan's body had been removed from the site of the lynching. Only a charred hand remained. Later that day, Jordan's burned corpse turned up twenty-six miles away in Isle of Wight County. The furor surrounding the lynching and removal of Jordan's body prompted Governor Trinkle to travel to Waverly, where he addressed a group of the town's leading citizens and called upon them to preserve order and to think of the state's reputation. The county sheriff and deputies told the governor that Jordan had confessed and had been identified by the white woman he reportedly attacked. They insisted that the mob had moved so swiftly that they had no time to act. The chief executive exonerated local officials of any blame but urged the commonwealth's attorney to find those persons who were responsible.[28]

In the *Norfolk Virginian-Pilot*, Louis Jaffé urged readers not to consider lynchings "inevitable." He called upon white Virginians to denounce mob violence within the Old Dominion as fervently as they responded to crimes farther South. Jaffé predicted correctly, as it turned out, that no one in Sussex County would be punished for the lynching and argued that only the force of public opinion could bring an end to the epidemic. In particular, he called upon schools, churches, and politicians to instill in all civilized beings a commitment to the belief "that one accused of a crime, no matter how horrible or fearsome, must have his hour in an established court and that only the law itself may punish him."[29]

The *Richmond News Leader* seconded Jaffé's condemnation of the lynching. Regardless of the validity of the charges against Jordan, reasoned the Richmond paper, each spasm of violence in the Old Dominion would only encourage further lawlessness. "Men can not take liberties with one part of the law," explained the daily, "and not feel less respect for the rest." The *News Leader* reminded the people of Sussex County that Jordan's lynching was a murder, no matter how outraged they felt, and that individuals could not absolve themselves of responsibility by hiding amongst the mob. In conclusion, the *News Leader* emphasized the degree to which the mob murder constituted a "deep humiliation to Virginia."[30]

While Virginia's white press condemned Jordan's death as a stain on civilized society and a blot on Virginia's reputation, black Virginians dissected the lynching in their own terms. The *St. Luke's Herald* contradicted claims that the white woman had identified Jordan. Nevertheless, wrote the Richmond paper, "Judge Lynch sentenced him to be loaded with bullets and burned at the stake." The weekly concluded that Waverly had "prostituted law and order, and committed a whoredom with the forces of lawlessness by burning a human being at the stake. This bloodstain can never be removed." W. L. Davis, identifying himself as a resident of "Lynchingburg, Virginia," referred to the disproportionate number of Christian churches in Waverly that had instilled a curious notion of courage in their members. Davis mocked the "courageous and death defying Christian gentlemen, armed only with shotguns, pistols, bludgeons and clubs" who captured a single black man, "hung him to a tree, riddled him with bullets and burned his body. He who tells me this was not the embodiment, the perfection, and the acme of human courage, errs and most grievously so." The writer told of encountering a young white man several days after the lynching who lamented, "'I didn't get there until about forty minutes after it was all over; I'd like to have been there to help 'em put it in him.'" Two white children listened to the latecomer with rapt attention.[31]

Each lynching elicited growing support for state intervention, albeit for a variety of reasons. White representatives of the Women's Missionary Council of the Methodist Episcopal Church appealed to Governor Trinkle to put an end to lynching by securing the "prosecution and conviction of the guilty parties at whatever cost." James Weldon Johnson of the NAACP suggested to the chief executive that the Waverly lynching had provided further evidence of the need for a federal antilynching law, an unthinkable proposition for the South that ultimately led a number of white Virginians to advocate state legislation as a reasonable alternative. H. S. Parker of Norfolk beseeched Trinkle to protect "my helpless Race" but also warned that bitterness, hatred, and enmity on the part of whites would eventually "burn its way through the walls of meekness and obedience and burst forth into a dreadful conflict that you and I will regret."[32]

Not all constituents who wrote the governor shared Parker's concerns. H. C. Spangler of Roanoke, a white man, expressed regret that a lynching had occurred and asked, "But who should wonder?" Citing a recent case in Franklin County, he argued that mob rule would continue so long as certain judges and courts refused to adequately punish black criminals. "The masses of the people demand justice," explained Spangler, "and if the courts fail to give justice they must resort to mob violence to satisfy the natural revenge that demands the average man who has any grit and red blood in him." Spangler guessed that even Trinkle would sanction mob rule if a court failed to punish a man guilty of a grave offense against his own family. No doubt Spangler's ability to express regret yet at the same time support lynching epitomized the enormous task that faced Louis Jaffé and others committed to ending mob violence. Even more frightening to antilynching advocates, however, must have been the realization that young children understood the dynamics of lynching; just weeks after Jordan's lynching, an armed posse in Bristol responded to the claim of an eleven-year-old girl that she had been attacked by a black man. The mob encountered no African Americans to bring before the girl, who later admitted that she had made up the story to avoid punishment for being late to school.[33]

By November 1925, as Louis Jaffé recognized that his efforts to sway public opinion were unlikely to put an end to lynching, the editor began to embrace the power of state government as an effective weapon in ending mob law. Noting the inaction of local officials in King and Queen in 1923 and in Sussex in 1925, Jaffé drew inspiration from the actions of North

A Melancholy Distinction

Carolina's governor, Angus McLean, who had called out the state militia to protect a black prisoner threatened by a mob in Asheville. In addition, McLean ensured that members of lynch mobs were actually punished, accomplishing what Virginia's governors had only discussed. In a series of editorials published in early 1926, Jaffé urged Virginia's state leaders to emulate McLean's approach.[34]

A particularly gruesome lynching in the summer of 1926 intensified Jaffé's campaign for state involvement. In the early morning hours of August 15, 1926, a masked mob of fifty, some dressed as women, broke into the Wythe County jail in Wytheville and shot to death Raymond Bird, a thirty-one-year-old black man, who had been accused of assaulting two daughters of his employer. According to an Associated Press report, the mob shot Bird, beat his head "into a pulp," tied a rope around his neck, attached his corpse to a waiting automobile, dragged his body nine miles to the scene of his alleged assaults, strung his body to a tree, and filled his body with more bullets.[35]

White newspapers throughout Virginia joined to condemn the lynching, which appeared to set a new precedent for savagery and barbarity. The *Newport News Times-Herald* attacked a newspaper in the southwestern part of the state, near Wytheville, that attempted to justify the lynching. Louis Jaffé's paper argued that the lynchers could be caught with a concerted effort among local officials and the proper leadership of Governor Harry Byrd. Roanoke's two papers agreed, citing the example of North Carolina's governor in successfully prosecuting mob members. Other papers emphasized the most recent blot on Virginia's good name. The *Richmond News Leader* opined that "it was not the 'Virginia way' to put on masks, to hide individual identity in a mob, to hang some wretch in the dark of the moon, and then to slink away in blood guiltiness." The *Richmond Times-Dispatch* also denounced the attack but then turned a blind eye by adding that no one need feel sympathy for Bird if he was guilty of the alleged crimes, because in that case the "mob only hastened the punishment that surely would have been meted out to him promptly if the community had been content to permit the law to take its course."[36]

Although the reaction of the white press elicited praise from black citizens, newspapers, and organizations such as the NAACP, not one white newspaper raised doubt as to Raymond Bird's guilt. The *Baltimore Afro-American*, on the other hand, reported critical facts that challenged Bird's guilt and were known to local officials as well as the governor. Several weeks after Bird's death, the *Afro-American* reported that the middle daughter of Grover Grubb, the white Wythe County farmer who employed Bird, had given birth to Bird's baby several weeks before the lynching. The Maryland paper added that the girl had failed in an attempt to put the baby up for adoption, but that Bird had found a home for their child with black friends. Furthermore, the *Afro-American* revealed that Grubb's oldest daughter was about to give birth to a second child of Bird's. The pair of births supported the contention of another black newspaper, the *Richmond Planet*, that the Grubb family had been mixing with African Americans for over ten years.[37]

Governor Harry Byrd learned of these and other crucial details in a confidential letter from Stuart Campbell, an attorney in Wytheville who had been hired by Grover Grubb to press charges against Bird for sexual assault. According to Campbell, Grubb owned a small farm of sixty acres but worked at a sawmill, which kept him away from home six days a week. Raymond Bird lived nearby and had worked for Grubb for five years. The Wytheville attorney speculated that shortly after starting work for Grubb, Bird "began playing with the older girls, carrying them about and scuffling with them." On July 23, only weeks before the lynching, Grubb's middle daughter had indeed given birth to a child of mixed blood. Furthermore, Grubb's oldest daughter expected to give birth in September and had named Bird as the father of her child as well. The oldest daughter admitted that she and Bird had been "intimate" on a number of occasions, while the middle daughter acknowledged only two or three such encounters. Campbell emphasized that the girls' parents remained unaware of either pregnancy until after the birth of the middle daughter's child, a stunning lapse made credible only by the father's absence from home six days a week and his wife's mental incapacity.[38]

Once his middle daughter gave birth to a mulatto child, Grover Grubb apparently figured out that his oldest daughter also carried a child of Raymond Bird's. He then traveled to Wytheville and swore out a warrant that charged Bird with raping his two oldest girls. Authorities arrested Bird and set August 13 as the date for a preliminary hearing. The day before the scheduled hearing, Grubb and his second daughter consulted H. M. Heuser, the commonwealth's attorney, who advised the father that the facts did not warrant a charge of rape, but that he might be able to successfully prosecute Bird for a lesser offense. The following day, Grubb asked Campbell to join the prosecution, but for the second time an attorney informed Grubb that a rape charge could not be sustained.[39]

Only at this point, on the verge of seeing his case collapse, did Grubb allege that Bird had also attacked his youngest daughter, not yet a teenager. According to Campbell's subsequent investigation, the youngest daughter claimed that a few days before July 23, Bird picked her up in the barn, carried her into the woods, and began to remove her clothes. When she started crying, Bird apparently "told her that he was only playing with her and let her go." Grubb's youngest daughter later claimed to have told her oldest sister what had happened, but the oldest daughter chose not to tell her father until after he failed to bring rape charges against Bird, a rather suspicious sequence of events that challenges the veracity of the entire story. Grubb and a neighbor also suggested, in Campbell's words, that "if this negro was turned loose the people of the community would take the law into their own hands," but that public feeling might be sated "if substantial punishment could be had in the case of the youngest girl." Before a court met to consider the allegations, however, Bird was lynched.[40]

The inaction of the Wythe County sheriff and commonwealth's attorney in the wake of the mob attack led others to conclude that only a state investigation would result in any indictments. Stuart Campbell described the sheriff as "a man of no initiative" and noted that he and the commonwealth's attorney "seem unable to arouse themselves." Despite a pledge from Commonwealth's Attorney Heuser to present the names of all known participants to a grand jury, Judge Horace Sutherland concluded that local officials were incapable of action. Like Campbell, the jurist raised the possibility of bringing in outside investigators but suggested "that none of the Wythe County officers be advised of it for fear they may be in sympathy with those responsible for the crime." A reluctant governor expressed his willingness to send assistance, but only "upon invitation of the local authorities."[41]

As Harry Byrd considered the wisdom of appointing a state investigator, Louis Jaffé for the first time raised the possibility of passing legislation that would make lynching a state crime. In a letter to the governor, the Norfolk editor argued that lynching involved the "violent death of many innocent people" and that, at the very least, it desecrated "the most inviolable of natural human rights—the right to one's life until it is forfeited to society by offenses duly proved and assessed by established judicial agencies." Adding that the lynching of Raymond Bird included "a touch of savagery" that humiliated all Virginians, Jaffé asked if "the time has arrived for the State of Virginia to declare by appropriate enactment that lynching, being fundamentally an assault on the authority of the Commonwealth and a negation of its police power, is a matter of direct State concern?" No doubt aware of the governor's deep reluctance to interfere in local matters, Jaffé cited as precedent the successful state campaign to eliminate dueling several decades earlier.[42]

Although Byrd did not respond to Jaffé, he did eventually appoint Joseph Chitwood of Roanoke and Leon M. Bazile of the attorney general's office as special prosecutors. Wythe County authorities, however, accepted

Byrd's offer of assistance with the utmost reluctance and relented only on the understanding that all evidence would be presented to a local grand jury. The difficulty in forcing local authorities to act prompted some observers, black and white, to conclude that the Wytheville lynching constituted the best possible argument for a federal antilynching law.[43]

Despite the additional team of prosecutors, who brought numerous witnesses before a panel of grand jurors, and despite the instruction of the judge to consider charges of perjury against all witnesses, the grand jury indicted only one person, Floyd Willard, described as a young farmer. At his trial, prosecutors presented five witnesses, all of them from adjacent Grayson County, a clear sign that Willard's Wythe County neighbors had proved unwilling to cooperate. Each witness testified that Willard, while on a hunting trip, had described in detail the manner in which the mob had lynched Bird. The defendant, however, claimed to have been in bed throughout the murder. His wife and children corroborated his story, and other leading citizens testified to his character. A jury acquitted Willard after only ten minutes of deliberation.[44]

Governor Harry Byrd evinced no particular proclivity to endorse a state antilynching law in the wake of Raymond Bird's death or Floyd Willard's acquittal. But when a lynch mob struck in the Old Dominion for the third year in a row, Louis Jaffé pushed the hesitant governor to act. In the early morning hours of November 30, 1927, a mob estimated at three to four hundred people drove in seventy-five to one hundred automobiles to the jail at Whitesburg, Kentucky, used hacksaws, axes, and railroad ties to gain entrance, removed Leonard Woods to a platform on the Virginia-Kentucky border that had been erected for a celebration, pumped as many as six hundred bullets into his body, poured gasoline on his corpse, and burned him as if upon a funeral pyre.[45]

For days and weeks, authorities quibbled over whether to charge the lynching in Kentucky or Virginia. Sheriff P. H. Kennedy of Wise County, Virginia, telegrammed Governor Byrd that "Leonard Woods was lynched by Kentucky mob. Act did not occur on Virginia soil." Commonwealth's Attorney Harry L. Moore of Letcher County, Kentucky, on the other hand, concluded that Woods died on the Virginia side and that mob leaders lived in Wise County. Virginia's governor condemned the lynching but appeared satisfied with Sheriff Kennedy's version of events and asserted that "Virginia has no legal jurisdiction."[46]

Wherever Woods actually died, circumstances suggest that a Virginia mob lay behind the gruesome murder. Woods had been arrested in connection with the death of Hershel Deaton, a thirty-five-year-old white man who lived in Wise County, Virginia, but worked in a Kentucky mine.

Taken from a Kentucky jail by a Virginia mob, Leonard Woods was lynched in the early morning hours of November 30, 1927. In an apparent effort to confuse authorities as to jurisdiction, the mob lynched Woods on a platform that had been erected on the Virginia-Kentucky border. The third mob death in Virginia in three years, the lynching led to the passage of an anti-lynching law the following year. (Courtesy of the James Allen Collection, Robert W. Woodruff Library, Emory University)

News reports indicated that the bulk of the mob came from Deaton's neighborhood, a likely fact in light of numerous studies that have pointed to the role of family and neighbors in mob leadership and membership. One specific report stated that Woods actually leaned against a railing on the Virginia side of the platform while his assassins pumped his body full of lead from the Kentucky side. It seems entirely logical that Woods's executioners planned his death on the border precisely to frustrate efforts at punishment; after all, two citizens of Wise County had been sent to jail for lynching just a few years earlier.[47]

While authorities debated the details of the lynching and attempted to pass responsibility for punishing mob members, Virginia's white press responded with disgust. The *Lynchburg News* condemned the rise in mob murders in Virginia at a time when lynchings throughout the South had declined. The daily applauded the response of the *Coalfield Progress*, published in Norton near the scene of the lynching, which encouraged a rapid and thorough response by law enforcement officials. The *News* asserted that "mob rule can be checked and beaten back only if the people of the commonwealth are sufficiently aroused to the danger to fight mob rule as they would fight the plague." The failure to punish mob members for the lynching of James Jordan in 1925 and Raymond Bird in 1926, however, indicated to the Lynchburg paper that the majority of Virginians who claimed to abhor mob rule "do not hate it enough to fight at the insidious approach of the menace."[48]

As further evidence that white Virginians lacked the inclination to end mob vengeance, the *Lynchburg News* cited an unusual case in which white citizens of Isle of Wight County actually retaliated against local officials for preventing a lynching. On October 15, 1927, authorities in Isle of Wight arrested Shirley Winnegan, a black male, for raping and killing a fourteen-year-old white girl the day before. Although the accused maintained his innocence throughout the ordeal and noted that he had previously "had some trouble" with the black teenager who placed him near the scene of the crime, white authorities and citizens in Isle of Wight never questioned Winnegan's guilt. Aware that the brutality of the crime had fostered talk of a lynching, Sheriff W. H. Chapman sent his prisoner to the more secure Petersburg jail. A mob estimated at a thousand forced the sheriff to disclose Winnegan's whereabouts, threatened him with violence if he called Petersburg authorities, and headed to that city. Commonwealth's Attorney George Whitley warned officials in Petersburg, who moved Winnegan to Richmond. The determination of the mob was fueled in part by reports that Winnegan had been judged legally insane the previous August and might therefore avoid the death penalty in a court of law.[49]

Residents of Isle of Wight turned their wrath on the sheriff and commonwealth's attorney. At a mass meeting held two weeks before the November elections, those in attendance recommended that voters repudiate the nominations of Chapman and Whitley, both of whom had easily won in the Democratic primary. The angry residents blamed the sheriff in particular for not properly committing Winnegan to an insane asylum after the August hearing. One report indicated that the asylum in Petersburg did not have enough room for Winnegan, quite possible given Virginia's grossly underfunded public welfare system; another report indicated that Chapman had not considered Winnegan dangerous.[50]

Louis Jaffé responded to the mass meeting with a call to his Tidewater neighbors not to punish those who had upheld the law. He lamented that no one would have sought to turn the two officials out of office had they

A Melancholy Distinction

failed to do their duty and let the lynching occur. "Under such an administration of justice," he concluded, "nobody would be safe, no rights would
be assured and orderly judicial process would give way to the rule of the
mob." In a private letter to Harry Byrd, Jaffé explained that he did not
know either Chapman or Whitley, but that "it is repugnant to me to think
that they should be made to suffer for doing what was their plain duty —
for doing something that civilized people should applaud instead of condemn." In a direct appeal to the governor, Jaffé asked Byrd to use his influence among leading citizens of Isle of Wight and not to allow Winnegan
to be returned to the county without heavy guard. Byrd, however, abdi-
cated all responsibility and refused to intervene, informing Jaffé that he
had been advised that any efforts on his part would not be welcomed and
would work against the two local officials.[51]

Just days before the election, a second lunacy commission met and ruled
Shirley Winnegan sane and therefore competent to stand trial. The findings prompted a clearly relieved governor to write Jaffé that the "political
situation in Isle of Wight appears to be greatly improved." Offering no
specifics, Byrd added that "we have done everything possible in a judi-
cious manner." Jaffé agreed that the decision of the sanity commission had
eased tensions, and both men expressed hope that Chapman and Whitley
would be reelected. Only the state's black press challenged the validity of
the second lunacy commission's verdict. Referring to the hostile and fever-
ish atmosphere that suffused the commission's deliberations, the *Norfolk
Journal and Guide* opined that "what every true lover of justice wants to see,
even in spite of the most provoking circumstances, is that the same official
courage which saved this man from a lynching at the hands of an infuriated mob, follow and protect him from a possible judicial lynching."[52]

Byrd and Jaffé, however, misread the situation. Despite the lunacy commission's reversal, which cleared the way for a sentence of death, Isle of
Wight voters threw the sheriff and commonwealth's attorney out of office.
Cognizant that voters remained enraged at not being able to exact vengeance with their own hands, Circuit Court Judge B. D. White ruled that
"the minds and judgments of the people are warped and prejudiced to
such an extent that neither an impartial jury can be obtained nor a fair
trial had." White therefore moved Winnegan's trial to Richmond, where
a jury of businessmen deliberated for ninety minutes before sentencing
him to death. Two months later, after a failed appeal, Shirley Winnegan
died in the electric chair.[53]

Although electoral results in Isle of White County confirmed that the
lynching spirit remained strong in the Old Dominion, Winnegan's sen-

tence satisfied white Virginians such as Louis Jaffé whose primary concern had been to avoid an extralegal lynching. Convinced of the accused's guilt, few white Virginians questioned the soundness of the lunacy commission's deliberations. The decision of the trial judge to move the proceedings to Richmond further bolstered a sense that the legal system had worked as intended. The death of Leonard Woods at the Virginia border, however, obviated whatever sense of self-satisfaction the Winnegan jury had provided white Virginians. Coming within hours of Winnegan's sentencing, the Woods lynching provided Louis Jaffé the leverage he needed to move state officials to consider an antilynching law. In a private letter in which he referred specifically to the murder of Leonard Woods, Jaffé pleaded with Governor Byrd to "find the means of forcing a showdown on this outrage." The editor of the *Norfolk Virginian-Pilot* reminded the chief executive that he had urged him the previous year to consider a law that would make lynching a state crime and asked if he might "take a step in this direction at the next General Assembly." The following day Byrd replied that he would like to discuss the matter with Jaffé, but he expressed reservations about such a law's compatibility with the state constitution.[54]

Sensing reluctance on the part of the governor, Jaffé used his editorial page to condemn the inaction of local authorities and to urge publicly that Byrd take action. In a derisive tone, the editor commented that "once more the publicists and the politicians of the State are dusting off the special invectives reserved for the denunciation of lynching." He noted the relief of authorities who claimed that Leonard Woods was killed in Kentucky and added that "the disgrace stinks across the boundary line." Quoting Byrd's own denunciation of the recent lynching, Jaffé despaired that "these moral revulsions are never supported by action" as "coroners' juries enter their usual findings of 'death at the hands of persons unknown.'"[55]

Reiterating comments expressed to Byrd more than a year before, Jaffé compared the task of outlawing lynching with the campaign to eliminate dueling in the nineteenth century. The editor argued that, as had been the case with dueling at one time, "lynching goes unpunished in Virginia because, deny it as one will, it commands a certain social sanction." Consequently, those opposed to lynching had "to stamp the unwritten code from which it draws its sanction as loathsome and poisonous." Jaffé explained that the eradication of mob violence mandated laws that punished not only the principal participants but all persons who "advise, encourage or promote" lynching. The Norfolk editor urged the commonwealth to strip mob members of the right to vote and hold office, and he argued for strict fines and punishments in addition to those for murder. "In short,"

A Melancholy Distinction

concluded Jaffé, "lynching must be recognized as a State cancer, requiring direct State action. It must be rid of its social cachet and stamped with the State's curse."[56]

As Jaffé and others had predicted, local authorities in Wise County made no serious efforts to punish those responsible for the murder of Leonard Woods. But by December 1927, the month after Woods's death, such inactivity no longer met the approval of all local leaders or the silence of the rest of the state. Editors in Norfolk, Richmond, and Lynchburg loudly condemned the lynching, while Wise County publisher Bruce Crawford went so far as to use his newspaper, *Crawford's Weekly*, to start a fund to prosecute and convict those involved in the lynching. Residents of Wise County expressed shock at Crawford's initiative, when neither the governor of Kentucky nor the governor of Virginia showed any inclination to take action. Directly challenging his own neighbors and subscribers, Crawford assumed that Woods would have been found guilty in the murder of Hershel Deaton but argued that the lynching constituted "an orgy of murder in which every man who fired an unnecessary shot—and only the first one was necessary to kill the Negro—gave vent to an impulse which usually seeks only a pretext for an outlet." Crawford expressed amazement that so many supposedly enlightened people in Wise accepted the action of the mob and felt no shame. The editor concluded that "to justify that lynching is to set a dangerous precedent. It is to forego trial by jury, to confess we are not civilized enough to make and enforce just laws, and to revert to a primitive state that gives the lie to all our claims to Christian enlightenment and human progress."[57]

A number of readers took umbrage at the editor's comments. He received complaints in the mail and over the phone and weathered a campaign to encourage the cancellation of subscriptions. Undeterred, Crawford expanded his attack and denounced newspaper editors throughout the state whose indifference allowed lynching to flourish. Specifically excepting the *Norfolk Virginian-Pilot* and the *Richmond News Leader*, he cited papers such as the *Roanoke Times* that downplayed the severity of mob infractions at the same time they magnified individual murders. He lamented this "disposition to see the devil in the individual more readily than in the group" and reiterated that "the members of a mob who actually take part in the killing and dismembering or burning of a human being derive a satisfaction from the orgy not inspired by motives of justice."[58]

Crawford's boldness no doubt reflected growing support for Jaffé's campaign. Throughout December and early January, the Norfolk editor continuously pushed his call for an antilynching law. In private, he consulted frequently with the governor and urged him to overcome his concerns about violating local authority. The chief executive sought the advice of the governor of North Carolina with regard to the feasibility of forcing counties or localities to pay money to the relatives of people lynched within their boundaries. Finally, on January 16, 1928, Harry Byrd asked the Virginia General Assembly to pass an antilynching law. Byrd emphasized that crimes such as rape, which often incited mobs, had been and would continue to be prosecuted effectively in Virginia, but he declared that "mob law is anarchy." Terming the existing code "insufficient," Byrd asked for a law "more drastic in order that it may be dreaded by those who permit their inflamed passions to drive them into crimes of mob violence."[59]

Byrd asked the legislature to declare lynching "a specific State offense" that would allow the attorney general to prosecute lynchings, in addition to local authorities; to force counties or cities in which a lynching occurred to pay $2,500 to the lawful heirs of the person lynched; and to authorize the governor to spend whatever money he considered necessary and appropriate to bring members of a mob to justice. Carefully guarding himself against charges of violating local authority, Byrd added that "it should be made clear that declaring lynching as a specific State offense does not take away the constitutional rights of accused citizens for trial in localities where the crime was committed." The governor's caveat no doubt limited the likelihood that white Virginians would be convicted of lynching; friends and neighbors rarely recognized guilt in such cases.[60]

Byrd's proposal drew the enthusiastic support of newspapers throughout the state. Louis Jaffé later commented that prior to the governor's address only his paper had called for state legislation; a number of other newspapers eventually joined the campaign. Virginia's largest black newspaper praised Byrd's proposal and commented upon its similarities with suggestions put forward by Jaffé in the *Virginian-Pilot*. The *Norfolk Journal and Guide* added that such a law would finally recognize lynching "as the foul and infamous crime that it is, and that it be accorded a place of particular atrocity in the catalog of crimes." In addition, Norfolk's black weekly argued that such a state law would prove far preferable to a federal law since it created an "enforcement machinery" that the federal government could not match.[61]

African Americans throughout Virginia and the United States praised Byrd. The Knights of Pythias in Washington, D.C., and a representative of the American Church Institute for Negroes sent words of thanks. The Reverend Daniel Hays of Baltimore commended the governor for his "brave and timely utterance." The Reverend W. J. G. McLinn of Norfolk termed Byrd's statement "the best ever produced by any executive, either State or Federal" and exclaimed that Virginia's passage of the act would do more to combat lynching than would the Dyer federal antilynching bill. The Reverend J. B. Askew, also of Norfolk, added that Byrd's position rendered him the "greatest Governor in America today."[62]

In private, a number of whites expressed reservations about Byrd's proposal. W. H. Tinsley of Salem estimated that 90 percent of mob members paid no taxes. Therefore, he wondered, "should the tax payers, who generally are as much opposed to mob law as you and I be made to pay a debt created by parties who as a rule will not pay one cent." Clearly Tinsley did not agree with Louis Jaffé, Bruce Crawford, and others who implicated all whites in the crime of lynching. Congressman Patrick Henry Drewry of Virginia's Fifth District seconded Tinsley's concern and told Byrd that "you have made a mistake in advocating a penalty on localities where lynchings might occur." The congressman considered that "to penalize innocent people for something that they knew nothing about would be manifestly unfair." Drewry complained that Virginia's congressional delegation had unanimously opposed the Dyer federal antilynching bill, in part because it contained just such a clause, but that Byrd's bill would compromise future opposition.[63]

Responding to such objections, Byrd indicated privately that he would not insist on the $2,500 fine levied against a locality in which a lynching occurred. The chief executive informed Drewry that he had changed his proposal so that the lawful heirs of a lynched person had "the right to recover from the county by due process of law which will mean, of course, trial before a local jury." No doubt both men understood the reduced likelihood of a local jury finding for the plaintiff; such a judgment would require jurors to levy fines against themselves. In addition, Byrd played to the gravest concern of Drewry and other white constituents when he emphasized that, in fact, his bill would forestall the adoption of federal legislation.[64]

Despite the governor's tempered advocacy, no member of the General Assembly introduced an antilynching bill for more than two weeks after Byrd addressed the legislature. As a result of the delay, Louis Jaffé wrote the governor that "I am moved to uneasiness by the failure of anybody in the Legislature to introduce a bill carrying your recommendations." In particular, the editor worried that further delay would play into the hands of opponents and, at best, result in a bill left to die in committee at the end of the session. In an effort to bolster Byrd's fortitude and commitment, Jaffé noted that he had closely followed the reaction of the press to Byrd's proposal and seen not one "adverse comment from any first class paper." The Norfolk editor also massaged the governor's ego, adding that Byrd stood to gain the "homage of every thoughtful student of public affairs in the United States" if the legislature passed a bill that would free "Virginia from the recurring lynching disgrace."[65]

Finally, on February 3, Senators James Barron of Norfolk and Cecil Connor of Leesburg introduced an antilynching measure. Two weeks later, to the general satisfaction of Virginia's press, the state senate passed the bill 32 to 0 with eight abstentions. Although grateful that the senate had taken a step toward "outlawing this crowning infamy of the century," Richmond's black newspaper lamented that the legislature had "extracted the teeth" from Byrd's original proposal by removing the penalty provision, a sentiment shared by the *Richmond News Leader*. On March 1, the house of delegates concurred with the senate's version by a margin of 74 to 5; a noticeable twenty-one delegates abstained. On March 14, Harry Byrd signed into law the nation's strictest antilynching measure and the first that directly termed lynching a state crime.[66]

The statute's enactment elicited another round of congratulatory letters addressed to Virginia's governor. Mrs. M. C. Lawton of Brooklyn, a self-described "old Virginian," applauded Byrd's "blow at lawlessness and barbarity which should be followed by other Southern States." She added that "as an apostle of justice, you have blazed the way for other State Executives who have not lifted their voices as yet in protestation against the infamous crime of lynching." Judge James H. Ricks of Richmond's Juvenile and Domestic Relations Court also congratulated Byrd but acknowledged that he, too, was disappointed that the $2,500 indemnity feature had not been retained.[67]

Several months after the passage of Virginia's antilynching law, a mob in Houston, Texas, lynched a black man just before that city was to host the 1928 Democratic National Convention. The attack prompted Louis Jaffé to wire Byrd and U.S. senator Carter Glass, both in Roanoke for the Virginia Democratic Convention. The Norfolk editor specifically requested that the two party leaders press for a state platform that included strong language in support of Virginia's recently enacted statute and a national platform that urged the individual states to adopt similar antilynching laws. Neither official responded to Jaffé's proposals, and the state convention ignored the lynching issue. The following day, however, Louis Jaffé unleashed an editorial entitled "An Unspeakable Act of Savagery," in which he concluded that "we have not yet arrived at that social abhorrence of this crime that must precede its practical extinction. . . . the rise and fall of the lynching curve is governed by racial passions that remain still

Louis Jaffé, editor of the *Norfolk Virginian-Pilot* from 1919 until his death in 1950, won a Pulitzer Prize for his campaign to end lynching. (Courtesy of the *Norfolk Virginian-Pilot*)

to be brought under civilized control." That editorial won Jaffé a Pulitzer Prize.[68]

Although specifically citing Jaffé's editorial response to the Houston lynching, the Pulitzer committee clearly intended to reward his long-term commitment to the denunciation of lynching in Virginia and in the South and his role in the passage of Virginia's antilynching law. P. B. Young, the editor of the *Norfolk Journal and Guide*, began his letter of recommendation by stating that "I doubt if 'disadvantaged groups' without regard to class or race, have a warmer or more effective advocate than Mr. Jaffé has proved to be." In particular, Young cited Jaffé's persistent willingness to address issues of labor, education, health, and recreation that especially affected Norfolk's black and poor populations. He commended Jaffé's campaign against the Ku Klux Klan but concluded that "his most outstanding achievement was his anti-lynching law. His was the first paper in the State to propose an anti-lynching law, the first to submit a tentative outline of such a measure . . . and it was his courageous and convincing advocacy of the bill after it was introduced that aided most in bringing to Virginia the distinction of being the first Southern State to adopt an antilynching law." Young added that Jaffé's legislative success came only after years of making "the reception of such a movement possible by building up through convincing editorial treatment an invulnerable case against this particular social cancer."[69]

Guided by Louis Jaffé's resolve more than by his own commitment, Harry Byrd did sign the Old Dominion's antilynching statute into law. Over time, however, Byrd's advocacy of the measure seemed to be determined more by pride of Virginia's reputation than by concern for the well-being of the commonwealth's black populace. Despite his own initial ambivalence, Byrd came to recognize that the antilynching law provided positive publicity and aided in the recruitment of new industry and jobs. Conversely, Byrd and other state boosters—industrialists, journalists, and public officials—recognized that the law needed to be seen as effective. To this end, they insisted that Virginia never suffered another lynching after the passage of the 1928 act, a claim that occasionally flew in the face of common sense.[70]

On September 15, 1932, a white farmhand living near the border of Fauquier and Warren Counties reportedly found hanging from a tree the body of Shadrack Thompson, a black man who had been the subject of an intense search since the middle of July. Thompson had been accused of attacking Mr. and Mrs. Henry Baxley, who had employed him until several weeks before the alleged assault, and seriously injuring Mrs. Baxley, whose wounds left her hospitalized for weeks and subject to "horrible mental pictures" of the assailant. For reasons that were not explained, authorities only reached Thompson's body three hours after it was discovered, long after a mob had reached the scene and set fire to the corpse. According to initial reports, officials succeeded in saving the corpse's head and some clothing from flames and thereby identified the victim. The coroner ruled Thompson's death a suicide; news reports emphasized that the rope from which he hung had been in his possession the day before he attacked the Baxleys, and the commonwealth's attorney speculated that Thompson had assembled a pile of rocks, used them to reach the limb from which he tied the rope, and then jumped from the rock pile. F. F. Hall, a Warrenton police officer, offered his opinion that Thompson must have fled into the woods soon after attacking the Baxleys, understood the severity of his situation, and hanged himself.[71]

Several days later, however, doubts surfaced as to whether or not Thompson had taken his own life. The *Washington Evening Star* reported that a hole in the victim's head appeared to be that of a bullet and that his corpse had been mutilated before being set afire. In addition, the paper noted that Fauquier residents apparently removed teeth from the body and took them home as souvenirs. An editorial in the *Richmond News*

Leader asked, "Was It a Lynching?" The paper reasoned that the distance of Thompson's body from the scene of the attack on the Baxleys and the time that had passed since his disappearance made it likely that he had killed himself. On the other hand, the Richmond daily stressed that few blacks ever committed suicide and that "persons who find a dead body hanging from a tree in the woods are not apt to set fire to it before notifying the sheriff." The *News Leader* encouraged a full investigation because "Virginia is increasingly jealous of her good name as a state that protects even the worst criminal from the madness of the mob, and she is determined to enforce to the letter her stringent anti-lynching law."[72]

After a thorough investigation by one of its correspondents, the *Richmond News Leader* concluded that Shadrack Thompson had not been lynched. The *News Leader* acknowledged that a crowd had burned the body and removed teeth as souvenirs "in the post-mortem orgy" but concluded that "there has not developed the slightest evidence that Thompson technically was lynched." The Richmond daily based its findings on the word of Dr. George H. Davis, the coroner and "the last man in the county open to suspicion of bearing false witness." Davis claimed to have had "plenty of time to make a complete examination" before the mob arrived and set the corpse afire. He admitted that he, too, had wondered if Thompson had in fact hanged himself, and he made his examination with that question in mind. But Davis found that Thompson's hands had not been tied and that his clothing showed no signs of rearrangement, both indications that no struggle had taken place. Most important, according to Davis, Thompson had been dead at least several weeks, and his body bore no signs of a bullet hole, of mutilation, or of any other kind of antemortem injury.[73]

The coroner insisted that Thompson had "hanged himself and for a good reason." He acknowledged to the *News Leader* that the victim would have been lynched if the mob had found him alive, "but he was not lynched, unless the burning of a corpse is a lynching." Davis revealed that after he had completed his examination a crowd that eventually numbered more than 150 gathered throughout the night. The coroner, however, gave no indication that law enforcement personnel were ever present, an odd omission given the size of the mob and the circumstances. As citizens of Fauquier County fought for teeth and other souvenirs, Davis retrieved the skull; the *News Leader* reported that the skull and rope had been exhibited publicly in Warrenton for several days after the "bonfire."[74]

The *News Leader*'s investigator reported that no rumors of a lynching had circulated prior to the discovery of Thompson's body, but that in the days following the burning scores of Fauquier residents claimed to have lynched Thompson. Apparently so many people gave credence to these rumors that Judge J. R. H. Alexander impaneled a grand jury. On October 3, the jurors ruled not only that Thompson had died at his own hands, but that they "could find no evidence as to who burned the body." Although initial accounts of Thompson's death in the *News Leader* had said only that he had been sought in connection with an attack on the Baxleys, the grand jury report made clear that he had been sought for raping Mrs. Baxley after attacking her husband.[75]

In an editorial accompanying the results of the investigation, the *Richmond News Leader* expressed satisfaction at the verdict. Acknowledging that "the whole affair, surely, is no credit to Virginia" and that "[s]uch ghoulishness disgraces the state," the paper's editors sounded relieved to conclude that "the case is not one to be written down on the dark roll of lynching." The *News Leader* sent the results of its investigation to officials from Tuskegee Institute, who published an annual compilation of national lynching statistics, and reiterated that Thompson's case could not be considered a lynching "unless the term 'lynching' can be applied to violence against a long-dead corpse." Nevertheless, in December the NAACP, acting in conjunction with Tuskegee, listed Shadrack Thompson's death as one of eleven lynchings in 1932.[76]

Within days, Harry Byrd joined Fauquier officials and others in protesting the NAACP's findings. At first the former chief executive sought to use third parties to influence the organization. He asked Louis Jaffé to contact NAACP officials and have them change their ruling. Byrd also wrote George Milton of the *Chattanooga News* and a member of the Southern Commission to Study Lynching and made a similar request. Byrd explained to Milton that "we do not want to be charged with a lynching which did not occur." He reminded both editors that Virginia had not had a lynching since the passage of the 1928 antilynching law.[77]

Milton, not familiar with the circumstances of Thompson's death, politely forwarded Byrd's letter to Walter White of the NAACP. Douglas Southall Freeman, perhaps also responding to a request from Byrd, went a step further and assured White that his organization's ruling had been in error. Freeman noted that "here in Virginia we have been very jealous of our good name in avoiding mob violence" and described the steps that his paper had taken in ruling the death a suicide. Walter White responded to Milton that the NAACP had ruled the death a lynching only after speaking with individuals in the vicinity and concluding that "there seemed no proof" of a suicide.[78]

Frustrated by the position of the NAACP, Harry Byrd eventually wrote directly to Walter White. Emphasizing, perhaps even exaggerating, his own leadership in the state's antilynching movement, Byrd insisted that a careful examination of the facts, especially as outlined by the *News Leader*, would lead White to the proper conclusion. In response, White acknowledged that the evidence did not appear definitively to point toward either a lynching or a suicide. But the NAACP official remained particularly troubled that the burning and disfigurement of the body were more indicative of mob violence than of suicide, a salient point that Byrd did not address in his zeal to protect the Old Dominion's reputation.[79]

Over the course of the next week, Walter White received two letters from Roy Flannagan, the reporter who had conducted the *Richmond News Leader*'s investigation. Flannagan insisted that "I went to Fauquier county firmly convinced that this man had been lynched. I returned just as firmly convinced that he had not been." Reviewing the evidence contained in his *News Leader* article, a report that White had not read, the reporter told the NAACP official that, in addition to the facts that pointed to a suicide, he considered it significant that no reports of a lynching surfaced until after the discovery and burning of the body. Flannagan opined that "not even a very small lynching gang could keep such a secret, particularly while the fugitive was being sought everywhere in the hills." Furthermore, Flannagan believed firmly that Thompson "had every reason to kill himself. He was being hunted like a fox with no means of finding food and no family, not even a Negro family would have helped him because of the atrocious nature of his crime." The Richmond reporter noted that few blacks lived in the western part of Fauquier County, making it nearly impossible for Thompson to hide. He concluded that Thompson "was intelligent enough to know that any one of a dozen posses would have tortured and killed him if they had caught him, and that every man in three counties was on the lookout for every stray Negro."[80]

Unlike Byrd and Fauquier officials who objected to the NAACP's ruling, Flannagan flayed local officials for failing to protect Thompson's body. He wrote White, "I described the unspeakable outrage against the corpse in plain words in my report, and neither I nor any other citizen can defend the people of Fauquier and Warren counties against a charge of barbarism." At the same time, Flannagan made clear his belief that Thompson killed himself. He concluded by telling White that "I believed also that the man was lynched—until I spent four days interviewing crackerbox liars and fishing with village Rip Van Winkles who launched the lynching stories. On assignment from my paper and at the personal request of the governor I hunted for a lynching as no man ever hunted before—and failed to find it."[81]

Despite the conviction of Flannagan, Freeman, and other elites who insisted that Thompson had committed suicide, James Hardy Dillard, a leading white proponent of black educational programs and an early member of the cic, confided to Walter White that "personally I am convinced it was a lynching." Writing from his home in Charlottesville, Dillard expressed particular dismay that "the gentlemen who write so emphatically of their conviction that the case was not a lynching do not in their letters give very distinctly the ground of this conviction." Ultimately, he advised White to report the matter officially "as a doubtful one," and the executive secretary of the naacp concurred.[82]

In May 1935 the people of Fauquier County again turned to the suicide explanation as a means of avoiding a charge of lynching. According to the *Richmond Planet*, a group of enraged whites cornered Nelson Pendleton, a twenty-five-year-old black man accused of assaulting a white woman. The mob, "armed it is said, with rifles," either killed Pendleton or forced him to kill himself. According to the *Planet*, "The coroner immediately returned a verdict of suicide. It is patent to every sensible person that this suicide yarn has been overworked in Warrenton and vicinity." More to the point, Richmond's black newspaper derided the propensity of state and local officials to accept the coroner's verdict "in order to save Virginia the disgrace of being listed with the lynch states of this Union. . . . Virginia may stand by and in self-complacency assert that the Byrd law precludes lynching in this state, but the rest of the country will not believe this last suicide story." L. R. Reynolds, the director of the Virginia cic, had accepted the suicide verdict in Thompson's death but agreed with the *Planet* that "it looks a little bit 'fishy' to me that this Nelson Pendleton . . . should be found another suicide."[83]

One year after the death of Nelson Pendleton, residents of Gordonsville confirmed that the lynching spirit remained alive in the Old Dominion. William Wales, a black man, and his sister Cora owned land in the town situated in the Orange County foothills of the Blue Ridge Mountains. For several years, Wales had never left his property, apparently afraid that whites would attempt to take away the land he had refused to sell. His reclusiveness and propensity for walking the perimeters of his property while armed led Sheriff William B. Young to attempt to serve him a warrant to appear before a lunacy commission. Wales refused to comply and shot the sheriff to death. In response, 2,000 whites surrounded Wales's home and pumped as many as 10,000 rounds of ammunition into the dwelling over the course of seven hours. Finally, as the house burned around them, Wales and his sister were forced to the windows, where they were killed. Over the course of the next few days, men, women, and children hacked at the remains and combed through the ashes for souvenirs.[84]

A Melancholy Distinction

Initial reports of the confrontation in the white press indicated that Mrs. George Zinn, a wealthy white widow living near Wales, had sought his arrest for threatening her with a gun. No doubt such rumors allowed the mob to justify the attempt of the sheriff to arrest Wales in the first place. But in the aftermath Zinn insisted that Wales had never once bothered her. She had on occasion seen him walking around with a gun but never did she feel unsafe. The Old Dominion's two major black newspapers reported that Wales suffered no malady other than a fear of bodily harm and a belief that whites would try to take his land, both rooted in prior experience. A brother had been slain by his girlfriend, who acted on the orders of white men. In addition, the town of Gordonsville had several years earlier condemned some of Wales's property in order to build a town cemetery. William Wales was determined to hold on to his remaining land at any cost.[85]

Although the coroner ruled that Wales and his sister died as a result of resisting arrest, black newspapers and the NAACP emphasized that the mob had not been deputized and that the Wales siblings would certainly have been lynched had they surrendered. Walter White sent Gertrude Stone of Washington, D.C., to investigate the deaths of William and Cora Wales. He asked her to take care to disguise the purpose of her visit, to examine the possibility that certain whites had been motivated by a desire to steal away the Wales farm, and on balance to "determine whether we can legitimately classify the killings as lynchings." P. B. Young informed Stone that his reporters had discovered that J. R. Yaeger, a Gordonsville official and deputy sheriff, had sworn out the arrest warrant against William Wales. Young described Yaeger as a "rather rabid person" who "led the element engaged in the shooting which refused to make any effort to capture the Wales' alive."[86]

After several days in Gordonsville, during which a Klan-sponsored cross burning occurred on the Wales property, Gertrude Stone concluded that she had not "found anything which will permit us to classify this as a lynching—all the spirit and intent was there, but it was a 'legal' case" in which close to two hundred police officers had been on the scene. While Stone's findings meant that Virginia's reputation remained officially unsullied for another year, she did uncover a number of unfounded rumors that whites had circulated to sanction their own barbarity. The investigator asked Walter White to contact a surviving sister in New York to shed light on stories that William Wales had spent time in prison in New York or New Jersey, a rumor that allowed whites to think of him as a "'bad nigger,'" and that he had deserted a wife and three children in New Jersey.[87]

Walter White succeeded in contacting Julia Wales, the older sister of William and Cora and a resident of New York City. Julia told her interviewer that their father had settled in Orange County as a young man and worked there as a farmer and preacher. An ardent believer in education, Menoah Wales had persuaded the Episcopal Home Mission Board to establish a black high school in Gordonsville, where many of his eleven children went to school. Their father saved his money and used it to acquire property, raising "his family on the land which William and Cora died defending." According to Julia, many white people had tried to buy his land, but Menoah Wales had refused to sell.[88]

After their father's death another brother, James Wales, lived on the property with his sisters Cora and Elizabeth, the rest of the siblings having scattered to other regions. Julia recalled that James was "'smart and up and coming like his father.'" He owned and operated a variety of businesses throughout Orange County, bought a car before any other African American in the county, and purchased a significant amount of his own property. Jealous white neighbors poisoned and killed some of his cattle; undeterred, he opened a grocery store and an undertaking business. In May 1922 his girlfriend shot him to death. According to Julia, "It was common knowledge that white business men of Orange County had promised her $500 to put him on the spot but they only paid $100." She was later acquitted after three hung juries.[89]

James's death left his sisters Cora and Elizabeth alone on the farm. When Elizabeth died in January 1933, William chose to move from New Jersey to Gordonsville to help her with the farm and to provide protection. Contrary to newspaper reports at the time of his death, William Wales was forty-nine, not in his sixties. He had no history of mental illness and had never been in jail. He had worked on the docks in Newport News for many years until he and his wife and younger children moved to New Jersey to live with his eldest son and his son's wife. The siblings had vowed always to keep the land in the family.[90]

Although William and Cora Wales were never officially listed as lynching victims, their grisly deaths deserve special attention. Hardworking, industrious, thrifty, they had succeeded to a degree envied by many whites. William and Cora Wales were found guilty in Orange County of owning land coveted by whites such as the town official who fabricated accusations of lunacy. The fate of his brother James no doubt informed William Wales's decision to shoot the sheriff who came to arrest him on baseless charges. Once William killed the law enforcement officer, an orgy of hatred and jealousy was played out in a barbaric scene whose participants included impressionable children. In the aftermath, whites manufactured charges and stories in an attempt to justify their worst instincts. As expected, no whites were punished for their participation in the deaths of William and Cora Wales.

Ironically, state officials never used Virginia's antilynching law to punish a white person for crimes committed against an African American. Instead, the law was used only to punish whites for crimes against other whites. In 1930 prosecutors in Mecklenburg County successfully used the statute to charge John Hagood for his role in the beating of another white man. In September 1937 officials in Alleghany County used the antilynching statute against striking textile workers who attacked nonstrikers at the Industrial Rayon Corporation's plant in Covington. The convictions prompted the *Richmond News Leader* to proclaim that while "mass picketing and intimidation will not be countenanced in this State . . . the antilynching law was intended for the purpose indicated by its title." A statewide uproar over the misapplication of the antilynching law ultimately led to the pardon of those convicted in the Covington strike and to the passage of an act in the 1938 General Assembly that specifically exempted from the statute violence arising from labor disputes. Nevertheless, in 1948 Governor William Tuck ordered Attorney General J. Lindsay Almond to use the antilynching law to prosecute 178 striking union miners in Buchanan County for attacking non-union miners.[91]

The passage of Virginia's antilynching law represented a profound victory for staunch advocates such as Louis Jaffé. Its adoption emboldened some local officials to act more forcefully to prevent lynchings, as in Clifton Forge in November 1934.[92] But when mob violence did erupt, local and state authorities fought harder to protect the Old Dominion's name and image than they did to apply the punitive sections of the act. Authorities passed on each opportunity to prove the law's effectiveness and appeared more concerned with technical definitions of lynching than with eradicating the mob spirit. Furthermore, and perhaps most important, the majority of white supporters of Virginia's antilynching law failed to recognize that it would remain a hollow device so long as segregation remained an accepted way of life. In effect, the law's passage offered little of substance to address the most pressing daily concerns of African Americans and, in fact, allowed white elites the smug satisfaction of believing that they had fulfilled their paternalistic responsibilities.

Just months after the passage of the antilynching law, the caprices of electoral politics reminded black Virginians just how circumscribed their lives remained under Jim Crow. Serious differences split the Democratic Party during the 1928 presidential election, but supporters of both camps in Virginia found it easier to appeal for votes by turning the campaign into a referendum on race rather than a discussion of the issues. Once again, white elites turned on the faucet of racial antipathy when it furthered their own interests. But this time, African Americans in Virginia rejected the empty words of their self-proclaimed white friends and looked elsewhere to guarantee their basic rights of citizenship. Dominant whites soon discovered just how difficult the management of white supremacy had become.

7

The Erosion of Paternalism

CONFRONTING THE LIMITS OF MANAGED

RACE RELATIONS

> The Negroes of Richmond . . . , through their tolerance,
> through their refusal to countenance any act calculated to
> disturb the friendly relations existing between the races in
> Richmond and through their cooperation in every effort to
> promote the best interests of Richmond, have earned the
> reputation of being peaceful, useful and law-abiding citizens.
> . . . They have believed the assurances of the white people
> of Richmond that they are friends of the Negro, and have
> waited patiently for some evidence of this friendship. . . .
> [Richmond] is the only Southern city which offers a
> segregation ordinance as proof of the friendship of the
> whites for the blacks. — Statement of black residents
> of Richmond, 1929

The reservoir of interracial goodwill generated by the passage of the antilynching law evaporated within months as white Virginians turned the
1928 presidential campaign into an exercise in race-baiting. That year's
election divided white Virginians more than any other in the first half of
the twentieth century. Aroused by the twin issues of Prohibition and anti-
Catholicism, the Ku Klux Klan and the chief of the Virginia Anti-Saloon
League, Bishop James Cannon, led droves of male and female Democrats
to desert their party's standard-bearer, New York governor Al Smith, a
Roman Catholic and a wet. Although troubled by Smith's stand on Prohibition, a number of state leaders, including Governor Harry Byrd and

Senator Carter Glass, refused to abandon their party's nominee and condemned the religious bigotry of the anti-Smith faction. Deeply aware that the lack of enthusiasm among many reliable party functionaries spelled trouble for Smith's campaign, Democratic leaders attempted to win back deserting voters by finessing the most reliable card in their arsenal: race. The anti-Smith forces responded in kind, and by the time the fall campaign ended, each side had fought to expose the other as the greater threat to white supremacy.[1]

Thousands of Ku Klux Klan members joined the anti-Smith Democrats, not only because of their unwavering support of Prohibition and general hostility to Catholicism, but because of their intense opposition to the reform policies of Harry Byrd. In particular, the Klan objected to the short ballot, a measure that removed from the electorate and gave to the governor the power to appoint the state superintendent of public instruction, commissioner of agriculture, and treasurer. The short ballot, in effect, protected John M. Purcell, the Roman Catholic state treasurer whom the Klan had worked to defeat in 1925 and planned to target again in 1929. Byrd and other party leaders placed the short ballot before voters in June 1928. For weeks prior to the referendum, the Klan burned crosses, threw bombs, and threatened the governor with bodily harm. Nevertheless, the amendments passed, albeit by a narrow margin that confirmed for Democratic officials that a difficult and divisive fall campaign lay ahead.[2]

Soon after the June referendum, Jennings Cropper Wise, a leading Republican spokesperson and speechwriter, polled hundreds of people throughout the state in an effort to understand the position of the electorate. In every report, Wise concluded that respondents seldom mentioned the "negro question" and that "religion is the real basis of the opposition [to Smith]." According to the *Richmond News Leader*, an anonymous Democrat, a "Virginian of distinction," took a similar reading of the electorate's mood but determined to meet the crisis of defections by focusing on white supremacy. Such tactics drew the condemnation of the *News Leader*, which remarked that African Americans had kept themselves out of the campaign and could not be held responsible for divisions among whites. "It would speak exceedingly ill for the Southern Democrats in this hour of great opportunity," argued the Richmond daily, "if they put aside the real issues for the false." Not surprisingly, Norfolk's black paper congratulated the *News Leader* for its stand and added that, if involved at all, many blacks had decided to vote for the Democratic nominee.[3]

Tired of Republican lily-whitism, African Americans throughout the South and the nation began to migrate to the Democratic Party in greater numbers in 1928. In Virginia, blacks formed Negro Smith Clubs in Richmond, Farmville, Norfolk, and other parts of the state. While *Richmond Planet* editor John Mitchell continued to criticize the Democrats for accepting the white South's demands vis-à-vis segregation, his counterpart in Norfolk, P. B. Young, officially endorsed Al Smith on the editorial pages of the *Norfolk Journal and Guide*. The confirmation that some blacks had embraced the Democratic Party emboldened Virginia Republicans, who concluded that the Democratic machine could no longer charge Republicans with threatening white supremacy.[4]

In fact, as the campaign heated up, Republicans and anti-Smith Democrats challenged the racial credentials of their opponents by denouncing Smith's loyalty to Tammany Hall, New York City's Democratic machine. In a flyer entitled "Why Va. Voters Are for Hoover!," anti-Smith forces condemned Tammany's appointment of 276 blacks to key positions as a clear sign that the machine and its candidate stood for racial equality. The circular warned that Smith would impose his beliefs on Virginia and the South but insisted that "the White, Self-respecting, true Democrats of this State are not yet ready to surrender White Supremacy of the South to the negro-loving Tammany Tiger of the North." In addition, supporters of Republican candidate Herbert Hoover disseminated an inflammatory article reprinted from the *Fellowship Forum*, an anti-Catholic publication with ties to the Ku Klux Klan. Headlined "White Supremacy as Practiced by Tammany" and accompanied by a half-page photograph of a black civil servant dictating to his white secretary, the text derisively praised the image as a "beautiful picture of race equality," identified the civil servant as the leader of hundreds of thousands of black New Yorkers, and revealed that he was on a first-name basis with Al Smith. "If this picture isn't enough to nauseate any Anglo-Saxon of the South," concluded the broadside, "then there is little use for advocating white supremacy any longer."[5]

As opponents of Smith attacked his candidacy on racial lines, Governor Harry Byrd attempted to stem the flow of desertions from the Democratic Party. After insisting that numerous proponents of Prohibition in Virginia continued to support Smith, the chief executive addressed what he considered "the real issue in this campaign." A vote for Hoover, argued Byrd, threatened to subject Virginia to the whims of its sectional enemies in Congress. More specifically, Byrd cited Leonidas Dyer, a Republican member of Congress from Missouri, who backed a federal antilynching law and efforts to enforce the Fourteenth and Fifteenth Amendments. Byrd reminded his constituents that those amendments had been "designed to give the Negro equal rights with the white man." Recalling the threats posed by the Lodge Force Bill in the 1890s, Virginia's governor warned that Dyer had pledged that a victory for Hoover in the South would allow Congress to pass enforcement laws designed, in Dyer's words, to "'give millions of Negroes their constitutional rights as citizens and place them on an equality with all other races.'"[6]

Byrd made a half-hearted effort to take the high ground when he condemned "the rekindling in this campaign of old sectional fires." But given the tactics of his opponents, the governor urged Democrats to remember "the reconstruction days, when, under Republican State administration, thirty-five negroes, as representatives of the people, sat side by side with white gentlemen in the State capitol." The Republican Party, warned Byrd, had proved itself "out of sympathy with our traditions and our sentiments." As a parting shot, the governor accused Henry Anderson, who remained a leading voice in the state Republican Party, of recently advocating the liberalization of Virginia's election laws, "the effect of which would be to permit Negroes to vote."[7]

Despite Byrd's efforts, Smith opponents remained on the offensive. When Carter Glass attempted to defend Smith's record, Jennings Wise asked the senator what role he and other Democratic officials had played in the formation of the Negro Smith Clubs. In response to editorials in the Richmond papers reminding readers of the lessons of Reconstruction, Mrs. Jesse W. Nicholson, the president of the National Women's Democratic Law Enforcement League, told a group in Richmond that "if Al Smith is elected you may say good-bye to your Jim Crow cars, for he will do away with them inside of six months. For he has always been elected by the Negro vote in Harlem 'Nigger Heaven.'" According to one Republican, Democratic leaders in Roanoke became so desperate that they "organized a special drive under Ex-Governor Trinkle to raise the cry of negro rule and scare the bolters back." Ignoring the complicity of Hoover supporters in turning the campaign into a referendum on racial fears, this particular observer excoriated Democratic leaders for their willingness to "in cold blood deliberately agitate this dangerous question, stirring up as much hate and fury as possible."[8]

In the final days of the campaign, the NAACP issued a statement on behalf of a group of black leaders distressed by the climate in Virginia and the rest of the South. "'The emphasis of racial contempt and hatred which is being made in this campaign," began the statement, "is an appeal to the lowest and most primitive of human motives, and as long as this appeal successfully can be made there is for this land no real peace, no sincere religion, no national unity, no social progress even in matters far removed from racial controversy." The authors of the statement insisted, furthermore, that "in a civilized land in a Christian culture . . . limits must be put to race disparagements and separation and to campaigns of racial calumny."[9]

As if to underscore the wide gulf separating black and white Virginians, the *Norfolk Journal and Guide* published along with the NAACP statement a letter from Elizabeth Sutherland Young, a sixty-eight-year-old white resident of Norfolk. Clearly intent on offering a modicum of support to the black newspaper, Young assured the editor that the racial issue "is not taken seriously by persons of good common sense." Like so many whites of "good common sense," however, Young failed to comprehend the effect of three months of intense racial discourse; ideas, words, and actions produced serious consequences. In early August, for instance, Menalcus Lankford, the Republican candidate for Congress from Norfolk, had stated, "'We are not going to stand for Negroes in office in the South.'" Lankford, who won in November, was not known as a race-baiter, and white papers reported his speech as "'quiet and dispassionate.'" But as the *Journal and Guide* replied at the time, and as Young apparently failed to consider, "his words are in themselves an unfortunate appeal to intolerance, regardless of how dispassionately they were uttered." Norfolk's black press proved all too prescient when it warned that blacks would be savaged before the end of the coming political campaign.[10]

With the exception of Byrd and Glass, Democratic stalwarts exerted little effort on Smith's behalf. Consequently, the coalition of Republicans and anti-Smith Democrats proved too strong a combination to overcome, even for Virginia's Democratic machine. Hoover carried the commonwealth by nearly 25,000 votes. In the aftermath of the election, Louis Jaffé praised "the courage and magnanimity" of Harry Byrd in championing "the cause of intellectual and religious liberty." In fact, Jaffé deemed Byrd's advocacy "as in keeping with the finest Virginia traditions." The Norfolk newsman, however, avoided any mention of the propensity exhibited by Byrd and other Democratic leaders to resort to racial abuse when necessary. The finest Virginia traditions apparently did not extend to an understanding and awareness of the numbing consequences of repeated racial invective.[11]

Just months after Hoover's victory, Democrats and Republicans across the country looked to the Old Dominion, the only state in the nation holding a gubernatorial election in 1929. The coalition of Republicans and anti-Smith Democrats hoped to once again upend Virginia's political status quo, while anxious Democrats understood the importance of regaining the upper hand. The greatest concern facing the Democrats was how to win the votes of party members who had crossed over and voted for Hoover. Since state law prevented such persons from voting in the next Democratic primary, party officials began discussing the possibility of abolishing the primary in favor of a convention. Ultimately, however, the Virginia Democratic Central Committee asked for and received from the attorney general a ruling that differentiated between national and state elections and thus allowed Hoover Democrats back into the fold for the primary.[12]

Republicans and anti-Smith Democrats continued to rely on the strategy that had proved successful in 1928. In separate conventions, they selected William Moseley Brown, a young professor of psychology and education, to head the ticket. Possessing solid credentials as a dry Protestant who had opposed Al Smith, Brown ran on a platform that made every attempt to associate the state Democratic Party with the reviled policies of the national party and its standard-bearer. A reporter for the *Norfolk Journal and Guide* predicted that the coalition would succeed again in making race an issue, insofar as the mass of voters would believe claims that the Democrats intended to integrate public schools as Al Smith had done in New York. Democrats, however, picked a nominee whose predilections and reputation undercut Republican and anti-Smith claims. A committed Prohibitionist, Baptist layman, and former attorney general of Virginia, John Garland Pollard proved the antithesis of Al Smith. In addition, what became known as the "DePriest Affair" allowed Democrats to regain for themselves the political benefits of racial calumny.[13]

In mid-June headlines throughout Virginia and the South reported that Herbert Hoover's wife had held a White House tea for a group of congressional spouses, including the wife of Oscar DePriest, a black Republican congressman from Chicago. Although it was no more than a routine reception, southern politicians echoed the sentiments of a senator from Texas who declared the event a "recognition of social equality between the white and black races" that threatened "infinite danger to our white civilization." Closer to home, the *Norfolk Virginian-Pilot* reported that many political leaders in Virginia surmised that the Hoover administration could not have come up with a more effective means of ensuring a Democratic victory at the polls in November.[14]

Norfolk's leading white newspaper, on the other hand, attempted to downplay the significance of the White House reception. An editorial reminded readers that Theodore Roosevelt's invitation to Booker T. Washington to dine at the White House had not caused "the Caucasian race [to] suffer an impairment of its security." Furthermore, the Tidewater daily argued that the First Lady had made no attempt to encourage interracial mixing but had merely performed one of her official duties as the wife of the president. Nevertheless, acknowledged the paper, the event "is likely to have sententious reverberations, especially among the hell-raisers who are always ready to scent social danger where no social danger exists."[15]

African Americans in Virginia responded to the "DePriest Affair" in differing ways. Many shared the anger expressed by J. W. Grey of Norfolk, a former serviceman, who struggled to understand how newspapers could report the event as a crime. The incident opened up old wounds and led Grey to challenge the hypocrisy of whites. In particular, the former doughboy asked how whites could allow black mothers to cook their meals and black sisters and daughters to nurse white babies, without any sense of danger, and yet not tolerate the presence of Mrs. DePriest at a tea. "We have no desire to mix with the white race," insisted Grey, "but we do want justice, because we are human."[16]

Soon after the infamous White House reception, Oscar DePriest toured the Southeast and spoke in a number of cities, including Roanoke and Norfolk. Southern blacks had hailed DePriest's victory in 1928, especially since no black candidate had been elected to Congress since 1900. Not all African Americans, however, welcomed his appearance in the South. Many southern representatives in Congress had objected to his election from the start, claiming that DePriest was morally unfit to serve because he remained under indictment in Chicago for his involvement in a gambling operation. Objectors even refused to take the oath of office at the same time as DePriest, who was sworn in alone after every other member of Congress. When DePriest began speaking in various southern cities, Norfolk's black press argued that the congressman should have addressed only the circumstances of the White House tea, and that he had no business inflaming "racial hecklers" in the South. The *Norfolk Journal and Guide* added that DePriest's speeches threatened gains made by blacks in recent years.[17]

Other blacks in Virginia vehemently disagreed with the position taken by the *Journal and Guide*. Henry C. Davis denounced the hypocritical pretensions of civility that guided white elite discourse and expressed shock that a black newspaper would accept these arguments with such ease. The Norfolk resident explicitly rejected the suggestion that DePriest had "opened anew the bitter discussion of the race question in Southern newspapers for that is the one discussion which Southern newspapers never allow to close. Almost every day we read in the Norfolk dailies about Negro this, and Negro that, and Negro the other thing . . . and never a word of commendation and encouragement." Referring to Virginia's recently enacted antilynching law, Davis suggested that no law would prevent whites from lynching a black man or woman if whites felt strongly enough.[18]

As the fall campaign moved into high gear, Democrats used the "De-Priest Affair" in much the way that had been predicted. State senator Samuel Ferguson, a Democratic stalwart, raised the "bogey of Negro domination" in a campaign speech and warned that a vote for the coalition of Republicans and anti-Smith Democrats would imperil white supremacy. The *Norfolk Virginian-Pilot* chided the senator's choice of words and equated his threats with the efforts of anti-Smith forces in 1928. The Norfolk newspaper considered Ferguson's remarks an unfortunate diversion away from the recent achievements of the Democratic administration.[19]

Although the *Virginian-Pilot* might have preferred that candidates address issues considered more relevant to state government, the "DePriest Affair" took center stage, especially in the closing weeks of the campaign. Democrats released a circular that included a picture of DePriest and his wife, a copy of the invitation to the White House tea, and texts from several of DePriest's speeches, all accompanied by the claim that Republicans intended to abolish the poll tax. Few Virginians could have failed to understand the point of the flyer's authors. Republican leaders Henry Anderson and Jennings Wise vilified Democrats for producing the pamphlet and accused state officials of responsibility. Despite repeated denials from Democratic Party leaders, the Republicans produced affidavits proving that Clyde Saunders, a member of the Richmond Democratic Committee, had printed the circular and that various county, state, and Democratic Party officials had distributed it throughout the commonwealth. Wise later included members of the governor's staff among those responsible for the pamphlet's dissemination.[20]

Leading Republicans attempted to take the high road and accused Democrats of diverting attention from issues of real importance. Jennings Wise, according to one Richmond newspaper, argued that blacks ought to be left alone to cast their ballots for either party without being seen as a "menace." Such discourse, however, could not mask the complicity of Republicans in making race a preeminent campaign issue, especially when it was revealed that I. C. Trotman of Suffolk, an anti-Smith leader in 1928, had authored the DePriest circular. Angered that Republican and anti-Smith forces refused to pass a resolution condemning the White House tea, Trotman quit the coalition in June and remained a nonfactor until the appearance of the circular. The *Richmond Times-Dispatch* noted with irony that in 1928 Trotman had labored to save Virginia from the evils of Al Smith, all with the support of Republicans like Wise. In 1929, continued the paper, "the patriot took his new nightmare with him into the Democratic camp." Using "precisely the same tactics" that had proved so successful the year before, Trotman "got up a pamphlet, telling about how Virginia was going to be turned over to the black race, and sent it broadcast over the State."[21]

Trotman's flip-flop underscored the fragility of the coalition that had joined forces to defeat Al Smith in Virginia in 1928. Republicans sought to create a second party that would prove effective in challenging the traditional Democratic control of the state. But to win in 1928, the Republicans allied themselves with the followers of Bishop Cannon and the Ku Klux Klan. Numerous Republicans expressed a discomfort with this arrangement, yet the marriage held together and successfully exploited racial and religious prejudices to win. A year later, Bishop Cannon fled to Brazil in disgrace over improper financial dealings, and the anti-Smith coalition faced an opponent whose religious and racial beliefs were beyond question. In a post-election memorandum, Jennings Wise acknowledged that the defeat of the coalition in 1929 was "not altogether unfortunate for the Republican party, National and State." The future of the party, he believed, should not depend on the approximately 30,000 pro–Ku Klux Klan, anti-Smith voters such as Trotman, who had made the difference in 1928 but had subsequently realigned themselves with the Democrats.[22]

John Garland Pollard defeated his opponent in a landslide, reaffirming the strength of the Democratic machine in general and boss Harry Byrd in particular. In the days following Pollard's victory, an embittered anti-Smith Democrat on the Eastern Shore wrote to Republican leaders to complain about the hypocrisy of the Democrats. The writer explained that on the Saturday night prior to the election, the Democrats brought in former governor Trinkle "to yell nigger, nigger, nigger, DePriest, DePriest." Exactly one week later, in the same white high school auditorium, the same people invited "40 niggers" from Hampton Institute to sing and provide entertainment. Although not in the least bit enamored of such Democratic shenanigans, Richmond's black newspaper expressed "genuine satisfaction" that the Republican lily-whites had finally met their "Waterloo." The *Richmond Planet* reasoned that Republicans had done their best to make electoral inroads in 1928 by manipulating racial hatreds and fears but had now received appropriate comeuppance.[23]

The anecdote relayed by the Eastern Shore resident highlighted a recurring theme in Virginia, as well as southern, politics. Time and time again, white Virginians proved capable of hurling nasty invectives at their black neighbors, warning that the smallest breach of deference constituted social equality and endangered white supremacy. In the next breath, whites claimed to be the best friends of their black brethren and not to have meant what they said. Some white newspapers, including the *Richmond Times-Dispatch*, condemned the injection of racial rhetoric into the 1929 campaign but simultaneously dismissed it is a "shabby trick," a harmless charade in the theater of politics. The Richmond daily, in fact, emphasized that racial amity prevailed in the Old Dominion, as evidenced by the relative absence of violence that plagued other states and the fair treatment meted out by the courts and local governments.[24]

As usual, it remained the job of black leaders and the black press to remind white Virginians that the words uttered in the pursuit of political victory had real consequences. The *Norfolk Journal and Guide* directly challenged the conclusion of the white press "that all is well, in spite of the criminal assault upon a disadvantaged people that is made perennially in the name of a political campaign. It is idle to say that appeals to race prejudice do no harm to the race they are directed against." Furthermore, the black paper argued that employers and merchants throughout the state followed the lead set by the politicians and appealed to racial prejudice in a manner that injured black efforts to obtain jobs. A bakery in Norfolk "advertised over the radio that it employed only white help in the making of its white bread." A local laundry warned whites "that it is a menace to have clothes laundered by Negro washer-women." A union organized a boycott of a chain store that had hired black bricklayers to complete renovations. For its part, the *Richmond Planet* questioned the failure of whites to recognize the inherent immorality in a criminal justice system that handed out a suspended sentence to a white woman for shoplifting $13,000 worth of merchandise and, on the same day, sent a black woman to jail for thirty years for forging checks that totaled $29.[25]

As the decade of the 1920s came to an end, African Americans in Virginia had good reason to challenge the hollow assertions of elite whites who continued to embrace paternalism. In two successive years, race had played a significant role in the rhetoric, if not the outcome, of statewide elections. Although religion had been a major factor in the anti-Smith movement, those forces ultimately appealed to the racial prejudices of Virginia's white electorate. A year later, the Democrats successfully turned the tables on their opponents and made great use of the "DePriest Affair." The *Norfolk Journal and Guide* concluded that this "unholy assault upon our integrity and intelligence" threatened to destroy whatever gains had been made throughout the decade. Furthermore, the black newspaper rejected the claims of white elites that "racial hecklers" and "certain easily identifiable demagogues" were responsible for "these campaigns of hate." Instead, the *Journal and Guide* expressed profound disheartenment "that our Governor-elect Pollard, our ex-Governor Trinkle, our United States Senator Swanson and numerous others high in our political and civil life of the

State took up this DePriest circular and waved the red flag with as much satisfaction and with tremendously more effect than did the Trotman person who brazenly and exultantly came forward and claimed authorship of it." The entire experience led the paper to conclude that "the white people of the State have been so schooled in the psychology of Negro antipathy, that when the issue is raised it overshadows all others."[26]

As whites, both Republicans and Democrats, embraced racial invective to gain an electoral advantage in the 1928 and 1929 campaigns, African Americans in Virginia initiated two court cases aimed at breaking the paralyzing grip of "Negro antipathy." Buoyed by the decision of the U.S. Supreme Court in *Nixon v. Herndon*, blacks in Richmond sought to participate in the 1928 municipal Democratic primary. Barred by party policy, blacks filed suit in federal court and ultimately won a decision that opened doors, albeit only slightly at first, to black political participation. Only months later, African Americans in Richmond challenged a recently enacted segregation ordinance. The battle over the ordinance and a subsequent court challenge revealed potentially irreparable fault lines in the traditionally paternalistic relationship that guided the management of white supremacy in Richmond and the Old Dominion.[27]

In March 1927 the U.S. Supreme Court ruled in *Nixon v. Herndon* that state law could not bar African Americans from participating in party primaries. Reaction in Virginia was mixed. The *Norfolk Virginian-Pilot* reminded its readers that educational requirements would still limit the number of black voters but termed the decision "unquestionably an important contribution to the definition of political justice. In strict law and logic, the court's decision is, we believe, flawless." Once again out in front of other white opinion shapers in the state, the Tidewater daily recognized that the ruling would invalidate the arrangement in states like Virginia where party policy, not state law, prevented blacks from participating. "It is axiomatic," opined the *Virginian-Pilot*, "that if the Legislature itself is without power to make color the basis of eligibility to participate in a primary, it can not delegate the right to set up such a discrimination to anybody else."[28]

Others, however, argued precisely that this critical distinction should allow Virginia's law to stand. The *Richmond News Leader* quoted a number of lawyers who emphasized that Texas law specifically forbade blacks from voting in the Democratic primaries, while state law in Virginia made no such provision but rather allowed each party to determine the eligibility of participants. Other officials and leading Democrats suggested that if the federal courts were going to inject themselves into party activities, it might be best to abolish primaries and return to a convention system of nomination.[29]

In March 1928 six hundred blacks in Richmond decided to seek a court order to compel city officials to allow African Americans to vote in the following month's mayoral primary. State and city Democratic Party leaders expressed satisfaction with the current situation and, with help from the white press, reiterated the legality of Virginia law and Democratic Party policy. The *Richmond Times-Dispatch* went so far as to insist that a comparison between the Texas and Virginia laws revealed a "wide variance" and that "Virginia law itself does not discriminate in any way." As if to remind its readers of the essential purpose of the white primary, the Richmond daily speculated that as many as 5,000 qualified black voters, if allowed to participate, would hold the balance of power. Not surprisingly, Richmond's black press rejected any insinuation that the state could encourage or allow individuals to discriminate in a manner clearly off-limits to state authorities. The *Richmond Planet* emphasized, furthermore, that party officials were already agents of the state owing to the state's subsidization of party activities. On March 30, however, Judge Beverly Crump denied the petition of lead plaintiff James O. West, arguing that the Fourteenth and Fifteenth Amendments protected against discrimination practiced by representatives of the state, but that party primaries involved the actions of private officials.[30]

In the wake of Crump's decision, *Richmond News Leader* editor Douglas Southall Freeman urged white Democrats to recognize the changes taking place around them. African Americans, he argued, had lost all trust in the Republican Party. Educational and economic improvements for the state's black citizens had inspired a new sense of pride in self and in the community. Black leaders emphasized that badly needed municipal improvements would come only after African Americans began to vote. Consequently, black Virginians understood that their own well-being necessitated participation in Democratic primaries. Freeman acknowledged that many whites would continue to "insist vigorously that the Democratic party must be kept a 'white man's party,'" but the editor considered such resistance short-sighted, especially since few blacks were eligible to vote. In conclusion, Freeman admonished party leaders to recognize that in the coming years black illiteracy would continue to fall and greater numbers of black people would qualify to vote despite current impediments. "What will be done then?" asked the editor. "When the parties no longer can bar the Negro because he is illiterate, will they continue to bar him because he is a Negro?"[31]

The Erosion of Paternalism

Despite the adverse ruling from Judge Crump, James West attempted to vote in the Richmond mayoral primary on April 3. Although West met all the requirements necessary to vote in a general election, local officials barred him from casting a ballot in the primary, citing the 1924 "Primary Plan of the Democratic Party," which conferred that privilege on "all white persons qualified to vote." Represented by Richmond lawyers Joseph Pollard, who was black, and Alfred Cohen, who was white, and who in turn were aided by the national office of the NAACP, West filed suit in federal district court in the fall of 1928. Answering repeated claims that Virginia's law differed substantially from the Texas statute overruled the year before, NAACP attorney Louis Marshall wrote that "what has been done in Virginia is only to pursue in a roundabout manner the same vicious method of holding a primary as was sought to be effected in a more brutal, but more honest, fashion by the Legislature of Texas." Marshall's analysis cut to the heart of race relations in the Old Dominion: less brutal, but also less honest.[32]

On June 5, 1929, federal district court judge D. Lawrence Groner found that Virginia's primary law violated the Fourteenth and Fifteenth Amendments of the U.S. Constitution. In his decision, the judge rejected defense arguments that the actions of party officials constituted private rather than official conduct and noted that although the method of discrimination differed from that found in Texas, the result did not. Groner explicitly ruled that "the legislature cannot by delegation or otherwise give vitality to a claimed right which it is itself prohibited by the constitution from enacting into law." The jurist acknowledged that the effect of his ruling "may be to change a custom that has long obtained in the political system in effect in this state." But no matter how unpleasant the reaction of many white Virginians might be, Groner believed his ruling was the only option that satisfied "the performance of the duty evolving on this court."[33]

Reaction throughout the commonwealth varied along expected lines. Richmond's black newspaper praised the logic of Groner's decision as "impregnable." The *Norfolk Virginian-Pilot* wrote that Groner had concluded "what was apparent to nearly everybody that gave serious thought to the matter two years ago" when the Supreme Court ruled in *Nixon v. Herndon*. As it concluded then, the *Virginian-Pilot* reiterated that an end to the white primary would have little practical effect, insofar as few blacks would qualify to vote. But, added the Tidewater daily, the state's political situation would benefit from allowing African Americans to participate in the activities of both parties, rather than excluding them from primaries and leaving them susceptible to demagogic appeals in general elections. Norfolk's other daily, the *Ledger-Dispatch*, took a similar stand, emphasizing that "educational qualifications, poll-tax prepayment, registration and all the other requirements prescribed by state law are still in effect."[34]

Most white newspapers in Virginia, however, had reached a different conclusion in response to *Nixon v. Herndon* and remained uncertain how to digest Groner's ruling. The *Richmond Times-Dispatch*, in particular, appeared at a loss for words, incoherently opining that Groner's decision "did not consider specifically the attitude of the Democratic party in Virginia toward permitting Negroes to participate in its primaries." The *Petersburg Progress-Index*, reacting to criticism from a black newspaper in New York, went so far as to deny that the intent of the Democratic Party plan was to circumvent the Fourteenth and Fifteenth Amendments. Acknowledging reluctantly that Groner's decision represented sound legal thinking, the Petersburg paper stretched credulity when it argued that "there is not the faintest reason to believe that any democrat responsible in any degree for the adoption of this regulation excluding Negroes had any thought of violating the fourteenth and fifteenth amendments or of evading them." The *Portsmouth Star* took comfort in the fact that the appeals process would prevent blacks from participating in Democratic primaries for at least another year. The *Newport News Daily Press* held out hope that either the court of appeals or the U.S. Supreme Court would overturn Groner's decision.[35]

Several days after the announcement of Groner's decision, the *Richmond Times-Dispatch* attempted a fuller reckoning with the full implications of the ruling. Ultimately, however, the Richmond daily succeeded only in further highlighting the heightened uncertainty that had come to characterize managed race relations. First, as if to defend the commonwealth's reputation, the paper acknowledged that most people conceded the validity of Groner's opinion, but it insisted that many legal scholars noted a legitimate difference in the approaches taken by Texas and Virginia, a position supported by at least one contributor to the *Virginia Law Review*. Second, the editorial stated that the ruling would have no immediate effect because state officials intended to appeal. Third, the paper suggested that the state legislature take the "opportunity to enact some new law accomplishing by indirection what it has failed to accomplish otherwise," a clear invitation to devise a course of resistance cloaked in legalisms. Next, in an effort to satisfy one of the lawsuit's most critical contentions, the *Times-Dispatch* raised the possibility of abolishing state-financed primaries in favor of privately funded events. Despite its best efforts, Richmond's morning paper apparently failed to convince even itself of the legitimacy of these options, finally admitting that the exclusion of African Americans from party politics could no longer be achieved legally.[36]

The Erosion of Paternalism

Two months after Groner's ruling, African Americans throughout Virginia attempted to vote in the August gubernatorial primaries. The *Norfolk Journal and Guide* reported that George Walker, a prominent attorney in Norfolk, sought an order from a local judge to compel election officials to allow him to cast a ballot. Ignoring the recent decision by the attorney general that allowed Hoover Democrats to participate in the primary, the jurist refused Walker's request on the grounds that he admitted not having voted for Al Smith in the previous year's election. Reports indicated that throughout the state, in Portsmouth, Petersburg, Richmond, and Newport News, election judges prevented many African Americans, including James West, from voting.[37]

West's inability to vote in the August primary prompted another suit charging election officials with contempt and seeking damages of $5,000. In October, a jury awarded West $5, a sum agreed to by both parties in order to allow an appeal to go forward. Finally, in June 1930, the Fourth Circuit Court of Appeals upheld Groner's decision, commending his careful consideration and logical reasoning. In delivering the opinion of the court, Judge Elliott Northcott derided Virginia's primary scheme as clearly unconstitutional and remarked that "if all the political parties in the State of Virginia incorporated the same qualifications in their rules and regulations as did the Democratic Party, nobody could participate in the primary except white persons."[38]

The decision of the appellate court left some Democratic leaders speechless. The secretary of the Washington, D.C., branch of the NAACP asked Murray Hooker, the chairman of the Democratic State Central Committee, if qualified blacks in northern Virginia would be allowed to vote in the August 1930 primaries. The party chair, after consulting with Harry Byrd, chose not to reply at all. Some newspapers, led by the Norfolk dailies and the *Richmond News Leader*, urged Virginians to accept the Groner ruling, to acknowledge the justness of a desire among blacks for improved municipal services, and to understand that few blacks would qualify to vote in the cities, while virtually none would do so in the state's rural areas. The *News Leader* claimed that only "a deliberate policy of fascism" could circumvent the decision. Nevertheless, others in the Old Dominion acknowledged that the main purpose of the white primary was to ensure "the maintenance of the supremacy of the white voters of Virginia," particularly in counties with a majority black population, and urged the General Assembly to find a way to return to the old system of independently financed primaries. But unlike their brethren in Texas, who continued to pursue every imaginable legal option to bar blacks from the primary, Democratic leaders in Virginia chose a less confrontational path of resistance. Aware that few African Americans attempted to vote in the August primaries and determined that state and municipal treasuries continue to bear the cost of financing its primaries, Democratic Party officials chose not to appeal to the U.S. Supreme Court. In September, James West's victory became final and irrevocable, establishing an important precedent in the quest of black Virginians for full citizenship.[39]

The determination of James West and other African Americans to participate fully in the electoral process derived from a desire for autonomy and a recognition that political access was a prerequisite for bringing about meaningful change in their lives. In Richmond, where West lived, municipal officials had fashioned the politics of racial demagoguery into public policy more effectively than in any other city in the commonwealth. In the months between the invective-laden elections of 1928 and 1929, as West's case began its trip through the court system, city leaders in Richmond debated and then passed a residential segregation statute. Supporters of the ordinance, who had repeatedly denied African Americans a reasonable share of municipal resources, considered the measure a necessary response to blacks who had followed the pattern in Norfolk and elsewhere and had begun moving into formerly all-white neighborhoods.

Black encroachments into white residential districts were never as ubiquitous as claimed by proponents of Richmond's segregation ordinance. Nevertheless, African Americans did seek alternative living arrangements in response to the abject refusal of the city to provide essential services to black neighborhoods. Theodore W. Jones, a black resident of Leigh Street, made the case clear in a letter published in the *Richmond News Leader*. Referring to the blatant racial appeals made by Mayor Fulmer Bright, Jones argued that "local office holders or their appointees should not be commended or reelected who practice economy at the expense of Negro citizens." The city of Richmond had failed, he said, when it paved the portion of Leigh Street occupied by whites but refused the same improvement to black residents. Such a policy left African Americans who desired better living conditions few alternatives to moving into already-improved neighborhoods.[40]

Jones acknowledged that the movement of blacks into white neighborhoods often forced white neighbors to sell, a situation particularly hard on the "unfortunate white man, especially of small means, who has labored for years to pay for his home and his church." But, insisted Jones, whites had only themselves to blame. First, office holders failed to make improvements. Second, white real estate agents sold and rented to African Americans. Third, working and middle-class whites remained "unsympathetic

The Erosion of Paternalism

and unconcerned about the miserable living conditions forced upon the Negro, until their own neighborhoods are invaded by him." Dismissing the empty gestures so often tendered by white Virginians, Jones stressed that no lasting, meaningful friendship between the races would occur until whites in Richmond adopted a truly "equitable public policy." In effect, Jones argued that blacks would stay in their neighborhoods if their streets were swept and paved, their garbage collected, and their children provided access to parks and swimming pools, all services taken for granted by the city's white residents.[41]

Instead of acting to meet the needs and concerns expressed by Theodore Jones and endorsed frequently by the city's white press, Richmond's bicameral municipal government, comprised of a city council and board of aldermen, affirmed its commitment to white supremacy by enacting a residential segregation statute. Ever mindful that the U.S. Supreme Court had repeatedly ruled such ordinances unconstitutional, Alderman Henry W. Woody, an undertaker, proposed that the new ordinance bar persons from living next to each other who were prohibited from intermarrying by Virginia's Racial Integrity Act of 1924. The Richmond ordinance, therefore, never mentioned race or skin color. The intent, however, was unmistakable.[42]

Opponents of the proposed statute, both black and white, attempted to persuade the city council to appoint a commission of six citizens and three city officials to study the factors responsible for the movement of African Americans into white neighborhoods. The commission would have included representatives from the real estate commission, a member of the interracial committee, and at least two black citizens appointed by the mayor. Despite initial expressions of support, the council, which considered the matter before it went to the board of aldermen, rejected the plan.[43]

A week before the council held its first public hearing on the proposed ordinance, hundreds of African Americans gathered at the True Reformers Hall to pass a resolution of protest. Emphasizing that for decades they had complied faithfully with the basic terms of the paternalistic bargain, those in attendance issued a remarkable statement that questioned the sincerity of the city's white residents and brought into relief the contradictions inherent in managed race relations. Reminding white residents that "they have never been militant or assertive, even under the most extreme provocation," black citizens noted that for years they "believed the assurances of the white people of Richmond that they are friends of the Negro, and have waited patiently for some concrete evidence of this friendship." Instead, city administrators and white residents repeatedly and systematically responded with nothing but prejudice and intolerance. Recognizing all too well that the pathological failure of the city's whites underscored the complete emptiness of paternalism, those assembled warned that while in the past blacks "have hesitated to join national movements designed to resist oppressive anti-Negro legislation, feeling that Richmond's problem could be better solved by citizens of Richmond," African Americans in Richmond could make no such promise with regard to the future.[44]

As the council prepared to hold its first public hearing, Douglas Southall Freeman attempted to mobilize white public opinion against the measure. In an effort to guide Richmond whites to recognize the legitimacy of black grievances and aspirations, a critical first step in meeting paternalistic obligations, Freeman argued in private as well as on the editorial page of the *Richmond News Leader* that African Americans did not seek social or racial equality. He emphasized instead that the standard of living among African Americans had risen substantially since the First World War and that it therefore made sense that blacks sought better houses and cleaner streets. The editor of the *News Leader* acknowledged that a temporary depression might occur as neighborhoods changed hands, but he insisted that such drops in property values would not last. Freeman noted that aspiring blacks had actually improved the condition of some previously all-white neighborhoods.[45]

Segregation proponents appearing before the council's Ordinance Committee expressed no inclination to heed Freeman's advice, stating very clearly their intention to keep blacks out of white neighborhoods. Crawford C. Crouch, a school principal, argued that living conditions for blacks were not as bad as some had argued, that streets in black neighborhoods equaled those in many white parts of town, and that the city had provided blacks with outstanding educational and recreational facilities. Speaking on behalf of working-class and middle-class whites, he insisted that further encroachment would cause "calamity in the ranks of the whites who had put their all in little homes." The Reverend S. R. Orrell of the East End Baptist Church claimed that some blacks had left better homes in their own neighborhoods in order to move into white sections of town. Before long, he declared, African Americans would attempt to buy homes on Monument Avenue, a boulevard lined with fine homes and statues of Virginia's Civil War heroes.[46]

Numerous white elites, including *News Leader* publisher John Stewart Bryan, one of the most well-respected individuals in the city, vigorously fought the ordinance. With the exception of Lucy Randolph Mason, these whites couched their arguments in terms that embodied the essence of

Richmond native Lucy Randolph Mason (ca. 1920s) stood out among white elites who opposed the city's residential segregation ordinance in 1929. (Courtesy of the National Consumers' League Collection, Library of Congress)

managed race relations: equal parts white supremacy and white responsibility. Richard W. Carrington, the chairman of the Richmond branch of the Commission on Interracial Cooperation, spoke for most white elites when he confirmed his own belief in white supremacy. Carrington then articulated a deep sense of responsibility, which emanated precisely from this position of superiority and which, in the words of the *Richmond Planet*, "made it incumbent upon the dominant race . . . to justly exercise the powers entrusted to their hands and to treat the colored people fairly." Carrington and like-minded elites thus rejected the ordinance as an unnecessary and unconstitutional burden that only served to antagonize and destabilize relations between blacks and whites.[47]

Lucy Randolph Mason, on the other hand, refused to accept this coupling of white supremacy and white responsibility. Mason was a direct descendant of George Mason, the author of Virginia's Declaration of Rights (a precursor to the federal Bill of Rights), and her lineage placed her in ethereal company in the Old Dominion. But Mason rejected the very concept of white supremacy. As she once wrote to Gordon Blaine Hancock, her colleague on Richmond's interracial committee, "[I]n my thinking, there are no inferior or superior races or nations, but only some who have had more opportunity . . . to get a running start on their brothers. Really superior races would never exploit weaker peoples, for their superiority would rest on moral virtues."[48]

Guided by a deep reservoir of religious faith heavily influenced by the social gospel, Mason led a most unconventional life for a southern woman of her age, or any age, for that matter. Born in 1882, Mason committed herself at the turn of the century to fighting injustice of every sort: racial, class, and gender. In the 1910s and 1920s, she worked for the Richmond YWCA and the League of Women Voters. Mason labored hard on behalf of women's suffrage and supported striking textile workers in a state known for its hostility to unions. In the late 1920s, she assumed a leading role on Richmond's Negro Welfare Survey Committee, which argued for an expansion of educational and economic opportunities for African Americans and spawned the city's Urban League. In 1932, after the deaths of her father and her partner, also a YWCA reformer, a grieving Mason left Virginia to become general secretary of the National Consumers' League and later a leading organizer for the Congress of Industrial Organizations (CIO). In both positions, Mason joined the ranks of New Dealers who favored the use of federal power to improve horrendous working conditions, especially in the South. Lobbying for the CIO in the 1930s and 1940s, Mason confronted industrial and textile bosses known for their ability to intimidate and their willingness to beat, maim, and kill in order to prevent union organization. More than one observer noted that only a dignified, gray-haired, southern woman of impeccable breeding such as "Miss Lucy" could have escaped unharmed. Mason was, in the words of a Richmond friend, "a spirit consecrated, living on a plane far above that in which ordinary folk dwell."[49]

Blacks and whites alike recognized the uniqueness of Lucy Randolph Mason's unconditional commitment to social and racial justice. While genuinely appreciative that many white elites opposed the segregation ordinance and fought to improve the lives of blacks in general, African Americans understood that most whites offered deeply circumscribed support. Mason, by contrast, fought to create a more just society with no strings attached. When she left Richmond in 1932, black citizens of the city held a testimonial and praised her in terms reserved for no other whites. Speaking on behalf of the city's black social workers, Lucretia Jordan applauded Mason's "sense of fairness and justice," as well as her "dauntless courage" and willingness to absorb "harsh criticism, often from her friends." Indeed, a number of Mason's social peers found her "too militant," but her unmatched pedigree protected her from outright ostracism, and even many of those unable "to follow her in her well nigh prophetic

The Erosion of Paternalism

sight" begrudgingly offered their "respect and admiration." Writing on the eve of her departure from Richmond, Douglas Southall Freeman poignantly articulated the divide that separated Lucy Randolph Mason from those whites, himself included, most committed to managed race relations. "I admire her for her many splendid qualities," he wrote. "But most of all for the fact that she is not afraid of tomorrow."[50]

Not surprisingly, African Americans in Richmond noted Mason's appearance before the city council's Ordinance Committee with particular interest. Eschewing the propensity of her peers to declare their white supremacist credentials, Mason argued with clear conviction that morality and justice required the defeat of the residential segregation ordinance. Drawing upon her work with the Negro Welfare Survey Committee, Mason cited statistical evidence to challenge those who claimed that black living conditions were not so bad. The *Richmond Planet* noted that Mason's testimony "made a profound impression" on the city's black citizenry. G. H. Harris, a Richmond native who had taken up residence in Massachusetts, encouraged Mason to "pay no attention to the disapproval of your stand by some" and assured her that "God has seen your act, and knows your heart." In his weekly newspaper column, Gordon Blaine Hancock cited Mason as one of the South's true redeemers and praised her courage in facing the criticism of her peers; privately, he told Mason that he understood the "difficulty of [her] position" and assured her that he and other African Americans appreciated that her "constructive efforts" on their behalf far exceeded what other white Virginians offered.[51]

In a final plea before the Ordinance Committee, representatives of the Richmond Chamber of Commerce, the Real Estate Exchange, the Richmond Bar Association, the Ministerial Union, the Interracial Committee, and the Central Trades and Labor Council joined Douglas Southall Freeman and the *Richmond News Leader* in urging the council to delay voting on the statute; opponents called instead for a thorough study of the issues surrounding black living conditions. Alderman Woody, however, warned the committee that in just the past few weeks, since debate on the statute had begun, blacks had encroached further in sections of Church Hill and the situation for whites had turned desperate. In addition, Earnest Sevier Cox, a cofounder of the Anglo-Saxon Clubs, announced his support for the measure and expressed his belief that it would prove satisfactory to whites and blacks alike. He suggested that segregation in housing would work itself out as well as had segregation on streetcars, in schools, on railways, in theaters, and in churches. Expediency won out, and the proposal passed the committee by a unanimous vote.[52]

Following the committee's approval of the ordinance, Douglas Southall

Freeman attempted to distinguish between the proposed residential seg-regation ordinance and the state's other segregation statutes, opposing the one as not consistent with the others. In reference to the residential seg-regation statute, the editor of the *News Leader* wrote:

> Gentlemen who advocated its adoption failed to draw the distinction be-tween separation and segregation. Everybody desires separation of the races for the good of both, but separation is not promoted by a law that will arouse resentments before it can be invalidated by the courts. Segre-gation of the sort now proposed cannot be justified by citing segregation in streetcars, on trains, and in theaters. The existing segregation laws for transportation and public places rest on the theory that the accommoda-tion afforded the Negroes is as good as that allotted white people. Only on this ground have the "Jim Crow" laws been sustained. Will anyone con-tend for a moment that, in the larger sense of the word, this applies to residential segregation? Do the Negro districts get the same service from the city that the white districts receive?[53]

In the months ahead, Freeman would return to this distinction between separation and segregation in an attempt to rationalize and justify the racial status quo. His formulation, however, placed him on increasingly untenable ground and underscored the eroding authority of paternal-ism. Freeman seemed to ignore the inequities that many of the common-wealth's other segregation statutes had produced throughout society. Blacks and whites did ride the same streetcars and buses in most cities, but African Americans were prohibited from first-class railroad accommoda-tions and, perhaps most important, schools suffered from the same dis-parity in resources that plagued neighborhoods and homes. Surely Free-man could not have believed that existing segregation laws provided equal, albeit separate, facilities.

On the eve of the ordinance's passage, Freeman wrote an editorial in which he blamed the imminent approval of such a bad piece of legisla-tion on the failure of the city's elites to run for elective office and to vote. Citing the miserably low numbers needed to win election to the city coun-cil, Freeman essentially argued that the segregation statute would never have been considered had the right people been in office. The best white people in Richmond never failed to answer the call of business and in-dustry, complained Freeman, but they ignored the same call to serve in public office. In the context of Freeman's other editorials on the subject, this elitist argument made sense. Like many of his peers, the editor of the *News Leader* preferred a quiet separation of the races, not enforced legal segregation. Although correct to denounce the ordinance as unconstitutional and inflammatory, Freeman failed to acknowledge that its passage reflected a divergence of opinion among whites as to the most effective means of managing white supremacy. Residential segregation spoke to the anxieties of many working-class and poorer whites in a way that elites had never needed to understand; white elites did not feel threatened by black encroachment because African Americans did not move into exclusive white neighborhoods and were unlikely to compete with elites on the job market.[54]

After Richmond's segregation ordinance overwhelmingly passed both the city council and the board of aldermen, it arrived on the desk of Mayor Fulmer Bright for his signature. Silent up until this point, the NAACP cabled the mayor, declared the statute unconstitutional, cited Supreme Court precedent, and asked him to veto it. Bright responded that he would approve the law and, furthermore, that it had been "drawn in the best interest of both races." The mayor's response led James Weldon Johnson, the executive secretary of the NAACP, to reply that a "slight exercise of intelligence on the part of Richmond municipal government would have revealed to it that courts have already held such ordinances unconstitutional." The insult could not have been lost on Bright, especially after one newspaper concluded in its headline, "Richmond, Va. Mayor Is Dumb Says NAACP." The mayor replied to Johnson that "the spirit shown by your telegram only confirms me in my conviction that the principle involved in the segregation ordinance is highly desirable for the peace and social good order of our people."[55]

The mayor's signature left opponents with no alternative but to challenge its constitutionality in court, a course supported by both of the city's white newspapers. African Americans formed a Citizens' Defense Committee and appointed attorneys Joseph Pollard and Alfred Cohen, who also argued *West v. Bliley*, to lead their efforts. Early news reports emphasized that every black religious, civic, and social organization in the city, as well as a number of white individuals, had pledged financial support. The Citizens' Defense Committee divided the city into fifteen districts, assigning a leader and fund-raising goal to each. African American children did their part, selling buttons inscribed "Why Segregate Us?" Within a month, organizers succeeded in raising nearly $1,500 for the court challenge, roughly six times the amount raised to fight the white primary case.[56]

While both the *Richmond News Leader* and the *Richmond Times-Dispatch* opposed the ordinance, the *News Leader* was by far the more vocal in mobilizing white opinion to support a court challenge. From the outset, however, Douglas Southall Freeman caged his advocacy in very specific terms, never questioning the desirability of racial separation, but only the means. For Freeman, the ordinance engendered bitterness, threatened to erode the commitment of leading blacks and whites to civility and goodwill, and therefore "represented the wrong way of securing racial separation." Inasmuch as he recognized the necessity of legal action, Freeman worried that a court challenge, if not carefully monitored, might backfire and embolden African Americans in a manner that threatened the future of managed race relations. Consequently, Freeman stressed that capable local attorneys, known to the city's white elites, would direct the proceedings. The editor of the *News Leader* implied that NAACP lawyers were to stay out of Richmond. "It is bad enough to have a dispute of this kind," Freeman wrote. "It would be still worse to have it aggravated by the coming of outside lawyers who make a business of capitalizing race prejudices." The newspaper appeared especially pleased several days later to report that Richmond attorney Joseph Pollard had informed the national office of the NAACP that he and his staff were capable of handling the case on their own.[57]

White elites in the press and in business circles would have been delighted had they known of the frustration experienced by the national office of the NAACP in communicating with the Richmond branch. Walter White, the assistant secretary of the organization, told Richmond businesswoman and NAACP member Maggie Walker, "We are somewhat disturbed at our inability even to hear from our Richmond branch." He recounted repeated instances over the past few months when the national office had sought information regarding the segregation statute, only to hear nothing in response. Sensing resistance from African Americans in Richmond, White acknowledged that "we do not want to interfere in cases where we are not wanted but, on the other hand, we would be recreant to our duty if we would not continue our twelve-year fight against residential segregation."[58]

Several days later, White traveled to Richmond in an effort to revive the Richmond branch of the NAACP and to discover firsthand what was being done to fight the ordinance. White concluded immediately that as a result of the ineffective leadership of president C. V. Kelly, the Richmond branch was "absolutely dead." Kelly, in White's estimation, had failed to act when the ordinance was first proposed, or at any point along the way. Fortunately, Dr. Leon A. Reid had stepped into the breach and organized the Citizens' Defense Committee.[59]

During his visit, White found what he called a "rather peculiar situation" concerning support for the NAACP in Richmond. He emphasized the stark division among whites regarding the ordinance, noting the strong opposition of the press, the interracial commission, and "most of the upper class of whites." The NAACP official concluded that "the measure was jammed through the City Council at the insistence of a lower class of whites, most of them assumed to be of Klan membership or sympathy." Upper-class whites, in White's words, "seemed to feel very bitter because the Council ignored their request." Consequently, "a quiet proposal has been made to the colored people to the effect that if Richmond Negroes fight the ordinance these whites would clandestinely bring quiet pressure to bear and make up whatever deficit there was between the cost of the case and the amount raised by the Negroes themselves. One condition, however, was that the NAACP must be kept out of the case."[60]

While in Richmond, White discovered a great deal of disagreement among the city's African Americans concerning a response to this proposal. Some black citizens, according to the assistant secretary, "felt that they should go along with 'their good white people'; another faction felt that white people or no white people, the thing to do was to beat the ordinance and that could be most effectively done through the NAACP." White emphasized to the Citizens' Defense Committee that the national office "had no desire to control the case or take complete charge of it" but only wanted to ensure that the victories won in previous residential segregation cases would not be overturned. Furthermore, White noted that the national office "would enter into no clandestine arrangement" and could not take responsibility for the records or conduct of the case unless allowed to view all papers from the beginning. After a long discussion, the Citizens' Defense Committee voted to embrace White's position and accept the aid of the national office; several days later, the NAACP announced publicly that it would assist the attorneys fighting to overturn the Richmond ordinance.[61]

The involvement of the NAACP placed Douglas Southall Freeman in a difficult bind. He and other white elites had sought to keep NAACP lawyers at a distance, a concern that the NAACP attempted to side-step by announcing that it would participate only "in an advisory capacity." Freeman, however, recognized that the willingness of African Americans in Richmond to turn to the NAACP in any capacity, rather than rely solely on "their good white people," threatened the very fabric of managed race relations. Yet he also believed that the residential segregation ordinance had violated the paternalistic bargain. Consequently, Freeman concluded that he and other white elites had no alternative but to support the court

Douglas Southall Freeman, editor of the *Richmond News Leader* from 1915 until his retirement in 1949, in his home study. (Used with permission of the Virginia Historical Society)

challenge. In asking William Reed to make a financial contribution to the Citizens' Defense Committee, the editor of the *News Leader* sought to slow the growing independence of the city's black citizens and to fortify their fading commitment to "separation by consent."[62]

Although Reed ultimately sent Freeman a contribution, he did so reluctantly. While Freeman combined a commitment to white supremacy with a desire to apply basic standards of decency and justice to the lives of African Americans, Reed gave little thought to the living conditions of blacks in Richmond or to the role of public policy in perpetuating those conditions. Born in the midst of the Civil War, two decades before Freeman, the tobacco magnate "regretted very much that the segregation ordinance was introduced, as it just opened up an old sore, which was getting along . . . in fairly good shape." But unlike Freeman, Reed believed "that after the ordinance was passed by the Council, notwithstanding the fight that was made against it by some of our best citizens, it was possibly best to drop the whole matter, and I felt that bringing it up into court might further increase this bad feeling, even if the Negroes won, rather than let the ordi-

The Erosion of Paternalism

nance alone." No matter how unfair the statute, Reed expected African Americans to adjust to its implementation.[63]

While Freeman and Reed discussed the merits of a court challenge, the Citizens' Defense Committee precipitated a test case to do just that. On March 26, 1929, J. B. Deans, an insurance salesman and member of the committee's executive board, purchased a home and lot in a section of town reserved under the city ordinance for white persons. Several days later, Deans filed suit in federal district court, seeking an injunction against the city's enforcement of the statute. The petitioner argued that the city measure violated his fundamental property rights, and that although the statute "was enacted under the guise of a racial integrity ordinance," it constituted "nothing more or less than an ordinance segregating the white and colored races in their residences." Richmond city attorney James Cannon filed a counter motion, arguing that the ordinance was perfectly legitimate because it applied standards to blacks and whites in equal terms.[64]

On May 18, just weeks before his decision in *West v. Bliley*, Judge Lawrence Groner ruled that the Richmond ordinance did violate the Constitution as established by the U.S. Supreme Court. Unwilling to accept the jurist's opinion, the city appealed Groner's decision to the Fourth Circuit Court of Appeals. On January 14, 1930, Judges John J. Parker, Elliott Northcott, and Henry C. McDowell affirmed Groner's decision. The appeals court, like Groner, found wanting the city's argument that the Richmond statute differed from previously overturned ordinances in Louisville and New Orleans because it separated persons based on their inability to intermarry. "As the legal prohibition of intermarriage is itself based on race," ruled the panel, "the question here, in final analysis, is identical with that which the Supreme Court has twice decided in the cases cited." Instead, the court of appeals accepted the argument of Alfred Cohen, an attorney for Deans, who suggested, "'If it were once conceded that the legislature may lawfully, in the exercise of its police power, exclude a Negro from residence in a city square, if already occupied by the white race, than it would logically follow that it could deny him residence in every county of the state under like conditions, as the latter is only a matter of degree in the expanse of territory.'" In fact, a candidate for sheriff in Buchanan County in the mid-1930s ran on just such a platform.[65]

Municipal officials in Richmond lost their final battle in May 1930, when the U.S. Supreme Court upheld the ruling of the lower courts. The decision, according to the *Norfolk Journal and Guide*, affirmed "the right of the Negro race to purchase and live in homes of his choice in any part of

American cities just like any other United States citizen." Reports of the decision, in both white and black papers, noted that the case had figured in the recent confirmation hearings of John Parker. Between the court of appeals decision in January and the Supreme Court ruling in May, the U.S. Senate had rejected Parker's nomination for a seat on the nation's highest court. His opponents, spearheaded by the NAACP, had pointed to a statement Parker made during the 1920 gubernatorial campaign in North Carolina as evidence of his racial prejudice. Parker's supporters emphasized his decision in the *Deans* case to argue that he harbored no such animus.[66]

Alfred Cohen was particularly angered by Parker's rejection. In a scathing letter to *The Nation*, the Richmond attorney labeled as "indefensible" charges that the publication had leveled at the jurist. "You say that Judge Parker should not sit on the Supreme Court," wrote Cohen, "because cases affecting the rights of colored people will come before that court." But, he pointed out, Parker had ruled that Richmond's segregation ordinance had violated the rights of African Americans under the Fourteenth Amendment. As counsel for Deans, Cohen decried the magazine's "unfair attack upon an upright, courageous judge."[67]

Soon after the final defeat of Richmond's residential segregation ordinance, Douglas Southall Freeman asserted yet again his belief in "separation by consent." Freeman understood from the beginning that Richmond's ordinance would never be upheld by the courts. He objected to a measure that unnecessarily increased animosity between the races and threatened the stability essential to managed race relations. As he told his readers, "Much of the work done in the last twenty years for better understanding was undone in a few weeks—and all to no other purpose than to have the supreme court affirm the opinion of the federal circuit judges and thereby tell the city what it should have known already."[68]

Freeman was not, however, any less committed to the separation of the races than those who pushed the ordinance through the city council. He believed that "the separation of the residential districts of the two races is desirable from the standpoint of both." Freeman differed from proponents in the debate, therefore, not in the desirability of rigid separation, but in the means to separation. He argued consistently in his newspaper that lasting, meaningful separation of the races required a commitment from the city to provide African Americans with services similar to those in white sections of town. Furthermore, he acknowledged that blacks "who have the means and ambition to rise above the crowded squalor of dilapidated shacks" must have an opportunity to purchase homes in new neighborhoods. To this end, Freeman supported the efforts of the city's interracial commission to look for an "amicable solution" to the housing crisis that faced the city.[69]

Freeman's editorial and ideological construction depended upon a presumption that blacks and whites could remain separate and yet be treated equally. He argued this point repeatedly and at one point even insisted that legalized segregation on streetcars, trains, and in theaters depended upon this formulation. The proponents of Richmond's residential segregation ordinance, on the other hand, openly rejected calls for a more equal allocation of public funds. They believed passionately that public resources should benefit only those in power and advocated policies to achieve that vision. Freeman and like-minded white elites, while certainly advocating a more just treatment of African Americans, must have understood the inherent weakness of their own position. Freeman's insistence on defining a critical difference between separation and segregation rang hollow; gross inequalities pervaded nearly every aspect of life in Virginia's Jim Crow society and were nowhere so apparent as in the schools, segregated fully to the extent allowed by law, not by consent.

Decisions made in fighting Richmond's residential segregation ordinance signaled a critical break in the strategy of African Americans in Virginia. When members of the Richmond Citizens' Defense Committee voted to enlist the support of the NAACP, despite the stated preference of sympathetic white elites, they began a new era in their search for justice and citizenship. Tired of waiting for "their good white people" to enact meaningful change, blacks in Richmond and throughout Virginia defined their own course of action. As Joseph Pollard wrote soon after the Supreme Court ruled in the *Deans* case, "I am of the decided opinion that the time is now ripe to take advantage of the healthy sentiment prevailing in this City and State, to institute or reinstitute various branches of the National Association for the Advancement of Colored People, to whom, in the final analysis, colored people of the south must look to the defense and protection of their civil and political rights."[70]

This determination among African Americans to assert greater independence, combined with the growing frustrations of working-class and middle-class whites, undermined the paternalistic authority of white elites throughout Virginia, but especially in the state's urban areas. Many elites had long recognized a need to improve the living conditions of the Old Dominion's black citizens; a few even considered it an obligation. But paternalistic impulses failed to prevent the passage of the Racial Integrity Act and the Public Assemblages Act, which required segregated events even on the grounds of an already segregated college. Furthermore, as

African Americans had long recognized, elite whites could not participate in the denigration of blacks in order to pursue victory at the polls and then expect to place limits on racially exclusionist municipal policies. Consequently, efforts by white elites to promote "separation by consent" became more untenable each time a municipal or state administration ignored the needs and denied the rights of black citizens. Emboldened by their dual federal court victories in *West v. Bliley* and *Deans v. Richmond*, African Americans in Virginia pressed forward in the 1930s, determined to claim for themselves their rights as citizens. Shocked to discover that blacks no longer accepted the terms of paternalism, Virginia's white elites and self-described persons of goodwill found themselves increasingly unable to manage white supremacy.

8

Traveling in Opposite Directions

> It may be that white Virginians and the NAACP mean
> different things by "amicable race relations." . . . The test of
> "amicable race relations" is not whether whites and Negroes
> can remain friends while the Negro is at the little end of the
> horn, but whether they can remain friends when Negroes
> insist on sharing with whites the rights and advantages to
> which they are lawfully entitled and which the whites have
> illegally appropriated to themselves all these years.
> —CHARLES H. HOUSTON, 1935

The resolution of the *Deans* and *West* cases emboldened African Americans politically just as the onset of the Great Depression created greater economic uncertainty and suffering. Although the state's balanced economy eased the suffering of Virginians relative to other southerners, African Americans were hit the hardest and earliest in the Old Dominion, exacerbating already significant inequities that pervaded Virginia's management of white supremacy. In this crucible of increased political independence and economic marginalization, African Americans divided over tactics as a younger, sometimes radical, generation bristled at the caution of older, more conservative, black leaders. Nevertheless, black Virginians of all classes and ideological persuasions remained bound by a common determination to achieve equality of opportunity and the full recognition of their rights as citizens. To this end, African Americans challenged more forcefully the daily vestiges of Jim Crow, demanding better housing and living conditions, their fair share of federal relief payments and jobs, continued access to the ballot box, and more equitable educational opportunities.[1]

White extremists, including Walter Plecker and John Powell, rejected all such appeals. White supporters of state and local interracial commissions, by contrast, remained cognizant of the need to address black grievances yet became increasingly cautious, particularly as some black leaders questioned the civility and paeans to goodwill that had dominated interracial discourse in the 1920s. Before long, progressive white elites boxed themselves into an ideological corner, unable to cope with black assertions of independence that exposed the limitations and contradictions inherent in their paternalism. Confusing any call for equality with a desire for amalgamation, especially with regard to education, these whites soon echoed the same dire warnings favored by the most rabid advocates of white supremacy. As a result, conservative black leaders such as P. B. Young and Gordon Blaine Hancock found old ties to their white counterparts dangerously weakened.

By 1930, John Powell and Walter Plecker had turned their attention to the emerging importance of education as a litmus test in their crusade to maintain racial integrity. The specific aim of the 1924 Racial Integrity Act had been to prevent intermarriage between whites and blacks. Consequently, Plecker had devoted his efforts to ensuring that local registrars and clerks denied marriage licenses to such couples. The statistician, however, realized over time that all Virginians, especially those called to serve as jurors, did not accept his rigid interpretation of the law. In August 1926 a Rockingham County grand jury considered what would have been the first conviction for violating the law. Apparently the jury failed to convict, for in May 1928 the state's press announced that an Amherst County court had handed down the state's first conviction under the law when it found a white woman, Mary Hall Wood, guilty and sentenced her to two years in prison for marrying Mott Hamilton Wood, a mulatto. Several weeks later, her husband received the same sentence.[2]

The couple's arrest and conviction, apparently incited by a complaint from the bride's father, prompted the *Norfolk Journal and Guide* to remark that their "case would be a crowning comedy were it not so profoundly pathetic." According to the paper, Mott Wood was but one-sixteenth black, had been raised his entire life as white among white friends, and had "all the instincts and feelings of a white man." It seemed only natural to that newspaper that he choose to marry a white woman. But perhaps instead of marrying, suggested Tidewater's black paper, the couple should have raised a family outside of wedlock; in that case they would not have gone to the penitentiary. Soon after the couple's conviction, Governor Harry Byrd denied Mary Hall Wood's request for a pardon. Acknowledging that trial officials and a number of other prominent persons had supported her application, the governor determined that the applicant knew at the time of her marriage that her husband was legally black. "The necessity of racial integrity is so important," reasoned the governor, "that after mature consideration I find myself unable to act favorably on this application."[3]

In January 1929, five months after Byrd's denial of Mary Wood's appeal, the newspapers reported another violation of Virginia's ban on intermarriage. In this instance, James Reedy, white, and Lizzie Copp, "of alleged Negro extraction," were married in Hagerstown, Maryland, and then returned to their home in Shenandoah County. Since the Virginia statute specifically prohibited persons from marrying outside the state in an effort to avoid the law, authorities arrested and jailed the couple. A similar case occurred later that year in Phoebus, a small town near Hampton. Emil Umlauf, the town's former police chief, married Lizzie Whitehead, a black woman, in Brooklyn, New York. When they arrived back in Virginia, they too were arrested. Despite strong currents of ill will aimed at the pair by their neighbors, a jury found that they lacked evidence to prove that the Umlaufs had left the state for the purpose of marrying. In releasing the couple, an exasperated Judge Vernon Spratley, an ardent supporter of the Anglo-Saxon Clubs, ordered them to leave the jurisdiction that evening, explaining that their decision to marry rendered them "unfit for association with decent people." Turning to the former police chief, who remained unrepentant, Spratley added that "it was a mistake to endow you with the greater advantage and outlook that it gives to a white man."[4]

Walter Plecker recognized that the Umlauf jury had come to represent the norm, not the exception. Despite the support of adherents like Judge Spratley, Plecker complained that authorities around the state refused to prosecute violators of the law. He noted in a report that as many as fifty interracial couples a year wed outside the state and returned undisturbed, bolstered by the knowledge that no jury would choose to convict. Recognizing that sympathetic juries considered sentences of two to five years in the penitentiary too harsh, Plecker urged the General Assembly to reduce the penalty for violations of the Racial Integrity Act. The legislature rebuffed Plecker's suggestion to redefine the crime as a misdemeanor subject to no more than a year in jail, but it did lower the minimum sentence for a felony conviction to one year, leaving the maximum of five years in place.[5]

Although deeply annoyed with the unwillingness of juries to convict people for interracial marriage, Plecker had already shifted the focus of his efforts to the public schools and, more specifically, to defining certain children as black in order to keep them out of white schools. Since the mid-1920s, Plecker had informed school superintendents whenever he suspected that children with any black blood had enrolled in schools for whites. Despite the objections of parents, most of these children were expelled and left with no choice but to attend far inferior black schools. Furthermore, aggrieved parents could not appeal Plecker's decisions.[6]

As had been the case with intermarriage, individuals claiming to be Indian rather than black provided Plecker his greatest obstacle in ensuring racial purity within Virginia's schools. The statistician's relentless campaign against Virginia's Indians, however, eventually drew criticism from certain quarters. During its 1928 session, the Virginia senate killed yet another racial integrity bill because of perceptions that it involved an unfair attack on the state's Indians. Eighteen months later, Plecker sent a formal letter of complaint to A. Willis Robertson, chairman of the State Commission on Game and Inland Fisheries, in which he charged that M. D. Hart, the commission's executive secretary, had attacked and hindered efforts to reclassify many Indians as black. After a formal hearing, Robertson, later a U.S. senator, ruled that Hart had acted as a private citizen and not in an official capacity.[7]

Writing on the editorial page of the *Richmond News Leader*, Douglas Southall Freeman not only termed Robertson's ruling as "eminently correct" but seized the opportunity to launch a personal attack on Plecker. The editor of the *News Leader* had opposed the Public Assemblages Act and a revised racial integrity bill put forward in 1926, but he had refrained from publicly criticizing the principal authors of the measures, satisfying himself with a private denunciation of Plecker as a "childless, smileless Presbyterian elder." By 1929, however, Freeman understood that Plecker's crusade threatened to damage further the state's already strained race relations. Commenting as the *Deans* and *West* cases wound their way through the court system, Freeman warned that Plecker had exceeded his authority and "in his zeal for racial integrity, has gone farther, has become a propagandist, has sought to play upon emotions and prejudices, and to arouse ill-feeling to the end that new and more drastic laws be enacted." Leaving no doubt as to his own position, Freeman concluded that "the continued harassment of an inoffensive, isolated people, whose only desire is to be left alone, is a blot on the name of the state, and, indeed, savors of cruelty. It has gone too far."[8]

Plecker responded to the attack in a scathing, three-page letter. The statistician defended his practices, asserted that his findings could not be repudiated, and expressed concern that the *News Leader* consistently failed to report the truth. He recited for Freeman the genealogy of certain

Charles City and New Kent County Indians, insisted that they descended from black ancestors, and declared that the *News Leader*'s position boosted their efforts to intermarry with whites. On a matter of even greater practical concern, Plecker condemned the efforts of these families to have their children admitted into white schools. "Our law has defects which must be corrected," he added, "even if it does 'harass' these pretenders. Especially must our white schools be protected from becoming mixed." Plecker expressed further the hope that Freeman "may yet see the light, and be guided by it."[9]

The necessity of preserving racial integrity in order to maintain segregated schools assumed a level of critical importance as the General Assembly prepared to meet in January 1930. Revelations that a number of mixed-race children attended white schools in Essex County, and that local officials remained powerless to prevent it, provided advocates of a stricter law the means of persuasion that they had lacked in 1926 and 1928, when they were seen as unnecessarily harassing the state's Indians. The admitted fact of mixed schools, coming as African Americans in Virginia won important legal battles in *West v. Bliley* and *Deans v. Richmond*, redefined the terms of managed race relations in the Old Dominion. Not only did a much stricter racial integrity law pass the legislature that year without serious opposition, but, as became evident throughout the 1930s, white Virginians proved remarkably like-minded when debating the role of race in the public schools.[10]

The situation in Essex County first developed in 1928 as local school officials took steps to remove mixed-race children from the white schools. Officials in Essex succeeded in dismissing the children of one family but ran into trouble when a second family resisted, hired a lawyer, and filed suit. In the Circuit Court of Essex County, school officials acknowledged that the children in question had less than one-sixteenth black blood. Consequently, Judge Joseph W. Chinn ruled that the children could not be kept out of white schools. Chinn based his ruling on what racial integrity advocates had long understood as a loophole in the original legislation. The 1924 Racial Integrity Act defined a white person as an individual with "no trace whatsoever of any blood other than Caucasian," making an exception only for certain Indians. The act specifically prohibited the intermarriage of a white person with a nonwhite person but made no mention of the schools. The act also failed to define a black person. John Powell later testified that he assumed that all persons not deemed white would be classified black. But since the 1924 act did not specifically amend the 1910 act that termed blacks as persons with one-sixteenth or more black blood, an individual with less than one-sixteenth black blood could not

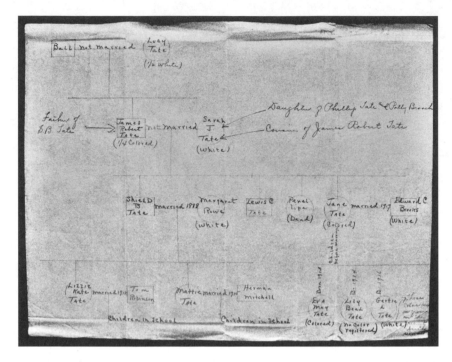

In 1928 Judge Joseph Chinn of the Essex County Circuit Court determined that the children of Lizzie Tate and Tom Robinson (see lower left) possessed less than one-sixteenth black blood and therefore had to be admitted into the county's white school. Chinn's ruling led the General Assembly to adopt a "one-drop" rule in 1930. (Courtesy of the Essex County Circuit Court)

be considered black and therefore could not be prevented from attending white schools.[11]

A reporter for the *Richmond Times-Dispatch* concluded that under Chinn's ruling "any child having less than one-sixteenth Negro blood, not only can attend a white school, but must attend it, and is by law prevented from attending a colored school." Furthermore, noted the journalist, the judge's opinion opened the door for persons with less than one-sixteenth black blood to attend any of Virginia's colleges or universities. In the wake of Chinn's decision, local officials understood that their only avenue of relief lay with the state legislature; consequently, the proposed measure defined as black "any person in whom there is ascertainable any Negro Blood," the so-called one-drop rule.[12]

As the General Assembly began deliberations on the revised statute, the same correspondent for the *Richmond Times-Dispatch* visited the Essex

Traveling in Opposite Directions

County schools that had sparked the controversy. One of the schools, a combined grade school and high school, enrolled 180 children, sixteen of whom had some black ancestry. The principal of the school acknowledged that he knew personally all of the children considered mixed and that all of the white students knew who they were. Such knowledge apparently made no difference to the children; blacks and whites, in the words of the reporter, "played together on terms of equality." The situation in a second school was more disturbing to officials. The last remaining one-room school in the county enrolled only twenty-four students, twelve boys and twelve girls. The superintendent of the county schools revealed that six of the boys and five of the girls definitely had black ancestors, and three other girls possibly did.[13]

The *Times-Dispatch*'s correspondent observed that of the fourteen boys and girls who either had or might have had black blood, "only one pupil would have impressed the casual observer as revealing traces" of black features, while the "remaining thirteen could have passed for white anywhere." The observer noted that during recess the "children trooped out and played together. There was apparent no consciousness of any racial barrier." School superintendent W. G. Rennolds insisted that both adults and children in the community understood which children were of mixed descent. The Richmond reporter echoed the belief shared by the superintendent and the commonwealth's attorney, James M. Lewis, that this particular aspect of the situation was most "tragic" and "shocking." The journalist noted that both men appeared especially concerned that so "many residents of the community have become accustomed to the fact that their children go to school with mix breeds, and show no resentment, active or passive."[14]

The seeming acceptance of the white parents whose children attended school with children of mixed racial ancestry only heightened in Rennolds and Lewis a determination to act on behalf of their constituents. The *Times-Dispatch* reporter emphasized that both men spoke of the racially mixed children in terms of great "sympathy" and evidenced no "racial prejudice," adding that Rennolds had served on the local interracial commission. Both men noted that the black schools did not want to admit these children, and that the county might have to open a new school for them. Nevertheless, they felt a need to make certain that only white children attended white schools. Rennolds acknowledged the impossibility of maintaining an absolute color line but expressed a determination to try. The Richmond journalist added that both men believed that the Racial Integrity Act's ban on intermarriage "cannot be hoped for if children of both races are permitted to go to school together and regard each other as equals over a period of eight or ten years." Equality, they insisted, ultimately led to intermarriage.[15]

In testimony before the General Assembly, proponents of a revised statute repeatedly cited the situation in Essex County. W. Leigh Carneal, a Richmond architect, echoed the thoughts of W. G. Rennolds, acknowledging that ultimate amalgamation appeared likely, but he considered the bill crucial to slowing the process. Richard Heath Dabney, a professor of history at the University of Virginia and the father of Virginius Dabney, referred to Egypt, Portugal, India, and Cuba as countries where racial mixing had destroyed civilizations. More specifically, he warned that a failure to pass the proposed statute would make it possible for persons with some black blood to gain admittance to the university, thereby threatening the bastion of white elite privilege.[16]

Unanimity among whites, however, was not to be found. Led by clergy who felt the measure again unfairly targeted Indians, a parade of opponents appeared before the legislature. The Dover Baptist Association, an organization that represented sixty-seven churches in Richmond and its outlying counties, including a number of Indian congregations, objected to the "recurring attempts to misrepresent and humiliate" the Pamunkey, Mattaponi, and Chickahominy Indians. Acting at the request of an aide to Walter Plecker, W. G. Rennolds wrote to one member of the organization and declared that "unless we can get some legislation, we might as well turn our schools over to both races and save the expense of a dual system of schools." Rennolds's complaint infuriated Hill Fleet, an officer in a Richmond publishing firm, who iterated that he was only concerned with protecting the Pamunkey, Mattaponi, and Chickahominy who had been "called Indians for the past fifty years." Fleet agreed that steps should be taken to stop those persons who tried to evade the law with unwarranted claims of Indian ancestry, but he denied the right of Rennolds and his cohorts to "throw those people out of education or any advantages that they might be able to enjoy; cut them loose from any kind of society and damn them as negro on account of the sins of their forefathers, just because one drop of negro blood flows in their veins." As if to punctuate his rejection of rigid racial integrity doctrine, Fleet added that "the milk of human kindness certainly ought to flow in their direction along with the cold blooded law."[17]

Nevertheless, the reality of mixed schools in Essex County overwhelmed such objections and the house of delegates passed the revised measure with little dissent. The Virginia senate amended the bill to allow those persons with at least one-fourth Indian blood and less than one-sixteenth black blood to remain classified as Indians, but only if they lived on a recognized reservation. In particular, this amendment protected the Pamunkey and Mattaponi, who had lived on reservations since the eighteenth century, but it did not extend to the Chickahominies of Charles City and New Kent Counties, who were said to have claimed Indian ancestry only after the passage of the first Jim Crow laws at the turn of the twentieth century. Virginia's 1930 Racial Integrity Act allowed for the bizarre possibility that two full-blooded siblings, one living on a reservation, one living outside such boundaries, would be classified as members of different races. The senate passed the amended version without a dissenting vote and the house soon concurred.[18]

The *Richmond Times-Dispatch* hailed the measure's passage as "A Long Fight Won" and lauded its "great objective" to "maintain the color line in the public schools." Richmond's morning paper commended the legislature for rejecting a suggestion that the issue be submitted to a commission for more thorough study. Before such an investigative body reported to the General Assembly, surmised the *Times-Dispatch*, "there would have been mixed public schools all over the State." In conclusion, the paper praised the efforts of John Powell and Earnest Cox, asserting that "those Virginians who feel that the maintenance of pure white public schools is a worthy thing will recognize their debt to the men who did this job for them." The emphasis of the *Times-Dispatch* underscored the degree to which the debate over racial integrity had shifted toward the schools, where it would remain for the next three decades.[19]

The *Richmond News Leader* and *Norfolk Virginian-Pilot* provided less generous assessments of the bill's adoption. The Norfolk daily concluded that the bill "involves for a limited group of our population a genuinely tragic predicament." The *News Leader* predicted "endless possibilities of controversy" between the Bureau of Vital Statistics and various Indians. "Even with these faults," concluded the paper in a tone that reflected the paternalistic ethos of editor Douglas Southall Freeman, "liberal Virginians are apt to accept the bill without a further fight, in the hope that it puts an end to the continuous agitation of the race question before the general assembly. Year after year this has gone on, to the distress of inoffensive people and to the impairment of better racial relations." The decision of Freeman and other "liberal" Virginians to accept the legislation rather than risk continued racial agitation reminded African Americans yet again of the emptiness of paternalism.[20]

As usual in racial matters in Virginia, it required the insight of the state's black press to underscore the depth of hypocrisy and delusion inherent in the passage of the new racial integrity measure. "Traced to its logical end it comes up against a pathetic and rather tragic impasse," editorialized the *Norfolk Journal and Guide*, "which will in reality constitute a defeat of its own purpose. For instance, if a person having only a trace of Negro blood is defined by fiat as a Negro in the face of all his nominally Caucasian instincts, associations, heritage, passions and emotions—in short, against his very nature itself, here is created a problem the ramifications of which are pathetic and delicate to contemplate. He is nominally white, biologically mixed, and legally Negro."[21]

The shifting focus of the racial integrity debate among white elites toward an emphasis on the state's public schools paralleled the emergence of education in the 1930s as the arena in which managed race relations became most deeply contested. Throughout the decade, the amity and professions of goodwill that had bound together white elites and leading blacks began to fray in response to a host of issues related to education. State and municipal authorities had ignored their constitutional mandate regarding black education for years, but when state officials formally institutionalized grossly unequal salary scales for black and white teachers, a younger generation of more vocal black educators fought back. Although the all-black Virginia Teachers Association yielded to conservative sentiment and waited until 1937 to endorse the NAACP's campaign for salary equalization, individual members violated the terms of paternalism much earlier when they rejected a long-standing pledge to accept "the salary received" without objection. Just months after the passage of the 1930 Racial Integrity Act, state superintendent of schools Harris Hart announced the establishment of a salary equalization fund intended to eliminate the disparity in pay between rural and urban teachers. The new scale, however, embedded in state policy lower salaries for black teachers: white teachers were to receive a minimum of $60 per month plus as much as $50 more per month based on their qualifications, while their black counterparts would receive a minimum of only $45 per month and not more than an additional $25 based on qualifications. The decision prompted the *Norfolk Journal and Guide* to acknowledge that the social conscience of white Virginians was not yet ready to demand equal pay for black and white teachers; nevertheless, the paper wondered how whites could continue to justify such a "gross disparity" in salaries.[22]

A gathering of six hundred black teachers issued a formal protest against the commonwealth's action. Thomas L. Dabney, the principal of a black school in Buckingham County and a professor at various black colleges throughout his life, led efforts to increase salaries for black teachers. Acting under the umbrella of the Buckingham County Teachers Association,

Traveling in Opposite Directions

Dabney collected the signatures of black teachers in twenty-five counties and five cities in support of a petition aimed at correcting the disparity. "Your grocer, doctor, landlord and the like do not sell their products and wares according to the color of their customers, but according to the general market price of such articles," remarked Dabney in an address to black teachers. "It is manifestly unjust to have to buy according to economics while earning money according to color!" Plummer Jones, the white superintendent of schools in Buckingham County, praised Dabney as a principal but warned a prospective employer in another county that his efforts might offend some whites and lead to friction. Dabney, on the other hand, told the *Richmond News Leader* that he did not intend for his activities to create ill feeling between blacks and whites, but that black teachers needed and deserved higher salaries.[23]

Despite Dabney's best efforts, Governor John Garland Pollard urged a 10 percent across the board pay cut in January 1932 for all teachers' salaries in an effort to avoid depression-related budget shortfalls. Black teachers had hoped that Pollard would reduce their salaries by a smaller percentage since they were already paid much less. The chief executive's refusal prompted one observer to conclude "that 'separate but equal' education is a shibboleth and a mockery."[24]

Although unsuccessful in their initial attempt to secure better salaries, Thomas Dabney and other African American teachers demonstrated a heightened interest in political engagement that reflected broader consequences of the *West* and *Deans* cases. While many whites comforted themselves by stressing that few blacks had actually voted in subsequent primaries, African Americans in cities throughout the commonwealth took their newly confirmed rights quite seriously. The commitment to civic leagues accelerated all over the state. Groups in Richmond, Petersburg, and Danville, often working in conjunction with churches and other organizations, discussed means of qualifying larger numbers of blacks for the franchise. Professor Luther P. Jackson of Virginia State College in Petersburg began releasing studies of black voter participation; Petersburg appeared at the bottom of his list, with only 2 percent of blacks qualified, while Danville topped the list with 14 percent, perhaps a reflection of that city's economic growth since the First World War. Theodore W. Jones of Richmond concluded that blacks were evincing a greater interest in local and state politics and placing less emphasis on national events. "It makes a difference to us in Richmond," he explained, "who is mayor and what his record is toward the Negro. It makes a difference to us as to the type and quality of the men who compose the common council, the board of education, the judges of our courts of law, and the man who is chief of police. These are officials whose acts, utterances and decrees affect for good or ill our daily lives." In Arlington County, Dr. Edward T. Morton, a former Republican denied a seat at the 1921 state convention, decided that blacks not only should vote but should govern as well; he declared himself a candidate for the county board of supervisors, becoming only the second African American in Virginia to run for elected office since 1903.[25]

Having firmly established their right to participate in the Democratic primaries, which at the time were tantamount to election, African Americans still had to contend with the whims and prejudices of individual registrars. In Newport News, blacks faced "no serious obstacles" to registering. One observer noted that R. R. Jones, the registrar, "is informed and helpful and it is reported very helpful to those Negroes who can hardly write in filling out their application to register." Jones's attitude no doubt reflected the influence of the shipyard's leadership, which, although paternalistic, had created a climate long considered more favorable in its attitude toward blacks than that found in most municipalities.[26]

Aspiring black voters in Hampton and Portsmouth, on the other hand, faced less-cooperative election officials. According to court records, Hampton registrar Thomas C. Allen rejected the application of W. E. Davis, a forty-eight-year-old black man, for his failure "to make application in proper form and to answer to the satisfaction of the registrar certain questions affecting his qualifications." Virginia statute required only that eligible persons, having paid all taxes and met all residency requirements, make an application in their own hand, including their "name, age, date and place of birth, residence and occupation at the time and for the one year next preceding, and whether he has previously voted, and, if so, the State, county, and precinct in which he voted last." In addition, all applicants were required to answer "on oath any and all questions *affecting his qualifications as an elector*." Typically, registrars handed whites a piece of paper and told them step-by-step what to write down; blacks, on the other hand, had to memorize all pertinent information in advance.[27]

Davis submitted to the registrar the following application, which included handwritten answers to Allen's questions:

Hampton, Va. Oct. 5, 1929

to the Registrar Courthouse
    Precinct Dear Sir I W. E. Davis hereby apply for Registration to vote in Courthouse Precinct Elizabeth City County. My age is 48 years was born at Jamesville, N. C. the 27 Day of May 1881, I now reside at 34 Union St in the

City of Hampton Va have lived there for the past 26 years my occupation is Skill Labor and have Been for the past 2 years I have never voted

Very Respectfully,
W. E. Davis

Queston. What is ment By Legal *Residenct* in Va
Answer. All persons Who have lived in the Stat—for one year are a Legal *Residenter*
Question. When is the Payment of Poll Tax Not *Requared*
Answer. After a *Pearson* have *obtaine* the age of sixty years
Question. What are the *Requisites* to enable one to Register in Va
Answer he will have to Be 21 years of age and a citizen—of the State for one year in the City Town or county for 6 *month* Precinct in which he *ofers* to vote 30 Days and Pay all State Tax for 3 years Back say for 1926, 27, 28.[28]

Elizabeth County Circuit Court Judge Vernon Spratley upheld Allen's refusal to register Davis, but the justices of the Virginia Supreme Court did not. The state's highest court ruled that although Davis's application revealed a lack of education, he had provided the necessary information. Furthermore, and of greater significance, the tribunal rejected the right of registrars to ask far-reaching questions that did not affect an applicant's qualifications. They granted that Allen's first question might prove relevant and concluded that, if so, Davis provided a correct response, no matter how poor his spelling and grammar. The justices found, however, that Allen's second and third questions "elicit no information" required by law. In essence, the court struck down the use of so-called understanding and education clauses, long a staple in the preservation of white primaries and white supremacy. Referring to Davis, Virginia's Supreme Court found that "neither his knowledge or lack of knowledge of these subjects, nor his proficiency or deficiency in education as disclosed by his answers to these questions, has any bearing on whether he is, or is not, entitled to register and vote."[29]

The decision in the *Davis* case proved every bit as critical to the participation of African Americans in Virginia politics as did the *West* case. Although no more than 6 percent of African Americans over the age of twenty-one voted in 1932, that number represented an increase over previous years and pointed the way toward future gains as African Americans pressed their rights of citizenship at the polling booth. In one locale after another, the decision placed the law firmly on the side of black voters. In Portsmouth, for instance, election judges prevented a Mr. Walker, an attorney, from voting in the 1931 primary because they said he voted Republican in the last election. Walker, however, took his case to a judge and "was given the privilege to return to the polls and cast my ballot." Frank L. Wilson, another black attorney, found his way to the polls barred by election judges Emmett Dean, M. M. Cain, and Lorenzo Cass for no other reason than that he was black. He, too, filed suit, won, and ended up voting before the day was over.[30]

Charles Butts, a black singer in Portsmouth, experienced enough frustration trying to register that he almost gave up, quite probably the intended object of the registrar's methods. "I knew beforehand," explained Butts, "that Mr. Parker, the registrar, was a violent Negro hater. He had made up his mind to keep as many Negroes out as possible." Four times the singer went to register, and each time he received a blank piece of paper. On the first occasion, Parker accepted his form but asked him how many people signed the Declaration of Independence, prompting Butts to remark that "these were civil government questions which one doesn't know unless one is in school constantly." The second time, the registrar announced that he was closed for the day, and on the third try, Parker claimed that Butts had not signed his name in enough places. Finally, recalled Butts, "I knew the machine was run at that time by Dr. Brooks, who was anti-Negro, and so I figured it would be best for me to take a politician along with me the last time I went. I took our ward leader, a man who was 'in the know.' I was registered this time. I almost got out of the notion of voting, though."[31]

Black women in Portsmouth faced the same obstacles. Mrs. Samuel E. Johns, like Butts, remembered that Parker "hated Negroes." Nevertheless, with the encouragement of her husband, she attempted to register. The registrar, however, also refused Johns on the grounds that she had not signed her name in the appropriate place and that she could not tell him how many people had signed the Declaration of Independence. Rather than giving up, though, Johns took her case to court. When her lawyer asked the registrar if he knew how many had signed the Declaration, Parker remained silent. The presiding judge found in her favor and Johns registered. Miss Quintelia Brown, a schoolteacher, wrote "Portsmouth, Virginia" on the blank form as her birthplace, but the registrar refused her on the grounds that she should have added "Norfolk County." She, too, took her case to court and won. Brown, however, encountered a new obstacle when she arrived at the polling place; election judges attempted to put her ballot in the box for her. She refused.[32]

Throughout the 1930s, registrars and election officials continued to hinder African American voters by employing nonviolent tactics that one observer labeled "courteous disfranchisement." By 1940 few such obstacles remained. Instead, whites relied almost exclusively on the poll tax to limit the black electorate, a function that levy served into the 1960s. The poll tax—due three consecutive years and six months in advance of any election or primary—proved especially debilitating to working-class and poor blacks in the midst of the Great Depression, although a number of laborers and domestics in the state's urban areas managed to register. On the whole, the tax remained so effective that leaders of the state Democratic Party ignored the wishes of some county officials and refused to exclude qualified black voters after the nation's highest court upheld a Texas white primary statute on the condition that the state not finance party activities. Aware that the number of registered African American voters in Virginia was growing, but secure in their ability to control the electorate, white Democrats preferred that the state government continue to fund their primaries. When the commonwealth's major white newspapers came out in favor of abolishing the poll tax, Democratic Party officials refused to consider the possibility.[33]

Although important, political gains in the 1930s offered African Americans insufficient protection against the capriciousness of Jim Crow. Despite the protestations of Douglas Southall Freeman and other white elites, white supremacy simply did not allow the coexistence of separate and equal in any aspect of life, from the most trivial to the most important. P. B. Young once described Jim Crowism as "not a set of laws" but rather "a state of mind" that infused the religion, philosophy, and literature of the South with "the phantom called 'social equality.'" As a result, according to the editor of Norfolk's black paper, "Jim Crowism has been enforced with the purpose of crushing the spirit, the pride, and the aspirations of Negroes. It has not accomplished these ends, for Negroes keep their heads erect despite the abuses and iniquities of Jim Crowism. But Jim Crowism has kept the spirit, the pride, and the aspirations of Negroes bruised and bleeding."[34]

Young did not have to look far for evidence to support his contention. The People's Service Store on Norfolk's Church Street practiced what the *Norfolk Journal and Guide* referred to as "a little orthodox discrimination to make their customers feel, perhaps, that there is a difference." Unlike most five-and-tens that served coffee to black and white customers in the same type of cup, soda jerks at People's poured coffee for whites in "a thin, delicately shaped and decorated china cup and saucer." Black customers, on the other hand, received their coffee in a thick mug, prompting one columnist to ask if the store's owners were under the impression "that their off-color customers drink coffee with a suction that is liable to crack the cup."[35]

The Association for the Preservation of Virginia Antiquities did its part to remind African Americans that their political rights extended only so far when it barred blacks from visiting historic Jamestown Island. Up until 1930, blacks had been allowed to visit the site without restriction, but when a group of tourists from New Jersey complained, the association decided that African Americans would be admitted only twice a year, and only in conjunction with Hampton Institute. After he was personally refused admission along with some friends, Richmond clergyman W. L. Ransome wrote the *Richmond News Leader* to express a feeling of "pain to know that Negroes are counted unworthy and unfit to stand on the soil to which their fathers were brought in 1619."[36]

While the actions of individual proprietors and organizations reminded black Virginians of their second-class standing, state and municipal officials remained responsible for the most glaring and pervasive inequities in education, housing, and recreational facilities. As increasing numbers of black students sought an education, overcrowding in some urban schools became so severe that black students were forced to attend on a part-time basis. In Norfolk, the plight of 2,000 part-timers appeared especially unjust in view of the situation at the all-white Henry Clay School, which was built for 1,000 students but had enrolled only 350. Ignoring the state constitution's guarantee of a public education for all students, school officials in Richmond simply chose not to enroll 200 black students when space became an issue. The situation in the counties mirrored that of the cities. In Southampton County, 2,000 white students attended eight accredited high schools; 4,000 black students crammed into one substandard facility. Throughout the state, African Americans had access to only one-twelfth of the high schools, even though they comprised one-fourth of the school-age population.[37]

Not only did the construction of black schools fail to keep pace with the demand for education, but the school facilities available to African Americans were generally older, often unsafe, and even combustible. Black children lacked access to modern textbooks and equipment, and their teachers were grossly underpaid. In Richmond, African Americans took special offense at the school board's absolute refusal before 1933 to employ black principals in the black schools. John J. Corson III, a white investigative reporter, left no doubt as to whom he blamed for the city's woeful record in educating its black citizens; Corson ridiculed the claim of school officials that African Americans evinced no real interest in their own training.[38]

Traveling in Opposite Directions

Despite repeated investigations in the 1910s and 1920s that urged an improvement in housing stock for African Americans, living conditions for most blacks remained intolerable. One federal official referred to the slums in Norfolk as the "worst" in the United States, while Corson cited housing in Richmond as "disgraceful, inhuman, pestilential and in a civic sense entirely too costly to be tolerated by the people of this city."[39]

Recreational facilities in the Old Dominion's urban areas also remained woefully inadequate. As the neighborhood surrounding the Hollywood Cemetery in Richmond became increasingly inhabited by African Americans, black and white members of the Negro Welfare Council suggested converting the adjacent Clark Springs Playground into use for black children. Oliver Sands, a white banker, saw no problem with black children using the playground or the cemetery, explaining that "'the living are much more important than the dead.'" A female member of the Hollywood Memorial Association, on the other hand, emphatically objected. "'Our Association considers our Confederate dead more important than any living person,'" she declared. "'We do not want a Negro playground within a mile of that cemetery.'" Opponents of the playground took seriously the mile-wide no-play zone, refusing to accept as a compromise a twelve-foot fence that would have prevented children in the park from spilling over into the cemetery. When asked if the Confederate memorialists would support a petition to the city council to establish a playground in a different location, a representative responded that "'we are not interested in securing playgrounds for Negroes; let those who are interested go to the Council and ask for them.'"[40]

The attitudes exhibited by members of the Hollywood Memorial Association underscored the obstacles that whites placed in the way of basic reform. No one understood this problem better than Louis Jaffé. For more than a decade, beginning in the mid-1920s, Jaffé worked to persuade the city of Norfolk to build a beachfront for the city's 65,000 black residents. On the pages of the *Norfolk Virginian-Pilot* and in private correspondence, the editor described the situation a "civic emergency" and asked his readers what would happen if the city's 115,000 white residents lost access to the half-dozen beach and resort facilities available to them. Jaffé implored city authorities to meet what he considered "a commanding moral obligation," made all the more urgent by the city's construction of yet another beachfront and park for whites.[41]

Jaffé and other supporters, black and white, finally prevailed upon the Norfolk city council to purchase land for a beach. Almost immediately, however, objectors arose and threatened the project. In the columns of the *Virginian-Pilot*, Jaffé described attempts to deny the area's expansive ocean facilities to blacks as a "gross injustice." He argued that hot weather was more punishing to African Americans than to whites because of their cramped living quarters. Noting that poor ventilation and sewage plagued black homes and that inadequate shade and a surfeit of dust characterized the unpaved streets in black neighborhoods, Jaffé reminded his readers that African Americans could "not escape to the shade and solace of nearby parks, because the entire public park system, with negligible exceptions, although paid for and maintained by taxing both races, is reserved for the use of the white race alone. These are the facts and however we may explain them we can not dispute them."[42]

Despite the protestations of what the *Norfolk Journal and Guide* referred to as a "howling mob of six or seven hundred misguided and prejudice ridden whites who all but reenacted the scene that furnished the background for Pontius Pilate's court when Christ was the defendant," the city council voted with only one objection to move forward with the beach project. White residents who lived within a few miles of the proposed beach, however, joined real estate investors in raising one objection after another. Otto Wells, whose company had put $1.5 million into the development of a beach and amusement park for whites several miles from the proposed black beach, feared that the presence of blacks on adjacent roadways would devalue his investment. Each round of objections forced the city council to reconsider the issue and ensured that African Americans in Norfolk spent another summer without beach access.[43]

Two years of legal delays culminated in city council members threatening to overturn the entire project. An exasperated *Norfolk Journal and Guide* exclaimed, "For months the Council's committee looked for a site and finally selected the one in question, and if there is a spot on the Atlantic seaboard that meets all the requirements of repression, segregation, Jim Crowism, and isolation, it is the site at Little Creek." Tidewater's black newspaper articulated the extent to which objectors had forced African Americans into the most out-of-the-way public spaces. "It can be reached through Norfolk's back door, through a section remote in contact with white developments," noted the paper. "In front of it is the Chesapeake Bay, to the right of it is a railroad terminal; to the left of it is a depression where there was once a creek. It is four miles from Ocean View, the Christian suburb of Norfolk that has fought it to death."[44]

In March 1932 a Norfolk judge ended the legal stall tactics. The judge's ruling, however, did not mean that the land was automatically turned into an adequate beachfront. In fact, Louis Jaffé and his allies on the city's interracial commission spent an additional three years pushing municipal officials to finish the project. Along with Douglas Gordon, editor of the *Norfolk Ledger-Dispatch*, and Eugene Diggs, a black attorney, Jaffé wrote the city council in October 1934 and urged the allocation of necessary funds to provide water, electricity, sewage, the construction of changing rooms, office space for a beach manager, and concession stands. As a last resort, the three representatives of Norfolk's interracial commission recommended that the council subcontract the project to private investors if the municipal treasury lacked the funds to make the improvements. Finally, in the summer of 1935, the city opened a modest facility for black residents. Two years later, authorities granted E. B. Davis, a white man, the rights to run the beachfront for private profit; the city provided next to no services.[45]

The establishment of a bathing beach for Norfolk's black citizenry took nearly a decade of active agitation to come to fruition. What originally appeared to some as an obvious necessity and moral imperative soon became embroiled in the bitter and spiteful politics and rhetoric of racial antagonism. The difficulty in convincing Norfolk's white populace to approve a beachfront for the city's black residents confirmed for Louis Jaffé the uncertain road that lay ahead in the amelioration of racial tension. In the midst of the beach affair, Jaffé told William Shands Mcacham, the editor of the *Danville Register* and a leading member of the state interracial commission, that "there is really not much new to say about interracial affairs in the South. All of us know the predicament and none of us know the answer. All we can think of is mitigations." Given that conundrum, Jaffé explained, newspapers and their editors had a responsibility to become fully informed about specific problems and grievances that oppressed African Americans in their daily lives. Furthermore, Jaffé considered it imperative to consider the perspective of those most affected and to fashion remedies wherever possible. To achieve that understanding, Jaffé maintained an open door to individual blacks and, in his mind, became knowledgeable about their most pressing concerns.[46]

Jaffé recognized that the thorough commitment to white supremacy of most whites, even those at the forefront of the interracial movement, ensured that "the problem of racial amelioration . . . is all exploratory and slow." The editor understood that he could not correct every injustice, but he never allowed his pragmatism to serve as an excuse for inaction. "All we, as newspaper editors, can hope to do is to attack the rightable wrongs," he told Meacham. "Some of the wrongs, I fear, are not rightable—not in this generation, at least. But many of them are. The problem is to discern them, identify them, conduct a sound reconnaissance to determine whether they can be righted without a fight so bitter that it will leave the atmosphere more poisoned than ever, and then to strike and keep on striking until the resistance gives way. And when that is done, to repeat the operation with another objective. Over and over again. Endlessly." But as Jaffé experienced first-hand, the most persistent advocacy faced long odds; he reminded one colleague that, despite the continual support of Norfolk's two white newspapers, "the politicians and Little Caucasians have managed to keep the beach tract unimproved and barren."[47]

Louis Jaffé did more than any white opinion-shaper in the Old Dominion to prod whites to recognize their moral responsibility to provide better services, improve health-related conditions, and end the stain of lynching. In his editorials and private correspondence, Jaffé revealed a more genuine and less paternalistic recognition of the humanity of the Old Dominion's black citizens than most of his peers. He deplored the unconscionable obstructionism and pure mean-spiritedness of those who prolonged the establishment of a black beach and called on state political leaders to recognize the effect of their words on the actions taken by other officials. Jaffé consistently sought to make segregation more humane and less odious, and he expressed no fear of the change certain to come. At the same time, he never questioned the rightness of segregation itself as an organizing ideology. Consequently, as historian Earl Lewis has concluded, Jaffé's advocacy allowed white elites "to maintain the social advantage that segregation brought without giving up the moral high ground."[48]

Furthermore, as Lewis emphasizes, the support of Jaffé and other white elites for a black beachfront underscored the irony that confronted African Americans who fought to improve their lives within the context of managed race relations. Given the vituperative objections of the so-called "Little Caucasians" to the most basic requests, blacks had no alternative but to ally with white elites. In return for their support, however, upperclass whites defined the terms of debate and expected African Americans to comply. But, to borrow Lewis's words, these "insidious expectations of civility" served first and foremost to protect white interests and "proved to be as limiting for blacks as the frontal attacks of the white working class."[49]

Although limited by such expectations, Jaffé far exceeded his contemporaries in proactively addressing black grievances. By contrast, most other urban paternalists reacted only if they sensed a threat to racial and social stability. In hindsight, and especially from a distance of more than sixty-five years, such distinctions might seem trivial, but African American contemporaries appreciated the difference. According to Jerry Gilliam, a railway mail clerk and the president of the Norfolk NAACP in the late 1930s, black residents of the city considered Jaffé one of the few reliable whites in their midst, a clear recognition that the editor's thoughts and actions distinguished him from other white elites, including those who lent their support to state and local interracial efforts.[50]

Most upper-class whites in Virginia, on the other hand, only begrudgingly acknowledged the need for interracial cooperation. For most, that meant an occasional gesture of goodwill, such as contributing funds for a black recreational center, but entailed a minimal commitment and certainly no recognition of the need for fundamental change. When Louis Jaffé first began work on the black bathing beach, for instance, he asked then-governor Harry Byrd to lend his name to the effort. The chief executive agreed but made it clear that he would not "undertake any responsibilities and duties." Byrd's attitude confirmed the conclusions of one observer who noted that "many excellent white people have preferred to 'let sleeping dogs lie'" rather than face the "ugly facts" that permeated Virginia's commitment to white supremacy.[51]

This prevailing penchant for neglect and the inherent conservatism of Virginia's upper class meant that the Commission on Interracial Cooperation proceeded with caution, that its work was "done quietly," and that the number of committed members remained low. In fact, throughout the 1920s and 1930s the Virginia CIC struggled to boost membership. In August 1934 the organization prevailed upon Harry Byrd, by then Virginia's junior U.S. senator, to invite targeted Virginians of distinction to join the CIC's Citizens' Committee of One Thousand. The most powerful political personality in the state from the mid-1920s until his death in 1966, Byrd remarked that "Virginia has good understanding between the two races on her soil. You know what an asset this is. We must keep it so. Happily we have a quiet conservative group tugging at this task." As a CIC member himself, Byrd asked other Virginians to help him ensure that "the same high spirit and idealism" continue to define the commonwealth's interracial efforts.[52]

For Byrd, who epitomized the commitment of white elites to managed race relations, conservative leadership foreclosed the possibility of any reform deemed meaningful to the state's black citizenry. Not a demagogue in the tradition of the Deep South's most virulent race-baiters, Byrd denounced mob savagery and the Ku Klux Klan. The senator, however, spoke not as an advocate of racial or social justice, but as a guarantor of social order. Byrd, whose success as a businessman matched his political acumen, was concerned first and foremost with maintaining a stable, low-wage labor force that, combined with low taxes, would encourage the growth of business and preserve the social and economic position of the

Members of the Virginia Commission on Interracial Cooperation (ca. 1940) include Gordon Blaine Hancock (back row, far left) and P. B. Young (next to last row, third from right). (Used with permission of the Valentine Museum/ Richmond History Center)

state's upper class. William Reed, Byrd's closest confidant, summed up this view when he told Byrd, "We must keep Virginia like she is without any changes."[53]

The decision itself to bring Byrd on as chair of the membership drive reflected the extent to which the cic operated within the narrow confines of upper-class conservatism. The commission's leadership understood that most white elites needed to feel confident that the organization's agenda was controlled by faithful adherents to the racial status quo. Byrd provided such assurance, as did pamphlets sent out by the cic that emphasized "Virginia's way of handling social matters—sanely and conservatively." To an extent, the membership drive succeeded. Beginning with 120 active men and women of both races in the early 1930s, the commission added 800 new members, more than 125 of whom were ministers, in response to Byrd's invitation. By 1939 the cic claimed over 1,500 members, all representative "of the economic, educational, religious, and civic leadership of the Commonwealth."[54]

Traveling in Opposite Directions

Throughout the 1930s, black and white Virginians continued to meet and discuss issues of mutual concern. African Americans, however, were fully cognizant that Virginia's elite power brokers actually hindered meaningful reform. Wiley Hall, the secretary of the Richmond Urban League, described the thorough and very conservative social control practiced by Richmond's and Virginia's leading white citizens. White members ensured that the league stuck to a program deemed "practical" for the community. Hall explained to an interviewer that his board had an even mix of white and black members but that whites did not serve for long, preferring to quit rather than become embroiled in any controversial matters. According to Hall's interviewer, whites "think it is a fine thing to come on the Board, and as long as the organization is run without too much conflict with local mores, they go along; otherwise they quit. Appeasement is their policy."[55]

Hall emphasized the thoroughly paternalistic attitude of Richmond's most liberal and progressive whites. He mentioned Mary Munford, a member of the Richmond school board and the state interracial committee, as one of those "liberals willing to work for Negroes but not to work with Negroes." Munford reportedly once said that "'white people here know what is best for our Negroes and when we feel that they're ready for it, we're going to give it to them without them asking or fighting for it.'" As a result of the success of whites in asserting this level of control, Hall found it impossible to appeal directly to black leaders for help on Urban League proposals. Instead, he had to ask "responsible whites" to approach other blacks on his behalf. On balance, Hall considered the paternalistic approach of white elites to be "sincere," but "naive."[56]

J. M. Tinsley, a Richmond dentist and the first president of the statewide NAACP Conference of Branches, described white elites in decidedly harsher terms. Referring to interracial organizations as "camouflage," Tinsley explained that the "strategy of whites is to praise local Negroes and tell them they are the best in the world." In Tinsley's opinion, no truly dependable whites remained in the city; only Lucy Randolph Mason and John Corson did not "backfire under pressure," and both, unfortunately, had left Richmond to live and work elsewhere.[57]

After conducting research on behalf of black sociologist Ralph Bunche, James Jackson concluded that "the white 'leading citizens' of the city maintain a watchful surveillance over all Negro life and keep a careful tab on all Negro leadership aspirants." A Richmond native, Jackson referred to the local interracial commission as a "spy court" whose members expended a great deal of energy "in selecting, grooming and promoting" acceptable black leaders. White elites, according to Jackson, limited their support to black leaders who would "frustrate all genuine movements which may take root among the Negro people and that seek to tilt the balance of 'racial harmony' away from the status quo toward equal rights."[58]

This expectation of compliance placed a number of African American leaders in an awkward position, especially as challenges to their leadership intensified after 1930. At the depth of the Great Depression, Communist Party and labor activists made inroads in cities such as Norfolk and Richmond. Addressing basic economic issues that affected all unemployed workers, black and white alike, radicals preached a vision of class solidarity that transcended the South's color line. White elites, of course, disdained the Communist message, while middle-class and professional blacks expressed deep distrust of any organization that threatened to exacerbate racial tension. Aided by federal relief dollars and jobs programs that blunted radical impulses, black clergy and other leaders considered safe by whites reasserted their control. Although no more than several hundred black Virginians joined the Communist Party, the organization's presence proved far more influential than the numbers would indicate. Not only did the radicals contribute to a new language of protest that ultimately extended to the black populace at large, but, as J. M. Tinsley and Wiley Hall both pointed out, an active Communist Party in parts of Virginia actually bolstered the legitimacy of the NAACP and Urban League. Both organizations appeared more reasonable, and therefore less threatening to whites, when compared to the demands made by the Communists. Hall even suggested that "one Communist Party demonstration here [in Richmond] is worth a month of Urban League activity."[59]

Although united in their opposition to the Communists and other radicals, middle-class and professional African Americans soon divided over the most appropriate and effective means of attacking Jim Crow. Even those who opposed the Communist Party recognized that the radicals had received significant support in part because years of interracial cooperation had failed to alleviate the persistence of neglect and inequality. In Richmond, black newspaper columnist Josephus Simpson derided the passivity of African Americans and the futility of their interracial diplomacy. Seventy years after the end of the Civil War, Simpson declared, "the problems of the day call for new methods shaped to meet the exigencies of the times." Simpson warned that whites would not change their racial attitudes in the foreseeable future and that African Americans must therefore seize the initiative and insist on their rights as citizens. In Norfolk, black elites formally split into two competing camps. One, led by P. B. Young and Eugene Diggs, preferred to work with white allies on the interracial

Traveling in Opposite Directions

commission and to follow the same strategy that had ultimately produced a bathing beach, hospital, and school gymnasium. A second faction, led by local NAACP officials Jerry Gilliam and Ione Diggs, considered such accomplishments insufficient. Gilliam, a champion of working-class blacks, and Diggs, who "abhorred the civility" at the heart of managed race relations, encouraged African Americans to put less faith in their supposed white friends and to make their voices heard if they hoped to enact change. As a result of such advocacy, a number of white elites came to distrust Gilliam and Diggs; one particularly prominent white Virginian, long considered a racial moderate in the state, went so far as to call Gilliam a "hoodlum" while specifically praising Young.[60]

Like local officials Gilliam and Diggs, the NAACP as an organization evolved throughout the 1930s into a source of great consternation to white Virginians. Earlier in the decade, the state's whites had praised the NAACP, especially with regard to its defense of George Crawford, a black caretaker accused of murder in Loudoun County. Douglas Southall Freeman, in particular, applauded NAACP chief counsel Charles Houston for his demeanor at trial and compared him favorably with the antagonistic and bombastic representatives of the International Labor Defense (ILD). The legal arm of the Communist Party, the ILD had outmaneuvered the NAACP in the infamous case of the Scottsboro Boys and had attempted to gain control of Crawford's case. Freeman, who had advocated for years on behalf of a more equitable criminal justice system, surmised that ILD lawyers would have attacked the integrity of white supremacy itself, while Houston confined his defense to the facts of the case. For Freeman, the resolution of Crawford's trial, in which the defendant was found guilty but spared the electric chair, represented a triumph of managed race relations. Before long, however, he and other leading whites would discover that the NAACP and its members intended to challenge white supremacy in more fundamental terms.[61]

Beginning with two branches in Falls Church and Richmond in 1915, the NAACP struggled to make headway in the Old Dominion. The national office of the NAACP repeatedly chartered chapters in cities such as Norfolk and Alexandria that subsequently fell apart due to inactivity. Specific local issues, including the Richmond residential segregation ordinance, and national concerns, such as the fate of the Scottsboro Boys, slowly galvanized support for the organization. By 1935 the number of local chapters had risen to twenty, and the Virginia State Conference of Branches was established to further increase membership and coordinate strategy. In Richmond, by far the largest chapter, annual campaigns sought as many as 2,000 new members. Within fifteen years, sixty branches carried on the work of the NAACP throughout the state.[62]

The rise in membership reflected, and further contributed to, an increase in black activism. In 1933 African Americans in Suffolk sued, albeit unsuccessfully, to force the school board to provide a high school education for their children. A year later, local residents in Alexandria, where black students had to travel to Washington, D.C., if they wanted to continue school beyond the eighth grade, were more successful. In Richmond, the NAACP successfully pressured the A&P grocery store chain to hire more black clerks. A short time later, African Americans in the state capital threatened court action if the city council approved another playground for whites while black schools remained so underfunded. Their action prompted the *Richmond News Leader* to announce that "the servile tradition is dead among Negroes."[63]

While each of these incidents reflected a heightened independence among African Americans, it was Alice Jackson's application to the University of Virginia that shook the foundations of managed race relations and permanently altered the contours of interracial cooperation in the Old Dominion. The daughter of a Richmond druggist and his wife, Jackson received her bachelor's degree from Virginia Union University in 1934 and began master's work in English at Smith College in Massachusetts. In August 1935 she sought admission to the University of Virginia's graduate program in French; if admitted, Jackson would have become the first African American to attend the school. Set within the context of the NAACP's broader attack on all-white graduate and professional schools in the South, Jackson's petition met with strong resistance from those white elites who had most vigorously championed African American advancement in other areas. To these whites, and some blacks, Jackson's assertiveness and relationship with the NAACP violated paternalism's mandate that whites dictate the pace of change. In denouncing her application, those whites considered most progressive in racial matters began to echo the familiar discourse of the most rabid advocates of white supremacy.[64]

Activism appeared to run in the Jackson family. By the time Alice applied to the University of Virginia, her brother James had assumed a leadership role in an interracial student group that openly advocated an end to segregation; later in the decade, as a member of the Southern Negro Youth Congress, he was arrested while picketing on behalf of striking tobacco stemmers. Alice Jackson's petition came on the heels of the NAACP's groundbreaking legal victory in the case of Donald Gaines Murray, an Amherst College graduate who sought admission to the law school at the

University of Maryland. Like Virginia, Maryland barred African Americans from its graduate and professional schools. Murray rejected the state's offer of scholarship aid to attend law school at Howard University in Washington, D.C., insisting that the state itself must provide equal opportunities for all students. When a judge agreed, Murray became the first African American to enroll at the University of Maryland and the NAACP won a crucial first victory in its assault on segregated education, a campaign that came to fruition two decades later in *Brown v. Board of Education*.[65]

Black and white Virginians recognized from the outset that the NAACP's victory in the *Murray* case had influenced Jackson's decision to apply to the University of Virginia. Not surprisingly, black newspapers applauded her determination to procure for African Americans the same rights and privileges of citizenship, including educational opportunity, that white Virginians enjoyed. Without endorsing the NAACP, the generally conservative *Norfolk Journal and Guide* explained that the civil rights organization had a "perfect case" only because of the persistent inequality of black schools. By contrast, Douglas Southall Freeman opined on the pages of the *Richmond News Leader* that Jackson and the NAACP were "badly advised" in forcing the matter, while the *Richmond Times-Dispatch* announced that the relevant question "is not what the Negro has an abstract 'right' to do, but what it is wise for him to attempt." Like a number of other white opinion shapers in the Old Dominion, the *Times-Dispatch* professed to support an increase in funding for African American schools but rejected the threat of court proceedings, in the event that Jackson was denied admission, as likely to arouse interracial hostilities. In support of its position, the *Times-Dispatch* quoted at length an article by Theodore Jones, a black resident of Richmond and frequent critic of that city's white authorities. Jones urged African Americans to agitate for better elementary and secondary schools but warned that any advance toward integration would antagonize "the best white people of Virginia" and would undermine the "promotion of more friendly relations between the races."[66]

White officials debated how best to respond to Jackson's application. Initially, officials at the University of Virginia hinted that they might deny Jackson admission on a technicality, noting that the Association of American Universities had not accredited her undergraduate institution. Meanwhile, L. R. Reynolds, the director of Virginia's Commission on Interracial Cooperation, informed university president John Newcomb that a number of black members of the commission had guided Jackson's appeal. Reynolds urged Newcomb to postpone a decision until January, when Reynolds and other white members of the interracial commission planned to ask the General Assembly to provide funds for African Americans to attend out-of-state graduate and professional schools. Ultimately, the Board of Visitors of the University of Virginia determined that "the education of white and colored persons in the same schools is contrary to the long established and fixed policy of the Commonwealth of Virginia." Without further explanation, the board rejected Jackson's application.[67]

With the denial of Jackson's request for admission, attention shifted to the NAACP. Chief legal counsel Charles Houston outlined the organization's strategy and quipped that while white elites in Virginia had praised his veracity in the Crawford case, he wondered how they would respond when he revealed "the truth about southern education." With the exception of a small number of radical students at the University of Virginia who supported Jackson's petition on grounds of equal opportunity, most white Virginians roundly condemned a court challenge. Anticipating Houston's next move, the chief editorial writer and later editor of the *Richmond Times-Dispatch*, Virginius Dabney, decried "such belligerent efforts . . . to force Negroes into institutions hitherto used by the whites." Beyond his generic denunciation of the NAACP, Dabney raised a more fundamental concern at the root of white supremacist ideology, warning that even the slightest amount of integration in any of the commonwealth's schools might lead to "racial amalgamation."[68]

Dabney's introduction of the shibboleth of white supremacy shocked, saddened, and disappointed those who had come to recognize him as a fair voice of southern progressivism. Born in 1901 into an aristocratic Virginia family, Dabney emerged in the late 1920s and early 1930s as a critic of southern religious, cultural, and political backwardness. In 1932 Dabney authored *Liberalism in the South*, a book whose publication cemented his reputation as a leading southern liberal. Unlike an earlier generation of southern reformers who envisioned rigid and thorough social control as necessary for regional advancement, Dabney and his cohorts recognized that future progress depended upon the integration of African Americans into civic life. In words hailed by the black press as "courageous," Dabney remarked in 1931 that African Americans had made tremendous strides in recent years, both in educational and economic terms, and that whites ought to recognize that both races stood to benefit from such advances. Instead, bemoaned Dabney, "as soon as a Negro begins dressing decently and exhibiting evidences of education there are always whites to protest that he is 'uppish' or 'putting on airs.' Nothing would be more to the taste of this white element than to have all members of the black race remain in ignorance, poverty and squalor." In addition, Dabney derided the injustice inherent in southern election laws that "are drawn on the theory that it is better for the most ignorant and depraved white man to cast a ballot than for the most highly educated Negro to do the same thing."[69]

In supporting the political, economic, and educational advancement of African Americans, Dabney called specifically on white southerners to recognize paternalism as an "outmoded" form of social control. Acknowledging the "genuine affection" of "often honorable and respected citizens" who conceived of African Americans in childlike terms, Dabney sought "to counteract the paternalistic philosophy, which holds that the Negro is always happier, always better off, always better cared for when his 'white folks' are supervising him, guiding him and controlling him." As an alternative, Dabney called on white southerners to recognize the capacity of African Americans to reach their potential as full citizens. At first glance, Dabney's attitude toward paternalism appears incongruous with his opposition to Alice Jackson's petition. But in fact, as historian John Kneebone has articulated, southern liberals never questioned the correctness or necessity of the color line but rather tilted it from the horizontal to the vertical, encouraging greater equality, but only within the bounds of segregation. Along with like-minded compatriots, Dabney denounced the rabble-rousers and cheap politicians who encouraged racial violence and fostered gross inequality, but he remained adamant that segregation be maintained as a bulwark against social equality and miscegenation. Furthermore, his belief that African Americans ought to supervise, guide, and control their own lives had limits. As early as 1933, Dabney began to express grave concern that "a radical Negro element" refused to work with white southern liberals such as himself. Over time, his definition of radical would expand to include not only Communist revolutionaries and northern agitators but indigenous supporters of the NAACP as well. Dabney himself, it turned out, preferred that white southerners manage the pace of change. As it became increasingly clear in the latter half of the 1930s that such change threatened segregation itself, Dabney revealed that he was far more southern than liberal.[70]

A number of African Americans upbraided Dabney for his editorial on the Jackson case, none more explicitly than *Richmond Planet* columnist Josephus Simpson, who denounced Dabney for instilling fears of racial amalgamation that clouded the real issues. As Simpson reminded Dabney, miscegenation occurred not in response to the admission of a few blacks into all-white schools, but as a result of forced intercourse between white men and black women. Simpson challenged those who considered the South's customs "inviolate" and ridiculed the "so-called peaceful relations now extant in the South as a one-sided affair in which the black gives all and receives nothing." Instead, argued Simpson, truly amicable relations required the full recognition of African Americans as citizens. Given that the best white Virginians and southerners had failed for seventy years to provide economic, political, legal, and educational equality, Simpson pledged to fight for the "annihilation of the damnable system of legal segregation and discrimination."[71]

Several months after the University of Virginia denied admission to Alice Jackson, state officials devised a two-pronged strategy to head off further applications from African Americans and to minimize the threat of lawsuits. First, in December, the State Board of Education authorized Virginia State College, a black institution in Petersburg, to establish a graduate school. In March, the General Assembly passed the 1936 Educational Equality Act, which provided scholarship assistance for qualified black students to attend universities outside the state. Under the terms of the law and with state assistance, thirty African Americans, including Alice Jackson, attended out-of-state graduate schools in the fall of 1936. The popularity of the scholarship program, however, left the NAACP without a second plaintiff, a necessary back-up in the event that Jackson's petition was dismissed. Consequently, the civil rights organization dropped the appeal. Likening the thirty recipients of state aid to Judas, Josephus Simpson castigated their decision to capitulate to Virginia's Jim Crow system of education.[72]

While angry at African Americans as a whole for lacking the courage to see the Jackson case through to the end, Simpson placed particular blame on the shoulders of traditional black leaders who had the support of white elites. In deeply personal terms, Simpson attacked Gordon Blaine Hancock and other black leaders who continued to stress the necessity of interracial cooperation and goodwill. Refusing to accept the "sop" to equal education offered in the wake of the Jackson case, Simpson urged black Virginians to litigate, protest, strike, and picket.[73]

Despite Simpson's assertions, Hancock and like-minded African Americans leaders, such as P. B. Young, did not merely do the bidding of their white acquaintances. Hancock and Young sought the same ends as Simpson but believed cooperation was essential to the attainment of first-class citizenship. Both men vigorously defended themselves against the charges lobbed their way by more confrontational African Americans but simultaneously came to question the efficacy of biracialism. Tired of the empty promises that spewed forth from white colleagues on the interracial commission, and deeply aware that the condemnation of mob violence had not addressed the unremitting daily effects of white supremacy, Hancock implored southern whites to recognize that only genuine fraternalism could guarantee racial amity. Not yet ready to disavow the civility central to managed race relations, but equally cognizant that separate would never be equal, Hancock and Young found themselves "travelling in opposite directions" from their white colleagues in the interracial movement. Before long, they joined an emerging chorus of African Americans who demanded no less than "the end of all official Jim Crow regulations and practices." In the process, white elites in the Old Dominion awoke to the stunning realization that they had mistaken African American forbearance as contentment; as it turned out, white elites never understood the thoughts, desires, or aspirations of their black neighbors.[74]

9

Too Radical for Us

THE PASSING OF MANAGED RACE RELATIONS

> Any effort to force the abolition of segregation, over the
> protest of a strongly hostile white South, is bound to do far
> more harm than good to the Negro. If I were a Negro, I
> should wish the system done away with, but I hope I should
> have the intelligence to realize that no lasting benefit would
> result, so long as the great majority of white southerners were
> ranged in opposition. —VIRGINIUS DABNEY, 1943

> Negro southerners may strike blows at the segregation
> laws forever, but final victory can never come until
> white southerners unite with them.
> —LUTHER P. JACKSON, 1944

Throughout the late 1930s and early 1940s, African Americans in Virginia hastened their attack on the foundations of white supremacy, driving an ever-widening wedge between black and white advocates of managed race relations. While willing to acknowledge the reasonableness of certain black demands, Virginius Dabney and like-minded white elites could not envision a future without segregation. For a time, black leaders such as P. B. Young and Gordon Blaine Hancock continued to embrace civility and cooperation as essential to African American progress. Ultimately, however, even the most cautious black leaders acknowledged publicly that separate would never be equal and that African Americans would never lead even remotely full lives as long as segregation governed the laws and customs of the commonwealth and the region. As the United States plunged into World War II, white elites labeled African Americans who demanded their rights as citizens and the most rabid white southerners as equal threats to racial harmony and social order. The inability of self-proclaimed whites of goodwill to distinguish morally or intellectually between the two underscored the emptiness of paternalism and the limits of managed race relations.

Just weeks before Alice Jackson applied for admission to the University of Virginia, Gordon Blaine Hancock noted in a newspaper column that no white politician would treat the demands of black constituents seriously until African Americans voted in sufficient numbers to command respect. White Virginians, of course, preferred to keep black Virginians out of politics altogether, but political leaders and their cronies were first and foremost interested in winning elections, maintaining power, and holding onto the perks of office. As Norman Hamilton, the editor of the *Portsmouth Star*, explained, "Few white people in the community are in favor of Negroes voting. You know this is the south and the only kind of people interested in the Negro vote are the professional machine politicians who buy it and cannot therefore honestly say they are in favor of it." Consequently, as African Americans began to vote in larger, albeit still relatively small, numbers, and especially as blacks continued to shift their allegiance to the party of Franklin Roosevelt and the New Deal, white candidates competed for African American votes.[1]

As Hamilton experienced firsthand, however, white politicians had to exercise great care in soliciting black support. The editor of Portsmouth's daily ran for Congress from Virginia's Second District in 1936 and 1938, both times battling Colgate Darden, a future governor and president of the University of Virginia. Darden had first won election to Congress in 1932 and was easily reelected two years later. Supported fully by the state Democratic machine, known more popularly as the Organization, as well as by his wife's DuPont fortune, Darden faced an unexpected challenge from Hamilton in the 1936 primaries. A firm supporter of Franklin Roosevelt, Hamilton broke from Organization insiders over their opposition to the New Deal. Throughout the campaign, both sides engaged extensively in the illegal but common practice of paying the poll taxes of otherwise unqualified voters. Hamilton operatives complained that the Darden campaign's "orgy of poll tax payments" set a new standard of chicanery in a district known for its shameful political history; while perhaps not as deep-pocketed, Hamilton's campaign proved as adept at recruiting new voters. Cobbling together a coalition of pro–New Deal Democrats, labor unionists, African Americans, radicals, and Republicans, Hamilton defeated Darden by less than 1,800 votes.[2]

Although neither Hamilton nor Darden appears to have specifically solicited black votes in 1936, both sides recognized in the aftermath that African Americans had played a significant role in the outcome of the election. In a district in which an estimated 1,300 blacks voted in Portsmouth alone, state senator and later lieutenant governor Saxon Holt expressed grave concern that African Americans, who had registered to vote in greater numbers than ever before, provided the margin of victory. During Hamilton's term in office, African American constituents, male and female, repeatedly reminded the congressman of the significance of their support. Members of black civic clubs in particular attempted to parlay their perceived group strength into patronage appointments.[3]

Aware of the need to capture African American votes again in 1938, Hamilton established a campaign office in the center of Portsmouth's black district and hired young black women to staff it. Recognizing a prime opportunity to exploit the situation to their own ends, Darden's managers hired photographers to document the scene and printed pictures of the black women working in Hamilton's office along with captions that included "'Look Hamilton's a nigger lover!,' 'See the niggers are set up better than your own people by him,' 'If you vote for Hamilton, niggers will be teaching your children soon!'" Darden forces reportedly distributed 10,000 copies of the circular throughout the district's rural areas, as well as sections of Portsmouth and Norfolk inhabited by poorer whites. Although Hamilton's congressional record had centered on providing services and relief that benefited the entire district, Darden's campaign successfully portrayed Hamilton as favoring blacks. Such tactics surely cost Hamilton votes among the white electorate.[4]

In addition to frightening white voters, the Darden campaign simultaneously attempted to purchase black votes. Talmedge Johnson, a grocer and recent college graduate, received a visit from Darden supporters. These functionaries, whom Johnson referred to as "DuPont paid men," offered to give him enough money to pay for a master's degree in business administration. When the young ward leader told the men that while in college he had discovered that extracurricular activities cost as much as tuition, and that new clothes were a must, the Darden supporters agreed to cover all costs. "'All they wanted,'" claimed Johnson, "'was for me to get the 200 votes in our civic league and the people they influenced to vote for Colgate W. Darden, Jr. I refused all of their offers.'" According to Thomas Reid, a prominent black attorney in Portsmouth, the Darden campaign spent $50,000 in the city buying and influencing votes; Reid himself, according to one interviewer, was offered $500 to "turn away from the Hamilton forces."[5]

Not satisfied with buying black votes, Darden advocates attempted to woo black voters by challenging the sincerity of Hamilton's concern for African Americans. Ignoring the Darden campaign's own appeals to racial prejudice, black supporters of Colgate Darden circulated a flyer entitled "How Does Norman Hamilton Really Feel about Colored People?" The attack centered on the passage of the Wagner–Van Nuys antilynching act in the House of Representatives the previous year, a vote for which Hamilton was not present.[6]

The flyer castigated Hamilton for missing the vote, an opportunity "to voice his disapproval of Mob Law." Furthermore, the flyer claimed, when asked about the vote by a Norfolk newspaper, the congressman answered, "I WAS NOT PRESENT TO VOTE ON THE BILL, BUT IF I HAD BEEN THERE I WOULD HAVE VOTED 'NAY' AS LOUD AS I COULD." The leaflet asked, "DOES HE ALSO BELIEVE THAT THE PRIVILEGE TO LYNCH NEGROES IS SACRED, AND OUGHT NOT BE DENIED BY FEDERAL LAW?" Finally, the Darden circular concluded, "The injury done to the Colored citizens of the Second Congressional District by Mr. Hamilton in failing to be present when the issue of 'Rope and Faggot vs. Law and Order' was being decided was not enough for him. Mr. Hamilton added to that injury the INSULT of publicly declaring that he would have voted 'Nay . . . as loud as I could.' 'NAY' says Mr. Hamilton to the Colored People, 'NAY — AS LOUD AS I COULD.' THAT'S WHY YOU SHOULD VOTE FOR COLGATE W. DARDEN. . . . He Believes in Fair Play." Although considered a racial moderate throughout his political career, Colgate Darden never intimated that he would have supported a federal antilynching statute; he was a loyal member of the state political organization that consistently opposed even the thought of federal intervention.[7]

During the 1938 contest both the Hamilton and the Darden forces grappled not only with the impact of the size of the black electorate, but also with the importance of race as an issue. While simultaneously catering to the racial fears of white voters, Darden solicited black votes as well, some with dubious assertions, others with cash. Although it is impossible to know the precise impact of each prong of his attack, Darden defeated Hamilton by just 1,547 votes. Dissatisfaction among labor unionists and New Dealers may well have cost Hamilton even more votes than did Darden's racial strategy, but Hamilton himself remained convinced that the inflammatory circular was a major cause of his failure to capture a second term.[8]

If Darden's strategy represented a new reality in Virginia politics, Carter Glass refused to participate. In the fall of 1936, the author of Virginia's disfranchisement statute contributed $500 to the congressional campaign of Clifton A. Woodrum, the representative of Virginia's Sixth District,

**How Does Norman Hamilton
Really Feel about Colored People?**

||| MR. VOTER: Before You Cast Your
Ballot, Ask Yourself These Questions:

1. **WHAT WAS MR. HAMILTON'S ATTI-
TUDE ON THE ANTI-LYNCHING BILL?**

2. **WHAT DID HE SAY ABOUT IT?**

3. **DOES HE ALSO BELIEVE THAT THE
PRIVILEGE TO LYNCH NEGROES IS
SACRED, AND OUGHT NOT BE DENIED
BY FEDERAL LAW?**

— Here Are the Answers —

When the House of Representatives passed the Wagner-Van Nuys "Anti-
Lynching" Bill at the last session of Congress, Mr. Hamilton was NOT there to
voice his disapproval of Mob Law.

That was not all. Not for Mr. Hamilton.

When a Norfolk daily paper, shortly afterwards, asked Mr. Hamilton about
his vote on the Anti-Lynching Bill, he replied:

"I WAS NOT PRESENT TO VOTE ON THE BILL, BUT IF I HAD BEEN
THERE I WOULD HAVE VOTED "NAY" AS LOUD AS I COULD."

The injury done to the Colored citizens of the Second Congressional District
by Mr. Hamilton in failing to be present when the issue of "Rope and Faggot vs.
Law and Order" was being decided was not enough for him.

Mr. Hamilton added to that injury the INSULT of publicly declaring that he
would have voted "Nay . . . as loud as I could."

"NAY" says Mr. Hamilton to the Colored People, "NAY — AS LOUD AS I
COULD."

THAT'S WHY YOU SHOULD VOTE FOR

COLGATE W. DARDEN

For Congressman From The Second Congressional District

• **He Believes In Fair Play** •

Subject to the Democratic Primary, August 2

ISSUED BY COLORED FRIENDS OF COLGATE W. DARDEN

Supporters of Colgate Darden released this attack on
Norman Hamilton during the 1938 Democratic primary
campaign for Congress in the Second District. (Used
with permission of the Ralph J. Bunche Papers, Department of Special Collections, Young Research Library,
UCLA)

which included Glass's native Lynchburg. Virginia's senior senator explained that he offered his contribution "purely from a personal standpoint and because you have been exceptionally friendly to me." But, continued Glass, "I desire to insist upon a single reservation and that is that
no part of my contribution be used to qualify negro voters." Glass knew as
well as anyone that even presumably honest politicians turned a blind eye
to the illegal payment of poll taxes, but he drew a line at the inclusion of
African Americans in such schemes. Explaining that the commonwealth
"spent thirty-seven years after the Civil War trying to eliminate negroes

Colgate Darden gets a lift from his supporters after his victory over Norman Hamilton in August 1938. (Courtesy of the Berjes Collection, Norfolk Public Library)

from elections and this State went to the trouble and expense of a Constitutional Convention for this purpose," Glass concluded that he did "not want to have anything to do with any effort to qualify negro voters." A note in Glass's handwriting indicated that Woodrum acceded to the senator's wishes.[9]

Despite Glass's most fervent wishes and thorough efforts, African Americans participated in the electoral process. Although the Democratic Party continued to officially restrict its primary to whites as late as 1947, qualified African Americans voted in all primaries and elections. Self-interest guided both white politicians and black voters. Darden and other white officials recognized the potential impact of black voters and courted them accordingly. Blacks had their own reasons for supporting white candidates. In the 1939 primaries in Hampton, approximately 350 members of a local black voters league helped reelect Alvin Massenburg to the house of delegates, despite the fact that he had authored the state's Public Assemblages Act thirteen years earlier. Paul N. Williams, the president of the Elizabeth City County Civic League, explained that his organization backed Massenburg because the local postmaster promised to appoint a few blacks as letter carriers in return for the group's support. He kept his promise and hired four black mailmen that fall.[10]

If the cauldron of African American dissatisfaction and activism had been simmering for the better part of a decade, it came to a boil in 1939 as black plaintiffs initiated lawsuits across the state that challenged the persistence of institutionalized and state-sanctioned inequality. The most prominent case had its origins in Norfolk in the fall of 1938 when Aline Black, a high school chemistry teacher, asked the school board for a pay increase commensurate with the salary of similarly qualified white teachers; at the time, the city paid a white janitor at Black's school more than any black teacher. When the school board rejected her request, the NAACP filed suit on Black's behalf, alleging that the city's race-based pay scale violated the due process and equal protection clauses of the Fourteenth Amendment.[11]

The action represented a culmination of the struggle initiated nearly a decade earlier by Thomas Dabney and the Buckingham County Teachers Association. As early as 1935, state and national NAACP officials contemplated bringing such a suit but chose not to proceed without the support of the all-black Virginia Teachers Association. Finally, in 1937, conservatives in the teachers' organization gave way and agreed to establish a fund to support such litigation. In broader terms, the Norfolk salary equalization case constituted the latest step in the NAACP's campaign to dismantle segregation in the nation's public schools. Following the decision of the U.S. Supreme Court in *Missouri ex. rel. Gaines v. Canada*, in which the high court ruled for the first time that state officials had to provide professional school facilities for black students equal to those available to whites, the Norfolk case extended this strategy to one particular aspect of elementary and secondary education.[12]

Not surprisingly, white officials and citizens opposed the lawsuit as audacious and inappropriate. Lutrelle Palmer, the principal of the black high school in Newport News, noted that "many of our white friends say we are setting back Negro education in Virginia twenty years by going to the courts on the salary question." Such whites argued that blacks ought "to wait for sympathetic white elements to achieve this for them." African Americans in Virginia, however, had waited long enough; as Wiley Hall of Richmond exclaimed, "Until we get to the point where we are willing to make people mad, we can't make any progress. The policy of appeasement can produce no further results."[13]

Black's decision to file suit was not necessarily an easy one, especially as white authorities reminded her of the consequences. In June 1939, Cir-

On June 25, 1939, Norfolk schoolchildren led a demonstration against the firing of Aline Black, a plaintiff in an NAACP salary equalization suit. (NAACP Records, Library of Congress. The author wishes to thank The Crisis Publishing Co., Inc., the publisher of the magazine of the National Association for the Advancement of Colored People, for the use of this work.)

cuit Court Judge Allan Hanckel denied Black's petition. Before her lawyers had an opportunity to argue an appeal before the Virginia Supreme Court of Appeals, the city announced that it would not renew Black's contract for the following year, effectively firing her after twelve years of service. If white officials in Norfolk had hoped to stifle dissent among African Americans, they badly miscalculated. In fact, Black's termination so enraged African Americans in Norfolk that those who otherwise disagreed over tactics and strategy found common ground. P. B. Young and his frequent nemesis, local NAACP president Jerry Gilliam, joined forces to organize a massive demonstration of protest. After black schoolchildren marched through Norfolk's streets carrying banners and placards that equated the school board with Hitler and Mussolini, thousands of African Americans crammed into St. John's A.M.E. Church to listen to speeches by national NAACP officials Walter White and Thurgood Marshall.[14]

Recognizing that African Americans in Norfolk considered Black's firing a question of "elementary human justice" and sensing that her termination threatened to undermine managed race relations in the city, the *Norfolk Virginian Pilot* urged the school board to recognize Black's First Amendment right to protest and to reconsider its decision. Whether or not one agreed with the legal merits of her claim, reasoned the Tidewater daily, Black possessed a right to pursue the matter in court. At the same time, in an attempt to provide cover for beleaguered white officials in Norfolk, the *Virginian-Pilot* shifted blame to state authorities in Richmond who, according to the paper, favored Black's termination in order to stem the threat of similar suits all over the state.[15]

Just days after African Americans in Norfolk took to the streets over the firing of Aline Black, the national membership of the NAACP gathered in Richmond for the organization's weeklong annual meeting. Addressing many of the convention's 5,000 delegates, chief counsel Charles Houston discussed the far-reaching implications of the Supreme Court's recent decision in *Gaines v. Canada*. In that case, Lloyd Gaines sought admission to the law school at the University of Missouri. When the registrar advised him to accept a state scholarship to attend an out-of-state institution, an arrangement similar to the one established in Virginia in the wake of Alice Jackson's application to the University of Virginia, Gaines refused and subsequently was denied admission on account of his race. Much to the chagrin of white elites in general and Virginius Dabney in particular, Houston urged his audience to recognize that, in rejecting Missouri's position, the high court granted African Americans the authority to accept nothing less than admission to the same graduate and professional schools attended by whites. "There can be no compromise now upon this question," exclaimed Houston. "It is not a question of wanting to sit in the same classroom with white students. It is a question of vindicating one's citizenship."[16]

Houston's remark completely vexed Virginius Dabney. Throughout the late 1930s, the self-described "seeker after justice for the Negro" had consistently urged whites to recognize the benefits to themselves of African American progress, had endorsed efforts to provide blacks with better facilities, and had spoken in favor of federal antilynching legislation. His support of the salary equalization campaign in Norfolk followed naturally. At the same time, Dabney expected African Americans, and especially their leaders, not to make requests that he and other white elites deemed unreasonable. Houston's embrace of the Supreme Court decision in *Gaines*, however, served to repudiate what Dabney and other white elites had considered a fair compromise: an increase in state funding for black graduate and professional opportunities, albeit in segregated or out-of-

Too Radical for Us

state institutions. African Americans, of course, saw nothing equitable in the arrangement and were delighted when the nation's high court agreed.[17]

Although Houston limited his remarks to a discussion of graduate and professional schools, Dabney accurately gauged that the same logic might be extended to undergraduate, secondary, and ultimately elementary education. The Richmond editor claimed that the issue would soon be "whether the South's system of segregated education is to be destroyed from top to bottom, and both races mingled indiscriminately all the way from the elementary grades to the graduate and professional schools." Just as he had declared when Alice Jackson applied to the University of Virginia, Dabney predicted that the NAACP's strategy would lead to racial amalgamation, a possibility that led him to announce that the organization's program had become "far too radical for us."[18]

While Dabney grossly exaggerated fears of miscegenation, he correctly perceived that African Americans no longer considered segregation compatible with first-class citizenship, even in a tactical sense. Blacks understood that separate had never been, nor would ever be, equal. Whites acknowledged no other alternative. African Americans repeatedly denied that they sought social equality, a shibboleth most often used by whites to warn against racial amalgamation. But, as Earl Lewis has articulated, blacks "did not define social equality as interracial social mingling" and, in fact, found such a notion "totally foreign." African Americans did, however, demand equal pay, equal access to education and public facilities, and an equal chance at earning a living regardless of race. In this sense, blacks across the South and the nation were demanding social equality. Consequently, Virginius Dabney and his peers on city and state interracial commissions found themselves unable to cope with the central contradiction of managed race relations: how to balance the fairer treatment of African Americans with a commitment to white supremacy when increased fairness pointed toward legal, political, educational, and economic equality. Although Dabney was far more progressive than most of his contemporaries, his response to Charles Houston indicated that the accumulated weight of a half-century of empty promises could no longer be papered over. White paternalists had run out of options as black Virginians refused to wait any longer for substantive change.[19]

For Samuel Wilbert Tucker, a twenty-six-year-old black attorney in Alexandria, Charles Houston's words reinforced his own determination to dismantle the most fundamental inequities of white supremacy in the northern Virginia hamlet of his birth. In fact, as Virginius Dabney drafted a response to Houston, white elites in Alexandria scrambled covertly to stymie Tucker's efforts to force the city's public library to admit African Americans. For nearly a year, the young civil rights attorney pushed and prodded, filed lawsuits, and ultimately masterminded an act of civil disobedience that prefigured the tactics of the civil rights movement, all in an effort to hasten the full realization of African American citizenship. In the process, Tucker eloquently challenged the essential assumptions of paternalism and put white elites on notice that they could no longer manage race relations in the manner to which they had become accustomed.

The Alexandria of the 1920s in which Samuel Wilbert Tucker came of age was less segregated in residential terms than cities such as Norfolk and Richmond. Tucker, for instance, told an interviewer later in life that he grew up in a neighborhood in which black and white children lived close to one another and played together frequently. But as he quickly pointed out, Jim Crow pervaded the lives of blacks and whites in Alexandria, just as it did throughout Virginia and the South. Nowhere did this disparity appear more evident to Tucker than when he reached the eighth grade. Despite funding two secondary schools for its white students, Alexandria provided no high school for its black residents. Consequently, Tucker and his classmates who wished to continue school had no alternative but to travel across the Potomac River to Washington, D.C., where they claimed district residency in order to "bootleg" a high school education. As an adult, Tucker continued to feel the pain caused by such inequities, remarking, "That was the first kind of scar. We knew that something was wrong with it, there was a public high school within sight of my home that white children attended as a matter of course."[20]

Tucker's lifelong commitment to education and civil rights no doubt germinated from the example set by his parents. His mother, a teacher, and his father, a real estate agent and charter member of the Alexandria NAACP, were fiercely devoted to the formal and informal education of their children. Both parents instilled in their offspring a deep sense of self-worth and a determination to challenge anyone who attempted to limit their potential. Tucker's legal education began before he hit his teens. Under the tutelage of Tom Watson, who shared office space with his father, Samuel Tucker came to appreciate the possibilities and intricacies of the law. By the time he was fourteen, Tucker had written his first deeds and, on at least one occasion, had prepared Watson's clients for court.[21]

That same year, Samuel Tucker discovered a taste for civil disobedience. In June 1927, along with his older brother George, younger brother Otto, and a friend, Tucker boarded a streetcar in the District of Columbia to return to Alexandria. Reversible seats allowed the four youths to face one another. As soon as the trolley crossed the river and became subject to Virginia's Jim Crow laws, a white woman, Lottie May Jernigan, demanded that the young men give up the seat that now faced backwards and that she believed was designated for whites. The Tucker brothers refused to move. Upon arrival in Alexandria, Jernigan swore out a warrant, charging the boys with disorderly conduct, assault, and abusive language. The police court levied no fine against Otto, who was only eleven at the time, but fined Samuel $5 plus court costs and George Tucker $50 plus costs, claiming that as the oldest he should have known better. On appeal, however, an all-white jury found the young men not guilty.[22]

After graduating from Armstrong High School in 1929, Tucker enrolled at Howard University at a most propitious time. During Tucker's tenure at Howard, Charles Houston established the nation's first training program in civil rights law, while school chaplain Howard Thurman, who in the mid-1930s became one of the most outspoken American proponents of Mahatma Gandhi's campaign of nonviolent resistance, emphasized the necessity of linking faith and social justice. Although destined to enter the legal profession, Tucker skipped law school altogether after receiving his bachelor's degree. Instead, under the continued guidance of Tom Watson, he passed the Virginia bar exam in December 1933, just six months after graduating from college. Not yet twenty-one, Tucker had to wait until June 1934 to begin practicing law.[23]

After a two-year stint in the Civilian Conservation Corps, Tucker returned to Alexandria in 1938 and began a sustained assault on the city's Jim Crow system. In particular, Tucker focused on Alexandria's library, located just two blocks from his home. Peeved that the library would not allow him a card and borrowing privileges, Tucker found an accomplice in George Wilson, a retired Army sergeant. On March 17, 1939, Tucker and Wilson entered the public library, where Tucker filled out an application for a card on behalf of Wilson. An assistant librarian informed the pair that the city library board had instructed her "not to issue cards to colored persons." A week later, city librarian Katharine Scoggin, who was not present when Tucker and Wilson applied for the card, confirmed the correctness of her assistant's interpretation. On the job only two months, Scoggin iterated the policies set by her superiors and added that "effort is being made at the present time to provide library service to colored people, but as yet nothing definite has been accomplished."[24]

Records show that the city's library board had indeed discussed the "question of the colored library" as early as March 1937 as the city prepared to open its first public library. Ultimately, however, no steps were taken to provide facilities for Alexandria's black residents. Instead, in August 1937, a new public facility opened its doors to "all persons of the white

Samuel Wilbert Tucker
(ca. 1950) engineered
the 1939 Alexandria
library sit-down strike.
(Courtesy of Stephen J.
Ackerman and the
Tucker Family)

race living in the City of Alexandria and to all persons of the white race
who are taxpayers in Alexandria." In addition, the library allowed whites
who did not live in Alexandria and were not taxpayers to use the facility
for a fee of $1.50 per year. White people who did not live in Alexandria
were allowed access to the new library; black residents and taxpayers were
not.[25]

Just four days before Tucker requested a borrower's card for George
Wilson, the library board renewed its discussions with regard to a facility
for black citizens. No doubt Tucker's efforts spurred city and library officials to a greater sense of urgency. Board members considered several options that included providing books for an expanded library at the black
Parker-Gray School, building an annex to the white library, or erecting
an entirely separate branch. The librarian preferred an annex that would
be open two afternoons and two evenings per week, while the city manager favored a separate building. The Alexandria interracial committee
seconded the library board's preference for an annex but objected to suggestions that a separate entrance be built. While city officials debated the
merits of the various options, Tucker filed suit on Wilson's behalf and
asked the Alexandria Corporation Court to command and compel the
librarian to issue a card to the plaintiff. The *Washington Tribune*, a black

Too Radical for Us

newspaper, acknowledged that plans for a black library were being discussed but opined that in terms of convenience, comfort, or availability of quality books "such accommodations will not be equal to those of white readers."[26]

Although Tucker's advocacy on behalf of George Wilson occurred concurrently with the NAACP's litigation in the Aline Black case, Tucker and Wilson acted entirely on their own and not with the aid of any organization. In fact, Tucker noted years later that Charles Houston had not considered libraries as a place to test segregation statutes. But once Tucker initiated proceedings against authorities in Alexandria, Houston invited the young lawyer to his office in Washington, D.C., to ensure that he prepared the most effective case possible. At a hearing in July, just days after Houston delivered the speech before the NAACP in Richmond that so disturbed Virginius Dabney, Tucker argued that Alexandria's library "was maintained by the taxes of all of the citizens" and that blacks, therefore, "had a right to the use of its facilities." As the city attorney of Alexandria, thirty-one-year-old Armistead Boothe represented the librarian, Katharine Scoggin. Although library rules and regulations barred blacks, no state law or municipal ordinance specifically forbade both races from using the same facility; the 1926 Public Assemblages Act only mandated that the races be segregated within the building. Boothe, therefore, attempted to have Wilson's suit thrown out on a technicality, claiming that the plaintiff had not specifically asserted or proven his citizenship at the time he applied for the card. Tucker objected to the argument as an ill-disguised attempt to sidestep the fundamental issue at the heart of their complaint, namely that Wilson's "right as a bona-fide citizen had been denied to him." While Alexandria's white newspaper covered the facts of the hearing and avoided discussions of its larger significance, the region's black press speculated that "the case, if won, will have far-reaching influence upon other municipal facilities, which are now used exclusively for white residents."[27]

In the wake of the July proceedings, Corporation Court Judge William Woolls withheld a ruling in an attempt to give city and library officials time to figure out how to resolve the matter. Soon thereafter, the city council met in special session and authorized the city manager to prepare a report on the cost and feasibility of erecting a separate branch for black residents. Although the NAACP stepped forward to offer Tucker help at this point, the young attorney apparently kept his own counsel. All too cognizant of what the city's white elites intended to do and not at all interested in a Jim Crow library, Samuel Tucker decided to force a confrontation with white authorities.[28]

On Monday, August 21, 1939, the *Alexandria Gazette* reported that the British were fortifying their coastal defenses as Germany increased pressure on Poland. Hitler spoke only seven miles from the Polish border. A little closer to home, and perhaps less important to the future of the world, renovations were finished at the People's Drug Store, the Alexandria Light Infantry returned from its summer training, and heat and humidity returned after a brief respite. That same day, five young black residents of Alexandria—Otto Tucker, Edward Gaddis, Morris Murray, William Evans, and Clarence Strange, all between the ages of eighteen and twenty-two—entered the public library one at a time and asked for a borrower's card. Rather than leaving when refused, each took a book from the stacks, sat quietly, and read. Meanwhile, a sixth participant—fourteen-year-old Robert Strange, the younger brother of Clarence—ran back and forth between the library and Samuel Tucker's office to update the counselor as events unfolded.[29]

The police eventually arrived and asked the young men to leave. When one of the officers announced the five would be arrested if they did not depart, one of the young men replied, according to the *Washington Tribune*, "Well, we are staying." More than an hour after entering the library, the five were escorted out by police, only to find a crowd of two to three hundred onlookers plus reporters and photographers; a media-savvy Samuel Tucker had thoroughly planned what the newspapers called a "sit-down" strike, a term used widely in the late 1930s to describe labor protests.[30]

Although all parties remained civil and no hint of violence ever arose, the decision to take part in the protest was not easy and required significant courage. In fact, as many as eleven young men initially agreed to participate, but half of them backed out at the last minute, more than likely at the insistence of their parents. Meeting in secret over the course of ten days, Tucker prepared the five protesters to a fault, instructed them what to wear, how to act, and what questions to ask. Each arrived at the library well dressed. When refused a card, the young men politely drew out the librarian until told that cards were not issued to African Americans. At that point, instead of objecting, the young men had been coached by Tucker to "say thank you, go to the stack, pick up a book, any book, and go to the table and sit down and start reading. Next person goes in, and same thing but don't go to the same table, everyone goes to a different table, so they can't be talking to each other." Throughout the entire episode, they remained quiet, orderly, and polite. The Alexandria police responded in a similar manner. According to Samuel Tucker, Morris Murray later remarked that "everything went all so politely, that one would have thought I [Tucker] had also told the police what to do." Apparently one

Too Radical for Us

On August 21, 1939, William Evans, Otto Tucker, Edward Gaddis, Morris Murray, and Clarence Strange (left to right, with an unidentified police officer) were arrested at the whites-only Alexandria library after demanding borrowing privileges. (Used with the permission of the Alexandria Museum of African American Culture)

of the young men, upon being placed under arrest, said "Thank you" and put his book back on the shelf. William Evans remembered being "too afraid at the particular time to do any reading," but Morris Murray later expressed regret that the arrest came when it did because he was enjoying his book and wanted to finish.[31]

Shock, amazement, and general uncertainty pervaded the actions of city and library officials throughout the protest and subsequent court proceedings; the possibility of such defiance simply had not occurred to white Alexandrians. The slow response of the police, as well as their polite handling of the young men, led Samuel Tucker to conclude that city officials "didn't know what in the world to do." When reports arrived at city hall that the protest was under way, officials desperately sought a solution, apparently uncertain what laws, if any, the young men had actually violated. Ultimately, city manager Carl Budwesky gave the order to arrest the protesters on a charge of disorderly conduct.[32]

The five young men appeared the next day before Judge James Reece Duncan in Alexandria's Police Court. Tucker had coached the five so well that preliminary court testimony made it clear that a charge of disorderly conduct would be difficult to sustain. The arresting officers acknowledged that they witnessed "no disorder," prompting Tucker to ask if "they were disorderly because they were black." At the behest of City Attorney Armistead Boothe, who had been out of town the previous day and thus not privy to the decision to arrest the five demonstrators, Judge Duncan postponed the trials one week to allow him time to consider the charge. In its coverage of the proceedings, the *Washington Tribune* prophetically remarked, "It is the belief in Alexandria that the court is marking time on the case until the city council has had time to work out plans for providing colored residents of the city with library facilities."[33]

Soon after the arrests, the library board, whose officers included the city attorney, met in emergency session to discuss the "latest developments." On August 28, a statement credited to the board's president, Mrs. Albert A. Smoot, but drafted by Boothe, appeared in the *Alexandria Gazette*. Emphasizing that it had acted responsibly to meet the needs of Alexandria's black citizens, the board noted that it had raised the possibility of constructing a black library two years earlier, but that "prominent colored citizens" had expressed a greater desire for a boys' club and a community center. Furthermore, the board accepted the city council's verbal pledge to furnish a library for black residents "when the demand arose." In the opinion of the board, however, African Americans in Alexandria had only recently asked for a library, at which time the board and council had renewed discussions on the matter. But before the board had sufficient time to respond, "over-zealous persons" had filed suit.[34]

The response of the library board highlights the assumptions that underlay so much of the ideology that governed the management of white supremacy in Virginia. The members of the board accepted as their responsibility the provision of a library for blacks but clearly believed that they should determine how and when such a facility was built. Consequently, citizens such as Samuel Tucker, who went outside established channels and tried to hasten the process, were branded as "over-zealous." The dual system required by segregation meant that black residents had to choose

Too Radical for Us

between a boys' club, community center, and library; whites in Alexandria certainly never faced such a choice.

When the trials resumed on August 29, the revelation that one of the defendants had hired a white lawyer caused a temporary stir. Unbeknownst to Samuel Tucker, William Evans, the youngest of the defendants, was on probation for an assault conviction. No doubt concerned that his son's record threatened to land him in jail on the most recent charges, Evans's father accepted the aid of his employer, attorney Brooke Howard, who represented William free of charge. Adopting a strategy at odds with Tucker's, Howard asked that Evans's case be called first because he "did not wish his client to be compelled to abide by the decision of any of the other defendants." Under questioning from Howard, Evans testified that he went to the library at the request of Otto Tucker, but that Samuel Tucker had planned the entire demonstration. Howard's attempt to direct responsibility away from Evans and onto the older Tucker prompted Judge Duncan to ask, in a tone reminiscent of the library board's, whether Tucker "did not think that there could have been a more peaceful way" to handle the matter. Tucker reminded the judge that he was not on trial.[35]

Evans's father need not have worried. Neither the prosecutor nor other city officials had any interest in sending the young men to jail. Boothe, who had won election in 1938 with significant black support, understood the weakness of the charges and would have preferred that they had never been brought. In particular, the city attorney recognized that Tucker stood on firm legal ground since no ordinance specifically excluded blacks from the library. Consequently, Boothe first tried to ignore the constitutional issue raised by Tucker and defended the city's action on grounds of custom. When Judge Duncan failed to respond favorably, Boothe found himself in a bit of a jam. No doubt sensing the weakness of his position, and by implication the weakness of segregation itself, Boothe claimed "with much embarrassment" that Virginia had been forced to ratify the Fourteenth Amendment and, therefore, was not bound to recognize its guarantees of due process and equal protection. Although Boothe and Tucker forged a friendship during the course of the trial that deepened over the years, the prosecutor's remark deeply offended Tucker and other African Americans. Clearly aware of the legal flaccidity of his argument, Boothe concluded with a nod to one of the major tenets of managed race relations, arguing that the defendants—and their lawyer—should have taken into consideration the steps being taken by "the proper authorities." The question of disorderly conduct still unresolved, Judge Duncan asked Tucker and Boothe to file briefs relative to a charge of "committing a breach of the peace."[36]

While the two attorneys prepared their responses, black and white citizens of Alexandria discussed the case and its implications. Florence Murray, a columnist for the *Washington Tribune*, noted that the sit-down strike had divided some blacks along generational lines. Older African Americans, explained Murray, worried that "the 'agitation' will bring about bad feeling which might even invite danger," while younger blacks "contend that the justice of the fight for civil rights will hurt no one and will cause the leading white citizens of the town to have more respect for their more than 5,000 colored fellow citizens." Wise, focused, and driven beyond his twenty-six years, Samuel Tucker clearly articulated a strategic vision that resonated with this younger generation.[37]

Boothe and Tucker filed their briefs in mid-September. The city attorney cited case law to support a charge of either disorderly conduct or breach of peace. Tucker, on the other hand, passionately argued that the five young men had a right to be in the library and that no statute prohibited them from exercising that right. Although certainly not known at the time, the briefs submitted by Tucker and Boothe marked the end of judicial proceedings in the sit-down strike. Throughout the fall of 1939, Judge Duncan repeatedly granted continuances, never officially dismissing the charges, but never bringing the matter back before his court.[38]

Meanwhile, in mid-September, Judge William Woolls issued his first ruling in the case of George Wilson's application for a library card. The jurist denied Wilson's petition, accepting Boothe's argument that Wilson had not identified himself as a tax-paying citizen, but he did not rule that Wilson's color excluded him from using the library. In fact, Woolls specifically acknowledged that Wilson was "entitled to use and enjoy the facility of the library." In October, the jurist allowed Wilson to amend his original petition and claim an assertion of citizenship at the time of application.[39]

On January 10, 1940, William Woolls rendered his second and final decision in the Wilson case. The judge again denied the petition on a most dubious technicality, explaining that Samuel Tucker rather than Wilson had filled out the application. At the same time, however, Woolls declared explicitly that since the city council had not provided a separate facility for African Americans, it must allow black citizens and taxpayers to use the white library, as long as they followed the proper application procedures. Blacks and whites both read the decision as evidence that city officials would have to open the doors of the public library to African Americans. Even the *Alexandria Gazette* reported that the decision "seemingly paved the way for colored use of the Alexandria library."[40]

Two days after Woolls's decision, however, the Alexandria City Council dashed such possibilities when it approved funds for a new facility for African Americans. Although the council had discussed the matter for months, the timing of its action could not have been a coincidence. In the wake of Woolls's ruling, an ever-growing number of black citizens applied for borrower's cards and expected to receive them. The library board met twice in emergency session and determined that cards would be issued to black residents, but only for use at the new library, scheduled for completion in March. City manager Carl Budwesky expressed his confidence that African Americans in Alexandria understood that a separate facility was in the "public interest" and would be "willing to wait this short time longer."[41]

For Samuel Tucker, however, the vindication of African American citizenship was not negotiable. The twenty-six-year-old lawyer eloquently denounced the refusal of officials to accept the implications of Woolls's ruling. In a short note to city librarian Katharine Scoggin, Tucker wrote, "I refuse and will always refuse to accept a card to be used at the library to be constructed and operated at Alfred and Wythe Streets." Tucker reiterated his displeasure to city manager Budwesky, explaining that "our position is well fortified by those fundamental rights of the citizen which exist as the basis and foundation of government. Any attempt at segregation contravenes the basic and underlying principle of the common law." In closing, Tucker told the city manager that he and George Wilson "consider the offer of a substitute [card] . . . as adding no more than insult to the injury applicants now suffer through delay—occasioned solely because they are Negroes."[42]

Once challenged by black protesters and by the implications of judicial rulings, white officials in Alexandria moved quickly to build a separate library facility for the city's black residents. Although never equal in terms of its inventory to the white library on Queen Street, the Robert Robinson library opened in April 1940. Reflecting the essence of white paternalism as well as a selective memory, the *Alexandria Gazette* editorialized that "the opening of the Robert Robinson library for the use of colored persons is excellent evidence of the desire and the willingness of Alexandria to be helpful to the race and to assist them in becoming better educated and worth while members of the community." One wonders how long it would have taken for that "desire and willingness" to have manifested itself had Samuel Tucker, George Wilson, and the five young protesters not acted as they did.[43]

Although the black press and many other African Americans hailed the opening of the Robinson library as a "great victory," Samuel Tucker felt otherwise. The young attorney fought for and expected government to serve all its citizenry, black and white alike. He desired nothing less than equal access to the Alexandria library. Consequently, for Tucker, who was sidelined for a month with the flu and thus unable to continue his fight, the city's erection of a separate and unequal structure represented nothing more than a source of "consternation and disgust."[44]

On the surface, Samuel Tucker's crusade to integrate the Alexandria library failed. White elites in Alexandria stalled the court proceedings for months, and in the case of the five young men, indefinitely, until they could figure out how to address the challenge posed by the young civil rights attorney. But, in fact, the events in Alexandria in 1939–40 dealt a blow to the city's paternalistic race relations. No matter how genuinely white elites in Alexandria may have felt a "desire and willingness" to help their black neighbors, they imagined only a world in which they, the white power brokers, controlled that relationship. By the eve of the Second World War, however, Samuel Tucker and African Americans across Virginia and the South had, to paraphrase historian Bryant Simon, broadcast their refusal to endure the slights and humiliations of segregation in silence and instead "announced that they intended to grab hold and not let go of long-denied freedoms."[45]

For L. R. Reynolds, the director of the Virginia Commission on Interracial Cooperation, Tucker's frontal attack on segregation reflected a troubling development in the Old Dominion's race relations. In defending the membership and tactics of his organization, Reynolds told black sociologist Ralph Bunche that the interracial commission based its appeal on moral suasion and the "reasonableness of requests" rather than the lawsuits, pressure, and demands favored by the NAACP and other "radicals." Reynolds expressed particular concern that the young protesters in Alexandria had challenged their exclusion from the library by demonstrating and going to court rather than allowing the local interracial commission "to work out a reasonable solution." But as Tucker undoubtedly understood, Reynolds and other white elites had developed a rather elastic definition of "radical," along with an exceedingly circumscribed conception of "reasonable."[46]

Two years later, as he tendered his resignation from the Virginia CIC in order to take a defense-related job, Reynolds attempted to reconcile his stewardship of interracial cooperation with the increasingly evident frustrations of African Americans. "I have tried," he explained, "to conform to Virginia's way of doing things—quietly and by process of evolution,

Too Radical for Us

rather than revolution." Reynolds acknowledged that such gradual change seemed painfully "slow to those who see and feel the injustice of intolerance and discrimination" and even speculated that the state CIC's executive committee might soon decide that "the time has come when the speed limit should be revised upward." In the meantime, however, Reynolds spoke for the vast majority of white Virginians when he expressed his personal conviction that a speedier course of action would only exacerbate racial tension and animosity.[47]

Throughout the fall of 1939 and into 1940, Reynolds and other white elites looked aghast as African Americans in general, and the NAACP in particular, intensified their attack on white supremacy. In Norfolk, NAACP officials jumpstarted the salary equalization campaign that had fizzled after the school board fired Aline Black. When Thurgood Marshall determined that Black's termination prevented her from continuing as the plaintiff, the NAACP found itself without a litigant. No doubt afraid of losing their jobs as well, Black's peers refused to join the lawsuit until Melvin O. Alston, a commerce teacher at Booker T. Washington High School and the head of the local teachers' association, agreed to become the new petitioner. In February 1940, Circuit Court Judge Luther Way delivered his opinion. Ignoring the issue of unequal pay, the jurist ruled against Alston on the ground that he had waived his right to petition the court when he signed his contract with the school board. In June, however, the Fourth Circuit Court of Appeals reversed Way. Judge John J. Parker, who sat on the panel that overturned Richmond's residential segregation ordinance ten years earlier, wrote on behalf of his colleagues that the fixing of teachers' salaries did constitute state action and that Norfolk's dual, race-based pay scale violated the Fourteenth Amendment. When the U.S. Supreme Court refused to hear the city's appeal, Parker's decision became law and the case was remanded to a lower court for settlement.[48]

When officials in Norfolk proposed to phase in salary equalization over three years, NAACP attorneys urged the Norfolk teachers not to accept the compromise, fearing that the offer was but a tactic to delay implementation of the court's directive. Black leaders Lutrelle Palmer and P. B. Young, on the other hand, spoke in favor of the city's proposal. Palmer, the principal of Newport News's black high school and the president of the Virginia Teachers Association, argued that the settlement provided a precedent that would eventually benefit all black teachers. Young, whom Earl Lewis has described as "always the conservative militant and always pragmatic," suggested that black teachers accept the city's offer, but only in exchange for a new, badly needed, elementary school. The editor of the *Norfolk Journal and Guide*, who himself had been labeled an "agitator" for supporting the equalization suit, recognized the compromise as an opportunity to restore an ethos of civility to the city's race relations.[49]

The decision of black teachers in Norfolk to accept the compromise infuriated Thurgood Marshall. The NAACP's lead attorney on the *Alston* case denounced the timidity of local black leaders and held them responsible for "the most disgraceful termination of any case involving Negroes in recent years." In particular, Marshall worried that the acceptance of the city's offer would dampen the courage of teachers throughout Virginia to file similar suits. Marshall's critique made clear that African Americans in Virginia remained divided over the most effective tactics and strategies to employ in their fight against white supremacy. Some black leaders, like Young and Palmer, remained wedded to civility as the most pragmatic means of accomplishing their ends, while others, such as Samuel Tucker, considered legal rights beyond compromise. The gap between the two camps, however, soon narrowed, especially in the eyes of white elites.[50]

Despite Marshall's concerns, the resolution of Norfolk's salary equalization campaign did not lessen the willingness of African Americans in the Old Dominion to demand equity. Instead, in the wake of the *Alston* decision, lawsuits sprang up all over the state. In the cities of Petersburg, Danville, and Richmond, as well as Chesterfield, Mecklenburg, and Goochland Counties, black lawyers affiliated with the NAACP challenged white authorities to equalize teacher salaries and school facilities. Officials acquiesced in some locales, while judges adjudicated other disputes. Oliver Hill, who trained under Charles Houston at Howard Law School, spent nearly every weekend traveling across Virginia, drumming up community support for the NAACP's campaign. A friend of Samuel Tucker's as an undergraduate and later his law partner, Hill cited the two years prior to America's entrance into the Second World War as the crucible of the Virginia NAACP's frontal assault on white supremacy. In fact, according to Hill, the war served not as a catalyst for the civil rights movement, but rather as a hindrance that interrupted and interfered with work already under way.[51]

If the late 1930s constituted scene one of the first act of the civil rights movement, as historian Adam Fairclough has argued and Oliver Hill's testimony confirms, then the opening act of white southern resistance to change must also be set in these years. For every lawsuit that NAACP attorneys filed and for every assertion of independence that violated the terms of managed race relations, white power brokers and opinion-shapers resisted. Throughout the Old Dominion, officials attempted to forestall additional equalization suits by threatening to postpone the construction of new facilities or the much-needed repairs of old buildings. Nowhere, however, did school authorities contest an equalization suit as ferociously as in Newport News. Not only did that city's school board and superintendent ignore a federal court order for two years until ruled in contempt, but they complied only after terminating the contracts in June 1943 of three black teachers and three black principals, including Lutrelle Palmer.[52]

Irony suffused the decision to fire Palmer. A teacher and principal in Newport News since 1920, Palmer had been considered safe by most whites. In 1939 the *Richmond Times-Dispatch* said as much when it named Palmer to its "honor roll" of distinguished Virginians. As the Virginia Teachers Association began to press for salary equalization in the late 1930s, Palmer reassured the group's membership that "the broad humanitarian sentiment that has been cultivated among the white people of the state" ensured that black teachers would not lose their jobs. Thurgood Marshall's blistering critique of Palmer and P. B. Young, in fact, reflected his own refusal to believe in the authenticity of such sentiment.[53]

Palmer, however, was no sycophant. A pragmatist like Young, the principal of Huntington High School believed that, at the time, he could accomplish more by working within the system of segregation than by attacking it directly. In explaining his educational philosophy, Palmer acknowledged that "we must take frankly into account that the school serves a segregated and underprivileged people who have not yet been admitted to full citizenship." Not satisfied with the status quo, however, Palmer maintained "an unshakable faith in democracy" and remained absolutely committed to overcoming existing barriers. Within the confines of his school, Palmer fought segregation in less obvious, but psychologically important terms. When white residents of Newport News expressed an interest in attending Huntington High athletic events, for example, the principal refused to provide segregated seating. Rather than sit next to black patrons, the interested parties chose to stay home.[54]

That the Newport News school board fired an African American leader of Lutrelle Palmer's temperament signified the extent to which the Second World War radically altered the already shifting terms of interracial cooperation. As the United States entered World War II, white southerners stumbled over themselves to assert their patriotism and to support the war effort. Blacks throughout the South and the nation rallied around the flag with substantial vigor as well but simultaneously pointed to the hypocrisy of fighting for freedom overseas when racial segregation and discrimination remained a way of life at home. Led by A. Philip Randolph of the Brotherhood of Sleeping Car Porters, African Americans threatened to march on Washington, D.C., demanding an end to hiring discrimination in defense-related industries and the abolition of segregation in the armed forces. Although not previously associated with such tactics, the NAACP and Urban League lent their support to the proposed march. Confronted with the possibility of 100,000 black protesters in the nation's capital, Franklin Roosevelt signed an executive order that banned job discrimination in defense industries. Although FDR left untouched the matter of segregation in the military, march leaders declared victory and called off the demonstration.[55]

Such assertiveness on the part of African Americans completely paralyzed Virginius Dabney and a host of other white southerners previously deemed liberal. As rumors of impending interracial violence swirled around Richmond, Dabney expressed alarm at what he termed an "increasingly dangerous situation" and excoriated blacks "to accept that real improvement in race relations can only come by gradual evolution." Mark Ethridge, the publisher of the *Louisville Courier-Journal*, condemned the "all or nothing" attitude of black protesters and warned that "there is no power in the world—not even all the mechanized armies of the earth, Allied and Axis—which could now force the Southern white people to the abandonment of the principle of social segregation." While recognizing the economic benefits that the war effort had bestowed on the South, John Temple Graves warned southern blacks not to fall prey to northern agitators and radicals who promised rapid and momentous social change. "Segregation in the South is not going to be eliminated," insisted the editor of the *Birmingham Age-Herald*. "That is a fact to be faced." In response to what he considered hysterical utterances, NAACP executive secretary Walter White quipped that "the highest casualty rate of the war to date seems to be that of Southern white liberals. For various reasons they are taking to cover at an alarming rate—fleeing before the onslaught of the professional Southern bigots."[56]

In this context, much to the distress of white Virginians, seemingly reliable black leaders questioned the gradualist approach that had governed interracial cooperation in the Old Dominion. P. B. Young encouraged African Americans to support the war but used the pages of the *Norfolk Journal and Guide* to condemn the multiple injustices at the heart of its prosecution. In addition, Young denounced the propensity of Virginius Dabney and like-minded whites to insist on controlling the pace of reform. "This is no time to be conservative," declared Young. "Help us get some of the blessings of democracy here at home first before you . . . tell

Too Radical for Us

us to go forth and die in a foreign land." Wartime developments likewise heightened the expectations of Young's ideological soulmate, Gordon Blaine Hancock. Without specifically calling for the abolition of segregation, the Richmond cleric and sociology professor warned of grave consequences if white elites failed to replace paternalism and its empty promises with a genuine commitment to concrete reform.[57]

Unable to conceive of an alternative to managed race relations, Virginius Dabney struggled to remain relevant by attempting to seize what historian John Kneebone has characterized as "the rational middle ground." With greater frequency and urgency, the editor of the *Richmond Times-Dispatch* identified white extremists and black protesters as equal threats to civic order and insisted that tempered gradualism alone, guided by white elites such as himself, would ensure "the steady progress of the Negro" and prevent an all-out race war. Dabney's concern reflected a devolution in his attitude toward the NAACP and its leadership. The civil rights organization, he felt, played an important and commendable role in improving the lives of African Americans, but only insofar as it proceeded within the confines of segregation. Consequently, as Walter White pointed out, Dabney began "seeing things under the bed" from the moment that Charles Houston announced in June 1939 that the NAACP would be satisfied with nothing less than the full vindication of African American citizenship. What Houston wrought, White's deputy Roy Wilkins embellished when he announced that blacks and whites belonged "on a plane of absolute political and social equality." Beside himself with consternation, Dabney responded with a warning that black agitators and white rabble-rousers threatened to precipitate the "worst internal clashes since Reconstruction, with hundreds, if not thousands, killed and amicable race relations set back for decades."[58]

Dabney's formulation failed to distinguish morally between the nonviolent, legally based aspirations of black protesters and the threat or actual use of force employed by white extremists. But even within the confines of his equation, Dabney assumed different standards of behavior for whites and blacks. The Richmond newsman accepted as inevitable that certain white southerners would react violently to black demands. Consequently, without condoning such violence, Dabney disproportionately blamed African Americans for creating the conditions that threatened to accelerate out of control. Firmly convinced that black leaders ought to retreat from their demands rather than risk bloodshed, Dabney warned African Americans that their assertiveness threatened to drive him and other sympathetic whites "into the opposition camp."[59]

Dabney's proclamation deeply offended long-time black allies such as P. B. Young, a colleague for years on the state interracial commission.

Young angrily challenged Dabney's failure to address the fundamental pressures and inequities under which African Americans labored. "You merely point to alarm and predict violence and bloodshed," Young wrote. "Can't you offer something rational and human which would avert the dire things you predict?" Furthermore, according to the *Norfolk Journal and Guide* editor, Dabney's preoccupation with the potential for violence foreclosed the possibility of genuine advancement for African Americans. In a stinging personal rebuke to Dabney, Young added that "while your language is always cultured and your attitude dignified," in contrast with the coarse language and brutal attitudes of the worst southern demagogues, "the result is the same."[60]

Journalist Thomas Sancton, a white native of New Orleans who moved to New York during the war, attacked Dabney along lines similar to Young's. In particular, Sancton denounced the tendency of Dabney and other white elites to blame all racial tension on black militants and rabidly racist lower-class and working-class whites. As Sancton understood and historian John Kneebone has articulated, white elites in the South regularly employed these bogeymen as an excuse to postpone reform and to allow themselves to maintain the moral high ground. Expressing greater faith in non-elite whites and blacks than the genteel editor of the *Times-Dispatch*, Sancton urged Dabney to direct his message toward a more culpable class of white southerners. Referring specifically to "well-to-do housewives who sit around talking their snide talk" about uppity blacks, Sancton declared that "someone has got to tell these people straight to their faces even though it means insulting them that . . . a change of attitude is damn well demanded of them by virtue of every soldier who is risking and giving his life to keep this country worth living in."[61]

Young and Sancton, in effect, recognized and exposed the fundamental weakness, the inherent limitation, of Dabney's devotion to managed race relations. In articles, editorials, and private correspondence penned throughout the war years, Dabney admitted that racial discrimination was incompatible with democratic ideals. On an intellectual level, he recognized the legitimacy of black grievances, especially given the absolute failure of white southerners to provide equal facilities. Nevertheless, Dabney suffered the same debilitating disease that afflicted the most crass and violent white southerners: he could not free himself from an emotional and ideological attachment to white supremacy. Whenever the legal rights of African Americans came into conflict with the wishes and customs of the white South, Dabney defined himself as a segregationist. Consequently, his brand of southern progressivism—characterized by a repudiation of bigotry and an emphasis on the fairer treatment of blacks—lost credibility;

Dabney lamented in private correspondence that some blacks now derided him as a "pale dishwater liberal."[62]

Traveling ever farther in opposite directions, black and white supporters of the Commission on Interracial Commission made a final attempt to reestablish common ground. In April 1942 Gordon Blaine Hancock led the way when he called upon "white men and women who are not afraid to be called 'Nigger Lovers' and Negroes who are not afraid to be called 'Uncle Toms'" to adopt a new "Southern Charter" that guaranteed African Americans a living wage, equitable educational opportunities, and the right to vote. Over the course of the next six months, Hancock directed a committee of thirteen black Virginians, including P. B. Young, Lutrelle Palmer, and Virginia State College professor Luther P. Jackson, who carefully considered the most effective means of implementing such a blueprint. While agreeing to convene a conference in order to present a slate of demands to white southerners, the organizing committee differed sharply over the composition of delegates. Concerned that white southerners would otherwise dismiss their efforts as the work of northern militants, Hancock successfully urged the committee to limit participation to southern blacks, a decision that led northern blacks and the northern press to vilify Hancock as a lackey for Dabney and other whites.[63]

In the face of intense criticism, fifty-nine black leaders, all but three of them men, gathered in Durham, North Carolina, on October 20 and organized themselves into the Southern Conference on Race Relations. In a statement commonly known as the "Durham Manifesto," the delegates rejected the old terms of racial cooperation as overly "paternalistic and traditional" and "not compatible with the manhood and security of the Negro." Addressing white southerners but also mindful of their northern black critics, conference participants declared themselves "fundamentally opposed to the principle and practice of compulsory segregation." While significant in its total rejection of segregation, the statement did not foreclose the possibility of continued cooperation. In fact, a majority of delegates, again led by Hancock and Young, eschewed an outright assault on Jim Crow and acknowledged a pragmatic willingness to work with white southerners to end segregation gradually. But despite what Hancock's biographer refers to as the "purposeful ambiguity" of the manifesto, southern black leaders iterated in no uncertain terms that they expected white southerners to envision and accept a future devoid of white supremacy.[64]

Most of the white men and women who populated the South's interracial councils, however, ignored this last point and chose to view the declaration as a thoughtful, rational document that contained an implied acceptance of segregation. Relieved to be able to claim that their black colleagues had spoken in such reasonable terms, white interracialists recognized that a constructive response offered the best evidence of their own good faith. Acknowledging the legitimacy of the Durham statement's specific demands, which included an end to the poll tax, greater economic opportunity, equal pay for equal work, and improved housing and educational facilities, whites prepared to convene their own conference in order to issue a formal statement. But after a series of delays postponed the gathering for several months, Hancock began to question the seriousness with which whites approached the task, while P. B. Young warned that further delays might incite a group of blacks in North Carolina who threatened to call a meeting of black leaders from all over the United States.[65]

Finally, on April 8, 1943, nearly six months after the Durham conference, 113 white southerners—mostly newspaper editors, clergy, and educators who supported the CIC—convened in Atlanta. Ambivalence surrounded the convocation, as 80 percent of the 550 invitees failed to show up. Praising the Durham Manifesto as "free from any suggestion of threat and ultimatum," those assembled in Atlanta offered assurance of their "desire to cooperate" in fostering better race relations. Delegates to the Atlanta conference acknowledged that white southerners violated the rights of their black neighbors in multiple ways. They denied, however, that any inherent unfairness plagued the laws that governed the southern states, blaming instead the maladministration of such laws. In conclusion, the delegates reiterated a favorite quodlibet of managed race relations, remarking that future progress depended upon the cooperation of persons of "determined good will" devoted to "evolutionary methods" and not "ill-founded revolutionary movements which promise immediate solutions."[66]

The Atlanta statement eventually received the support of more than three hundred prominent white southerners, including Virginius Dabney and Virginia's wartime governor, Colgate Darden. In effect, the statement allowed signatories to acknowledge that segregation had imposed unfair hardships on African Americans, while simultaneously affirming their belief in the viability of segregation itself. As historian Ray Gavins has noted, supporters of the Atlanta compact, although distinct in their approach and sentiments from the mass of white southerners, "committed themselves to nothing except cultivating an atmosphere of understanding, cooperation, and mutual respect."[67]

Expecting to be met halfway in the wake of the Durham statement, black leaders such as Hancock denounced the moral emptiness of the gesture proffered in Atlanta. In a personal visit with Dabney, Hancock impugned the failure of the Atlanta conferees to at least consider the possibility of a future without segregation. Black leaders in Durham had accepted a gradual dismantling of Jim Crow but left no doubt that the South's statutes and ordinances were, in fact, unjust. Years of experience had taught black southerners that separate could never be equal. The same passage of time, unfortunately, had prepared their white neighbors for no alternative. In fact, referring to the Atlanta meeting, Dabney remarked that "many conservative white people are fearful that such movements as this have the destruction of segregation as an ultimate objective." Rather than accepting the possibility of such change and preparing the white South accordingly, Dabney opted "to allay such fears."[68]

Amid this atmosphere of heightened disappointment and distrust, representatives of the Durham and Atlanta conferences assembled in Richmond in June 1943. Black delegates appeared intent on pushing their white colleagues to act more aggressively; whites, in turn, resented the pressure and their inability to control the agenda. Uneasy with the implications of his own participation, Virginius Dabney declined an offer to preside over the proceedings. In his place, P. B. Young served as chair while Hancock delivered the keynote address. Tired of "counseling patience and the elusive consolations of social evolution," Hancock challenged white interracialists to offer something other than empty promises. Only a genuine manifestation of southern liberalism, he warned, would prevent black southerners from embracing the call of northern black militants.[69]

The implied threat of Hancock's address terrified M. Ashby Jones, a white minister from Atlanta and a founding member of the CIC in 1919. In a tone suffused with paternalism, the Atlanta clergyman cautioned black delegates that they would lose the support of well-intentioned whites if they asked for too much, too soon. Black participants, in turn, objected vociferously. As the Richmond conference teetered on the brink of dissolution, University of North Carolina sociologist Howard Odum sublimated threats of a walk-out by objecting to the tone and substance of Jones's remarks. Odum then prevailed upon the delegates to commit themselves to the establishment of a new regional council that would recognize the "importance of affirmative action, without which we will fall short of our hopes and possibilities." By invoking the need to establish methods and procedures for interracial cooperation in "accord with our professed principles of Christianity and democracy," Odum's resolution deftly acknowledged what the Atlanta statement did not: the possibility of the eventual demise of Jim Crow.[70]

In the aftermath of the chaotic meeting, uncertainty reigned with regard to the viability of continued cooperation. Determined to make clear to white participants that Jones's attitude was "'no longer acceptable,'" Young disavowed his former ally in terms readily applicable to managed race relations as a whole. "'In my estimation,'" wrote the Norfolk editor, "'Dr. Jones is dead and ought to be buried and forgotten.'" For his part, Hancock bristled that "unless white leaders are willing to risk something . . . we are hopelessly lost in a morass of confusion." Meanwhile, Dabney and other increasingly cautious whites fretted over the scope of Odum's new organization. Offered a chance to cochair the planning session, Dabney declined, prompting charges of cowardice from Young. Jessie Daniel Ames, a cic stalwart since the 1920s, worried that black leaders expected more than she was prepared to support. Despite sympathy for Ames's position, Dabney recognized the absolute necessity of maintaining a dialogue with southern black leaders lest they turn to the "'radical Northern leadership of the Walter White caliber.'" Consequently, he decided to join representatives of the Durham and Atlanta conferences who voted in August to establish the Southern Regional Council (src). Adopting a tone similar to that which characterized the Richmond statement, the src dedicated itself to constitutional and democratic guarantees of "equal opportunity" for all African Americans without specifically taking a position on Jim Crow. In November, the cic provided for its own demise, folding its membership and resources into the new council as of January 1, 1944.[71]

As plans were finalized for the establishment of the Southern Regional Council, Virginius Dabney surprised blacks and whites in the South and the North when he urged the commonwealth of Virginia to repeal its laws mandating segregation on common carriers. In an editorial published on November 13 in the *Times-Dispatch*, Dabney argued that wartime conditions had produced "well-nigh intolerable friction" on streetcars and buses in Richmond, Norfolk, Portsmouth, and Newport News. The rationing of fuel and tires, a ban on pleasure driving, and the migration of thousands of newcomers into these cities had, in fact, stretched urban transportation systems to the breaking point, especially during rush hour. Forced to sit or stand in the rear of common carriers, African American riders had to push their way through aisles packed with whites. Instead of keeping the races apart as intended, Dabney explained, this particular segregation statute actually had the opposite effect and had become a "constant source of trouble, irritation, and bad feeling."[72]

To an extent, Dabney recognized and hoped to address what few white southerners cared to understand. As Swedish social scientist Gunnar Myrdal concluded in his massive study of American race relations, *An*

Too Radical for Us

American Dilemma, "It is a common observation that the Jim Crow car is resented more bitterly among Negroes than most other forms of segregation." Black passengers chafed in particular against the often arbitrary enforcement of Jim Crow transportation statutes, which at times appeared to serve only as an incessant and gratuitous reminder of white superiority. Throughout the war, especially as buses and streetcars became more crowded, these slights intensified.[73]

As Dabney prepared his editorial, African Americans such as Sarah Davis increasingly resisted such affronts. A resident of Norfolk whose experience with a white driver proved all too typical, Davis boarded a city bus in June 1943 and occupied the only available seat, located between two white passengers toward the front of the bus. Meanwhile, additional white passengers sat in the back of the bus in seats normally assigned to black riders. The driver ordered Davis to move, and when she asked where she should sit, he replied, "I don't care where you sit, as long as you get up and get on in the back of the bus." At no point did the driver request that one of the white passengers in the rear of the bus exchange seats with Davis, an arrangement that she later testified would have been acceptable to her. Unwilling to move, she was arrested and fined. Davis, however, fought back and appealed her conviction to the Virginia Supreme Court. Ultimately, the commonwealth's highest court issued an opinion whose logic affirmed the essence of managed race relations. Upholding the constitutionality of the state's segregation statutes, the justices simultaneously declared that the driver had enforced the statute in a discriminatory manner. "It is necessary to the validity of segregation statutes," wrote the court, "that there be no discrimination either in their terms or in their enforcement." Although ruling in Davis's favor on the merits of the particular case, the court effectively allowed white Virginians to continue to adhere to the principle of separate but equal. African Americans, on the other hand, understood from experience that such equality remained illusory.[74]

Intent on eliminating the discriminatory application of the state's segregation statutes in order to save the laws themselves, Dabney wrote a second editorial eight days after the first in which he defined the repeal of segregation on common carriers as "the truly conservative course" in race relations. Dabney initially offered his proposal as a simple and logical means of lessening tension, but in his second piece he presented the abolition of Jim Crow on streetcars and buses as absolutely necessary to the continued management of white supremacy. Discussing at length the deliberations that took place in Durham, Atlanta, and Richmond, the editor of the *Times-Dispatch* warned that whites must immediately provide "evidence" of goodwill to black leaders in the South who labored intensively

Virginius Dabney, editor of the *Richmond Times-Dispatch* for more than three decades before his retirement in 1969, at his office (ca. 1940). (Courtesy of the Virginius Dabney Papers [#7690], Albert and Shirley Small Special Collections Library, University of Virginia)

to minimize the influence of radical northerners. "Unless we meet them halfway," he wrote, "it will be difficult, if not impossible, for them to retain control over their people." Dabney urged his readership to recognize that the future of white supremacy required "reasonable concessions," and that the repeal of segregation on common carriers not only would provide such evidence but would constitute the "greatest single step toward race relations taken in any Southern State for decades."[75]

Whether he liked it or not, Dabney's editorials drew the enthusiastic praise of his most caustic critics—militant editors in the North and leaders of the NAACP. Not surprisingly, black leaders in the South added their support. White newspapers in the South, on the other hand, met Dabney's challenge with a chilly silence; only a small paper in Kinston, North Carolina, even bothered to respond. For his part, Douglas Southall Freeman privately expressed his belief that Dabney should not have agitated the issue. Even closer to home, Dabney came under intense pressure from elite women in Richmond who complained to his wife that his proposal had

Too Radical for Us

made it more difficult to control and keep their domestic servants. Politicians throughout the state kept their own counsel, but when the General Assembly convened in January, no one offered a bill to repeal segregation on the state's common carriers.[76]

Hundreds of readers, on the other hand, responded to Dabney's two editorials. The editor admitted that the letters he received did not accurately represent white opinion in Virginia, but he nevertheless felt gratified that whites in favor of his proposal outnumbered opponents three to one. Needless to say, black correspondents were nearly unanimous in their praise. Dabney's supporters, many of them women, interpreted the issue as a matter of basic fairness and emphasized the need to live up to democratic principles, especially while at war with a fascist enemy. Quite a few individuals acknowledged that the war itself had led them to rethink the wisdom and necessity of segregation. Drawing upon several common themes, opponents virulently denounced Dabney. Some argued in what were essentially class terms, asserting that only those who did not depend on public transportation could have supported the proposal. In an editorial note, Dabney refuted such charges and claimed that he rode Richmond's buses and streetcars every day. The most intense feeling came from opponents who accused Dabney of creating an opening wedge that would just as logically lead to the abolition of segregation in other areas and, ultimately, to interracial marriage.[77]

No doubt aware that he negotiated uncertain terrain, Dabney felt the need to defend himself against such charges. Reiterating that he favored the abolition of segregation on common carriers only because the laws no longer functioned as intended, Dabney insisted that "the *Times-Dispatch* is not advocating the repeal of any of these laws except those covering urban streetcars and busses." In fact, Dabney warned his readers that the greatest threat to segregation was not his proposal, but the general failure of white southerners to accept their own responsibilities with a sense of purpose. "There can be no conceivable moral or legal justification for our dual system, under a democratic government, unless *absolutely equal facilities are provided for both races*," the editor concluded. "The whole series of hateful oppressions which segregation has come to connote must not be allowed to continue one day longer than necessary."[78]

In a private exchange with Louis Jaffé, Dabney expanded on these themes in terms that hint at the deepest motivations behind his editorial campaign. Without professing an ideological attachment to segregation, the editor of the *Norfolk Virginian-Pilot* conveyed to Dabney his own determination that segregation on common carriers "ought to be terminated as soon as practicable." Jaffé looked forward to the day when that might occur but concluded that segregation on streetcars and buses could not yet be abolished peacefully. Dabney defined pragmatism in different terms. Not only did he accept the abolition of Jim Crow on buses and streetcars as a practical means of alleviating tension, he did so precisely to protect the legitimacy of segregation as an organizing ideology. Dabney recognized that a failure to affirm segregation's compatibility with democratic values and principles meant that "it is just as logical to argue against it in the public schools," a possibility that had preoccupied Dabney, much to his horror, ever since Alice Jackson applied for admission to the University of Virginia. In attempting to show his black neighbors that "we are not stalling them off with nothing but fine words," Dabney undoubtedly recognized and embraced an opportunity to repair the damage done to his reputation during the war years. But of greater concern to Dabney, his editorial campaign against Jim Crow transportation constituted a plea to the white South to cut its losses, retrench, and protect what remained most important: segregation in the schools.[79]

Epilogue

> I can remember [my grandfather] speaking of something
> and saying, "Before they Jim Crowed us." . . . So at an early
> age I knew it had not always been this way. Segregation was
> not God-ordained.—SAMUEL WILBERT TUCKER, 1979

In 1944, at the height of a distinguished public life in which he served as a
congressman, governor, and president of the University of Virginia, Colgate Darden met with P. B. Young to discuss a plan to create regional institutions of higher learning for African Americans; the proposal had been
devised by whites to bring the southern states into compliance with the
Supreme Court's *Gaines* decision without incurring the prohibitive costs
associated with the establishment of separate institutions in each state. As
Virginia's governor at the time, Darden had a particular interest in finding
an affordable solution that in no way threatened segregation. As a prac-
titioner of managed race relations, he depended upon black leaders like
Young to lend their support. But as Darden remembered their exchange,
Young calmly and without rancor informed him that "none of that is going
to satisfy us. What we are against is segregation, and we are never going
to come to terms with anything that maintains it."[1]

Young's retort stunned Darden. Not until that moment did Virginia's
chief executive comprehend the depth and intensity of African American dissent. Although more thoughtful than most of his contemporaries,
Darden had failed to recognize that blacks who abided by the terms of
managed race relations throughout the 1920s and into the 1930s did so for
tactical and pragmatic reasons. He admired Young for his emphasis on

goodwill, civility, and gradualism and mistakenly believed that he understood Young's aspirations and temperament. Thus reassured about the management of white supremacy in the Old Dominion, Darden never imagined that reasonable black leaders such as Young would completely repudiate segregation. "It didn't occur to me that it would ever be a matter that I would have to give any consideration in my lifetime," he recalled years later. "I projected that ahead some centuries."[2]

As governor, Darden had exhibited a genuine commitment to justice and an interest in the lives of the state's black citizens. Soon after his inauguration in January 1942, he agreed to consider a commutation request from Odell Waller, a black sharecropper sentenced to death in 1940 for killing his white landlord after the landlord attempted to cheat Waller out of his share of the wheat harvest. No one questioned that Waller killed the landlord, but conflicting testimony suggested that he might have acted in self-defense. Nevertheless, an all-white jury sentenced him to death. Enough doubt persisted, however, that Darden's predecessor stayed the execution to allow for an appeal. Eventually Waller's case garnered national attention, as an example of some of the inequities inherent in the southern criminal justice system. Although Darden ultimately refused the petition and Waller was executed in July 1942, the governor generally earned plaudits for methodically reviewing the evidence in a case that few expected him to consider at all.[3]

On the surface, Darden's handling of the matter appeared consistent with his commitment to managed race relations; his willingness to review Waller's appeal was sufficient to ensure that he appeared fair without actually having to overturn the death sentence. At least one contemporary observer, however, surmised that the governor had ultimately been swayed less by a sense of fairness than by "his resentment of the broad interest in the case, which brought Virginia's system of justice and his own role under public scrutiny." In his statement denying a commutation, Darden gave little attention to the significant support that Waller received from Virginians, black and white; instead, the governor emphasized that a false and slanderous propaganda campaign directed from outside the state "'had been carried on without any regard to the facts in this case.'" Darden warned that such distortions were bound "'to sow racial discord at a critical time when every loyal citizen should strive to promote unity.'" Long a staple of white southern resistance to change, such denunciations of outsiders and northerners as unnecessarily meddling in the South's race relations soon assumed an added urgency.[4]

On balance, Darden's consideration of the Waller case enhanced his image among black Virginians. The governor earned further praise several months later when he accepted an invitation to meet with black leaders in Norfolk, an offer extended to every new chief executive but routinely refused in the past. At the meeting, Darden listened attentively and gave assurances that he, too, recognized the need to improve black living conditions and access to meaningful work. The following spring Darden signed the Atlanta Statement, the only governor and the highest profile white southerner to do so.[5]

Darden's concern for blacks, however, always remained bound by his commitment to segregation. The decision of black leaders in Norfolk in the fall of 1942 not to directly discuss segregation affirmed for Darden the wisdom of his approach to managed race relations. The ambiguous language of the Atlanta Statement served much the same purpose. P. B. Young's repudiation of Jim Crow finally forced Darden to acknowledge that a crisis of paternalism had undermined the essence of managed race relations, while simultaneously reinforcing the need for such relations. Unable to imagine that segregation itself was wrong, Darden reacted to Young's announcement with a heightened emphasis on the need for immediate and genuine equalization in all aspects of civic life. Certainly, reasoned Darden, Young did not object to segregation but to the inequality and discrimination that so pervaded it in practice. In public and private, Darden urged Virginians to recognize that for too long segregation had been used not to separate, "but to act as a shield for exploitation and oppression." Darden returned to this theme repeatedly over the course of the next decade, never wavering from his belief that segregation need not be discriminatory.[6]

The luxury of time, however, was not available to Darden and other white elites. For too long, segregation had entailed outright exclusion for African Americans; professions of goodwill had resulted in few schools, parks, playgrounds, or jobs, and housing conditions remained subhuman. By 1944, the ever-cautious Young had grown tired of waiting for the substantiation of African American citizenship. Simultaneously, Gordon Blaine Hancock expressed his own impatience when he contributed to a compendium of essays entitled *What the Negro Wants*, a volume in which fourteen black writers unanimously condemned segregation and, in effect, renounced managed race relations. The unequivocal stand taken by the authors so troubled the publisher of the collection, W. T. Couch of the University of North Carolina Press, that he appended an introduction in which he defended segregation and praised those African American leaders of a previous generation who accepted the inevitability of the dual system. Virginius Dabney, among others, praised Couch's essay and regretted that African Americans now appeared of one mind on the issue.[7]

The evolution of Young and Hancock toward an open rejection of segregation signaled the denouement of managed race relations. Throughout the 1920s and early 1930s, black leaders in Virginia accepted a certain level of white control as the necessary price of economic and educational uplift. But in the late 1930s and 1940s, urged on by a younger generation of activists, black Virginians developed new strategies that centered on political and legal challenges to the cancerous inequities of white supremacy. In Norfolk, the NAACP won a landmark salary equalization case. In Alexandria, Samuel Tucker directly challenged the constitutionality of segregation itself. In Richmond, African Americans helped defeat mayor Fulmer Bright in 1940 and then elected Oliver Hill to the city council eight years later. This new course did not evolve overnight, and all African Americans were not immediately supportive; nevertheless, each assertion of independence further eroded the ability of white elites to manage race relations on their own terms.[8]

The walls of white supremacy did not come crumbling down with the end of managed race relations. The commonwealth's governing class remained firmly in control of all electoral, lawmaking, and budgetary functions. Black political power remained relatively insignificant throughout the state, and African Americans continued to live in poorer neighborhoods and attend far inferior schools. But without the assent of black Virginians, the middle ground long claimed by white elites such as Colgate Darden and Virginius Dabney evaporated. White proponents of managed race relations found themselves on the defensive, under attack not only from critics in the North, but also from a new generation of southerners committed to the radical notion that segregation in any guise was not compatible with essential principles of democracy and human equality.

Grounded in the activities of the NAACP, the Southern Conference for Human Welfare, the Southern Negro Youth Congress, and other organizations shunned or at least kept at arm's length by practitioners of managed race relations, a "new southern liberalism," as Patricia Sullivan has written, began to take hold during the Second World War. By the time the war drew to a close, these new southern liberals openly rejected the gradualist approach favored by Dabney, Darden, and their cohort. No white southerner expressed this point of view as powerfully as did author Lillian Smith. Writing in the *New Republic*, Smith ignored the politicians and the majority of white southerners who predictably opposed any meaningful steps toward equality for African Americans. Instead, she condemned the silence and ambivalence of white southerners who supported a better deal for blacks but continued to defend segregation. "I cannot endure the idea so many liberals hold that segregation must change slowly," Smith wrote. "I believe it can change as rapidly as each of us can change his own heart." Labeling white supremacy a disease that distorted and crippled the personalities of all southerners, black and white, Smith wondered if, in fact, many sympathetic whites hoped its eradication "will take a long time—*because we do not know what we shall do* with our own fears and hates when we can no longer take them out on the Negro or on some other scapegoat."[9]

The themes so eloquently put forward by Smith resonated with the editor of the *Flat Hat*, the student newspaper at William and Mary College in Williamsburg. In February 1945 senior Marilyn Kaemmerle stunned faculty, trustees, and alumni of the college when she wrote on the occasion of Abraham Lincoln's birthday that emancipation remained a job only "half-done." Leaving no doubt as to the importance of war-related rhetoric in reconfiguring notions of freedom, justice, and citizenship, the native of Michigan implored whites to educate "ourselves away from the idea of White Supremacy, for this belief is as groundless as Hitler's Nordic Supremacy nonsense. We are injuring our personalities with arrogance, we are blocking our own emotional growth. Not until we eliminate Nazi race tactics in our own everyday life can we hope for a victory which will bring peace." Rejecting the assumption of superiority that guided white attitudes toward blacks, Kaemmerle opined in the *Flat Hat* that "Negroes should be recognized as equals in our minds and hearts. For us, this means that Negroes should attend William and Mary; they should go to our classes, participate in college functions, join the same clubs, be our roommates, pin the same classmates, and marry among us."[10]

A handful of faculty and most of the student body defended Kaemmerle. Even southern students most offended by her words tended to recognize her right to freedom of speech. Most white southerners, on the other hand, did not hear Kaemmerle when she added that her suggestions "cannot and should not be done today, or tomorrow—but perhaps the next day." Instead, most whites responded only to her advocacy of integration and intermarriage. Telegrams denouncing Kaemmerle's perfidy flooded in from around the state and region. Without delay, the school's trustees ordered the administration to take control of student publications. Merchants in Williamsburg threatened to withhold advertising if Kaemmerle remained in her post. Rumors abounded that heavy-handed state political leaders, with the assent of Harry Byrd, had discussed cutting the college's appropriations. Bowing to intense pressure as the incident garnered national attention, college president John Pomfret dismissed Kaemmerle from her post and forced students to accept faculty supervision of future publications.[11]

As he had done consistently ever since Alice Jackson applied to the University of Virginia a decade earlier, Virginius Dabney recoiled from any suggestion that left open the possibility of interracial marriage. Terming Kaemmerle's editorial "a juvenile and ill-considered outburst" certain to do "immense harm to the course of better race relations," Dabney wrote in the *Richmond Times-Dispatch* that "while Miss Kaemmerle was evidently laboring under the delusion that she was furthering the cause, what she actually did, when she advocated ultimate intermarriage between whites and blacks, was to place a serious hazard in the way of interracial progress." Furthermore, added Dabney, in language that echoed Colgate Darden's response to the Waller case, Kaemmerle's editorial offered proof that nonnative southerners lacked "sufficient understanding of interracial problems to contribute to their solution." The *Norfolk Journal and Guide* responded that Kaemmerle had spent four years in Williamsburg and could not be dismissed as an outsider just because she advocated a more progressive conception of race relations.[12]

An ever-widening gulf separated individuals such as Lillian Smith and Virginius Dabney and clouded the initial deliberations of the Southern Regional Council. Dabney in particular attempted to move the src toward an explicit acceptance of segregation. An uneasy truce reigned as the src declined to commit itself one way or the other, a decision that pleased no one. Smith refused to join the organization so long as it tolerated segregation. African Americans such as Young and Hancock expressed profound disillusionment and questioned the sincerity of their white colleagues. Uncomfortable with the implications of continued involvement, whites such as Jessie Daniel Ames retreated to the sidelines, bringing to an end more than two decades of interracial activism. Also wary of the influence of new southern liberalism, Dabney nevertheless retained his membership, ever fearful that militant black leaders stood ready to step into the breach if the best southern whites and blacks did not work together.[13]

As the src struggled to determine its course, Dabney assumed an increasingly defensive posture. Writing for a national audience, he again warned outsiders against undue interference in the South's affairs. Dabney insisted that southerners such as himself considered it a top priority to eliminate racial injustice, but not at the risk of offending the pride or incurring the wrath of the region's whites. Such change, he argued, had to be handled delicately and from within. Not surprisingly, Dabney objected vociferously to the October 1947 findings of President Harry Truman's Committee on Civil Rights. Although the committee's report acknowledged that constitutional restrictions limited the reach of the federal government in the enforcement of civil rights, it nevertheless undermined the legitimacy of the South's dual system. Stressing the failure of the separate but equal doctrine, the report concluded that "there is no adequate defense of segregation" and called for the "elimination of segregation . . . from American life." To this end, the committee recommended the passage of federal laws aimed at the eradication of lynching and the poll tax, as well as the abolition of segregation in the armed services, on interstate transportation, and throughout Washington, D.C. Once a proponent of a federal antilynching statute, Dabney no longer considered such legislation necessary. On record as opposed to the poll tax, the editor of the *Times-Dispatch* insisted that such matters be left to the states.[14]

The release of the report ensured that civil rights, or, more precisely, white opposition to civil rights, dominated southern discourse in 1948. William Tuck, Darden's lieutenant governor and his successor as chief executive, responded with a legislative initiative designed to keep Truman's name off the ballot in Virginia. The Democratic State Central Committee supported Tuck's effort and unanimously adopted a resolution that condemned the president's efforts to "abolish the barriers of segregation and social division recognized by the leaders of both races to be most conducive to the maintenance of peaceable and friendly relations between the races."[15]

As he waited for the Virginia legislature to respond formally to the resolution, Douglas Southall Freeman revealed the extent to which his views and attitudes about race had remained essentially fixed for two decades. Throughout his professional career, Freeman had expressed satisfaction with Virginia's management of white supremacy. In the late 1920s, Freeman objected to a residential segregation ordinance because he knew it would not pass constitutional muster and would only serve to heighten friction. As an alternative, he offered "separation by consent" as the most effective means of maintaining the racial status quo. Twenty years later, in a nod to the South's critics, Freeman acknowledged that white Virginians and white southerners had failed to meet their responsibilities. The editor of the *Richmond News Leader* for more than thirty years, Freeman explained that "whites must be prepared to pay for their insistence on separate schools and separate transportation. The equality must be real, and if real, it will be expensive."[16]

Despite such recognition, Freeman urged African Americans to forgo legal challenges and instead "to trust to the processes of time and to the triumph of fair play in the human heart" for the redress of their grievances. Whatever the shortcomings of the white South, white elites expected blacks to wait patiently and, if necessary, to wait some more. In fact, no sooner had Freeman acknowledged the failings of the white South than he urged blacks to "reconcile themselves to the fact that segregation is not going to be abandoned in schools or in transportation, and that the line is to be drawn as strictly as ever between civil rights and social privilege." Freeman warned with chilling foresight that the white South would "obstruct to the utmost" any attempt to force the issue.[17]

The white South's inability and unwillingness to meet even the minimum responsibilities it set for itself, however, had eroded any possibility of consent on the part of African Americans. As Gordon Blaine Hancock iterated in a devastating attack on Virginius Dabney, white inaction and mistreatment had left blacks with no choice but "to sue for everything." And sue they did. By 1948, equalization cases clogged the dockets of Virginia's courts. The gross inferiority of African American schools proved all the more untenable given the emergence of education as the most important, debated, and talked about political issue in the state after 1945. Pressured by parents and children of both races to improve the quality of education, state and local officials struggled frantically to comply within the confines of a dual system. One of the more desperate, and unworkable, solutions entailed black teachers and students swapping schools with white teachers and students. Not surprisingly, white parents and students exhibited little enthusiasm for that suggestion.[18]

Meanwhile, African Americans used the federal courts to further chip away at the edifice of white supremacy. In June 1950 the U.S. Supreme Court ruled unanimously in *Sweatt v. Painter* that a Texas law school for blacks, hastily established to meet the Court's edict in *Gaines v. Canada*, did not satisfy the statutory requirement to provide a facility equal to the law school for white students. While the Supreme Court did not specifically strike down segregation in graduate and professional schools, it achieved as much by setting an unattainable standard for equalization, announcing that such difficult-to-measure features as alumni prestige, faculty reputation, and tradition would henceforth be taken into consideration.[19]

Within weeks of the Supreme Court's decision in *Sweatt v. Painter*, Gregory Swanson applied for admission to the University of Virginia's law school. Colgate Darden, the president of the university since 1947, and law school dean F. D. G. Ribble both recognized that the ruling in *Sweatt* had eliminated any reasonable justification for denying admission to Swanson. While both men privately expressed a willingness to accept the inevitable, alumni and state legislators exerted intense pressure to maintain an all-white student body. Ultimately, the Board of Visitors, who had final say in the matter, chose not to incur the wrath of either group, both of which provided critical sources of funding. Specifically citing the state constitution's prohibition against racially mixed schools, the board denied Swanson's application. In effect, the Board of Visitors insulated the university against the recriminations of angry alumni and legislators by forcing the courts to settle the matter. In early September, Judges John Paul, John Parker, and Morris Soper of the Fourth Circuit Court of Appeals did just that; Gregory Swanson entered the University of Virginia later that month without incident.[20]

In the wake of Swanson's matriculation, Darden addressed an annual gathering of southern governors. Drawing a sharp distinction between elementary and secondary education, on the one hand, and professional and graduate education on the other, Darden accepted limited integration in graduate and professional schools as the only practical means of complying with Supreme Court mandates. Certainly, the former chief executive reasoned, southern states could not absorb the exorbitant cost of creating separate graduate schools for a handful of black applicants, especially when the Supreme Court had set increasingly strict standards for equalization. Darden also urged the South's governors to recognize the absolute necessity, and more pressing concern, of providing meaningful and immediate equalization in order to maintain segregation in the elementary and secondary schools. Segregation, he reiterated, had for too long served as an excuse to humiliate and exploit blacks. A failure on the part of white southerners to tax themselves to pay for an equitable dual system, he warned, would lead to federal intervention.[21]

As Darden and other whites throughout the Old Dominion and the South awoke to the realization that only a thorough commitment to equalization could head off integration, the NAACP switched tack and challenged segregation itself. Throughout the 1930s and 1940s, the NAACP had won a series of court rulings that challenged the constitutionality of inequality in graduate and professional schools without attacking segregation directly. But after the *Sweatt* ruling in 1950, the civil rights organization decided to cease filing equalization suits and to seek instead the abolition of segregation in the public schools at all levels, from graduate and professional to secondary and elementary. In the spring of 1951, NAACP attorneys in Virginia initiated proceedings against the school board of Prince Edward County, one of five suits from around the South ultimately bundled together into *Brown v. Board of Education*. Virginius Dabney's greatest fear, so clearly articulated more than a decade before in his response to Charles Houston, had come to fruition.[22]

Attorneys for the Prince Edward school board understood implicitly that Colgate Darden—sincere, thoughtful, well respected by both blacks and whites, a former governor, and leading educator—represented their best hope to defend the validity of segregation. When the case came before a panel of federal district court judges, Darden appeared as the key witness for the defendants. In his testimony, Darden spoke in the deeply paternalistic language so central to managed race relations, never conceiving of the issue in terms of the constitutional rights of Virginia's black citizens but rather in terms of what benefits whites were willing to grant to blacks. The former governor deplored the horrid conditions of the black schools in Prince Edward County and insisted that whites had not only the capacity but an obligation to provide equal opportunities to black students. He refused to accept, however, that segregation itself guaranteed discrimination; instead, Darden expressed publicly his belief that a dual system could be made equal, and that such a system served the best interests of both races.[23]

In response to the NAACP's shift in strategy, the Southern Regional Council finally ended its eight-year dance of ambiguity. Late in 1951, as lawyers for the NAACP and Prince Edward County prepared their arguments, the SRC acknowledged what Colgate Darden could not: that segregation and equality were not compatible. In a statement of policy and aims entitled "Toward the South of the Future," the SRC specifically pledged itself to the creation of a South "where segregation will be recognized as a cruel and needless penalty on the human spirit, and will no longer be imposed; where, above all, every individual will enjoy a full share of dignity and self-respect, in recognition of his creation in the image of God." Without hesitation, Virginius Dabney resigned from the SRC, unwilling to lend his support to an organization that openly repudiated segregation. Dabney's tortured ordeal, to paraphrase historian John Kneebone, had finally come to an end.[24]

Soon thereafter, a more circumspect Colgate Darden submitted his own resignation to the council. Writing to SRC executive director George Mitchell in July 1953, Darden acknowledged yet again that for too long segregation had been used "as a shield for discrimination and oppression. For this there is no justification or excuse." Nevertheless, he remained firmly opposed to the abolition of segregation, especially in the primary and secondary schools. A decent man who cared genuinely about the welfare of the commonwealth's citizenry, Darden tragically lacked the insight, or the courage, to free himself from the confines of his heritage. Darden continued to insist that the South could eliminate discrimination and provide "an equality of opportunity" while remaining segregated, yet he knew perfectly well that white southerners lacked the will or inclination to do so.[25]

Less than a year after Darden's resignation from the src, the U.S. Supreme Court delivered its opinion in *Brown v. Board of Education*. In ruling that racial segregation in public education did indeed violate the Fourteenth Amendment's guarantee of equal protection, the Court rejected the concept of managed race relations championed by Darden and so many white southerners. Political leaders in Virginia scrambled to devise a response. Governor Thomas Stanley actually called black leaders, including P. B. Young and Oliver Hill, to the state capitol and asked them to ignore the Supreme Court's ruling. Stanley hoped that these black leaders would urge African Americans around the state to abide by the state's segregation laws. While Stanley's request may have made sense in the context of managed race relations in which whites dictated the pace of change, black leaders such as Young had repudiated the paternalistic bargain a decade before and had no intention of negotiating away the hard-won recognition of their citizenship.[26]

Stanley eventually appointed a panel dominated by the state's most conservative legislators, most of whom hailed from the Southside counties with the highest concentration of African Americans, to consider the matter. After a year of mostly behind-the-scenes maneuvering, the Gray Commission, named for its chairman, put forward a plan with two essential features. The first called for local option, a device intended to meet the Supreme Court's review by allowing minimal integration in certain parts of the state while ensuring the indefinite perpetuation of segregation in any community or locale that chose not to integrate. As a safety valve, the Gray plan also recommended that the electorate amend the state constitution to allow for tuition grants that would enable public funds to be used for private education by families who objected to sending their children to integrated schools.[27]

Ultimately unwilling to accept even token integration, Virginia's political leadership jettisoned local option and followed Harry Byrd down a path of massive resistance. In the summer of 1956, the state legislature adopted a series of school-closing laws that required the governor to close any school that enrolled even a single black student. The key provision passed the state senate by a vote of twenty-one to seventeen; that the seventeen votes represented a larger percentage of the state's population than the twenty-one underscores the extent to which malapportionment and rural overrepresentation influenced Virginia's political response to *Brown*. With the eyes of the South and the nation on the Old Dominion, federal judges responded to NAACP suits in the fall of 1958 and ordered black students into white schools in Norfolk, Charlottesville, and Warren County. Virginia chose to close the affected schools rather than integrate; nearly 13,000 white students went without public schooling for the next few months.[28]

While Virginia's massive resistance laws reflected the disproportionate political power of rural interests, most white elites in the state's urban areas initially went along or, at best, remained silent. Few white elites in Virginia embraced the position taken by the *Norfolk Virginian-Pilot*, the only major white newspaper in the state that urged compliance with the *Brown* decision from the outset. Louis Jaffé had died in 1950, but Lenoir Chambers proved himself an able successor as he characterized the Supreme Court ruling as a "'superb appeal to the wisdom, intelligence, and leadership of the Southern States'" and expressed his hope that Virginia would "'rise to leadership in the probably long and difficult task.'" When the state chose an alternative course, Chambers denounced massive resistance and ultimately won a Pulitzer Prize for his stand. The *Richmond News Leader* staked out the other end of the ideological spectrum. Douglas Southall Freeman had also died, four years after turning over the helm of the *Richmond News Leader* to James J. Kilpatrick in 1949. Young and ambitious, Jack Kilpatrick attached his fortunes to the mighty Byrd machine and implored the white South to interpose its will against the faulty logic of "'that inept fraternity of politicians and professors known as the United States Supreme Court.'" Kilpatrick championed resistance until the end.[29]

The very whites who most enthusiastically embraced managed race relations found themselves caught between their own devotion to segregation and an eventual recognition of the legal futility of continued resistance. Openly critical of the *Brown* decision, Virginius Dabney simultaneously urged compliance with the law while supporting efforts to delay and circumvent its implementation, so long as such efforts remained legal and nonviolent. Consequently Dabney, like Colgate Darden, supported the Gray plan. Both men, on the other hand, considered massive resistance a futile course of action but did little to oppose it. The editor of the *Times-Dispatch* claimed later in his life that his publisher, who thoroughly supported massive resistance, constrained his ability to speak out editorially. More than likely, however, Dabney himself remained deeply conflicted. He recognized the idiocy of further resistance yet could not accept the implications of the Supreme Court's rulings. Referring to integration as the first step toward intermarriage and one likely to induce "turmoil, conflict, and even chaos" in the educational system, Dabney defended Virginia's course to a national audience just weeks prior to the school closings in the fall of 1958. Consistent in his abhorrence of even the threat of violence, Dabney insisted that massive resistance was not an invitation to violence but, in fact, a "legal, peaceful, and honorable" alternative to the disorder certain to accompany integration.[30]

Not until 1959, when federal and state courts ruled Virginia's school-closing laws unconstitutional, did Dabney and most urban white elites move gradually toward accepting the inevitability of mixed schools. Prominent urban businessmen and lawyers, including future Supreme Court justice Lewis F. Powell Jr., did play an important role in moving Virginia governor J. Lindsay Almond Jr. away from his embrace of massive resistance. But these business elites, the very people who stood to gain the most from managed race relations, remained silent until the eleventh hour, unwilling to challenge the state's political hierarchy. Even when they did inject themselves into the debate, these elites did so in order to protect the state's reputation—an absolute necessity for continued industrial development—rather than out of any commitment to justice for African Americans. Consequently, even after Virginia retreated from massive resistance in 1959, dominant whites made sure that integration proceeded at a glacial pace. White elites in Virginia, however, could no longer presume to speak for their black neighbors. Blacks throughout Virginia and the South understood all too well what Martin Luther King Jr. so eloquently recognized in his "Letter from Birmingham City Jail": "[T]he Negro's great stumbling block in his stride toward freedom is not the White Citizens' Councilor or the Ku Klux Klanner, but the white moderate, who is more devoted to 'order' than justice; who prefers a negative peace which is the absence of tension to a positive peace which is the presence of justice." It is hard to imagine a more fitting epitaph for managed race relations.[31]

Thirty years after the Supreme Court outlawed segregation in the nation's public schools, Virginius Dabney referred to massive resistance as an "aberration" from Virginia's history of good race relations. The response of the commonwealth's leaders and white citizens, he wrote, "was untrue to its heritage." But Dabney knew as well as anyone that massive resistance was not an aberration at all. No matter how often white elites in Virginia disavowed racial violence or affirmed their affinity and professed their goodwill for their black neighbors, they remained deeply committed to white supremacy. John Powell and Walter Plecker represented the most extreme manifestation of white supremacy in the Old Dominion, but their essential message resonated with a majority of white Virginians. As long as whites controlled the pace and extent of change without interference, they "could be remarkably friendly," as Adam Fairclough has written. Some whites even took the responsibilities of managed race relations quite seriously. But when African Americans rejected the terms of managed race relations, as they did in Virginia with heightened intensity from the late 1920s on, their supposed white friends proved less accommodating. Afraid of the future, white Virginians clung to a system ordained by them alone and in the process gave the lie to the myth of racial harmony and goodwill in the Old Dominion.[32]

Notes

The following abbreviations are used throughout the notes.

AG	*Alexandria Gazette*
BEP	Harry Flood Byrd Sr. Executive Papers, LVA
DSF	Douglas Southall Freeman
DSFP-LC	Douglas Southall Freeman Papers, LC
DSFP-UVA	Douglas Southall Freeman Papers, UVA
ELT	E. Lee Trinkle
GBH	Gordon Blaine Hancock
HFB	Harry Flood Byrd Sr.
HFBP	Harry Flood Byrd Sr. Papers, UVA
JCW	Jennings Cropper Wise
JCWP	Jennings Cropper Wise Papers, VHS
JEG	James E. Gregg
JP	John Powell
JPP	John Powell Papers, UVA
LC	Library of Congress, Washington, D.C.
LIJ	Louis Isaac Jaffé
LIJP	Louis I. Jaffé Papers, UVA
LVA	Library of Virginia, Richmond
NAACP-LC	National Association for the Advancement of Colored People Papers, LC
NAACP-Mfm.	National Association for the Advancement of Colored People Papers, microfilm
NJG	*Norfolk Journal and Guide*
NVP	*Norfolk Virginian-Pilot*
RDMPC	Records of the Virginia Division of Motion Picture Censorship, LVA
RJB	Ralph J. Bunche
RJBP	Ralph J. Bunche Papers, Charles E. Young Research Library, University of California at Los Angeles
RNL	*Richmond News Leader*
RTD	*Richmond Times-Dispatch*

SWT   Samuel Wilbert Tucker
TEP   E. Lee Trinkle Executive Papers, LVA
UVA   Albert and Shirley Small Special Collections Library, University of Virginia, Charlottesville
VD   Virginius Dabney
VDP   Virginius Dabney Papers, UVA
VHS   Virginia Historical Society, Richmond
WAP   Walter A. Plecker
WSC   Walter Scott Copeland
WT   *Washington Tribune*

INTRODUCTION

1 DSF to William T. Reed, Mar. 26, 1929, section 1, William T. Reed Family Papers, VHS.
2 Ibid. (quotation); "Separation by Consent," *RNL*, May 20, 1930, 8.
3 Heinemann, *Depression and New Deal*, 1–2; "Not the Virginia Way," *RNL*, Feb. 9, 1926, 8; "In the Virginia Way," *RNL*, Feb. 26, 1926, 8; "This Is Not Like Virginia," *RNL*, Sept. 4, 1926, 8; Key, *Southern Politics*, 19–35 (quotation on 32 n. 11). Key notes that blacks in Virginia also believed that governance should be left to the upper classes (35). On the more physically oppressive kind of race relations found elsewhere in the South, see McMillen, *Dark Journey*, and Hale, *Making Whiteness*.

   As both a term and a concept, "paternalism" has been used to describe a wide range of behaviors and attitudes. At its core, paternalism entails a belief in the social, cultural, intellectual, emotional, and often racial superiority of one individual or group who presumes to act in the best interest of another individual or group in exchange for the subordinate party's compliance. Historians of the antebellum South such as Eugene Genovese have placed paternalism at the heart of master-slave relations in such a manner as to resemble the relationship between parents and children. Kenneth Stampp, on the other hand, emphasizes the brutality of slavery rather than its paternalism. See Genovese, *Roll, Jordan, Roll*, and Stampp, *The Peculiar Institution*.

   Paternalism has also figured prominently in the work of labor historians. Specifically rejecting rural, planter-based paternalism as a model for modern industrial relations, Douglas Flamming deemphasizes the centrality of "patriarchy, noblesse oblige, and personalism." Instead, he defines mill village paternalism as "official company policies, which provided nonwage benefits to workers, sought to create a distinctive corporate culture, and regulated the living environment of the millhands and their families." See Flamming, *Creating the Modern South*, xxvi–xxviii, 120–41 (second quotation on 121), and 360–61 n. 10 (first quotation).

   I have attempted to discuss paternalism throughout this study in the evolving terms employed by contemporary Virginians, white and black. Most white elites in Virginia in the 1920s and 1930s did speak of noblesse oblige and imagined their paternalism as a means of simultaneously ensuring order, promoting rudimentary uplift, and affirming their own rose-colored view of antebellum race relations. In this respect, most contemporary white Virginians would have recognized the paternalism described by William Alexander Percy. Writing well into the twentieth century, the Mississippian described blacks known personally to him in the most intimate and affectionate terms yet simultaneously disparaged them as inferior while reluctantly accepting his burden to protect and defend them. See Percy, *Lanterns on the Levee*, esp. chap. 23.

Soon after the publication of Percy's book in 1941, Virginius Dabney rejected "the paternalistic philosophy which holds that the Negro is always happier, always better off, always better cared for when his 'white folks' are supervising him, guiding him and controlling him." While acknowledging the benevolence that guided Percy and many white southerners, Dabney emphasized that other paternalists could be quite brutal. (Virginians repeatedly emphasized the benevolence of their paternalism vis-à-vis that of other southerners.) Dabney's denunciation of paternalism, however, was not entirely consistent and certainly did not entail a rejection of segregation. Recognizing that white elites in the cities lacked the intimate contact so central to rural-based paternalism, Dabney continued to insist that whites should control the pace of the change that was certain to come as blacks in the South's growing and ever more anonymous cities chafed against the constraints imposed by paternalism. With the erosion of paternalism, Dabney and other urban elites struggled to construct an alternative method of managing race relations. See Dabney, "Paternalism in Race Relations Is Outmoded," 1, 4 (quotation on 4). For more on Dabney and managed race relations, see Chapter 9.

4 Chafe, *Civilities and Civil Rights*, 6–9 (quotations on 8). Chafe's discussion of the "progressive mystique" and the tension between "civilities and civil rights" in North Carolina has had a profound influence on my understanding of the attitudes of elite whites in Virginia and their management of white supremacy.

5 On the New South in general, see Woodward, *Origins of the New South*; Ayers, *Promise of the New South*; Gaston, *New South Creed*; and Tindall, *Emergence of the New South*. On urbanization and economic modernization in Virginia, see Earl Lewis, *In Their Own Interests*; Silver, *Twentieth-Century Richmond*; and Wilkinson, *Harry Byrd*, esp. chap. 6. Wilkinson emphasizes the effect that urbanization from 1940 to 1960 had on the state's politics and race relations. While Wilkinson is certainly correct in his assessment, the emphasis here is on the evolutionary nature of that change that began decades earlier.

6 "Richmond's Humiliation," editorial from the *NVP*, reprinted in *NJG*, July 30, 1927, 12.

7 "Too Radical for Us," *RTD*, July 17, 1939, 10.

8 See Dabney, *Virginius Dabney's Virginia*, xviii–xix. On massive resistance, see Bartley, *Rise of Massive Resistance*; Lassiter and Lewis, *Moderates' Dilemma*;

Robbins L. Gates, *Making of Massive Resistance*; Muse, *Virginia's Massive Resistance*; Wilkinson, *Harry Byrd*, chap. 5; and Heinemann, *Harry Byrd of Virginia*, chap. 17.

My emphasis on understanding white southern resistance in the 1950s in the context of the 1920s and 1930s draws upon the work of scholars who have located the origins of the civil rights movement in the decades prior to the 1950s. See Sullivan, *Days of Hope*; Norrell, *Reaping the Whirlwind*; Egerton, *Speak Now against the Day*; and Fairclough, *Race and Democracy*.

9 Lassiter and Lewis, *Moderates' Dilemma*, esp. 1–4; Chafe, *Civilities and Civil Rights*; Pratt, *The Color of Their Skin*; Lassiter, "Rise of the Suburban South," esp. the introduction and pt. 1; and Wilkinson, *Harry Byrd*.

10 See Wilkinson, *Harry Byrd*; Pulley, *Old Virginia Restored*; and Key, *Southern Politics*, 19–35.

11 In this sense, the situation in Virginia differed from that described by Glenda Gilmore in North Carolina. Gilmore argues that in the wake of disfranchisement, middle-class black women, not men, served as the primary liaisons to white elites. Although middle-class black women in Virginia were very active, played an important role on interracial commissions, and contributed in many of the ways described by Gilmore, I see no evidence in Virginia that their activities replaced those of their husbands, brothers, sons, and fathers. See Gilmore, *Gender and Jim Crow*. On black elites and their often-troubled relationship with working-class and poor blacks, see Gaines, *Uplifting the Race*, esp. 1–17.

12 DSF, "Virginia—A Gentle Dominion," 69 (first quotation); Pulley, *Old Virginia Restored*; Wynes, *Race Relations in Virginia*; Key, *Southern Politics*, 19–35 (second quotation on 26).

13 DSF, "Virginia—A Gentle Dominion," 70 (quotations). These same sentiments were expressed by black and white Virginians interviewed by Alexander Heard in the late 1940s. As a research assistant for V. O. Key, Heard conducted the interviews with a promise of anonymity, and therefore scholars may not quote or reveal the names of sources. All material relevant to this work can be found in "Virginia Interviews," box 10, Southern Politics Collection, Alexander Heard Library, Vanderbilt University.

14 DSF to William T. Reed, Mar. 26, 1929, section 1, Reed Family Papers, VHS; "Separation by Consent," *RNL*, May 20, 1930, 8; Gignilliat, "The Thought of Douglas Southall Freeman"; Dickson, "The Divided Mind of Douglas Southall Freeman."

15 For more on Mason, see Salmond, *Miss Lucy of the CIO*, and Mason, *To Win These Rights*.

16 Heinemann, *Harry Byrd of Virginia*; Wilkinson, *Harry Byrd*.

17 Bowie, *Sunrise in the South*.

18 Leidholdt, *Editor for Justice*.

19 Kneebone, *Southern Liberal Journalists*; Nitschke, "Virginius Dabney of Virginia"; Sosna, *In Search of the Silent South*, 121–39; Egerton, *Speak Now against the Day*, 137–39.

20 Gavins, *Perils and Prospects*; Earl Lewis, *In Their Own Interests*; Suggs, *P. B. Young, Newspaperman*.

21 DSF, "Virginia—A Gentle Dominion," 70 (first quotation); Gavins, *Perils and Prospects*, 41 (second quotation).

22 Kirby, *Darkness at the Dawning*, 177–81.

23 Wynes, "Evolution of Jim Crow Laws," 416 (first quotation); Dan T. Carter, "From Segregation to Integration," 409 (second quotation). In his survey of the field, Carter refers to studies of Georgia and Virginia that suggest that the onset of segregation statutes at the turn of the twentieth century reflected the "racial self-confidence" of white southerners. The argument here, by contrast, is that the laws passed in Virginia in the 1920s and 1930s reflected a lack of such confidence.

24 Woodward, *Strange Career of Jim Crow* and *Origins of the New South*; Gaston, *New South Creed*; Kousser, *Shaping of Southern Politics*.

25 Tindall, *Emergence of the New South*, 160 (quotation); Williamson, *Crucible of Race*, 1–7, 234–41.

26 Hale, *Making Whiteness*, 144 (quotation). Likewise, historians of Virginia have portrayed race relations in mostly static terms. Focusing unremitting attention on the handful of individuals who dominated the state's politics and for whom white supremacy was a given, scholars have assumed that little of significance changed in the state's race relations in this period. In his study of Virginia during the Great Depression, for instance, Ronald Heinemann concludes that the political hegemony of the Democratic Party in Virginia ensured that race relations remained unaffected by New Deal policies and programs. See Heinemann, *Depression and New Deal* and *Harry Byrd of Virginia*; Younger and Moore, *Governors of Virginia*, esp. 220–305; Willis, "E. Lee Trinkle and the Virginia Democracy"; Hopewell, "An Outsider Looking In"; Hawkes, "Career of Harry Flood Byrd." While I disagree with Heinemann's conclusion that "no change in race relations occurred" (*Depression and New Deal*, 185), I am not arguing that the changes that did take place were a result of New Deal policies and programs. As discussed in Chapters 8 and 9, I emphasize the extent to which the significant changes that took place in the 1930s and 1940s were the result of developments that predated the New Deal.

CHAPTER ONE

1 Buni, *Negro in Virginia Politics*, 1–3 (quotation on 2).

2 Moger, "Virginia's Conservative Political Heritage," 319–20, and "Origin of the Democratic Machine," 183–209.

3 Dailey, *Before Jim Crow*, 24–31; Moger, "Virginia's Conservative Political Heritage," 320–21 (quotation on 320), and "Origin of the Democratic Machine," 184; Buni, *Negro in Virginia Politics*, 3–4.

4 Dailey, *Before Jim Crow*, 27–46; Moger, "Origin of the Democratic Machine,"

184–85 (quotation on 185, taken from Charles C. Pearson, *The Readjuster Movement in Virginia* [New Haven: Yale University Press, 1917]), and "Virginia's Conservative Political Heritage," 321–22.

5 Dailey, *Before Jim Crow*, 40–68 (first quotation on 45; second quotation on 48).

6 Ibid., 78–102.

7 Ibid., 103–26; Moger, "Origin of the Democratic Machine," 185–91; Buni, *Negro in Virginia Politics*, 4–6.

8 Moger, "Origin of the Democratic Machine," 191–203 (quotation on 191); Buni, *Negro in Virginia Politics*, 6–8; Wynes, *Race Relations in Virginia*, 55; VD, *Virginia: The New Dominion*, 430. Hal Flood, a stalwart in the Democratic Party, explained that the Anderson-McCormick election law, passed in 1894, made it possible for Democratic election judges "when the polls were closed to turn everyone out of the election room until they had an opportunity to make the number of ballots in the ballot box tally with the number of names on the poll book. In the black counties this enabled them to change the ballots to suit themselves. This was done in many instances to save those counties from Negro domination." Kousser, *Shaping of Southern Politics*, 172 (quotation).

9 Buni, *Negro in Virginia Politics*, 8–9; Moger, "Origin of the Democratic Machine," 199 n. 61.

10 Buni, *Negro in Virginia Politics*, 8–9 (first quotation on 9); Wynes, *Race Relations in Virginia*, 85–87 (second and third quotations on 86).

11 Buni, *Negro in Virginia Politics*, 12; Pulley, *Old Virginia Restored*, 164–68. On the threat of the Populists, who failed to make significant inroads in Virginia, see Pulley, *Old Virginia Restored*, 53–57.

12 Pulley, *Old Virginia Restored*, 52–53; Moger, "Origin of the Democratic Machine," 207. For more on the "courthouse cliques" in the twentieth century, see Wilkinson, *Harry Byrd*, esp. chap. 1.

13 Wynes, *Race Relations in Virginia*, 51–55; Kousser, *Shaping of Southern Politics*, 172–75 (quotation on 173); Dailey, *Before Jim Crow*, 160–62.

14 Pulley, *Old Virginia Restored*, 57–65 (quotation on 57); Wynes, *Race Relations in Virginia*, 56; Buni, *Negro in Virginia Politics*, 14; Kousser, *Shaping of Southern Politics*, 173–75; *Williams v. Mississippi*, 170 U.S. 213 (1898).

15 Pulley, *Old Virginia Restored*, 66–72; Kousser, *Shaping of Southern Politics*, 175–81.

16 Pulley, *Old Virginia Restored*, 72–75; Wynes, *Race Relations in Virginia*, 57–61, 146–47.

17 Wynes, *Race Relations in Virginia*, 62–67 (quotations on 63); Pulley, *Old Virginia Restored*, 76–77; Kousser, *Shaping of Southern Politics*, 177–81; Dailey, *Before Jim Crow*, 160–64.

18 Statement of Carter Glass, *Report of the Proceedings and Debates of the Constitutional Convention*, 3076–77.

19 Buni, *Negro in Virginia Politics*, 21–27; Pulley, *Old Virginia Restored*, 77–91; Kousser, *Shaping of Southern Politics*, 180–81; Key, *Southern Politics*, 19–20 (quotation on 20). On the refusal of the constitutional convention to sub-

mit its work for ratification, see *Report of the Proceedings and Debates of the Constitutional Convention*, 291–307.

20 Pulley, *Old Virginia Restored*, 111–13, 127–31, 152–54; Buni, *Negro in Virginia Politics*, 33 (quotation).

21 Wynes, *Race Relations in Virginia*, 95–96. According to Adams's testimony, the five hundred men were part of an informal group whose members had taken it upon themselves, at their own expense, to survey the situation throughout the South.

22 Ibid., 96–97.

23 Brundage, *Lynching in the New South*, 144–60 (quotation on 157). The conclusions of Wynes and Brundage support the contention of Joel Williamson that "conservatives" in Virginia never lost power to "radicals." See Williamson, *Crucible of Race*, 234–41, 287.

24 Wynes, *Race Relations in Virginia*, 73–78, 110 (quotations on 110); Guild, *Black Laws of Virginia*, 144–48; Buni, *Negro in Virginia Politics*, 33–48; Earl Lewis, *In Their Own Interests*, 68–69.

25 Earl Lewis, *In Their Own Interests*, 1–28 (quotation on 3); Meier and Rudwick, "Boycott Movement against Jim Crow Streetcars," 267–89; Dailey, *Before Jim Crow*, 165–67.

26 Gavins, "Urbanization and Segregation," 257–73; Suggs, "Black Strategy and Ideology," 161–90; Earl Lewis, *In Their Own Interests*, 66–75; Suggs, *P. B. Young, Newspaperman*; Elsa Barkley Brown, "Womanist Consciousness," 610–33.

27 Grantham, "Contours of Southern Progressivism," 1035–59 (first quotation on 1045); Link, *Paradox of Southern Progressivism*, xii, 58–78 (second and third quotations on 59); Woodward, *Origins of the New South*, 369–95; Kousser, *Shaping of Southern Politics*, 229–31; Pulley, *Old Virginia Restored*. Kousser and Pulley, in particular, emphasize the self-interest of reformers in Virginia and the South.

28 Link, *Paradox of Southern Progressivism*, xii, 58–78; Wheeler, *New Women of the New South*, 100–132 (quotation on 131). It is no accident that throughout the twentieth century, white reformers continued to link the need for a better deal for black southerners with the possibilities of regional development. See Ayers, "Southern Chronicle," 189–202.

29 Link, *Paradox of Southern Progressivism*, 64–70 (quotation on 65); Wheeler, *New Women of the New South*, 100–112. Wheeler cites a poem entitled "A Southern Symphony," authored by Lila Meade Valentine's husband but based on both their experiences, as a fascinating example of white elite attitudes about slavery and emancipation (109). Scientific racism constituted just one of the "permissions to hate" that signaled the North's acquiescence to southern law and custom in the management of race relations. See Woodward, *Strange Career of Jim Crow*, 69–82 ("permissions to hate" on 81).

30 Silver, *Twentieth-Century Richmond*, 13–14, 57–58; Gavins, *Perils and Prospects*, 41–42; Kneebone, *Southern Liberal Journalists*, xiii–xx, 3–20; Pulley, *Old Virginia Restored*, 132–51; Gilliam, "Making Virginia Progressive," 189–222; Moger, *Virginia: Bourbonism to Byrd*; Ferrell, *Claude A. Swanson*; Kirby,

Westmoreland Davis; Willis, "E. Lee Trinkle and the Virginia Democracy"; Hawkes, "Career of Harry Flood Byrd"; Heinemann, *Harry Byrd of Virginia*; Tindall, "Business Progressivism," 92–106.

31 Blanton, "Virginia in the 1920s," 19–23.

32 U.S. Bureau of the Census, *Fourteenth Decennial Census, 1920*, vol. 4, *Population: Occupations*, tables 9 and 11, and *Fifteenth Decennial Census, 1930, Population*, vol. 4, *Occupations by States*, "Virginia—Occupation Statistics," table 3. Between 1910 and 1920, the number of Virginians earning a living in agriculture dropped from 45 to 36 percent of the working population. By 1930, that number had fallen another 4 percent. The number engaged in manufacturing, on the other hand, rose from 20 to more than 24 percent between 1910 and 1930. While decisions made in Virginia, particularly the refusal to float a bond issue to build roads, ensured that the state's increase in manufacturing would not match the rate of manufacturing growth in North Carolina, the Old Dominion's overall economy remained much less dependent on agriculture than that of its neighbor to the south. In 1920 more than half of North Carolina's population remained tied to the farm economy.

33 Blanton, "Virginia in the 1920s," 37–68. For the significance of mill villages in other parts of the South, see Hall et al., *Like a Family*; Tullos, *Habits of Industry*; Flamming, *Creating the Modern South*; and Simon, *Fabric of Defeat*.

34 Blanton, "Virginia in the 1920s," 1–10.

35 Hershman, "Shrinking Black Belt," 93–97; U.S. Bureau of the Census, *Fourteenth Decennial Census, 1920*, vol. 3, *Population*, table 9. Significant numbers of blacks, however, did live throughout the central and northern Piedmont. As recently as 1900, Culpeper had a majority-black population, and several counties in the northern Piedmont had black populations that exceeded one-quarter. In 1900 thirty-six counties in the state had majority-black populations; by 1920 that number had fallen to twenty-three, all of them in the Tidewater and Southside, but forty-five counties and cities had black populations that exceeded 40 percent and sixty-two counties and cities had black populations greater than 30 percent.

Although Virginia had a readily ascertainable black belt dependent on cheap labor, the commonwealth's diverse economy contributed to a rate of tenant farming lower than that of its southern neighbors. A Commerce Department study in conjunction with the 1920 census concluded that two-thirds of cotton farmers in the United States toiled as tenants while less than half of tobacco farmers did so. Those raising vegetables and food crops were even less likely to be tenants. Consequently, in Virginia in 1920, only 26 percent of farmers were listed as tenants; 35 percent of those were black. In North Carolina, by contrast, 44 percent of farmers were tenants, and 46 percent of tenant farmers were black. Farther south, the rates of tenancy exceeded one-half and even approached two-thirds in Georgia and Mississippi. The vast majority of tenant farmers in South Carolina, Georgia, Alabama, Mississippi, and Louisiana were black. See U.S. Bureau of the Census, *Farm Tenancy in the United States, 1920*, Census Monographs 4 (Washington, D.C.: Government Printing Office, 1924), 33, and *Fourteenth Decennial Census, 1920*, vol. 6, *Agriculture*, pt. 2, table 1.

36 Blanton, "Virginia in the 1920s," 109–36.

37 Ibid.; U.S. Bureau of the Census, *Sixteenth Decennial Census, 1940*, vol. 2, *Population*, pt. 7, table 5, "Urban, Rural-Nonfarm, and Rural-Farm Population, by Race, Nativity, and Sex, for the State: 1910–1940," 135, and table 4, "Race, by Nativity and Sex, for the State: 1850–1940," 134. Blanton, "Virginia in the 1920s," 120–23, provides a synopsis of Wilson Gee and John J. Corson III, *Rural Depopulation in Certain Tidewater and Piedmont Areas of Virginia* (Charlottesville: Institute for Research in the Social Sciences, 1929). For the enormous urban growth that occurred in Newport News, Petersburg, Portsmouth, and Roanoke, see *Fourteenth Decennial Census, 1920*, vol. 2, *Population*, table 17, "Color or Race, Nativity, and Parentage for Cities Having in 1920, from 25,000 to 100,000 Inhabitants: 1920, 1910, and 1900," 73. Norfolk and Richmond each had more than 100,000 inhabitants at this time.

38 Blanton, "Virginia in the 1920s," 109–36; U.S. Bureau of the Census, *Fourteenth Decennial Census, 1920*, vol. 3, *Population*, table 9; Earl Lewis, *In Their Own Interests*, 29–35.

39 VD, "Negroes and the Franchise: Their Participation in the Primaries," *RTD*, reprinted in *NJG*, Sept. 12, 1931, 7.

40 J. A. Brinkley to the editor, "A Dogged Ideal," *NJG*, Aug. 27, 1921, 4.

41 W. O. Saunders, article in *Collier's National Weekly*, reprinted as "W. O. Saunders Writes Interestingly on Phase of Negro Life in South," *NJG*, Jan. 5, 1924, 9.

42 Richard H. Bowling, "The Fun of Being a Negro," *NJG*, Oct. 9, 1927, 16.

43 Mary Burnley Gwathmey, manuscript of "Royal Purple Preferred," dated 1949 (first quotation on 25–26; all other quotations on 15; emphasis in original), folder "Sylvia Hill 1943–1959," box 52, Mary Burnley Gwathmey Family Papers, VHS. For more on the importance of the mammy in southern culture, see Hale, *Making Whiteness*, chap. 3.

44 Wayland, *History of Virginia*, 43–54 (first quotation on 43; second quotation on 53; third quotation on 53–54).

45 Ibid., 259–338 (quotation on 259).

46 Munford, *Virginia's Attitude toward Slavery*, 10–32 (first quotation on 10–11; second quotation on 11).

47 Ibid., 32–43 (first quotation on 32; second and third quotations on 42; fourth quotation on 43).

48 Ibid., 43–48 (all quotations on 48).

49 Ibid., 181, 208–13, 255–56, 263–83.

50 Bailey, "Free Speech and the Lost Cause," 237–66 (first and third quotations on 260; second quotation on 250).

51 On the New South era of Freeman's childhood and adolescence, see especially Woodward, *Origins of the New South*; Gaston, *New South Creed*; and Ayers, *Promise of the New South*. On the Lost Cause, see Wilson, *Baptized in Blood*, and Brundage, "White Women and the Politics of Historical Mem-

ory." On the New South and Richmond during Freeman's adolescence, see Gignilliat, "The Thought of Douglas Southall Freeman," 30–79, and Dickson, "The Divided Mind of Douglas Southall Freeman," 11–45. On Freeman and his affection for Robert E. Lee, see Edmunds, *Virginians Out Front*, 396–412, and Dumas Malone, "'This Quiet Man, Whose Tireless Pen Traced the Marches [of] . . . Great Captains': Douglas Southall Freeman," in Duke and Jordan, *A Richmond Reader*, 365.

52 Jones, "The Negro and the South," 5–6 (first quotation on 5), and "Approach to the South's Race Question," 40–41 (second quotation on 40); Earl Lewis, *In Their Own Interests*, 67.

53 Jones, "Approach to the South's Race Question," 41 (the terms "better class" and "lower class" are Jones's). For an assessment of Jones as a "benevolent paternalist," see Egerton, *Speak Now against the Day*, 48, 239.

54 Jones, "The Negro and the South," 10.

55 Jones, "Approach to the South's Race Question," 41.

CHAPTER TWO

1 Kneebone, *Southern Liberal Journalists*, 18; Tindall, *Emergence of the New South*, 53–64.

2 Kennedy, *Over Here*, 3–44; Jordan, "'Damnable Dilemma,'" 1562–83. The phrase "golden opportunity" appears in "Young Officers Win Applause," *NJG*, Aug. 4, 1917, 1.

3 "The Labor Problem South," *NJG*, Nov. 18, 1916, 7; Earl Lewis, *In Their Own Interests*, 29–32. On the Great Migration, see Grossman, *Land of Hope*; Emmett J. Scott, "Letters of Negro Migrants," 290–340; and Adero, *Up South*.

4 Suggs, *P. B. Young, Newspaperman*, 36; "Should Negroes Leave the South," *NJG*, Oct. 21, 1916, 4; "Labor Should Stand Firm," *NJG*, Mar. 24, 1917, 1. In almost every weekly issue from October 1916 to May 1917, Young stressed the migration and his preference for its end. The Great Migration only left the front page when preparations for war assumed center stage.

5 "Richmond Negroes Pledge Loyalty," *NJG*, Apr. 7, 1917, 1; "War Has Been Declared," *NJG*, Apr. 7, 1917, 4; "Echoes of East St. Louis," *NJG*, July 14, 1917, 1, 4; "The Right of Free Speech," *NJG*, Aug. 18, 1917, 4 (quotation). Miner's letter originally appeared in the *Richmond Planet* but was also carried by the *Norfolk Journal and Guide*.

6 "Close Ranks," *Crisis* 16 (July 1918): 111 (quotation); Jordan, "'Damnable Dilemma,'" 1562–83; David Levering Lewis, *W. E. B. Du Bois*, 555–56.

7 Details of black participation in the war effort and white reaction to that participation can be found in virtually every county and city report submitted to the Virginia War History Commission. See Davis, *Virginia Communities in War Time: First Series* (quotation from Mecklenburg County on 266) and *Virginia Communities in War Time: Second Series*.

8 Mrs. W. B. Goodwyn, "Greensville County in War Time," in Davis, *Virginia*

Communities in War Time: First Series, 206; "A Mob Leader Is Boycotted," *NJG*, Oct. 6, 1917, 1.

9   "Springarn on War Training," *NJG*, Mar. 17, 1917, 1 (quotation); "Senator Vardaman's Queer Notion," *NJG*, Sept. 22, 1917, 4.

10 "Fluvanna County in War Time," in Davis, *Virginia Communities in War Time: First Series*, 149 (quotation); J. Douglas Smith, "Black Troops, White Business: Petersburg and Camp Lee during World War I," unpublished seminar paper, in possession of the author.

11 "Norfolk Offers Colored Regiment," *NJG*, Apr. 14, 1917, 1; "Thousands Enrolled on Registration Day," *NJG*, June 9, 1917, 1; "Fine Record of Negro Regiment," *NJG*, June 23, 1917, 1 (first quotation); "Asks Broader Army Service," *NJG*, June 16, 1917, 1; Wynn, *From Progressivism to Prosperity*, 170–95; W. E. B. Du Bois, "Returning Soldiers," *Crisis* 18 (May 1919): 13–14 (second quotation); Jordan, "'Damnable Dilemma,'" 1583; Tindall, *Emergence of the New South*, 157.

12 James D. Fife to Ella K. Fife, Feb. 2, 1918; Ella K. Fife to Mrs. S. A. G. S. Fife, Aug. 7, 1918; Ella K. Fife to M. W. Fife, Nov. [28], 1918, box 1, Ella K. F. Freudenberg Papers, UVA.

13 Responses of Willis Brown Godwin and William Franklin Banks, folder "Elizabeth City County (Colored)," response of Judge Goodwin, folder "Dinwiddie County (Colored)," response of James Waverly Crawley, folder "Petersburg (Colored)," Virginia War History Commission Questionnaires, LVA.

14 C. M. Long, "Observation on My Southern Trip," *NJG*, Jan. 6, 1923, 6; S. H. Williamson to the editor, "Race Relations Sunday," *NJG*, Feb. 17. 1923, 4 (quotation); Tindall, *Emergence of the New South*, 151–56; Tuttle, *Race Riot*.

15 Tindall, *Emergence of the New South*, 175–82; Kneebone, *Southern Liberal Journalists*, 24–25, 75–77; Ellis, "Commission on Interracial Cooperation"; McDonough, "Men and Women of Good Will"; Sosna, *In Search of the Silent South*, 20–41; Egerton, *Speak Now against the Day*, 47–51.

16 Kneebone, *Southern Liberal Journalists*, 24–25; Tindall, *Emergence of the New South*, 175–82; Link, *Paradox of Southern Progressivism*, 249–67; Bowie, *Sunrise in the South*; Ellis, "Commission on Interracial Cooperation"; McDonough, "Men and Women of Good Will." The importance of religion as a motivating factor for many CIC members should not be underestimated. Lucy Randolph Mason, a member of the Virginia CIC and one of the few southern elites to actually condemn segregation, once indicated that she would have become a priest, like her father, had she been a man. See Storrs, *Civilizing Capitalism*, 68–70; Mason, *To Win These Rights*; and Salmond, *Miss Lucy of the CIO*.

17 Kneebone, *Southern Liberal Journalists*, 24–25; Tindall, *Emergence of the New South*, 175–82; Link, *Paradox of Southern Progressivism*, 249–67; Bowie, *Sunrise in the South*; Ellis, "Commission on Interracial Cooperation"; McDonough, "Men and Women of Good Will."

18 Virginia Education Commission, *Virginia Public Schools, Education Commission's Report to the Assembly of Virginia*, 198.

19 Cartoon entitled "The Right Solution—Let It Flow," *NJG*, July 2, 1921, 4; "Real and Unreal Race Adjustment," *NVP*, reprinted in *NJG*, Feb. 4, 1922, 4 (quotation).

20 Address of the Reverend Russell Bowie in "Robert E. Lee vs. the Ku Klux Klan," *NJG*, Feb. 5, 1921, 3 (first quotation); "Says New Appreciation of Each Other's Worth by Races Is Necessary," *NJG*, July 19, 1924, 1 (second quotation).

21 R. W. Miles, "Recent Instances of Inter-racial Cooperation," file 230, reel 55, CIC Papers; "Races Work for Cooperation," *NJG*, Nov. 12, 1921, 1.

22 Minutes of the Virginia CIC, Nov. 7, 1924, file 229, reel 55, CIC Papers; "For Harmony between Races," *NJG*, Oct. 8, 1921, 1; Mrs. Lee Britt to Dr. J. T. Martin, quoted in letter from R. W. Miles to Will W. Alexander, May 15, 1922, file 230, reel 55, CIC Papers.

23 Mrs. G. Harvey Clarke, "The Negro in the Home," file 230, reel 55, CIC Papers.

24 Ibid.

25 GBH interview by RJB, Richmond, Va., Oct. 18, 1939, folder 6, "Field Notes: Southern Trip, Bk. 1," box 85, RJBP. On Hancock, see Gavins, *Perils and Prospects*.

26 John J. Corson III, "Negroes Living in Intolerable Conditions Here," *RNL*, Sept. 19, 1931, 1, 18 (quotation); Negro Welfare Survey Committee, *The Negro in Richmond*; Silver, *Twentieth-Century Richmond*, 97–129; Earl Lewis, *In Their Own Interests*, 120–22. Corson's article was the first in an eleven-part series that ran in the *Richmond News Leader* between September 19 and October 1, 1931, in which he studied living conditions in black sections of Richmond and found essentially the same conditions as those discussed by Weber in 1913 and by Charles L. Knight, a University of Virginia researcher, in 1927. The quotation from the Weber study is taken from Corson's synopsis. See Chapter 8, note 39, for a full citation of the eleven-part series.

27 "Are Rebuked for Showing Bad Housing," *NJG*, May 14, 1921, 1; "Streets in White Sections Oiled; Negroes Forgotten," *NJG*, June 11, 1932, 8; "Many Streets Now Impassable in Colored Sections of the City," *NJG*, Mar. 18, 1922, 1; "The Negroes Want This More Than Parks or Playgrounds," *RNL*, Apr. 9, 1928, 8 (first quotation); interview with Frank C. Hartman, May 25, 1995, in Department of Community Planning, *Ridge Street Oral History Project*, 30–38; interview with Margie Linton Ix and Lucy Bell Linton Watson, Feb. 16, 1995, ibid., 61–66 (second quotation); interview with Pocahontas Sellers, Mary Sellers Carter, and Virginia Carter, Aug. 13, 1994, ibid., 111–13.

28 "Playgrounds for Colored Children," *NJG*, Apr. 9, 1921, 4 (quotation); "City Will Purchase Land for Park," *NJG*, Mar. 18, 1922, 1; Earl Lewis, *In Their Own Interests*, 81–85.

29 John P. Pitt to the editor, *NVP*, July 25, 1923, reprinted as "Asks for Park Facilities for All the People," *NJG*, Aug. 4, 1923, 1 (quotations); "A Plea for Fair Play," *NJG*, Aug. 4, 1923, 10; Earl Lewis, *In Their Own Interests*, 81–85.

30 "The Suggested Park Site," *NJG*, Aug. 11, 1923, 10 (first quotation); "When

Do We Get the Park?," *NJG*, Feb. 18, 1928, 16; Earl Lewis, *In Their Own Interests*, 81–85 (second and third quotations on 82).

31 Tindall, *Emergence of the New South*, 152–54 (quotation on 153).

32 Robert T. Kerlin, "An Open Letter to the Governor of Arkansas," *The Nation* 112 (June 15, 1921): 847–48, copy on frames 0933–34, pt. 3, series A, "Legal Department Records, 1919–1940," reel 18, NAACP-Mfm.

33 Ibid.

34 "Some Corrections from the Record," frames 0967–69, pt. 3, series A, reel 18, NAACP-Mfm.

35 Robert T. Kerlin to Herbert J. Seligmann, Aug. 12, 1921, frames 0936–37, "Some Corrections from the Record," frame 0968, both in pt. 3, series A, reel 18, NAACP-Mfm.

36 Robert T. Kerlin to Herbert J. Seligmann, Aug. 17, 1921, frames 0939–40, pt. 3, series A, reel 18, NAACP-Mfm.

37 Robert T. Kerlin to Board of Visitors, [handwritten date Aug. 19], frames 0941–42, pt. 3, series A, reel 18, NAACP-Mfm. On the University Commission on Southern Race Questions, see Tindall, *Emergence of the New South*, 175–77, and Culley, "Muted Trumpets."

38 Robert T. Kerlin to Board of Visitors, frames 0942–47 (quotation), pt. 3, series A, reel 18, NAACP-Mfm; Kerlin, *Voice of the Negro*.

39 Robert T. Kerlin to Board of Visitors, frame 0947, pt. 3, series A, reel 18, NAACP-Mfm.

40 Statement of the Board of Visitors signed by Lewis E. Steele, frame 0954 (first quotation), Robert T. Kerlin to Herbert Seligmann, Aug. 24, 1921, frame 0959, Kerlin to Seligmann, Aug. 25, 1921, frame 0964 (second quotation), pt. 3, series A, reel 18, NAACP-Mfm. Over the course of the next several years, on the other hand, state and federal courts did stay the executions and then overturn the convictions of the tenant farmers in Arkansas. See Tindall, *Emergence of the New South*, 154.

41 "Strafing the Protester," *NVP* (quotation), and "The Discharge of Colonel Kerlin," *RTD*, both reprinted in *NJG*, Sept. 3, 1921, 4.

42 "The Kerlin Case," *Southern Workman* 50 (Dec. 1921): 529–32 (quotation on 531); Kneebone, *Southern Liberal Journalists*, xvii–xx.

43 Minutes of the *News Leader* Current Events Class, June 12, 1922, folder "1922 Fe–Oc, 1922 Oc–1923 March," box 177, DSFP-LC. Freeman led the class from 1918 until his death in 1953. The meetings allowed him an opportunity both to shape and to solicit opinions from the city's elites. See Gignilliat, "The Thought of Douglas Southall Freeman," 296, and Dickson, "The Divided Mind of Douglas Southall Freeman," 99–100.

44 Tindall, *Emergence of the New South*, 182; Egerton, *Speak Now against the Day*, 48; Dunbar, *Against the Grain*, vii–viii (quotation); Bellamy, "If Christ Came to Dixie," 33–42.

45 Buni, *Negro in Virginia Politics*, 73–74; Lebsock, "Woman Suffrage and White Supremacy," 62–100 (quotation on 75). For a more comprehensive view of women's suffrage and race in the South, see Wheeler, *New Women of the New South*, esp. 100–132.

46 Lebsock, "Woman Suffrage and White Supremacy," 82–85; "Negro Women Continue to Outnumber White in Attempting to Qualify," *RNL*, Sept. 18, 1920, 1; "Registration Office Gets Assistance; Women Swamp Place; Race Segregation," *RNL*, Sept. 17, 1920, 1; "Richmond Women Register at Rate of 578 in One Day . . . Maggie Walker Protests," *RTD*, Sept. 21, 1920, 1; Buni, *Negro in Virginia Politics*, 75–80. On Walker's varied life as a bank president, newspaper publisher, and activist, see Elsa Barkley Brown, "Womanist Consciousness."

47 "Virginia's Assembly Will Stand Firm," *RNL*, Sept. 2, 1919, 6 (first quotation); Lebsock, "Woman Suffrage and White Supremacy," 85 (second quotation); "Negro Women Continue to Outnumber White in Attempting to Qualify," *RNL*, Sept. 18, 1920, 1 (third and fourth quotations).

48 A. W. Hunton, "General Statements," frames 0481–83, pt. 4, "The Voting Rights Campaign, 1916–50," reel 2, NAACP-Mfm.

49 Ibid.

50 Ibid.

51 Statement of Mrs. Allen Washington, frame 0479, pt. 4, reel 2, NAACP-Mfm. Washington accompanied Isham to the registrar's office and relayed both her experience and that of Isham to Hunton.

52 Ibid.

53 Statement of Mrs. G. W. Fields, frame 0480, A. W. Hunton, "General Statements," frames 0481–83, pt. 4, reel 2, NAACP-Mfm.

54 A. W. Hunton, "General Statements," frames 0481–83, statement of Mrs. G. W. Fields, frame 0480, statement of Mrs. Allen Washington, frame 0479, pt. 4, reel 2, NAACP-Mfm.

55 Henry W. Anderson, "Freedom in Virginia: An Address . . . Delivered before the Republican State Convention at Norfolk, July 14, 1921," 5–6, 9, copy in folder A, box 354, HFBP.

56 HFB to John Harper, Mar. 23, 1921 (first quotation), folder "1921 Correspondence H–I," box 72, William F. Keyser to HFB, Oct. 11, 1921 (second quotation), folder "1921 Correspondence William F. Keyser," box 72, HFB to Mrs. R. T. Barton (third quotation), folder "1921 Correspondence B," box 71, HFBP.

57 "Slurring a Race for Political Party Gain," *NJG*, Apr. 2, 1921, 4 (first quotation); Anderson, "Freedom in Virginia," 5–6, 9 (second quotation on 6), copy in folder A, box 354, HFBP; Buni, *Negro in Virginia Politics*, 81–83.

58 Anderson, "Freedom in Virginia," 19–25, copy in folder A, box 354, HFBP. Anderson's language echoed the terms of Booker T. Washington's 1895 speech at an international exposition in Atlanta. Speaking at a time when racial violence had reached appalling proportions, Washington sought to establish terms under which blacks and whites might at least coexist peacefully. Washington pledged that blacks would seek to better themselves economically and educationally but would stay out of politics. White southerners openly embraced this essentially accommodationist approach, which became known as the Atlanta Compromise, and Washington became the recognized

leader of African Americans until his death in 1915. See Woodward, *Origins of the New South*, 350–68.

59 Gignilliat, "The Thought of Douglas Southall Freeman," 289–94 (first quotation on 292); "The Republican Convention," *RNL*, July 15, 1921, editorial page (second quotation).

60 "The Republican Convention," *RNL*, July 15, 1921, editorial page. For more on the emergence of segregation as a function of the modern industrial state, see Cell, *Highest Stage of White Supremacy*.

61 Buni, *Negro in Virginia Politics*, 79–81; "Republican Convention Barred Afro-Americans," *NJG*, July 16, 1921, 1; "Two GOP Tickets in Field Certain," *NJG*, Sept. 3, 1921, 1.

62 "Sentiment in Favor of Nationwide Protest," *NJG*, July 23, 1921, 1; "The Republican State Convention," *NJG*, July 23, 1921, 4 (quotation).

63 Suggs, *P. B. Young, Newspaperman*, 45–62 (quotation on 45); Earl Lewis, *In Their Own Interests*, 25–26, 64–65.

64 "'He Is a Man Who Would Walk into the Jaws of Death to Serve His Race': John Mitchell, Jr.," in Duke and Jordan, *A Richmond Reader*, 325–28; Meier and Rudwick, "Boycott Movement against Jim Crow Streetcars," 267–89; Gaines, *Uplifting the Race*, 88 (quotation); John Mitchell Jr. to ELT, Nov. 10, 1923, folder M (4), box 7, TEP. For more on the "New Negro," whose generic name came from the 1925 publication of a book of that name, see Tindall, *Emergence of the New South*, 157–59; Gaines, *Uplifting the Race*, 224–60; David Levering Lewis, *When Harlem Was in Vogue*, esp. chap. 4; and Tuttle, *Race Riot*, esp. chap. 7.

65 "The Republican State Convention," *NJG*, July 23, 1921, 4; "Colored Republicans Will Name Full State Ticket," *NJG*, July 23, 1921, 1; "Full Colored Ticket Named in Richmond," *NJG*, Sept. 10, 1921, 1; Suggs, *P. B. Young, Newspaperman*, 50–51 (quotation on 51); Buni, *Negro in Virginia Politics*, 84–87.

66 "Candidate Newsome's Smoke Screen," *NJG*, Oct. 8, 1921, 4 (first quotation); Thomas Newsome, letter to the editor, "The Republican Split in Virginia," *NJG*, Oct. 8, 1921, 4; "The Issue Clearly Defined," *NJG*, Oct. 15, 1921, 4; "Pollard, Newsome and Williams, Colored Republicans' Heavy Artillery, Arouse Class Hatred in Race in Bitter Speeches," *NJG*, Oct. 22, 1921, 1 (third quotation); Buni, *Negro in Virginia Politics*, 84–87 (second quotation on 85); Suggs, *P. B. Young, Newspaperman*, 50–51.

67 Press release from Democratic Campaign Headquarters, Sept. 16, 1921, folder 3, section 13, Carter C. Wormeley Papers, VHS. On lily-white Republicanism as a response to women's suffrage in North Carolina, see Gilmore, "False Friends and Avowed Enemies," 219–38.

68 "Promises Fair Deal to Race as Governor," *NJG*, Oct. 8, 1921, 1.

69 Press release from Democratic Campaign Headquarters, dated Oct. 17, 1921, byline Oct. 18, 1921, folder 2, section 13, Wormeley Papers, VHS.

70 ELT and H. D. Flood to Henry W. Anderson, Oct. 27, 1921, issued as press release from Democratic Campaign Headquarters, Oct. 28, 1921, folder 1, section 13, Wormeley Papers, VHS.

71 Claude A. Swanson to H. D. Flood, Oct. 29, 1921, released by Democratic Campaign Headquarters, Nov. 1, 1921, folder 2, section 13, Wormeley Papers, VHS.

72 Buni, *Negro in Virginia Politics*, 87–89 (quotation on 89); Earl Lewis, *In Their Own Interests*, 87; Gavins, *Perils and Prospects*, 87.

73 Gilmore, "False Friends and Avowed Enemies," 220–32; Buni, *Negro in Virginia Politics*, 87–99, 106–23; Suggs, *P. B. Young, Newspaperman*, 52–63; LIJ to Mark Sullivan, Sept. 27, 1921 (quotation), folder "1921 Sullivan, Mark," box 2, LIJP (#9924-i). Leading Republicans, in the wake of their victory in the 1928 presidential election, confirmed the validity of Louis Jaffé's comment that white Republicans intended to absorb the black vote without paying for it. Jennings Cropper Wise wrote Henry Anderson that "[w]e are particularly fortunate in owing no political debts to the Negroes so that we are free to stress our moral obligation to them." See JCW to Henry W. Anderson, Nov. 8, 1928, section 5 letterbook, 37–39, JCWP. As Glenda Gilmore argues with regard to North Carolina in "False Friends and Avowed Enemies," and as I am suggesting here with regard to Virginia, the migration of African Americans in the South to the party of Franklin Roosevelt and the New Deal must be understood in the particular context of southern racial politics in the 1920s and 1930s and not merely as a by-product of the Great Depression and New Deal. For the most influential work that emphasizes the role of the Depression and New Deal in this process, see Weiss, *Farewell to the Party of Lincoln*.

74 William Anthony Aery, Publications Secretary, Hampton Institute, to ELT, Nov. 1922, folder "Msc Corr A (3-1)," box 1, TEP; "Inter-racial Meeting Held in State Capitol," *NJG*, Mar. 31, 1923, 3 (first quotation); "Governor Addresses Inter-racial Meeting," *RTD*, Mar. 26, 1923, 12 (second quotation).

75 "Well Said," *NJG*, Jan. 10, 1925, 12 (first quotation); "Richmond's Colored Citizens," *RTD*, reprinted in *NJG*, Feb. 12, 1921, 4 (second quotation); ELT to A. N. Johnson, Mar. 6, 1923 (third quotation), folder J (2), box 6, John Mitchell Jr. to ELT, Nov. 10, 1923 (fourth quotation), folder M (4), box 7, TEP.

76 Link, *Paradox of Southern Progressivism*, 260–61; Gavins, *Perils and Prospects*, 41; Silver, *Twentieth-Century Richmond*, 11–12, 121–29.

77 Guild, *Black Laws of Virginia*, 144–45, 150; Wynes, "Evolution of Jim Crow Laws," 421; *Virginia Railway and Power Company v. Sarah A. Deaton*, 147 Va. 577 (1927) (first quotation); Commonwealth of Virginia, *Acts of Assembly, 1930*, 343–44 (all other quotations).

78 Roscoe Lewis interview by RJB, Hampton, Va., Oct. 2, 1939 (first and second quotations), folder 6, "Field Notes: Southern Trip, Bk. 1," box 85, RJBP; *Virginia Railway and Power Company v. Sarah A. Deaton*, 147 Va. 578 (third quotation).

79 Kelley, *Race Rebels*, chap. 3; "Violates Jim Crow Law and Gets a Fine," *NJG*, July 30, 1921, 1. In addition, Kelley writes eloquently about the multiple ways in which blacks protested against and resisted the injustices of Jim Crow without overtly violating the law. See *Race Rebels*, chaps. 2 and 3.

80 Interview with Elizabeth Snyder Carter, July 19, 1994, in Department of Community Planning, *Ridge Street Oral History Project*, 23–27 (first quotation); "On a Journey," *NJG*, Aug. 1, 1931, editorial page (second quotation).

81 *Virginia Railway and Power Company v. Sarah A. Deaton*, 147 Va. 576, 578–80 (quotation on 579).

82 Wynes, *Race Relations in Virginia*, 73–76, 148; Silver, *Twentieth-Century Richmond*, 3–14, 97–129.

83 Guild, *Black Laws of Virginia*, 147–48; *Buchanan v. Warley*, 245 U.S. 60 (1917); *Hopkins v. City of Richmond*, 117 Va. 692 (1915); *Irvine v. City of Clifton Forge*, 124 Va. 781 (1918); Earl Lewis, *In Their Own Interests*, 68–69; Silver, *Twentieth-Century Richmond*, 33–40, 59, 113–25.

84 "Are Rebuked for Showing Bad Housing," *NJG*, May 14, 1921, 1.

85 "Brambleton Is in Eruption Again: Near White Family Ordered to Move Out," *NJG*, July 14, 1923, 5; Earl Lewis, *In Their Own Interests*, 77–78.

86 "55,868 Colored People in the City of Norfolk," *NJG*, Jan. 20, 1923, 1; "Brambleton Is in Eruption Again," *NJG*, July 14, 1923, 1, 5; Earl Lewis, *In Their Own Interests*, 77-78.

87 "Brambleton Is in Eruption Again," *NJG*, July 14, 1923, 5; Earl Lewis, *In Their Own Interests*, 77–78.

88 "Brambleton Is in Eruption Again," *NJG*, July 14, 1923, 1 (quotation); Earl Lewis, *In Their Own Interests*, 77–78.

89 "Brambleton Is in Eruption Again," *NJG*, July 14, 1923, 1, 5 (quotations on 1); Earl Lewis, *In Their Own Interests*, 77–78.

90 "Brambleton Is in Eruption Again," *NJG*, July 14, 1923, 5; Earl Lewis, *In Their Own Interests*, 77–78.

91 Chalmers, *Hooded Americanism*, 231 (quotation); Buni, *Negro in Virginia Politics*, 101–4.

92 Chalmers, *Hooded Americanism*, 230; Cuthbert, "A Social Movement," 101–18; "The Chief and the Klan," *NVP*, Sept. 18, 1921, 6; "White Ministers Would Not Help Check Ku Klux," *NJG*, May 7, 1921, 1; "Roanoke Bars Ku Klux Klan," *NJG*, Feb. 12, 1921, 1 (quotation).

93 Wade, *Fiery Cross*, 249–50; "Ku Klux Klan Attend Funeral," *NJG*, Feb. 25, 1922, 1; "$100 Contribution to Mrs. E. S. Pierce by Ku Klux Klan," *RNL*, Aug. 1, 1923, 1; "Week's News in Brief," *NJG*, Jan. 5, 1924, 1; "Busmen and Klansmen to Play Sunday," *AG*, May 26, 1927; Craig and Silver, "'Tolerance of the Intolerant,'" 213–22.

94 Suggs, *P. B. Young, Newspaperman*, 59–60; "Father Warren, Here, Sheds Light on Kidnapping," *RNL*, Sept. 8, 1926, 1, 9; "Father Warren Unharmed When Carried Off by Band of Robed and Hooded Men," *NJG*, Sept. 4, 1926, 1; "Kidnappers Scurry under Hail of Shot," *NJG*, Sept. 1, 1923, 1 (quotation). On the violence and terrorism of the Ku Klux Klan in the 1920s in other parts of the South and the United States, see Feldman, *Politics, Society, and the Klan*; MacLean, *Behind the Mask of Chivalry*; Wade, *Fiery Cross*, bk. 2; and Blee, *Women and the Klan*.

95 "Race Antagonism a Case of 'Nerves,'" *RTD*, July 30, 1919, 6; "Stick to the Mummery," *NVP*, Dec. 26, 1920 (first and second quotations), reprinted in

NJG, Jan. 1, 1921; Ku Klux Klan #31, Franklin, Virginia, to Editor, *NVP*, July 24, 1922 (third quotation), "A Charter Member of the KKK" to LIJ, Sept. 18, 1921 (fourth quotation), and Threat to LIJ, July 15, 1921 (fifth quotation), folder "1920–1924 Correspondence: Ku Klux Klan," box 1, LIJP (#9924-e); Cuthbert, "A Social Movement."

CHAPTER THREE

1 "Post No. 1, Anglo-Saxon Clubs, Has 400 Members," *RNL*, June 5, 1923, 18 (quotation). For more on Powell's career as a pianist and composer, see Ward, "Life and Works of John Powell," and Whisnant, *All That Is Native and Fine*, chap. 3.
2 See Sherman, "'The Last Stand,'" 69–92 (all quotations on 69). The racial extremism and histrionics of the leaders of the Anglo-Saxon Clubs have also attracted the attention of scholars interested in the connection between the 1924 Racial Integrity Act, the major legislative achievement of the organization, and *Loving v. Virginia*, the 1967 Supreme Court decision that outlawed three centuries of miscegenation statutes in the United States. See *Loving v. Virginia*, 388 U.S. 1 (1967); Wadlington, "The *Loving* Case," 1189–1223; and Lombardo, "Miscegenation, Eugenics, and Racism," 421–52. Lombardo draws upon Wadlington's more wide-ranging essay and emphasizes the influence that the "science" of eugenics had on proponents of Virginia's anti-miscegenation crusade. In part, Lombardo's purpose is to challenge historians of the eugenics movement who have not paid much attention to the connection between eugenics and anti-miscegenation laws. See "Miscegenation, Eugenics, and Racism," 424 n. 15. Gregory Michael Dorr, a historian of the eugenics movement in Virginia, successfully answers Lombardo's challenge in "Assuring America's Place in the Sun," 257–96. Legal historian Paul Finkelman does not discuss the Anglo-Saxon Clubs or Virginia's twentieth-century miscegenation laws but does examine such efforts in Virginia in the seventeenth and eighteenth centuries. See Finkelman, "Crimes of Love, Misdemeanors of Passion," 124–35. Historian Peter Wallenstein touches upon Virginia's 1924 Racial Integrity Act in an insightful piece that looks more broadly at the regulation of interracial marriage in Virginia and Alabama from the end of the Civil War to the *Loving* decision. See Wallenstein, "Race, Marriage, and the Law of Freedom," 371–437, and "Right to Marry," 37–41. For a comparison of miscegenation statutes throughout the United States, see Pascoe, "Miscegenation Law," 44–69; Murray, *States' Laws on Race and Color*; and Mangum, *Legal Status of the Negro*, esp. chap. 1.
3 Showalter, "Virginia—A Commonwealth That Has Come Back," 439 (first quotation); Clark, *Stuffed Peacocks*, 68 (second quotation). Douglas Southall Freeman once described eastern Virginians, who dominated the state in political, social, economic, and cultural terms, as "Shintoists" for whom "genealogy makes history personal" and "kinship to the eighth degree is usually recognized." See Freeman's introduction to Works Progress Administration,

Virginia, 4. For more on Lady Astor, born Nancy Langhorne in central Virginia, see Fox, *The Langhorne Sisters*.

4 JP to William T. Reed, Jan. 24, 1921, section 1, William T. Reed Family Papers, VHS. For more on Reed and his influence, see Fry, "Senior Advisor," 445–69.

5 "Post No. 1, Anglo-Saxon Clubs, Has 400 Members," *RNL*, June 5, 1923, 18 (quotation). On the Ku Klux Klan and its lack of support among Democratic officials in Virginia, see Chalmers, *Hooded Americanism*, 230–35. On the Klan in the 1920s, see MacLean, *Behind the Mask of Chivalry*; Leonard J. Moore, *Citizen Klansmen*; Wade, *Fiery Cross*, esp. bk. 2; Feldman, *Politics, Society, and the Klan*; and Blee, *Women of the Klan*.

6 "Ku Klux Klan Here Acts to Break Up Order in Nation," *RTD*, Oct. 18, 1922, 1, 6 (first, second, and third quotations on 1; fourth quotation on 1, 6).

7 Ibid., 6; "Ku Klux Klan Fined $1000," *RNL*, Oct. 30, 1922, 1; "Ku Klux Klan Is Fined $50 by Va. Corp. Commission," *RNL*, Apr. 13, 1923, 1; "Klan's Suit Here Is Compromised," *RNL*, June 7, 1923, 1.

8 "Ku Klux Klan Here Acts to Break Up Order in Nation," *RTD*, Oct. 18, 1922, 1, 6; "Post No. 1, Anglo-Saxon Clubs, Has 400 Members," *RNL*, June 5, 1923, 18. In a letter to Dr. Stuart McGuire written on Jan. 1, 1925, Powell insisted that "I am not a leader, nor even a member of the Ku Klux Klan. The Anglo-Saxon Clubs are in no way connected with the Klan. In fact the men who originated the Clubs were so strongly opposed to the Klan that they took it into the Courts and stopped its activities in the state for more than a year." See JP to Dr. Stuart McGuire, Jan. 1, 1925, folder 2, box 56, JPP.

9 "Post No. 1, Anglo-Saxon Clubs, Has 400 Members," *RNL*, June 5, 1923, 18; JP, "Is White America to Become a Negroid Nation?," *RTD*, July 22, 1923, Sunday Magazine, 2 (quotations), and Earnest Sevier Cox, "Is White America to Become a Negroid Nation?," *RTD*, July 22, 1923, Sunday Magazine, 2. It is not entirely clear why Powell and Cox ceased to discuss immigration by July 1923, well in advance of the passage of the Native Origins Act in 1924. Virginia's population hovered between 98 and 99 percent native-born throughout the 1920s. It is possible that Virginians simply did not respond to fears over immigration in the same way that they did to concerns over racial mixing. Powell and Cox may have sensed this and tailored their arguments accordingly. See U.S. Bureau of the Census, *Fourteenth Decennial Census, 1920*, vol. 2, *Population*, 33 (table 7), and *Fifteenth Decennial Census, 1930, Population*, vol. 3, pt. 2, *Montana–Wyoming*, 1141 (table 2).

10 JP, "Is White America to Become a Negroid Nation?," *RTD*, July 22, 1923, Sunday Magazine, 2 (quotations); Sherman, "'The Last Stand,'" 70–71.

11 Williamson, *New People*, 112–15, 126–29; U.S. Bureau of the Census, *Fourteenth Decennial Census, 1920*, vol. 2, *Population*, 16–18 (quotation on 16). For more on the variability of census enumerations and racial designations, see Bynum, "'White Negroes' in Segregated Mississippi," 247–76, esp. 255, 261.

12 Gregory Michael Dorr, "Assuring America's Place in the Sun," 257–96 (first quotation on 258; second quotation on 262; third quotation on 259).

13 Ibid., 257–96; *Buck v. Bell*, 274 U.S. 200 (1927); Kevles, *In the Name of Eu-*

genics, 110–12; Peter Hardin, "Segregation's Era of Science," *RTD*, Nov. 26, 2000, A1; Minutes, *News Leader* Current Events Class, Mar. 10, 1924 (quotation), folder "1923 Ap–De and 1924," box 177, DSFP-LC. On the support of the Bureau of Vital Statistics for the 1924 sterilization measure, see WAP, "Racial Improvement," *Virginia Medical Monthly*, Nov. 1925, 486–89, copy in folder "Bureau of Vital Statistics," box 43, TEP. In February 2001 the Virginia General Assembly voted to express "profound regret" over the state's involvement in eugenic sterilization. See Peter Hardin, "Legislature Acknowledges Harm Caused by Eugenics," *RTD*, Feb. 25, 2001, A11.

14 Gregory Michael Dorr, "Assuring America's Place in the Sun," 265 n. 23; WAP to Ivey Lewis, Oct. 29, 1926, Lewis to WAP, Nov. 9, 1926, folder "1926 Letters," box 1, Ivey Foreman Lewis Papers, UVA; Lewis to WAP, Oct. 18, 1929 (quotations), folder "Pl–Pz," box 13, DSFP-LC. For more on the national eugenics movement and the Anglo-Saxon Clubs, see Sherman "'The Last Stand,'" 71–74; Lombardo, "Miscegenation, Eugenics, and Racism," 422–25; Thomson, "Racism and Racial Classification," 102–38; and Reilly, *Surgical Solution*, 72–74.

15 JP, "Is White America to Become a Negroid Nation?," *RTD*, July 22, 1923, Sunday Magazine, 2. With reference to Powell's opportunistic use of eugenics, Paul Lombardo rightly concludes that "the true motive of the Racial Integrity Act of 1924 was the maintenance of white supremacy and black economic and social inferiority—racism, pure and simple. It was an accident of history that eugenic theory reached its peak of acceptability in 1924 so as to be available as a respectable veneer with which to cover ancient prejudice. For Powell, Plecker, and their ilk, eugenical ideology was not a *sine qua non* for legislation, but merely a coincidental set of arguments that provided intellectual fuel to the racist fires." See Lombardo, "Miscegenation, Eugenics, and Racism," 425.

16 Cox, "Is White America to Become a Negroid Nation?," *RTD*, July 22, 1923, Sunday Magazine, 2.

17 JP, "Is White America to Become a Negroid Nation?," *RTD*, July 22, 1923, Sunday Magazine, 2.

18 Ibid.

19 "Racial Integrity," *RTD*, July 22, 1923, 4.

20 Sherman, "'The Last Stand,'" 75–76 (quotation on 75). See also form letters designed by Plecker for use by the commissioner of revenue, dated July 26, 1923, and by the local registrar, dated June 22, 1922, folder 1, box 56, JPP.

21 At the end of the nineteenth century, twenty-six states throughout the United States, mostly in the South and West, prohibited interracial marriage; ultimately at least thirty-eight states adopted such laws, although only sixteen southern states retained such statutes by the time of the *Loving* decision in 1967. See *Loving v. Virginia*, 388 U.S. 1 (1967); Bardaglio, *Reconstructing the Household*, 176–89; Pascoe, "Miscegenation Law," 44–69; Finkelman, "Crimes of Love, Misdemeanors of Passion," 124–35; Williamson, *New People*, 97–98; and Mangum, *Legal Status of the Negro*, 1–17. More than likely, members of the Anglo-Saxon Clubs would have cited the situation that Vic-

toria Bynum has described in "'White Negroes' in Segregated Mississippi" as proof of the necessity of a "one-drop" rule. Bynum discusses the acquittal of Davis Knight, a "white negro" who acknowledged having black blood, but who could not be convicted under Mississippi's miscegenation law because it defined blackness according to a "one-eighth" rule.

22   Letter from a local registrar to WAP, July 28, 1923 (quotation), and WAP to Senator M. B. Booker, Feb. 15, 1924, folder 1, box 56, JPP.

23   "Constitution of the Anglo-Saxon Club[s] of America: Adopted in Convention at Richmond, Va., October 13, 1923" (first and second quotations), folder 7, box 56, JPP; Sherman, "'The Last Stand,'" 76 (third quotation, originally drawn from the Anglo-Saxon constitution). The number of posts is gleaned from an undated letter from Lawrence T. Price requesting support for legislation and from a letter from JP to Stone Deavours dated Apr. 20, 1925. Powell indicates that there were twenty-four posts at the time of the convention; Price's letter lists twenty-five posts just a short time afterward. The Powell letter is in folder 2, box 56, and the Price letter is in folder 7-c, box 56, JPP.

24   JP to Stone Deavours, Apr. 20, 1925, W. C. Neill (member of Georgia legislature) to James C. Davis (member of Georgia legislature), May 19, 1925, Davis to JP, May 25, 1925, JP to Davis, May 30, 1925, all in folder 2, box 56, JPP; Davis to JP, Aug. 22, 1927, and "Addresses of W.R.I. Club of Richmond, Virginia, 1926," both in folder 3, box 56, JPP; *Richmond City Directory, 1926*; *Social Register, 1919*; Handy, *Social Recorder of Virginia*; Mangum, *Legal Status of the Negro*, 6–8. The establishment of Anglo-Saxon chapters in the North (at the University of Pennsylvania and Columbia University, and on Staten Island) reflected the presence of leading eugenicists in those locales. There is no evidence that those posts were ever active. Richard Sherman notes quite accurately that Powell himself evinced little interest in the nuts and bolts of running the organization and left day-to-day operations to Lawrence T. Price, a doctor in Richmond. See Sherman, "'The Last Stand,'" 76. Former Richmond journalist Parke Rouse includes Mrs. E. Randolph (Maude) Williams among Richmond's most important "dowagers." Williams and a number of her relatives and friends appear on the list of members of the Women's Racial Integrity Club. See Rouse, *We Happy WASPs*, 204.

25   M. H. Bettinger to JP, Oct. 13, 1923 (first quotation), M. O. Williams to JP, Nov. 1, 1923, Williams to Dr. Lawrence T. Price, Jan. 31, 1924 (second and third quotations), folder 1, box 56, JPP.

26   *The Virginia Tech*, Jan. 10, 1924 (quotation), and Mrs. Reid Brockenbrough to JP, Feb. 2, 1924, folder 1, box 56, JPP. The article in question was highlighted, either marked for Powell's attention or by Powell himself. In addition, check marks were placed next to some of the specific suggestions.

27   W. S. Gooch to JP, Apr. 14, 1924, and Gooch to JP, Apr. 18, 1924, folder 1, box 56, JPP.

28   Bellamy, "If Christ Came to Dixie," 37–40; Tindall, *Emergence of the New South*, 183 n. 160.

29   Bellamy, "If Christ Came to Dixie," 33–42 (quotations on 37); Egerton, *Speak*

Now against the Day, 124–26; Dunbar, *Against the Grain*, 18–45; Tindall, *Emergence of the New South*, 183 n. 160.

30 Commonwealth of Virginia, *Acts of Assembly, 1924*, 535 (first quotation); Sherman, "'The Last Stand,'" 77 (second quotation); Guild, *Black Laws of Virginia*, 35. The issue of registration only applied to persons born before June 14, 1912. All persons born after that date were already registered according to the provisions of a 1912 statute that established the Bureau of Vital Statistics. See Sherman, "'The Last Stand,'" 78. Because Virginia's 1924 statute defined white persons for the first time, the act had the effect of outlawing for the first time marriages between whites and Asians. Before 1924, state law defined only black persons, and therefore all Asians were considered white. See Wallenstein, "Race, Marriage, and the Law of Freedom," 409.

31 "Powell Asks Law Guarding Racial Purity," *RTD*, Feb. 13, 1924, 1; "Citation of Cases: Showing Racial Amalgamation and Decadence of Racial Sense," folder 7, box 56, JPP; Lothrop Stoddard, "To All Whom This Statement May Concern," Feb. 1, 1924, Franklin Giddings to JP, Feb. 5, 1924, Madison Grant to JP, Feb. 1, 1924, folder 1, box 56, JPP; Sherman, "'The Last Stand,'" 77–78; Thomas L. Dabney, "Views and Reviews," *NJG*, Feb. 23, 1924, 7, 9 (quotation on 9).

32 "Race Amalgamation Will Be Discussed," *RNL*, Feb. 20, 1924, 4; "Race Amalgamation Bill Passed in Va. Legislature," *Richmond Planet*, Mar. 1, 1924, 1; *Richmond Planet*, Feb. 23, 1924, 4 (quotation), reprinted in Thomson, "Racism and Racial Classification," 128; *NJG*, Mar. 15, 1924, 12, cited in ibid., 132.

33 GBH to the editor, *RNL*, Feb. 23, 1924, 19 (first and second quotations); WAP to Stone Deavours, Apr. 15, 1925 (third quotation), folder 2, box 56, JPP. Douglas Southall Freeman actually sent a copy of Hancock's letter to Powell and asked if he thought the newspaper should print it. Powell's response is unrecorded. Freeman's action is remarkable and suggests the depth of Powell's influence at the time. Freeman later denounced the lengths to which Walter Plecker went in enforcing the statute, but he never objected to the principle behind the measure. See DSF to JP, Feb. 14, 1924, folder 1, box 56, JPP. For more on Hancock, see Gavins, *Perils and Prospects*.

34 Sherman, "'The Last Stand,'" 78; Pascoe, "Miscegenation Law," 59 (first quotation); E. H. Anderson to ELT, Apr. 17, 1924 (second quotation), folder "Bureau of Vital Statistics," box 43, TEP. Thirteen of forty senators and nineteen of one hundred delegates actually abstained from voting at all. The reasons for this are not entirely clear. See Commonwealth of Virginia, *Journal of the Senate, 1924*, Feb. 27, 1924, 476–77, and *Journal of the House of Delegates, 1924*, Mar. 8, 1924, 774–75.

35 "To Further Aims of Racial Law," *RTD*, Mar. 19, 1924, 2.

36 WAP to ELT, Apr. 19, 1924, folder "Bureau of Vital Statistics," box 43, TEP; WAP to Stone Deavours, Apr. 15, 1925, WAP to Sen. Morris Shepherd, Mar. 12, 1925, JP to Hon. George H. Roberts, Feb. 28, 1925, folder 2, box 56, WAP to Earnest S. Cox, Aug. 9, 1924, folder 1, box 56, JPP.

37 "Instructions to Local Registrars and Other Agents in Administration of Law," *Virginia Health Bulletin, Department of Health* 16, extra no. 1 (Mar. 1924): 1–3, copy in folder 7, box 56, JPP; WAP, "Birth Registration and Racial Integrity Law," *Virginia Journal of Education* 18 (Sept. 1924): 13 (first and second quotations). In his "Instructions," Plecker defined "mulatto" as the offspring of white and colored parents, "quadroon" as the offspring of mulatto and white, and "octoroon" as the offspring of quadroon and white. He used "mixed" and "issue" to refer to any person having a mixture of white and black blood in which white predominated. "That is the class," he warned, "that should be reported with the greatest care, as many of these are on the borderline, and constitute the real danger of race intermixture" ("Instructions to Local Registrars," 2). It is ironic that Plecker insisted that persons with even a trace of black blood would continue to "present clear marks of colored ancestry" ("Birth Registration," 13), while Powell had cited as evidence for the need of a Racial Integrity Act his own difficulty in being able to tell who was black or white.

38 WAP to Mrs. Robert Cheatham, Apr. 30, 1924 (first quotation), WAP to Mary Gildon (second quotation), folder 1, box 56, JPP. Plecker copied these letters on a single sheet and sent it to Powell; he added the third quotation at the top of this copy.

39 WAP to R. N. Anderson, July 31, 1924, folder 1, box 56, JPP.

40 H. H. Sorrells to WAP, Apr. 25, 1924, WAP to Clerks of Rockbridge, Amherst, Augusta Counties, Apr. 29, 1924, folder 1, box 56, JPP.

41 WAP to Earnest S. Cox, Aug. 9, 1924, WAP to JP, July 30, 1924, folder 1, box 56, JPP.

42 WAP to W. E. Sandidge, Oct. 4, 1924, folder 1, box 56, JPP; J. David Smith, *Eugenic Assault on America*, 71; Sherman, "'The Last Stand,'" 80. Governor Trinkle, essentially silent up until this point, wrote Willis Robertson, the commonwealth's attorney for Rockbridge County, a future U.S. senator, and the father of evangelist Pat Robertson, that "this law is a new one and I regard it of vital importance. There are a great many of our real substantial white people who fought hard for the Bill and are doing all they can to help out in this situation over the State." See ELT to A. Willis Robertson, Oct. 6, 1924, folder "Bureau of Vital Statistics," box 43, TEP.

Just as census takers did not apply uniform standards in determining who was black and who was mulatto (see note 11, above), evidence exists that "colored" may have sometimes referred specifically to blacks but at other times designated any nonwhite person. See Mangum, *Legal Status of the Negro*, 4–5. In addition, no consistent definition of "Indian" existed in the nineteenth century; racial designations depended upon the whims of enumerators. Furthermore, many of the records in Virginia counties with large Indian populations burned or were lost at various points during the century. Thus, any attempt to document the racial classification of persons with Indian ancestry is fraught with difficulty. See Rountree, *Pocahontas's People*, 188–90.

43 WAP to Silas Coleman (quotation), WAP to ELT, WAP to A. Willis Robertson, WAP to A. T. Shields, all dated Nov. 7, 1924, folder "Bureau of Vital Statistics," box 43, TEP.

44 "Woman, Listed Negroid, Wins Right to Be Called 'White,'" *RNL*, Nov. 18, 1924, 1, 4 (first quotation on 1, 4; second, third, fourth, and fifth quotations on 4; final quotation on 1); J. David Smith, *Eugenic Assault on America*, 71–73; Sherman, "'The Last Stand,'" 80–81.

45 U.S. Senate, *Reports of the Immigration Commission*, vol. 5, *Dictionary of Races and Peoples*, 30–33; Jacobson, *Whiteness of a Different Color*, 78–80; JP, "Is White America to Become a Negroid Nation?," *RTD*, July 22, 1923, Sunday Magazine, 2.

46 "Woman, Listed Negroid, Wins Right to Be Called 'White,'" *RNL*, Nov. 18, 1924, 4; "Testing the Racial Integrity Law," *RTD*, Nov. 20, 1924, 6; J. David Smith, *Eugenic Assault on America*, 74 (quotation).

47 JP to Henry Holt, Apr. 6, 1925, folder 2, box 56, JPP; John Kneebone, "In Jim Crow's Lifetime: Race in Virginia before the Civil Rights Movement" (talk delivered at the Virginia Historical Society, Apr. 19, 1996); WAP to JP, June 29, 1946, folder 6, box 56, JPP; J. David Smith, *Eugenic Assault on America*, 69–70. I am grateful to John Kneebone, who personally inspected these records, for sharing his conclusions.

48 Rountree, *Pocahontas's People*, 188–218; DeMarce, "'Verry Slitly Mixt,'" 5–13; "Chief Cook's Lament," *Richmond Planet*, Feb. 11, 1928, 4 (quotation). Even prior to the Civil War, many mixed-race Virginians understood the social and political benefits of claiming Indian rather than black ancestry. See Peter Wallenstein, "Indian Foremothers," 57–73. The desire among some ethnic groups to hide or deny black ancestry, born no doubt of the realities of racial discrimination and oppression, continues into the twenty-first century. Contentious debates continue to swirl over the racial ancestry of the Melungeons, a group of mixed-race people in western Virginia and eastern Tennessee and Kentucky. Walter Plecker considered the Melungeons, like all mixed-race persons in Virginia in the 1920s, to have African ancestors. The Melungeons themselves denied this at the time, and many of them continue to do so today. See Henige and Wilson, "Viewpoint: Brent Kennedy's *Melungeons*," 270–98; DeMarce, "Looking at Legends—Lumbee and Melungeon"; and Carol Morello, "Beneath Myth, Melungeons Find Roots of Oppression," *Washington Post*, May 29, 2000, A1.

49 J. David Smith, *Eugenic Assault on America*, 71–81; WAP to Samuel Adams, Dec. 11, 1924, folder 1, box 56, JPP; WAP to C. W. Garrison, Jan. 5, 1925, and WAP to the editor of *RTD*, Apr. 28, 1925, folder 2, box 56, JPP; DeMarce, "'Verry Slitly Mixt,'" 9. DeMarce says in her study that "not all bearers of the family names mentioned here are of tri-racial ancestry; many of the names were common among white settlers in the Upper South." Plecker, however, relying on lists of such names to prove his allegations, assumed that all persons with the same surname in a given community shared a common racial heritage. Plecker did confide to an out-of-state correspondent that the classification of tri-racial individuals often proved difficult. "One of our local reg-

istrars," relayed the statistician, "told us that they have a comb which hangs in their church. If it passes through the hair of an applicant he is an Indian, if not, he is a negro." See WAP to Harry E. Davis, Oct. 4, 1924, folder 1, box 56, JPP.

50 "Stenographic Report of an Interview Regarding the So-Called 'Indians' of Charles City County between Mr. E. H. Marston of Charles City County and Dr. W. A. Plecker, State Registrar, Held in the Bureau of Vital Statistics, February 1925," 1; "A Statement of the Origin of the So-Called 'Indians' of Charles City County, as Given by Mr. George H. Marston, brother of Mr. E. H. Marston . . . (in February 1925)"; "Mr. D. F. Rudisill, local registrar at Roxbury, gives us Hill Adkins' Reason for not Joining the 'Tribe,' February 1925" (quotation), all in folder 2, box 56, JPP. Anthropologist Helen Rountree acknowledges that the advent of Jim Crow laws did, in fact, spur the Chickahominies to organize formally and to assert their "Indianness." But Rountree also documents that the Chickahominies had been encouraged to seek formal recognition in the early 1890s by a white anthropologist and the chief of the Pamunkey Indians, one of two tribes living on state-recognized reservations. Thus, while Plecker's interpretation appears to be based on a kernel of truth, he clearly relied upon a distorted interpretation of events. See Rountree, *Pocahontas's People*, 212–15.

51 "Stenographic Report of an Interview Regarding the So-Called 'Indians' of Charles City County, February 1925," and "The description of the Comb Test of William Archer Jones when he applied for admission into the 'tribe' as told by William Archer Jones to Mr. George H. Marston. Mr. Marston is giving the description to the Bureau of Vital Statistics, February 1925," folder 2, box 56, JPP; WAP to W. M. Steuart, Director, United States Bureau of the Census, Jan. 14, 1925, folder "Bureau of Vital Statistics," box 43, TEP; WAP to Steuart, Nov. 20, 1928, WAP to Steuart, Aug. 30, 1929, folder "Health—Bureau of Vital Statistics," box 24, BEP; "Aid Indians in School Request," *RNL*, Feb. 14, 1924, 5.

52 "At an Interview between William Archer Thaddeus Jones and Hon. Albert O. Boschen Held in the Office of the Bureau of Vital Statistics the Following Questions Were Asked and Answered, January 31st, 1925," and Clarence Jennings to Albert O. Boschen, Jan. 27, 1925, folder 2, box 56, JPP.

53 WAP to W. M. Steuart, Director, United States Bureau of the Census, Jan. 14, 1925, folder "Bureau of Vital Statistics," box 43, TEP; WAP to Steuart, Nov. 20, 1928 (quotation), WAP to Steuart, Aug. 30, 1929, folder "Health—Bureau of Vital Statistics," box 24, BEP.

54 WAP to Georgia Fraser, Mar. 16, 1925, WAP to ELT, Oct. 5, 1925, folder "Bureau of Vital Statistics," box 43, TEP; "Places Indians in Negroid Class," *RNL*, July 2, 1925, 1, 16; "Indian Warfare Starts over Race Classification," *NJG*, July 11, 1925, 1; "Threats to Lead to Arrests Here," *RNL*, July 22, 1925, 4; Sherman, "'The Last Stand,'" 78–79.

55 ELT to E. P. Bradby, Dec. 1, 1925 (first quotation), ELT to WAP, Dec. 1, 1925 (second quotation), folder "Bureau of Vital Statistics," box 43, TEP. Trinkle's claim that he knew nothing of Plecker's intentions seems dubious at best.

After Plecker first broached the subject in October, Trinkle advised him to consult with the director of legislative services about preparing new bills for the 1926 General Assembly. See ELT to WAP, Oct. 5, 1925, folder "Bureau of Vital Statistics," box 43, TEP.

56 WAP to ELT, Dec. 2, 1925, ELT to WAP, Dec. 4, 1925 (first quotation), WAP to ELT, Dec. 5, 1925 (second quotation), folder "Bureau of Vital Statistics," box 43, TEP; J. David Smith, *Eugenic Assault on America*, 76; "Real Indians Family Says, Not Negroes," *RTD*, Jan. 29, 1929, 3.

57 WAP to Hiram Smith, Nov. 19, 1925, folder "Bureau of Vital Statistics," box 43, TEP; photograph of Trinkle with Chief Cook and his daughter, *RTD*, Nov. 12, 1925, 9; WAP to HFB, Dec. 2, 1925, folder "1925 Correspondence Ph–Pl," box 90, HFBP. Plecker wrote to Byrd, "For our office to succeed in its struggles to keep these people where they belong, it is necessary for us to have the support of other branches of government."

58 Ennion G. Williams to WAP, Dec. 10, 1925, ELT to W. L. Kerr, May 12, 1925, ELT to W. McDonald Lee, Commissioner of Fisheries, Dec. 12, 1925, folder "Bureau of Vital Statistics," box 43, TEP; "Give Grounds for Ousting Plecker," *RNL*, Apr. 2, 1925, 26.

59 Virginia State Board of Health, Bureau of Vital Statistics, *Eugenics in Relation to the New Family and the Law on Racial Integrity: Including a Paper Read before the American Public Health Association*, 2d ed. (Richmond, 1925), copy in folder "Bureau of Vital Statistics," box 43, TEP. The language of Plecker's warning, explicitly urging young white men not to join "of themselves to females of a lower race," challenges the conclusions of historian Lisa Lindquist Dorr in "Arm in Arm," 143–66. Lindquist Dorr argues that the "key" to Virginia's 1924 Racial Integrity Act was "prescribing the behavior and attitudes of Virginia's white women" (143–44). She adds that Powell and Plecker acted in response to a fear "that social interactions between whites and blacks, specifically between white women and black men, had increased sharply in Virginia during the early 1920s" (143). More specifically, she argues that Powell and Plecker worried that men of unknown racial ancestry "targeted the most innocent victims—presumably naive, young, modern women newly free from traditional familial supervision" (156). Many white Virginians, however, blamed white men, not black men, for whatever miscegenation did occur. Douglas Southall Freeman, for example, argued that it was the "bad habits" of "good-for-nothing" white men who pursued black women that caused the trouble (Minutes, *News Leader* Current Events Class, Nov. 24, 1924, folder "1923 Ap–Dc and 1924," box 177, DSFP-LC). Furthermore, the *Johns* and *Sorrells* cases involved white men marrying women whom Plecker considered part black. These were not modern women, freed from the constraints of family, but relatively isolated individuals who lived in rural communities with extended families. Powell and Plecker certainly objected to any form of interracial mixing, and Plecker's remarks included a warning to white women as well, but neither Plecker's admonition nor his experience in enforcing the Racial Integrity Act support Lindquist Dorr's thesis that white women were the main targets.

60 "Virginia Health Officer Brands Colored Races as Incapable of Attaining Highest Civilization," *NJG*, Feb. 14, 1925, 7; "The Nordic Craze," *NJG*, Feb. 14, 1925, 12 (quotation); "Give Grounds for Ousting Plecker," *RNL*, Apr. 2, 1925, 26; "Plecker Aroused by Blow Aimed at Racial Law," *RTD*, Mar. 31, 1925, 1; "It Is Political Censorship," *RNL*, Apr. 2, 1925, 8; "Steps Are Taken by Labor Bureau to Oust Dr. Plecker," *NJG*, Apr. 4, 1925, 1.

61 Virginia State Board of Censors, *1923 Censorship Law and Rules and Regulations* (Richmond, 1923), 3, copy in folder "Motion Picture Censorship," box 44, BEP; *Report of the Virginia State Board of Censors, July 1, 1924, to June 30, 1925* (Richmond, 1925), 2 (quotation), copy in folder 23, box 45, RDMPC. In April 1927 the act that reorganized the state government renamed the Board of Censors the Division of Motion Picture Censorship and placed it under the jurisdiction of the Department of Law. For a more complete discussion of the activities of the Division of Motion Picture Censorship, see J. Douglas Smith, "Patrolling the Boundaries of Race."

62 Cripps, *Slow Fade to Black*, 170–202 (quotation on 170).

63 Henry T. Sampson, "Micheaux Film Corporation: Oscar Micheaux," in *Blacks in Black and White*, 142–69 (quotation on 142).

64 Regester, "Black Films, White Censors," 162–64 (first and second quotations on 162; third and fourth quotations on 164).

65 On the board's deliberation on previous Micheaux films, *Birthright* and *Son of Satan*, see J. Douglas Smith, "Patrolling the Boundaries of Race," esp. 279–85.

66 "Films Rejected In Toto since August 1922," 4, folder 94, box 54, RDMPC; Memo on *The House behind the Cedars* (quotation), folder 9, box 54, RDMPC; Henry T. Sampson, "Micheaux Film Corporation: Oscar Micheaux," in *Blacks in Black and White*, 322; JP to Arthur James, July 8, 1925, folder 2, box 56, JPP. For more on Louise Burleigh Powell, see Norfleet, "Louise Burleigh Powell," 22–28.

67 Memo on *The House behind the Cedars*, folder 9, box 54, RDMPC.

68 Telegram from Oscar Micheaux to Virginia Board of Censors, Mar. 13, 1925, Oscar Micheaux to Virginia Motion Picture Censors, Mar. 13, 1925, Evan Chesterman to Micheaux, Oct. 18, 1925, folder 9, box 54, RDMPC. Micheaux made extensive cuts to his nine-reel picture, including the elimination of the entire second reel that apparently dealt with the "hardships and social disadvantages suffered by negroes," a phrase that appears in a handwritten list of eliminations attached to the letter of Oct. 18, 1925.

69 Oscar Micheaux to Virginia Motion Picture Censors, Mar. 13, 1925, folder 9, box 54, RDMPC.

70 "Films Rejected In Toto since August 1922," 4, folder 94, box 54, RDMPC; Evan Chesterman to Oscar Micheaux, Oct. 18, 1925, folder 9, box 54, RDMPC.

71 Statement of Louise Burleigh (first and second quotations), folder "1926 Jan–June," box 3, JPP; JP to Arthur James, June 6, 1925 (third quotation), folder 2, box 56, JPP; J. David Smith, *Eugenic Assault on America*, 51–52.

72 JP to Arthur James, June 6, 1925 (quotations), JP to James, July 8, 1925,

folder 2, box 56, JPP; Statements of Earnest S. Cox and Louise Burleigh, folder "1926 Jan–June," box 3, JPP; J. David Smith, *Eugenic Assault on America*, 52–54.

73 "Ex-Welfare Chief, Arthur James, Dies," *RTD*, Feb. 14, 1985.

74 Schuyler, *Black No More*, 35 (first quotation), 81 (second quotation).

75 Ibid., 119 (first quotation), 120 (second quotation), 122 (third quotation).

76 Minutes, *News Leader* Current Events Class, Nov. 24, 1924, folder "1923 Ap–Dc and 1924," box 177, DSFP-LC; "Negroes Want Racial Integrity, Too," *Richmond Planet*, Feb. 11, 1928, 4 (quotation); George S. Schuyler to John Mitchell, Feb. 13, 1928, reprinted in *Richmond Planet*, Feb. 25, 1928, 1.

CHAPTER FOUR

1 JEG to William Howard Taft, Sept. 3, 1925, reel 276, William Howard Taft Papers; Minutes, *News Leader* Current Events Class, Feb. 8, 1926, folder "*News Leader* Current Events Class, Minutes (1926)," box 176, DSFP-LC; Sherman, "'Teachings at Hampton Institute,'" 281; Wolters, "Rites of Passage," 239 (first quotation); "Integrity of the Anglo-Saxon Race," *Newport News Daily Press*, Mar. 15, 1925, 4 (all other quotations).

2 "Integrity of the Anglo-Saxon Race," *Newport News Daily Press*, Mar. 15, 1925, 4.

3 JEG to WSC, Mar. 17, 1925, folder "Miscellaneous Correspondence 3-1," box 77, BEP, copy of letter reprinted in "Virginia Editor Sees Menace in Education of Race," *NJG*, Mar. 28, 1925, 3.

4 *Newport News Daily Press*, Mar. 20, 1925, reprinted in "Virginia Editor Sees Menace in Education of Race," *NJG*, Mar. 28, 1925, 3.

5 JEG to ELT, July 11, 1925, folder "Hampton Institute," box 21, TEP; JEG to William Howard Taft, Sept. 3, 1925, reel 276, Taft Papers; Sherman, "'Teachings at Hampton Institute,'" 282.

6 "Error Attempts to Dethrone Truth," *NJG*, Mar. 28, 1925, 12.

7 "Virginia Editor Sees Menace in Education of Race," *NJG*, Mar. 28, 1925, 3 (first quotation); Pulley, *Old Virginia Restored*, 132–51; Wolters, "Rites of Passage," 240; Grace Copeland to ELT, July 21, 1925, folder "Hampton Institute," box 21, TEP; Fairclough, "'Being in the Field of Education and Also Being a Negro,'" 65–91 (second quotation on 75; third quotation on 76).

8 "What About Black Mammy's Children?," *NJG*, Apr. 4, 1925, 12; WSC, letter to the editor of the *Northampton Progress*, Mar. 14, 1922 (quotation), copy in folder "1908–1954 Newspaper Clippings," box 4, WSC Papers, UVA.

9 WSC to JEG, no date, folder "1919–1928 Speeches," box 3, WSC Papers, UVA.

10 WSC, letter to the editor of the *Northampton Progress*, Mar. 14, 1922, copy in folder "1908–1954 Newspaper Clippings," box 4, WSC Papers, UVA; "What About Black Mammy's Children?," *NJG*, Apr. 4, 1925, 12. On the founding of Hampton Institute as a vocational training ground for black laborers, see Engs, *Freedom's First Generation*, 139–60. Raymond Wolters details the

struggles of students to demand a more academic and less vocational education. Although James Gregg appeared sympathetic, he moved slowly in order not to antagonize white supporters of the school who might have considered the shift offensive. Resistance on the part of the administration ultimately led to a student strike in October 1927. See Wolters, "Rites of Passage," 230–75.

11 JEG to William Howard Taft, Sept. 3, 1925, reel 276, Taft Papers; Grace B. Copeland to ELT, [Apr. 23, 1925; date not on letter but gleaned from response] (all quotations), folder C (8-7), box 2, TEP.

12 ELT to Grace B. Copeland, May 5, 1925 (first quotation), folder C (8-7), box 2, TEP; JEG to ELT, July 11, 1925, folder "Hampton Institute," box 21, TEP; JEG to William Howard Taft, Sept. 3, 1925, reel 276, Taft Papers; "The Anglo-Saxon at Bay," *Crisis* 30 (May 1925): 10–11; "Social Equality at Hampton," *Crisis* 30 (June 1925): 59–60 (block quotation); Sherman, "'Teachings at Hampton Institute,'" 282–83.

13 "Social Equality at Hampton," *Crisis* 30 (June 1925): 60.

14 Henley Guy, Hampton, Va., to JP, Apr. 9, 1925, folder 2, box 56, JPP; Sherman, "'Teachings at Hampton Institute,'" 282; "John Powell to the Rescue," *NJG*, May 9, 1925, 12. Powell's absence from Richmond from January through April is also mentioned in a letter from JP to Arthur James, June 6, 1925, folder 2, box 56, JPP.

15 Elizabeth Norfleet, interview by author, Charlottesville, Va., Dec. 28, 1996. In a letter to William Howard Taft, James Gregg confirmed the essence of Norfleet's recollection. Gregg described Grace Copeland as an "intimate friend" of Powell's who, along with the pianist, "put Colonel Copeland up to writing the two editorials." See JEG to William Howard Taft, Sept. 3, 1925, reel 276, Taft Papers.

16 William Pickens, "Yelling Murder and Doing All the Murder," *NJG*, Apr. 4, 1925, 12; "The Tuskegee-Hampton $5,000,000 Endowment," *NJG*, Apr. 4, 1925, 12; ELT to Homer Ferguson, May 15, 1925 [two separate letters] (first quotation), Ferguson to ELT, May 18, 1925 (second quotation), folder "Hampton Institute," box 21, TEP.

17 ELT to JP, May 29, 1925, folder "Bureau of Vital Statistics," box 43, TEP; ELT to JP, June 15, 1925, ELT to JEG, July 8, 1925 (quotations), folder "Hampton Institute," box 21, TEP.

18 JEG to ELT, July 11, 1925 (quotation), folder "Hampton Institute," box 21, TEP; Sherman, "'Teachings at Hampton Institute,'" 284–85.

19 Lawrence T. Price, Chairman, Anglo-Saxon Clubs of America, to ELT and others, July 10, 1925 (quotations), folder "Hampton Institute," box 21, TEP; "Asks Southerners Quit Endowment Fund Committee," *NJG*, July 18, 1925, 1.

20 Sherman, "'Teachings at Hampton Institute,'" 286–87.

21 Telegram from *RTD* to ELT, July 14, 1925, folder "Hampton Institute," box 21, TEP; "South Looks to Dr. Gregg," *RNL*, July 15, 1925, 8 (quotations).

22 WSC to ELT, July 16, 1925, folder "Hampton Institute," box 21, TEP.

23 Grace B. Copeland to ELT, July 21, 1925, folder "Hampton Institute," box 21, TEP.

24 "Mixed Faculties in Negro Schools," *NJG*, July 25, 1925, 12. The *Virginian-Pilot* editorial was quoted in the same issue.

25 On Hampton Institute as a school whose mission fit safely within the boundaries of paternalism, see Engs, *Freedom's First Generation*, 138–60, and Schall, *Stony the Road*. On the student strike at Hampton in 1927, see Wolters, "Rites of Passage," 230–75. Wolters argues persuasively that the decision of Hampton administrators and trustees to acquiesce in southern white demands and not push Hampton too quickly in the direction of a liberal arts curriculum contributed to the student strike.

26 ELT to JEG, Aug. 7, 1925, JEG to ELT, Aug. 18, 1925, ELT to WSC, Aug. 7, 1925 (quotation), WSC to ELT, Aug. 15, 1925, ELT to WSC, Aug. 17, 1925, folder "Hampton Institute," box 21, TEP; Sherman, "'Teachings at Hampton Institute,'" 287–88; "Why Don't They Stay Away?," *NVP*, Nov. 16, 1925, 4.

27 Young, "William Howard Taft and Hampton Institute," 149–50 (first quotation on 149); Sherman, "'Teachings at Hampton Institute,'" 288; "Want More Laws to Separate Races," *NJG*, Dec. 5, 1925, 1 (second quotation). Throughout his life, James Lawrence Blair Buck remained committed to both educational and interracial issues. In the late 1950s, he served as president of the Virginia Committee for Public Schools, a grassroots organization that fought to keep the public schools operating in the face of massive resistance. See Hershman, "Massive Resistance Meets Its Match," 107–11.

28 *Newport News Star*, Dec. 3, 1925, editorial page (first and second quotations), clipping in folder "Race Separation," box 24, James E. Gregg Collection, Hampton University Archives; Young, "William Howard Taft and Hampton Institute," 150 (third, fourth, and fifth quotations).

29 Commonwealth of Virginia, *Acts of Assembly, 1926*, 945–46; Dodson, *General Assembly of the Commonwealth of Virginia*, 115; Paul N. Williams, President, Elizabeth City County Civic League, interview by RJB, Oct. 22, 1939, folder 6, "Field Notes: Southern Trip, Bk. 1," box 85, RJBP.

30 Sherman, "'Teachings at Hampton Institute,'" 288–89; "Separation of the Races," *RTD*, Jan. 23, 1926, reprinted in "Our Friends Have the Courage of Their Convictions," *NJG*, Feb. 6, 1926, 12. The *Richmond Times-Dispatch* made essentially the same argument several days after the hearing in the house of delegates. See "Race Separation," *RTD*, Jan. 28, 1926, editorial page, copy in folder "1908–54 Newspaper Clippings," box 4, WSC Papers, UVA.

31 Sherman, "'Teachings at Hampton Institute,'" 288–89; "Oppose Bill to Separate Races in Public Halls," *NJG*, Feb. 6, 1926, 1; "Race Separation Advocates Win," *RTD*, Jan. 27, 1926, 1; "Chamber Opposes Racial Measure in Legislature," *RNL*, Feb. 2, 1926, 2; "Chamber Deplores Racial Legislation in the Virginia Assembly," *Richmond Planet*, Feb. 7, 1926, 1.

32 "The Opposition Grows," *NVP*, Feb. 15, 1926, 4 (first and second quotations); editorial from *Lynchburg News* reprinted in "Spirit of the Press," *NJG*, Feb. 6, 1926, 12 (third quotation); LIJ to Junius Fishburne, Feb. 6, 1926 (fourth, fifth, and sixth quotations), Fishburne to LIJ, Feb. 8, 1926 (seventh quotation),

folder "Correspondence of LIJ with Junius Fishburne," box 1, LIJP (#9924-d). Jaffé also editorialized against the legislation on Jan. 30 and Feb. 8, 1926.

33 "The Opposition Grows," *NVP*, Feb. 15, 1926, 4; "The Racial Bills," *RNL*, Feb. 8, 1926, 8; Minutes, *News Leader* Current Events Class, Feb. 8, 1926, 2–3 (quotations on 3), folder "Minutes (1926)," box 176, DSFP-LC; "State Papers Condemn Race Bills," *NJG*, Feb. 20, 1926, 1, 7.

34 "Race Segregation Bill Is Opposed," *RNL*, Feb. 9, 1926, 1; "Anti-Racial Law Would Hurt Work," *RNL*, Feb. 20, 1926, 4 (quotations); "The Leading White Citizens Make Protest," *Richmond Planet*, Feb. 20, 1926, 1; "Copy of Resolutions Passed by the Methodists Preachers Meeting, Richmond, Va.," J. F. Love to "My Dear Senator," Mar. 10, 1926, and other supporting documents, folder "Virginian Interracial Commission/Committee, 1922–1945," box 35, Adele Goodman Clark Papers, Special Collections and Archives, James Branch Cabell Library, Virginia Commonwealth University.

35 "The Leading White Citizens Make Protest," *Richmond Planet*, Feb. 20, 1926, 1, 4 (quotation on 4); "Allege Vast Negro Conspiracy in Support of Race Separation Bill," *NJG*, Feb. 20, 1926, 1, 7; Sherman, "'Teachings at Hampton Institute,'" 290–91.

36 "Allege Vast Negro Conspiracy in Support of Race Separation Bill," *NJG*, Feb. 20, 1926, 1, 7; J. A. Rogers, "'Color' Psychology Amazingly Revealed in State Legislature," *NJG*, Feb. 27, 1926, 1, 9 (first and third quotations on 9; second quotation on 1); Sherman, "'Teachings at Hampton Institute,'" 290–91; Wolters, "Rites of Passage," 240. It should be noted that Rogers's account is the only one that this author has found in which Copeland reportedly used the word "nigger."

37 J. A. Rogers, "'Color' Psychology Amazingly Revealed in State Legislature," *NJG*, Feb. 27, 1926, 1.

38 Ibid., 1, 9 (first quotation on 1; second and third quotations on 9).

39 J. A. Rogers, "Virginia 'Nordic Blood Purists' Reveal Their Scheme to J. A. Rogers," *NJG*, Mar. 6, 1926, 1, 8 (quotations on 1). For more on the Chicago race riot of 1919, see Tuttle, *Race Riot*.

40 WAP to ELT, Jan. 2, 1926, folder "Bureau of Vital Statistics," box 43, TEP; "Integrity Act Affects 20,000, Whites Claim," *RNL*, Feb. 8, 1926, 1; "Bill Brands 63 'First Families' of Va. 'Colored,'" *RNL*, Feb. 9, 1926, 1; Minutes, *News Leader* Current Events Class, Feb. 8, 1926, 3, folder "Minutes (1926)," box 176, DSFP-LC; note to editor, *RNL*, n.d., folder "1925 Racial Bills," box 13, DSFP-UVA. The list of unnamed individuals threatened with racial reclassification is taken from "Integrity Act Affects 20,000, Whites Claim" and "Bill Brands 63 'First Families' of Va. 'Colored.'" The Anglo-Saxon Clubs also supported a resolution encouraging the colonization of blacks back to Africa, but it garnered little support or attention. See "Negro Colony Bill Supported by Cox," *RNL*, Jan. 23, 1926, 26, and Sherman, "'The Last Stand,'" 85–87.

41 "Amend New Racial Integrity Measure," *RNL*, Feb. 9, 1926, 1; "Racial Integrity Bill Reported Out," *RTD*, Feb. 12, 1926, 5; "Racial Integrity Bill Compli-

cated," *RNL*, Feb. 13, 1926, 1, 23; "Says Racial Bill Modifies The Law," *RNL*, Mar. 1, 1926, 1, 27; "The Bill 'As Is' and 'As Was,'" *RNL*, Mar. 2, 1926, 8; R. H. Pitt to HFB, Mar. 8, 1926 (first quotation), folder "General Assembly 1926—Bills Before," box 22, BEP; "Killed," *Religious Herald*, Mar. 18, 1926, 11 (second and third quotations); Dodson, *General Assembly of the Commonwealth of Virginia*, 175, 180, 199; JP, "The Last Stand" (thirteen-part series), *RTD*, Feb. 16, 1926, 7, Feb. 17, 1926, 7, Feb. 18, 1926, 14, Feb. 19, 1926, 9, Feb. 20, 1926, 5, Feb. 22, 1926, 8, Feb. 23, 1926, 8, Feb. 24, 1926, 7, Feb. 25, 1926, 7, Feb. 26, 1926, 7, Feb. 27, 1926, 5, Mar. 1, 1926, 14, Mar. 2, 1926, 20; Sherman, "'The Last Stand,'" 85–87.

42 "Give Approval to Separation of Races Bill," *RNL*, Feb. 20, 1926, 1; LIJ to JEG, Feb. 26, 1926, folder "1926–29 Correspondence of LIJ with James E. Gregg," box 1, LIJP (#9924-d); JEG to R. E. Blackwell, Mar. 1, 1926 (quotations; emphasis in original), folder "General Assembly 1926," box 22, BEP.

43 WSC to the editor, "Pass the Massenburg Bill," *RTD*, Mar. 4, 1926, editorial page; "The Massenburg Bill," *RTD*, copies of both in folder "1908–1954 Newspaper Clippings," box 4, WSC Papers, UVA. Copeland's daughter commented that cultural offerings in Hampton and Newport News, aside from what was offered at the Institute, were "arid." Elizabeth Norfleet, interview with the author, Charlottesville, Va., Dec. 28, 1996.

44 Young, "William Howard Taft and Hampton Institute," 150 (first and second quotations); "Race Bill Defense by Noted Citizens," *RNL*, Mar. 3, 1926, 26 (third and fourth quotations), copy in folder "Virginia Interracial Commission/Committee, 1922–1945," box 35, Adele Goodman Clark Papers, Special Collections and Archives, James Branch Cabell Library, Virginia Commonwealth University. The article in the *Richmond News Leader* lists twenty-six white elites, including several of the city's top lawyers and William T. Reed, a powerful player in the Democratic Party.

45 Sherman, "'Teachings at Hampton Institute,'" 290–92 (quotation on 292); Young, "William Howard Taft and Hampton Institute," 151–52. Historian Raymond Pulley writes about the educational reform work of Copeland and the Munfords in *Old Virginia Restored*, 132–51. For more on Mary-Cooke Branch Munford, see Bowie, *Sunrise in the South*.

46 JP to WSC, Mar. 4, 1926 (first and second quotations), JP to Mrs. B. B. Munford, Mar. 5, 1926 (third, fourth, and fifth quotations), folder "1903, 1921–26 Correspondence of WSC," box 1, WSC Papers, UVA; Sherman, "'Teachings at Hampton Institute,'" 292–93.

47 JEG to Mrs. B. B. Munford, Mar. 13, 1926, folder "Munford, Mrs.," box 24, James E. Gregg Collection, Hampton University Archives; William Howard Taft to Mary-Cooke Branch Munford, Mar. 15, 1926 (two separate letters; all quotations from the longer of the two), item 249, folder "William Howard Taft, 1857–1930," Mary-Cooke Branch Munford Family Papers, VHS.

48 William Howard Taft to Mary-Cooke Branch Munford, Mar. 15, 1926, item 249, folder "William Howard Taft, 1857–1930," Munford Family Papers, VHS; Sherman, "'Teachings at Hampton Institute,'" 294–95; Dr. J. Wilton Hope to HFB, Mar. 23, 1926 (quotation), folder "General Assembly 1926—

Bills Before," box 22, BEP. Pitt's role and position appear somewhat puzzling. In a letter to Byrd just one week before the meeting, Pitt urged the governor to quietly oppose the other racial integrity bill before the General Assembly in 1926. He even asked Byrd to veto it if necessary, calling it the creation of a band of "partisans" who were "laboring under a kind of obsession." However, Pitt specifically excluded the Massenburg Bill from his request, intimating that he and friends for whom he spoke were not as concerned with its outcome. R. H. Pitt to HFB, Mar. 8, 1926, folder "General Assembly 1926—Bills Before," box 22, BEP.

49 Sherman, "'Teachings at Hampton Institute,'" 295 (quotation); Commonwealth of Virginia, *Journal of the Senate, 1924*, Feb. 27, 1924, 476–77. The senate records show that Byrd joined twelve others in not voting on final passage of the Racial Integrity Act. In addition, Byrd never went on record opposing the act.

50 "Virginia Adopts a New Segregation of Races Law," *NJG*, Mar. 13, 1926, 1; Richard H. Bowling, "Hampton Not to Blame," *NJG*, Mar. 13, 1926, 14; J. H. Baynes, letter to the editor, *NJG*, Mar. 27, 1926, 12; A. Dodson McWilliams, letter to the editor, *NJG*, Mar. 20, 1926, 14.

51 "The Rising Tide of Prejudice," *The Nation* 122 (Mar. 10, 1926): 247.

52 Sherman, "'Teachings at Hampton Institute,'" 296 (first and second quotations); Wolters, "Rites of Passage," 244–45 (third quotation); Young, "William Howard Taft and Hampton Institute," 153. Sherman, Wolters, and Young all quote from the same letter from Robert Moton to James Gregg, dated Mar. 25, 1926.

53 Young, "William Howard Taft and Hampton Institute," 153–54; Sherman, "'Teachings at Hampton Institute,'" 298; copy of terms of new policy, approved June 8, 1926, folder "H.I. Notice to Students, Alumni, and Employees," box 24, James E. Gregg Collection, Hampton University Archives.

54 William Howard Taft to Mary-Cooke Branch Munford, Dec. 28, 1926 (first and second quotations), item 249, folder "William Howard Taft, 1857–1930," Munford Family Papers, VHS; George Mallison to JP, quoted in J. David Smith, *Eugenic Assault on America*, 45 (third quotation).

55 Young, "William Howard Taft and Hampton Institute," 154 (first quotation); Wolters, "Rites of Passage," 246–58 (second quotation on 248).

56 Wolters, "Rites of Passage," 230–75 (quotation on 268); Young, "William Howard Taft and Hampton Institute," 154–57. Copeland died on July 24, 1928, only nine months after the strike. In 1949, more than twenty years after Copeland's death, the Virginia Press Association named its most prestigious honor the W. S. Copeland Award for Journalistic Integrity and Community Service. In July 2000, however, Copeland's name was stricken from the award in response to an article in the *Richmond Times-Dispatch* that reported his leadership in the crusade for the Public Assemblages Act. See Peter Hardin, "Honored Editor Fought Racial Equality," *RTD*, July 23, 2000, A1, and "VPA Award's Name Change Is Approved," *RTD*, July 27, 2000, A1. For more on black activism on college campuses other than Hampton in the 1920s, see the remaining chapters in Wolters, *New Negro on Campus*. On

the "New Negro," see David Levering Lewis, *When Harlem Was in Vogue*, chap. 4, and Tuttle, *Race Riot*, chap. 7; see also Chapter 2, note 64, above.

57 Grace B. Copeland to HFB, Oct. 17, 1927, folder "Hampton Institute," box 24, BEP.

58 In 1930 the legislature extended Jim Crow to buses; in 1936, to waiting rooms in bus stations; in 1944, to waiting rooms in airports. See Wynes, "Evolution of Jim Crow Laws," 421.

CHAPTER FIVE

1 *Plessy v. Ferguson*, 163 U.S. 537 (1896).

2 Heinemann, *Harry Byrd of Virginia*, chaps. 2–3; Fry, "Senior Advisor," 445–69. Reed's name appeared on the list of Richmond elites who publicly supported racial integrity and public assemblages legislation in 1926. See "Race Bill Defense by Noted Citizens," *RNL*, Mar. 3, 1926, 26.

3 HFB, speech to Democratic State Central Committee, folder "Speech—State Democratic Meeting: Gubernatorial Pledges 1925," box 356, HFBP. Byrd's two predecessors as governor, Westmoreland Davis and E. Lee Trinkle, spoke about many of the same fiscal issues emphasized by Byrd. But it was Byrd who hung his reputation on making government more like business and pledged the rest of his considerable political life to that end. In addition to Heinemann, see Moger, *Virginia: Bourbonism to Byrd*; Kirby, *Westmoreland Davis*; Willis, "E. Lee Trinkle and the Virginia Democracy"; and Hawkes, "Career of Harry Flood Byrd" For more on Byrd and the business progressives of the 1920s, see Tindall, "Business Progressivism," 92–106.

4 "Keynote Speech of Hon. H. F. Byrd, Democratic Nominee for Governor, Delivered at Harrisonburg, Va., October 19, 1925," 13 (first quotation), folder "Gubernatorial Campaign: Keynote Speech, Oct. 1925," box 356, HFBP; "Democratic Politics in Virginia," *NJG*, Oct. 31, 1925, 14 (second quotation); cartoon entitled "Riding the Usual Hobby," *NJG*, Oct. 31, 1925, 14.

5 "Keynote Speech of Hon. H. F. Byrd, Democratic Nominee for Governor, Delivered at Harrisonburg, Va., October 19, 1925," 5, folder "Gubernatorial Campaign: Keynote Speech, Oct. 1925," box 356, HFBP; "Governor Harry F. Byrd on Education: From His Inaugural Address," *Virginia Journal of Education* 19 (Feb. 1926): 239 (first quotation); constitutional mandate quoted in O'Shea, *Public Education in Virginia*, 337 (second quotation).

6 Virginia Education Commission, *Virginia Public Schools, Education Commission's Report to the Assembly of Virginia*, 41–42, 199–209 (quotation on 209). For more on education in Virginia at this time, see Link, *A Hard Country*, esp. chap. 8.

7 "Keynote Speech of Hon. H. F. Byrd, Democratic Nominee for Governor, Delivered at Harrisonburg, Va., October 19, 1925," 5, folder "Gubernatorial Campaign: Keynote Speech, Oct. 1925," box 356, HFBP; O'Shea, *Public Education in Virginia*, 332–51.

8 O'Shea, *Public Education in Virginia*, 279–92 (quotation on 292). A growing

number of educators in Virginia recognized the same inadequacies noted in the O'Shea report. In particular, the University of Virginia issued a series of county surveys, edited by rural economist and sociologist Wilson Gee, that described many of the same inequalities in education. The tone of most of these reports, however, failed to match that of the O'Shea report, which clearly did not shy away from placing blame with the Old Dominion's political leadership. See Gee, *Economic and Social Survey of Albemarle County*, 52–62; Ferebee and Wilson, *Economic and Social Survey of Princess Anne County*, 48–55; Mundie, *Economic and Social Survey of King and Queen County*, 45–54; Warner, *Economic and Social Survey of Clarke County*, 76–93; and Deck and Heaton, *Economic and Social Survey of Loudoun County*, 72–81.

9 "State Senate for Compulsory Education," *NJG*, Mar. 11, 1922, 1; O'Shea, *Public Education in Virginia*, 281; Address of Forbes Norris to the *News Leader* Current Events Class, Sept. 21, 1933, folder "Minutes (1933)," box 176, DSFP-LC; Commonwealth of Virginia, *Annual Report of the Superintendent of Public Instruction of the Commonwealth of Virginia: School Year 1925-1926* (Richmond, 1927), 98–99.

10 "Comparative Showing of Education in the South," *NJG*, Aug. 12, 1922, section 2, 1; "Schools Open with Serious Overcrowding," *NJG*, Sept. 16, 1922, 1; "Aggravated Discrimination," *NJG*, Feb. 24, 1923, 4; "Elimination of Free School Books," *NJG*, Dec. 8, 1923, 10; "Public High Schools for Negroes," *Southern Workman* 53 (July 1924): 305–11.

11 Cartoon entitled "Making Progress Despite Their Handicap," *NJG*, Sept. 26, 1925, 12; "Grossly Unjust Division of School Funds Is Alleged in Norfolk County," *NJG*, July 25, 1925, 7; "Norfolk County's Shame," *NJG*, July 25, 1925, 12. For an example of the pronouncements of white officials who emphasized minor progress over gross disparity, see W. D. Gresham, "The Work of the Negro Supervisors in Virginia," *Virginia Journal of Education* 15 (Oct. 1921): 51–52; "Problems of Education Being Rapidly Solved in the State of Virginia," *NJG*, Jan. 31, 1925, 7; and "Negro Education Gaining in State, *RNL*, Oct. 23, 1928, 17.

12 Letter to the editor from "An Interested Citizen," *NJG*, Oct. 3, 1925, 12; "The Deep Creek School Situation," *NJG*, Oct. 3, 1925, 12; "Inequalities of Educational Opportunity in Brunswick County," *NJG*, Mar. 12, 1927, 12.

13 "Lengthen the School Terms in the Rural Districts," *NJG*, May 17, 1924, 12; A. M. Proctor, "N. C. Newbold and Negro Education," *Southern Workman* 53 (Aug. 1924): 367–71, reprinted as "Negro Education in North Carolina," *NJG*, Aug. 16, 1924, 7; "Forward Stride in Education," *NJG*, Nov. 22, 1924, 12 (quotation); "Negro Education in North Carolina Aids Race Amity," *NJG*, July 18, 1925, 8; "Schools May Get More Funds," *NJG*, Oct. 3, 1925, 1; "Higher Education of Negro Entails Small Outlay in Virginia," *NJG*, Mar. 13, 1926, 1; "North Carolina—The Fifth Division," *NJG*, Dec. 25, 1926, 12; Link, *Paradox of Southern Progressivism*, 242–47; Leloudis, *Schooling the New South*, 177–228.

14 VD interview by RJB, Oct. 18, 1939 (first and second quotations), folder 6, "Field Notes: Southern Trip, Bk. 1," box 85, RJBP; James Jackson, "Memo-

randum on Richmond, Va." (third quotation), folder 44, "Bunche *Political Status of the Negro*, James Jackson's Field Notes, Richmond, Va., Memo," box 85, RJBP. Bright continued as mayor until he was defeated in 1940.

15 Silver, *Twentieth-Century Richmond*, 10–14, 54–93 (quotation on 90). Bright's commitment to minimal government expenditures was so intense that he refused to request or accept most available federal aid during the Great Depression (ibid., 130–31).

16 Minutes, *News Leader* Current Events Class, July 18 and July 25, 1927, folder "Minutes 1926 Sept.–1927 Sept.," box 178, DSFP-LC; "Richmond's Humiliation," editorial from *NVP*, reprinted in *NJG*, July 30, 1927, 12 (quotation).

17 "Richmond Daily Starts Drive For Playground For Colored Children," *NJG*, June 14, 1924, 1; "Richmond Sees The Need," *NJG*, June 21, 1924, 12; "What Negroes Want," *Richmond Planet*, Apr. 14, 1928, 4; "To Advise Negro Playground Here," *RNL*, Jan. 31, 1929, 8; "Build Concrete Swimming Pool," *RNL*, Apr. 13, 1929, 4; "Richmond Has One of Best of Negro Amusement Parks," *RNL*, Aug. 5, 1929, 6.

18 Lutrelle F. Palmer, principal of Huntington High School, interview by RJB, Oct. 22, 1939 (first quotation), folder 6, "Field Notes: Southern Trip, Bk. 1," box 85, RJBP; Wilhelmina Jackson, "Memorandum on Newport News" (second quotation), folder 31, "Bunche *Political Status of the Negro*, W. Jackson's Field Notes: Newport News Memorandum," box 85, RJBP. The black high school in Newport News was built in 1919 and was named for Collis Huntington.

19 Wilhelmina Jackson, "Memorandum on Newport News" (quotation), folder 31, "Bunche *Political Status of the Negro*, W. Jackson's Field Notes: Newport News Memorandum," box 85, RJBP; Wallenstein, "'These New and Strange Beings,'" 209–12.

20 Earl Lewis, *In Their Own Interests*, 79–85.

21 "Do We Accept Segregation without Protest?," *NJG*, May 30, 1925, 12.

22 "Another Crisis Up as Colored Buy in Brambleton," *NJG*, Mar. 21, 1925, 1; Earl Lewis, *In Their Own Interests*, 77–79.

23 "An Ordinance to Provide for the Separation of White and Negro Residential Communities within the City of Norfolk, and Providing Penalty for Violation," frame 0895 (quotation), pt. 5, "The Campaign against Residential Segregation, 1914–55," reel 4, NAACP-Mfm; "Supreme Court Will Pass upon City Ordinance," *NJG*, Sept. 26, 1925, 1; "Virginia Town Reverses Itself on Segregation," *NJG*, Oct. 31, 1925, 1; "Segregation Law Talk in Portsmouth," *NJG*, Oct. 16, 1926, 1.

24 Press release, "Norfolk, Va., Segregation Law Declared Unconstitutional," Feb. 26, 1926, frame 0887, pt. 5, reel 4, NAACP-Mfm.; "Police Court Test Strikes Blow at Law," *NJG*, Feb. 20, 1926, 1; "Segregation Ruled Invalid by Hanckel," *NJG*, Mar. 27, 1926, 1; Earl Lewis, *In Their Own Interests*, 77–79; Suggs, *P. B. Young, Newspaperman*, 57–59.

25 Press release, "Norfolk Branch NAACP Fights Segregation Ordinance," July 9, 1926, frames 0898–99 (quotation on 0899), pt. 5, reel 4, NAACP-Mfm.; "Justice Spindle Hears Argument on Segregation," *NJG*, July 3, 1926, 1, 5. It

is not entirely clear why the second case was even granted standing in court given the result in *Edwards v. Falls*, decided in March 1926 in the Norfolk Circuit Court. Edwards, however, did distinguish in correspondence with the national office of the NAACP between the nature of the first case, in which he had sued a white, Jewish man, and the second case, in which whites in Brambleton tried to enforce the ordinance against a black man. See David H. Edwards to Walter White, June 23, 1926, frame 0900, pt. 5, reel 4, NAACP-Mfm.

26 Press release, "Norfolk Judge Declares Segregation Ordinance Invalid for Second Time," July 23, 1926, frames 0888, 0897, pt. 5, reel 4, NAACP-Mfm.; "Spindle Again Rules against Segregation," *NJG*, July 17, 1926, 1; "Segregation Law Nailed by Roanoke Court," *NJG*, July 24, 1926, 1 (quotation); "Decision Sustains Ruling of Local Courts," *NJG*, Mar. 19, 1927, 1. The New Orleans case was *Harmon v. Tyler*, 273 U.S. 668 (1927).

27 "Bus Men Wage Fight on Unified Transportation," *NJG*, Oct. 17, 1925, 1; "V.E.P. Prepares for Complete Bus Service," *NJG*, Nov. 21, 1925, 8.

28 "Fate of Unified Bus Ordinance to Be Decided Today," *NVP*, Nov. 17, 1925, 1; "Bus Men Wage Fight on Unified Transportation," *NJG*, Oct. 17, 1925, 1; "The Bus Transportation Problem," *NJG*, Oct. 17, 1925, editorial page; "Traction Company to Continue All Routes," *NJG*, Oct. 24, 1925, 1; "Power Company Employs Many Colored Men," *NJG*, Oct. 31, 1925, 1; "Says Unified Plan Improves Service to All," *NJG*, Nov. 7, 1925, 1.

29 "Sees Traction Monopoly in Unified Plan," *NJG*, Nov. 7, 1925, 1, 8; "New Bus Ordinance vs. Present Transportation Facilities," *NJG*, Nov. 7, 1925, 7; "Busmen Say the System Best for Race Relations," *NJG*, Nov. 14, 1925, 1 (quotation).

30 "Denies Ordinance Would Mix Races or Increase Fare," *NVP*, Nov. 17, 1925, 1.

31 "Curtailed Bus Service Annoyance to Number of Uptown Residents," *NJG*, Jan. 23, 1926, 1, 8; "Power Company Announces Bus Operating Plan," *NJG*, Feb. 13, 1926, 1, 6 (first quotation on 1); "Did Not Approve Entire Bus Plan," *NJG*, Feb. 13, 1926, 1, 6 (second quotation on 1; third quotation on 6); "Protest City Manager's Bus Arrangement," *NJG*, Feb. 3, 1926, 2.

32 "Curtailed Bus Service Annoyance to Number of Uptown Residents," *NJG*, Jan. 23, 1926, 1, 8 (first quotation on 8); "Why? Norfolk, Why?," *NJG*, July 10, 1926, 12 (second quotation).

33 "St. Joseph's Fosters Splendid Community Center for Colored People Here," *NJG*, Apr. 19, 1924, 6.

34 "Father Warren, Here, Sheds Light On Kidnapping," *RNL*, Sept. 8, 1926, 1, 9; "Father Warren Unharmed When Carried Off by Band of Robed and Hooded Men," *NJG*, Sept. 4, 1926, 1.

35 "Father Warren, Here, Sheds Light On Kidnapping," *RNL*, Sept. 8, 1926, 1, 9 (quotation on 9); "Father Warren Unharmed When Carried Off by Band of Robed and Hooded Men," *NJG*, Sept. 4, 1926, 1.

36 Princess Anne County was among those parts of Virginia with the most active Klan. See Chalmers, *Hooded Americanism*, 230–31.

37 "Kluxery in Princess Anne," *NVP*, Sept. 3, 1926, 6 (first quotation); James E. Allen to HFB, Sept. 3, 1926 (second quotation), folder "Miscellaneous Correspondence A-1," box 70, BEP; "No Investigation in Kidnapping of Norfolk Priest," *RNL*, Sept. 2, 1926, 1; "May Seek Aid of Governor," *RTD*, Sept. 3, 1926, 1; "Ready to Act in Kidnap Case," *RTD*, Sept. 4, 1926, 1; "Father Warren, Here, Sheds Light on Kidnapping," *RNL*, Sept. 8, 1926, 1, 9; "Say Some of Abductors of Priest Known," *NJG*, Sept. 11, 1926, 1; "Judge White Flays Kidnappers of Catholic Priest in Charge," *RTD*, Sept. 14, 1926, 2.

38 "Norfolk Council Enacts Anti-Mask Law," *NJG*, Sept. 11, 1926, 1; "Rev. Bowling Preaches on Father Warren," *NJG*, Oct. 2, 1926, 11.

39 LIJ, editorial, *NVP*, Dec. 3, 1927, copy in folder "1925–1949: Young, P. B.," box 1, LIJP (#9924-j).

40 LIJ, "Some Thoughts on a Common Problem," speech delivered at the Attucks Theater, Nov. 27, 1927, 8–9, folder "1920–75: Articles and Speeches," box 1, LIJP (#9924-l)

41 Ibid., 12–17.

42 Ibid., 7.

43 "Borah Would Have Party Declaration on 15 Amendment," *Lynchburg News*, Nov. 16, 1927, 1; "Can Not Frighten South by Threats, Says Senator," *Lynchburg News*, Nov. 16, 1927, 1 (quotation). Adopted in the wake of the Civil War, the Fourteenth Amendment guaranteed all persons, regardless of race, "due process" and the "equal protection" of the nation's laws, thereby according citizenship to all former slaves and protecting these rights against violation by the state governments. The Fifteenth Amendment prohibited national and state authorities from denying individuals the right to vote "on account of race, color, or previous condition of servitude." In response, white southerners adopted understanding clauses, literacy tests, poll taxes, property requirements, and a host of other mechanisms to disfranchise black voters.

44 "Can Not Frighten South by Threats, Says Senator," *Lynchburg News*, Nov. 16, 1927, 1.

45 Ibid., 3.

46 "The Fourteenth and Fifteenth Amendments," *Newport News Daily Press*, Nov. 18, 1927, 4. The *Danville Register* and the *Norfolk Virginia-Pilot* also criticized Glass, while the *Richmond Times-Dispatch* and the *Roanoke Times* defended his position.

47 "Nullification of the Fifteenth Amendment," *Newport News Daily Press*, Nov. 22, 1927, 4.

48 "Why the Heathen Rage," *Lynchburg News*, Nov. 23, 1927, 6 (first quotation); "Nullification," *Roanoke Times*, reprinted in *Lynchburg News*, Nov. 27, 1927, 6; "Nullification of the Fifteenth Amendment," *Newport News Daily Press*, Nov. 27, 1927, 4; "Does Virginia 'Nullify'?," *Lynchburg News*, Nov. 29, 1927, 6; "The Suffrage Laws and Prohibition," *Newport News Daily Press*, Nov. 30, 1927, 4 (all other quotations); letter from "A Democratic Voter" to the editor, *Lynchburg News*, Dec. 1, 1927, 6.

49 LIJ to WSC, Nov. 28, 1927, folder "1922–1927 Correspondence of LIJ with WS Copeland," box 3, LIJP (#9924-b).

50 *Congressional Record*, 70th Cong., 1st sess., 1928, vol. 69, pt. 2:1848–53 (first quotation on 1850; second quotation on 1852–53).

51 Ibid., 1853. A magazine article in the late 1930s mentioned that Bruce frequently accompanied Glass to the prizefights. See James, "Gentleman from Virginia," 17.

52 *Congressional Record*, 70th Cong., 1st sess., 1928, vol. 69, pt. 2:1854–64 (first quotation on 1861; second and third quotations on 1863).

53 J. J. Taylor, "Senator Glass Apology," *Religious Herald*, Mar. 29, 1928, 8.

54 Sidney Sutherland, "The 14th, 15th, and 18th Amendments," *Liberty* 5 (Apr. 28, 1928): 34.

55 "Senator Carter Glass," *NJG*, May 5, 1928, 16 (first and second quotations); "Senator Glass Speaks Plainly," *Richmond Planet*, Apr. 28, 1928, 4 (third quotation).

56 "The 14th, 15th, and 18th Amendments," *Liberty* 5 (May 26, 1928): 73–74 (first and second quotations); "In Fairness to Senator Glass," *NJG*, May 12, 1928, 16; "Senator Glass Revealed in a Better Light," *NJG*, May 19, 1928, 16 (third quotation).

57 "Says Senator Glass Is Consistent," *NJG*, May 19, 1928, 16.

58 "Gordon Hancock Answers Mr. Glass," *NJG*, May 19, 1928, 16.

59 "South Is Changing View of the Negro, Declares Editor Douglas Gordon," *NJG*, Feb. 18, 1928, 1, 5.

CHAPTER SIX

1 J. Douglas Smith, "'When Reason Collides with Prejudice,'" 12.

2 NAACP, *Thirty Years of Lynching*, 34–35, 41, 99–101; Raper, *Tragedy of Lynching*, 483; Brundage, *Lynching in the New South*, 281–83. According to the NAACP study, North Carolina lynched fewer blacks than Virginia in the years 1889 to 1918. The NAACP and Raper both provide figures that show that after 1900 fewer blacks were lynched in Virginia than in North Carolina. The claim that no blacks were lynched in Virginia from 1906 to 1916 comes from Brundage, the most recent and thorough account of lynchings in Virginia. The NAACP figures list three additional lynchings of blacks in Virginia, one each in 1910, 1912, and 1915. Brundage provides the more authoritative account because his work is more recent and more thoroughly focused on Virginia and Georgia. Virginia mobs also lynched fifteen whites between 1880 and 1930, although all but one of those occurred during the nineteenth century.

3 Brundage, *Lynching in the New South*, 140–90 (quotation on 172).

4 Ibid., 281–83. George Tindall used the term "business progressivism" to describe the philosophy embodied by Harry F. Byrd, governor of Virginia from 1926 to 1930. Byrd and others stressed efficiency and fiscal soundness in state government and actively used governmental policy, especially regarding labor and taxation, to induce industrial development. The elimination of lynching was considered important in creating the proper atmosphere to

attract industry and business to Virginia. See Tindall, "Business Progressivism," 92–106, and *Emergence of the New South*, esp. 219–53. On the efforts of the antilynching efforts of the CIC and the Association of Southern Women for the Prevention of Lynching (ASWPL), see Hall, *Revolt against Chivalry*.

5 Edwin H. Gibson to Westmoreland Davis, Dec. 2, 1918, folder "Lynching," box 16, Westmoreland Davis Executive Papers, LVA. Needless to say, not all black men accused of raping or sexually assaulting white women were lynched. Lisa Lindquist Dorr places lynching within the broader context of punishments meted out to blacks in Virginia for rape and sexual assault. See Lisa Lindquist Dorr, "Black-on-White Rape and Retribution," 711–48.

6 Edwin H. Gibson to Westmoreland Davis, Dec. 2, 1918, folder "Lynching," box 16, Davis Executive Papers, LVA; "The First Lynching in Culpeper in 40 Years," *Culpeper Exponent* (quotation), copy on frame 0789–90, pt. 7, "The Anti-Lynching Campaign, 1912–1955," series A, "Investigative Files, 1912–1953," reel 19, NAACP-Mfm.

7 Westmoreland Davis to Edwin H. Gibson, Dec. 10, 1918, Gibson to Davis, Dec. 2, 1918, folder "Lynching," box 16, Davis Executive Papers, LVA.

8 Moses A. Summons to Westmoreland Davis, Dec. 17, 1918, folder "Lynching," box 16, Davis Executive Papers, LVA.

9 Ibid.

10 Ibid.

11 Wade H. Thompson to Westmoreland Davis, Feb. 15, 1919, folder "Lynching," box 16, Davis Executive Papers, LVA.

12 Ibid.; U.S. Bureau of the Census, *Fourteenth Decennial Census, 1920*, vol. 3, *Population*, table 9; "The First Lynching in Culpeper in 40 Years," *Culpeper Exponent* (quotation), copy on frame 0789–90, pt. 7, series A, reel 19, NAACP-Mfm.

13 John M. Royall to James Weldon Johnson, Aug. 29, 1920, and *Danville Register*, Aug. 28, 1920 (included with letter from Royall), frames 0907–11, pt. 7, series A, reel 19, NAACP-Mfm. Walter F. White wrote Royall several weeks later and thanked him for the information on Allen but indicated that the NAACP had secured no further information. See Walter F. White to John M. Royall, Sept. 24, 1920, frame 0906, pt. 7, series A, reel 19, NAACP-Mfm. Fitzhugh Brundage does not include Allen's death in his tally of lynchings in Virginia. See Brundage, *Lynching in the New South*, 281–83. A number of African American veterans of World War I, some of them still in uniform, were lynched during and in the years immediately following the war. See McMillen, *Dark Journey*, 30–31, and Tuttle, *Race Riot*, 22.

14 C. R. McCorkle to Westmoreland Davis, Nov. 16, 1920, 1–2, folder "Lynching," box 16, Davis Executive Papers, LVA.

15 Ibid., 2–3.

16 Ibid., 3–4.

17 C. R. McCorkle to Westmoreland Davis, Aug. 16, 1921, Davis to McCorkle, Aug. 19, 1921, folder "Lynching," box 16, Davis Executive Papers, LVA; "First Convicted Va. Lyncher Goes to Penitentiary," *NJG*, Jan. 6, 1923, 7 (first

quotation); "Wise County Man Must Serve Year for Leading Mob," *NJG*,
Mar. 17, 1923, 1 (second quotation); Pardon Files of Shaler B. Tate and A. L.
Napier, Commonwealth of Virginia, Secretary of the Commonwealth, Executive Papers, Oct. 6, 1923, LVA; Commonwealth of Virginia, Secretary of
the Commonwealth, Executive Journals, 1922–26, 172, 294–95, LVA.

18 "First Convicted Va. Lyncher Goes to Penitentiary," *NJG*, Jan. 6, 1923, 7;
"Attack on Wise Jail Results in Death of Two Men," *Bluefield (W.Va.) Daily-
Telegraph*, Dec. 7, 1920, "Wise Negro Is Removed to Roanoke," *Lynchburg
News*, Dec. 7, 1920, copies of both on frames 0795–96, pt. 7, series A, reel 19,
NAACP-Mfm.; "Anti-Lynching Fight Starts," editorial from *Grand Rapids
(Mich.) Herald*, reprinted in *NJG*, Jan. 1, 1921, 1.

19 "Negro Is Taken from Jail and Lynched by Mob," *Johnson City (Tenn.) Staff*,
Aug. 3, 1921 (quotation), "Virginians Lynch Negro," *New York Times*, Aug. 4,
1921, both on frames 0885, 0889, pt. 7, series A, reel 19, NAACP-Mfm.; Aide
to Governor Westmoreland Davis to B. A. Lewis, Commonwealth's Attorney for Brunswick County, Aug. 3, 1921, folder "Lynching," box 16, Davis
Executive Papers, LVA; "Fear Lynching by Mob, Bring Negro to Richmond
Jail," *RTD*, Aug. 4, 1921, 1, 9.

20 Dvorak, "Louis I. Jaffé," 15–21.

21 "Negro Seized and Shot to Death in King and Queen," *RNL*, Oct. 13, 1923,
1; "King and Queen Mob Kills Negro," *RTD*, Oct. 14, 1923, 1, 16 (quotation
on 16).

22 "Lynching Arouses Governor Trinkle," *RNL*, Oct. 15, 1923, 1 (first quotation); ELT to John R. Saunders, Oct. 15, 1923, ELT to Judge Fleet, Oct. 15,
1923 (second quotation), ELT to Judge Clagett B. Jones, Oct. 15, 1923, ELT
to W. H. Eubank, Oct. 15, 1923 (third quotation), Eubank to ELT, Oct. 17,
1923 (fourth and fifth quotations), all in folder "King and Queen Lynching,"
box 27, TEP.

23 Handwritten list of names and notations relating to King and Queen lynching, folder "King and Queen Lynching," box 27, TEP.

24 "Virginia's Shame," *NJG*, Oct. 27, 1923, 10.

25 "Besmirching a Good Record," *NVP*, Oct. 15, 1923, 6, reprinted in *NJG*,
Oct. 20, 1923, 10.

26 "Lynching and Enlightenment," *NVP*, reprinted in *NJG*, Jan. 10, 1925, 12
(quotations); Dvorak, "Louis I. Jaffé." Dvorak explores Jaffé's inability to connect lynching with the underlying assumptions of segregation and white supremacy on pages 30–32, 66–68.

27 "Mob Storms Jail, Lynches Man on Street," *RTD*, Mar. 21, 1925, 1, 2. The brutality of Jordan's death was quite common in the twentieth-century South.
See Allen, *Without Sanctuary*.

28 "Lynched Man's Body Is Stolen from Scene," *RTD*, Mar. 22, 1925, 1, 10.

29 "To Virginia's Shame," *NVP*, reprinted in *NJG*, Mar. 28, 1925, 12 (quotations); Dvorak, "Louis I. Jaffé," 22–23; "Charred Body of Mob Victim Buried
in Potters Field," *NJG*, Mar. 28, 1925, 1.

30 "The Waverly Lynching," *RNL*, Mar. 21, 1925, 8.

31 "Waverly, Virginia, Accursed," *St. Luke's Herald*, reprinted in *NJG*, Apr. 4, 1925, 12 (first and second quotations); W. L. Davis, letter to the editor, *NJG*, Apr. 4, 1925, 12 (all other quotations).

32 Telegram from the Women's Missionary Council of the Methodist Episcopal Church to ELT, Mar. 24, 1925 (first quotation), telegram from James Weldon Johnson of the NAACP to ELT, Mar. 21, 1925, H. S. Parker to ELT, Mar. 22, 1925 (second and third quotations), folder L (5), box 6, TEP.

33 H. C. Spangler to ELT, May 8, 1925 (quotations), folder S (9), box 9, TEP; "Story of Attack by Colored Man on School Girl, Fake," *NJG*, Apr. 25, 1925, 1.

34 Dvorak, "Louis I. Jaffé," 23–24, 29–32.

35 "Masked Mob Storms Jail, Kills Negro," *RTD*, Aug. 16, 1926, 1, 9; "Governor Regrets Negro's Lynching in Wythe County," *RNL*, Aug. 16, 1926, 1 (quotation).

36 Editorials from *Norfolk Virginia-Pilot*, *Norfolk Ledger-Dispatch*, *Roanoke Times*, *Roanoke World-News*, *Newport News Times-Herald*, *Newport News Daily Press*, *Petersburg Progressive-Index*, all reprinted in "Virginia Press Flays Bird Lynchers; Wants Members Punished," *NJG*, Aug. 28, 1926, 1, 7; "A Dark Disgrace to Virginia," *RNL*, Aug. 16, 1926, 8 (first quotation); "Law and Order Outraged," *RTD*, Aug. 17, 1926 (second quotation), copy on frame 1049, pt. 7, series A, reel 19, NAACP-Mfm.

37 James Weldon Johnson to the editors of the *Lynchburg News*, *Norfolk Virginian-Pilot*, *Roanoke World-News*, *Roanoke Times*, *Richmond News Leader*, *Richmond Times-Dispatch*, *Norfolk Journal and Guide*, Sept. 22, 1926, frames 0997–1003, W. Taylor Staples, Shawsville, Va., to James Weldon Johnson, Aug. 20, 1926, frames 0968–71, "Baby Born to Girl before Va. Lynching," *Baltimore Afro-American*, Sept. 11, 1926, copy on frames 1063–64, all in pt. 7, series A, reel 19, NAACP-Mfm.

38 Stuart B. Campbell to HFB, Aug. 20, 1926, 1–2, folder "Wytheville Lynching," box 69, BEP.

39 Ibid., 2–3.

40 Ibid.

41 Ibid., 4–5 (first quotation); Campbell to HFB, Aug. 28, 1926 (second quotation), H. M. Heuser to HFB, Aug. 23, 1926, Judge Horace Sutherland to HFB, Aug. 24, 1926 (third quotation), HFB to Heuser, Aug. 25, 1926 (fourth quotation), HFB to Sutherland, Aug. 25, 1926, all in folder "Wytheville Lynching," box 69, BEP.

42 LIJ to HFB, Aug. 30, 1926, folder "1924–1930 Correspondence of LIJ with HFB," box 2, LIJP (#9924-b).

43 Telegram from Joseph Chitwood to HFB, Aug. 30, 1926, HFB to Chitwood, Aug. 31, 1926, folder "Wytheville Lynching," box 69, BEP; "Modern 'Murdrum,'" *RNL*, Aug. 31, 1926, 8; "The State Is Powerless to Punish Lynchers," *NJG*, Sept. 4, 1926, 12; "Southern Sentiment for Federal Anti-Lynching Law," *NJG*, Oct. 23, 1926, 14. Throughout the 1920s, Congressman Leonidas Dyer of Missouri introduced a bill making lynching a federal crime. On January 26, 1922, the House of Representatives passed his bill by a vote of 231 to 119, but a filibuster led by southern senators killed it in the Senate.

See *Congressional Record*, 67th Cong., 2d sess., 1922, vol. 62, pt. 2:1795. Dyer reintroduced the bill for years, but southerners continued to defeat it.

44 "Wythe Lynching Shames State, Asserts Court," *RTD*, Sept. 2, 1926, 1, 14; "Grand Jury's Probe Sinking into Mob Law," *RTD*, Sept. 3, 1926, 1; "Bird Lynching Inquiry Drags," *RTD*, Sept. 4, 1926, 1, 8; "Investigation into Mob Lynching of Negro at Wytheville in Full Swing," newspaper from Kingsport, Tenn., Sept. 2, 1926, "Bird Investigation at Wytheville Adjourned," *Bristol (Va.) Courier*, copies on frames 1041, 1043, pt. 7, series A, reel 19, NAACP-Mfm.; "Indict Lone Farmer in Lynching," *NJG*, Jan. 15, 1927, 1; "Jury Quickly Frees Willard in Mob Killing," *RTD*, July 20, 1927, 1; "Wythe Continues Seeking Mobbers," *RNL*, July 20, 1927, 1, 9; "Alleged Lyncher Is Freed," *NJG*, July 23, 1927, 1.

45 "Mob Takes Life of Negro Held as Va. Man's Slayer," *RNL*, Nov. 30, 1927, 1; "Byrd Condemns Negro Hanging as 'Dastardly,'" *RTD*, Dec. 1, 1927, 1.

46 Telegram from P. H. Kennedy to HFB, Dec. 1, 1927 (first quotation), folder "Lynchings," box 43, BEP; "Sheriff Wires Byrd Lynchers from Kentucky," *RNL*, Dec. 2, 1927, 1 (second quotation).

47 "Mob Takes Life of Negro Held as Va. Man's Slayer," *RNL*, Nov. 30, 1927, 1; "Byrd Condemns Negro Hanging as 'Dastardly,'" *RTD*, Dec. 1, 1927, 1.

48 "The People Can End Lynching," *Lynchburg News*, Dec. 3, 1927, 6.

49 "Smithfield Negro Protected Here," *RTD*, Oct. 17, 1927, 1; "Colored Aid in Capture," *NJG*, Oct. 22, 1927, 1–2; "Threatened by Lynchers," *Richmond Planet*, Oct. 22, 1927, 1; "White Girl Murdered," *Richmond Planet*, Oct. 29, 1927, 1 (quotation).

50 "Isle of Wight Can't Afford It," *NVP*, Oct. 26, 1927, 6; "The Isle of Wight Crime," *NJG*, Oct. 29, 1927, 16; "Isle of Wight Officers Defeated as Out-growth of Smithfield Murder," *NVP*, Nov. 9, 1927, 1–2; "Shirley Winnegan Sentenced to Die in Electric Chair," *Richmond Planet*, Dec. 3, 1927, 1, 4.

51 "Isle of Wight Can't Afford It," *NVP*, Oct. 26, 1927, 6 (first quotation); LIJ to HFB, Oct. 26, 1927 (second quotation), HFB to LIJ, Oct. 31, 1927, folder "Miscellaneous Correspondence J-1," box 75, BEP.

52 HFB to LIJ, Nov. 5, 1927 (first and second quotations), LIJ to HFB, Nov. 7, 1927, HFB to LIJ, Nov. 8, 1927, folder "1924–1930 Correspondence of LIJ with HFB," box 2, LIJP (#9924-b); "Conflicting Lunacy Findings," *NJG*, Nov. 12, 1927, 16 (third quotation); "Shirley Winnegan Sentenced to Die in Electric Chair," *Richmond Planet*, Dec. 3, 1927, 4.

53 "Isle of Wight Officers Defeated as Outgrowth of Smithfield Murder," *NVP*, Nov. 9, 1927, 1–2; "Officers Who Frustrated Lynching Punished by Defeat for Re-Election," *NJG*, Nov. 12, 1927, 1–2; "Negro Given Change Venue," *Lynchburg News*, Nov. 12, 1927, 2 (quotation); "Winningham Trial Opens in Hustings," *RNL*, Nov. 29, 1927, 1–2; "Winningham to Die for Slaying Girl," *RNL*, Nov. 30, 1927, 1–2; "Winningham Plea for Stay Is Lost," *RNL*, Jan. 14, 1928, 18; "Winningham Pays in Electric Chair," *RNL*, Jan. 25, 1928. A number of newspapers, such as those cited here, misspelled Winnegan's name as Winningham. In the race for commonwealth's attorney, voters cast seventeen more ballots for A. E. S. Stephens, a young Smithfield attorney, than

for the incumbent, but the victor refused to serve given the circumstances. Two years later, voters sent Stephens to the house of delegates. He served in that body for a number of years before moving over to the state senate. In 1953 and 1957 he was elected lieutenant governor, and in 1961 he lost a race for governor.

54 "The People Can End Lynching," *Lynchburg News*, Dec. 3, 1927, 6; LIJ to HFB, Dec. 1, 1927 (quotation), HFB to LIJ, Dec. 2, 1927, folder "1924–1930 Correspondence of LIJ with HFB," box 2, LIJP (#9924-b).

55 "What to Do about Lynching?," *NVP*, Dec. 4, 1927, 6 (quotations), reprinted in "The *Norfolk Virginian-Pilot* and the Virginia Anti-Lynching Law," 3, folder "1920–1975 Articles and Speeches," box 1, LIJP (#9924-l); Dvorak, "Louis I. Jaffé," 48–51.

56 "What to Do about Lynching?," *NVP*, Dec. 4, 1927, 6 (quotations), reprinted in "The *Norfolk Virginian-Pilot* and the Virginia Anti-Lynching Law," 3, folder "1920–1975 Articles and Speeches," box 1, LIJP (#9924-l); Dvorak, "Louis I. Jaffé," 48–51.

57 "After Two Weeks," *Crawford's Weekly*, reprinted in *NJG*, Dec. 17, 1927, 16.

58 "Mob Sympathizers Criticize Editor Who Flayed Lynching," *NJG*, Dec. 24, 1927, 1; "Are Virginia Editors Superficial?," *NJG*, Feb. 4, 1928, 16 (quotations).

59 LIJ to HFB, Dec. 11, 1927, and "Lynching Must Stop," address of HFB, Jan. 16, 1928 (quotations), both in folder "1924–1930 Correspondence of LIJ with HFB," box 2, LIJP (#9924-b); HFB to A. W. McLean, Jan. 9, 1928, folder "Lynching," box 43, BEP.

60 "Lynching Must Stop," address of HFB, Jan. 16, 1928 (quotation), folder "1924–1930 Correspondence of LIJ with HFB," box 2, LIJP (#9924-b); "Urges Anti-Lynching Law," *New York Times*, Jan. 17, 1928, 20; "Gov. Byrd Asks State Lynching Law," *NJG*, Jan. 21, 1928, 1.

61 "The *Norfolk Virginian-Pilot* and the Virginia Anti-Lynching Law," 4, folder "1920–1975 Articles and Speeches," box 1, LIJP (#9924-l); "State Anti-Lynching Law Proposed," *NJG*, Jan. 21, 1928, 14 (quotations).

62 Edward W. Bundy, Grand Chancellor, Knights of Pythias, to HFB, Jan. 18, 1928, Rev. Daniel W. Hays to HFB, Jan. 17, 1928 (first quotation), Rev. W. J. G. McLinn to HFB, Jan. 17, 1928 (second quotation), Rev. J. B. Askew to HFB, Jan. 17, 1928 (third quotation), folder "Lynching," box 43, BEP; Wallace A. Battle, Field Secretary, American Church Institute for Negroes, to HFB, Mar. 4, 1928, folder "General Assembly Bills 3–1," box 20, BEP.

63 W. H. Tinsley to HFB, Jan. 24, 1928 (first quotation), folder "Lynching," box 43, BEP; Patrick Henry Drewry to HFB (second and third quotations), folder "General Assembly Bills 3–3," box 20, BEP.

64 HFB to W. H. Tinsley, Jan. 26, 1928, folder "Lynching," box 43, BEP; HFB to P. H. Drewry, Feb. 3, 1928, folder "General Assembly Bills 3–3," box 20, BEP.

65 LIJ to HFB, Feb. 3, 1928, folder "1924-1930 Correspondence of LIJ to HFB," box 2, LIJP (#9924-b).

66 Telegram from HFB to LIJ, Feb. 6, 1928, folder "1924–1930 Correspondence of LIJ to HFB," box 2, LIJP (#9924-b); Commonwealth of Virginia, *Journal*

of the Senate, 1928, 129, 213, 293, 331, 353, 527, 647, 768, 803; Commonwealth of Virginia, *Journal of the House of Delegates, 1928,* 424, 516, 542, 638–39, 783, 905, 928; Commonwealth of Virginia, *Acts of Assembly, 1928,* 715–16, copy in folder "Lynching," box 86, John Garland Pollard Executive Papers, LVA; "Senate Passes Anti-Lynching Bill by 32–0," *RNL,* Feb. 17, 1928, 1; "Senate Passes Anti-Lynching and Fee Bills," *RTD,* Feb. 18, 1928, 1; "The Anti-Lynching Bill," *Richmond Planet,* Feb. 25, 1928, 4 (quotations); "A Law to Protect Virginia's Honor and Good Name," *RNL,* Feb. 18, 1928, 8.

67 Mrs. M. C. Lawton to HFB, Mar. 3, 1928 (quotations), Judge James H. Ricks to HFB, Mar. 10, 1928, folder "General Assembly 1928, 2–2," box 20, BEP.

68 Telegram from LIJ to HFB, Carter Glass, and State Senator James S. Barron, June 21, 1928, folder "1924–1930 Correspondence of LIJ with HFB," box 2, LIJP (#9924-b); "The *Norfolk Virginian Pilot* and the Virginia Anti-Lynching Law," folder "1920–1975 Articles and Speeches," and "An Unspeakable Act of Savagery," *NVP,* June 22, 1928 (quotation), copy in folder "1926–1943 Articles and Speeches by LIJ," both in box 1, LIJP (#9924-l).

69 P. B. Young to Edwin Alderman, Jan. 22, 1929 (quotations), folder "1925–1949 Young, P. B.," box 1, LIJP (#9924-j); Everett Ewing, "Romances of American Journalism: Stories of Success Won by Leaders of the Press," *Editor and Publisher The Fourth Estate,* June 1, 1929, copy in folder "1920–1975 Articles and Speeches," box 1, LIJP (#9924-l). Ewing's article elaborates on many of the points in Young's letter.

70 In his study of the NAACP's antilynching campaign, Robert Zangrando paraphrases sociologist John Shelton Reed, who determined, in Zangrando's words, that "advocates of industrialism . . . rallied to suppress violence or the evidence of violence that might damage the region's image and retard its growth." See Zangrando, *NAACP Crusade against Lynching,* 11.

71 "Attacker of Two Is Found Hanging; And Body Burned," *Washington Evening Star,* Sept. 16, 1932, 1, copy on frame 0912, pt. 7, series A, reel 19, NAACP-Mfm.; "Body Of Suspect Found," *RNL,* Sept. 16, 1932, 1, 28; Henry L. Baxley to HFB, n.d. (quotation), Baxley to HFB, July 24, 1932, folder "Baxley, H. L.," box 111, HFBP; HFB to John Garland Pollard, Sept. 15, 1932, Baxley to Pollard, Sept. 16, 1932, folder "Lynching," box 86, Pollard Executive Papers, LVA.

72 "Suicide Doubted in Death of Man," *Washington Evening Star,* Sept. 19, 1932, copy on frame 0915, pt. 7, series A, reel 19, NAACP-Mfm.; "Was It a Lynching?," *RNL,* Sept. 20, 1932, 8 (quotations).

73 "Find Va. Lynching Stories Baseless," *RNL,* Oct. 7, 1932, 1, 28.

74 Ibid.

75 Ibid.

76 "Not a Lynching," *RNL,* Oct. 7, 1932, 8 (quotations); "Tuskegee Makes Inquiries about Thompson Case," *RNL,* Oct. 28, 1932, 2; "Officials Deny Fauquier Case Was Lynching," *RTD,* Dec. 28, 1932, 2.

77 HFB to LIJ, Dec. 29, 1932, folder "1930–1947 Correspondence of LIJ with HFB," box 2, LIJP (#9924-b); HFB to George F. Milton, Dec. 29, 1932, frame 0924 (quotation), pt. 7, series A, reel 19, NAACP-Mfm.

78 George F. Milton to Walter White, Jan. 2, 1933, frame 0923, DSF to White, Jan. 6, 1933, frame 0936 (first quotation), White to Milton, Jan. 11, 1933, frame 0922 (second quotation), pt. 7, series A, reel 19, NAACP-Mfm.

79 HFB to Walter White, Jan. 23, 1933, White to HFB, Jan. 24, 1933, frames 0927–28, pt. 7, series A, reel 19, NAACP-Mfm.

80 Roy Flannagan to Walter White, Jan. 26, 1933, frames 0940–41 (first quotation), White to Flannagan, Feb. 2, 1933, frame 0939, Flannagan to White, Feb. 3, 1933, frames 0946–48 (all other quotations), pt. 7, series A, reel 19, NAACP-Mfm.

81 Roy Flannagan to Walter White, Feb. 3, 1933, frames 0946–48, pt. 7, series A, reel 19, NAACP-Mfm.

82 Walter White to James H. Dillard, Jan. 17, 1933, frame 0932, Dillard to White, Jan. 25, 1933, frame 0938 (first quotation), White to Dillard, Feb. 2, 1933, frame 0937, Dillard to White, Feb. 17, 1933, frame 0945 (second and third quotations), pt. 7, series A, reel 19, NAACP-Mfm. On the NAACP's ultimate ruling in the case, see Walter White to the *Baltimore Afro-American*, July 5, 1933, frame 0949, pt. 7, series A, reel 19, NAACP-Mfm. R. E. Blackwell, the president of Virginia's CIC and a Fauquier native, was among those who deplored the actions of the mob but felt it unfair to classify Thompson's death as a lynching. See L. R. Reynolds to DSF, Jan. 25, 1933, folder "1932–33 Thompson, Shadrack Case," box 16, DSFP-UVA.

83 "Was It a Suicide?," *Richmond Planet*, May 24, 1935, editorial page (all quotations but the final one); L. R. Reynolds to DSF, Jan. 25, 1933, folder "1932–33 Thompson, Shadrack Case," box 16, DSFP-UVA; L. R. Reynolds to George C. Peery (final quotation), folder "Lynching," box 59, George C. Peery Executive Papers, LVA.

84 "Bold Stand Costs 3 Lives at Gordonsville," *Richmond Planet*, May 23, 1936, 1; "Ominous Calm Pervades Gordonsville on Sabbath, Guide Reporter Discovers," *NJG*, May 23, 1936, "Faced Lynching If Taken Alive by Va. 'Posse,'" *NJG*, copies of both on frames 0850–52, pt. 7, series A, reel 19, NAACP-Mfm.

85 "Bold Stand Costs 3 Lives at Gordonsville," *Richmond Planet*, May 23, 1936, 1; "Ominous Calm Pervades Gordonsville on Sabbath, Guide Reporter Discovers," *NJG*, May 23, 1936, "Faced Lynching If Taken Alive by Va. 'Posse,'" *NJG*, copies of both on frames 0850–52, pt. 7, series A, reel 19, NAACP-Mfm. The *Richmond Times-Dispatch* was among those papers reporting that Wales had threatened Mrs. Zinn with a gun. See "Fatal Battle at Gordonsville Had Inception 10 Years Ago," *RTD*, May 17, 1936, 1, 14.

86 "Bold Stand Costs 3 Lives at Gordonsville," *Richmond Planet*, May 23, 1936, 1; "Ominous Calm Pervades Gordonsville on Sabbath, Guide Reporter Discovers," *NJG*, May 23, 1936, "Faced Lynching If Taken Alive by Va. 'Posse,'" *NJG*, copies of both on frames 0850–52, pt. 7, series A, reel 19, NAACP-Mfm.; Walter White to Gertrude Stone, May 26, 1936 (first quotation), P. B. Young to Stone, May 27, 1936 (second and third quotations), frames 0842–46, pt. 7, series A, reel 19, NAACP-Mfm.

87 Gertrude Stone to Walter White, May 31, 1936, frames 0860–61, pt. 7, series A, reel 19, NAACP-Mfm.

88 "Facts about the Family History and Life of the Late William and Cora Wales," interview with Julia Wales, June 2, 1936, frames 0866–69, pt. 7, series A, reel 19, NAACP-Mfm.

89 Ibid.

90 Ibid.

91 Petition of J. L. Hagood in the Supreme Court of Appeals of Virginia, *J. L. Hagood v. Commonwealth of Virginia*, 157 Va. 918 (1932); Hagood Commutation File, box 579, "November 23 to December 8, 1932," Record Group 13, Executive Branch, Secretary of the Commonwealth, Executive Papers, 1866–1962, LVA; Fry, "Rayon, Riot, and Repression," 13–18; "Jail Terms Are Imposed in Strike Case," *RTD*, Sept. 29, 1937, 1; "Review Covington Cases," *RNL*, Sept. 29, 1937, 8 (quotation); "Buchanan Sheriff Says Tuck's Idea 'Wrong' in Mine Case Accusation," *RNL*, June 12, 1948, 1; "Governor Tells Almond to Prosecute 178 Men in Antilynch Violation," *RTD*, June 12, 1948, 1, 4.

92 On the successful efforts to prevent a lynching in Clifton Forge in November 1934, see LIJ to George C. Peery, Nov. 21, 1934, Peery to LIJ, Nov. 22, 1934, folder "1934–1937 Peery, George C.," box 2, LIJP (#9924-g), and "Report of an Investigation in the Matter of Philip Jones, Nannie Jones, John Pryor, and C. Arthur Smith, Jr., Parties Being Held in the Henrico County Jail in Connection with the Death of Alice B. Hill and Ellen Hill of Clifton Forge, Va.," frames 0800–0833, pt. 7, series A, reel 19, NAACP-Mfm.

CHAPTER SEVEN

1 Sweeney, "Rum, Romanism, and Virginia Democrats," 403–31; Patterson, "Fall of a Bishop," 493–518. On several occasions, Douglas Southall Freeman referred to the lackluster support that many Democratic officials provided Smith's campaign. See Minutes, *News Leader* Current Events Class, Oct. 22, 1928, folder "1927 Oc–De, 1928 Ja–No," box 178, DSFP-LC, and DSF, unpublished biography of John Stewart Bryan, 441–42, VHS.

2 Sweeney, "Rum, Romanism, and Virginia Democrats," 405; "Klan Registers Disapproval at Byrd's Speech," *RTD*, May 25, 1928, 1; "Klan Sheet Warns Amendments 'Bad,'" *RTD*, May 30, 1928, 1; "Threatening Letter Mailed to Governor Promises Flogging," *RTD*, June 8, 1928, 1; "Klan Disclaims Threat to Flog Governor Byrd," *RTD*, June 9, 1928, 1; "Gov. Byrd Is Sent Letter of Violence," *AG*, June 9, 1928, 1; Ferrell, *Claude A. Swanson*, 143–49; Chalmers, *Hooded Americanism*, 233–35. As Ferrell points out, Byrd became suspicious in 1931 that Claude Swanson, Virginia's senior U.S. senator, had helped finance the Klan's campaign against him and his supporters. Swanson, at best a lukewarm supporter of the short ballot, lived in Pittsylvania County, which overwhelmingly rejected the amendments. He also owned considerable stock in the Chatham Savings Bank, which had loaned money to the Klan in 1928. Although Byrd had no direct evidence that tied Swanson to the loan, his suspicions only soured his already strained relationship with the senator. After

Swanson joined Franklin D. Roosevelt's cabinet in 1933, Byrd was appointed to his Senate seat. In addition to Ferrell, see "Suit for $2,900 Filed against Ku Klux Klan," *RTD*, Sept. 18, 1931, 1; HFB to William T. Reed, Sept. 22, 1931, and Reed to HFB, Sept. 24, 1931, folder 20, section 1, William T. Reed Family Papers, VHS.

3 Results of Personal Canvass by JCW, section 4 letterbook, 127–33 (first and second quotations), JCWP; "The Negro Is Not an 'Issue' in This Campaign," *RNL*, Aug. 1, 1928, 8 (third quotation); "Virginia Daily Hits Race Issue: Flays It in Political Campaign," *NJG*, Aug. 5, 1928, 1.

4 Wilhelmina Jackson, "Memorandum on Norfolk, Va.," 14–15, folder 29, "Bunche *Political Status of the Negro*, W. Jackson Notes: Norfolk Memorandum," box 85, RJBP; James Jackson, "Memorandum on Richmond, Va.," appendix 4, interview with M. A. Norrell, folder 44, "Bunche *Political Status of the Negro*, James Jackson's Field Notes, Richmond, Va., Memo," box 85, RJBP; handwritten note, section 9 scrapbook, 92, JCWP; Dr. J. D. Eggleston to JCW, Oct. 16, 1928, section 4 letterbook, 378–79, JCWP; letter to the editor, *RTD*, July 22, 1928, copy in section 9 letterbook, 32, JCWP; Buni, *Negro in Virginia Politics*, 97–101; Suggs, "Black Strategy and Ideology," 176. On the migration of African Americans to the Democratic Party in North Carolina in 1928, see Gilmore, "False Friends and Avowed Enemies." As mentioned in Chapter 2, note 73, Gilmore challenges the narrative put forward by Weiss in *Farewell to the Party of Lincoln* that emphasizes the influence of the Great Depression and New Deal on the migration of African Americans to the Democratic Party.

5 "Why Va. Voters Are for Hoover!," copy in Minute Book, Blue Ridge Council #3, folder 2, box 3, Papers of Junior Order United American Mechanics, Rockingham County, LVA; "Local Republicans Raise Race Question in 'Whispering' Campaign," *NJG*, Oct. 20, 1928, 1; "White Supremacy as Practiced by Tammany," section 9 scrapbook, 89, JCWP. At the height of the 1928 campaign, members of the *News Leader* Current Events Class referred to the *Fellowship Forum* as having been "taken over" by the Klan. See Minutes, *News Leader* Current Events Class, Oct. 8, 1928, folder "Minutes (1928)," box 176, DSFP-LC.

6 "The Real Issue in This Campaign: What the Continuation of Our Government Means to Virginia," radio speech delivered by HFB, Oct. 1, 1928, 2–4 (quotations), folder "Speech—Presidential Campaign—1928," box 357, HFBP; Sweeney, "Rum, Romanism, and Virginia Democrats," 420–21. In 1890 Congressman Henry Cabot Lodge introduced legislation that provided for strict federal oversight of elections. Considered by southerners to be as potentially threatening as the most severe Reconstruction-era legislation, the bill was defeated in 1891. The measure's defeat contributed to a sense in the South that the federal government would not oppose disfranchisement. See Woodward, *Origins of the New South*, 254–55, 321–49.

7 "The Real Issue in This Campaign," radio speech delivered by HFB, Oct. 1, 1928, 5–8 (quotations), folder "Speech—Presidential Campaign—1928," box 357, HFBP.

8 Buni, *Negro In Virginia Politics*, 99; "Projects Negro Question into Campaign Here," *RTD*, Sept. 29, 1928 (first quotation), copy in section 9 scrapbook, 86, JCWP; letter by unidentified author, section 4 letterbook, 262–63 (second and third quotations), JCWP. It is quite possible that Wise is the author of this letter.

9 "Leaders Protest Race Issue in Campaign: See Danger in Race Rancor," *NJG*, Nov. 3, 1928, 1.

10 Elizabeth Sutherland Young, letter to the editor, *NJG*, Nov. 3, 1928, 16 (first quotation); "Guide's Prophecy Being Fulfilled," *NJG*, Aug. 4, 1928, 12 (all other quotations).

11 Heinemann, *Harry Byrd of Virginia*, 93–94; Sweeney, "Rum, Romanism, and Virginia Democrats," 403–31; LIJ to HFB, Jan. 1, 1929 (quotations), folder "1924–1930 Correspondence of LIJ with HFB," box 2, LIJP (#9924-b).

12 Alvin L. Hall, "Virginia Back in the Fold," 280–302; "Say Democrats May Drop State Primary System," *RNL*, Nov. 12, 1928, 16; Heinemann, *Harry Byrd of Virginia*, 96. Throughout the 1940s, 1950s, and 1960s, Byrd and his supporters pointed to this ruling to justify their support of Republican presidential candidates. For more on Byrd and his "golden silences" with regard to Democratic presidential nominees, see Heinemann, *Harry Byrd of Virginia*, 243–44, 262–64, 315, 368–70, 380, 406, 411–13.

13 Alvin L. Hall, "Virginia Back in the Fold," 280–96; Heinemann, *Depression and New Deal*, 3; "Sit Quietly in the Boat," *NJG*, July 6, 1929, editorial page.

14 "White House Tea Hurts Chances of Republican Party in South," *NVP*, June 16, 1929, 1–2.

15 "Recalling the Booker Washington Incident," *NVP*, June 16, 1929, 6.

16 "An Ex-Service Man Resents Slurs upon Mrs. DePriest," *NJG*, June 22, 1929, editorial page.

17 "DePriest Will Be Asked to Step Aside When Congress Convenes," *NJG*, Apr. 13, 1929, 1; "Hail Congressman DePriest," *NJG*, Apr. 20, 1929, editorial page; "DePriest Should Stop Talking," *NJG*, July 13, 1929, editorial page (quotation).

18 "Approval of DePriest," *NJG*, July 27, 1929, editorial page.

19 "The Bogey of Negro Domination," *NVP*, reprinted in *NJG*, Oct. 12, 1929, editorial page.

20 "Virginia G.O.P. Irate at DePriest Circular," *Washington Post*, Oct. 29, 1929; "Wise Assails Political Use of Race Issue," *RTD*, Oct. 29, 1929, "Democrats Deny Issuing Pamphlet as to DePriest," [*RTD*], Oct. 29, 1929, "Circulation of Pamphlets Laid at Door of Committee," *RTD*, Nov. 1, 1929, all in section 10 scrapbook, JCWP; JCW, "The Gubernatorial Election in Virginia, 1929: Influence of the Ku Klux Klan and the Race Issue," section 6 letterbook, JCWP; "Political Trickery," *Richmond Planet*, Nov. 2, 1929, editorial page.

21 "Jennings Wise Sees Solution of Race Issue," *RTD*, Oct. 25, 1929 (first quotation), copy in section 10 scrapbook, JCWP; "Poetic Justice," *RTD*, Nov. 3, 1929 (all other quotations), copy in section 6 letterbook, 420, JCWP.

22 Letter with unreadable signature to Jennings [Tim] Wise, Oct. 11, 1928, section 4 letterbook, 352–53, JCWP; Henry A. Wise to JCW, Nov. 9, 1929, sec-

tion 6 letterbook, 355–61, JCWP; JCW, "The Gubernatorial Election in Virginia, 1929: Influence of the Ku Klux Klan and the Race Issue," section 6 letterbook, 319–30 (quotation on 329), JCWP; Alvin L. Hall, "Virginia Back in the Fold." For information on Bishop Cannon, see Heinemann, *Harry Byrd of Virginia*, 98, and Patterson, "Fall of a Bishop," 493–518.

23 Letter from an "anti-Smith" to JCW and Henry Anderson (first and second quotations), section 6 letterbook, 373–75, JCWP; "The Lily-Whites Meet Waterloo in Virginia Election," *Richmond Planet*, Nov. 9, 1929, 1 (third quotation); "The Result," *Richmond Planet*, Nov. 9, 1929, editorial page.

24 "Recalling a Painful Episode," *NJG*, Dec. 7, 1929, editorial page.

25 Ibid. (quotations). For the reference to the *Planet* and the disparity in sentencing, see Minutes, *News Leader* Current Events Class, June 14, 1926, folder "Minutes (1926)," box 176, DSFP-LC.

26 "Race Psychosis in Virginia Politics," *NJG*, Nov. 9, 1929, editorial page (all quotations but the final one); "Pollard Landslide in Virginia Aided by Note of Repression," *NJG*, Nov. 9, 1929, 1, 5 (final quotation).

27 *Nixon v. Herndon*, 273 U.S. 536 (1927).

28 Ibid.; "The Outlawing of Racial Primaries," *NVP*, reprinted under "Reaction of State Press to Court's Decision Temperate," *NJG*, Mar. 12, 1927, 1, editorial page.

29 "Lawyers Doubt Texas Ruling Will Hurt Va.," *RNL*, Mar. 8, 1927, 1.

30 Untitled column, *Richmond Planet*, Mar. 3, 1928, 4; "Barring Negro Democrats Here," *Richmond Planet*, Mar. 31, 1928, 4; "Negro Democrats To Ask Writ Here," *RNL*, Mar. 21, 1928, 1, 24; "Will Resist Court Action by Negroes," *RTD*, Mar. 23, 1928, 1, 5 (quotations on 1); "Denies Negroes Primary Ballot," *RNL*, Mar. 30, 1928, 1–2.

31 "The Democratic Party and the Virginia Negro," *RNL*, Apr. 2, 1928, 8.

32 *James O. West, Plaintiff, against A. C. Bliley, William Boltz, and William Ricker, Defendants*, Amended Complaint, frames 1000–1054, Louis Marshall to W. T. Andrews, May 26, 1928, frames 1032–35 (quotation on frame 1035), pt. 4, "The Voting Rights Campaign, 1916–1950," reel 4, NAACP-Mfm.; "Bright Wins, Disgruntled Negro Democrats Angry," *Richmond Planet*, Apr. 7, 1928, 1; "Sues the Judges," *Richmond Planet*, Apr. 21, 1928, 4; Hine, *Black Victory*, 92–93.

33 "Groner Rules Va. Primary Statute Not Legal," *RNL*, June 5, 1929, 1, section 2, 23 (first quotation on section 2, 23; second and third quotations on 1); *James O. West v. A. C. Bliley et al.*, 33 F.2d 177 (E.D. Va. 1929); "Judge Groner," *Richmond Planet*, June 8, 1929, 1; Hine, *Black Victory*, 93–94.

34 "Judge Groner in the Limelight," *Richmond Planet*, June 8, 1929, 4; editorials from *NVP* and *Norfolk Ledger-Dispatch* reprinted in "Virginia Press Comments on Judge Groner's Democratic Primary Ruling," *NJG*, June 15, 1929, editorial page.

35 Editorials from *RTD*, *Petersburg Progress-Index*, *Portsmouth Star*, and the *Newport News Daily Press* reprinted in "Virginia Press Comments on Judge Groner's Democratic Party Ruling," *NJG*, June 15, 1929, editorial page.

36 "Negroes and the Primary," *RTD*, June 9, 1929, editorial page (quotations), copy on frame 0077, pt. 4, reel 5, NAACP-Mfm.; F.G.D., "Notes: Constitutional Law—Elections—Statute Authorizing Political Party to Disqualify Voters in Primary Election," *Virginia Law Review* 16 (Dec. 1929): 193–97.

37 "Colored Voters Participate in State Primary," *NJG*, Aug. 10, 1929, 1, 13; "Newport News Man Sues for Heavy Damages," *NJG*, Aug. 17, 1929, 1; "Primary Again in Court," *NJG*, Aug. 17, 1929, editorial page.

38 "Election Judges to Face Charges," *RNL*, Aug. 14, 1929, 1; "Plea Is Filed in Litigation over West Case," *RTD*, Aug. 14, 1929, 1–2; "James O. West Wins Damages in Primary Suit," *Richmond Planet*, Oct. 26, 1929, 1; "Judge Groner Is Expected to Act in Next Few Days," *RNL*, Oct. 28, 1929, 2; "Gets Judgment in Democratic Primary Case," *NJG*, Nov. 2, 1929, 1; "U.S. Appeals Court Rules for Negro in Primary Vote," *RTD*, June 14, 1930, 1; *Bliley et al. v. West*, 42 F.2d 101–3 (1930) (quotation on 103).

39 J. Murray Hooker to HFB, May 20, 1930, with enclosure, A. S. Pinkett to Hooker, May 16, 1930, HFB to Hooker, May 21, 1930, folder "1930 Hooker, J. Murray," box 97, HFBP; "The Negro and the Primary," *RNL*, June 16, 1930, 8 (first quotation); "Negroes and the Primary," *RNL*, Sept. 16, 1930, 8; "Return of Old State Primary Plan Is Sought," *RNL*, Sept. 18, 1930, 1, 29 (second quotation on 1); "The Primary and the Negro," *RNL*, Sept. 19, 1930, 8; "Negro Allowed Democrat Vote in Va. Primary," *RNL*, Sept. 15, 1930, 1; Buni, *Negro in Virginia Politics*, 119–20; Hine, *Black Victory*, 93–94, 101–2. As Democratic Party leaders recognized, the role of the state in financing party primaries proved crucial in meeting the objections of the courts. In 1935 the U.S. Supreme Court allowed a revised Texas white primary statute that specifically prohibited the state from financing party activities, thus clearing the way for the Court to rule Texas's primary a private affair. See *Grovey v. Townsend*, 295 U.S. 45 (1935), and Hine, *Black Victory*, 167–87. In 1944 the Supreme Court reversed itself and overturned all white primary statutes. See *Smith v. Allwright*, 321 U.S. 649 (1944), and Hine, *Black Victory*, 212–32. The oft-repeated claims among Virginia whites that few blacks would vote proved true in 1930, although less so in later years. Only 10,000 out of 385,000 voting-age blacks cast ballots in Virginia in 1930, and most of them continued to support Republicans. See Buni, *Negro in Virginia Politics*, 120.

40 "You Who Are Troubled about Negro Encroachments, Please Read This," *RNL*, Sept. 7, 1927, 8. The authors of the most authoritative study of urban planning and race in Richmond argue that black encroachment never approached the levels claimed by proponents of "racial zoning." See Silver, *Twentieth-Century Richmond*, 113, and Silver and Moeser, *Separate City*, 26–27.

41 "You Who Are Troubled about Negro Encroachments, Please Read This," *RNL*, Sept. 7, 1927, 8.

42 "Will Review Segregation Law in City," *RNL*, Nov. 14, 1928, 1.

43 "Special Group to Make Study of Segregation," *RNL*, Dec. 6, 1928, 15; "Race Segregation Study Plan Lost," *RNL*, Dec. 21, 1928, 6.

44 "No Segregation Wanted," *Richmond Planet*, Jan. 12, 1929, 1, 8; "Negroes Protest Projected Plan of Segregation in City," *RTD*, Jan. 9, 1929, 1–2 (quotations).

45 "Study the Measure More in All Its Phases," *RNL*, Jan. 14, 1929, 12; "Do It by Conference, Not by Ordinance," *RNL*, Jan. 15, 1929, 8; Minutes, *News Leader* Current Events Class, Feb. 4, 1929, folder "Minutes (1929)," box 176, DSFP-LC.

46 "Action Delayed Again on Plan of Segregation," *RTD*, Jan. 15, 1929, 1, 6 (quotation); "Facts versus Fiction," *Richmond Planet*, Jan. 26, 1929, 4.

47 "Action Delayed Again on Plan of Segregation," *RTD*, Jan. 15, 1929, 1, 6; "Segregation Ordinance Blocked," *Richmond Planet*, Jan. 19, 1929, 1, 8; "Interdenominational Ministerial Alliance Holds Big Meeting," *Richmond Planet*, Jan. 19, 1929, 1, 8 (quotation on 8).

48 Lucy Randolph Mason to GBH, Mar. 6, 1932, frame 122, reel 62, Lucy Randolph Mason Papers.

49 Storrs, *Civilizing Capitalism*, 68–70; Sullivan, *Days of Hope*, 96–97; Salmond, *Miss Lucy of the CIO*; Mason, *To Win These Rights*; Negro Welfare Survey Committee, *The Negro in Richmond*; Jane Purcell Guild to Lucy Randolph Mason, Jan. 28, 1932, frame 1476 (quotation), reel 65, Mason Papers.

50 "Dedicated to Lucy Randolph Mason by the Negro Citizens of Richmond, Virginia, July 17, 1932," frames 1453–61 (first, second, and third quotations on frame 1456), Katherine Hawes, Testimonial to Lucy Randolph Mason, Jan. 1932, frame 1480 (fifth and sixth quotations), DSF, Testimonial to Lucy Randolph Mason, frame 1474 (final quotation), all on reel 65, Mason Papers; L. R. Reynolds to Lucy Randolph Mason, Sept. 6, 1932, frame 145 (fourth quotation), reel 62, Mason Papers.

51 "Action Delayed Again on Plan of Segregation," *RTD*, Jan. 15, 1929, 1, 6; "Segregation Ordinance Blocked," *Richmond Planet*, Jan. 19, 1929, 1, 8 (first quotation on 8); G. H. Harris to Lucy Randolph Mason, Feb. 2, 1929, frame 10 (second and third quotations), GBH to Lucy Randolph Mason, Feb. 5, 1929, frame 11 (fourth and fifth quotations), reel 62, Mason Papers; GBH, "Redeeming the South," *NJG*, Feb. 2, 1929, editorial page.

52 "Do It by Conference, Not by Ordinance," *RNL*, Jan. 15, 1929, 8; "How Shall Richmond Apply Justice to the Negroes?," *RNL*, Jan. 28, 1929, 8; "Segregation Proposal Wins Unanimously in Council Committee," *RNL*, Feb. 1, 1929, 1, 3; "Segregation Ordinance Passes Committee," *Richmond Planet*, Feb. 2, 1929, 1, 8.

53 "Richmond Will Yet Find the Better Way," *RNL*, Feb. 1, 1929, 8.

54 "All Bad Ordinances Go Back to This State of Affairs," *RNL*, Feb. 4, 1929, 8.

55 "Segregation Is Passed by Common Council, Only 2 Negative Votes," *RTD*, Feb. 5, 1929, 1–2; "Segregation Is Passed; Only 2 Negative Votes," *RNL*, Feb. 5, 1929, 1–2; "Segregation Is Approved Unanimously by Alderman," *RTD*, Feb. 13, 1929, 1; "The Richmond Liberal-Minded White Folk Oppose Race Hatred," *Richmond Planet*, Feb. 9, 1929, 1, 8; press release, "Richmond Mayor Asked to Veto New Segregation Ordinance," Feb. 14, 1929, frame 0786, telegram from J. Fulmer Bright to James Weldon Johnson, Feb. 14,

1929, frame 0787 (first quotation), press release, "Richmond City Government Challenged on Segregation Issue by NAACP," Feb. 15, 1929, frame 0789, telegram from Johnson to Bright, Feb. 15, 1929, frame 0790 (second quotation), "Richmond, Va. Mayor Is Dumb Says NAACP," *Baltimore Afro-American*, [n.d.], frame 0859, telegram from Bright to Johnson, Feb. 16, 1929, frame 0791 (third quotation), all in pt. 5, "The Campaign against Residential Segregation, 1914–55," reel 2, NAACP-Mfm.

56 "Segregation and the Courts," *RNL*, Feb. 5, 1929, 8; "Negroes Here Plan Fight on Segregation," *RNL*, Feb. 15, 1929, 1; "Richmond's Segregation Ordinance," *Buffalo (N.Y.) Progressive Herald*, Mar. 2, 1929, copy in folder "Cases Supported: Richmond, Va. Residential Segregation Case," box D-68, Group I-D, NAACP-LC; "Segregation Money Coming in Rapidly," *Richmond Planet*, Mar. 9, 1929, 1, 8; "Segregation to Be Fought to Finish," *Richmond Planet*, Mar. 16, 1929, 1; Hine, *Black Victory*, 94. For a list of the more than fifty black organizations active in Richmond at the time, see "List of Organizations in Richmond, Va.," frames 0908–9, pt. 5, reel 4, NAACP-Mfm.

57 "A Diversion, Not a Defeat," *RNL*, Feb. 13, 1929, 8 (quotations); "A Diversion, Not a Defeat," *Richmond Planet*, Feb. 16, 1929, 4; "Negroes Here Plan Fight on Segregation," *RNL*, Feb. 15, 1929, 1.

58 Walter White to Maggie Walker, Feb. 21, 1929, frames 0904–5 (quotations), pt. 5, reel 4, NAACP-Mfm.; James Weldon Johnson to C. V. Kelly, Nov. 24, 1928, frames 0845–46, pt. 5, reel 2, NAACP-Mfm.

59 "Memorandum: Visit of Assistant Secretary to Richmond, Virginia, February 25, 1929," Feb. 26, 1929, frame 0806, pt. 5, reel 2, NAACP-Mfm.

60 Ibid., frame 0807 (quotations), Walter White to Moorfield Storey, Feb. 27, 1929, frame 0810, pt. 5, reel 2, NAACP-Mfm.

61 "Memorandum: Visit of Assistant Secretary to Richmond, Virginia, February 25, 1929," Feb. 26, 1929, frame 0807 (quotations), Walter White to Moorfield Storey, Feb. 27, 1929, frame 0810, press release, "NAACP to Help Fight Richmond, Va., Segregation," Mar. 1, 1929, frame 0811, pt. 5, reel 2, NAACP-Mfm.; "NAACP to Help in Richmond Segregation Fight," *NJG*, Mar. 9, 1929, section 2, 1.

62 DSF to William T. Reed, Mar. 26, 1929, section 1, Reed Family Papers, VHS. On Reed and his influence on Harry Byrd and the Democratic Party, see Fry, "Senior Advisor," 445–69.

63 William T. Reed to DSF, Mar. 30, 1929, DSF to Reed, Apr. 24, 1929, DSF to Reed, Apr. 30, 1929, section 1, Reed Family Papers, VHS.

64 Petition of *J. B. Deans v. The City of Richmond*, In the District Court of the United States for the Eastern District of Virginia (quotations), frames 0822–34, pt. 5, reel 2, NAACP-Mfm; "Negro Land Owner's Attorneys Ask Injunction to Restrain City," *RTD*, Mar. 30, 1929, 1, 3; "Ask Dismissal of Segregation Bill Fight Here," *RNL*, Apr. 12, 1929, 1, 30; "Segregation Plea in U.S. Court," *Richmond Planet*, Apr. 6, 1929, 1; "The Segregation Case," *Richmond Planet*, Apr. 20, 1929, 4; "Segregation Case Is Argued before U.S. Court," *Richmond Planet*, May 11, 1929, 1, 8.

65 "Segregation Opponents Win First Skirmish," *RTD*, May 19, 1929, 1–2;

"Richmond Segregation Law Invalid," *NJG*, May 25, 1929, 1; "Unconstitutional, Segregation Law Has Been Annulled," *Richmond Planet*, May 25, 1929, 1; "Appeal Filed in Ruling on Segregation," *RTD*, Aug. 13, 1929, 1, 3; "City Files Brief on Racial Tangle," *RNL*, Sept. 27, 1929, 1, 34; "Appeal Brief in Segregation Case Is Filed," *NJG*, Oct. 5, 1929, 1; *City of Richmond et al. v. Deans*, 37 F.2d 713 (1930) (first quotation); "Segregation Loses," *Richmond Planet*, Jan. 18, 1930, 1; "Segregation Law Is Again Ruled Invalid," *NJG*, Jan. 18, 1930, 1; "Richmond's Segregation Law Is Held Illegal," *RNL*, Jan. 14, 1930, 1, 21; "Residential Segregation Law Invalid, High Court Rules Again: Richmond Case Verdict Affects Property Rights," *NJG*, May 24, 1930, 1, 15 (second quotation); "Would Ban Negroes from Virginia County," *NJG*, Nov. 2, 1935, 11. For the U.S. Supreme Court ruling that invalidated a residential segregation ordinance in Louisville, Kentucky, see *Buchanan v. Warley*, 245 U.S. 60 (1917); for the Supreme Court opinion that invalidated New Orleans's statute, see *Harmon v. Tyler*, 273 U.S. 668 (1927).

66　*City of Richmond et al. v. Deans*, memorandum decision 281 U.S. 704 (1930); "City Segregation Bill Held Invalid by Supreme Court," *RTD*, May 20, 1930, 1–2; "Residential Segregation Law Invalid, High Court Rules Again: Richmond Case Verdict Affects Property Rights," *NJG*, May 24, 1930, 1, 15 (quotation); "Court Refuses Second Hearing on Segregation," *RTD*, May 27, 1930, 1.

67　Alfred E. Cohen, letter to the editor, *The Nation*, May 7, 1930, frame 0915 (quotations), pt. 5, reel 2, NAACP-Mfm. For a full account of the events surrounding Parker's nomination and rejection in the Senate, see Kluger, *Simple Justice*, 141–44. As Kluger notes, Parker figured prominently in a number of segregation cases throughout the 1930s, 1940s, and 1950s. Despite the role played by the NAACP in his confirmation defeat, Parker usually ruled in favor of the NAACP's position.

68　"Separation by Consent," *RNL*, May 20, 1930, 8.

69　Ibid. (first and second quotations); Richard W. Carrington to Members, Richmond Committee on Interracial Cooperation, May 29, 1930 (third quotation), folder "Virginia Interracial Commission/Committee, 1922–1945," box 35, Adele Goodman Clark Papers, Special Collections and Archives, James Branch Cabell Library, Virginia Commonwealth University.

70　Joseph R. Pollard to W. T. Andrews, May 24, 1929, frames 0882–83, pt. 5, reel 2, NAACP-Mfm.

CHAPTER EIGHT

1　Heinemann, *Depression and New Deal*, 1–43; Earl Lewis, *In Their Own Interests*, 110–66; Gavins, *Perils and Prospects*, 51–75; Martin-Perdue and Perdue, *Talk about Trouble*.

2　"First Test Case under New Race Integrity Law," *NJG*, Aug. 28, 1926, 1; "Appeal Likely from Two-Year Term in Prison," *RTD*, May 4, 1928, 1; "Test Case Looms in Virginia Racial Integrity Law," *NJG*, May 12, 1928, 1; "Two Convicted under Racial Integrity Act," *NJG*, June 23, 1928, 1.

3 "Mott Wood's Crime," *NJG*, June 23, 1928, 16 (first quotation); "Byrd Refuses Pardon under Va. Racial Law," *RNL*, Aug. 31, 1928 (second quotation).

4 "Charge Woman Is Part Negro: Jail Newlyweds," *RTD*, Jan. 17, 1929, 3 (first quotation); "Former Police Chief Weds Colored Woman, Arrested," *NJG*, Nov. 23, 1929, 1, 5; "Judge Lectures Acquitted Mixed Marriage Pair," *NJG*, May 10, 1930, 1 (second and third quotations).

5 "Plecker Claims Racial Integrity Statute Is Violated in Virginia," *RTD*, Apr. 10, 1931, 16; "Negroid Baby Registry as White Noted," *RTD*, Sept. 29, 1931, 1; "Advocates of Race Integrity Are All Het Up," *NJG*, Oct. 3, 1931, 1, 4; "Urges That Race Law Be Modified," *RNL*, Dec. 30, 1931, 1; "Miscegenation Status Reduced in Senate Bill," *RTD*, Jan. 29, 1932, 4; Commonwealth of Virginia, *Acts of Assembly, 1932*, 68; Wallenstein, "Race, Marriage, and the Law of Freedom," 409–10.

6 Abraham Branham, Lexington, Va., to HFB, July 3, 1926, folder "Vital Statistics, Bureau of," box 68, BEP; WAP to Kate Robinson, Dec. 11, 1926, folder "Letters 1923–28 'P,'" box 1, William Gregory Rennolds Papers, LVA.

7 "Real Indians, Family Says, Not Negroes," *RTD*, Jan. 29, 1929, 3; "Race Integrity Bill Beaten in Senate by Vote of 26 to 13," *RTD*, Feb. 14, 1928, 1–2; Sherman, "'The Last Stand,'" 88–89; "Indians Fear Classification among Negroes," *RTD*, Sept. 10, 1929, 14; "Find Hart Acted as Private Citizen," *RNL*, Sept. 20, 1929, 1, 26.

8 Minutes, *News Leader* Current Events Class, Feb. 8, 1926, 2 (second quotation), folder "Minutes (1926)," box 176, DSFP-LC; "Rights as Citizens Not Lost by State Officers," *RNL*, Sept. 21, 1929, 8 (all other quotations).

9 WAP to DSF, Oct. 22, 1929, folder "Health — Bureau of Vital Statistics," box 24, BEP.

10 "New Racial Integrity Measure Is Offered," *RTD*, Jan. 17, 1930, 1.

11 Decision of Judge Joseph W. Chinn, Sept. 22, 1928, and papers pertaining to "In Re Petition of Robinson et al. to County School Board: Petition and Appeal to Circuit Court of Essex County, June Term, 1928," Chancery Order Book 8, 220, Circuit Court of Essex County; "Investigator Finds Mixed Schools in Essex County," *RTD*, Jan. 26, 1930, 1; handwritten speech of JP in favor of House Bill No. 2, introduced 1928, folder 3, box 56, JPP; Commonwealth of Virginia, *Acts of Assembly, 1924*, 535 (quotation). I am grateful to the Honorable Joseph E. Spruill Jr., judge of Virginia's Fifteenth Judicial Circuit, for locating the Essex County Court records.

12 "Investigator Finds Mixed Schools in Essex County," *RTD*, Jan. 26, 1930, 2 (first quotation); "New Racial Integrity Measure Is Offered," *RTD*, Jan. 17, 1930, 1 (second quotation).

13 "Investigator Finds Mixed Schools in Essex County," *RTD*, Jan. 26, 1930, 2.

14 Ibid.

15 "Essex Acts to Prevent Mixed Races in Schools," *RTD*, Jan. 27, 1930, 1–2 (quotations); L. R. Reynolds, Director of Virginia CIC, to William Gregory Rennolds, Apr. 19, 1928, folder "Letters 1923–28 'R,'" box 1, Rennolds Papers, LVA.

16 "Substitute Bill Being Sought by Its Opponents," *NJG*, Feb. 8, 1930, sec-

tion 2, 1, 7. Richard Heath Dabney, in fact, had for decades warned that granting rights and privileges to blacks would lead to an increase in racial tension. In 1901 he authored a lengthy article in the *Richmond Times* that praised the loyalty of blacks as slaves but warned against "political, social, and industrial equality." See folder "1901 article by R. Heath Dabney on the Negro Problem in *Richmond Times* and other material on the subject," box 2, VDP.

17 Dover Baptist Association, "A Statement in Regard to Senate Bill, No. 49" (first quotation), W. G. Rennolds to R. Hill Fleet, Jan. 27, 1930 (second quotation), Fleet to Rennolds, Jan. 31, 1930 (third, fourth, and fifth quotations), folder 4, box 2, Rennolds Papers, LVA; Estelle Marks to W. G. Rennolds, Jan. 24, 1930, folder 7, box 2, Rennolds Papers, LVA.

18 "Virginia Racial Integrity Bill Passes House," *NJG*, Feb. 15, 1930, 3; "Race Integrity Bill Is Passed by Delegates," *RNL*, Feb. 11, 1930, 1; "Race Integrity Bill Passed by a Large Vote," *RTD*, Feb. 14, 1930, 1, 6; Sherman, "'The Last Stand,'" 90.

19 "A Long Fight Won," *RTD*, Feb. 12, 1930, 8 (quotations). On the *Richmond News Leader*'s support of a commission, see "Refer the Racial Bills," *RNL*, Feb. 11, 1930, 8.

20 *NVP* editorial quoted in "Latest Racial Integrity Bill Is Now a Law," *NJG*, Feb. 22, 1930, 8 (first quotation); "May This Be the End of It!," *RNL*, Feb. 14, 1930, 8 (second and third quotations).

21 "Virginia's 1930 Edition of Racial Integrity," *NJG*, Feb. 15, 1930, editorial page.

22 Picott, *History of the Virginia Teachers Association*, 95–108 (first quotation on 102); Harris Hart to all Division Superintendents of Schools, May 15, 1930, copy in folder 6, box 2, Rennolds Papers, LVA; "Disparity in Teachers' Pay," *NJG*, May 24, 1930, editorial page (second quotation). The disparity in salaries between rural and urban teachers and the need for an equalization fund was most clearly documented in a series published by the University of Virginia's School of Rural Economics. See *University of Virginia News Letter*, Oct. 1, Oct. 15, Nov. 1, Nov. 15, Dec. 1, and Dec. 15, 1929.

23 "Teachers Hit Salary Inequalities," *NJG*, May 9, 1931, 1, 15; "Further Discrepancies in Va. School Outlays Are Revealed," *NJG*, May 9, 1931, 11; "More Pay for Teachers," *NJG*, June 20, 1931, editorial page; "A Justifiable Claim," *NJG*, Nov. 28, 1931, editorial page; "Teachers Back Move for Higher Salary Scale," *NJG*, Dec. 5, 1931, 1, 15; "Negro Teachers Salaries Small," *RNL*, Dec. 5, 1931, 10; "Cuts in Teachers Pay Described: Low Salaries in the South Attacked," *NJG*, Jan. 23, 1932, 3 (quotation); "Citizen Voters League Wins against School Board in Appointment of Principal," *NJG*, Sept. 10, 1932, 9.

24 "Gov. Pollard Would Cut All Salaries," *NJG*, Jan. 23, 1932, 1; "Separate But Equal," *NJG*, Feb. 13, 1932, editorial page (quotation).

25 VD, "Negroes and the Franchise: Their Participation in the Primaries," *RTD*, reprinted in *NJG*, Sept. 12, 1931, 7; "Call Issued for Political Talk at Petersburg," *NJG*, Feb. 18, 1928, 1; "Voters League Rouses Citizens of Richmond, Va.," *NJG*, June 6, 1931, 2; "New Civic League Promotes Citizenship,"

NJG, Mar. 19, 1932, 1; "Danville Has Largest Number of Negro Voters," *NJG*, July 16, 1932, 9; "Business Men of Danville, Va., Forging Strong Link in Race's Chain of Economic Progress," *NJG*, July 14, 1923, 7; Theodore W. Jones, letter to the editor, "The Race on Trial," *NJG*, Apr. 2, 1932, editorial page (quotation); "Candidacy of Va. Physician Creates Furor," *NJG*, Aug. 8, 1931, 1. In 1920 a Mr. Press, an attorney, apparently ran for city council in Newport News. See Wilhelmina Jackson, "Memorandum on Newport News, Virginia," 7–8, folder 31, "Bunche *Political Status of the Negro*, W. Jackson's Field Notes: Newport News Memorandum," box 85, RJBP, and Gavins, "Hancock, Jackson, and Young," 470–77.

26 Wilhelmina Jackson, "Memorandum on Newport News, Virginia," 7–8, folder 31, "Bunche *Political Status of the Negro*, W. Jackson's Field Notes: Newport News Memorandum," box 85, RJBP. On the Democratic primaries in the twentieth century, see Sabato, *Democratic Party Primary*.

27 *W. E. Davis v. Thomas C. Allen, Registrar*, 157 Va. 84, 86, 88 (1931) (emphasis added). The discriminatory tactics faced by Davis in Hampton were familiar to aspiring black voters in Richmond. See Frazer, "How Does It Feel to Be Colored?," 10. I am indebted to Brent Tarter at the Library of Virginia for bringing the Frazer piece to my attention.

28 *Davis v. Allen*, 157 Va. 84, 86–87. Italics appear in the trial record; presumably these are the misspellings emphasized by the registrar.

29 Ibid., 84–91 (quotations); "Registrars' Subterfuge Held Illegal," *NJG*, Oct. 10, 1931, 1, 15.

30 Buni, *Negro in Virginia Politics*, 112–27; Wilhelmina Jackson, "Memorandum on Portsmouth, Va.," 3–5 (quotation), folder 12, "Bunche *Political Status of the Negro*, W. Jackson's Field Notes, Portsmouth Memorandum and Map," box 85, RJBP; "Judge B. D. White Rules against Color Barrier," *NJG*, Aug. 8, 1931, 1.

31 Wilhelmina Jackson, "Memorandum on Portsmouth, Va.," 6, folder 12, "Bunche *Political Status of the Negro*, W. Jackson's Field Notes, Portsmouth Memorandum and Map," box 85, RJBP.

32 Ibid., 7.

33 Buni, *Negro in Virginia Politics*, 112–34; Earl Lewis, *In Their Own Interests*, 147; *Grovey v. Townsend*, 295 U.S. 45 (1935); "Texans Win Vote Point," *NJG*, Apr. 6, 1935, 1, 10; "Va. County Is in Favor of Lily-Whitism," *NJG*, June 8, 1935, 1; "No Ban on Voting in Campbell Co. during Primary," *NJG*, Aug. 17, 1935, 1; "Voting Strength Doubled," *Richmond Planet*, Dec. 14, 1935, 1; "Voting Interest in Petersburg Growing," *NJG*, Dec. 14, 1935, 11; "Mayor Bright," *Richmond Planet*, Apr. 11, 1936, 12. The phrase "courteous disfranchisement" appears in the "Virginia Interviews," box 10, Southern Politics Collection, Alexander Heard Library, Vanderbilt University. The interviews were conducted with a guarantee of anonymity, which remains a condition for examining them. Hence, no material quoted here from this collection can be attributed by name.

34 "Jim Crowism at Its Worst," *NJG*, Aug. 15, 1931, editorial page.

35 Virginius, "Coffee Cups and Racial Integrity," *NJG*, Feb. 21, 1931, 1.

36 "Barred from Jamestown," *NJG*, Oct. 4, 1930, editorial page; "Negroes Should Be Admitted to Jamestown," *RNL*, Sept. 2, 1930, 10 (quotation).

37 "A Reasonable and Just Request," *NJG*, May 16, 1931, editorial page; P. B. Young to LIJ, Nov. 4, 13, 1931, folder "1925–1949 Young, P. B.," box 1, LIJP (#9924-j); "Nearly 200 Richmond Children Refused Admission to Public School for Lack of Space," *NJG*, Jan. 30, 1932, 3; "Portsmouth School Official Urges Congestion Relief," *NJG*, Oct. 8, 1932, 8; "One-Twelfth of Virginia's High Schools Available for Colored Students, Altho Negro Population One-Fourth of Total," *NJG*, Oct. 8, 1932, 7; Report of 12th Annual Meeting, 1931, frame 229, reel 55, CIC Papers.

38 "Richmond's Serious School Condition," *Richmond Planet*, June 1, 1935, 1; "Richmond's Negro Schools Needing Better Equipment," *RNL*, May 26, 1930, 15; "Low Wage, No Advancement Hurts Negro as Teacher," *RNL*, May 27, 1930, 7; "Richmond Negro Schools Need Greater Facilities," *RNL*, May 28, 1930, 14; "Better Equipment Is Need of Negro Schools in City," *RNL*, May 29, 1930, 7. Richmond finally hired a black principal for a black school in 1933. See "Negroes Will Be Allowed to Head Schools of Race," *RNL*, Mar. 25, 1933, 2; "For Better School Morale," *RNL*, Mar. 25, 1933, 8; and "Negro Principals for Two Schools," *RNL*, July 29, 1933, 2.

39 Earl Lewis, *In Their Own Interests*, 121; "Negroes Living in Intolerable Conditions Here," *RNL*, Sept. 19, 1931, 1, 18 (quotation on 1). Corson described the results of his investigation in an eleven-part series that ran in the *Richmond News Leader* from Sept. 19, 1931, through Oct. 1, 1931. See "Negroes Living in Intolerable Conditions Here," *RNL*, Sept. 19, 1931, 1, 18; "Every Richmond Section Sorely Affected by Conditions Prevailing in Crime-Breeding Slums Where Negroes Live," *RNL*, Sept. 20, 1931, 7; "Old Age, Decay and Neglect Combine to Make Houses in Poorer Negro Sections Unfit for Human Occupancy," *RNL*, Sept. 22, 1931, 3; "Squalid Interior of Many Negro Homes Makes Jail and Almshouse Real Relief," *RNL*, Sept. 23, 1931, 9; "Sanitary Facilities in Richmond's Negro Hovels So Poor as to Put Premium on Decency and Health," *RNL*, Sept. 24, 1931, 6; "Unpaved Streets and Rubbish-Littered Yards Add to Bad Conditions in Poor Negro Sections," *RNL*, Sept. 25, 1931, 6; "Better Plumbing and Building Codes Needed to Wipe Out Richmond's Slums," *RNL*, Sept. 26, 1931, 2; "Overcrowded Conditions in Poorer Negro Homes Means Lowering of Morals and Breeding of Crime," *RNL*, Sept. 28, 1931, 9; "Shiftless Negro Tenants and Avaricious Owners Combine to Make Living Conditions Almost Tragic," *RNL*, Sept. 29, 1931, 4; "Incomes of Many Negroes So Small They Can Eke Out Only Barest Living," *RNL*, Sept. 30, 1931, 8; and "Comprehensive City Plan Is Needed to Rid Richmond of Slum Conditions," *RNL*, Oct. 1, 1931, 4.

40 "Richmond Women Indignantly Quit Meeting Which Tried to Open Clark Springs to Negro Children," *NJG*, Feb. 27, 1932, 9.

41 "65,000 Norfolkians Without a Beach," *NVP*, Feb. 20, 1929, 6 (quotations). For the earliest discussion of the need for a beach, see unsigned memos, dated July 30 and Aug. 10, 1925, addressed to S. Heth Tyler and the City Council, folder "1919–1949 'Tampa' through 'Tyler,'" box 2, LIJP (#9924-i). In all like-

lihood, Jaffé authored these memos. At the very least, the editor had begun discussions around this time regarding the need for a black beach and parks. See letter from Jaffé, Douglas Gordon, and Eugene Diggs to City Council of Norfolk, Oct. 8, 1934, folder "1930–35 Negro Bathing Beach," box 2, LIJP (#9924-f), which states that the Norfolk Interracial Commission had begun discussions about a beach around 1926.

42 "Norfolk's Christmas Gift to Her Negro Citizens," *NJG*, Jan. 4, 1930, editorial page; "Expected Objection to Beach Site," *NJG*, Jan. 11, 1930, editorial page; "A Plea for Justice," *NVP*, Jan. 14, 1930, 6 (quotations).

43 *NJG*, Jan. 18, 1930, 1 (quotation); "We Are Grateful," *NJG*, Jan. 18, 1930, editorial page; LIJ to Capt. Joseph D. Wood, Jan. 14, 1930, Wood to LIJ, Jan. 17, 1930, folder "1920–1949 W. Wiggins–Wyatt," box 1, LIJP (#9924-j); Otto Wells to Walter Truxton, Jan. 11, 1930, Wells to LIJ, Jan. 14, 1930, LIJ to Wells, Feb. 3, 1930, Wells to LIJ, Feb. 4, 1930, folder "1926, 1930 Wells, Otto—Wells Amusement Co.," box 1, LIJP (#9924-j); "Delay Now Seen as Probable in Beach Project," *NJG*, Feb. 1, 1930, section 2, 1, 4; editorial from *Norfolk Ledger-Dispatch*, reprinted as "Another Protest, Of Course," *NJG*, Mar. 8, 1930, editorial page; "Beach Assured: Will Be Ready by Next Season," *NJG*, June 28, 1930, 1; "Opposition to Bathing Beach Here Renewed," *NJG*, July 12, 1930, 1; LIJ and Douglas Gordon to the State Corporation Commission, Sept. 25, 1930, folder "1930–35 Negro Bathing Beach," box 2, LIJP (#9924-f); "Beach Objectors at Ocean View Adding Red Tape," *NJG*, Jan. 3, 1931, 1; "Bathing Beach Case to Be Heard by Supreme Court," *NJG*, June 13, 1931, 1.

44 "Proposal of City Manager Is Voted Down," *NJG*, Jan. 30, 1932, 1; "Beach Project May Be Killed," *NJG*, Feb. 6, 1932, 1; "The Beach on the Brink," *NJG*, Feb. 6, 1932, editorial page (quotations); Earl Lewis, *In Their Own Interests*, 144–46.

45 "Beach Opponents Give Up Fight: Court Rules City's Title Legal, Valid," *NJG*, Mar. 12, 1932, 1, 15; "A Legal and Moral Victory," *NJG*, Mar. 12, 1932, editorial page; LIJ to L. H. Windholz, Chairman, Norfolk Public Works Committee, June 21, 1933, LIJ, Douglas Gordon, Eugene Diggs to the City Council of Norfolk, Oct. 8, 1934, folder "1930–35 Negro Bathing Beach," box 2, LIJP (#9924-f); Memo Re: Bathing Beach, folder A, box 1, LIJP (#9924-k); Earl Lewis, *In Their Own Interests*, 144–46.

46 LIJ to William Shands Meacham, Nov. 9, 1934, folder "1927–49, Meacham, Wm. Shands," box 1, LIJP (#9924-f). On Meacham and the CIC, see "Virginia Interracial Commission," *Southern Workman* 64 (July 1935): 199–201.

47 LIJ to William Shands Meacham, Nov. 9, 1934 (first and second quotations), folder "1927–49, Meacham, Wm. Shands," box 1, LIJP (#9924-f); LIJ to Raymond Bottom, Feb. 14, 1935 (third quotation), folder "1924–1925 Correspondence of LIJ with Bl–Bo," box 1, LIJP (#9924-b).

48 Earl Lewis, *In Their Own Interests*, 148.

49 Ibid., 144–47 (first quotation on 147; second quotation on 144).

50 Jerry O. Gilliam interview by RJB, Oct. 21, 1939, folder 6, "Field Notes: Southern Trip, Bk. 1," box 85, RJBP.

51 LIJ to HFB, Mar. 29, 1929, HFB to LIJ, Apr. 3, 1929 (first quotation), folder "1924–1930 Corres. of LIJ with HFB," box 2, LIJP (#9924-b); "1930: The Present Situation in Race Relations," frames 979–85 (second and third quotations on frame 985), reel 53, CIC Papers.

52 "Report of the Findings Committee," Apr. 30, 1930, frame 1424 (first quotation), "A Message to the Citizens' Committee of One Thousand," frame 1675, both on reel 55, CIC Papers; L. R. Reynolds to Will Alexander, May 19, 1934, frame 524, HFB to A Citizens' Committee of One Thousand, frame 815 (second and third quotations), both on reel 53, CIC Papers.

53 William T. Reed to HFB, Aug. 8, 1931, folder 20, section 1, William T. Reed Family Papers, VHS.

54 1934 Interracial Plan, frames 1644–50 (first quotation on frame 1646), "The Interracial Commission at Work," frames 1675–81, "Going Forward Together," frame 1657 (second quotation), all on reel 55, CIC Papers; "1930: The Present Situation in Race Relations," frames 979–87, reel 53, CIC Papers.

55 Wiley Hall, Secretary, Urban League of Richmond, interview by RJB, Oct. 18, 1939, folder 6, "Field Notes: Southern Trip, Bk. 1," box 85, RJBP.

56 Ibid.

57 Dr. J. M. Tinsley interview by RJB, Oct. 18, 1939 (quotations), folder 6, "Field Notes: Southern Trip, Bk. 1," box 85, RJBP; NAACP, *Virginia State Conference of Branches*, 14.

58 James Jackson, "Memorandum on Richmond, Va.," folder 44, "Bunche *Political Status of the Negro*, James Jackson's Field Notes, Richmond, Va., Memo," box 85, RJBP.

59 Earl Lewis, *In Their Own Interests*, 126–66; Wiley Hall interview by RJB, Oct. 18, 1939 (quotation), Dr. J. M. Tinsley interview by RJB, Oct. 18, 1939, folder 6, "Field Notes: Southern Trip, Bk. 1," box 85, RJBP.

60 Simpson, "Are Colored People in Virginia a Helpless Minority?," 373–75, 381 (first quotation on 381); Suggs, *P. B. Young, Newspaperman*, 61–62; Earl Lewis, *In Their Own Interests*, 135–48 (second quotation on 148); "Virginia Interviews" (third quotation), box 10, Southern Politics Collection, Alexander Heard Library, Vanderbilt University. The terms of access to the Southern Politics Collection prohibit the identification of any source by name.

61 Suggs, *P. B. Young, Newspaperman*, 110–15; Gignilliat, "The Thought of Douglas Southall Freeman," 328–40. On the fight between the ILD and the NAACP over the defense of the Scottsboro Boys, see Goodman, *Stories of Scottsboro*, and Dan T. Carter, *Scottsboro*. For African Americans as a whole, the most significant aspect of the Crawford case was Houston's challenge to the all-white jury system that pervaded Virginia and the South. Although Houston ultimately agreed not to force the constitutional issue during Crawford's trial, a number of localities in Virginia added African Americans to their juror rolls in advance of the U.S. Supreme Court's decision in *Norris v. Alabama*, 294 U.S. 587 (1935). See "Negroes Here to Be Put on Grand Juries," *RNL*, Aug. 9, 1933, 1; "Negroes on Grand Juries, *RNL*, Aug. 9, 1933, 8; "Negro Is Chosen for Grand Jury," *RNL*, Sept. 28, 1933, 2; and "Negroes Drawn for Jury List in Nansemond," *RNL*, Apr. 17, 1934, 1, 20.

62 Buni, *Negro in Virginia Politics*, 127; Brundage, *Lynching in the New South*, 365 n. 8; NAACP, *Virginia State Conference of Branches*, 14–15; folder "Alexandria, Va., 1919–1939," box G-206, Group I–Branch Files, NAACP-LC; Suggs, *P. B. Young, Newspaperman*, 61–62; "NAACP Begins Drive for 2000 Local Members," *Richmond Planet*, Oct. 6, 1934, 1; "Richmond Branch of NAACP Reviews Its Program on Eve of Annual Membership Drive," *NJG*, Nov. 2, 1935, 11; "Richmond Branch NAACP Opens Fall Membership Drive," *Richmond Planet*, Oct. 10, 1936. I am grateful to Larissa Smith, who has shared with me her research on the growth of the NAACP in the 1930s. For more on the NAACP in the 1930s and 1940s, see Larissa M. Smith, "Where the South Begins."

63 "Negro Education Facilities Issue," *RNL*, Nov. 22, 1933, 6; folder "Alexandria, Va., 1919–1939," box G-206, Group I–Branch Files, NAACP-LC; Dr. J. M. Tinsley interview by RJB, Oct. 18, 1939, folder 6, "Field Notes: Southern Trip, Bk. 1," box 85, RJBP; "Plea Tonight Opens Negro School Battle," *RNL*, Jan. 21, 1936, 1, 13; "The Negroes' Tomorrow," *RNL*, Mar. 27, 1936, 8 (quotation).

64 "Negro Plans Battle in Court to Enter University of Virginia," *RTD*, Aug. 27, 1935, 1, 3.

65 Sullivan, *Days of Hope*, 82–83; Maurice Gates, "Negro Students Challenge Social Forces," 232–33, 251; Cohen, *When the Old Left Was Young*, 218–19; Love, "Cigarette Capital of the World," 187–204; "First Negro to Enter Md. State University," *NJG*, Sept. 28, 1935, 1; Kluger, *Simple Justice*, 186–96. Alice Jackson's brother is the same James Jackson who later conducted research for Ralph Bunche and is quoted above.

66 "Our Educational Dilemma and Proposed Court Action as Remedy," *NJG*, Aug. 31, 1935, 8; "Let Us Understand Each Other," *NJG*, Sept. 7, 1935, 8 (first quotation); "Some Observations on the Discriminatory Public Education System—and Some Recent History," *NJG*, Sept. 14, 1935, 11; "NAACP to Stress the Right of Negroes to Enter State Colleges," *Richmond Planet*, Sept. 7, 1935, 1; "Badly Advised," *RNL*, Aug. 28, 1935, editorial page (second quotation); "Futile and Unwise," *RTD* (third quotation), in "Virginia Editors on the Question of Negroes at the University of Virginia," *NJG*, Sept. 7, 1935, 8; "Dislikes Association's Militant Methods," *Richmond Planet*, Sept. 14, 1935, 1; "Negro Plans Battle in Court to Enter University of Virginia," *RTD*, Aug. 27, 1935, 1, 3 (fourth and fifth quotations on 3).

67 "Admission May Be Denied Girl on Technicality," *NJG*, Aug. 31, 1935, 1; Gavins, *Perils and Prospects*, 95–96; "Application Referred to Board," *Richmond Planet*, Sept. 21, 1935, 1; "Final Decision in Univ. Case Up to Trustees," *NJG*, Sept. 21, 1935, 1; "Application of Negro Student Rejected by University Board," *RTD*, Sept. 20, 1935, 1 (quotation); "Board Rejects Application of Richmond Girl," *NJG*, Sept. 28, 1935, 1.

68 Houston, "Educational Inequalities Must Go!," 300–301, 316; Houston, "Cracking Closed University Doors," 364, 370, 372; "Board Rejects Application of Richmond Girl," *NJG*, Sept. 28, 1935, 11 (first quotation); "University of Virginia Case Now before the NAACP," *Richmond Planet*, Sept. 28, 1935, 1;

"Student Group at U. of Va. Hits Inequalities," *NJG*, Oct. 12, 1935, 11; "White Students Protest U. of Va. Discrimination," *Richmond Planet*, Oct. 12, 1935, 1; Sullivan, *Days of Hope*, 82–83; "Best for Both Races," *RTD*, Sept. 21, 1935, 6 (second and third quotations). On Houston's life, see McNeil, *Groundwork*.

69 Kneebone, *Southern Liberal Journalists*, xiii–xx, 3–73; Nitschke, "Virginius Dabney of Virginia," 1–130; VD, "Negroes and the Franchise: Their Participation in the Primaries," *RTD*, reprinted in *NJG*, Sept. 12, 1931, 7 (second and third quotations); "A New Version of the Negro in Politics," *NJG*, Sept. 12, 1931, editorial page (first quotation).

70 VD, "Paternalism in Race Relations Is Outmoded," 1, 4 (all quotations except the final one on 4); Nitschke, "Virginius Dabney of Virginia," 77–91 (final quotation on 78); Kneebone, *Southern Liberal Journalists*, 74–96; R. Charlton Wright, "Southern White Man and the Negro," 175–94. In his attack on paternalism, Dabney cited William Alexander Percy's *Lanterns on the Levee* as the quintessential statement on paternalism (see Introduction, note 3, above). In part, Dabney's views on paternalism reflected the influence of Jessie Daniel Ames, the general field secretary of the CIC, who laid out her views in a fascinating letter to Dabney. See Jessie Daniel Ames to VD, Apr. 10, 1942, folder "1943 — Negroes — Atlanta, Durham, Richmond Conferences (1)," box 5, VDP. Like Dabney, Ames was seen as a racial progressive in the 1920s and 1930s but retreated to the sidelines in the 1940s as African Americans demanded an end to Jim Crow. For more on Ames, see Hall, *Revolt against Chivalry*.

71 Josephus Simpson, "An Open Letter to the Times Dispatch," *Richmond Planet*, Sept. 28, 1935, 1–2 (all quotations); "A Scare-Crow in Defense of Jim Crow," *Richmond Planet*, Sept. 28, 1935, 12; "Go Forward NAACP and Fight It," *Richmond Planet*, Sept. 7, 1935, 1.

72 "Va. State Grad Study Approved," *NJG*, Dec. 21, 1935, 1, 10; "Graduate Instruction at State College," *NJG*, Dec. 21, 1935, 8; "Negro Education Bill Is Proposed," *RNL*, Feb. 17, 1936, 1; Commonwealth of Virginia, *Acts of Assembly, 1936*, 561; "30 Negroes Ask Va. School Aid," *RNL*, July 27, 1936, 1, 20; "University of Virginia Case," *Richmond Planet*, Nov. 30, 1935, 1; "U. of Va. Fight Discussed by Chas. Houston," *NJG*, Dec. 7, 1935, 11; "NAACP to Press Suits," *Richmond Planet*, Dec. 21, 1935, 1; "NAACP's Position on Rights of Negroes in Tax-Supported Schools," *Richmond Planet*, Jan. 11, 1936, 1; "Fear Cold Feet in Jackson Case," *Richmond Planet*, June 20, 1936; "Charles H. Houston Says NAACP Ready to Go on with Educational Fight," *Richmond Planet*, June 27, 1936, 1; "30 Receive Aid under Virginia's Jim Crow Set-Up," *Richmond Planet*, Aug. 8, 1936, 1.

73 Josephus Simpson, "Sidewalks of the South," *Richmond Planet*, Dec. 20, 1935, 12; "Simpson's Protest," *Richmond Planet*, Dec. 20, 1935, 12.

74 Gavins, *Perils and Prospects*, 76–99 (first quotation on 96); GBH, "Between the Lines," *NJG*, Nov. 30, 1935, 8; Henry Dolphin, chairman of the Tidewater Anti-Lynch Conference, to Mayor Slover of Norfolk, Nov. 5, 1933 (second quotation), folder "Lynching," box 86, John Garland Pollard Executive Papers, LVA.

CHAPTER NINE

1 Buni, *Negro in Virginia Politics*, 115, 142; Wilhelmina Jackson, "Memorandum on Portsmouth, Va.," 9–10 (quotation), folder 12, "Bunche *Political Status of the Negro*, W. Jackson's Field Notes, Portsmouth Memorandum and Map," box 85, RJBP.

2 "Challenge Casts Doubt on State's At-Large Election," *RTD*, Oct. 12, 1932, copy in section 12, JCWP; election returns from *Culpeper Exponent*, Dec. 11, 1932, copy in section 13, JCWP; Wilhelmina Jackson, "Memorandum on Portsmouth, Va.," 1–2, 24, folder 12, "Bunche *Political Status of the Negro*, W. Jackson's Field Notes, Portsmouth Memorandum and Map," box 85, RJBP; Charles A. Russell to Norman Hamilton, July 7, 1936, Russell to Hamilton, Dec. 10, 1936, folder "Rossiter, Rear Admiral to Ryle, James," box 16, Norman Hamilton Papers, LVA; untitled, undated campaign memo (quotation), miscellaneous folder 9, R. B. Duncan to the editor of the *Star*, n.d. [1938], miscellaneous folder 3, both in box 25, Hamilton Papers, LVA; "Whether Hamilton or Darden Is Beneficiary Clouded in Doubt," *RNL*, Aug. 5, 1936, 1, 21. For more on the opposition of Organization leaders to the New Deal, see Heinemann, *Depression and New Deal* and *Harry Byrd of Virginia*, 159–222; Creel, "Byrd Song," 21, 30–31.

3 Saxon Holt to HFB, Aug. 17, 1936, HFB to Holt, Aug. 22, 1936, HFBP; Eight Wards Civic Club to Norman Hamilton, Mar. 24, 1937, folder "Red Cross–Renshaw, Winston R.," box 16, Hamilton Papers, LVA; Negro Women's Democratic Club to Norman Hamilton, Feb. 17, 1938, folder "Negro Women's Dem. Club–Norfolk Advertising Board," box 14, Hamilton Papers, LVA. I am indebted to Brent Tarter of the Library of Virginia for bringing the Holt-Byrd correspondence to my attention.

4 Wilhelmina Jackson, "Memorandum on Portsmouth, Va.," 24–25 (quotations), folder 12, "Bunche *Political Status of the Negro*, W. Jackson's Field Notes, Portsmouth Memorandum and Map," and "Memorandum on Norfolk, Va.," 18, folder 29, "Bunche *Political Status of the Negro*, W. Jackson Notes: Norfolk Memorandum," both in box 85, RJBP; Buni, *Negro in Virginia Politics*, 142–43.

5 Wilhelmina Jackson, "Memorandum on Portsmouth, Va.," 27–28, folder 12, "Bunche *Political Status of the Negro*, W. Jackson's Field Notes, Portsmouth Memorandum and Map," box 85, RJBP.

6 Campaign memo, "How Does Norman Hamilton Really Feel about Colored People? Issued by Colored Friends of Colgate W. Darden," folder 30, "Bunche *Political Status of the Negro*, W. Jackson Notes: Norfolk Memorandum, Miscellaneous Field Materials and Maps," box 85, RJBP.

7 Ibid. Emphasis in original.

8 Wilhelmina Jackson, "Memorandum on Portsmouth, Va.," 1–2, folder 12, "Bunche *Political Status of the Negro*, W. Jackson's Field Notes, Portsmouth Memorandum and Map," box 85, RJBP; "Smith, Darden Win in Primary; Dodd Trails 1 to 3," *RTD*, Aug. 3, 1938, 1, 6; Friddell, *Colgate Darden*, 60–61; Buni, *Negro in Virginia Politics*, 143.

9 Carter Glass to Clifton A. Woodrum, Sept. 29, 1936, copy in folder "Glass, Carter," box 139, HFBP. I am indebted to Professor James Sweeney of Old Dominion University for bringing this letter to my attention.

10 Buni, *Negro in Virginia Politics*, 124–64; "Virginia Interviews," box 10, Southern Politics Collection, Alexander Heard Library, Vanderbilt University; Paul N. Williams interview by RJB, Oct. 22, 1939, folder 6, "Field Notes: Southern Trip, Bk. 1," box 85, RJBP.

11 Earl Lewis, *In Their Own Interests*, 155–59; Parramore, *Norfolk: The First Four Centuries*, 317–19; Wilkerson, "Negro School Movement in Virginia," 17–20.

12 "Court Test of Va. Teachers' Pay Planned," *NJG*, June 22, 1935, 1; W. P. Milner to Walter White, Feb. 2, 1935, folder "Virginia State Conference, 1935–37," box G-206, Group I–Branch Files, NAACP-LC; Picott, *History of the Virginia Teachers Association*, 108; Earl Lewis, *In Their Own Interests*, 157; Kluger, *Simple Justice*, 187–217; *Missouri ex. rel. Gaines v. Canada*, 305 U.S. 337 (1938). In *Murray v. Maryland*, cited in Chapter 8, the Maryland Supreme Court made the same determination as the U.S. Supreme Court in *Gaines v. Canada*, but Maryland authorities chose not to appeal to the U.S. Supreme Court. Hence, the nation's highest court ruled on the matter for the first time in *Gaines v. Canada*.

13 Lutrelle Palmer interview by RJB, Oct. 22, 1939 (first and second quotations), Wiley Hall, Secretary, Urban League of Richmond, interview by RJB, Oct. 18, 1939 (third quotation), folder 6, "Field Notes: Southern Trip, Bk. 1," box 85, RJBP.

14 "Virginia Teacher Loses in Lower Court; Appeals," *Crisis* 46 (July 1939): 213–14; "To Hold Protest Meeting, Parade," *NJG*, June 24, 1939, 1; "1,900 Sign Petition to Reappoint Fired Teacher," *NJG*, July 1, 1939, 1; Earl Lewis, *In Their Own Interests*, 159–60; Suggs, "Black Strategy and Ideology," 183.

15 "Let the School Board Reconsider," *NVP*, June 27, 1939, editorial page, reprinted as the "Editorial of the Month" in *Crisis* 46 (Sept. 1939): 275.

16 "30th Annual Conference in Richmond, Va.," *Crisis* 46 (Sept. 1939): 278–79; Thurgood Marshall, "Equal Justice under Law," *Crisis* 46 (July 1939): 199–201; "Too Radical for Us," *RTD*, July 17, 1939, 10 (quotation).

17 "Too Radical for Us," *RTD*, July 17, 1939, 10.

18 Ibid.

19 Earl Lewis, *In Their Own Interests*, 156.

20 Higginbotham, "Conversations with Civil Rights Crusaders," 38; Ackerman, "Trials of S. W. Tucker," 16 (quotations).

21 SWT and Otto Tucker interview by William Elwood, Alexandria, Va., Feb. 18, 1985, 853–61; Julia Tucker (wife of Samuel Tucker) and Oliver Hill interview by John Whaley Jr., Richmond, Va., Feb. 28, 1995, 1–10, Virginia Black History Archives, Special Collections and Archives, James Branch Cabell Library, Virginia Commonwealth University; folder "Alexandria, Va., 1919–1939," box G-206, Group I–Branch Files, NAACP-LC.

22 SWT and Otto Tucker interview by Elwood, 864; Ackerman, "Trials of S. W. Tucker," 16–17; *City of Alexandria v. Wm. Tucker and Geo. Tucker* (1927),

Criminal Case No. 1621, Corporation Court, City of Alexandria; Minute Book 25, 396, Corporation Court, City of Alexandria.

23 Ackerman, "Trials of S. W. Tucker," 16–17; Julia Tucker and Oliver Hill interview by Whaley, 9–11.

24 SWT interview by A. Leon Higginbotham Jr., Richmond, Va., May 24, 1986, 884; SWT to Katharine Scoggin, Mar. 25, 1939 (first quotation), Scoggin to SWT, Mar. 28, 1939 (second quotation), box 98, Special Collections Clipping File, Lloyd House, Alexandria Library.

25 Minutes, Alexandria Library Association, 1931–47, 150, 153, 158 (first quotation on 150), Lloyd House, Alexandria Library; Brandt, *Alexandria, Virginia, Library*, 25 (second quotation). Between 1794 and 1937 Alexandria's library facilities were considered private.

26 Minutes, Board of Directors, Alexandria Library Society: January 1938–October 1947, 26–33, Lloyd House, Alexandria Library; Corporation Court of the City of Alexandria, Proceedings in the Case of *George Wilson v. Katharine H. Scoggin*, Law #2599; "Suit Filed against Alexandria Librarian for Use of Facilities," *WT*, May 13, 1939, 1 (quotation).

27 SWT and Otto Tucker interview by Elwood, 874; Corporation Court of the City of Alexandria, Proceedings in the Case of *George Wilson v. Katharine H. Scoggin*, Law #2599; "Library Suit in Alexandria Given Hearing," *WT*, July 15, 1939, 2 (first and second quotations); "Technicalities Hold Up Alexandria Library Case," *WT*, July 22, 1939, 9 (third and fourth quotations); "Argument to Use Library Is before Court," *AG*, July 10, 1939, 1.

28 "Library for Colored to Be Studied," *AG*, Aug. 5, 1939, 1; "Ordinance," *AG*, Aug. 9, 1939, 9; "Alexandria City Council Ponders Library Annex," *WT*, Aug. 12, 1939, 3.

29 "5 Arrested at City Library," *AG*, Aug. 21, 1939, 1; "Quintet Arrested for Library 'Sit Down,'" *WT*, Aug. 26, 1939, 1; "Five Colored Youths Stage Alexandria Library Sit-Down," *Washington Post*, Aug. 22, 1939, 3; SWT and Otto Tucker interview by Elwood, 870; SWT interview by Higginbotham, 884; William Evans interview by William Elwood and Seth Graves, Washington, D.C., Feb. 18, 1985, 280; "Pioneer Sit-In Is Recalled," *Alexandria Journal*, Dec. 6, 1990, 1.

30 "5 Arrested at City Library," *AG*, Aug. 21, 1939, 1; "Quintet Arrested for Library 'Sit-Down,'" *WT*, Aug. 26, 1939, 1 (quotations); "Five Colored Youths Stage Alexandria Library Sit-Down," *Washington Post*, Aug. 22, 1939, 3; SWT and Otto Tucker interview by Elwood, 870; SWT interview by Higginbotham, 884; Evans interview by Elwood and Graves, 280; "Pioneer Sit-In Is Recalled," *Alexandria Journal*, Dec. 6, 1990, 1. For an example of a "sit-down" strike in Virginia that involved labor agitation, see Fry, "Rayon, Riot, and Repression," 3–18.

31 SWT and Otto Tucker interview by Elwood, 868–70 (first, second, and third quotations); Evans interview by Elwood and Graves, 276–81 (fourth quotation); Ackerman, "Trials of S. W. Tucker," 14–17.

32 SWT and Otto Tucker interview by Elwood, 870, 873.

33 "Quintet Arrested for Library 'Sit-Down,'" *WT*, Aug. 26, 1939, 1–2 (quota-

tions); "Decision Is Deferred on Library Case," *AG*, Aug. 22, 1939, 1; SWT and Otto Tucker interview by Elwood, 873.

34 Minutes, Board of Directors, Alexandria Library Society: January 1938–October 1947, 34, Lloyd House, Alexandria Library; "City Library Board Outlines Position on Colored Branch," *AG*, Aug. 28, 1939, 1, 9 (quotations).

35 "Opinions Are Asked in Use of Library," *AG*, Aug. 29, 1939, 1; "Decision in Alexandria Library Case Delayed: City Prosecutor Raps 14th, 15th Amendments," *WT*, Sept. 2, 1939, 1–2 (quotations). I am indebted to Stephen J. Ackerman, who interviewed William Evans's sister and shared with me the connection between Howard and the older Evans.

36 Ackerman, "Trials of S. W. Tucker," 17; Julius Newman, "In and Around Alexandria," *Chicago Defender*, Nov 11, 1939, 11 (first quotation); "Opinions Are Asked in Use of Library," *AG*, Aug. 29, 1939, 1 (second and third quotations); "Decision in Alexandria Library Case Delayed: City Prosecutor Raps 14th, 15th Amendments," *WT*, Sept. 2, 1939, 1–2; SWT and Otto Tucker interview by Elwood, 873; SWT interview by Higginbotham, 884–85. I am grateful to Stephen J. Ackerman for sharing with me the article from the *Defender*. Boothe later distinguished himself as one of the few white politicians in Virginia who urged compliance with the Supreme Court's *Brown* decision. On his career in the General Assembly and his opposition to massive resistance, see J. Douglas Smith, "'When Reason Collides with Prejudice.'"

37 Florence Murray, "Alexandria Library Case Grows Daily in National Importance," *WT*, Sept. 2, 1939, 2.

38 "Legal Briefs Being Finished in Alexandria Library Case," *WT*, Sept. 9, 1939, 1; "Youths Innocent, Police Unlawful, Argues Tucker in Library Case," *WT*, Sept. 16, 1939, 2; "Library Case Still Hangs Fire in Alexandria," *WT*, Oct. 28, 1939, 1; "Jury Will Hear Library Case in Alexandria," *WT*, Dec. 2, 1939, 1; "Colored Resident Denied Writ to Force Library Privileges," *AG*, Jan. 11, 1940, 1; Ackerman, "Trials of S. W. Tucker," 17.

39 William Woolls to Armistead Boothe and SWT, Sept. 12, 1939 (quotation), in files of *George Wilson v. Katharine H. Scoggin*, Law #2599, Corporation Court, City of Alexandria; "Deny Petition for Writ in Library Case," *AG*, Sept. 12, 1939, 1; "Wilson Denied Library Card in Alexandria," *WT*, Sept. 16, 1939, 1; "Library Case Still Hangs Fire in Alexandria," *WT*, Oct. 28, 1939, 1; "Jury Will Hear Library Case in Alexandria," *WT*, Dec. 2, 1939, 1; "Lawyer's Tardiness in Court Delays Va. Public Library Case," *WT*, Dec. 9, 1939, 1; "Hearing on Library Case Is Continued," *AG*, Dec. 4, 1939, 1; Ackerman, "Trials of S. W. Tucker," 17.

40 Corporation Court of the City of Alexandria, Proceedings in the Case of *George Wilson v. Katharine H. Scoggin*, Law #2599, and *George Wilson v. Katharine Scoggin*, Law #2599, Minute Book 29, 139; "Colored Resident Denied Writ to Force Library Privileges," *AG*, Jan. 11, 1940, 1 (quotation); "Judge's Decision Opens Library in Alexandria," *WT*, Jan. 13, 1940, 1.

41 "Hearing on Library Case Is Continued," *AG*, Dec. 4, 1939, 1; "Fund for Colored Library Is Passed on First Reading," *AG*, Jan. 13, 1940, 1; "Ap-

proval of Library Fund Due Tomorrow," *AG*, Jan. 22, 1940, 1; "Inclement Weather Delays Construction Work on New Library," *AG*, Jan. 25, 1940, 1; "Library Branch Work to Start," *AG*, Feb. 5, 1940, 1; Minutes, Board of Directors, Alexandria Library Society: January 1938–October 1947, 44–46, Lloyd House, Alexandria Library; "Alexandria Officials Welsh in Library Case: Applicants Still Denied Right to Use Facilities," *WT*, Feb. 3, 1940, 9 (quotations). Armistead Boothe, who reportedly told Samuel Tucker in the wake of Woolls's ruling that he would urge city officials to comply with the "spirit" of the ruling, had resigned from the library board in December 1939. See "Judge's Decision Opens Library in Alexandria," *WT*, Jan. 13, 1940, 1, and Minutes, Board of Directors, Alexandria Library Society: January 1938–October 1947, 40, Lloyd House, Alexandria Library.

42 SWT to Katharine Scoggin, Feb. 13, 1940 (first quotation), SWT to Carl Budwesky, Feb. 13, 1940 (second and third quotations), box 98, Special Collections Clipping File, Lloyd House, Alexandria Library; "Alexandria Officials Welsh in Library Case: Applicants Still Denied Right to Use Facilities," *WT*, Feb. 3, 1940, 9; Ackerman, "Trials of S. W. Tucker," 17–18.

43 "Colored Library Addition Rapidly Nearing Completion," *AG*, Mar. 4, 1940, 1; "New Library Construction Is Under Way," *AG*, Mar. 6, 1940, 1; "Library Branch Near Completion," *AG*, Mar. 20, 1940, 1; "New Colored Library Branch to Open to Public Tomorrow," *AG*, Apr. 22, 1940, 1; "Colored Library Opens," *AG*, Apr. 23, 1940, 1; "Alexandria's Colored Library," *AG*, Apr. 27, 1940, 4 (quotation); SWT interview by Higginbotham, 886.

44 SWT interview by Higginbotham, 884–85 (quotation on 885), reprinted in Higginbotham, "Conversations with Civil Rights Crusaders," 39; Ackerman, "Trials of S. W. Tucker," 17–18.

45 Simon, "Race Reactions," 241.

46 L. R. Reynolds, Director, Virginia CIC, interview by RJB, Oct. 19, 1939 (first quotation), folder 6, "Field Notes: Southern Trip, Bk. 1," box 85, RJBP; RJB, "The Programs, Ideologies, Tactics, and Achievements of Negro Betterment and Interracial Organizations: A Research Memorandum," 467–68 (second and third quotations), book 3, box 81, RJBP.

47 "Statement of the Director, L. R. Reynolds," Feb. 4, 1942, frames 696–703 (quotations on frame 703), reel 53, CIC Papers.

48 Earl Lewis, *In Their Own Interests*, 160–63; Kluger, *Simple Justice*, 214–17; Parramore, *Norfolk: The First Four Centuries*, 319, 329–30; *Alston v. School Board of City of Norfolk*, 112 F.2d 992 (1940), cert. denied 311 U.S. 693 (1940).

49 Earl Lewis, *In Their Own Interests*, 163–65 (first quotation on 163); Wilhelmina Jackson, "Memorandum on Norfolk, Va.," 18 (second quotation), folder 29, "Bunche *Political Status of the Negro*, W. Jackson Notes: Norfolk Memorandum," box 85, RJBP; Parramore, *Norfolk: The First Four Centuries*, 329–30.

50 Earl Lewis, *In Their Own Interests*, 164–65.

51 Wilkerson, "Negro School Movement in Virginia," 18–29; Higginbotham, "Conversations with Civil Rights Crusaders," 13–14; Julia Tucker and Oliver Hill interview by Whaley, 19–20, 32–38.

52 Fairclough, *Race and Democracy*, xii; Kluger, *Simple Justice*, 216; Wilkerson, "Negro School Movement in Virginia," 19–20; Picott, *History of the Virginia Teachers Association*, 120. In addition to Fairclough's, other notable studies that emphasize the importance of the 1930s in laying the groundwork for the civil rights movement include Norrell, *Reaping the Whirlwind*; Sullivan, *Days of Hope*; and Egerton, *Speak Now against the Day*.

53 Works Progress Administration, *Virginia: A Guide to the Old Dominion*, 85–86 (first quotation); Picott, *History of the Virginia Teachers Association*, 111–20 (second quotation on 113).

54 Fairclough, "'Being in the Field of Education,'" 84 (quotations); Lutrelle Palmer interview by RJB, Oct. 22, 1939, folder 6, "Field Notes: Southern Trip, Bk. 1," box 85, RJBP.

55 Kneebone, *Southern Liberal Journalists*, 196–214; Sullivan, *Days of Hope*, 133–68; Earl Lewis, *In Their Own Interests*, 167–98; Gavins, *Perils and Prospects*, 100–127.

56 VD to P. B. Young, May 21, 1942 (first and second quotations), VD to Thomas Chappelle, June 25, 1943, folder "1942–43, Negroes: Editorial 1," box 6, VDP; VD, *Across the Years*, 162–63; Odum, *Race and Rumors of Race*, 53–104; Kneebone, *Southern Liberal Journalists*, 197–99 (third and fourth quotations on 198); Ayers, "Southern Chronicle," 194–97 (fifth and sixth quotations on 195); White, "Decline of Southern Liberals," 43 (seventh quotation); Matthews, "Virginius Dabney, John Temple Graves," 405–20; Sosna, *In Search of the Silent South*, 127–33.

57 Gavins, *Perils and Prospects*, 112–17 (quotations on 115).

58 Kneebone, *Southern Liberal Journalists*, 201–9 (first quotation on 201); Sullivan, *Days of Hope*, 164; Sosna, *In Search of the Silent South*, 127–33; White, "Decline of Southern Liberals," 43–46 (third quotation on 44); VD, "The Negro and His Schooling," 459–68, and "Nearer and Nearer the Precipice," 94–100 (second quotation on 98; fourth and fifth quotations on 94).

59 Kneebone, *Southern Liberal Journalists*, 201–9; VD, "Nearer and Nearer the Precipice," 94–100 (quotation on 98), and "The Negro and His Schooling," 467.

60 Kneebone, *Southern Liberal Journalists*, 208–9; P. B. Young to VD, Jan. 20, 1943 (first and second quotations), P. B. Young to VD, Jan. 12, 1943 (third and fourth quotations), folder "1942–1943 Negroes: Editorial 1," box 6, VDP; Sosna, *In Search of the Silent South*, 132–33.

61 Sosna, *In Search of the Silent South*, 137–39 (quotations on 138); Kneebone, *Southern Liberal Journalists*, 198–99, 212. For this concept of the "bogeyman," I have relied on Kneebone, who discusses it in terms of the "cruelly Negrophobic poor white" (212).

62 VD to P. B. Young, May 21, 1942, folder "1942–43, Negroes: Editorial 1," VD to Alice Ware, Jan. 18, 1943 (quotation), folder "1943–44 Negro: Survey Graphic, etc.," both in box 6, VDP; VD, "The Negro and His Schooling," 459–68, and "Nearer and Nearer the Precipice," 94–100; White, "Decline of Southern Liberals," 43–46; Kneebone, *Southern Liberal Journalists*, 196–214; Matthews, "Virginius Dabney, John Temple Graves," 405–20.

63 Hancock, "Needed . . . A Southern Charter for Race Relations," 1, 3 (quotation on 3), copy on frame 1348, reel 30, CIC Papers; Kneebone, *Southern Liberal Journalists*, 203–4; Gavins, *Perils and Prospects*, 117–22.

64 Hancock, "Race Relations in the United States," 239 (first quotation); "A Basis for Interracial Cooperation and Development in the South: A Statement by Southern Negroes (Durham Conference Statement)," Oct. 1942, reprinted in Bond and Lewis, *Gonna Sit at the Welcome Table*, 147–53 (second quotation on 147); Gavins, *Perils and Prospects*, 122–27 (third quotation on 127); Kneebone, *Southern Liberal Journalists*, 203–5; Egerton, *Speak Now against the Day*, 304–7; McDonough, "Men and Women of Good Will," 206–51.

65 Gavins, *Perils and Prospects*, 128–38; Kneebone, *Southern Liberal Journalists*, 205.

66 "Statement of Conference of White Southerners on Race Relations (Atlanta Statement)," Apr. 8, 1943 (quotations), reprinted in Bond and Lewis, *Gonna Sit at the Welcome Table*, 154–55; Gavins, *Perils and Prospects*, 138–39; McDonough, "Men and Women of Good Will," 206–51.

67 Gavins, *Perils and Prospects*, 139–40 (quotation on 140).

68 VD to P. B. Young, Apr. 17, 1943 (quotations), folder "1942–43 Negroes: Editorial 1," box 6, VDP; Gavins, *Perils and Prospects*, 140; McDonough, "Men and Women of Good Will," 238–39.

69 Gavins, *Perils and Prospects*, 140–44 (quotations on 143); Kneebone, *Southern Liberal Journalists*, 205–6; Sullivan, *Days of Hope*, 165–66.

70 "Resolutions of the Collaboration Committee," Richmond, Va., June 16, 1943 (quotations), reprinted in Bond and Lewis, *Gonna Sit at the Welcome Table*, 156–57; Gavins, *Perils and Prospects*, 144–45; Kneebone, *Southern Liberal Journalists*, 205–6.

71 Gavins, *Perils and Prospects*, 143–45 (first and second quotations on 145); GBH to Jessie Daniel Ames, June 25, 1943 (third quotation), VD to Ames, July 2, 1943, VD to Ames, July 14, 1943, Ames to VD, July 16, 1943, all in folder "1943—Negroes—Atlanta, Durham, Richmond Conferences (1)," box 5, VDP; Kneebone, *Southern Liberal Journalists*, 205–7; Sosna, *In Search of the Silent South*, 133–34 (fourth quotation on 134); "Resolution Launching the Southern Regional Council," Aug. 4, 1943 (fifth quotation), reprinted in Bond and Lewis, *Gonna Sit at the Welcome Table*, 159–60.

72 "To Lessen Race Friction," *RTD*, Nov. 13, 1943, 4 (quotations); Armstrong, *Study of an Attempt*, 62–67, 77–79; Tyler-McGraw, *At the Falls*, 274; Earl Lewis, *In Their Own Interests*, 189–91.

73 Myrdal, *An American Dilemma*, 635, quoted in Armstrong, *Study of an Attempt*, 78; Earl Lewis, *In Their Own Interests*, 189–91.

74 *Sarah B. Davis v. Commonwealth of Virginia*, 182 Va. 760 (1944) (first quotation on 760; second quotation on 765); "Virginia's High Court Will Review Bus Segregation Case," *NJG*, Dec. 4, 1943, 1, 10; "'Move Back' Segregation Law Set Back," *NJG*, Dec. 25, 1943, 2; Earl Lewis, *In Their Own Interests*, 189–91. On the eventual abolition of Jim Crow transportation statutes, see Barnes, *Journey from Jim Crow*.

75 "The Conservative Course in Race Relations," *RTD*, Nov. 21, 1943, section 4, 2.

76 "An Historic Proposal for the Public Welfare," *NJG*, Nov. 20, 1943 (national edition), 6; Armstrong, *Study of an Attempt*, 59–71; Kneebone, *Southern Liberal Journalists*, 209–12; Gavins, *Perils and Prospects*, 147; Sosna, *In Search of the Silent South*, 134–36.

77 This synopsis of responses comes from an examination of the 138 letters that Dabney published in "Voice of the People" on the *Richmond Times-Dispatch*'s editorial page between November 16 and December 9, 1943, as well as more than one hundred unpublished letters found in folder "1943, Segregation—columns—editorials—Voice of People—unused letters," box 6, VDP. See also VD to Stuart B. Gibson, Dec. 3, 1943, folder "1943 Segregation Correspondence," box 6, VDP.

78 "Why Only Cars and Busses?," *RTD*, Nov. 27, 1943, 6 (emphasis in original).

79 LIJ to VD, Nov. 15, 1943 (first quotation), VD to LIJ, Nov. 16, 1943 (second and third quotations), folder "1927–1949 Correspondence of LIJ with VD," box 3, LIJP (#9924-b); Kneebone, *Southern Liberal Journalists*, 209–11; Sosna, *In Search of the Silent South*, 135–37.

EPILOGUE

1 Friddell, *Colgate Darden*, 84.

2 Ibid.

3 Sherman, *Case of Odell Waller*; Hamer, "Modest Forward Step," 10–13.

4 Murray, *Autobiography of a Black Activist*, 150–76 (quotations on 171). Pauli Murray worked tirelessly on behalf of the Workers Defense League (WDL), the object of Darden's ire, to raise money for Waller's appeal. A black native of Baltimore who had moved to New York, Murray described the WDL as "a nonpartisan civil rights organization inspired by Norman Thomas and A. Philip Randolph." In her autobiography, Murray recounts the frequency with which she had to rebut charges that the WDL was a communist organization. See ibid., 7, 134–35 (quotation on 134–35).

5 Hamer, "Modest Forward Step," 13–17; Gavins, *Perils and Prospects*, 139–40.

6 Hamer, "Modest Forward Step," 13–26; "Governor Darden Raps Segregation as Abuse Cover-Up," *Pittsburgh Courier*, Jan. 6, 1945, 9 (quotation).

7 Singal, *War Within*, 296–301; Egerton, *Speak Now against the Day*, 271–74; Kneebone, *Southern Liberal Journalists*, 202.

8 Silver and Moeser, *Separate City*, 57–61. For the most complete look at African American activism in Virginia during the twenty-five years before the *Brown* decision, see Larissa M. Smith, "Where the South Begins."

9 Sullivan, *Days of Hope*, 164–68 (first quotation on 167); Lillian Smith, "Addressed to White Liberals," 331–33 (second and third quotations on 332; emphasis in original). In *Days of Hope*, Sullivan provides the most thorough account available of the individuals and organizations that provided the impetus for this "new southern liberalism."

10 "Lincoln's Job Half-Done," *Flat Hat*, reprinted in *NJG*, Feb. 17, 1945 (home edition), 1.

11 Ibid. (quotation); "William and Mary College Ousts Student Editor for Race Views," *NJG*, Feb. 17, 1945 (home edition), 1; "The Face of Tradition," *Newsweek* 25 (Feb. 26, 1945): 85–86; "The Case of the *Flat Hat*," *Commonweal* 41 (Feb. 23, 1945): 460; "Jefferson's Heirs," *Time* 45 (Feb. 26, 1945): 64; "Plea for Negro Halts William-Mary Paper," *New York Times*, Feb. 12, 1945, 21; "Fight Press Curb at William, Mary," *New York Times*, Feb. 13, 1945, 25; "Ask 'Censor' Forum at William and Mary," *New York Times*, Feb. 14, 1945, 14; "Students Reverse Paper Suspension," *New York Times*, Feb. 15, 1945, 17.

12 VD editorial in *RTD*, reprinted in "Mixed Reaction in Comment on Editorial," *NJG*, Feb. 17, 1945 (home edition), 1–2 (quotations on 1); editorial on incident at William and Mary, *NJG*, Feb. 17, 1945 (home edition), 8. The *Norfolk Virginian-Pilot* essentially ignored the substance of Kaemmerle's editorial and instead criticized the response of the college's president and trustees. See "Mixed Reaction in Comment on Editorial," *NJG*, Feb. 17, 1945 (home edition), 1–2.

13 Kneebone, *Southern Liberal Journalists*, 206–14; Gavins, *Perils and Prospects*, 148–57; Sosna, *In Search of the Silent South*, 152–63; Hall, *Revolt against Chivalry*, 255–66.

14 VD, "Is the South That Bad?," 9–10, 84–88; President's Committee on Civil Rights, *To Secure These Rights*, 139–73 (quotations on 166); Nitschke, "Virginius Dabney of Virginia," 182–84; Sosna, *In Search of the Silent South*, 149–52.

15 "Central Democratic Committee Attacks Civil Rights Program, Praises Governor Tuck's Stand," *RTD*, Mar. 7, 1948, section 2, 1, 4 (quotation), cited in J. Douglas Smith, "'When Reason Collides with Prejudice,'" 8–9. Tuck's bill ultimately failed, and Truman carried Virginia in the November election. The president, however, lost five southern states to the Dixiecrat candidate, Strom Thurmond. On the Dixiecrats, see Frederickson, *Dixiecrat Revolt*.

16 "Separation by Consent," *RNL*, May 20, 1930, 8 (first quotation); "Virginia and Civil Rights," *RNL*, Feb. 25, 1948, 12 (second quotation).

17 "Virginia and Civil Rights," *RNL*, Feb. 25, 1948, 12.

18 GBH to VD, Nov. 15, 1948, cited in Gavins, *Perils and Prospects*, 157 (quotation); Andrew B. Lewis, "Wandering in Two Worlds"; "Mixed School Classes Held Possible in Gloucester, King George under Court's Ruling," *RNL*, July 30, 1948, section B, 1–2; "We Must Pay for Separate Schools," *RNL*, Aug. 6, 1948, 10; Wilkerson, "Negro School Movement in Virginia," 20–24; Virginia Educational Commission, *Virginia Public School System*.

19 *Sweatt v. Painter*, 339 U.S. 629 (1950).

20 Hamer, "Modest Forward Step," 27–46.

21 Ibid., 46–53.

22 Kluger, *Simple Justice*, esp. 451–507; Wilkerson, "Negro School Movement in Virginia," 24–29; Andrew B. Lewis, "Wandering in Two Worlds."

23 Colgate Darden's testimony in *Dorothy E. Davis v. County School Board of*

Prince Edward County, Virginia, in Hamer, "Modest Forward Step," 54–69; Kluger, *Simple Justice*, 480–507.

24 "Toward the South of the Future," *New South* 6 (Dec. 1951): 1–2 (quotation on 2), copy on frames 349–50, reel 217, Southern Regional Council Papers; Egerton, *Speak Now against the Day*, 523–69; Kneebone, *Southern Liberal Journalists*, 211–20; Sosna, *In Search of the Silent South*, 162–69; Hancock, *Perils and Prospects*, 158–60.

25 Colgate Darden to George S. Mitchell, July 25, 1953 (quotations), frames 617–18, reel 12, Southern Regional Council Papers. I am indebted to Paul M. Gaston for bringing Darden's letter to my attention, and to Cathy Mundale, reference archivist at the Atlanta University Center's Robert W. Woodruff Library, for finding the letter in the Southern Regional Council Papers.

26 Robbins L. Gates, *Making of Massive Resistance*, 30.

27 Lassiter and Lewis, introduction to *Moderates' Dilemma*, 1–21; Muse, *Virginia's Massive Resistance*, 15–18; Robbins L. Gates, *Making of Massive Resistance*, 62–85. Local option was the essential feature of North Carolina's Pearsall plan, which met the approval of federal courts by allowing minimal amounts of integration in select areas. See Lassiter and Lewis, *Moderates' Dilemma*, 1–4, 15.

28 Lassiter and Lewis, *Moderates' Dilemma*; Heinemann, *Harry Byrd of Virginia*, 325–54; Robbins L. Gates, *Making of Massive Resistance*; Muse, *Virginia's Massive Resistance*, esp. 30–32 for an analysis of the key vote in the state senate. As I mentioned in the Introduction, rural interests in North Carolina's legislature did not enjoy such disproportionate power as in the Virginia General Assembly. Consequently, North Carolina opted for a response to *Brown* that reflected the interests of an urban elite.

29 Editorials from *Norfolk Virginia-Pilot* and *Richmond News Leader* quoted in Muse, *Virginia's Massive Resistance*, 95. For more on Chambers, see Leidholdt, *Standing before the Shouting Mob*. On Kilpatrick, see Thorndike, "'The Sometimes Sordid Level.'" For a look at the handful of political leaders who urged compliance with *Brown*, see J. Douglas Smith, "'When Reason Collides with Prejudice.'"

30 VD, "Virginia's 'Peaceable, Honorable Stand,'" 51–52, 55–56 (first quotation on 51; second quotation on 56); Robbins L. Gates, *Making of Massive Resistance*, 96 n. 6; Hamer, "Modest Forward Step," 115; Sosna, *In Search of the Silent South*, 168–69.

31 Lassiter and Lewis, introduction to *Moderates' Dilemma*, 17–18; Martin Luther King Jr., "Letter from Birmingham City Jail," in Washington, *Testament of Hope*, 289–302 (quotation on 295). On Lewis Powell and his role in the end of massive resistance and the integration of the Richmond schools, see Jeffries, *Justice Lewis F. Powell*, and Pratt, *The Color of Their Skin*.

32 VD, *Virginius Dabney's Virginia*, xviii–xix (first quotation on xix; second quotation on xviii); Fairclough, *Race and Democracy*, xvii (third quotation).

Bibliography

MANUSCRIPT COLLECTIONS

Alexandria, Virginia

Alexandria Museum of African American Culture
    1939 Library Sit-Down Strike Clipping File
Lloyd House, Alexandria Library
    Minutes, Alexandria Library Association
    Minutes, Board of Directors, Alexandria Library Society
    Special Collections Clipping File

Charlottesville, Virginia

Albert and Shirley Small Special Collections Library, University of Virginia
    Harry Flood Byrd Sr. Papers
    Walter Scott Copeland Papers
    Virginius Dabney Papers
    Douglas Southall Freeman Papers
    Ella K. F. Freudenberg Papers
    Louis Isaac Jaffé Papers
    Ivey Foreman Lewis Papers
    John Powell Papers
    Howard Worth Smith Papers

Hampton, Virginia

Hampton University Archives
    James E. Gregg Collection

Los Angeles, California

Charles E. Young Research Library, University of California at Los Angeles
    Ralph J. Bunche Papers

Nashville, Tennessee

Alexander Heard Library, Vanderbilt University
    Southern Politics Collection

Norfolk, Virginia

Norfolk State University
   Colgate W. Darden Papers

Richmond, Virginia

Library of Virginia
   E. Griffith Dodson Papers
   Executive Papers of
       Harry Flood Byrd Sr., 1926–30
       Westmoreland Davis, 1918–22
       George C. Peery, 1934–38
       John Garland Pollard, 1930–34
       E. Lee Trinkle, 1922–26
   Norman Hamilton Papers
   Junior Order United American Mechanics, Rockingham County, Papers
   William Gregory Rennolds Papers
   Secretary of the Commonwealth, Executive Papers
   Virginia Division of Motion Picture Censorship Records
   Virginia War History Commission Papers
Special Collections and Archives, James Branch Cabell Library, Virginia
       Commonwealth University
   Adele Goodman Clark Papers
   Samuel Wilbert Tucker Collection
   Virginia Black History Archives
Virginia Historical Society
   Roy Catesby Flannagan Papers
   Mary Burnley Gwathmey Family Papers
   Mary-Cooke Branch Munford Family Papers
   William T. Reed Family Papers
   Jennings Cropper Wise Papers
   Carter C. Wormeley Papers

Washington, D.C.

Library of Congress
   Douglas Southall Freeman Papers
   National Association for the Advancement of Colored People Papers

MANUSCRIPT COLLECTIONS ON MICROFILM

Commission on Interracial Cooperation Papers
Lucy Randolph Mason Papers, in Operation Dixie: The CIO Organizing
   Committee Papers, 1946–53
National Association for the Advancement of Colored People Papers

Southern Regional Council Papers
William Howard Taft Papers

NEWSPAPERS

Alexandria Gazette
Crisis
Lynchburg News
Newport News Daily Press
Newport News Star
New York Times
Norfolk Journal and Guide
Norfolk Ledger-Dispatch
Norfolk Virginian-Pilot
Pittsburgh Courier
The Religious Herald
Richmond News Leader
Richmond Planet
Richmond Times-Dispatch
Washington Post
Washington Tribune

GOVERNMENT DOCUMENTS, PAMPHLETS, AND REPORTS

Circuit Court of the County of Essex, Virginia. Chancery Order Book 8, 1928.
Commonwealth of Virginia. *Acts of Assembly*, 1924, 1926, 1928, 1930, 1932, 1936.
———. *Journal of the House of Delegates*, 1924, 1928.
———. *Journal of the Senate*, 1924, 1928.
Commonwealth of Virginia. State Board of Education. "Annual Report of the Superintendent of Public Instruction." *Bulletin* 6 (October 1923).
———. "Annual Report of the Superintendent of Public Instruction." *Bulletin* 9 (October 1926).
———. "Annual Report of the Superintendent of Public Instruction." *Bulletin* 12 (November 1929).
———. "Annual Report of the Superintendent of Public Instruction." *Bulletin* 13 (September 1930).
———. "Annual Report of the Superintendent of Public Instruction." *Bulletin* 14 (November 1931).
———. "Gloucester County, Virginia: Educational Survey Report." *Bulletin* 11 (August 1928).
———. "High and Elementary Textbook List, 1925-1927." *Bulletin* 7 (April 1925).

————. "Louisa County, Virginia: Educational Survey Report." *Bulletin* 10 (May 1928).

————. "State Course of Study, High Schools of Virginia: History and Social Science." *Bulletin* 8 (July 1925).

Corporation Court of the City of Alexandria. Minute Books 25 and 29.

————. Proceedings in the Case of *George Wilson v. Katharine H. Scoggin*, Law #2599.

O'Shea, M. V. *Public Education in Virginia: Report to the Educational Commission of Virginia of a Survey of the Public Educational System of the State.* Richmond: Davis Bottom, Superintendent of Public Printing, 1928.

"Report of Citizens' Committee on Consolidation and Simplification in State and Local Governments." Richmond: Commonwealth of Virginia, 1929.

Report of the Proceedings and Debates of the Constitutional Convention, State of Virginia, held in the City of Richmond, June 12, 1901, to June 26, 1902. Richmond, 1906.

U.S. Bureau of the Census. *Fourteenth Decennial Census of the United States, 1920.*

————. *Fifteenth Decennial Census of the United States, 1930.*

————. *Sixteenth Decennial Census of the United States, 1940.*

U.S. Congress. *Congressional Record.* 67th Cong., 2d sess., 1922, and 70th Cong., 1st sess, 1928.

————. House of Representatives. *Contested Election Case of Paul v. Harrison.* 67th Cong., 2d sess., 1922. H. Rept. 1101, pts. 1 and 2.

————. Senate. *Reports of the Immigration Commission.* Vol. 5, *Dictionary of Races or Peoples.* 61st Cong., 2d sess., 1910. S. Doc. 662. Washington, D.C.: Government Printing Office, 1911.

Virginia Education Commission. *Virginia Public Schools: A Survey of a Southern State Public School System.* Yonkers-on-Hudson, N.Y.: World Book Company, 1921.

————. *Virginia Public Schools, Education Commission's Report to the Assembly of Virginia: Survey Staff's Report to the Education Commission.* Richmond: Everett Waddey Company, 1919.

Virginia Educational Commission. *The Virginia Public School System: Report of the Virginia Educational Commission, 1944.* Richmond: Division of Purchase and Printing, 1944.

FEDERAL AND STATE COURT CASES

Alston v. School Board of City of Norfolk, 112 F.2d 992 (1940), cert. denied 311 U.S. 693 (1940).

Bliley et al. v. West, 42 F.2d 101 (1930).

Brown, Felix J., et al. v. City of Richmond et al., 204 Va. 471 (1963).

Brown v. Board of Education of Topeka, 347 U.S. 483 (1954).

Buchanan v. Warley, 245 U.S. 60 (1917).

Buck v. Bell, 274 U.S. 200 (1927).

City of Richmond et al. v. Deans, 37 F.2d 712 (1930), mem. decision 281 U.S. 704 (1930).

Davis, Dorothy E. v. County School Board of Prince Edward County, 103 F.Supp. 337 (1952), 347 U.S. 483 (1954).

Davis, Sarah B. v. Commonwealth of Virginia, 182 Va. 760 (1944).

Davis, W. E. v. Thomas C. Allen, Registrar, 157 Va. 84 (1931).

Grovey v. Townsend, 295 U.S. 45 (1935).

Hagood, J. L. v. Commonwealth of Virginia, 157 Va. 918 (1932).

Harmon v. Tyler, 273 U.S. 668 (1927).

Hopkins v. City of Richmond, 117 Va. 692 (1915).

Irvine v. City of Clifton Forge, 124 Va. 781 (1918).

Keith, Bascomb v. Commonwealth of Virginia, 165 Va. 705 (1935).

Loving v. Commonwealth of Virginia, 388 U.S. 1 (1967).

Missouri ex. rel. Gaines v. Canada, 305 U.S. 337 (1938).

Morgan, Irene v. Commonwealth of Virginia, 328 U.S. 373 (1946).

Naim v. Naim, 350 U.S. 985 (1956).

Nixon v. Condon, 286 U.S. 73 (1932).

Nixon v. Herndon, 273 U.S. 536 (1927).

Plessy v. Ferguson, 163 U.S. 537 (1896).

Smith v. Allwright, 321 U.S. 649 (1944).

Sweatt v. Painter, 339 U.S. 629 (1950).

Virginia Railway and Power Company v. Sarah A. Deaton, 147 Va. 576 (1927).

West, James O. v. A. C. Bliley et al., 33 F.2d 177 (E.D. Va. 1929), 42 F.2d 101 (1930).

INTERVIEWS

Dabney, Virginius. Richmond Community Interviews. Videotaped recording. Box 9: Race Relations, Valentine Museum/Richmond History Center, Richmond, Va.

Evans, William. Interview by William Elwood and Seth Graves. Washington, D.C., February 18, 1985. Transcript courtesy of William Elwood.

Hill, Oliver, and Henry Marsh. Richmond Community Interviews. Videotaped recording. Box 9: Race Relations, Valentine Museum/Richmond History Center, Richmond, Va.

Martyn, Katharine Scoggin. Interview by author. Tape recording. Falls Church, Va., June 24, 2000.

Norfleet, Elizabeth. Interview by author. Tape recording. Charlottesville, Va., December 28, 1996.

Thomas, Elsie. Interview by author. Tape recording. Alexandria, Va., June 24, 2000.

Tucker, Julia, and Oliver Hill. Interview by John Whaley Jr. Richmond, Va.,
February 28, 1995. Transcript in the Virginia Black History Archives, Special
Collections and Archives, James Branch Cabell Library, Virginia Common-
wealth University.

Tucker, Samuel. Interview by A. Leon Higginbotham Jr. Richmond, Va.,
May 24, 1986. Transcript courtesy of William Elwood.

Tucker, Samuel Wilbert. Richmond Community Interviews. Videotaped
recording. Box 9: Race Relations, Valentine Museum/Richmond History
Center, Richmond, Va.

Tucker, Samuel Wilbert, and Oliver Hill. Interview by William Elwood. Richmond, Va., October 1987. Transcript courtesy of William Elwood.

Tucker, Samuel Wilbert, and Otto Tucker. Interview by William Elwood.
Alexandria, Va., February 18, 1985. Transcript courtesy of William Elwood.

SECONDARY SOURCES

Abbot, C. M. "Relative Emphasis in the Teaching of American History." *Virginia Journal of Education* 23 (February 1930): 239–42, 267–68.

Ackerman, Stephen J. "The Trials of S. W. Tucker." *Washington Post Magazine*,
June 11, 2000, 14–18, 24–25, 28–29.

Adero, Malaika, ed. *Up South: Stories, Studies, and Letters of This Century's
African-American Migrations*. New York: New Press, 1993.

Allen, James. *Without Sanctuary: Lynching Photography in America*. Santa Fe,
N.M.: Twin Palms Publishers, 2000.

Armstrong, Nancy. *The Study of an Attempt Made in 1943 to Abolish Segregation
of the Races on Common Carriers in the State of Virginia*. Publications of the
University of Virginia Phelps-Stokes Fellowship Papers, no. 17, 1950.

Ayers, Edward L. *The Promise of the New South*. New York: Oxford University
Press, 1992.

———. "A Southern Chronicle: The *Virginia Quarterly Review* and the American South, 1925–2000." *Virginia Quarterly Review* 76 (Spring 2000): 189–202.

Bailey, Fred Arthur. "Free Speech and the Lost Cause in the Old Dominion."
Virginia Magazine of History and Biography 103 (April 1995): 237–66.

Bardaglio, Peter W. *Reconstructing the Household: Families, Sex, and the Law
in the Nineteenth-Century South*. Chapel Hill: University of North Carolina
Press, 1995.

Bardolph, Richard, ed. *The Civil Rights Record: Black Americans and the Law,
1849–1970*. New York: Thomas Y. Crowell, 1970.

Barnes, Catherine A. *Journey from Jim Crow: The Desegregation of Southern
Transit*. New York: Columbia University Press, 1983.

Bartley, Numan V. *The Rise of Massive Resistance: Race and Politics in the South
during the 1950s*. Baton Rouge: Louisiana State University Press, 1969.

Barton, Beth Lynne. "'A Harmonious People': Virginia Democrats and Disfranchisement, 1890–1905." M.A. thesis, University of Virginia, 1987.

Bell, Derrick A., Jr. *Race, Racism, and American Law*. Boston: Little, Brown, 1973.

Bellamy, John Stark. "If Christ Came to Dixie: The Southern Prophetic Vision of Howard Anderson Kester, 1904–1941." M.A. thesis, University of Virginia, 1977.

Bernardi, Daniel, ed. *The Birth of Whiteness: Race and the Emergence of U.S. Cinema*. New Brunswick, N.J.: Rutgers University Press, 1996.

Black, Earl, and Merle Black. *Politics and Society in the South*. Cambridge, Mass.: Harvard University Press, 1987.

Blanton, S. Walker, Jr. "Virginia in the 1920s: An Economic and Social Profile." Ph.D. diss., University of Virginia, 1969.

Blee, Kathleen M. *Women of the Klan: Racism and Gender in the 1920s*. Berkeley: University of California Press, 1991.

Boles, John B., and Evelyn Thomas Nolen. *Interpreting Southern History: Historiographical Essays in Honor of Sanford W. Higginbotham*. Baton Rouge: Louisiana State University Press, 1987.

Bond, Horace Mann. "The Extent and Character of Separate Schools in the United States." *Journal of Negro Education* 4 (July 1935): 321–27.

Bond, Julian, and Andrew B. Lewis, eds. *Gonna Sit at the Welcome Table*. New York: American Heritage, 1995.

Boothe, Armistead L. "Civil Rights in Virginia." *Virginia Law Review* 35 (November 1949): 928–75.

Bowie, Walter Russell. *Sunrise in the South: The Life of Mary-Cooke Branch Munford*. Richmond: William Byrd Press, 1942.

Brandt, Beverly Seehorn. *The Alexandria, Virginia, Library: Its History, Present Facilities, and Future Program*. Alexandria, Va.: self-published, 1951.

Browder, Walter Gordon, and Linwood Everett Lunsford. *An Economic and Social Survey of Dinwiddie County*. University of Virginia Record Extension Series, vol. 22, no. 4, October 1937.

Brown, Elsa Barkley. "Uncle Ned's Children: Negotiating Community and Freedom in Postemancipation Richmond, Virginia." Ph.D. diss., Kent State University, 1994.

———. "Womanist Consciousness: Maggie Lena Walker and the Independent Order of Saint Luke." *Signs* 14 (Spring 1989): 610–33.

Brown, Elsa Barkley, and Gregg D. Kimball. "Mapping the Terrain of Black Richmond, 1852–1915." *Journal of Urban History* 21 (March 1995): 296–346.

Brown, William Henry. *The Education and Economic Development of the Negro in Virginia*. Publications of the University of Virginia Phelps-Stokes Fellowship Papers, no. 6, 1923.

Brundage, W. Fitzhugh. *Lynching in the New South: Georgia and Virginia, 1880–1930*. Urbana: University of Illinois Press, 1993.

————. "White Women and the Politics of Historical Memory in the New South, 1880–1920." In *Jumpin' Jim Crow: Southern Politics from Civil War to Civil Rights*, edited by Jane Dailey, Glenda Elizabeth Gilmore, and Bryant Simon, 115–39. Princeton, N.J.: Princeton University Press, 2000.

————, ed. *Under Sentence of Death: Lynching in the South*. Chapel Hill: University of North Carolina Press, 1997.

Buni, Andrew. *The Negro in Virginia Politics, 1902–1965*. Charlottesville: University Press of Virginia, 1967.

Bustard, C. A. "John Powell: His Talent and His Mystique." *Albemarle Magazine* 4 (May–June 1981): 45–48.

Bynum, Victoria E. "'White Negroes' in Segregated Mississippi: Miscegenation, Racial Identity, and the Law." *Journal of Southern History* 64 (May 1998): 247–76.

Campbell, Edward D. C., Jr. *The Celluloid South: Hollywood and the Southern Myth*. Knoxville: University of Tennessee Press, 1981.

Carter, Dan T. "From Segregation to Integration." In *Interpreting Southern History: Essays in Honor of Sanford W. Higginbotham*, edited by John B. Boles and Evelyn Thomas Nolen, 408–33. Baton Rouge: Louisiana State University Press, 1987.

————. *Scottsboro: An American Tragedy*. Baton Rouge: Louisiana State University Press, 1969.

Carter, J. B. H., et al. *An Economic and Social Survey of Accomac County*. University of Virginia Record Extension Series, vol. 13, no. 9, March 1929.

Carter, Luther J. "Desegregation in Norfolk." *South Atlantic Quarterly* 58 (Autumn 1959): 507–20.

Cash, W. J. *The Mind of the South*. New York: Vintage Books, 1941.

Catlett, Clay, and Elliott G. Fishburne. *An Economic and Social Survey of Augusta County*. University of Virginia Record Extension Series, vol. 12, no. 7, January 1928.

Cell, John W. *The Highest Stage of White Supremacy: The Origins of Segregation in South Africa and the American South*. New York: Cambridge University Press, 1982.

Chafe, William H. *Civilities and Civil Rights: Greensboro, North Carolina, and the Black Struggle for Freedom*. New York: Oxford University Press, 1980.

Chalmers, David M. *Hooded Americanism: The History of the Ku Klux Klan*. 3d ed. Durham, N.C.: Duke University Press, 1987.

Chambers, Lenoir, and Joseph E. Shank. *Salt Water and Printer's Ink: Norfolk and Its Newspapers, 1865–1965*. Chapel Hill: University of North Carolina Press, 1967.

Chappell, David L. *Inside Agitators: White Southerners in the Civil Rights Movement*. Baltimore: Johns Hopkins University Press, 1994.

Chesnutt, Charles. *The House behind the Cedars*. 1900. Reprint, London: The X Press, 1995.

Clark, Emily. *Stuffed Peacocks*. New York: Alfred A. Knopf, 1927.

Clinton, Catherine, and Michele Gillespie, eds. *The Devil's Lane: Sex and Race in the Early South*. New York: Oxford University Press, 1997.

Cohen, Robert. *When the Old Left Was Young: Student Radicals and America's First Mass Student Movement, 1929–1941*. New York: Oxford University Press, 1993.

Cook, Samuel R. *Monacans and Miners: Native American and Coal Mining Communities in Appalachia*. Lincoln: University of Nebraska Press, 2000.

Corson, John Jay, III. *An Economic and Social Survey of Charles City County*. University of Virginia Record Extension Series, vol. 14, no. 1, July 1929.

Couvares, Francis G., ed. *Movie Censorship and American Culture*. Washington, D.C.: Smithsonian Institution Press, 1996.

Cowardin, Edward M., Jr. "John Powell's Concert Career: A Critical and Biographical Overview." *Albemarle Magazine* 4 (May–June 1981): 50–55.

Craig, John M., and Timothy H. Silver. "'Tolerance of the Intolerant': J. A. C. Chandler and the Ku Klux Klan at William and Mary." *South Atlantic Quarterly* 84 (Spring 1985): 213–22.

Creel, George. "Byrd Song." *Collier's Weekly*, August 21, 1937, 21, 30–31.

Cripps, Thomas. *Slow Fade to Black: The Negro in American Film, 1900–1942*. New York: Oxford University Press, 1977.

Culley, John J. "Muted Trumpets: Four Efforts to Better Race Relations, 1900–1919." Ph.D. diss., University of Virginia, 1967.

Cuthbert, Nancy B. "A Social Movement: The Norfolk Klan of the Twenties." *Virginia Social Sciences Journal* 2 (1967): 101–18.

Dabney, Thomas L. "Interracial Frontiers." *The Southern Workman* 64 (January 1935): 8–12.

Dabney, Virginius. *Across the Years: Memories of a Virginian*. Garden City, N.Y.: Doubleday, 1978.

———. *Below the Potomac: A Book about the New South*. New York: D. Appleton–Century, 1942.

———. "Is the South That Bad?" *Saturday Review of Literature* 29 (April 13, 1946): 9–10, 84–88.

———. *Liberalism in the South*. Chapel Hill: University of North Carolina Press, 1932.

———. "Nearer and Nearer the Precipice." *Atlantic Monthly* 171 (January 1943): 94–100.

———. "The Negro and His Schooling." *Atlantic Monthly* 169 (April 1942): 459–68.

———. "Paternalism in Race Relations Is Outmoded." *Southern Frontier* 3 (July 1942): 1, 4.

———. "Richmond's Quiet Revolution." *Saturday Review* 47 (February 29, 1964): 18–19, 28.

———. "The South Marches On." *Survey Graphic* 32 (November 1943): 441–43, 462.

———. *Virginia: The New Dominion*. Garden City, N.Y.: Doubleday, 1971.

———. "Virginia's 'Peaceable, Honorable Stand.'" *Life*, September 22, 1958, 51–52, 55–56.

———. *Virginius Dabney's Virginia: Writings about the Old Dominion*. Chapel Hill: Algonquin Books, 1986.

Dailey, Jane. *Before Jim Crow: The Politics of Race in Postemancipation Virginia*. Chapel Hill: University of North Carolina Press, 2000.

———. "Deference and Violence in the Postbellum Urban South: Manners and Massacres in Danville, Virginia." *Journal of Southern History* 63 (August 1997): 553–90.

Dailey, Jane, Glenda Elizabeth Gilmore, and Bryant Simon, eds. *Jumpin' Jim Crow: Southern Politics from Civil War to Civil Rights*. Princeton, N.J.: Princeton University Press, 2000.

Davis, Arthur Kyle, ed. *Virginia Communities in War Time: First Series*. Publications of the Virginia War History Commission, Source Vol. 6. Richmond, 1926.

———, ed. *Virginia Communities in War Time: Second Series*. Publications of the Virginia War History Commission, Source Vol. 7. Richmond, 1927.

Deck, Patrick A., and Henry Heaton. *An Economic and Social Survey of Loudoun County*. University of Virginia Record Extension Series, vol. 10, no. 10, June 1926.

DeCorse, Helen Camp. *Charlottesville—A Study of Negro Life and Personality*. Publications of the University of Virginia Phelps-Stokes Fellowship Papers, no. 11, 1933.

DeMarce, Virginia. "Looking at Legends—Lumbee and Melungeon: Applied Genealogy and the Origins of Tri-racial Isolate Settlements." *National Genealogical Society Quarterly* 81 (March 1993): 24–45.

———. "'Verry Slitly Mixt': Tri-racial Isolate Families of the Upper South—A Genealogical Study." *National Genealogical Society Quarterly* 80 (March 1992): 5–35.

Department of Community Planning, Charlottesville, Va. *Ridge Street Oral History Project: A Supplement to the Survey of the Ridge Street Historic District and Proposal for Local Designation*. Charlottesville: Preservation Piedmont for the City of Charlottesville, 1995.

Dickson, Keith Dean. "The Divided Mind of Douglas Southall Freeman and the Transmission of Southern Memory." Ph.D. diss., University of Virginia, 1998.

Dierenfield, Bruce J. *Keeper of the Rules: Congressman Howard W. Smith of Virginia*. Charlottesville: University Press of Virginia, 1987.

Directory of Business and Professional Women in Richmond, Virginia, 1921. Richmond: Virginia Federation of Business and Professional Women's Clubs, 1921.

Dodson, E. Griffith. *The General Assembly of the Commonwealth of Virginia, 1919–1939*. Richmond: Commonwealth of Virginia, 1939.

Dollard, John. *Caste and Class in a Southern Town*. New Haven, Conn.: Yale University Press, 1938.

Dorr, Gregory Michael. "Assuring America's Place in the Sun." *Journal of Southern History* 66 (May 2000): 257–96.

———. "Principled Expediency: Eugenics, *Naim v. Naim*, and the Supreme Court." *American Journal of Legal History* 42 (April 1998): 119–59.

Dorr, Lisa Lindquist. "Arm in Arm: Gender, Eugenics, and Virginia's Racial Integrity Acts of the 1920s." *Journal of Women's History* 11 (Spring 1999): 143–66.

———. "Black-on-White Rape and Retribution in Twentieth-Century Virginia: 'Men, Even Negroes, Must Have Some Protection.'" *Journal of Southern History* 66 (November 2000): 711–48.

Doyle, Bertram Wilbur. *The Etiquette of Race Relations in the South: A Study in Social Control*. Port Washington, N.Y.: Kennikat Press, 1937.

Duke, Maurice, and Daniel P. Jordan, eds. *A Richmond Reader, 1733–1983*. Chapel Hill: University of North Carolina Press, 1983.

Dulaney, Ben Bane. *An Economic and Social Survey of Washington County*. University of Virginia Record Extension Series, vol. 17, no. 6, December 1932.

Dunbar, Anthony P. *Against the Grain: Southern Radicals and Prophets, 1929–1959*. Charlottesville: University Press of Virginia, 1981.

Dvorak, James Patrick, Jr. "Louis I. Jaffé: A Southern Liberal's Critique of Lynching." M.A. thesis, University of Virginia, 1990.

Dykeman, Wilma, and James Stokely. *Seeds of Southern Change: The Life of Will Alexander*. New York: W. W. Norton, 1962.

Edmunds, Pocahontas Wight. *Virginians Out Front*. Richmond: Whittet and Shepperson, 1972.

Egerton, John. "The Pre-*Brown* South." *Virginia Quarterly Review* 70 (Autumn 1994): 603–22.

———. *Speak Now against the Day*. New York: Alfred A. Knopf, 1994.

Eisenberg, Ralph. *Virginia Votes, 1924–1968*. Charlottesville: Institute of Government, University of Virginia, 1971.

Ellis, Ann Wells. "The Commission on Interracial Cooperation, 1919–1944: Its Activities and Results." Ph.D. diss., Georgia State University, 1975.

Engs, Robert. *Freedom's First Generation: Black Hampton, Virginia, 1861–1890*. Philadelphia: University of Pennsylvania Press, 1979.

Fairclough, Adam. "'Being in the Field of Education and Also Being a Negro . . . Seems . . . Tragic': Black Teachers in the Jim Crow South." *Journal of American History* 87 (June 2000): 65–91.

———. *Race and Democracy: The Civil Rights Struggle in Louisiana, 1915–1972*. Athens: University of Georgia Press, 1995.

Feldman, Glenn. *Politics, Society, and the Klan in Alabama, 1915–1949*. Tuscaloosa: University of Alabama Press, 1999.

Ferebee, E. E., and J. Pendleton Wilson Jr. *An Economic and Social Survey of*

Princess Anne County. University of Virginia Record Extension Series, vol. 8, no. 9, May 1924.

Ferrell, Henry C., Jr. *Claude A. Swanson of Virginia: A Political Biography.* Lexington: University Press of Kentucky, 1985.

Fine, Richard. "Roy Flannagan: Richmond's 'Reporter's Reporter.'" *Richmond Quarterly* 6 (Spring 1984): 19–23.

Finkelman, Paul. "Crimes of Love, Misdemeanors of Passion: The Regulation of Race and Sex in the Colonial South." In *The Devil's Lane: Sex and Race in the Early South,* edited by Catherine Clinton and Michele Gillespie, 124–35. New York: Oxford University Press, 1997.

Fishwick, Marshall. *A New Look at the Old Dominion.* New York: Harper and Brothers, 1959.

Flamming, Douglas. *Creating the Modern South: Millhands and Managers in Dalton, Georgia, 1884–1984.* Chapel Hill: University of North Carolina Press, 1992.

Fox, James. *The Langhorne Sisters.* London: Granta Books, 1998.

Frazer, Emmet M. "How Does It Feel to Be Colored?" *Commonwealth* 12 (June 1945): 10.

Frederickson, Kari A. *The Dixiecrat Revolt and the End of the Solid South, 1932–1968.* Chapel Hill: University of North Carolina Press, 2001.

Freeman, Douglas Southall. "In Memoriam: John Stewart Bryan." *Virginia Magazine of History and Biography* 53 (January 1945): 57–63.

———. Unpublished biography of John Stewart Bryan in holdings of Virginia Historical Society.

———. "Virginia: A Gentle Dominion." *The Nation* 119 (July 16, 1924): 68–71.

Friddell, Guy. *Colgate Darden: Conversations with Guy Friddell.* Charlottesville: University Press of Virginia, 1978.

Fry, Joseph A. "Rayon, Riot, and Repression: The Covington Sit-Down Strike of 1937." *Virginia Magazine of History and Biography* 84 (January 1976): 3–18.

———. "Senior Advisor to the Democratic 'Organization': William Thomas Reed and Virginia Politics, 1925–1935." *Virginia Magazine of History and Biography* 85 (October 1977): 445–69.

Gaines, Kevin. *Uplifting the Race: Black Leadership, Politics, and Culture in the Twentieth Century.* Chapel Hill: University of North Carolina Press, 1996.

Gaston, Paul M. *The New South Creed: A Study in Southern Mythmaking.* New York: Alfred A. Knopf, 1970.

Gates, Maurice. "Negro Students Challenge Social Forces." *Crisis* 42 (August 1935): 232.

Gates, Robbins L. *The Making of Massive Resistance: Virginia's Politics of Public School Desegregation, 1954–1956.* Chapel Hill: University of North Carolina Press, 1964.

Gavins, Raymond. "Hancock, Jackson, and Young: Virginia's Black Triumvirate, 1930–1945." *Virginia Magazine of History and Biography* 85 (October 1977): 470–86.

————. *The Perils and Prospects of Southern Black Leadership: Gordon Blaine Hancock, 1884–1970.* Durham, N.C.: Duke University Press, 1977.

————. "Urbanization and Segregation: Black Leadership Patterns in Richmond, Virginia, 1900–1920." *South Atlantic Quarterly* 79 (Summer 1980): 257–73.

Gee, Wilson, et al. *An Economic and Social Survey of Albemarle County.* University of Virginia Record Extension Series, vol. 7, no. 2, October 1922.

Genovese, Eugene D. *Roll, Jordan, Roll: The World the Slaves Made.* New York: Pantheon Books, 1974.

Gignilliat, John L. "The Thought of Douglas Southall Freeman." Ph.D. diss., University of Wisconsin–Madison, 1968.

Gilliam, George H. "Making Virginia Progressive: Courts and Parties, Railroads and Regulators, 1890–1910." *Virginia Magazine of History and Biography* 107 (Spring 1999): 189–222.

Gilmore, Glenda Elizabeth. "False Friends and Avowed Enemies: Southern African Americans and Party Allegiances in the 1920s." In *Jumpin' Jim Crow: Southern Politics from Civil War to Civil Rights*, edited by Jane Dailey, Glenda Elizabeth Gilmore, and Bryant Simon, 219–38. Princeton, N.J.: Princeton University Press, 2000.

————. *Gender and Jim Crow: Women and the Politics of White Supremacy in North Carolina, 1896–1920.* Chapel Hill: University of North Carolina Press, 1996.

Glass, Carter. "The 14th, 15th, and 18th Amendments." *Liberty* 5 (May 26, 1928): 73–74.

Glass, Robert, and Carter Glass. *Virginia Democracy.* 3 vols. Springfield, Ill.: Democratic Historical Association, 1937.

Goodman, James. *Stories of Scottsboro.* New York: Pantheon, 1994.

Grantham, Dewey. "The Contours of Southern Progressivism." *American Historical Review* 86 (December 1981): 1035–59.

Greenberg, Jack. *Race Relations and American Law.* New York: Columbia University Press, 1959.

Gretlund, Jan Nordby, ed. *The Southern State of Mind.* Columbia: University of South Carolina Press, 1999.

Grossman, James R. *Land of Hope: Chicago, Black Southerners, and the Great Migration.* Chicago: University of Chicago Press, 1989.

Guild, June Purcell. *Black Laws of Virginia.* Richmond: Whittet and Shepperson, 1936. Reprint, New York: Negro Universities Press, 1969.

Hale, Grace Elizabeth. *Making Whiteness: The Culture of Segregation in the South, 1890–1940.* New York: Pantheon, 1998.

Hall, Alvin L. "Virginia Back in the Fold: The Gubernatorial Campaign and Election of 1929." *Virginia Magazine of History and Biography* 73 (July 1965): 280–302.

Hall, Jacquelyn Dowd. *Revolt against Chivalry: Jessie Daniel Ames and the*

Women's Campaign against Lynching. New York: Columbia University Press, 1979.

Hall, Jacquelyn Dowd, et al., eds. *Like a Family: The Making of a Southern Cotton Mill World*. Chapel Hill: University of North Carolina Press, 1987.

Hall, Kermit L., ed. *The Oxford Companion to the Supreme Court of the United States*. New York: Oxford University Press, 1992.

Hamer, Mark H. "A Modest Forward Step: Colgate W. Darden and the School Desegregation Crisis." B.A. thesis, University of Virginia, 1988.

Hancock, Gordon Blaine. "Needed . . . A Southern Charter for Race Relations." *Southern Frontier* 3 (April 1942): 1, 3.

———. "Race Relations in the United States: A Summary." In *What the Negro Wants*, edited by Rayford W. Logan, 217–47. Chapel Hill: University of North Carolina Press, 1944.

Handy, Henry Brantly, ed. *The Social Recorder of Virginia*. Richmond: Social Recorder of Virginia, 1928.

Hardin, Peter. "'Documentary Genocide': Families' Surnames on Racial Hit List." *Richmond Times-Dispatch*, March 5, 2000, A1, A10–11.

———. "Seeking Sovereignty: Indians Face Barriers, See Benefits in Quest." *Richmond Times-Dispatch*, March 6, 2000, A1, A6.

Hawkes, Robert Thomas, Jr. "The Career of Harry Flood Byrd, Sr., to 1933." Ph.D. diss., University of Virginia, 1975.

———. "The Emergence of a Leader: Harry Flood Byrd, Governor of Virginia, 1926–1930." *Virginia Magazine of History and Biography* 82 (July 1974): 259–81.

Haws, Robert, ed. *The Age of Segregation: Race Relations in the South, 1890–1945*. Jackson: University Press of Mississippi, 1978.

Heinemann, Ronald L. *Depression and New Deal in Virginia: The Enduring Dominion*. Charlottesville: University Press of Virginia, 1983.

———. *Harry Byrd of Virginia*. Charlottesville: University Press of Virginia, 1996.

———. "Virginia in the Twentieth Century: Recent Interpretations." *Virginia Magazine of History and Biography* 94 (April 1986): 131–60.

Henige, David, and Darlene Wilson. "Viewpoint: Brent Kennedy's *Melungeons*." *Appalachian Journal* 25 (Spring 1998): 270–98.

Hershman, James H., Jr. "Massive Resistance Meets Its Match: The Emergence of a Pro–Public School Majority." In *The Moderates' Dilemma: Massive Resistance to School Desegregation in Virginia*, edited by Matthew D. Lassiter and Andrew B. Lewis, 104–33. Charlottesville: University Press of Virginia, 1998.

———. "A Shrinking Black Belt and Virginia's Massive Resistance: A Note." *Virginia Social Science Journal* 20 (Winter 1985): 93–97.

Hewitt, Nancy A., and Suzanne Lebsock, eds. *Visible Women: New Essays on American Activism*. Urbana: University of Illinois Press, 1993.

Higginbotham, A. Leon, Jr. "Conversations with Civil Rights Crusaders." *Virginia Lawyer* 37 (February 1989): 11–16, 37–41.

Hine, Darlene Clark. *Black Victory: The Rise and Fall of the White Primary in Texas*. Millwood, N.Y.: KTO Press, 1979.

Holland, C. W., Jr., N. L. Holland, and W. W. Taylor. *An Economic and Social Survey of Northampton County*. University of Virginia Record Extension Series, vol. 12, no. 5, November 1927.

Hopewell, John Stanley. "An Outsider Looking In: John Garland Pollard and Machine Politics in Twentieth Century Virginia." Ph.D. diss., University of Virginia, 1976.

Houston, Charles H. "Cracking Closed University Doors." *Crisis* 42 (December 1935): 364, 370, 372.

————. "Educational Inequalities Must Go!" *Crisis* 42 (October 1935): 300–301, 316.

Hughes, Langston. "Cowards from the Colleges." *Crisis* 41 (August 1934): 226–28.

Irwin, Marjorie Felice. *The Negro in Charlottesville and Albemarle County*. Publications of the University of Virginia Phelps-Stokes Fellowship Papers, no. 9, 1929.

Jackson, Kenneth. *The Ku Klux Klan in the City, 1915–1930*. New York: Oxford University Press, 1967.

Jackson, Walter A. *Gunnar Myrdal and America's Conscience: Social Engineering and Racial Liberalism, 1938–1987*. Chapel Hill: University of North Carolina Press, 1990.

Jacobson, Matthew Frye. *Whiteness of a Different Color: European Immigrants and the Alchemy of Race*. Cambridge, Mass.: Harvard University Press, 1998.

James, Marquis. "The Gentleman from Virginia." *Saturday Evening Post* 210 (August 28, 1937): 16–17, 35–36, 39.

Jeffries, John C., Jr. *Justice Lewis F. Powell, Jr.* New York: Scribners, 1994.

Johnson, Charles S. *Patterns of Negro Segregation*. New York: Harper and Brothers, 1943.

Johnson, Franklin. *The Development of State Legislation Concerning the Free Negro*. 1918. Reprint, Westport, Conn.: Greenwood Press, 1979.

Jones, M. Ashby. "The Approach to the South's Race Question." *Journal of Social Forces* 1 (November 1922): 40–41.

————. "The Negro and the South." *Virginia Quarterly Review* 3 (January 1927): 1–12.

Jordan, William. "'The Damnable Dilemma': African-American Accommodation and Protest during World War I." *Journal of American History* 81 (March 1995): 1562–83.

Judkins, Shirleen Teresa. "The Massenburg Law, 1925–26: Virginia Segregation at the Crest." M.A. thesis, University of Virginia, 1977.

Kelley, Robin D. G. *Race Rebels: Culture, Politics, and the Black Working Class*. New York: Free Press, 1994.

Kennedy, David. *Over Here: The First World War and American Society*. New York: Oxford University Press, 1980.

Kennedy, Stetson. *Jim Crow Guide to the U.S.A.* London: Lawrence and Wishart, 1959.

Kerlin, Robert T. *The Voice of the Negro.* 1920. Reprint, New York: Arno Press, 1968.

"The Kerlin Case." *Southern Workman* 50 (December 1921): 529–32, 561–70.

Kevles, Daniel J. *In the Name of Eugenics: Genetics and the Uses of Human Heredity.* New York: Alfred A. Knopf, 1985. Reprint, Cambridge, Mass.: Harvard University Press, 1997.

Key, V. O., Jr. *Southern Politics in State and Nation.* New York: Alfred A. Knopf, 1949. Reprint, Knoxville: University of Tennessee Press, 1984.

Kirby, Jack Temple. *Darkness at the Dawning: Race and Reform in the Progressive Era South.* Philadelphia: J. B. Lippincott, 1972.

———. *Westmoreland Davis: Virginia Planter-Politician, 1859–1942.* Charlottesville: University Press of Virginia, 1968.

Kluger, Richard. *Simple Justice.* New York: Vintage Books, 1975.

Kneebone, John T. *Southern Liberal Journalists and the Issue of Race, 1920–1944.* Chapel Hill: University of North Carolina Press, 1985.

Kousser, J. Morgan. *The Shaping of Southern Politics: Suffrage Restriction and the Establishment of the One-Party South, 1880–1910.* New Haven, Conn.: Yale University Press, 1974.

Kuznets, Simon, and Dorothy Swaine Thomas. *Population Redistribution and Economic Growth in the United States, 1870–1950.* Philadelphia: American Philosophical Society, 1957.

Larson, Edward J. *Sex, Race, and Science: Eugenics in the Deep South.* Baltimore: Johns Hopkins University Press, 1995.

Lassiter, Matthew D. "The Rise of the Suburban South: The 'Silent Majority' and the Politics of Education, 1945–1975." Ph.D. diss., University of Virginia, 1999.

Lassiter, Matthew D., and Andrew B. Lewis, eds. *The Moderates' Dilemma: Massive Resistance to School Desegregation in Virginia.* Charlottesville: University Press of Virginia, 1998.

Lawson, Steven F. *Black Ballots: Voting Rights in the South, 1944–1969.* New York: Columbia University Press, 1976.

Leap, William Lester. *Red Hill—Neighborhood Life and Race Relations in a Rural Section.* Publications of the University of Virginia Phelps-Stokes Fellowship Papers, no. 10, 1933.

Lebsock, Suzanne. "Woman Suffrage and White Supremacy: A Virginia Case Study." In *Visible Women: New Essays on American Activism*, edited by Nancy A. Hewitt and Suzanne Lebsock, 62–100. Urbana: University of Illinois Press, 1993.

Leidholdt, Alexander S. *Editor for Justice: The Life of Louis I. Jaffé.* Baton Rouge: Louisiana State University Press, 2002.

———. *Standing before the Shouting Mob: Lenoir Chambers and Virginia's*

Massive Resistance to Public-School Integration. Tuscaloosa: University of Alabama Press, 1997.

Leloudis, James L. *Schooling the New South: Pedagogy, Self, and Society in North Carolina, 1880–1920*. Chapel Hill: University of North Carolina Press, 1996.

Lewis, Andrew B. "Wandering in Two Worlds: Race, Education, and Citizenship in Virginia since 1945." Ph.D. diss., University of Virginia, 2000.

Lewis, David Levering. *W. E. B. Du Bois: Biography of a Race*. New York: Henry Holt, 1993.

———. *When Harlem Was in Vogue*. New York: Alfred A. Knopf, 1981. Reprint, New York: Penguin Books, 1997.

Lewis, Earl. *In Their Own Interests: Race, Class, and Power in Twentieth-Century Norfolk, Virginia*. Berkeley: University of California Press, 1991.

Link, William A. *A Hard Country and a Lonely Place: Schooling, Society, and Reform in Rural Virginia, 1870–1920*. Chapel Hill: University of North Carolina Press, 1986.

———. *The Paradox of Southern Progressivism, 1880–1930*. Chapel Hill: University of North Carolina Press, 1992.

Logan, Rayford W., ed. *What the Negro Wants*. Chapel Hill: University of North Carolina Press, 1944.

Lombardo, Paul A. "Miscegenation, Eugenics, and Racism: Historical Footnotes to *Loving v. Virginia*." *University of California, Davis, Law Review* 21 (1988): 421–52.

Love, Richard. "The Cigarette Capital of the World: Labor, Race, and Tobacco in Richmond, Virginia, 1880–1980." Ph.D. diss., University of Virginia, 1998.

McDonough, Julia Anne. "Men and Women of Good Will: A History of the Commission on Interracial Cooperation and the Southern Regional Council, 1919–1954." Ph.D. diss., University of Virginia, 1993.

MacGregor, Morris J., and Bernard C. Nalty, eds. *Blacks in the United States Armed Forces: Basic Documents*. Vol. 4, *Segregation Entrenched, 1917–1940*. Wilmington, Del.: Scholarly Resources, 1977.

McKenney, Carlton. *Rails in Richmond*. Glendale, Calif.: Interurban Press, 1986.

MacLean, Nancy. *Behind the Mask of Chivalry: The Making of the Second Ku Klux Klan*. New York: Oxford University Press, 1994.

McMillen, Neil R. *Dark Journey: Black Mississippians in the Age of Jim Crow*. Urbana: University of Illinois Press, 1989.

McNeil, Genna Rae. *Groundwork: Charles Hamilton Houston and the Struggle for Civil Rights*. Philadelphia: University of Pennsylvania Press, 1983.

Mangum, Charles S., Jr. *The Legal Status of the Negro*. Chapel Hill: University of North Carolina Press, 1940.

Martin-Perdue, Nancy J., and Charles L. Perdue Jr., eds. *Talk about Trouble: A New Deal Portrait of Virginians in the Great Depression*. Chapel Hill: University of North Carolina Press, 1996.

Mason, Lucy Randolph. *To Win These Rights: A Personal Story of the CIO in the South*. New York: Harper and Row, 1952. Reprint, Westport, Conn.: Greenwood Press, 1970.

Matthews, John Michael. "Virginius Dabney, John Temple Graves, and What Happened to Southern Liberalism." *Mississippi Quarterly* 45 (Fall 1992): 405–20.

Meier, August, and Elliot Rudwick. "The Boycott Movement against Jim Crow Streetcars in the South, 1900–1906." In *Along the Color Line: Explorations in the Black Experience*, edited by August Meier and Elliot Rudwick, 267–89. Urbana: University of Illinois Press, 1976.

Moeser, John V., and Christopher Silver. "Race, Social Stratification, and Politics: The Case of Atlanta, Memphis, and Richmond." *Virginia Magazine of History and Biography* 102 (October 1994): 519–50.

Moger, Allen W. "The Origin of the Democratic Machine in Virginia." *Journal of Southern History* 8 (May 1942): 183–209.

———. *Virginia: Bourbonism to Byrd, 1870–1925*. Charlottesville: University Press of Virginia, 1968.

———. "Virginia's Conservative Political Heritage." *South Atlantic Quarterly* 50 (July 1951): 318–29.

Moore, Leonard J. *Citizen Klansmen: The Ku Klux Klan in Indiana, 1921–1928*. Chapel Hill: University of North Carolina Press, 1991.

Moore, Virginia. *Virginia Is a State of Mind*. New York: E. P. Dutton, 1943.

Mundie, Joseph Ryland. *An Economic and Social Survey of King and Queen County*. University of Virginia Record Extension Series, vol. 9, no. 10, July 1925.

Munford, Beverly B. *Virginia's Attitude toward Slavery and Secession*. Richmond: L. H. Jenkins, 1909.

Murray, Pauli. *The Autobiography of a Black Activist, Feminist, Lawyer, Priest, and Poet*. Knoxville: University of Tennessee Press, 1989. Originally published as *Song in a Weary Throat: An American Pilgrimage* (New York: Harper and Row, 1987).

———. *States' Laws on Race and Color*. 1950. Reprint, Athens: University of Georgia Press, 1996.

Muse, Benjamin. *Virginia's Massive Resistance*. Bloomington: Indiana University Press, 1961.

Myrdal, Gunnar. *An American Dilemma: The Negro Problem and Modern Democracy*. New York: Harper and Row, 1944.

National Association for the Advancement of Colored People. *Thirty Years of Lynching in the United States*. New York: Arno Press, 1969.

———. *Virginia State Conference of Branches: 25th Anniversary, 1935–1960*. Richmond: NAACP, 1960.

Negro Welfare Survey Committee. *The Negro in Richmond, Virginia*. Richmond: Richmond Council of Social Agencies, 1929.

Nickel, Lehman, and Cary J. Randolph. *An Economic and Social Survey of Fair-*

fax County. University of Virginia Record Extension Series, vol. 8, no. 12, August 1924.

Nitschke, Marie Morris. "Virginius Dabney of Virginia: Portrait of a Southern Journalist in the Twentieth Century." Ph.D. diss., Emory University, 1987.

Norfleet, Elizabeth Copeland. "Louise Burleigh Powell: An Artist in the World of the Theatre, on Stage, and behind the Scene." *Richmond Quarterly* 6 (Fall 1983): 22–28.

Norrell, Robert J. *Reaping the Whirlwind: The Civil Rights Movement in Tuskegee*. New York: Alfred A. Knopf, 1985.

OBrion, Catherine Greer. "The Black Community's Struggle for Education in Fredericksburg, Virginia, 1905–1963." M.A. thesis, University of Virginia, 1990.

Odum, Howard W. *Race and Rumors of Race: The American South in the Early Forties*. Chapel Hill: University of North Carolina Press, 1943. Reprint, with a new introduction by Bryant Simon, Baltimore: Johns Hopkins University Press, 1997.

Palmore, Joseph R. "The Not-So-Strange Career of Interstate Jim Crow: Race, Transportation, and the Dormant Commerce Clause, 1878–1946." *Virginia Law Review* 83 (1997): 1773–1817.

Parramore, Thomas C., with Peter C. Stewart and Tommy L. Bogger. *Norfolk: The First Four Centuries*. Charlottesville: University Press of Virginia, 1994.

Pascoe, Peggy. "Miscegenation Law, Court Cases, and Ideologies of 'Race' in Twentieth-Century America." *Journal of American History* 83 (June 1996): 44–69.

Patterson, Michael S. "The Fall of a Bishop: James Cannon, Jr., *versus* Carter Glass, 1909–1934." *Journal of Southern History* 39 (November 1973): 493–518.

Percy, William Alexander. *Lanterns on the Levee: Recollections of a Planter's Son*. 1941. Reprint, Baton Rouge: Louisiana State University Press, 1993.

Peters, J. S., and W. F. Stinespring. *An Economic and Social Survey of Rockingham County*. University of Virginia Record Extension Series, vol. 9, no. 1a, September 1924.

Picott, J. Rupert. *History of the Virginia Teachers Association*. Washington, D.C.: National Education Association, 1975.

Pinchbeck, Raymond B. *The Virginia Negro Artisan and Tradesman*. Publications of the University of Virginia Phelps-Stokes Fellowship Papers, no. 7, 1926.

Plecker, Walter A. "Birth Registration and Racial Integrity Law." *Virginia Journal of Education* 18 (September 1924): 13.

———. "Virginia's Vanishing Race." Synopsis of unpublished manuscript in holdings of Virginia Historical Society.

Pocket Directory and Guide of Richmond, Virginia, 1927.

Powell, John. "Lectures on Music." *Rice Institute Pamphlet* 10 (July 1923): 107–63.

Pratt, Robert A. *The Color of Their Skin: Education and Race in Richmond, Virginia, 1954–89*. Charlottesville: University Press of Virginia, 1992.

President's Committee on Civil Rights. *To Secure These Rights: The Report of the President's Committee on Civil Rights*. New York: Simon and Schuster, 1947.

Pulley, Raymond. *Old Virginia Restored: An Interpretation of the Progressive Impulse*. Charlottesville: University Press of Virginia, 1968.

Rable, George C. "The South and the Politics of Antilynching Legislation, 1920–1940." *Journal of Southern History* 51 (May 1985): 227–46.

Raper, Arthur. *The Tragedy of Lynching*. Chapel Hill: University of North Carolina Press, 1933.

Redding, J. Saunders. "A Negro Speaks for His People." *Atlantic Monthly* 171 (March 1943): 58–63.

Reed, John Shelton. "Mixing in the Mountains." *Southern Cultures* 3 (Winter 1997): 25–36.

Regester, Charlene. "Black Films, White Censors: Oscar Micheaux Confronts Censorship in New York, Virginia, and Chicago." In *Movie Censorship and American Culture*, edited by Francis G. Couvares, 159–86. Washington, D.C.: Smithsonian Institution Press, 1996.

Reilly, Philip R. *The Surgical Solution: A History of Involuntary Sterilization in the United States*. Baltimore: Johns Hopkins University Press, 1991.

Richmond, Virginia, City Directory, 1926. Richmond: Hill Directory Company, 1926.

Rise, Eric. *The Martinsville Seven: Race, Rape, and Capital Punishment*. Charlottesville: University Press of Virginia, 1995.

"The Rising Tide of Prejudice." *The Nation* 122 (March 10, 1926): 247.

Rountree, Helen C. *Pocahontas's People: The Powhatan Indians of Virginia through Four Centuries*. Norman: University of Oklahoma Press, 1990.

Rouse, Parke. *We Happy WASPs: Virginia in the Days of Jim Crow and Harry Byrd*. Richmond: Dietz Press, 1996.

Rudwick, Elliot M. "Section A: Oscar DePriest and the Jim Crow Restaurant in the United States House of Representatives." *Journal of Negro Education* 35 (1966): 77–82.

Sabato, Larry. *The Democratic Party Primary in Virginia: Tantamount to Election No Longer*. Charlottesville: University Press of Virginia, 1977.

Salmond, John A. *Miss Lucy of the CIO: The Life and Times of Lucy Randolph Mason, 1882–1959*. Athens: University of Georgia Press, 1988.

Sampson, Henry T. *Blacks in Black and White: A Source Book on Black Films*. Metuchen, N.J.: Scarecrow Press, 1995.

Schall, Keith L., ed. *Stony the Road: Chapters in the History of Hampton Institute*. Charlottesville: University Press of Virginia, 1977.

Schuyler, George S. *Black No More*. 1931. Reprint, New York: Modern Library, 1999.

———. "The Caucasian Problem." In *What the Negro Wants*, edited by Rayford W. Logan, 281–98. Chapel Hill: University of North Carolina Press, 1944.

Scott, Daryl Michael. *Contempt and Pity: Social Policy and the Image of the Dam-*

aged Black Psyche, 1860–1996. Chapel Hill: University of North Carolina Press, 1997.

Scott, Emmett J. "Letters of Negro Migrants of 1916–1918." *The Journal of Negro History* 4 (October 1919): 290–340.

Sherman, Richard B. *The Case of Odell Waller and Virginia Justice, 1940–1942*. Knoxville: University of Tennessee Press, 1992.

―――. "'The Last Stand': The Fight for Racial Integrity in Virginia in the 1920s." *Journal of Southern History* 54 (February 1988): 69–92.

―――. "The 'Teachings at Hampton Institute': Social Equality, Racial Integrity, and the Virginia Public Assemblage Act of 1926." *Virginia Magazine of History and Biography* 95 (July 1987): 275–300.

Showalter, William Joseph. "Virginia—A Commonwealth That Has Come Back." *National Geographic* 55 (April 1929): 403–503.

Silver, Christopher. *Twentieth-Century Richmond: Planning, Politics, and Race*. Knoxville: University of Tennessee Press, 1984.

Silver, Christopher, and John V. Moeser. *The Separate City: Black Communities in the Urban South, 1940–1968*. Lexington: University Press of Kentucky, 1995.

Simon, Bryant. *A Fabric of Defeat: The Politics of South Carolina Millhands, 1910–1948*. Chapel Hill: University of North Carolina Press, 1998.

―――. "Race Reactions: African American Organizing, Liberalism, and White Working-Class Politics in Postwar South Carolina." In *Jumpin' Jim Crow: Southern Politics from Civil War to Civil Rights*, edited by Jane Dailey, Glenda Elizabeth Gilmore, and Bryant Simon, 239–59. Princeton, N.J.: Princeton University Press, 2000.

Simpson, Josephus. "Are Colored People in Virginia a Helpless Minority?" *Opportunity* 12 (December 1934): 373–75, 381.

Singal, Daniel J. *The War Within: From Victorian to Modernist Thought in the South, 1919–1945*. Chapel Hill: University of North Carolina Press, 1982.

Smith, Charles Henry Edward. "The Jim Crow Laws of Virginia, 1900–1930." M.A. thesis, Virginia State College, 1964.

Smith, Howard Worth. *Our Paternal Hearth*. Self-published, n.d. Copy in possession of author.

Smith, J. David. *The Eugenic Assault on America: Scenes in Red, White, and Black*. Fairfax, Va.: George Mason University Press, 1993.

Smith, J. Douglas. "The Campaign for Racial Purity and the Erosion of Paternalism in Virginia, 1922–1930: 'Nominally White, Biologically Mixed, and Legally Negro.'" *Journal of Southern History* 68 (February 2002): 65–106.

―――. "Patrolling the Boundaries of Race: Motion Picture Censorship and Jim Crow in Virginia, 1922–1932." *Historical Journal of Film, Radio, and Television* 21 (August 2001): 273–91.

―――. "'When Reason Collides with Prejudice': Armistead Lloyd Boothe and the Politics of Desegregation in Virginia, 1948–1963." *Virginia Magazine of History and Biography* 102 (January 1994): 5–46.

Smith, John David, ed. *Racial Determinism and the Fear of Miscegenation, Post-1900: Race and the 'Negro Problem.'* Pt. 2. New York: Garland Publishing, 1993.

Smith, Larissa M. "Where the South Begins: Black Politics and Civil Rights Activism in Virginia, 1930–1951." Ph.D. diss., Emory University, 2001.

Smith, Lillian. "Addressed to White Liberals." *New Republic* 111 (September 18, 1944): 331–33.

Smith, Stuart W., ed. *Douglas Southall Freeman on Leadership*. Shippensburg, Pa.: White Mane Publishing, 1993.

Social Register: Richmond, Charleston, Savannah, Augusta, Atlanta, 1919. New York: Social Register Association, 1918.

Sosna, Morton. *In Search of the Silent South: Southern Liberals and the Race Issue*. New York: Columbia University Press, 1977.

Stampp, Kenneth M. *The Peculiar Institution: Slavery in the Ante-Bellum South*. New York: Alfred A. Knopf, 1956.

Stevens, George Raymond. *An Economic and Social Survey of Roanoke County*. University of Virginia Record Extension Series, vol. 15, no. 1, July 1930.

Storrs, Landon R. Y. *Civilizing Capitalism: The National Consumers' League, Women's Activism, and Labor Standards in the New Deal Era*. Chapel Hill: University of North Carolina Press, 2000.

Stribling, T. S. *Birthright*. New York: Century Company, 1922.

Suggs, Henry Lewis. "Black Strategy and Ideology in the Segregation Era: P. B. Young and the *Norfolk Journal and Guide*, 1910–1954." *Virginia Magazine of History and Biography* 91 (April 1983): 161–90.

———. *P. B. Young, Newspaperman: Race, Politics, and Journalism in the New South, 1910–1962*. Charlottesville: University Press of Virginia, 1988.

Sullivan, Patricia. *Days of Hope: Race and Democracy in the New Deal Era*. Chapel Hill: University of North Carolina Press, 1996.

Sutherland, Sidney. "The 14th, 15th, and 18th Amendments." *Liberty* 5 (April 21, 1928): 7–10.

———. "The 14th, 15th, and 18th Amendments." *Liberty* 5 (April 28, 1928): 27–34.

Sweeney, James R. "Rum, Romanism, and Virginia Democrats: The Party Leaders and the Campaign of 1928." *Virginia Magazine of History and Biography* 90 (October 1982): 403–31.

Tarter, Brent. "A Flier on the National Scene: Byrd's Favorite-son Presidential Candidacy of 1932." *Virginia Magazine of History and Biography* 82 (July 1974): 282–305.

Tate, Leland Burdine. *An Economic and Social Survey of Russell County*. University of Virginia Record Extension Series, vol. 16, no. 1, July 1931.

Thomson, Brian William. "Racism and Racial Classification: A Case Study of the Virginia Racial Integrity Legislation." Ph.D. diss., University of California at Riverside, 1978.

Thorndike, Joseph J. "'The Sometimes Sordid Level of Race and Segregation':

James J. Kilpatrick and the Virginia Campaign against *Brown*." In *The Moderates' Dilemma: Massive Resistance to School Desegregation in Virginia*, edited by Matthew D. Lassiter and Andrew B. Lewis, 104–33. Charlottesville: University Press of Virginia, 1998.

Tindall, George B. "Business Progressivism: Southern Politics in the Twenties." *South Atlantic Quarterly* 62 (Winter 1963): 92–106.

———. *The Emergence of the New South, 1913-1945*. Baton Rouge: Louisiana State University Press, 1967.

"Toward the South of the Future: A Statement of Policy and Aims of the Southern Regional Council." *New South* 6 (December 1951): 1–2.

Tullos, Allen. *Habits of Industry: White Culture and the Transformation of the Carolina Piedmont*. Chapel Hill: University of North Carolina Press, 1989.

Tuttle, William M., Jr. *Race Riot: Chicago in the Red Summer of 1919*. New York: Atheneum, 1970.

Tyler-McGraw, Marie. *At the Falls: Richmond, Virginia, and Its People*. Chapel Hill: University of North Carolina Press, 1994.

U.S. Congress. House Committee on Rules. *Hearings on the Ku Klux Klan, 1921*. New York: Arno Press, 1969.

Vogt, George Leonard. "The Development of Virginia's Republican Party." Ph.D. diss., University of Virginia, 1978.

Wade, Wyn Craig. *The Fiery Cross: The Ku Klux Klan in America*. New York: Oxford University Press, 1987.

Wadlington, Walter. "The *Loving* Case: Virginia's Anti-Miscegenation Statute in Historical Perspective." *Virginia Law Review* 52 (1966): 1189–1223.

Wallenstein, Peter. "Indian Foremothers: Race, Sex, Slavery, and Freedom in Early Virginia." In *The Devil's Lane: Sex and Race in the Early South*, edited by Catherine Clinton and Michele Gillespie, 57–73. New York: Oxford University Press, 1997.

———. "Race, Marriage, and the Law of Freedom: Alabama and Virginia, 1860s–1960s." *Chicago-Kent Law Review* 70 (1994): 371–437.

———. "The Right to Marry: *Loving v. Virginia*." OAH *Magazine of History* 9 (Winter 1995): 37–41.

———. "'These New and Strange Beings': Women in the Legal Profession in Virginia, 1890–1990." *Virginia Magazine of History and Biography* 101 (April 1993): 193–226.

Ward, Ronald David. "The Life and Works of John Powell." Ph.D. diss., Catholic University, 1973.

Warner, Paul L. *An Economic and Social Survey of Clarke County*. University of Virginia Record Extension Series, vol. 9, no. 12, August 1925.

Washington, James M., ed. *A Testament of Hope: The Essential Writings and Speeches of Martin Luther King, Jr*. New York: Harper Collins, 1986.

Wayland, John W. *A History of Virginia for Boys and Girls*. New York: Macmillan Company, 1925.

Weisiger, Minor Tompkins. "E. R. Combs: Chief of the Byrd Organization." M.A. thesis, University of Virginia, 1979.

Weiss, Nancy J. *Farewell to the Party of Lincoln: Black Politics in the Age of FDR*. Princeton, N.J.: Princeton University Press, 1983.

Wheeler, Marjorie Spruill. *New Women of the New South: The Leaders of the Woman Suffrage Movement in the Southern States*. New York: Oxford University Press, 1993.

Whisnant, David E. *All That Is Native and Fine: The Politics of Culture in an American Region*. Chapel Hill: University of North Carolina Press, 1983.

White, Walter. "Decline of Southern Liberals." *Negro Digest* 1 (January 1943): 43–46.

Wilkerson, Doxey A. "The Negro School Movement in Virginia: From 'Equalization' to 'Integration.'" *Journal of Negro Education* 29 (Winter 1960): 17–29.

Wilkinson, J. Harvie, III. *Harry Byrd and the Changing Face of Virginia Politics, 1945–1966*. Charlottesville: University Press of Virginia, 1968.

Williamson, Joel. *The Crucible of Race: Black-White Relations in the American South since Emancipation*. New York: Oxford University Press, 1984.

———. *New People: Miscegenation and Mulattoes in the United States*. New York: Free Press, 1980.

Willis, Leo Stanley. "E. Lee Trinkle and the Virginia Democracy, 1876–1939." Ph.D. diss., University of Virginia, 1968.

Wilson, Charles Reagan. *Baptized in Blood: The Religion of the Lost Cause, 1865–1920*. Athens: University of Georgia Press, 1980.

Wolters, Raymond. "Rites of Passage: Hampton Institute Becomes a College." In *The New Negro on Campus: Black College Rebellions of the 1920s*, 230–75. Princeton, N.J.: Princeton University Press, 1975.

Woodward, C. Vann. *Origins of the New South, 1877–1913*. Baton Rouge: Louisiana State University Press, 1951.

———. *The Strange Career of Jim Crow*. 3d ed. New York: Oxford University Press, 1974.

———, ed. *A Southern Prophecy*. Boston: Little, Brown, 1964.

Woofter, Thomas. *The Basis of Racial Adjustment*. Boston: Ginn and Company, 1925.

Works Projects Administration in the State of Virginia. *The Negro in Virginia*. New York: Hastings House, 1940. Reprint, Winston-Salem, N.C.: John F. Blair, 1994.

———. *Virginia: A Guide to the Old Dominion*. New York: Oxford University Press, 1940.

Wright, Gavin. *Old South, New South: Revolutions in the Southern Economy since the Civil War*. New York: Basic Books, 1986.

Wright, George C. *Racial Violence in Kentucky, 1865–1940: Lynchings, Mob Rule, and 'Legal Lynchings.'* Baton Rouge: Louisiana State University Press, 1990.

Wright, R. Charlton. "The Southern White Man and the Negro." *Virginia Quarterly Review* 9 (April 1933): 175–94.

Wynes, Charles E. "The Evolution of Jim Crow Laws in Twentieth Century Virginia." *Phylon* 28 (Winter 1967): 416–25.

———. *Race Relations in Virginia, 1870–1902*. Charlottesville: University Press of Virginia, 1961.

Wynn, Neil A. *From Progressivism to Prosperity: World War I and American Society*. New York: Holmes and Meier, 1986.

Young, Howard V., Jr. "William Howard Taft and Hampton Institute." In *Stony the Road: Chapters in the History of Hampton Institute*, edited by Keith L. Schall, 125–62. Charlottesville: University Press of Virginia, 1977.

Younger, Edward, and James Tice Moore, eds. *The Governors of Virginia, 1860–1978*. Charlottesville: University Press of Virginia, 1982.

Zangrando, Robert L. *The NAACP Crusade against Lynching, 1909–1950*. Philadelphia: Temple University Press, 1980.

Index

of Virginia branches of, 241, 243–
46; attacks segregated education,
244–48, 272–73, 292–97
National Consumers' League, 208
Native Origins Act, 317 (n. 9)
Negro Organization Society, 67
Negro Smith Clubs, 190–92
Negro Welfare Council, 235
Negro Welfare Survey Committee,
208–9
Newbold, Nathan C., 136
Newcomb, John, 245
New Deal, 251, 303 (n. 26), 314
(n. 73), 346 (n. 4)
New Kent County, Va., 95, 223
"New Negro," 14, 44, 127, 313 (n. 64)
Newport News, Va., 138–39, 230, 273
Newport News Daily Press, 57, 107,
109, 112–13, 152, 202
Newport News Shipbuilding and
Drydock Company, 47, 113, 138
Newport News Times-Herald, 167
News Leader Current Events Class,
56, 118, 122, 311 (n. 43)
Newsome, Thomas, 64
New South, 5, 307 (n. 51)
Nicholson, Mrs. Jesse, 192
Nineteenth Amendment, 57
Nixon v. Herndon, 199, 201–2
Norfleet, Elizabeth Copeland, 112
Norfolk, Va.: and World War I, 31–
32, 42, 139, 145; and local CIC, 47,
236; residential segregation in, 50,
71, 140–42; segregated facilities
in, 50–51, 235–38; and Brambleton dispute, 71–73, 140–41; race
relations in, 139–43; segregated
transportation system of, 142–44;
segregated education in, 234; and
salary equalization case, 256–58,
271–73, 288
Norfolk County, Va., 92, 135–36
Norfolk Journal and Guide, 44, 151–
52, 233; and segregation, 51, 70,
215–16; on elections, 62–63, 193–

95, 198–99; on eugenics and racial
integrity bills, 88, 99–100, 220,
226–27; and Hampton Institute,
109–18 passim, 120, 125; and Jim
Crow education, 134–36, 228, 245;
and emptiness of paternalism, 139–
40, 198–99; on lynching, 163, 173,
176; on *Flat Hat*, 290
Norfolk Kiwanis Club, 50
Norfolk Ledger-Dispatch, 60, 119,
201–2
Norfolk Virginian-Pilot, 41, 55, 137,
152, 369 (n. 12); and controversy
leading to Public Assemblages Act,
115–18; on lynching, 167, 175; on
primaries and elections, 194–96,
199, 201; and racial integrity, 227;
on firing of Aline Black, 258; and
massive resistance, 296
Norris v. Alabama, 358 (n. 61)
North Carolina, 4–5, 9, 14, 32, 60,
135–36, 301 (n. 4), 302 (n. 11), 306
(nn. 32, 35), 313 (n. 67), 314 (n. 73),
337 (n. 2), 370 (nn. 27, 28)
Northcott, Elliot, 203, 215
Northumberland County, Va., 43
Norton, Va., 172

Odum, Howard, 279–80
"One-drop" rule, 84, 224
Orrell, S. R., 206
O'Shea Commission, 133–34, 333
(n. 8)

Painter, Robert, 93
Palmer, Lutrelle, 138, 256, 271–73,
277
Parker, H. S., 166
Parker, John J., 215–16, 271, 293, 352
(n. 67)
Parrish, J. Scott, 118
Passing, 72, 77, 80, 91, 98, 103, 121
Paternalism: of white elites in Vir-
ginia, 4–5, 29–30, 37–38, 47, 51, 62,
67–68, 110, 239–42, 300–301 (n. 3),

Robinson, John, 62
Robson, William, 158
Rockbridge County, Va., 92, 95–96
Rockefeller, John D., Jr., 112
Rockingham County, Va., 220
Rogers, J. A., 120–21
Roosevelt, Franklin, 251, 274, 314 (n. 73)
Roosevelt, Theodore, 194
Rosenwald Fund, 134
Rountree, Helen, 323 (n. 50)
Royall, John M., 159, 338 (n. 13)
Russell County, Va., 91

St. Luke's Herald, 165
Sancton, Thomas, 276
Sands, Oliver, 235
Saunders, Clyde, 196
Saunders, W. O., 33–34
Schuyler, George, 104–5, 107
Scientific racism, 30, 81–82, 305 (n. 29)
Scoggin, Katharine, 261, 269
Scottsboro Boys, 243
Secession, 35–36
Segregation, 4, 9, 15, 20, 22, 28, 30, 49–51, 108; in transportation, 28, 68–70, 142–44, 260–61; in recreational facilities, 50–51, 138, 235–37; call to abolish, on common carriers, 280–84
—in education, 8, 13, 134–36, 217, 234, 354 (n. 22); and racial integrity, 220–26; and Alice Jackson case, 244–47; and Norfolk salary equalization case, 256–58, 271–73; in Alexandria, 260–70; NAACP and Prince Edward County schools, 293–95
—in residential districts, 28; in Richmond, 3–4, 71, 204–18, 235; in Norfolk, 70–73, 140–42, 235; and ordinances in Louisville and New Orleans, 141–42, 215, 352 (n. 65) *See also* Jim Crow; Public Assemblages Act

Seligmann, Herbert, 53
Shenandoah County, Va., 221
Shepherd, Morris, 90
Sherman, Richard, 319 (n. 24)
Shields, A. T., 92
Simon, Bryant, 270
Simpson, Josephus, 242, 247–48
Sisk, Lelia, 157–58
Slavery, 10, 30, 35–36
Smith, Al, 189–91, 193–94, 196–97, 203
Smith, Hiram, 98
Smith, Lillian, 288–90
Smith v. Allwright, 349 (n. 39)
Smoot, Mrs. Albert, 266
Snobbcraft, Arthur, 105
Social equality, 21, 38, 107–24 passim, 259, 275
Sons of Confederate Veterans, 37
Soper, Morris, 293
Sorrells, Atha, 93–95, 324 (n. 59)
Southampton County, Va., 36, 234
Southern Baptist Convention, 119
Southern Committee to Study Lynching, 182
Southern Conference for Human Welfare, 288
Southern Conference on Race Relations, 277
Southern Negro Youth Congress, 244, 288
Southern Regional Council (SRC), 280, 290, 294–95
Southern Workman, 55
Southside, 9, 23, 25, 32, 134, 295
Spangler, H. C., 166
Spindle, R. B., 141
Spratley, Vernon, 221, 231
Springarn, Joel, 44
Stampp, Kenneth, 300 (n. 3)
Stanley, Thomas, 295
Stephens, A. E. S., 341–42 (n. 53)
Sterilization, 82, 108, 318 (n. 13)
Stockton, W. I., Jr., 79
Stoddard, Lothrop, 81, 88
Stone, Gertrude, 185